AF669752

EARLY BUDDHIST THEORY OF KNOWLEDGE

BUDDHIST TRADITION SERIES

VOLUME 29

Early Buddhist Theory of Knowledge

K.N. JAYATILLEKE

MOTILAL BANARSIDASS PUBLISHERS
PRIVATE LIMITED • DELHI

5th Reprint : Delhi, 2015
First Indian Edition: Delhi, 1963

ISBN: 978-81-208-0619-1

MOTILAL BANARSIDASS
41 U.A. Bungalow Road, Jawahar Nagar, Delhi 110 007
8 Mahalaxmi Chamber, 22 Bhulabhai Desai Road, Mumbai 400 026
203 Royapettah High Road, Mylapore, Chennai 600 004
236, 9th Main III Block, Jayanagar, Bengaluru 560 011
8 Camac Street, Kolkata 700 017
Ashok Rajpath, Patna 800 004
Chowk, Varanasi 221 001

Printed in India

by RP Jain at NAB Printing Unit,
A-44, Naraina Industrial Area, Phase I, New Delhi–110028
and published by JP Jain for Motilal Banarsidass Publishers (P) Ltd,
41 U.A. Bungalow Road, Jawahar Nagar, Delhi-110007

DEDICATION

ukkādhāro manussānaṃ niccaṃ apacito mayā.

(I shall always revere the Torchbearer of Mankind.)

—*Sutta Nipāta,* 336

FOREWORD

The present work forms an important contribution to the solution of a number of problems more in particular pertaining to the earliest developments of Indian philosophy. In 1925 P. Tuxen observed that in any future exposition of the history of this philosophy two factors should predominate: 1. the relation of early Buddhism to Indian thought; 2. the correlation of the latter to the Indian science of grammar.[1] In 1927 the famous Russian Buddhologist Stcherbatsky made the significant statement that even after a century of scientific study of Buddhism in Europe, we were still in the dark about the fundamental teachings of this religion and its philosophy. At the current state of inquiry—thanks to the assiduous and penetrating efforts of many scholars in West and East—a good deal of this 'darkness' has been dispelled. Yet, there are still various gaps in our knowledge to be filled. For one thing, even though we are at present fairly well acquainted with the later developments of systematic Indian philosophy, there is still much uncertainty about the actual origin and incipient formative stages, i.e. the 'pre-history' of its logical and epistemological and, to a less extent, of its linguistic aspects. For another, even to-day too many misconceptions about the exclusively mystic and recondite nature of this philosophy continue to prevail, especially in non-professional circles. For the sphere of thought indicated by the collective name of 'Indian Philosophy' is extremely complex. Indeed, in terms of the history of ideas, its chief attraction must be sought, not only in its spiritual and cultural unity or in the perennial truths of its monistic-idealistic metaphysics, but rather in its rich diversity. For this is indicative of its long development including an ever deepening confrontation with fundamental philosophical problems. This complexity has led to highly divergent value judgments on the part of Western philosophers as well as professional scholars, mostly of an earlier generation. They included those who regarded the very term 'Indian philosophy' as a 'contradictio in adjecto' and its teachings as vaguely indefinite displays of dreamy thoughts, lacking in clear-cut concepts and proper definitions. However, other scholars were convinced that it had reached a very high standard of development. Stcherbatsky (e.g.) stated that, in addition to its systems of empirical idealism and spiritual monism, it had produced an intricate logic and a remarkable

[1] Cf. P. Tuxen, Zur Darstellung der indischen Philosophie, A.O., vol. IV, p. 118 f; Th. Stcherbatsky, Conception of Buddhist Nirvāṇa, Leningrad 1927, p. l; id. Madhyānta-Vibhaṅga, Leningrad, 1936, p. IV; H. Zimmer, Philosophies of India, London 1951, p. 27 f; K. Kunjunni Raja, Indian Theories of Meaning, Madras-Adyar, 1963. B. Faddegon, The Vaiçesika-System, Amsterdam 1918, p. 12.

epistemology and that the principal lines of its development showed parallels with those of Western philosophy, including rationalism and empiricism. Even though valid objections may be adduced to the theory of 'parallel development', there are at present few doubts about the 'high standard'. Among other things, it is a fact that the consistent investigation of logical fallacies and contradictions, on the basis of exact canons of reason, form an essential part of nearly all the systems, orthodox and heterodox. And, in the words of Faddegon, already in early Vaiśeṣika we find a purely theoretical attitude of mind and not 'that craze for liberation' which dominates nearly all forms of Indian thought . . . Rather, it is the theoretical desire for a correct classification and system of definition. The variety of opinion, mentioned above, is to a large extent induced by the problems of Indian, i.e. Sanskrit, Pali and Prakrit, philosophical language which—as shown in a number of recent publications—is itself correlated to the terminology and categories of the highly developed Indian science of grammar. Especially, the correct interpretation of the intricate technical terminology presents many difficulties. In many cases, the same terms have different connotations, or altogether different meanings, within different contexts and, historically, at the successive periods of their application. Indeed, already in ancient India, both the grammarians and the philosophers were concerned with the problems of meaning and important works were written on this subject. Long before this happened in the West, 'semantics' became a fundamental part of the Indian philosophical discipline. Thus, in addition to a careful historical consideration of the semantic theories, only a meticulous textual analysis, on an extensive comparative basis, can produce valid interpretations of Indian philosophical ideas in European languages which are both comprehensible and 'intrinsic'. Moreover, to give adequate meaningful renderings of the difficult texts, even a thorough grounding in modern philosophical analysis is nowadays an indispensable prerequisite.

A further problem which has engaged the attention of scholars is the exact position which early Buddhism occupied in the development of Indian thought, the more so as it was regarded by some of them as a 'foreign body' in Indian philosophy. Moreover, they were of the opinion that the purely philosophical quality of the Pali canon was surprisingly deficient. Again, Stcherbatsky stated that the Pali-school of Buddhologists entirely overlooked the system of philosophy which is present on every page of the Pali canon. In his opinion, Buddhist authors played a leading part in the development of Indian epistemology. This is certainly established for the later school of Dignāga and Dharmakīrti and their followers. Stcherbatsky's views are largely confirmed by the present work which is primarily concerned with the earlier period. Dr Jayatilleke, who had the privilege of being admitted to Wittgenstein's classes, is that rare combination of accomplished philologist, historian and methodic philosopher. His book goes far beyond the indication of its title. On the basis of a profound analysis of the relevant earlier and later texts as well as a critical re-examination of the works of his predecessors in the field, he traces with great ingenuity and scholarly thoroughness the epistemological foundations of Pali canonical thought, from the Vedic period onwards. His fully connected account sheds new light, not only on the problems of the earlier period which have engaged the attention of scholars during the past forty years, but also on those of the later developments. Moreover, with regard to the present day conflict of metaphysics versus logical and linguistic analysis, the book contains valuable material which elucidates from the Indian point of view some of the basic problems of this conflict.

D. Friedman

FOREWORD BY SERIES EDITOR

Jayatilleke's work is a magnificent coverage of early Buddhism in a theoretical sense, of judicious comparisons with other Indian philosophical systems, and evaluation of Western interpreters. Here the theory of meaning is carefully worked out in each paragraph as the author deals with important issues while sensitively using words.

It is a pleasure to include this work in the Buddhist Tradition series. The present editor has possessed Jayatilleke's initial edition (1963) for many years and has frequently consulted it with admiration for its fine standard of discourse on germane topics.

New York City, 1996 ALEX WAYMAN

PREFACE

The origins of the Indian empiricist tradition and its development in Early Buddhism are largely unknown to Western scholarship, despite the fact that T. W. Rhys Davids at a very early date compared Buddhism with Comtism[1] and Radhakrishnan went so far as to say that 'Early Buddhism was positivist in its outlook and confined its attention to what we perceive'.[2] However, modern Western thinkers, who have dipped into the literature of Buddhism, have sometimes been struck by its analytical and positivist turns of thought. H. H. Price, who was the Wykeham Professor of Logic at the University of Oxford, remarked that 'there are indeed some passages in the early part of the *Questions of King Milinda* which have a very modern ring, and might almost have been written in Cambridge in the 1920's'.[3] Aldous Huxley was of the opinion that Early Buddhism for the most part respected the principle of verification and confined its statements to verifiable propositions. In his own words: 'Among the early Buddhists, the metaphysical theory (i.e. of Brahman of the Upanishads) was neither affirmed nor denied, but simply ignored as being meaningless and unnecessary. Their concern was with immediate experience, which, because of its consequences for life, came to be known as "liberation" or "enlightenment". The Buddha and his disciples of the southern school seemed to have applied to the problems of religion that "operational philosophy" which contemporary scientific thinkers have begun to apply in the natural sciences . . . Buddha was not a consistent operationalist; for he seems to have taken for granted, to have accepted as something given and self-evident, a variant of the locally current theory of metempsychosis. Where mysticism was concerned, however, his operationalism was complete. He would not make assertions about the nature of ultimate reality because it did not seem to him that the corresponding set of mystical operations would admit of a theological interpretation'.[4]

Huxley's qualification that 'the Buddha was not a consistent operationalist' may not have been made had he been aware of the epistemological basis and the nature of the Buddha's positivism and had he not been misled by scholars to think that the Buddha had dogmatically accepted the doctrine of rebirth from the prevalent tradition (v. Ch. VIII).

[1] *Origin and Growth of Religion*, London, 1881, p. 31.

[2] S. Radhakrishnan, *Indian Philosophy*, Vol. II, London, 1931, p. 472.

[3] 'The Present Relations between Eastern and Western Philosophy' in *The Hibbert Journal*, Vol. LIII, April 1955, p. 229.

[4] *Grey Eminence*, London, 1942, pp. 47-8.

Our findings about the Early Buddhist theory of knowledge are based primarily on the source material afforded by the Pali Canon, studied historically and philosophically in the light of the contemporary, earlier and later literary evidence bearing on the subject. The literary, linguistic, ideological, sociological and historical evidence still points to the high antiquity and authenticity of the Pali Canon[1], although what we learn from it about Early Buddhism may have to be supplemented and, perhaps, even modified at times in the light of what we can glean from the other literary traditions of Buddhism[2]. We may refer here to the recent opinion of a student of religion, Dr Robert H. Thouless, who says that 'it seems more likely that Hīnayāna was Buddhism as originally taught and the Mahāyāna was a product of development and conventionalisation'[3].

The present work seeks to evaluate the thought of the Pāli Canon from a new point of view and in the light of new material. In it an attempt is made to uncover the epistemological foundations of Pāli Canonical thought. One of the main problems of epistemology is that of the means whereby our knowledge is derived. In this work the questions pertaining to the means of knowledge known to, criticized in and accepted by the Buddhism of the Pāli Canon are fully discussed. A comprehensive survey of the historical background (Chs. I, II and III) was indispensable for this purpose partly because this throws considerable light on the Buddhist theory of knowledge and also because part of the material for the study of this background is to be found in the Canon itself.

Apart from the inquiry into the means of knowledge, a number of questions relating to the problem of knowledge have been dealt with. Thus we have endeavoured to show the kind of logic adopted by the Buddhists in contradistinction to that of the Jains (Ch. VII). While Wittgenstein's[4] imaginary tribes played hypothetical language games showing the various possibilities in the use of language, we find here actual instances in which different systems of logic were employed in order to cope with certain conceptual situations. We have also investigated the rôle of analysis, the theories of meaning and truth and the problem of the limits of knowledge, as they appear in the Canon.

[1] v. *Dialogues of the Buddha*, Part 1, Tr. T. W. Rhys Davids, SBB., Vol. II, London, 1956, pp. ix-xx; cp. M. Winternitz, *A History of Indian Literature*, Tr. S. Ketkar and H. Kohn, University of Calcutta, 1933, p. 18.

[2] E. Lamotte grants a primitive core of remarkably uniform material common to the Pali Nikāyas and the Āgamas, v. *Histoire du bouddhisme indien*, Vol. I, Louvain, 1958, p. 171. For a sceptical view, v. J. Brough, *The Gāndhāri Dharmapada*, London, 1962, pp. 31 ff.

[3] "Christianity and Buddhism" in *Milla wa-Milla*, No. 2, November 1962, p. 3.

[4] The author had the privilege of being admitted to Wittgenstein's classes held in his rooms at Whewell's Court, Trinity College, Cambridge, in the years 1945-47.

The student of Indian philosophy should find here material pertaining to the 'prehistory' of systematic Indian logic and epistemology and the origins of the Indian empiricist tradition. A student of Greek thought may be able to see in these pages some parallel developments to his own field, as well as the differences. Of particular interest to the student of Western philosophy would be Chapters VI and VII dealing with 'Analysis and Meaning' and 'Logic and Truth' respectively, the anticipation of two theorems of the propositional calculus (Ch. VIII, sections 702–710), the theory of causation (Ch. IX, sections 758–782), the empiricism of the Materialists (Ch. II) and the Buddhists (Ch. IX).

I would express my gratitude to Dr D. L. Friedman for patiently reading through this thesis and offering many valuable comments, criticisms and suggestions. I am also grateful to him for introducing me to literature pertaining to this subject which I had failed to consult at the time of writing my first draft. My thanks are also due to Professor A. L. Basham, who evinced an interest in this work and very kindly read through the whole of Chapter III. I must also place on record my indebtedness to Professor O. H. de A. Wijesekera of the University of Ceylon, from whom I learnt the first lessons in research, and who encouraged me to work on this subject.

I am grateful to Mr D. J. Kalupahana, my pupil and colleague who was kind enough to undertake the task of preparing the index and to my wife and other colleagues and friends for assisting me with the proof-reading and advice. I must also thank the University of Ceylon, which with the generous assistance of the Asia Foundation defrayed a small portion of the cost of this publication.

University Park, Peradeniya, Ceylon.
19 May 1963 K. N. JAYATILLEKE

CONTENTS

ABBREVIATIONS

A. Aṅguttara Nikāya
AA. Aṅguttara Nikāya Aṭṭhakathā, i.e. Manorathapūraṇī
A.A.S. Āṇanda Āśrama Series
ABORI. Annals of the Bhandarkar Research Institute
Ait. Ār. Aitareya Āraṇyaka
Ait. Br. Aitareya Brāhmaṇa
AO. Acta Orientalia
Ār. Āraṇyaka
Ard. Mag. Ardha Māgadhi
AV. Atharvaveda
BEFEO. Bulletin de l'Ecole Française d'Extrême-Orient
BHS. Buddhist Hybrid Sanskrit
Br. Brāhmaṇa
Bṛh. Bṛhadāraṇyaka Upaniṣad
Ch. Chāndogya Upaniṣad
Comy. Commentary
CPD. Critical Pali Dictionary
C.S. Caraka Saṃhitā
D. Dīgha Nikāya
DA. Dīgha Nikāya Aṭṭhakathā, i.e. Sumaṅgalavilāsinī
Dh. Dhammapada
DhS. Dhammasaṅgaṇī
DPPN. Dictionary of Pali Proper Names
ERE. Encyclopaedia of Religion and Ethics
G.S. The Book of the Gradual Sayings, *v.* Aṅguttara Nikāya
HIP. History of Indian Philosophy
HOS. Harvard Oriental Series
IHQ. Indian Historical Quarterly
IP. Indian Philosophy
It. Itivuttaka
J. Jātaka
JA. Journal Asiatique
JAOS. Journal of the American Oriental Society
JPTS. Journal of the Pali Text Society
JRAS. Journal of the Royal Asiatic Society
Kaṭha. Kaṭha Upaniṣad
Kauś. Kauśītaki Upaniṣad
Kauś. Br. Kauśītakī Brāhmaṇa
Khp. Khuddakapāṭha
K.S. The Book of the Kindred Sayings, *v.* Saṃyutta Nikāya
Kvu. Kathāvatthu
KvuA. Kathāvatthuppakaraṇaṭṭhakathā
M. Majjhima Nikāya
MA. Majjhima Nikāya Aṭṭhakathā, i.e. Papañcasūdanī
Manu. Manusmṛti
Mait. Maitrī Upaniṣad
M.L.S. Middle Length Sayings, *v.* Majjhima Nikāya
M.S. Mīmāṃsā Sūtra
Muṇḍ. Muṇḍaka Upaniṣad
Nd.I. Mahāniddesa

Nd.II. Cullaniddeṣa
N.B. Nyāya Bhāṣya
N.S. Nyāya Sūtra (SBH. Edition)
NS. *v.* N.S.
O.U.P. Oxford University Press
P. Pali
PAS. Proceedings of the Aristotelian Society
PIPC. Proceedings of the Indian Philosophical Congress
Praśna. Praśna Upaniṣad
PTS. Pali Text Society
PU. The Principal Upaniṣads, Ed. S. Radhakrishnan
Pug. Pañ. Puggalapaññatti
PvA. Petavatthu Aṭṭhakathā, i.e. Paramatthadīpanī
Rām. Rāmāyana
RV. Ṛgveda
S. Saṃyutta Nikāya
SA. Saṃyutta Nikāya Aṭṭhakathā, i.e. Sāratthappakāsinī
Sam. Samavāyāṅga Sūtra
ŚB. Śatapatha Brāhmaṇa
SBB. Sacred Books of the Buddhists
SBE. Sacred Books of the East
SBH. Sacred Books of the Hindus
Ś.Br. *v.* ŚB.
SDS. Sarvadarśanasaṃgraha
S.K. Sāṅkhya Kārikā
Skr. Sanskrit
S.P.S. Sāṅkhya Pravacana Sūtra
Sn. Suttanipāta
SnA. Súttanipāta Aṭṭhakathā, i.e. Paramatthajotikā II
Sū. Sūtrakṛtāṅga
Śvet. Śvetāśvatara Upaniṣad
Tait. Taittirīya Upaniṣad
Tait. Br. Taittirīya Brāhmaṇa
Th. I Theragāthā
Th. II Therīgathā
Toev. Toevoegselen op't Woordenboek van Childers, H. Kern
U.C.R. University of Ceylon Review
Ud. Udāna
UdA. Udāna Aṭṭhakathā, i.e. Paramatthadīpanī
Vbh. Vibhaṅga
VbhA. Vibhaṅga Aṭṭhakathā, i.e. Sammohavinodanī
Vin. Vinaya
V.S. Vaiśeṣika Sūtras
Y.B. Yogabhāṣya
Y.S. Yogasūtras

CHAPTER I

THE HISTORICAL BACKGROUND I—VEDIC

(1) When we consider the history of thought in Greece, we find that metaphysics first develops out of mythology[1] and it is only when metaphysical speculation attains a certain maturity and results in the formulation of a variety of theories that an interest is shown in the problem of knowledge and epistemological questions are first mooted.[2] If we turn to the Indian context we can trace an analogous though by no means an identical development.

(2) The intense speculative interest, which is so evident in the tenth book (maṇḍala) of the Ṛgveda persists as an undercurrent in the period of the Brāhmaṇas and issues forth in the theories and intuitions of the Upaniṣads, whether we consider them a linear development in Vedic thought or as being due to the impact of an external element, Aryan or non-Aryan. Contemporaneous with the Middle[3] or Late Upaniṣads or perhaps even later, we find the existence of schools of thought which either broke away from the Vedic tradition or grew up in isolation from and in opposition to it. The thought of this period displays a wide variety of views. It was probably during this period, which is coeval with or immediately prior to the rise of Jainism and Buddhism that there arose the first questionings about the nature, scope and validity of knowledge, resulting in the emergence of the Sceptics (Ard. Mag. aṇṇāṇiā = Skr. ajñānikāḥ; P. amarāvikkhepikā,

[1] *v.* J. Burnet, *Greek Philosophy—Thales to Plato,* London, 1943, pp. 3 ff.

[2] Note that Book I in Burnet's work (*op. cit.*) dealing with the pre-Socratics is entitled 'the World' (p. 15) and Book II from the Sophists onwards 'Knowledge and Conduct' (p. 103).

[3] We shall be using the term 'Early Upaniṣads' to denote the 'Ancient Prose Upaniṣads', 'Middle Upaniṣads' for the 'Metrical Upaniṣads' and 'Late Upaniṣads' for the 'Later Prose Upaniṣads' in Deussen's classification; *v. The Philosophy of the Upanishads,* tr. Rev. A. S. Gedden, pp. 23–5.

v. infra, 147, 158) and the epistemological and logical theories peculiar to Materialism, Ājīvikism, Jainism and Buddhism.

(3) When a metaphysical theory is fairly well developed, there is a tendency to inquire into the grounds of its truth. Similarly, where there are a number of conflicting theories about a particular problem, it would be natural to ask which of them was true. Both these queries lead to an investigation of the nature of truth and knowledge, which may give rise to logical and epistemological doctrines. This seems to have been the general pattern according to which interest was first stimulated and advances made in the solution of the problem of knowledge both in India as well as in Greece.

(4) In this survey of the Vedic period we shall be concerned with what the Vedic (Brāhmaṇic and Upanisadic) thinkers assumed or thought were the means of knowledge and in the origin and nature of reasoning as we find it in this literature. Both these questions shall be considered in the light of their bearing on the thought of the Pāli Canon.

(5) The Ṛgveda does not betray any awareness of the nature of problems of knowledge. If we accept the naturalistic explanation, the Ṛgvedic gods were probably fashioned on the analogy of ourselves by positing wills behind the dynamic forces of nature but there is no indication whatsoever that the thinkers were consciously employing an argument from analogy. The mechanical and organic views of creation[1] seem to have been similarly arrived at, although here the analogies with some observable facts of nature are more evident at least to the reader. The tendency on the part of the mind to look for simpler explanations in place of the more complex is perhaps responsible for the emergence of monotheistic and monistic tendencies[2] in the last phase of Ṛgvedic thought.

(6) Interest is almost invariably focused on the outer world and it is rarely that we meet with a thinker in an introspective mood though we find an instance of a person who asks himself in a sceptical tone: 'I do not clearly know what I am like here; bewildered and bound with a mind, I wander' (na vi jānāmi yadivedām asmi niṇyaḥ[3] saṃnaddho

[1] Radhakrishnan, *Indian Philosophy*, I, pp. 99 ff. [2] *Op. cit.*, pp. 89 ff.

[3] We have followed the commentators in translating this term; Mādhava takes it to mean 'concealed' (antarhitaḥ, *v.* fn. 2) and Sāyaṇa following him says, 'the term "ninyaḥ" denotes what is concealed (and means here that) he is concealed, i.e. has a bewildered mind (antarhitanāmaitat antarhito mūḍhacittaḥ).'

manasā carāmi, RV. 1.164.37). Mādhava, the pre-Sāyaṇa commentator of the Vedas,[1] interprets this statement to mean '"I do not clearly know", i.e. I do not understand whether I am this (world), being beyond nature (*prakṛti-*); thoroughly bound by a mind attracted by objects and being concealed, I wander'.[2] While Mādhava speaks in terms of Sāṅkhya philosophy (*v. prakṛti-*), Sāyaṇa tries to give an explanation, consistent with the philosophy of Advaita Vedānta, when commenting on this statement he explains it as: 'I do not know that I am that which is the existent, the intelligent and the blissful (saccịdānando)'.[3] Both commentators take 'idam' to mean 'the universe' and Sāyaṇa makes this quite explicit (yadivedaṃ yadapīdaṃ *viśvam* asmi, *loc. cit.*). These interpretations, based as they are on later philosophies, are inadmissible for the Ṛgveda and we have tried to render the sentence literally taking 'idam' in its adverbial sense to mean 'here'.[4] With the exception of Wilson who as usual follows Sāyaṇa closely,[5] the translations of scholars bring out the sceptical nature of the utterance. Griffith has: 'What thing I truly am, I know not clearly: mysterious, fettered in my mind I wander'[6] and Geldner renders it as; 'Ich verstehe nicht was dem vergleichbar ist, was ich bin. Ich wandele, heimlich mit dem Denken ausgerüstet.'[7] Prasad denies that this verse betrays any scepticism,[8] but translates it as: 'I do not know whether I am like this, ignorant, prepared I go about'. Here the translation of 'saṃnaddho manasā' as 'prepared' is in contradiction with 'ignorant', but even this translation which differs from that of Sāyaṇa reflects a little of the sceptical mood of the original, though Prasad prefers to call this ignorance rather than scepticism (*v. op. cit.*, pp. 24, 28).

[1] *v.* Ṛgarthadīpikā on Ṛgvedasaṃhitā by Mādhava, ed. L. Sarup, Vol. I Lahore, 1939, Preface, p. 15. The pre-Mādhava commentary (*v. op. cit.*, p. 16) of Skandhasvāmin pertaining to this section is not available in print.

[2] Na vi jānāmi na vijānāmi yadapyaham idam asmi prakṛteḥ paraḥ viśayaparena manasā samyakbaddhaḥ antarhitaḥ carāmi, *op. cit.*, Vol. II, Lahore, 1940, pp. 326, 327.

[3] Yo'yaṃ saccidānando' sti so aham asmī ti na vijānāmi, *loc. cit.*

[4] *v.* Macdonell, *A Vedic Grammar for Students*, p. 210, Section 178, 2(a).

[5] 'I distinguish not if I am this all: for I go perplexed and bound in mind', H. H. Wilson, *Rigveda Sanhitā*, Vol. II, Poona, 1925, p. 77.

[6] R. T. H. Griffith, *The Hymns of the Ṛgveda*, Vol. I, Benares, 1889, p. 291.

[7] K. F. Geldner, *Der Rigveda, Ubersetzt und Erlautert*, Göttingen, 1923, Vol. I, p. 211.

[8] *History of Indian Epistemology*, 2nd ed. Delhi, 1958, pp. 20 ff.

(7) The very few stanzas which strike a sceptical note deserve a special mention.[1] Here for the first time there is an expression of doubt about the possibility of knowing certain things and a dim awareness that some sort of evidence was necessary before we can afford to make factual assertions. What evidence is there for the existence of Indra unless someone has seen him? One stanza in a hymn says, 'One and another say, "there is no Indra". Who hath beheld him? Whom then shall we honour?'[2] Who again can be sure about the fact or nature of creation when no one has beheld the spectacle, 'Who has seen that the Boneless One bears the Bony, when he is first born? Where is the breath, the blood and the soul of the earth? Who would approach the wise man to ask this?' (Ko dadarśa prathamaṃ jāyamānaṃ, asthanvantaṃ yad anasthā vibharti, bhūmya asur asṛgātmā kva svit, ko vidvāṃsam upagāt praṣṭum etat. RV. 1.164.4). It will be noticed that the author of this statement is the same as the person who felt uncertain about himself (*v. supra*, 6). Now Prasad has questioned the propriety of concluding that these questions suggest an attitude of scepticism and says that 'either they are simply meant to introduce a discussion, or at the most they indicate a confession of ignorance on the part of the individual, who puts them' (*op. cit.*, p. 24). Prasad is quite right in pointing out that this hymn contains the subject matter of a *brahmodya* (*v. infra*, 46) at which questions of this type were asked, but if we examine the nature of this question itself, it will be seen that it cannot be explained away as a confession of ignorance on the part of the author. The question expresses the puzzlement of one who cannot understand (in a philosophical sense) how a Boneless Being can produce a Bony offspring—an apparent contradiction. Quite apart from the contradictory nature of this statement, what evidence was there to believe in it. People doubted the existence of Indra because they could not see him and the Nāsadīya hymn poses the problem, 'the gods are posterior to this creation: if so, who knows whence it evolved?' (arvāg devā'sya visarjanenātha ko veda yata ābabhūva, RV. 10.129.6). Surely it is in this same sceptical spirit that it is asked, ko dadarśa . . .? (who has seen . . .?), meaning thereby 'who could have seen this spectacle for us to know that it did really happen?'. The fact that the author of this hymn doubts his own nature and confesses in all humility

[1] For a collection of sceptical stanzas in the Ṛgveda, *v.* Radhakrishnan and Moore, *A Source Book of Indian Philosophy*, pp. 34–36.

[2] N'endra astī ti nema u tva āha, ka īṃ dadarśa kamabhi ṣṭavāma, RV. 8.100.3 (=8.89.3, Griffith's Translation).

that he is 'asking these questions out of immaturity and ignorance' (pākaḥ pṛcchāmi manasāvijānan, 1.164.5) does not mark him off as an ignoramus, any more than Socrates could be deemed to be ignorant because he confessed that he knew nothing.

(8) The Scepticism of the Nāsadīya hymn (RV. 10.129), which has been unanimously accepted by scholars,[1] is denied by Prasad[2] following Sāyaṇa. The hymn ends on a sceptical note according to the usually accepted interpretation[3] and the question as to whether this is scepticism or not depends on the interpretation given to this last stanza, which reads:

Iyam viśṛṣṭir yata ābabhūva
Yadi vā dadhe yadi vā na
Yo' syādhyakṣaḥ parame vyomant .
So aṅga veda yadi vā na veda, 10.129.7.

Let us consider Sāyaṇa's explanation, especially since Prasad claims that it agrees with his.[4] Commenting on the first two lines Sāyaṇa says: 'The Highest Self which is the material cause from which this creation (i.e. this diverse creation variegated by way of its mountains, rivers, oceans, etc.) has evolved, i.e. has arisen, is indeed the One who either bears, i.e. sustains or does not sustain this; and thus, who else indeed would be capable of sustaining it: if (anyone) sustains it, it must be the Lord Himself, who would sustain it and no other'.[5]

[1] In addition to the translators we may mention Keith, *Religion and Philosophy of the Vedas*, HOS., Vol. 32, p. 435; Ranade, *A Constructive Survey of Upanishadic Philosophy*, p. 3; Barua, *History of Pre-Buddhistic Indian Philosophy*, p. 16; Winternitz, *Geschichte der indischen Litterature*, Vol. I, pp. 87, 88.

[2] *Op. cit.*, pp. 25 ff.

[3] Griffith translates,

'He the first origin of this creation, whether he formed it all or did not form it,
Whose eye controls this world in highest heaven, he verily knows it, or perhaps he knows not'.

Op. cit., Vol. IV, p. 368.

[4] Cp. Prasad, '. . . compare Sāyaṇa's interpretation of the verse which agrees with that of mine' (*op. cit.*, p. 27, fn. 1).

[5] Yata upādānabhūtātparamātmana iyam viśṛṣṭir vividhā girinadīsamudrādirūpeṇa vicitrā śṛṣṭir ābabhūvājāta so'pi kila yadi vā dadhe dhārayati yadi vā na dhārayati evañ ca ko nāmānyo dhartuṃ śaknuyāt yadi dhārayedīśvara eva dhārayennānya iti, *op. cit.*, Vol. 6, p. 410.

In the light of this comment Sāyaṇa's translation of the first two lines would be as follows:

> 'That (Highest Self) from whom this creation arose,
> Either sustains it or does not sustain it.'

The comment on the next two lines is as follows: 'The Highest Lord who is such a person does indeed ("indeed" in the sense of "as is well known") know, i.e. understands: if he does not know, i.e. does not understand, who else indeed would know: the sense is that the omniscient Lord alone would know about this creation and no other'.[1] This implies the following translation of the last two lines:

> 'He who is the Lord in the highest heaven;
> He verily knows, if (anyone else) does not know'.

Sāyaṇa's translation of the first two lines is unobjectionable from the point of view of grammar and syntax though his contention is that the second line means, 'the (Highest Self) alone sustains it and no one else', which is not apparent from even his literal rendering of the sentence. But his translation of the fourth line is clearly at variance with grammar, for he alters the subject of the verb 'veda' of the second sentence from 'saḥ' to 'ka anyaḥ' (understood) without any support from the original. If we have misunderstood Sāyaṇa in attributing to him such an unwarranted periphrasis, he is at least translating this line as 'he verily knows or does not know' and interpreting it to mean 'it is only he who knows and no one else', although it is evident that this sentence cannot mean this either in a literal or a figurative sense. Now Prasad, speaking of the second and fourth lines of this verse, observes, 'These two clauses do not express doubt or ignorance, but mean and that quite in accordance with idiom that it is only He who bore it, and no body else and it is He who knows it and no body else respectively' (*op. cit.*, p. 27, fn. 1), but he does not translate the verse or explain how the only possible literal translation can idiomatically mean what he and Sāyaṇa try to make it mean. It is evident that Sāyaṇa is really trying to explain the verse away rather than to interpret what it strictly meant since he could not countenance the claim that the sacred scriptures contained statements sceptical about the knowledge or power of the deity but we cannot be led by these considerations.

[1] Īdṛśo yaḥ parameśvaraḥ so aṅga aṅgeti prasiddhau so'pi nāma veda jānāti, yadi vā na veda na jānāti ko nāma anyo janīyāt sarvajña īśvara eva taṃ śṛṣṭiṃ jāniyāt nānya ityarthaḥ, *op. cit.*, Vol. 6, p. 471.

(9) The scepticism of this hymn is interesting not merely because it ends on a sceptical note but because it does so, after taking account of almost every possibility with regard to the problem of the origin of the world. If we consider the problem in the abstract at the purely philosophical level, we can say that we can either know the answer to this question or we cannot.[1] If we say we can know the answer, we can suggest either that the world was created or it was not. If we say that the world was created, we can say that it was created out of Being or Non-Being. If we say it is out of Being we may say that it is created either out of matter or out of spirit. An analysis of the hymn reveals that all these suggestions are implicit in it, although it offers its own theory tentatively by trying to synthesize the concepts of Being and Non-Being, of matter and of spirit. We may diagrammatically represent the alternatives considered in the hymn in the light of its statements as follows:

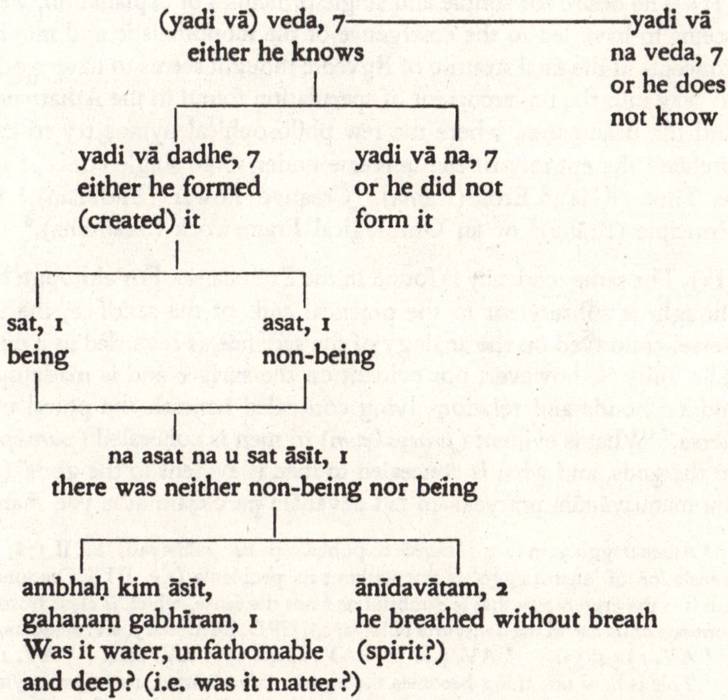

[1] We are leaving out the possibility that the question is meaningless in the Positivist's sense of the term.

(10) Despite the (to us) dogmatic presentation of his own theory, the sceptical conclusion, after taking account of almost all the possible answers to this question, nearly approaches scepticism with regard to the possibility of knowledge in respect of the problem of the origin of the world. This scepticism which is based on the consideration that 'since the gods came after the creation (śṛṣṭi-, *lit.* emission, emanation) no one knows how the world began' (arvāg devāsya visarjanenātha ko veda yata ābabhūva, 6) because no one was there to *behold* the spectacle (cp. ko. *dadarśa* ... ?, *supra*, 7), is soon forgotten in the orthodox tradition. However, it leaves its mark in (or is rediscovered by?) Buddhism, where Brahmā, reputed to be 'the creator', (sajitā, D. I.18 < śṛj-i-tā(5) = Skr. śraṣṭā: cp. kattā, nimmātā, *loc. cit.*) is said to be ignorant of his own origin (*loc. cit.*, *v. infra*, 645). Moreover, it is said that 'it is not possible to conceive of the beginning of the world: a first cause (*lit.* prior end) cannot be known'.[1]

(11) The desire for simple and single principles of explanation, which seems to have led to the emergence of the monotheistic and monistic concepts in the final stratum of Ṛgvedic thought seems to have worked its way into the undercurrent of speculation found in the Atharvaveda and the Brāhmaṇas, where the few philosophical hymns try to comprehend the entirety of the universe under some single concept such as Time (Kāla),[2] Eros (Kāma),[3] Creative Power (Brahman),[4] Life Principle (Prāṇa)[5] or an Ontological Framework (Skambha).[6]

(12) The same tendency is found in the Brāhmaṇas. For although here thought is subservient to the practical ends of the sacrifice, the universe, conceived on the analogy of the sacrifice, is regarded as a unity. The unity is, however, not evident on the surface and is made up of hidden bonds and relations lying concealed beneath the plural universe.[7] 'What is evident (*pratyakṣam*) to men is concealed (*parokṣam*) to the gods, and what is concealed to men is evident to the gods' (yad vai manuṣyānāṃ pratyakṣam tad devānāṃ parokṣam atha yan manuṣ-

[1] Anamataggo'yaṃ . . . saṃsāro pubbākoṭi na paññāyati, S. II.178; the translation of 'anamataggo' is not without its problems (*s.v.* PTS. Dictionary) but it is the etymology that is doubtful and not the sense, which is clear from the contexts of its use in the Saṃyutta Nikāya; cp. CPD. Dictionary, s.v. anamatagga.

[2] AV. 19.54, 53. [3] AV. 9.2. [4] AV. 19.42. [5] AV. 11.4. [6] AV. 10.7.

[7] This is how one thing becomes the mystic name (nāma), the mystic symbol (rūpa), the mystic body (tanu) and the mystic bond (bandhu) of another. For examples and references to Brāhmaṇic literature see Ranade and Belvalkar, *History of Indian Philosophy*, II, pp. 62–5.

yānām parokṣam tad devānām pratyakṣam, Tāṇḍyamahābrāhmaṇa, 22.10.3). In the Ṛgveda there was a primitive conception of causality underlying the idea of ṛta which seems to have denoted the 'course of things' or the observable physical order of the world before it acquired a moral and theological connotation. But in the Brāhmaṇas, which value 'what lies beyond the sphere of the senses' (parokṣa-),[1] the conception of a causal order gives way to that of a magical order.[2]

(13) It is in the Brāhmaṇas that we find developed what became for orthodoxy the supreme source of knowledge—the revealed scriptural text. As Ranade and Belvalkar say, 'the Brāhmaṇas came to invest the mantras with the character of divine revelation. They are at times spoken of as eternally self-subsistent and coeval with God-head—if not actually prior to Him. At other times—and especially *in the newer Brāhmaṇa texts* (*underlining* mine)—they are described as creations of Prajāpati, the head of the whole pantheon'.[3] The hymns are said to be seen, learned or found generally by some special insight on the part of the seers and not made or composed by them.[4]

(14) The reasoning in the Brāhmaṇas is analogical and centres round the symbolism of the sacrifice. The analogies are remote. A fanciful etymology, a myth, legend or a vague similarity is sufficient to establish a connection between two things.[5] An explanation to be satisfactory has to be made in terms of a sacrificial analogy. Examples of typically Brāhmaṇic reasoning may be found at ŚB. 11.4.1.12–15, which describes the debate between Uddālaka Āruṇi and Svaidāyana Gautama. The following are two arguments found there: (1) Atha *yad*apuro'nuvākyakā prayājā bhavanti, *tasmād* imāḥ prajā'dantakā jāyante, i.e. and *since* the fore-offerings are without preliminary formulae, therefore creatures are born here without teeth, 11.4.1.12, (2) atha *yad*ājyahaviṣaḥ prayājā bhavanti *tasmāt* kumārasya retaḥ siktanna sambhavaty udakamivaiva bhavaty udakam iva hyājyam, i.e.

[1] The expression parokṣapriyā hí devāḥ, i.e. the gods love what is not evident, is common in the Brāhmaṇas; *v. op. cit.*, p. 63.

[2] Oldenberg, *Religion des Veda*, pp. 315 ff., 321 ff.; Keith, HOS., Vol. 32, pp. 379 ff.; Frauwallner, *Geschichte der indischen Philosophie*, Band I, pp. 41 ff. References to magic are found in the Ṛgveda and the Yajurveda as well, *v.* H. Lüders, Varuna, Band II, Göttingen 1959, pp. 509–45, *Die magische Kraft des Ṛta in den vedischen Mythen.*

[3] *Op. cit.*, p. 56.

[4] Keith, HOS., Vol. 32, p. 482.

[5] *v.* Ranade and Belvalkar, *op. cit.*, p. 63.

and *since* the fore-offerings have ghee for their offering material, a boy's seed is not productive but is like water since ghee is like water. This sounds utter balderdash, but just as much as a biological reason would be given today as to why a 'boy's seed is not productive', nothing short of a 'sacrificial' reason would have satisfied a Brāhmaṇic thinker. Anything to be understood had to be explained on a sacrificial analogy and discovering these analogies (bandhutā) was as much an art as the reasoning itself. The reasoning in the above argument may be exhibited as follows since much is taken for granted in the arguments:

1. Ghee fore-offerings are not productive (since ghee is like water—*v.* udakam iva hyājyam—and water is not productive in a biological sense)
2. Ghee fore-offerings are like the boy's seed (since both are at the beginning, ghee fore-offerings at the beginning of the sacrifice and the boy at the beginning of life)
3. Therefore, the boy's seed is not productive.

The form of this argument from analogy would be as follows:

1. *A* has the characteristic *p*
2. *A* is like *B*
3. Therefore, *B* has the characteristic *p*.

The remotest connection, natural or magical, between two things is sufficient for the Brāhmaṇas to draw the analogy that '*A* is like *B*' on the basis of which inferences are made.

(15) There is rarely any admission of the need for or possibility of doubt and investigation (mīmāṃsā)[1] is always carried out with the conviction that the correct interpretation of the revealed texts opens the door to all knowledge but there is mention of vicikitsā, or the doubt that premotes inquiry.[2] Vicikitsā or 'doubt' is in fact one of the recognized states of mind. The Śathapatha Brāhmaṇa says, 'wish, conception, *doubt*, faith, lack of faith, determination, lack of determination, shame, thought, fear—all this is mind' (kāmaḥ saṃkalpo *vicikitsā* śraddhāsraddhā dhṛtiradhṛtirhrīrddhīrbbhīr ity etat sarvam mana eva . . ., 14.4.3.9); thus, 'Pratardana . . . questions about his *doubt*' (Pratardanaḥ *vicikitsam* papraccha, Kauś. Br. 26.5). Of specific

[1] *v.* Keith, *Religion and Philosophy of the Vedas*, HOS., Vol. 32, p. 483.
[2] *Ibid.*

doubts there is mention of the doubt regarding man's survival in the next world.[1] Some of the doubts raised appear to be genuinely philosophical as when it is asked how the raw and red cow can yield hot white milk and how the boneless semen can produce creatures with bones[2] but the answers given in terms of sacrificial analogies are, needless to say, hardly satisfactory.

(16) In the Āraṇyakas knowledge comes to be greatly valued; where the knowledge of the symbolism of the ritual was what really mattered, the performance of the ritual itself may be dispensed with. The knowledge is not prized for its own sake but is invariably considered to be a means to an end. The usual formula would be that knowledge of *X* gives *Y*, where *X* may stand for some item of empirical or metaphysical knowledge and *Y* for anything from material gain to spiritual reward. Thus we have the following statement in the Aitareya Āraṇyaka: 'The Hotṛ mounts the swing, the Udgātṛ the seat made of Udumbara wood. The swing is masculine and the seat feminine and they form a union. Thus he makes a union at the beginning of the uktha in order to get offspring *He who knows this gets offspring and cattle*.'[3] The growing importance attached to knowledge, however, is such that everything had to be subordinated and one's entire life geared to this end by the time of the Upaniṣads.

(17) In the Upaniṣads there is a continuation of the theme that knowledge gives some kind of reward. He who knows (veda, Bṛh. 1.3.7.), for instance, the superiority of the breathing principle (prāṇa-) over the sensory and motor organs becomes his true self and the enemy who hates him is crushed (*loc. cit.*). There is, however, no explanation as to why this knowledge should give this specified result. One of the rewards is immortality, conceived in the earliest Upaniṣads as the escape from a second death (punar-mṛtyu-): 'He who knows that air is the totality of all individuals conquers repeated death.'[4]

(18) This great importance attached to knowledge paves the way for thinkers to speculate on the nature of reality and the problems of life without being hampered by the limitations of the Vedic tradition. The influence of the earlier mythology and theology is no doubt felt, but

[1] *v.* Keith, *Religion and Philosophy of the Vedas*, HOS., Vol. 32, p. 483.

[2] Ranade and Belvalkar, *op. cit.*, p. 73.

[3] Prenkhaṃ hotādhirohaty audumbarīm āsandim udgātā, vṛsā vai prenkho yoṣā sandī, tan mithunam eva, tad ukthamukhe karoti prajātyai. Prajāyate prajayā paśubhir *ya evaṃ veda*, Aitareya Āraṇyaka, 1.2.4.10,11.

[4] Vāyuḥ samaṣṭiḥ apa punar mṛtyuṃ jayati ya evaṃ veda, Bṛh. 3.3.2.

the thinkers bring a fresh mind to bear on the problems they seek to solve.

(19) The tendency especially on the part of Indian scholars to regard the Upaniṣads as presenting a single systematic and coherent philosophy on the basis of the interpretations and expositions of either Śaṅkara, Rāmānuja, Madhva or others has much obscured the independence and originality of the speculations of many thinkers of the Upaniṣadic tradition. Such an attitude fails to take account of the fact that although the Upaniṣadic thinkers owed allegiance to the Vedic tradition, they were free to theorize on matters and topics that fell outside the scope of that tradition. They not only belonged to separate schools but were often separated and isolated geographically. Besides, many generations would have lapsed between one outstanding teacher and another. We find evidence of conflicting theories, of the criticism and replacement of one theory by another and the influence of earlier views on later thinkers, who build on them. All this would not have been possible if there was a single uniform philosophy called the *vedānta*, which is unfolded on every page of the Upaniṣadic texts.

(20) If we examine the Upaniṣadic texts, considering the theories found in separate sections or ideological units separately, we would find that the thinkers of the Upaniṣads can be classified into two different categories. Firstly, there are those who found and propound their views by indulging in metaphysical speculation and rational argument not without a basis in experience, despite the earlier mythology weighing heavily on their minds. Secondly, there are those who profess their theories as an expression and interpretation of what they claim to have themselves experienced by the practice of yoga, although in the form in which they are presented they are dressed in a good deal of metaphysical clothing. The former set of thinkers are usually met with in the Early Upaniṣads while the latter are generally represented in the Middle and Late Upaniṣads, but no absolute division is possible since the rational metaphysicians are found in some of the Middle and Late Upaniṣads (e.g. Praśna) while references to yoga philosophy and practice are not entirely absent in the Early Upaniṣads.

(21) The difference between these two types of thinkers, namely the rational metaphysicians who found their theories on *a priori* and empirical reasoning and the contemplative intuitionists who claim to acquire special insights into the nature of reality by following certain techniques of mind control and culture, would be clearer if we take

samples of their theories and statements and examine the epistemological bases of their thought. Let us first consider some of the metaphysical theories and see on what kind of thinking and reasoning they are based.

(22) Let us take the philosophy of Uddālaka. His philosophy has been treated separately[1] by both Barua[2] as well as Ruben.[3] Ruben examines his ontology and calls it a 'hylozoistische Monismus',[4] and refers to Uddālaka as 'der alteste Materialist'[5] and as a 'Realist'.[6] Barua starts with his theory of knowledge and is inclined to call him an Empiricist. Since we are interested only in this aspect of his thought we may examine Barua's appraisal of it. He says; '... Uddālaka propounded an empirical theory of knowledge. Henceforth let no one speak, he asserts, of anything but that which is heard, perceived or cognized. He seems repeatedly to point out:—The only right method of scientific investigation into the nature of reality is that of inference by way of induction' (*op. cit.*, p. 138). Later Barua seems to qualify Uddālaka's claims to be a pure empiricist: 'According to his own showing the senses furnish us with sufficient indications from which the knowing mind can easily infer the nature and relations of things in themselves'.[7]

(23) Now the statement that Barua attributes to Uddālaka, namely 'henceforth let no one speak of anything but that which is heard, perceived or cognized' does not seem to bear the meaning that Barua gives to it, when we consider its literal translation in the context in which it appears. Uddālaka propounds the elements of his philosophy and then says, 'Verily, it was just this that the great householders and great students of sacred knowledge knew when they said of old, "no one will now mention to us what we have not heard, what we have not perceived, what we have not thought" ' (etaddha sma vai tad vidvāṃsa āhuḥ purve mahāśālā mahaśrotriyāḥ na no 'dya kaścana aśrutaṃ, amataṃ, avijñātam udāhariṣyatī ti, Ch. 6.4.5). This statement does not

[1] I.e. separately from the rest of Upaniṣadic thought.

[2] *A History of Pre-Buddhistic Indian Philosophy*, pp. 124–42.

[3] *Die Philosophen der Upanishaden*, Bern, 1947, pp. 156–77; cp. *Geschichte der Indischen Philosophie, Einführung in die Indienkunde*, Berlin, 1954, pp. 25–7, 81–94.

[4] *Die Philosophen der Upanishaden*, p. 166.

[5] *Geschichte der Indischen Philosophie*, p. 81.

[6] *Die Philosophen der Upanishaden*, p. 156.

[7] *Op. cit.*, p. 140; *v.* his subtitle, 'Uddālaka neither trusts nor yet distrusts the evidence of the senses'.

seem to convey anything more than that anyone who has grasped the theory set forth by Uddālaka knows all there is to be known and therefore no one can teach him, i.e. make him hear, think or understand anything new. It is a dogmatic assertion claiming finality for his philosophy. It does not mean, 'henceforth let no one speak ...' but 'today (adya) no one (na kaścana) will speak (udāhariṣyati) ...' and no epistemological significance can be attached to it.

(24) Whether Uddālaka is an empiricist or not can only be determined by examining the epistemic origin of his theory and when we do so, he appears to be basically a rationalist, who makes considerable use of empirical premises to illustrate his theory and serve as a basis for his metaphysical insights.

(25) Uddālaka for the first time in the history of Indian thought expressly suggests a proof of the reality of Being (sat) instead of merely assuming it, when he asserts, 'some say that ... from non-Being Being was produced. But, verily, my dear, whence could this be? ... how could Being be produced from Non-Being'? (taddhaika āhuḥ ... asataḥ saj jāyata. Kutas tu khalu, saumya, evam syāt ... katham asataḥ saj jāyeta, Ch. 6.2.1, 2).

(26) Having proved the reality of being by pure reasoning, Uddālaka had to explain how the world could have a plurality of things, if Being (sat) alone were real. If Being was the only reality, plurality is mere appearance. The different shapes and names that things have, cannot be real, for Being is the one and only substance that exists. This is illustrated by some empirical examples. When we see an object of clay, we know that its shape and name can be changed but its substance cannot be changed for 'the modification is merely a verbal distinction, a name, the reality is just clay' (vācārambhaṇaṃ vikāro nāmadheyam mṛttikety eva satyam, 6.1.4).

(27) It is not only the present plurality that has to be accounted for but the origin of this plurality. Here Uddālaka uncritically accepts the earlier mythological notions and says that Being *wishes* to multiply and procreate and produces heat (6.2.3). Heat (tejas) produces water (apas) and water food (annam) (6.2.3, 4). Empirical evidence is adduced in favour of this causal sequence,[1] where it is pointed out that when we

[1] Note that heat, water and food are in the relationship of root and sprout; '... with food for a sprout look for water as the root. With water as a sprout look for heat as the root'... annena śungenāpo mūlam anvicceha, abdhiḥ ... śuṅgena tejo mūlam anviccha, 6.8.4).

are hot, water (i.e. tears or perspiration) is produced (6.2.3) and that water in the form of rain produces food (6.2.4).

(28) Original being conceived as an active and animating principle now produces everything out of its three emergent products, heat, water and food (6.3.2). So all things are made out of these three constituents, which are called the three colours or forms (trīṇī rūpāṇi, 6.4.1) because heat is supposed to be red in colour, water white and food or earth dark (6.4.2), again presumably on empirical grounds. Man himself is therefore a product of these three forms. But how can the mind or voice be explained as a by-product of these three primary products? Uddālaka here speaks of the coarse (sthaviṣṭaḥ), medium (madhyamaḥ) and fine (aṇiṣṭhaḥ) constituents of these products (6.5) and argues that the finest essence of food moves upward on the analogy of butter moving upward when milk is churned (6.6.1) and becomes the mind. Food becoming mind is again proved empirically on the grounds that if you refrain taking food while drinking only water for some time you forget what is in your mind[1] (6.7.1–3). Physiological processes like hunger and thirst are likewise explained as being due to the interaction of the primary products. You are hungry (aśanā = *aś*-a-*nā*) because water leads off (*na*yanti) the food eaten (*aś*itam) (6.8.3). This argument is based on fanciful etymology and is reminiscent of the type of reasoning found in the Brāhmaṇas (*v. supra*, 14).

(29) We are therefore produced from Being though we do not know it (6.9.2). We also reach Being at death for in the process of dying there is a reversal of the process of production, the mind (the product of food) goes into breath (prāṇa, the product of water) and breath in turn to heat and heat into the highest deity, at which point he knows not (6.15.1–2), for he cannot recognize the people who gather round him (*loc. cit.*). What is empirically urged by observations made on the dying man is also rationally arrived at where it is suggested that the substance of our personality, constituting the mind, breath and voice are so completely mixed up on reaching homogeneous Being that there would be no separate mind to know that 'I am this one' (iyam aham asmi) or 'I am that one' (iyam aham asmi) so that we know not that we have reached Being (6.9.1, 6.10.1).

[1] This is one of the earliest experiments performed with the idea of testing a theory; cp. Ruben, 'Er liess seinen Sohn Śvetaketu fünfzehn Tage nicht fur einen Ritus, sondern als materialistiches Experiment fasten. . . ', *Geschichte der Indischen Philosophie*, p. 87.

(30) Uddālaka ought to have said in accordance with his metaphysics that all beings are produced from Being at birth without knowing it and subsequently reach Being at death without knowing it. But the necessity of assigning a special reward to knowledge as was the prevalent fashion of the times (*v. supra*, 16) probably makes him say inconsistently that those who do not know his theory become tigers, lions, etc., in the next life (6.9.3) while those who know his theory (which is assumed to be the truth) reach Being and are merged in it never to return, their belief in truth ensuring this just as much as he who speaks the truth is saved in a trial by ordeal (6.16.1–3).

(31) At the end of the lecture, Uddālaka's son understands (vijajñau, 6.16.3) the theory that was propounded. There is no suggestion or implication whatsoever that the theory was to be comprehended by the practice of special techniques such as yoga. It was merely this rational understanding that was considered necessary for ensuring the goal of reaching Being at death. The theory itself is clearly a product of reason and speculation, as we have shown. The reasoning is partly *a priori* and partly empirical, although the *a priori* reasoning is not consistent and the empirical conclusions not warranted by the evidence adduced. It is also necessary to note the impact of the earlier mythology and the Brāhmaṇic 'reasoning' on the thought of Uddālaka. When the Buddha says that there was a class of brahmins who propounded theories on the basis of reason and speculation (*v. infra*, 420 ff.), was he thinking of thinkers of the type of Uddālaka, whose name and the central theme of whose philosophy was known to the Jātakas?[1]

(32) Let us now consider another metaphysical theory which is a product of rational and empirical reasoning and which is attributed to Prajāpati in the section 8.7–12 of the Chāndogya Upaniṣad. Its interest for Buddhism lies in the fact that it contains a kind of reasoning, which is taken to its logical conclusion in Buddhism (*v. infra*, 39).

(33) The inquiry begins with the assumption that there is a soul (ātman) which has the characteristics, *inter alia*, of being free from death (vimṛtyuḥ), free from sorrow (viśokaḥ) and having real thoughts (satyasaṃkalpaḥ) (8.7.1). The problem is to locate this soul in one's personality.

(34) The first suggestion is that the soul may be the physical personality, which is seen reflected in a pan of water (8.8.1). But this

[1] *v.* Barua, *op. cit.*, pp. 125–7.

physical personality, it is argued on empirical grounds, is subject to death; 'it perishes in the wake of the perishing of this body' (asyaiva śarīrasya nāśam anv eṣa naśyati, 8.9.1). So this will not do (nāham atra bhogyam paśyāmi *loc. cit.*). This conclusion embodies a rational argument of the following sort: if *X* (the body, in this instance) has the characteristic not-*p* (i.e. not free from death), then it cannot be an instance of *A* (the ātman), which necessarily has (by definition, i.e. assumption) the characteristic *p*.

(35) The next suggestion is that the soul may be identified with the self in the dream-state (8.10.1). This escapes the objection against the previous suggestion for the dream-self 'is not slain when (the body) is slain' (na vadhenāsya hanyate, 8.10.2). The logic of the reasoning is as follows: here is an instance of *Y* (the dream-self), which has the characteristic *p* (free from death) and which therefore may be an instance of *A* which must have the characteristic *p*. But this suggestion too is turned down (*v.* nāham atra bhogyam paśyāmi, 8.10.2) for not only must *Y* have the characteristic *p* to be an instance of *A*, but it must also have the characteristic *q* (free from sorrow, viśokaḥ). But it is seen on empirical grounds that *Y* does not have the characteristic *q*: 'he comes to experience as it were what is unpleasant, he even weeps as it were' (apriyavetteva bhavati, api rodatīva, 8.10.2). Therefore, *Y* cannot be an instance of *A*.

(36) The next suggestion is that the soul may be identified with the state of deep sleep (8.11.1). This, it may be observed, escapes the objections against the two previous suggestions. The reasoning may be represented as follows: here is an instance of *Z* (the state of deep sleep), which has the characteristic *p* (free from death; *v.* etad amṛtam, this is immortal, 8.11.1) and also the characteristic *q* (free from sorrow or grief; *v.* samastaḥ samprasannaḥ . . . etad abhayam, being composed and serene . . . this is free from fear, 8.11.1) and which therefore may be an instance of *A*, which must have the characteristics *p* and *q*. But this suggestion too is turned down, (*v.* nāham atra bhogyam paśyāmi, 8.11.1) for not only must *Z* have the characteristics *p* and *q* to be an instance of *A*, but it must also have the characteristic *r* (real thoughts, satya-saṃkalpaḥ). But it is seen on empirical grounds (i.e. by introspection) that *Z* does not have the characteristic *r*; 'in truth he does not know himself with the thought "I am he" nor indeed the things here—he becomes one who has gone to destruction' (naha khalv ayam evaṃ sampraty ātmānaṃ jānāti, ayam aham asmī ti, no

evemāni bhūtāni, vināśam evāpīto bhavati, 8.11.1). The argument up to this point is that the ātman cannot be identified with any aspect of the personality, physical or psychological.

(37) Not satisfied with this purely negative conclusion empirically arrived at, the metaphysical assumption is then made that the ātman (not identifiable with its states) must be an unobservable entity (a pure ego[1]) within the personality with all its aspects. 'The body is mortal but is the support of the immortal bodiless ātman' (martyam ... idam śarīram ... tadasyāmṛtasyāśarīrasyātmano'dhiṣṭhānam, 8.12.1). Dogmatic utterances have now taken the place of rational arguments and Prajāpati now indulges in his own quota of Brāhmaṇic 'reasoning'. He sees an analogy between 'air, clouds, lightning and thunder' on the one hand and the ātman on the other, since both are bodiless (8.12.2) and argues that since the air, etc., 'reach the highest light and appear each with its own form' (paraṃ jyotir upasampadya svena svena rupeṇābhiniṣpadyante, 8.12.2), the ātman too, similarly (evam, 8.11.2), 'rises up from this body and reaches the highest light and appears in its own form' (asmāc charīrāt samutthāya paraṃ jyotir upasampadya svena rupeṇābhiniṣpadyate, 8.11.3).

(38) Incidentally, it is significant that elsewhere in the Upaniṣads the soul (ātman) is identified with the dream-state (Bṛh. 4.3.9, 10; Ch. 8.3.2) and with the state of deep sleep (Bṛh. 2.1.16–20) and therefore this theory constitutes a criticism of these earlier theories (*v. supra*, 19).

(39) It will be seen that the Buddha in advocating the theory of anattā follows a pattern of argument very similar to that used by Prajāpati here in the earlier part of his theory. The Buddha like Prajāpati takes various aspects of the personality and shows that none of them can be identified with the ātman, since they do not have the characteristics of the ātman. The following is a sample of such an argument:

Buddha—What think you? Is the physical personality permanent or impermanent? (Taṃ kiṃ maññasi? ... rūpaṃ niccaṃ vā aniccaṃ vā ti, M.I. 232)

Saccaka—It is impermanent (aniccaṃ ..., *loc. cit.*)

Buddha—Is what is impermanent sorrowful or happy? (Yam panāniccaṃ dukkhaṃ vā taṃ sukhaṃ vā ti, *loc. cit.*)

[1] On the use of this term, *v.* Broad, ***The Mind and its Place in Nature***, pp. 214 ff., 278 ff., 558 ff., and 603 ff.

Saccaka—Sorrowful (dukkhaṃ . . ., *loc. cit.*)

Buddha—Of what is impermanent, sorrowful and liable to change, is it proper to regard it as 'this is mine, this I am, this is my soul'? (Yam panāniccaṃ dukkhaṃ vipariṇāmadhammaṃ, kallan nu taṃ samanupassituṃ: etam mama, *eso'ham asmi*, eso me attā ti, M. I.233)

Saccaka—It is not (No h'idaṃ . . ., *loc. cit.*).

This same argument is now repeated for other aspects of the personality such as feeling (vedanā), ideation (saññā), etc. (*loc. cit.*). One may compare the expression used in the Pāli passage, *eso aham asmi* to indicate the identification, with the corresponding expression, *ayam aham asmi* (Ch. 8.11.1) used for the same purpose, in the Upaniṣad. The main difference in the attitude of Prajāpati and the Buddha is that the former assumes the existence of an ātman and on failing to identify it with any of the states of the personality, continues to assume that it must exist within it and is not satisfied with the results of the purely empirical investigation, while the latter as an Empiricist makes use of the definition of the concept of the ātman without assuming its existence (or non-existence) and is satisfied with the empirical investigation which shows that no such ātman exists because there is no evidence for its existence. Was it those who reasoned in this manner basing their reasoning on definitions (lakṣaṇa-), who were called *lakkhaṇa-vādā* (Nd. I.294; *v. infra*, 367)?

(40) Whether these Upaniṣadic theories were known to Buddhism and had an impact on the thought of Buddhism can only be determined in the light of evidence. It is worth noting that Prajāpati's theory of the state of the soul after death is utterly different from Uddālaka's. In the Brahmajāla Sutta there is a reference to a theory held by a school of brahmins (eke samaṇa-*brāhmaṇā*, D. I.30) to the effect that the soul after death has form (rūpī), is without defect (arogo, *lit.* without disease) and is conscious (saññī) (D. I.31). Prajapati's theory assigned all these characteristics to the soul after death. The soul has form since 'it appears in its own *form*' (svena *rūpe*ṇābhiniṣpadyate, 8.12.3). It is without defect or disease since it is said that 'when crossing that bridge (to the next world) if one is blind he becomes no longer blind, if he is sick he becomes no longer sick' (etaṃ setuṃ tīrtvāndhaḥ sann anandho bhavāti, viddhaḥ sann aviddho bhavati, Ch. 8.4.2). And the soul is conscious because if it so desires it becomes conscious of enjoyment with women, chariots or relations (8.12.3). According to Uddālaka's theory on the other hand the soul would be without form

(arūpī), without defect (arogo) and without consciousness[1] (asaññī) being merged in Being, which is another theory about the after-life ascribed to a school of brahmins in the Brahmajāla Sutta (*v.* D. I.32).

(41) Let us now briefly consider some aspects of the thought of Yājñavalkya. Yājñavalkya's importance for us lies in the fact that he too is a rationalist thinker, who popularized a double negative form of expression, used in the Buddhist texts. His theory of survival also seems to be known to Buddhism.[1]

(42) Yājñavalkya has been called a mystic (Mystiker)[2] by Ruben but this is misleading since there is no reason to believe that Yājñavalkya's theories are based on any kind of mystical experience as were the views of most of the thinkers of the Middle and Late Upaniṣads. Besides, another fact that has not been considered in the treatment of Yājñavalkya is that the teachings ascribed to him in different places in the Upaniṣads do not seem to be of a piece, consistent with each other. For instance, on the one hand the *neti neti* doctrine or the transcendent conception of Brahman, who is describable only in terms of negative epithets, is attributed to him (Bṛh. 3.9.26, 4.5.13) and on the other hand the pantheistic doctrine totally opposed to it to the effect that Brahman is 'made of this, made of that' (idammayaḥ adomaya iti, Bṛh. 4.4.5). The probable explanation for this is that several incompatible doctrines were put in the mouth of an outstanding teacher.

(43) We shall confine ourselves to Yājñavalkya of the *neti neti* doctrine and consider the passages ascribed to him in sections 2.4.1–14, 3.9.28 and 4.5.15 of the Bṛhadāraṇyaka Upaniṣad. Now Deussen quite rightly traces 'the primitive source of the entire conception of the unknowableness of the ātman'[3] to the statements ascribed to Yājñavalkya in this Upaniṣad, but it is equally necessary to emphasize the fact that the rational unknowability of the ātman is rationally arrived at and is not a product of mystic experience. In fact Deussen himself points this out when examining (Bṛh. 2.4.12–14= 4.5.13–15), the *locus classicus* of this doctrine, he says, 'On careful consideration two thoughts will be found to be implied here: (1) the supreme ātman is unknowable because he is the all-comprehending unity, whereas all

[1] Note his saying that on reaching Being after death, 'they know not, "I am this one", "I am that one" ' (Ch. 6.10.1).

[2] *Geschichte der Indischen Philosophie*, p. 95.

[3] *The Philosophy of the Upanishads*, Edinburgh, 1906, p. 79.

knowledge presupposes a duality of subject and object; but (2) the individual ātman also is unknowable because in all knowledge he is the knowing subject, consequently can never be the object'.[1] We agree with Deussen that two arguments are implicit in this passage, first that since reality is one and knowledge is dual, we cannot have knowledge of reality and second that the subject of knowledge cannot be known since it is never the object and 'thou canst not know the knower of knowing' (na vijñater vijñātāraṃ vijānīyāḥ, Bṛh. 3.4.2). This is reasoning and not mystic experience.

(44) Yājñavalkya's conception of the after-life is also a product of reasoning. At Bṛh. 3.9.28, he compares man to a tree. Now a tree when it is felled at the root grows up again from the root 'but when a man dies from what root can he grow up' (martyaḥ svin mṛtyunā vṛknaḥ kasmān mūlāt prarohati, 3.9.28.4). One cannot say it is from semen (retasa iti mā vocata, 3.9.28.5) for that is possible even while the person is living. The answer given is cryptic for it is said that 'when born he is not born again for who would again beget him' (jāta eva na jāyate, konvenaṃ *janayet punaḥ*, 3.9.28.7). This is a plain denial of the possibility of rebirth (*punar janman*) and his theory seems to be as he himself states that 'after death there is no consciousness' (na pretya[2] saṃjñāsti, 4.5.13). By this he means the absence of any sense-consciousness, since this is possible only by the presence of the sense-organs, the uniting place (ekāyanam) of the sense-data (3.5.12). But he is at the same time not denying that all consciousness is absent since the subject of consciousness, conceived by him as 'a mass of pure experience' (*ayam ātmā*, anantaro'bāhyaḥ, kṛtsnaḥ *prajñāna-ghana eva*, 4.5.13) persists. So the state of survival is one in which 'there is no saṃjñā' nor a lack of it, i.e. no asaṃjñā. Now in the Majjhima Nikāya (II.231) there is a reference to a school of recluses and brahmins who argued that 'the state of being neither conscious nor unconscious' (na-eva-saññā-na-asaññā) was a peaceful (santa-) and an excellent state (panītam) because on the one hand 'normal consciousness is defective, a disease, a thorn' (saññā rogo saññā gaṇḍo saññā sallam, *loc. cit.*) while 'unconsciousness is utterly bewildering' (asaññā *sammoho*). Yājñavalkya's conclusion is at least the same, though his

[1] *Op. cit.*, pp. 79, 80.

[2] In all the sixteen contexts (*s.v.* 'pre-' in Jacob, *Concordance to the Principal Upaniṣads*) in which this verbal form is used in the Bṛhadāraṇyaka Upaniṣad, the reference is to departure at death.

argument is somewhat different but we may observe the parallel between the use of sammoha in the Pāli passage with the use of *moha-* to denote the bewilderment of Maitreyi (mohāntam āpīpipat) when Yājñavalkya says that 'after death there is no consciousness' at which Yājñavalkya replies, 'I am not speaking of a state of bewilderment' (na vā are'ham *mohaṃ* bravīmi, 8.5.14) probably implying as in the Pāli passage to a state of utter blankness in which there is no consciousness at all.

(45) We have illustrated the use of reason by the Early Upaniṣadic thinkers by the examples of Uddālaka, Prajāpati and Yājñavalkya. While they give unmistakable evidence of the presence of reasoning during this period, the Chāndogya Upaniṣad, according to the interpretation of Śaṅkara, and the translations of Deussen, Hume and Radhakrishnan speaks of Logic (vakovākya-) as being one of the branches of study during this period (*v. infra*, 51). Before we can understand what is meant here by vakovākya- it is necessary to study the origins of the debate for there is reason to believe that it was in and out of these debates that the first conceptions of valid and invalid reasoning arose (*v. infra*, 348). Brough seems to believe otherwise when writing the ERE. article on Logic he says: 'The historical beginnings of logical theory are to be found in the racial dispositions and social conditions which gave occasion for the deliberate control of our trains of thought. In India, it appears to have originated with rules in ceremonial deliberation.'[1] He contrasts the example of India with that of Greece saying that 'in Greece it originated with canons of public debate and scientific instruction'.[2] Randle on the other hand commenting on the Kathāvatthu says that 'logic was preceded by attempts to schematize discussion, attempts which were inevitable in view of the habit of organized public discussion, which prevailed in early India but which could not succeed until the nerve of argument had been separated from the irrelevancies in which the early methodology had obscured it and plainly exposed in the formulation of the syllogism'.[3] We cannot wholly agree with either of these verdicts. If by 'logical theory' Brough meant the problems of epistemology then certainly some of these problems, such as whether testimony (śabda) was a genuine means of knowledge, the meaning of words and

[1] Vol. 8, p. 128. [2] *Ibid.*

[3] H. N. Randle, *Indian Logic in the Early Schools*, Oxford University Press, 1930, p. 14; cp. Th. Stcherbatsky, *Buddhist Logic*, Vol. I, pp. 27 ff.

propositions, the problem of universals may perhaps be ultimately traced to 'ceremonial deliberation' and a significant portion of this was contributed by the Grammarians (Vaiyākaraṇas) but the first awareness of the validity and invalidity of reasoning seems to have arisen out of the debate as much in India as in Greece. On the other hand, Randle seems to imagine that the only forms of valid reasoning must be syllogistic and it was probably this which led him to ignore the foreshadowings of some of the theorems of the propositional calculus in the Kathāvatthu (*v. infra*, 703–710).

(46) The debate in the Indian context seems to have its historical origins in the Vedic institution of the ***brahmodya***[1] (or ***brahmavadya***). A brief glance at the history of the brahmodya seems profitable in so far as it gives a picture of the origin and development of the debate. The earliest brahmodyas are riddles or religious charades which are to be found in the Ṛgveda (1.164, 8.29) or the Atharvaveda (9.9, 10). They frequently occur in the Brāhmaṇas.[2] Their general form is that of question and answer though sometimes the answers are cryptic or the questions presupposed.[3] When the sacrifice became the reigning institution in Brāhmaṇic society, the brahmodya was a minor diversion within it. Bloomfield calls it in this context 'a charade to enliven the mechanical and technical progress of the sacrifice by impressive intellectual pyrotechnics'.[4] Keith says, 'it is a feature of the Vedic sacrifice that at certain points are found Brahmodyas, discussions about the Brahman, the holy power in the universe. Such theosophical riddles are specially common at the horse sacrifice'.[5] The following is an example of such a brahmodya as related in the ŚB. (13.5.2.11 ff.):

11. They hold a Brahmodya in the Sadas . . .
12. *Hotṛ*—Who walketh singly? *Adhvaryu*—the sun.

[1] *v.* Keith, *Religion and Philosophy of the Vedas*, HOS., Vol. 32, pp. 344, 345, 435; A. Ludwig, *Der Rigveda oder die Heiligen Hymnen der Brahmana*, Band III, Prag, 1878, pp. 390 ff.; Bloomfield, *Religion of the Veda*, pp. 216 ff.; Bloomfield, 'The Marriage of Saraṇyū, Tvaṣṭar's Daughter', JAOS., Vol. 15, pp. 172 ff.; M. Haug 'Vedische Räthselfragen und Räthselsprüche', *Transactions of the Munich Academy*, 1875, pp. 7 ff. This last reference is quoted from Bloomfield, JAOS., Vol. 15, fn. ‡, and I have not been able to find this article in the libraries of London and Cambridge.

[2] These references are given in the article of Bloomfield, JAOS., Vol. 15, p. 172.

[3] Bloomfield, JAOS., Vol. 15, p. 172.

[4] *Religion of the Veda*, p. 215.

[5] HOS., Vol. 32, p. 435.

13. *Adhvaryu*—Whose light is equal to the sun?
Hotṛ—The Brahman.
15. *Udgātṛ*—Into what things has the spirit (puruṣah) entered?
Brahman—Into five things hath the spirit entered and they are established in the spirit: this I reply unto thee: not superior in wisdom art thou (to me).[1]

(47) These brahmodyas were uttered in the form of a dialogue, technically called *vākovākya* (*lit.* speech and reply? cp. vākovākye brahmodyaṃ vadanti, they utter the brahmodya in the form of a dialogue, ŚB. 4.6.9.20). These dialogues are formal and stereotyped and were probably learnt by heart. They seem to have been among the earliest passages to be so learnt for they are mentioned along with the study of just the ṛc, sāman and yajus (madhu ha vā ṛcah, ghṛtaṃ ha sāmāmṛtaṃ yajūṃsi, yaddha vā ayaṃ vākovākyam adhīte kṣīraudana-māṃsaudanau haiva tau, the Ṛc verses are honey, the Sāma verses ghee, and the Yajus formulae ambrosia, but when he utters the dialogue it is both milk and meat, ŚB. 11.5.7.5). Later the list of things to be studied becomes longer and includes vidyā, itihāsapurānam, etc. (ŚB. 11.5.6.8). But what is important is that a time seems to have come when the vākovākya was no longer a formal utterance but an *ex tempore* performance and the study of vākovākya- would have then become the study of the nature of discussion and debate, whereby one could outwit one's rival. It may be observed that this desire to outwit one's rival is already seen in the example we quoted above where it is said by the Brahman 'not superior in wisdom art thou (to me)'. Such a 'free' vākovākya- to which Sāyaṇa has drawn our attention[2] is to be found at ŚB. 11.4.1.12–15, which is not even a debate in a sacrificial session but an open contest for victory between Uddālaka Āruṇi and Svaidāyana Gautama. We have already studied samples of the reasoning found here (*v. supra*, 14).

(48) When we come to the Early Upaniṣads this analogical reasoning tends to lose its magical character (not altogether) and becomes more empirical, though here too the inferences are not strictly warranted by the observations made. Thus the observation that we perspire when it is hot was sufficient for Uddālaka to conclude that 'Heat causes Water'[3] (*v. supra*, 27). At this stage we noticed *a priori* reasoning as

[1] SBE., Vol. 44, pp. 388, 389.
[2] *v.* SBE., Vol. 5, p. 98, fn. 3.
[3] The Milesian philosophers seem to have been at the same stage of thought.

well, such as 'Being cannot come out of Non-Being' (*v. supra*, 25). Both these forms of reasoning were made use of to construct metaphysical theories. Vākovākya- at this stage of its development may have signified a general study of this kind of reasoning as well as of topics, which would help to make one a good debater.

(49) The debate at this stage seems to have been carried over from the sacrifice to the public assembly and become an institution important in itself and not a minor feature of a sacrificial session. Śvetaketu Āruṇeya goes for the purpose of debating to the assembly of the Pañcālas, which is called pañcālānaṃ pariṣadaṃ (Bṛh. 6.2.1) and pañcālānaṃ samitiṃ (Ch. 5.3.1). Sometimes the brahmins would go to the courts of kings to hold such debates. Yājñavalkya goes to king Janaka of Videha 'desirous of cattle' (the prize of the debate) and subtle questions (paśūn icchan aṇvantān, Bṛh. 4.1.1), and holds controversy with him. So does Bālāki come to Ajātaśatru (Kauś. 4.1) and debate with him. It was these assemblies of the brahmins and the kṣatriyas which came to be known as the brāhmaṇa-parisā and the khattiya-parisā respectively in the Pāli Nikāyas (*v. infra*, 349).

(50) But the debate on the sacrificial ground also seems to have continued without a break, though it was no longer a formal brahmodya but a heated contest. There is a description of such a debate at a sacrifice at Bṛh. 3.1–9, which Janaka attends and where he offers a prize to the victor (i.e. to the wisest brahmin, brahmiṣṭha). In the Mahābhārata, it is said describing the proceedings of a sacrifice that 'as the sacrifice progressed eloquent reasoners (vāgmino hetuvādinaḥ) put forward many theories based on reasoning (hetuvādān) with the intention of defeating each other'.[1] It is probably these brahmins who called the 'brahmins addicted to the debate' (brāhmaṇā vādasīlā) at Sn. 382 (*v. infra*, 375). It is also probably to them that the Mahāniddesa refers by the term *hetuvādā* (Nd. I.294) though the term need not be restricted to the brahmins.[2]

(51) We found that the term vākovākya- was used in the Brāhmaṇas to denote a branch of study and observed that at a certain stage in its development, it probably meant 'the study of the nature of discussion

[1] Tasmiñ yajñe pravṛtte 'pi vāgmino hetuvādinaḥ, hetuvādān bahūn āhuḥ, parasparajigīṣavaḥ, Śrīmānmahābhāratam, Aśvamedhaparva, 86.27, Ed. T. R. Krishacharya and T. R. Vyasacharya, Vol. 14, Bombay 1909, p. 103.

[2] The Materialists were called 'haitukāḥ', and probably the vitaṇḍavādins (casuists) as well; *v.* Das Gupta, *History of Indian Philosophy*, Vol. 3, p. 518.

and debate'. One of its latest occurrences is in the Chāndogya Upaniṣad (7.1.2: 7.2.1: 7.7.1), after which it does not occur at all in this sense in Indian literature. Śaṅkara commenting on this word explains it as *tarka-śāstram*[1] and vākovākya- is translated by Deussen[2] as 'Dialektik' and by Hume[3] and Radhakrishnan[4] as 'Logic'. This is by no means unreasonable, for the study of the debate may have led to or included at this time the study of 'the elements of reasoning' and so long as vākovākya- as 'logic' is not taken to mean what logic (nyāyaśāstra-, tarka-śāstra-) later came to denote there is no insuperable objection to this translation.

(52) That the brahmins were studying some kind of tarkaśāstra also appears to be confirmed by the evidence of the Pāli texts for here *lokāyata-* (D. I.11.88; A. I.163, 166; A. III.223; Vin. II.139; Sn. p. 105) is represented as one of the branches of study of the orthodox brahmins and this is explained as *vitaṇḍa-vāda-sattham*[5] or 'the science of casuistry' (DA. I.24: SnA. 447) or *vitaṇḍa-sattham*.[6] As Prof. Rhys Davids has shown, what is stated in the Canonical texts is confirmed by a passage in the Mahābhārata where 'at the end of a list of the accomplishments of learned Brahmans they are said to be masters of the Lokāyata'.[7] Thus both according to Śaṅkara as well as the Pāli texts, the early brahmins were making a study of the elements of reasoning or casuistry or debating topics and this is by no means intrinsically improbable, when we find that these brahmins were constructing the first rational metaphysical theories at this time.

(53) Faddegon has however questioned the translation of this whole passage by Deussen and Hume on the grounds that 'the commentator has tried to find in the Upaniṣad-text all sciences known in his time'[8] and dismisses the translation of vākovākya- as 'logic' as unsupported by the use of this word at ŚB. 11.5.7.5 (*op. cit.*, p. 47). He says 'we may conclude that vākovākya in the Chāndogya-Upaniṣad cannot yet

[1] Vakovākyam tarka-śāstram, Chandogyopaniṣad, Ānanda Āśrama Series No. 14, p. 393.

[2] *Sechzig Upanisads des Veda*, Leipzig, 1921, p. 174.

[3] *The Thirteen Principal Upanishads*, pp. 250, 251, 254.

[4] *The Principal Upanisads*, pp. 469, 470, 475.

[5] Lokāyatam vuccati vitaṇḍavādasattham.

[6] Abhidhānappadīpikā, 5.12, vitaṇḍasattham viññeyyaṃ yaṃ taṃ lokāyatam, *v.* Abhidhanappadīpikā, ed. Muni Jina Vijaya, p. 18.

[7] SBB, Vol. II, p. 169.

[8] B. Faddegon, The Catalogue of Sciences in the Chāndogya Upaniṣad, AO., Vol. 4, p. 44.

have signified logic, since this science was developed many centuries later as an outcome of the technical art of philosophical discussion' (*loc. cit.*). He suggests for it 'the general meaning of dialogue and metaphorically ability and smartness in debating' (*loc. cit.*) or 'the cleverness of arguing in dialogue' (*op. cit.*, p. 53). We would agree with Faddegon that vākovākyam could not have meant 'the elements of reasoning' at ŚB. 11.5.7.5 but the case is different with its latest use at Ch. 7.2.1, etc., after the institution of the brahmodya, as we have seen (*v. supra*, 46–50) underwent many changes. As for Faddegon's other argument discrediting almost the entirety of Śaṅkara's interpretations of this passage on the grounds that they are anachronisms, we would like to point out that Śaṅkara's exposition on the whole is corroborated by what the Pāli Nikāyas attribute to the brahmins as the arts and sciences studied by them. In fact, this independently supports the Chāndogya list itself by showing that it does not contain later interpolations. It shows that the catalogue of sciences in the Chāndogya as well as Śaṅkara's comments on the whole are to be trusted as giving a fair sample of Brāhmaṇic learning at least at the time of the Pāli Nikāyas. We may do this in the form of a table giving the Chāndogya catalogue, Śaṅkara's comment, the word in the Pāli Nikāyas which is the equivalent either of the Chāndogya catalogue or Śaṅkara's comment. We have indicated in brackets the equivalents found only in a Pāli Comy.:

Chāndogya list	*Śaṅkara's comment*	*Pāli equivalent*
1. ātharvanam caturtham	—	āthabbanaṃ, Sn. 927
2. itihāsapurānam pañcamam	bhāratapañcamānam	itihāsapañcamānaṃ D. I.88
3. vedānāṃ vedam	vyākaraṇam	veyyākaraṇa-, D. I.88
4. pitryam	śraddhā-kalpau	saddhe, D. I.97: keṭubha-, Sn. 1020
5. rāśi	gaṇitam	gaṇanā, D. I.11
6. daivam	utpātajñānam	utpātaṃ, D. I.8, v. 1
7. nidhim	mahakālādinidhiśāstram	?
8. *vākovākyam*	*tarkaśāstram*	*lokāyataṃ*=(*vitaṇḍavāda-satthaṃ*, DA. I.247)

Chandogya list	*Sankara's comment*	*Pali equivalent*
9. ekāyanam	nītiśāśtram	(nītisatthaṃ, DA. I.93)
10. devavidyā	niruktam	sivavijjā?, D. I.9
11. brahmavidyā	ṛgyajuḥsāmākhyasyavidyā	tevijjā, Sn. 594
12. bhūtavidyā	bhūtatantram	bhūtavijjā, D. I.8
13. kṣatravidyā	dhanurvedam	khattavijjā, D. I.9
14. nakṣatravidyā	jyotiṣam	nakkhattaṃ, Sn. 927
15. sarpa (vidyā)	gāruḍam	ahivijjā, D. I.8
16. devajanavidyā	gandhayukti-nṛtya-gīta-vādya-śilpa-	naccaṃ gītaṃ vāditaṃ, D. I.6

(54) We do not propose to scrutinize this list item by item, as it would divert us from our present problem. But if we examine this list as a whole, it would be noticed that five of the Pāli items (1, 2, 12, 13, 14) are identical in word and meaning with the Chāndogya list, while one of them (15) is identical in meaning and one (10) doubtful. Of the rest, no less than six Pāli items (3, 4, 5, 6, 11, 16) are more or less identical in language and sense with the comments of Śaṅkara. This lends authenticity to Śaṅkara's comments in that it shows that these sciences were cultivated by the brahmins at least during the time the Pāli Nikāyas were composed, if not earlier and Śaṅkara could therefore not have been making arbitrary comments particularly with regard to items 4, 5, 6, 11, 16, which have been questioned by Faddegon. All this implies that when Śaṅkara was commenting on vākovākya- as tarkaśāśtra- there is no reason to think that he was trying to find a place for tarkaśāśtra in this list, but that he was probably recording a genuine tradition, particularly when we observe that the Buddhists have credited the brahmins with making a study of what they in their poor opinion of them have called the vitaṇḍa-sattha or the 'art of casuistry'. The fact that when Pāli commentaries came to be written Lokāyata- exclusively meant Materialism is perhaps an added reason why the comment vitaṇḍa-sattha, quite independently of the corroboration from Brāhmaṇic sources is to be considered as preserving a genuine tradition.

(55) The etymology of the word lokāyata- however, does not even remotely suggest any connection with logic or casuistry. On the other hand, all the explanations of the etymology of the term by scholars[1]

[1] *v.* Chattopadhyaya, Lokāyata, *A Study in Ancient Indian Materialism*, New Delhi, 1959, pp. 1–4. Das Gupta, *A History of Indian Philosophy*, Vol. III, pp. 512 ff.

on the presumption that the word directly or indirectly means 'the philosophy of Materialism' are utterly mistaken since the earliest use of the word, as we have seen, does not at all betray such a connotation. As Prof. Rhys Davids was the first to point out in his study of the meaning of the term,[1] lokāyata as used in the Nikāyas is one of the branches of learning of the orthodox Vedic brahmins. Speaking of the context in which the word appears he says: 'The whole paragraph is complimentary. And though the exact connotation of one or two of the other terms is doubtful, they are all descriptive of just those things which a Brahman would have been rightly proud to be judged a master of. It is evident, therefore, that *the Dictionary interpretations of the word are quite out of place in this connection.*'[2] It is necessary to point this out since this statement seems to have fallen on deaf ears in the field of scholarship[3] and no attempt has been made to explain the meaning of this earliest use of the term.

(56) Prof. Rhys Davids himself suggested that the word 'probably meant Nature-lore—wise sayings, riddles, rhymes . . .' (*op. cit.*, p. 171). He even gave a list of passages in the Bṛhadāraṇyaka and Chāndogya Upaniṣads and the Aitereya Araṇyaka (*loc. cit.*), which he believed contained the subject-matter of lokāyata- and suggested rather half-heartedly that with the growth of this branch of learning it came to be associated with 'sophists and casuists' (*loc. cit.*). All this was pure surmise, based on his belief that loka- meant 'nature' and that lokāyata- meant the 'study of nature' and that there was evidence for this in the Upaniṣadic and Āraṇyaka literature. Against this, Tucci has pointed out that loka- by itself does not mean 'nature' in the Pāli literature and that for this purpose the word bhājana-loka is used.[4]

(57) It is surprising that Prof. Rhys Davids and after him all the scholars who discuss the meaning of lokāyata- missed both passages in the Nikāyas which could have given some information about the subject-matter of lokāyata, one occurring in the Saṃyutta Nikāya (II. 77) and the other in the Aṅguttara Nikāya (IV.428). The former is

[1] SBB., Vol. II, pp. 166–72. [2] *Op. cit.*, p. 166.

[3] E.g. Chattopadhyaya uncritically quotes Prof. Rhys Davids to show that the early brahmins studied lokāyata- in the sense of Materialism (*v. op. cit.*, p. 32) and says, 'Evidences like these perhaps indicate that we are in need of revising our notion of the Brāhmaṇa, particularly of the Brāhmaṇa of Buddhist India' (*op. cit.*, p. 33). 'A Sketch of Indian Materialism', PIPC., 1925, p. 40.

[4] 'A Sketch of Indian Materialism', PIPC., 1925, p. 40.

quoted by Dr Malalasekera in a paragraph he has written about the 'lokāyatikā brāhmaṇā' (*s.v.* DPPN.) ignoring the problem of the meaning of lokāyata altogether, while the latter passage which also mentions lokāyatikā brāhmaṇā (*loc. cit.*) is not mentioned by him as well.[1] In both these contexts, 'two lokāyata brahmins' (dve lokāyatikā brāhmaṇā) approach the Buddha. This expression is translated by Mrs Rhys Davids as 'two Brahmins wise in worldly lore' (K.S. II.53) and by Hare as 'two brahmins skilled in metaphysics' (G.S. IV.287). The Comy. to the Saṃyutta Nikāya explains lokāyatikā as 'one versed in Lokāyata or the science of casuistry' (lokāyatiko ti vitaṇḍasatthe lokāyate kata-paricayo, SA. II.76) and in the Aṅguttara Comy. the word is explained as 'students of Lokāyata' (lokāyata-paṭhakā, AA. IV.200). The term lokāyatika- seems to describe the brahmin who made a special study of that branch of Brāhmaṇic learning known at the time as Lokāyata.

(58) These doctrines are specified in the Saṃyutta context as follows:
(1) *Sabbaṃ* atthī ti, i.e. 'that everything exists', which is called the oldest (jiṭṭhaṃ, Skr. jyeṣṭham) lokāyata-doctrine.
(2) *Sabbaṃ* natthī ti, i.e. 'that nothing exists', called the second (dutiyam) lokāyata-doctrine.
(3) *Sabbaṃ* ekattan ti, i.e. 'that everything is a unity', called the third (third) lokāyata-doctrine.
(4) *Sabbaṃ* puthuttan ti, i.e. 'that everything is a plurality', called the fourth (catutthaṃ) lokāyata-doctrine.

(59) It may be observed that all these theories are about sabbaṃ or sarvam, which is found in the Upaniṣads to denote the 'cosmos' or the universe as a whole (*v. infra*, 65). It will also be seen that these four doctrines are presented in two *pairs* as thesis and anti-thesis: the second and the fourth are the anti-theses of the first and the third respectively. The Comy. explains that the first and the third are Eternalist views[2] (sassata-diṭṭhiyo) while the second and the fourth are Materialist views[3] (uccheda-diṭṭhiyo, lit Annihilationist views). This dialectical opposition in these pairs of views reminds us of the Vedic institution of the *brahmodya*, which found expression in the form of a

[1] Lokāyatika- is not even mentioned in the Volume of Indexes (A. VI) of the Aṅguttara Nikāya.

[2] Evam ettha sabbam atthi, sabbam ekattan ti imā dve pi sassata-diṭṭhiyo, SA., II, 76.

[3] Sabbam natthi, sabbam puthuttan ti imā dve uccheda-diṭṭhiyo, *ibid*.

vākovākya- (*v. supra*, 47), which was originally a dialogue and later a debate (dialectics) in which one tried to outstrip the other by arguments, designed to disprove one's opponent's thesis and prove his own. The other main deduction that we can make from the above passage is based on the commentarial identification of the second and the fourth views as those of the Materialists. This suggestion is confirmed by the fact that there is evidence of the existence at this time of these two schools of Materialists referred to, the pluralist school (or schools, *v. infra*, 115) and the nihilist pragmatic school, which we have argued was the school to which Dīghanakha belonged (*v. infra*, 334) and which adumbrates the later philosophy of Jayarāśi (*v. infra*, 116). The fact that Lokāyata is the term which later comes into currency as a general term for these Materialist schools of thought also supports this identification. If this is so, then the later use of the term Lokāyata to denote exclusively the Materialist doctrines is a one-sided application and development of a term, which had a wider coverage earlier, denoting as we see not only the Materialist doctrines but their anti-theses, the Eternalist doctrines as well. In fact, it may be noted that according to this passage the oldest lokāyata is not the Materialist doctrine but the eternalist doctrine.

(60) In the Aṅguttara context too, 'two lokāyata brahmins' (dve lokāyatikā brāhmaṇā), *loc. cit.*, meet the Buddha to discuss the problem of the extent of the cosmos (loka-). They say that Pūraṇa Kassapa and Nigaṇṭha Nātaputta are 'directly opposed to each other' (aññamaññaṃ vipaccanīkavādānaṃ, M. I.429) in regard to the views that they hold about the extent of the universe, one holding that 'the universe is finite' (antavantaṃ lokaṃ, *loc. cit.*) and the other that 'the universe is infinite' (anantaṃ lokaṃ, *loc. cit.*). It is possible that these two theses constituted a pair of lokāyata-doctrines, in which case loka- is here used in the sense of the 'cosmos' (*v. infra*, 65), and lokāyata would mean 'what relates to the cosmos' or the problems of the nature and extent of the cosmos, studied as debating topics and based on reasoning.

(61) The Laṅkāvatāra Sūtra[1] also records an encounter between the Buddha and a lokāyatika brahmin. This gives a long list of lokāyata-doctrines and although it is less reliable than the Nikāya passages with regard to what it tells us about Brāhmaṇical doctrines, we can nevertheless glean some information. This passage too has been ignored by scholars in discussing the meaning of lokāyata- and Suzuki has

[1] Ed. B. Nanjio, Kyoto, 1923, *Bibliotheca Otaniensis*. Vol. I, pp. 176–9.

consistently mistranslated the term as 'materialism'[1] though it is obvious from the context that it could not mean this. Here thirty-one lokāyata-doctrines are mentioned as follows:

(1) *Sarvaṃ* kṛtakam, i.e. everything is created, called the first lokāyata- theory (prathamaṃ lokāyatam).
(2) *Sarvaṃ* akṛtakam, i.e. nothing is created, called the second lokāyata- theory (dvitiyam lokayatam).
(3) *Sarvam* anityam, i.e. everything is impermanent.
(4) *Sarvam* nityam, i.e. everything is permanent.
(5) *Sarvam* utpādyam, i.e. everything is resultant.
(6) *Sarvam* anutpādyam, i.e. everything is not resultant, called the sixth lokāyata- theory (ṣaṣṭham lokāyatam).
(7) *Sarvam* ekatvam, i.e. everything is a unity.
(8) *Sarvam* anyatvam, i.e. everything is different (the world is a plurality).
(9) *Sarvam* ubhayatvam, i.e. the world is a duality.
(10) *Sarvam* anubhayatvam, i.e. the world is a non-duality.
*(11) *Sarvam* karaṇādhīnam, i.e. everything is subject to causation since they are seen to proceed from a diversity of causes (vicitra-hetu-prapatti-darśanāt).
(12) *Sarvam* avyākṛtam, i.e. everything is inexplicable.
(13) *Sarvam* vyākṛtam, i.e. everything is explicable.
(14) Asty ātmā, i.e. there is a soul.
(15) Nāsty ātmā, i.e. there is no soul.
(16) Asty ayaṃ *loko*, i.e. this world exists.
(17) Nāsty ayaṃ *loko*, i.e. this world does not exist.
(18) Asti paro *loko*, i.e. the next world exists.
(19) Nāsti paro *loko*, there is no next world.
*(20) Nāsty asti ca paro *loko*, i.e. there is and is no next world.
(21) Asti mokṣaḥ, i.e. there is salvation.
(22) Nāsti mokṣaḥ, i.e. there is no salvation.
(23) *Sarvam* kṣaṇikam, i.e. everything is momentary.
(24) *Sarvam* akṣaṇikam, i.e. nothing is momentary.
(25) Ākāśam pratisankhyānirodho nirvānam kṛtakam, i.e. space, non-wilful destruction and nirvāna are conditioned.
(26) Ākāśam pratisankhyānirodho nirvānam akṛtakam, i.e. . . . are not conditioned.
(27) Asty antarbhavaḥ, i.e. there is an intermediate existence.

[1] *v.* D. T. Suzuki, *The Lankavatāra Sūtra*, London, 1932, pp. 152–5.

(28) Nāsty antarbhavaḥ, i.e. there is no intermediate existence.
(29) Ājñāna-tṛṣṇā-karma-hetukam . . . tribhavam, i.e. the three-fold world is caused by ignorance, desire and karma.
(30) (tribhavam) ahetukam, i.e. the threefold-world is not caused: and it is said that 'this *pair* too constitutes *a lokāyata*' (*dvayamapy* etat . . . *lokayatam*).
*(31) Sva-sāmānya-lakṣaṇa-patitā sarva-bhāvāḥ, i.e. all things are classifiable under their specific and general characteristics.

(62) The section ends by saying that 'there is lokāyata as long as the mental activity of the dogmatic construction of the external world persists'.[1] This is an attempt to explain the origin of lokāyata-theories on the basis of the assumptions made in the Laṅkāvatāra Sūtra itself and it is therefore not very enlightening. Even the list cannot be considered to give us an account of Brāhmaṇic doctrines. For instance, theories (25) to (28) are topics on which, les sectes du petit véhicule, to use Bareau's expression[2] were divided. Thus the two theses, namely that 'there is an intermediate existence' and its opposite (*v.* 27, 28) are considered a pair of lokāyata-theories. This is a doctrine on which, as the Kathāvatthu (VIII.2) shows the Buddhist sects were divided and it was a subject of debate between the contending parties.[3] This use of lokāyata- to refer to the debating topics, mentioning thesis as well as anti-thesis, on which the Buddhist order was divided seems indirectly to throw some light on the earlier use of lokāyata to refer to the debating topics of the brahmins, on which opposing views were found within the orthodox circle of brahmins. It will be seen that all the above topics excepting (11), (20) and (31)—marked with an asterisk—are stated in the form of thesis and anti-thesis and the fact that they were considered in *pairs* appears to be confirmed by the statement made about (29) and (30) namely that '*this pair too* (*dvayamapy etat*) constitutes *a lokāyata*' (*v. supra*, 61). This would have been

[1] Yāvad . . . manovispanditaṁ bāhyārthabhiniveśavikalpasya tāval lokāyatam, *op. cit.*, p. 178.

[2] *v.* Andre Bareau, *Les Sectes Bouddhique du Petit Véhicule*, Publications de l'école Francaise d'extreme-orient, Saigon, 1955.

[3] As Bareau has shown (*op. cit.*) the Purvaśailas (p. 101), Vatsīputriyas (p. 119), the Sammatīyas (p. 124), the Sarvāstivādin Vaibhāṣikas (p. 142) and the Late Mahīśāsakas (p. 188) were of the view that an antarā-bhava exists, while the Mahāsaṅghikas (p. 68), the Vibhajyavādiṁs (p. 172), the Mahīśāsakas (p. 184), the followers of the Śāriputrābhidharmaśāstra (p. 194) and the Theravādins (p. 223) were of the opposite view.

unnecessary unless they were debating topics, representing the thesis upheld by one party and the anti-thesis defended by the opposing party. We may therefore surmise on this ground that the lokāyata-theories mentioned in the Saṃyutta Nikāya were probably stated in the form of thesis and anti-thesis (*v. supra*, 59) because they were the subjects of debate among those brahmins, whom the Suttanipāta has described as being 'addicted to the debate' (*v. infra*, 375).

(63) The passage in the Saṃyutta Nikāya said that the oldest lokāyata thesis was 'that everything exists' while according to the Laṅkāvatāra Sūtra, the first thesis was 'that everything was created'. Now creation theories have undoubtedly to be reckoned among the first cosmological theories or the first attempts to comprehend the origin.of the cosmos. That Being or sat was the primary cause or the ultimate reality of the universe appears to have been one of the earliest cosmological theories, which was probably followed not very much later by the theory that 'nothing' (asat, *v.* RV. 10.72, 2)[1] really exists and the Nāsadīya hymn probably attempted a synthesis of these two theories (*v. supra*, 9). Even if we treat these theories as pre-philosophical, we notice that the subject is treated at a philosophical level at Ch. 6.2.1. Here the two theories are clearly contrasted: one is that 'Being is the only reality' (sad eva . . . āsīt) and the other, which is quite clearly held by 'certain people' (taddhaika āhuḥ) in opposition to this theory is that 'nothing is real' (asad eva . . . āsīt). This may be deemed to be a reference to the nihilist school of lokāyata, which according to the Saṃyutta Nikāya held the tenet that 'nothing exists' (sabbaṃ natthi, *v. supra* 58) and which is described in the Laṅkāvatāra Sutra as the school which held that 'this world does not exist' (*v.* 17). The other pair of lokāyata-theses mentioned in the Saṃyutta Nikāya (i.e. sabbam *ekattam*; sabbam *puthuttam*) also appear to have had their origin in the Upaniṣadic period. The Bhagavadgīta speaks of 'some who worship with the offerings of knowledge with (theories) of unity as well as of plurality' (*jñāna*-yajñena cā'pyanye . . . upāśate *ekatvena pṛthaktvena*, 9.15). We may note here that ekatva- and pṛthaktva- in Sanskrit give rise to ekatta- and puthutta- in Pāli according to the usual phonological rules. Now the Īśā speaks of the absence of delusion on the part of those who see the universe as a unity (*ekatvam* anupaśyataḥ, 7) and the Kaṭha holding that 'there is no diversity in the universe' (neha nānāsti kiñcana, 2.1.11) criticizes 'those who see diversity in it'

[1] asataḥ sad ajāyata, RV. 10.72.2. 2

(mṛtyos sa mṛtyuṃ gacchati *ya iha nāneva paśyati, loc. cit.*); this criticism must have been directed against a pluralistic theory of the universe and it is likely that this is the Materialist theory mentioned at Kaṭha 1.2.6 (*v. infra,* 116) where it is said that 'he who thinks "this world exists, there is no other" *repeatedly comes under my* (i.e. *of Death*) *control*' (ayam loko nāsti para iti mānī, *punaḥ punar vaśam āpadyate me, loc. cit.*) for the same fate (cp. *mṛtyos sa mṛtyuṃ gacchati*) was held out against those who were convinced of a pluralistic theory of the universe.

(64) The main concepts of the lokāyata theses also appear in the Mūlapariyāya Sutta (M. I.1 ff.), which gives a list of categories or concepts having a cosmological significance. Mūlapariyāya has been translated by Miss Horner as 'synopsis of fundamentals' (M.L.S. I.3) but this translation does not make sense. We believe that mūla- here means the 'root cause' or the primary cause of the world. It is in this sense that the word is used at Aitareya Āraṇyaka 2.1.8.1, where the cosmological theory that water is the first or primary cause of the world is mooted and it is said that 'this (water) was the *root* (cause) and that (i.e. the world) was the *shoot*' (i.e. the effect) (etad vai *mūlam* adas *tūlam*). In this Sutta we observe that this theory, namely that water or āpa- is a mūla- or a root cause is mentioned along with a number of such cosmological theories. *Pariyāya* here probably means 'the nature of' as at Sn. 581.[1] Mūlapariyāya Sutta, therefore probably means 'the discourse on the nature of primary causes or concepts'. Among such causes or categories explaining the origin or the nature of the universe, we find the concepts of *ekatta-*, *nānatta-* (= puthutta- in sense), and *sabba-* (M. I.3).

(65) All this points to *loka-* in lokāyata meaning not 'nature' as Prof. Rhys Davids imagined but the 'cosmos'. It may be seen that in the Laṅkāvatāra list the lokāyata-theses were about *sarva-* (i.e. the cosmos) or *loka-*. The references in the Nikāyas confirmed this (*v. supra,* 60). Now the word loka- is used in a collective sense, to denote the entire universe and this sense is in fact clearly defined at Bṛh. 1.5.17, where it is said, ye vai ke ca lokāh, teṣām sarveṣāṃ *loka* ity ekatā, i.e. whatever worlds there are, they are all comprehended under the word 'world'. We also notice that in this same context loka- is used synonymously with *brahman:* tvam *brahma,* tvam yajña, tvam *loka* iti. Brahman is

[1] Tasmā dhīrā na socanti viditvā loka-*pariyāyaṃ*, i.e. therefore the wise do not grieve, knowing the *nature* of the world.

also sometimes used synonymously with sarva-: etad *brahma* etad *sarvam*, Bṛh. 5.3.1. In the light of all this evidence we may conclude that these lokāyata-theses were promulgated at the *brahmodyas* which, as we have shown, developed from a simple formal dialogue into a lively debate and it was probably in preparation for these debates that the lokāyata-theses would have been studied. They would have constituted the possible answers to problems about the cosmos, along with the reasons on which they were based. The study of the reasoning would have been at first not strictly divorced from the theories themselves and it is to these studies of the brahmins that we have to trace the beginnings of metaphysics as well as of logic and epistemology. A verse in the Mahābhārata describing the sage Nārada shows that logical studies (nyāya-) went hand in hand with the study of metaphysical concepts such as 'monism' (aikya-, cp. ekatta) and 'pluralism' (nānātva-, cp. puthutta) and that this was part of Vedic studies as a whole:

> *vedopaniṣadāṃ vettā ṛṣiḥ* suragaṇārcitaḥ
> itihāsa-purāṇa-jñaḥ, purākalpa-viśeṣakṛt
> *nyāyavid*dharmatattvajñaḥ ṣaḍangavid anuttamaḥ
> *aikya*-saṃyoga-*nānātva*-samavāya-viśāradaḥ,[1]
> Sabhāparva, 5.2-3.

This verse may very well reflect a time when the Nyāya or logical studies were accepted by orthodoxy and admitted into the rank of Vedic studies but in the light of the above evidence from the Buddhist Nikāyas, confirmed and corroborated by the Brāhmaṇic literature, we have to presuppose that there was a period when the study of lokāyata or the 'elements of metaphysics and reasoning' formed a part of Vedic studies. However, a time seems to have come when some of the lokāyata-theses propounded in the process, were seen to oppose or undermine the fundamental doctrines of the Vedic tradition and it no longer seemed desirable for orthodoxy to allow brahmins the free exercise of reason and speculation. Thus the rule was laid down that 'the brahmin who despises the roots (of Vedic tradition) because of his dependence on the science of reasoning (*hetu-śāstra-*) should be cast out by the good (brahmins) as a nihilist, who scorns the Vedas' (yo'vamanyeta

[1] 'The supreme sage who was revered by the gods, knew the Vedas and Upaniṣads, the histories and Purāṇas, was a specialist in ancient rituals, was versed in logic, the truths of justice and the six branches (of learning) and had an expert knowledge of the (concepts of) *monism*, conjunction, *pluralism* and inherence.'

te mūle hetuśāstrāśrayād dvijaḥ sa sādhubhir bahiṣkāryo nāstiko vedanindakaḥ: Manusmṛti II.11). At this time Lokāyata- as a branch of study would have been taboo to the brahmin orthodoxy and the word lokāyata survived to denote those very doctrines, which were opposed to Vedic teachings but which were once nurtured within the orthodox fold itself.

(66) This sense of lokāyata- appears to be preserved in the Arthaśāstra, where it is said to form part of anvīkṣikī or 'philosophy', comprising both metaphysics and logic: sāṃkhyam yogo lokāyatam ānvīkṣikī . . . hetubhir anvīkṣamānā ānvīkṣikī lokasyopakaroti,[1] i.e. Sāṃkhya, Yoga and Lokāyata (constitute) philosophy . . . by investigating with reasons it serves the world; the Comy. (modern) explains lokāyata here as 'the science of reasoning as taught by Brahma and Gārgya' (nyāya-śāstram Brahmagārgyoktam, Vol. I, p. 27). Ānvīkṣikī was rendered by Jacobi as 'philosophie'.[2] But Hacker in an article entitled 'Ānvīkṣikī'[3] has questioned this translation on the ground that since anvīkṣikī according to Kauṭilya's own comment means 'examining by reasons' and this is practised in *all* the sciences the term does not exclusively mean 'philosophy'. Yet he too admits that 'ānvīkṣikī or reasoning' is 'habitually applied to systems of philosophy because these cultivate argument and logical thinking' (*op. cit.*, p. 82) and his main objection is that these terms are 'never synonymous with philosophy' (*loc. cit.*). It does not therefore disprove our contention that lokāyata- in its earliest use meant the study of metaphysical topics along with the reasoning involved, with the idea of gaining success in debate.

(67) The ways of knowing recognized at this time are, as Keith has shown,[4] stated in the Taittirīya Āraṇyaka as pratyakṣa (perception), anumāna (inference), smṛti (scripture) and aitihya (tradition). Keith

[1] *The Arthaśāstra of Kauṭalya,* Ed. T. G. Śāstri, Vol. I, p. 27.

[2] *v.* 'Zur Frühgeschichte der indischen Philosophie' in *Sitzungberichte der Preussische Akademie der Wissenschaften,* Berlin, 1911, pp. 733 ff.; cp. A. Foucher, *Le Compendium des Topiques (Tarkasaṃgraha) D'Annambhaṭṭa,* Paris, 1949, who translates 'anvīkṣikī' as 'investigation rationelle' (Introduction, p. xi), which he says is 'complètement indépendante des textes sacrés et uniquement fondée sur l'expérience courante; et celle en embraissait, nous dit-on, le Sāṅkhya, le Yoga et le Lokāyata, toutes doctrines originairement agnostique et realistes' (*loc. cit.*). He classifies Nyāya and Vaiśeṣika under 'Lokāyata' (*loc. cit.*).

[3] Paul Hacker, 'Ānvīkṣikī' in, *Wiener Zeitschrift für die Kunde Sud- und Ostasiens und Archiv für indische philosophie,* Band II, 1958, pp. 55 ff.

[4] *Religion and Philosophy of the Vedas,* HOS., Vol. 32, p. 482.

thinks that this represents 'a late popular view',[1] but the use of the word smṛti- to denote 'scripture' rather than the late word 'śruti', the absence of the use of the word pramāṇa and the general context of the passage does not favour Keith's view.

(68) When we analyse the language of the Early Upaniṣads we find the use of three or four verbal forms juxtaposed to signify the ways of knowing accepted at the time. Thus at Ch. 7.24.1, 'paśyati . . . śṛnoti . . . vijānāti', seems to sum up the different ways of knowing things. The root dṛś- is used in the Early Upaniṣads predominantly to denote the 'seeing' of visual objects with the eye (cakṣuṣā rupāṇi *paśyati*, Bṛh. 3.2.5). In this sense it is found very frequently either singly[2] or in lists where visual sensing or perception is contrasted with other forms of sensing or sensory perception.[3] These lists do not however mention all the five senses. Bṛh. 2.4.14 mentions smelling (jighrati), seeing and hearing, while Bṛh. 4.5.15 refers to seeing, smelling, tasting (rasayati) and hearing and Bṛh. 4.3.31 and 4.4.2 add touching (spṛśati) to the list, making five in all. When the verbal forms of √dṛś- are used without mention of the other forms of sensing or sensory perception, it seems to denote not just visual sensing or perception but perception in general. Thus, seeing (dṛṣṭiḥ) is used to denote perception in general where it is defined that seeing in this instance consists in perceiving the warmth of the body by touch (Ch. 3.13.8). The fact that the forms of √dṛś- were used predominantly to denote visual perception is undoubtedly due to the simple fact that perhaps the largest number of our perceptions are visual perceptions so that the word for visual perception is gradually extended to denote perception in general.

(69) Yet auditory perception was precluded from being denoted by √dṛś- since the verbal forms of √śru had to be used side by side in contexts, where ways of knowing were referred to, because of the tremendous importance traditionally attached to hearing at this time. This importance is due undoubtedly to the respect and reverence in which the sacred scriptures were held and these scriptures could not be seen[4] but had to be learnt by hearing them from one's teacher. The veneration in which hearing and learning from teachers was held is clearly seen from one of the earliest references in the Upaniṣads. It is

[1] *Religion and Philosophy of the Vedas*, HOS., Vol. 32, p. 482.

[2] Bṛh. 1.3.4; 1.4.1; 1.5.3.; 5.4.3; Ch. 1.2.4; 2.4.7; 2.24.4; 3.6.1; 5.1.7; 5.12.1; 6.12.1; 7.11.1, etc.

[3] Bṛh. 2.4.14; 4.5.15; 4.3.31; 4.4.2.

[4] See, however, supra, 13.

said that the eye is one's human wealth for one finds it with the eye, but that the ear is his 'divine wealth' (śrotram daivam) for he hears it with his ear (Bṛh. 1.4.17). Here the divine wealth referred to is undoubtedly the sacred scriptures and the use of the epithet 'divine' to describe what is heard as opposed to what is seen is indicative of the authority attached to the former. It is important, however, to notice that even in the Early Upaniṣads when it came to a matter of deciding between the evidence of seeing and the testimony of report or hearing about matters of fact in the everyday world, the decision was made in favour of sight against hearing as being the more reliable. It is said: 'Truth is sight. Therefore if two persons come disputing, one saying "I saw" and the other "I heard" they should trust the one who says "I saw" (cakṣur vai satyam, . . . tasmād yad idānīṃ dvau vivadamānau eyātām aham adarśam, aham aśrauṣam iti. Ya evam brūyāt, aham adarśam iti tasmā eva śraddadhyāma, Bṛh. 5.14.4).' We find this idea persisting later in the Maitrī Upaniṣad, where it is said that 'here the evidence is what is observed (by the senses)' (atra dṛṣṭaṃ nāma pratyayam, 6.10). This is possibly the reason why the Taittīriya Āraṇyaka distinguishes between two kinds of knowledge obtained from hearing, namely what is authoritatively heard and remembered (smṛti), that is the sacred scriptures and what is learnt from report or tradition (aitihya) with regard to other matters, a distinction which led to the necessity to separate divinely revealed scripture (śruti) from fallible human tradition (smṛti).

(70) In addition to perception or hearing (or learning) there is mention of thinking (√man; vi + √jñā; ni + √dhyā) as a means of knowledge at this time. The verbal forms used cover the rational reflective sources of knowledge, which the Taittirīya Āraṇyaka appears to indicate by the word anumāna, i.e. reasoning, or inference. The thinking process is sometimes described by the single word vijānāti but at other times a distinction appears to be drawn between the two cognitive processes of mental conceiving and rational understanding, a distinction which is not very clear. We may list the references to ways of knowledge as reflected in the language of this period as follows:

Text	*seeing or perceiving*	*hearing or learning*	*mentally conceiving*	*rationally understanding*
Bṛh. 2.4.5, 4.5.6	draṣṭavyaḥ	śrotavyaḥ	mantavyaḥ	nididhyāsitavyaḥ

Text	*seeing or perceiving*	*hearing or learning*	*mentally conceiving*	*rationally understanding*
Bṛh. 3.4.2	paśyeḥ	śṛṇuyāḥ	manvīthāḥ	vijānīyāḥ
Ch. 3.13.8	dṛṣṭiḥ	śrutiḥ		
Ch. 6.1.3		śrutam	matam	vijñātam
Ch. 7.25.2	paśyan		manvānaḥ	vijānan
Ch. 7.26.1	paśyataḥ		manvānasya	vijānataḥ

(71) Let us consider an example. It is said that 'the ātman should be perceived (draṣṭavyaḥ), learnt of (śrotavyaḥ), conceived of (mantavyaḥ) and rationally understood (nididhyāsitavyaḥ) (Bṛh. 2.4.5, 4.5.6). This is put in the mouth of the Yajñavalkya, who is soon going to prove by rational arguments that the ātman cannot be apprehended by any of these standard ways of knowing (Bṛh. 2.4.14, 4.5.15), but if we consider this passage in the light of other passages bearing on it in this stratum of thought, we see that there were thinkers at this time who believed that the ātman could be known by all these usual ways of knowing. The ātman could be seen or empirically perceived if it was a matter of seeing your figure in a pan of water (Ch. 8.8.1) or of perceiving the warmth of the body (Ch. 3.13.8). It could be heard or heard of, if it was a case of hearing the sound as of a fire blazing on closing one's ears (Ch. 3.13.8) or of hearing about it from a teacher when 'what was not heard of' (aśrutam) presumably in the sacred scriptures becomes heard (śrutam bhavati) (Ch. 6.1.3). It could likewise be metaphysically conceived of and rationally understood by thinking (e.g. vijajñau, Ch. 6.16.3). It is significant that even Śaṅkara's comment on 'mantavyo nididhyāsitavyaḥ' (Bṛh. 4.5.6) is that it can be known through 'argument and reasoning' (tarkeṇopapattyā). This was the ātman of the Early Upaniṣads, that could be known by the then accepted ways of knowing, that is by perceiving empirical instances, by instruction, or by metaphysical reasoning or rationally demonstrated to be unknowable in these ways.

(72) These ways of knowing are recognized in the Buddhist texts which employ the same terminology to denote them. These terms occur mostly in contexts which criticize these very Upaniṣadic doctrines of the ātman. For example it is said that one should not regard as the ātman 'what is *seen, heard, thought of, understood* or attained . . .' (*diṭṭhaṃ sutaṃ mutaṃ viññātam* pattam . . ., M. I.135). If we leave out the last (pattam, which is a way of knowing recognized by the Middle and Late Upaniṣadic thinkers, *v. infra*, 73, 74) we notice that the others

are the same as the concepts occurring in the Upaniṣadic list. Likewise, in the Suttanipāta we find that the forms, '*diṭṭha-*, *suta-*, muta-' often used to denote the corresponding ways of knowing in the Upaniṣads (*v.* Sn. 793, 798, 802, 813, 901).

(73) While perception, scripture, and reasoning were regarded as the usual ways of knowing in this period, we find that the verbal forms from √dṛs- acquire a new meaning (other than that of sense-perception) in the Middle and Late Upaniṣads. The ātman now has to be directly seen but this cannot be done by means of *perception*[1] (*v.* prāptum śakyo na cakṣuṣā, i.e. one cannot attain it with the eye, Kaṭha, 2.3.12 cp. Kaṭha, 2.3.9, na cakṣuṣā paśyati kascanainam, i.e. no one sees it with the eye). Nor can it be had from the sacred *scriptures* (nāyam ātmā pravacanena labhyo, i.e. this soul is not to be attained by means of scriptural instruction, Kaṭha, 1.2.23). 'Manifold instruction' is of no avail (na *bahunā śrutena*, Kaṭha 1.2.23 = Muṇḍ. 3.2.3). The mention of manifold instruction (śrutena) as distinguished from scripture (pravacanena) is probably a reference to the diverse metaphysical theories about the ātman in the Early Upaniṣads. 'Nor is this apprehension attainable by *reasoning*' (naiṣā *tarkena* matir āpaneyā, Kaṭha, 1.2.9). The ātman is 'not to be reasoned about' (*atarkyaḥ*, Mait. 6.17, cp. Kaṭha, 1.2.8, anīyān hy *atarkyam* aṇupramāṇāt, i.e. for it is inconceivable being subtler than the subtle): it 'cannot be had by the *intellect*' (labhyo na *medhayā*, Kaṭha, 1.2.23 = Muṇḍ. 3.2.3). The traditional ways of knowing hitherto accepted are discarded as far as the knowledge of the ātman goes and 'seeing' acquires the new connotation of extrasensory perception. Thus the ātman which is hidden within all things and does not shine forth is *seen* (*dṛśyate*) by the subtle seers by their subtle awakened intuition (dṛśyate tvagryayā buddhyā sukṣmayā sukṣmadarśibhih, Kaṭha, 1.3.12). One *sees* (*paśyate*) while in meditative rapture (dhyāyamānaḥ) by the purification of knowledge (*jñāna-prasādena*) and not by any of the sense-organs (Muṇḍ. 3.1.8). As the Śvetāsvatara puts it, one would see (paśyet) God hidden as it were by practising the drill of meditation (dhyāna) (1.4). Here was a new way of knowing, unrecognized in the earlier tradition, acquired by means of meditation (dhyāna = P. jhāna) though the vision or revelation itself was said

[1] Cp. 'He is not grasped by the eye . . . *nor by the other sense-organs*' (na cakṣuṣā gṛhyate . . . nānyair devaiḥ, Kaṭha, 3.1.8).

to be due to the grace of ātman or God.[1] Thus by the time of the Middle or Late Upaniṣads the following ways of knowing appear to have been recognized, viz. (1) normal perception, (2) extrasensory perception, (3) scriptural or traditional authority and (4) reason.

(74) The word that is most frequently or almost invariably used to denote the knowledge derived from this means of extrasensory perception is *jñāna*. Thus it is said that the ātman is obtained 'by right knowledge' (samyag-jñānena, Muṇḍ. 3.15) or by the 'peace of knowledge' (jñāna-prasādena, Muṇḍ. 3.1.8) and those who obtain it are 'satisfied with their knowledge' (jñāna-tṛptāḥ, Muṇḍ. 3.2.5). This ātman or God as 'knower' is jñaḥ (Śvet. 6.2, 16, 17) and knowing God or having the right knowledge is denoted by verbal forms of √jñā (jñātvā, Kaṭha 1.2.16; 17; 2.3.8; Śvet. 1.11,2.16, 3.10; jñātum, Kaṭha 1.2.21). But the word jñāna is not entirely confined to this usage for at Kaṭha 2.3.10 it is used in the plural to mean the 'knowledge of the five senses' (yadā pañcāvatiṣṭhante *jñānāni* manasā saha, when the five sense knowledges together with the mind cease). Likewise other cognitive verbs are at times employed to denote the above sense but their occurrence is sporadic and very rare: e.g. matvā (Kaṭha 1.2.22), matiḥ (Kaṭha 1.2.9), viditvā (Kaṭha 2.1.2), viduḥ (Kaṭha 2.3.9), vidyām (Kaṭha 2.3.18) and veda (Śvet. 3.8).

(75) Although the contemplatives claimed a direct experience of reality totally different in character from any kind of metaphysical insight, it must be said that their description of these experiences is not without interpretation and is bound up with a good deal of metaphysics and theology. A knowledge of the Vedas was in theory no more necessary than it was in the earlier metaphysical phase.[2] But tradition could not be entirely done away with and particularly at a

[1] There is a doubt whether dhātuḥ praśādāt ought to be translated as 'through the grace of the Creator', since Śaṅkara interprets the phrase as 'dhātusampraśādāt', i.e. through the tranquillity of the senses, an interpretation which is supported by usage in this stratum of thought as Hume has shown (*op. cit.*, p. 350, fn. 1). But this does not alter the fact that it is to be conceived as a revelation as well, since it is expressly stated that the ātman reveals himself (Kaṭha 1.2.23; Muṇḍ 3.2.3.).

[2] In this phase it said, for instance, that Janaka has no metaphysical knowledge of what happens to him after death although he has 'mastered the Vedas' (adhītavedaḥ, Bṛh. 4.2.1); Śvetaketu Āruṇeya returns proud and conceited 'after studying all the Vedas' (sarvān vedān adhītya (Ch. 6.1.2) but without knowing the nature of reality (*loc. cit.*).

time when the growing influence of heterodox schools of thought was felt,[1] it would have seemed desirable for the teachers of the Vedic tradition to close their ranks and give a definite place to traditional Vedic learning. This was done by the expedient of saying that there were two kinds of knowledge, the higher and the lower and while this new way of knowledge was regarded as the higher knowledge, the Vedas are given a definite place in the scheme of things by calling it lower knowledge. Thus the Muṇḍaka says, 'two kinds of knowledge are to be known . . . the higher and the lower' (dve vidye veditavye . . . *parā* caivā*parā* ca, Muṇḍ. 1.1.4), the lower being the study of the Vedas and the ancillary sciences (*op. cit.*, 1.1.5) 'and the higher that by which the imperishable is apprehended' (atha parā yāya tad akṣaram adhigamyate, *loc. cit.*). The use of the word vedānta (veda + ānta, the end or consummation of the Vedas) to denote this higher knowledge (Muṇḍ. 3.2.6, Śvet. 6.22) also reveals the same attitude of maintaining the continuity with the Vedic tradition while regarding this knowledge as final.

(76) Thus by the time of the Late Upaniṣads there were three main schools of thought in the Vedic tradition. Firstly, there were the orthodox brahmins who believed in the supernatural revelation of the Vedas and held the Vedas to be the supreme source of all knowledge. Secondly, there were the metaphysicians of the Early Upaniṣadic period, who held that the highest knowledge was to be had by rational argument and speculation based on their faith in or acceptance of premises, which they believed in, either because they were traditionally unquestioned or because there were rational or empirical grounds for believing in them. Thirdly, there were the contemplatives, who believed that the highest knowledge was personal and intuitional and was to be had by an extrasensory perception, acquired partly by the practice of a technique, though dependent ultimately on the will of the ātman or Iśvara. Each of these forms of knowledge was believed to result in salvation, so that salvation was conceived to be possible, *inter alia*, (1) by one's metaphysical beliefs, (2) reliance on scripture, and (3) intuitional knowledge. When, therefore, the Buddha 'says that there is no salvation through metaphysical beliefs, revelation or intuitional knowledge' (na diṭṭhiyā, na sutiyā, na ñāṇena . . . visuddhim āha, Sn. 839), in speaking to a brahmin, it is probable that he was referring to the theories of the above three classes of thinkers (cp.

[1] Deussen, *op. cit.*, p. 70.

'the sage does not say that they are "experts" by virtue of their (metaphysical) beliefs, scriptural learning and intuitional knowledge' (na *diṭṭhiyā*, na *sutiyā*, na *ñānena*, muni . . . kusalā vadanti, Sn. 1078).

(77) During the close of this period we find in the Maitrī Upaniṣad the use of the word pramāṇa (a valid means of knowledge) in a technical sense and a growing realization that our claims to knowledge must be backed up by their being made on valid grounds. We talk about time but how do we know that such a thing called time exists. This Upaniṣad suggests that we measure or know time from observing the movements of the sun across the constellations. It is said: 'Because of its subtlety this (course of the sun) is the *proof* for only in this way is time *proved* (to exist)' (saukṣmyatvād etat *pramāṇam* anenaiva *pramīyate* hi kālaḥ, 6.14). This is followed by the significant statement that '*without a valid means of knowledge there is no apprehension of objects* (*lit.* of what is to be proved)' (*na vinā pramāṇena prameyasyopalabdhih, loc. cit.*). The importance attached to the study of the pramāṇas or the valid means of knowledge (the central problem of epistemology) in Indian thought may be gauged by the fact that every school of thought, orthodox or heterodox had its theory of pramānas. When the Greeks (Strabo) referred to Indian philosophers as the 'prāmāṇikā',[1] it is not clear whether this was a reference to all the Indian philosophers at the time (of whom they were aware of), who claimed to base their theories on valid means of knowledge or a class of 'epistemologists', who made a study of the valid means of knowledge; in any case it shows the importance of pramāṇas for Indian thinkers at this time, as confirmed by the reference in the Maitrī Upaniṣad. There is also a reference to pamāṇikā in the Aṅguttara Nikāya and since this is not far removed in time from the Maitrī Upaniṣad and the Greek reference, we may translate the term pamāṇikā as 'epistemologists' since it fits the context: 'In this matter the epistemologists[2](?) argue thus; this person and the other have identically

[1] They are described as a class of brahmins 'contentious and fond of argument' called the *Pramnai*; *v.* J. W. M'Crindle, *Ancient India*, p. 76. Cp. *The Cambridge History of India*, Vol. I, p. 421, where E. R. Bevan, the author of the article says, 'The people intended were undoubtedly the *prāmāṇikas*, the followers of the various philosophical systems, each of which has its own view as to what constitutes *pramāṇa* a "means of right knowledge".'

[2] The Comy. has 'those who form judgments with regard to individuals, judge, i.e. ought to weigh and consider' (puggalesu pamāṇa-gāhā pamiṇanti, pametuṃ tuletuṃ arahanti, AA. V.53). The PTS. translation reads, 'those who measure thus measure . . .' (G.S. V. 98).

the same traits, why then is one of them (considered) inferior and the other superior' (Tatra ... *pamāṇikā pamiṇanti*: 'imassāpi te'va dhammā aparassāpi te'va dhammā, kasmā nesaṃ eko hīno eko paṇīto ti' (A. V.140). The context indicates that pamāṇikā here are a class of people who judge the truth-value of a statement in the light of evidence and is therefore strongly suggestive of the sense we have given to it.

(78) In the above discussion we have assumed that Upaniṣadic thought was known to Buddhism and has had an impact on it. The problem of the relation between the Upaniṣads and Buddhism deserves to be reviewed in respect of three questions, (1) the question as to whether there was any contact between Buddhism and the Upaniṣads, (2) if there was contact at what point (chronological) did it occur, and (3) the question whether Buddhist thought can be considered as a continuation of or a reaction against the main trends of Upaniṣadic thought. We shall, of course, not attempt to answer any of these questions here, but it is necessary to state that with regard to the first question, we assume *contra* Thomas[1] that there was contact and the knowledge that Buddhism shows of Upaniṣadic thought would we believe justify our assumption. With regard to the second question we find that while many scholars are inclined to place the rise of Buddhism close to the period of the Kaṭha Upaniṣad[2] others prefer a date long after even the Late Upaniṣads (e.g. Maitrī) had been completed.[3] We would prefer to date the rise of Buddhism somewhat before the Maitrī Upaniṣad, which we believe refers to a rising Buddhist movement.

(79) Hume, while stating that 'the usual date that is thus assigned to the Upanishads is around 600 BC just prior to the rise of Buddhism',[4]

[1] *The History of Buddhist Thought*, p. 90; most scholars, however, have admitted influence of interaction—*v.* Hume, *The Thirteen Principal Upanishads*, pp. 6 f.; J. Przyluski and E. Lamotte, 'Buddhisme et Upaniṣad', BEFEO., Vol. 32, 1932, pp. 141–69; Helmuth von Glasenapp, 'Vedānta und Buddhismus', *Abhandlungen der Geistes- und Sozialwissenschaftlichen Klasse Jahrgang* 1950, pp. 1013 ff.

[2] *v.* Oldenberg, Buddha, Calcutta, 1927, pp. 53–8; J. Charpentier, 'The Kāṭhaka Upaniṣad', *Indian Antiquary*, Nov. 1928, p. 207; J. N. Rawson, *The Kaṭha Upaniṣad*, Oxford University Press, 1934, pp. 42–8.

[3] E.g. Ranade and Belvalkar, who speak of the necessity of postulating a period of thought-ferment between 'the end of the Upanishadic movement and the commencement of the Jain-Buddhistic movements' (*History of Indian Philosophy* Vol. 2, Poona, 1927, p. 443).

[4] *The Thirteen Principal Upanishads*, p. 6.

finds 'evidences of Buddhist influences'[1] in the Bṛhadāraṇyaka, Muṇḍaka and Praśna Upaniṣads.[2] The examples he gives are of a very doubtful character and can hardly be considered evidence of influence. Thus it is arbitrary to say that the *karma* doctrine at Bṛh. 3.2.13 is due to Buddhist influence and the few philological affinities that he has shown between the language of the early Buddhist texts and the Upaniṣads *ipso facto* prove little. Deussen on the other hand has rather indirectly suggested Buddhist influence on the Maitrī Upaniṣad. He speaks of 'the polemic against the heretics which is found in Maitr. 7.8–10',[3] and says that 'Brahmanism in view of the consequences which the attitude of the earlier Upanishads had entailed in Buddhism and similar manifestations, returns to its original position'.[4] Later he states more expressly that 'in the Maitr. Upan. is revived the ancient Vedic standpoint in regard to *tapas* in the presence of Buddhist and other errors'.[5]

(80) In the section in the Maitrī Upaniṣad, where this polemic occurs, there is a reference to a sect wearing a 'ruddy robe' (kaṣāya-, 7.8). It is said that they convert their opponents by 'rational arguments and examples' (tarkadṛṣṭānta-, *loc. cit.*), deny the doctrine of the soul (nairātmyavāda-, *loc. cit.*), call attention to 'a *dharma* which is destructive of the Vedas and orthodox scriptures' (vedādiśāstra-hiṃsaka-dharmābhidhyānam astv iti vadanti, 7.9) and 'whose goal is the mere attainment of pleasure' (ratimātram phalam asya, *loc. cit.*). We may take it that the reference could be either to the Materialists, the Ājīvakas, the Jains or the Buddhists. There would have been many sects other than the Buddhists wearing the red robe, although the Dhammapada seems to regard it almost as a distinctive feature of the Buddhist monk where it is said that 'he who dons the red robe, not free from stain and lacking in restraint and truth is not worthy of the red robe' (anikkasāvo *kāsāvaṃ* yo vattham paridahessati, apeto dama-saccena na so *kāsāvam* arahati, 9). Now the Materialists did not value *dharma*:[6] but not only is dharma one of the central concepts of Buddhism, the doctrine being known as 'the dharma' (= P. dhamma-, M. I.37), the Buddha is known to the brahmins, according to the evidence of the Pali Nikāyas as a 'teacher of the dharma' (dhamma-vādi-); we find the brahmin Assalāyana (Skr. Aśvalāyana) saying:

[1] *The Thirteen Principal Upanishads*, p. 6. [2] *Op. cit.*, pp. 6, 7.
[3] Deussen, *op. cit.*, p. 65. [4] *Ibid.* [5] *Op. cit.*, p. 70.
[6] *v.* D. Chattopadhyaya, Lokāyata, p. 228.

'the recluse Gotama is a dharma-vādin; dharma-vādins are difficult to argue with ...' (samaṇo ... Gotamo *dhammavādī*, dhammavādino ca pana duppaṭimantiyā bhavanti, M. II.147). The Ājīvakas and the Jains may have also had their dharma, but they retained the doctrine of the soul (even if their concept of a soul differed from that of the Upaniṣads: the Jains 'upheld the soul', āyāvāī = Skr. ātma-vādī, Ācārāṅga Sūtra, 1.1.5)[1] and neither the Jain nor any of the Ājīvaka doctrines could be called a *nairātmya-vāda* (a doctrine denying the soul), by which Buddhism was known. The reference, ratimātram phalam asya (mere pleasure is the fruit thereof) clearly rules out the Jains and most of the Ājīvakas, who were given to extreme forms of ascetism and shunned pleasure; it seems to suggest the Materialists but it should be noted that the Buddhists had a strong reputation of being hedonists at this time. The Buddhist texts say that it was the opinion of the 'other religious teachers and wandering ascetics' that 'the recluses who are sons of the Sakyan live in luxury (*lit.* are addicted to *pleasure*)' (. . . añña-titthiyā paribbājakā evaṃ vadeyyuṃ—'Sukhallikānuyogam anuyuttā samaṇā Sakya-puttiyā viharantī ti, D. III.130). This is confirmed by the Sūtrakṛtāṅga, where it is said that 'some men, Sramaṇas and Brāhmaṇas, who ignore and deny these true words, adhere (to their own tenets) and are *given to pleasures*' (SBE., Vol. 45, p. 236) and which according to the Comy. is a reference, among others, to the Buddhists (*loc. cit.*, fn. 2). Considering this evidence the inference is unmistakable that the reference is to a rising Buddhist movement and while the Maitrī forbids the brahmins to study what is not of the Veda (nāvaidikam adhīyītāyam, 7.10), it is noteworthy that there is much material in it which has a Buddhist flavour. The instances are too many for us to discuss here, but mention may be made of the contemplation of the organic substances of the body.[2] Similarly, the concept of 'the sheath of Brahma' (*brahma-kośa-*, 6.38), which of all the classical Upaniṣads appears only in the Maitrī, is known to Buddhism (e.g. kosāni viceyya kevalāni, dibbam mānusakañ ca *brahma-kosam*, Sn. 525), but it will be noticed that while

[1] *The Āyāraṃga Sutta*, ed. H. Jacobi, Part I—Text, London, 1882, p. 1.

[2] The Upaniṣad mentions *fifteen* organic substances (1.3) while the Buddhist texts mention *thirty-one* (M. I.57) and sometimes *thirty-two* (Khp. 2). The belief that the earliest list contains thirty-two items is a common mistake; *v.* Warder, Early Buddhism and Other Contemporary Systems, BSOAS., 1956, p. 51, fn. 1, 'the stock list of thirty-two organic substances of the body—to which the brain is appended ... as 33rd'.

the Buddhist text speaks of three kosa-s, the Maitrī has the concept of a four-fold kośa- (caturjālam brahmakośam, *loc. cit.*).

(81) We may conclude from the above that the rise of Buddhism is not far removed in time from, though it is prior to, the Maitrī Upaniṣad.

CHAPTER II

THE HISTORICAL BACKGROUND II—NON-VEDIC I—MATERIALISM

(82) The impact of Materialist thinking on the thought of the Canon is strong (*v. infra*, 637) and it therefore seems desirable to study the epistemological doctrines of the Materialists in so far as they seem to have a bearing on the thought of the Canon.

(83) It is customary to regard Materialism as a heterodox school, which grew up in violent opposition to Vedic thought, but our study of the concept of Lokāyata has shown that Materialist philosophy emerged within the Brāhmaṇical fold as part of its logical and metaphysical (lokāyata-) speculations. Even scholars, we notice, trace the origins of Materialist thinking to the thought of the Early Upaniṣadic period.

(84) Das Gupta, followed in this respect by Jadunath Sinha[1] and Chattopadhyaya,[2] finds 'references to the lokāyata doctrine (by which he means Materialism) . . . in the Chāndogya Upaniṣad VIII, 7, 8, where Virocana . . . went away satisfied with the view that the self was identical with the body';[3] but this is not full-fledged Materialism since this particular brand of *dehātmavāda*, as Das Gupta calls it (*loc. cit.*), entertains a belief in the after-life which is quite explicit (Ch. 8.8.5). Ruben, on the other hand, as we have seen (*v. supra*, 22) traces the origins of Materialism to the thought of Uddālaka even calling him a Materialist. There are undoubtedly certain materialistic trends in the thought of Uddālaka[4] but we must remember that his ultimate reality Being (sat) has the quality of sentience (tad aikṣata bahu syām, Ch. 6.2.3) and creatures in some sense survive bodily death (Ch. 6.9.2.3). It nevertheless could have furnished the germs of a Materialist philosophy if these inconsistencies were got rid of.

[1] *History of Indian Philosophy*, Vol. I, p. 230. [2] *Lokāyata*, p. 45.

[3] *A History of Indian Philosophy*, Vol. III, p. 528.

[4] Note his materialist conception of the mind (manas), which is formed of the finest essence of food (anna-) (Ch. 6.6.1).

(85) It is perhaps not without significance that the second school of Materialists (i.e. according to the interpretation of Śīlāṅka[1]) mentioned in the Sūtrakṛtāṅga (2.1.10=SBB. 2.1.22, Vol. 45, p. 343) makes use of Uddālaka's *a priori* premiss that 'Being cannot come out of Non-Being' (kathaṃ asataḥ saj jāyeta, Ch. 6.2.2) when it says, sato ṇatthi viṇāso asato ṇatthi sambhavo, which Jacobi translates, 'what is, does not perish, from nothing nothing comes' and which literally means, 'there is no destruction of Being, there is no origination of Non-Being'. If so Uddālaka would be the father of Indian Materialism, in the sense in which all Materialism, according to Burnet,[2] is said to depend on the theory of Parmenides, who was the first philosopher of Being in Greek thought to make use of this premiss.

(86) Finally, it will be noticed that the Materialists themselves seem to trace their doctrines to the Early Upaniṣads when they quote a statement attributed to Yājñavalkya in the Upaniṣads in support of their doctrines.[3] It is significant that this same Yājñavalkya asks a question which has materialistic implications when, comparing man to a tree, he says, 'a mortal when cut down by death by what root does he grow up? For if with its roots they should pull up a tree, it would not come into being again.'[4] We find this same analogy used in the Mahābhārata where, as the context shows, the materialist conclusion is clearly drawn: 'If the root of a tree that is cut down does not grow up again, though its seeds germinate, where is the person who having died comes back again.'[5] It is therefore highly significant when the commentary to the Dīgha Nikāya speaking of the epistemic origins of the materialistic theories says that some 'accept Materialism on the basis

[1] *On Sū.* 2.1.10, Vol. II, fol. 17, sa ca Sāṃkhyamatāvalambī . . . Lokāyatamatāvalambī vā nāstiko, i.e. he depends on the Sāṅkhya theory . . . or is a nāstika depending on the Materialist theory.

[2] *Early Greek Philosophy,* London and Edinburgh, 1892, pp. 194–5, Hegel, Erdmann, Schwegler *et al.* traced the origins of idealistic thought to Parmenides but Burnet says, 'Parmenides is not as some have said the father of idealism. On the contrary, all materialism depends upon his view'.

[3] 'tad āhuḥ, "*vijñānaghana evaitebhyo bhūtebhyaḥ samutthāya tānyevanuvinaśyati na pretya saṃjñāsti*" ti,' Sarvadarśanasaṃgraha, by Sāyana-Mādhava, Ed. V. S. Abhyankar, Second Edition, Poona, 1951, p. 5; the quotation is from Bṛh. 2.4.12.

[4] yat samūlam āvṛheyuḥ vṛkṣaṃ na punar ābhavet martyaḥ svin mṛtyunā vṛknaḥ kasmān mulāt prarohati, Bṛh. 3.9.28.6.

[5] Chinnasya yadi vṛkṣasya, na mūlam pratirohati, bījānyasya prarohanti mṛtaḥ kva punar eṣyati, Śrīmanmahābhāratam, Śāntiparva, 184.14, Ed. T. R. Krishnacharya and T. R. Vyasacharya, Vol. 12, Bombay, 1907, p. 294.

of such *arguments* as 'beings are like tree-leaves (or trees and leaves), which when they fall, do not grow up again'.[1]

(87) If Materialism grew up as a product of the incipient rational temper of this period, it is not surprising that references to this doctrine should be found by the time of the Kaṭha Upaniṣad, which mentions a class of people who hold 'this is the world, there is no other'[2] and deny survival.[3] Later, in the Śvetāśvatara Upaniṣad, it had to be reckoned among the theories current at that time, for here reference is made to several speculative theories about the nature of reality and one of them is the 'doctrine of elements' (bhūtāni, 1.2). This may be identified either with the Materialist theory in the Buddhist texts, which upheld the reality of the four elements, viz. earth, water, fire and wind (cātummahābhūta-),[4] or the Materialist doctrine mentioned in the Jain texts, which held that the five elements (pañcamahabbhūyā, Sū. 2.1.10), viz. earth, water, fire, wind and air were alone real and that all things were composed of them.

(88) Since we are concerned only with the epistemological theories propounded and the nature of the arguments adduced in support of their doctrines by the Materialists contemporary with the rise of Buddhism, we shall confine ourselves to these aspects of their doctrines. It is, however, difficult to determine with any degree of exactness what portion or proportion of these doctrines could have been contemporary with this period, since most of the informative accounts that we have of the Materialists are of a later date. We would therefore adopt the method of stating those doctrines, which we suspect have a bearing, direct or indirect, on the thought of this period, even when the form in which they are stated is comparatively late and then endeavour in the light of the material available from the Early Jain and Buddhist sources to sift what may be early from the late.

(89) When we consider the epistemological theories of the various schools of Materialists, we find that with regard to the opinions and theories held on the problem of the means of knowledge, it is possible to classify them into three groups, viz. (1) those who upheld the

[1] Yathā rukkhapaṇṇāni patitāni na puna virūhanti, evaṃ sattā ti ādinā *takkena* vā ucchedaṃ gaṇhanti, DA. I.120.

[2] ayaṃ loko nāsti para iti māni, 1.2.6.

[3] yeyam prete vicikitsā manuṣye 'stīyeke nāyamastīti caike, 1.1.20.

[4] Cp. attā rūpī cātummahābhūtiko, D. I.34; cātummahābhūtiko' yam puriso, D. I.55.

validity of perception alone and denied inference and other forms of knowledge, (2) those who upheld the validity and priority of perception, but admitted inference in a limited sense, denying other forms of knowledge, (3) those who denied all means of knowledge including perception.

(90) Group (1) is the best known. In Mādhava's (14th c.) Sarvadarśanasaṃgraha, which is the *locus classicus* for a clear and concise statement of what appears to be the widest known school of materialism, it is said that 'this school holds that perception is the *only* source of knowledge' (pratyakṣaikapramāṇavāditayā, p. 3). Earlier in the Sarvasiddhāntasaṃgraha of Śaṅkara (8th c.) it is stated that according to the Materialists 'only the perceived exists, the unperceived does not exist by reason of its never having been perceived'.[1] Perhaps, still earlier, in a reference to materialistic doctrines, where the account is not technical or elaborate, we find it said that the Materialists held perception to be the only source of knowledge: 'Understand, intelligent One, that no one exists hereafter; regard not that which is beyond the reach of your senses, but only that which is an object of perception'.[2] It is not possible to determine how early this reference in the Rāmāyaṇa could be but we find that the theory set forth here is associated with the Materialists and is criticized in the Pāli Nikāyas D. II.328, 330). Kassapa is here arguing with the kṣatriya Pāyāsi (*v. infra*, 136–9), who has performed a series of experiments, all based on the assumption that it is possible to verify the existence of a soul by sense-experience. This shows indirectly that the Materialists represented, could only be satisfied by the evidence of the senses. The argument of the Materialist is stated by his opponent as follows: 'I do not know this, I do not see this; *therefore* (tasmā) it does not exist' (Ahaṃ etaṃ na jānāmi, ahaṃ etaṃ na passāmi, tasmā tam natthī ti, *loc. cit.*). This is countered by the argument that it is wrong to infer from 'I do not see *X*' that '*X* does not exist'.[3] An example is given of a man born blind (jaccandho puriso) who says he cannot see black or

[1] pratyakṣagamyamevāsti nāstyadṛṣṭamadṛṣṭataḥ, 2.2.3. Ed. M. Rangācārya, Madras, 1909, p. 5.

[2] sa nāsti param ity etat kuru buddhiṃ mahāmate, pratyakṣam yat tad ātiṣṭha parokṣam pṛṣṭhataḥ kuru, Ayodhyākāṇḍa, 108.17, *v.* Ed. Śrīnivāsa Śāstri Kaṭṭi, Vol. 2, p. 992.

[3] Cp. Cowell, SDS., p. 14, 'when you deny the existence of an object on the ground of its not being perceived, you yourself admit an inference of which non-perception is the middle term'.

white forms (kaṇhasukkāni rūpāni), forms of various colours, the stars, the sun or the moon and argues that since he does not see them, such things do not exist. Pāyāsi is made to admit that such things do exist and that therefore the argument that what one does not see, does not exist, is false. We saw in the above quotation from the Rāmāyaṇa that it was implied that there was no hereafter, since the hereafter is beyond the reach of our senses (i.e. of perception) and therefore the hereafter does not exist. It is the logic of this same argument that is assailed here. The Materialist could, however, still maintain his case for perception by arguing that even though one may be blind, visible objects exist because they are perceived by others, whereas the other world is in principle unobservable by anybody and therefore cannot be presumed to exist. This objection is implied in the question that Pāyāsi proceeds to ask, viz. 'who tells you, Kassapa, that the gods exist' (ko pan'etaṃ bhoto Kassapassa āroceti atthi devā . . ., *loc. cit.*). What is meant is that in the case of physical objects we can go on the information of others who have perceptual evidence of them, even if we are blind but in the case of the hereafter we cannot expect such information since no one can be presumed to have any perceptual evidence of its existence. This is met by the rejoinder that the 'other world cannot be observed in the way he thinks by the human eye' (na kho . . . evaṃ paraloko daṭṭhabbo yathā tvaṃ maññasi iminā maṃsacakkhunā, *loc. cit.*) but that it is still observable by some by means of 'clear, paranormal, clairvoyant vision' (dibbena cakkhunā visuddhena atikkantamānusakena, *loc. cit.*). It is claimed that there are recluses and brahmins who devote their lives to meditating in the forest and developing their faculty of clairvoyant vision, whereby they can observe this world and the next (imam eva lokam passanti param eva, *loc. cit.*). The Materialist is not impressed by this argument since he repeats that he is still of the former opinion,[1] presumably because he does not believe in the possibility of extrasensory perception and further discussion on these lines is dropped.

(91) It is, however, clear from the above that the Materialists at this time attached great importance to perception as a means of knowledge,

[1] Kiñcā'pi bhavaṃ Kassapo evam āha, atha kho evam me ettha hoti; iti pi n'atthi paraloko, n'atthi sattā opapātikā, N'atthi sukaṭadukkaṭānaṃ kammānaṃ, phalaṃ vipāko ti, i.e. although the reverend Kassapa says so, I am still of the opinion that there is no other world, no surviving beings, and no result or effect of good or evil deeds. Later (D. I., p. 352) it is said that he was convinced by these arguments.

even if it is not clear whether they did hold that it was the only means of knowledge. It is not possible to ascertain whether the metaphysics of materialism preceded its epistemology or vice versa but there is undoubtedly an intimate connection between them. Śīlāṅka, the ninth-century[1] commentator on the Sūtrakṛtāṅga, seems to think that the denial of the unverifiables on the part of the Materialist is based on their epistemology and results from the acceptance of perception alone as the only means of knowledge. Speaking of the Materialists he says, 'they argue (pramāṇayanti) as follows: there is no soul apart from the (material elements such as) earth, etc., *because there is no means of knowledge to apprehend it* and the only means of knowledge is perception and not inference or the rest since with the latter there is no direct sense-contact with the object and error results; as a result of error and owing to the presence of obstacles they (i.e. these means of knowledge) would be of a defective nature and one cannot have confidence in any of them; it has been said that "one who runs on uneven ground groping his way about (*lit.* trusting on his hands, feet, etc.) depending largely on inference is bound to fall"—this is the characteristic of inference, scripture and the rest (of the means of knowledge) for (with them) one has to move as it were by groping one's way because there is no direct contact with objects; therefore, *perception is the only means of knowledge* (pratyakṣamevaikam pramāṇam) *and by means of it one cannot apprehend a soul different from the elements* and as for the consciousness (caitanyam) found in their midst, it manifests itself only when the elements come together in the form of a body like the intoxicating power when the ingredients are mixed'.[2] This passage tells us why the Materialists relied only on perception and how their philosophical beliefs depend on this. Perception is the only valid means of knowledge since the others are liable to error, as there is no direct sense-contact with the object in their case; therefore, there cannot be a self-identical soul since

[1] Glasenapp, *Der Jainismus*, p. 107.

[2] On Sū. 1.1.8, Vol. I, fol. 15, tathā (te) hi evam pramāṇayanti—na pṛthivyādi-vyatirikta ātmā'sti, tadgrāhakapramāṇābhāvāt, pramāṇam cātra pratyakṣameva, nānumānādikam tatrendriyeṇa sākṣādarthasya sambandhābhāvādvyabhicārasambhavaḥ, sati ca vyabhicārasambhave sadṛśe cābādhāsambhave dūṣitaṃ syād iti sarvatrānāśvāsaḥ, tathācoktam—'hastasparśādivāndhena, viṣame pathi dhāvatā anumānapradhānena, vinipāto na durlabhaḥ' anumānaṃ cātropalakṣaṇamāgamādīnām api, sākṣādartha sambandhābhāvāddhastasparśaneneva pravṛttiriti, tasmāt pratyakṣamevaikam pramāṇam, tena ca bhūtavyatiriktasyātmano na grahaṇam, yattu caitanyaṣ teṃūpalabhyate, tad bhūteṣv eva kāyākārapariṇateṣv abhivyajyate madyāṅgeṣu samuditeṣu madaśaktivad iti.

one cannot perceive it. This shows that their metaphysical beliefs had an epistemological basis according to this account of Śīlāṅka. It may be seen that from the earliest times the more sceptical minded were inclined to doubt or deny the existence of what they did not see. Much of Ṛgvedic scepticism was based on this principle (*v. supra*, 7). It would therefore not be implausible to suggest that the birth of the Materialist philosophy in India may have taken place when the principle that what one does not see does not exist, was more or less systematically worked out.[1]

(92) Whatever the views held by the Materialists contemporary with or prior to Early Buddhism, there is every reason to believe that group (1) taken as a whole denied the validity of inference altogether. This is evident from the accounts given of the Materialist criticisms of inference in Śāntarakṣita's Tattvasaṃgraha (1457–9), Kamalaśīla's Pañjikā (*ibid.*), Jayanta's Nyāyamañjarī[2] and the Sarvadarśanasaṃgraha (Ch. I). In this respect group (2) is in agreement with group (3), which also criticizes anumāna (inference). A fairly adequate account of these group (1) criticisms of inference have been given by Das Gupta[3] and Jadunath Sinha[4] and we do not propose to repeat this here. A brief account of the group (1) criticisms of inference as taught in the Nyāya school is given by Radhakrishnan and Moore[5] although the criticisms of Jayarāśi Bhaṭṭa are specifically directed against the conceptions of inference found both in the schools of the Nyāya as well as the Buddhists (*v. infra*, 105, 106). Of these accounts, Jayarāśi's criticisms are the most specific and elaborate while the simplest and the most general account appears to be that given in the Sarvadarśanasaṃgraha. The gist of the argument here is that inference cannot be shown to be a valid mode of knowledge unless it can be proved that there are good grounds for knowing the truth of universal propositions (vyāpti) as well as their necessity. Now universal propositions or universals cannot be known by perception, for perception whether external or internal (i.e. introspection) is of particulars, with which we are acquainted through sense-experience or introspection. They cannot be claimed to be known through inference for this would lead to infinite regress. It cannot be testimony for this is either a form of inference or implies

[1] Cp. those who did not believe in gods or sacrifices in the Ṛgveda (RV. 8, 70.7, 71.8; 10.38.3); these contexts mention the 'godless man' (adevaḥ).

[2] Ed. Pandit S. S. Nārāyana Śukla, Benares, 1936, pp. 108, 109; *v.* anumānaprāmāṇyākṣepaḥ.

[3] HIP., Vol. III, 533 ff. [4] HIP., Vol. I, 235 ff. [5] *Op. cit.*, pp. 236–46.

inference and if we accept testimony we would have to believe anything whatsoever on authority. Nor can it be analogy (upamāna) for this merely relates a name to a thing named. Likewise, the necessary connection between causes and effects asserted by universal propositions cannot be established and the connection may very well be a coincidence.

(93) It is obvious that even this simplest account is far too sophisticated to have its roots in the period of Early Buddhism. Does this mean that the criticism of inference is a later development and that in the earliest period inference of some kind was admitted along with perception? If the Materialists were among the first thinkers in India to argue and thus develop the tarkaśāstra—it seems *prima facie* unlikely that they would have discarded anumāna so early, especially after realizing that it was the mainstay of the hetuśāstra. They had to argue very sharply against their opponents and they would have cut the ground beneath their feet if they denied the logical basis of their reasoning altogether and admitted its total invalidity. When we examine the reasoning behind some of Pāyāsi's experiments (*v. infra,* 136–9) we notice that he makes use of inference, though it is inference based on sense-perception, despite his fundamental assumptions, namely that the soul is visible or has weight being mistaken. Besides, the argument of the Materialists is put by the Buddhist in the form '*etaṃ na jānāmi etaṃ na passāmi,* tasmā taṃ natthi' and we have some reason to believe that the phrase 'jānāmi passāmi' is used in the Buddhist texts (*v. infra,* 783) to denote 'perception and inductive inference based on perception' though Buddhism uses 'perception' in a wider sense to include extra-sensory perception. If this is so, then in the context of the Materialist this phrase should mean 'sense-perception and inductive inference'. In other words perception has priority as the basic means of knowing though inference also plays a limited part when what is inferred is in principle verifiable by sense-perception.

(94) Another reason for surmising that inference in this sense is possibly a part of the early doctrine of Materialism of at least one of the schools is that it appears to have been held by group (2), represented by the views ascribed to Purandara in Kamalasīla's Tattvasaṃgraha-pañjikā.[1] The statement ascribed to Purandara[2] is as follows:

[1] 1482–3, p. 41; *v.* Das Gupta, *op. cit.*, Vol. III, p. 536, fn. 2.

[2] Tucci has shown that Purandara was a 'Cārvāka-mate granthakāra' (an author of a book on Materialism); *v.* 'A Sketch of Indian Materialism', PIPC., 1925, p. 36.

Purandaras tv āha, lokaprasiddham anumānam Cārvākairapīṣyata eva yattu kaiscillaukikam mārgamatikramya anumānamucyate tanniṣiddhyate, i.e. Purandara says that it is well known that even the Materialists accept inference although they object to people (kaiścit) employing inference beyond the limits of sense-perception (*lit.* beyond the path of this world). This view attributed to Purandara is confirmed by the references made to him by the Jain commentator Vādideva Sūri who, as Das Gupta has pointed out,[1] quotes in his commentary Syādvādaratnākara (II.131) on his Pramāṇanayatattvālokālaṅkāra a sūtra of Purandara, viz. pramāṇasya gauṇatvād anumānādarthaniścayadurlabhāt, i.e. from the very nature of this means of knowledge, it is difficult to determine (the existence of transcendent) objects by means of inference(?). The sense of this sūtra is however made clear by Vādideva's comment, laukikahetūnām anumeyāvagame nimittaṃ sa nāsti tantrasiddheṣv iti na tebhyaḥ parokṣārthāvagamo nyāyyo 'ta idamuktam anumanād arthaniścayo durlabhaḥ. Das Gupta's translation of this passage appears to be more of the nature of a commentary than a translation.[2] We may translate it more or less literally as follows: 'since in transcendent proofs (tantrasiddheṣu, *lit.* what is proved in religious texts) the basis for inference is absent unlike in the case of perceptual inferences, a knowledge of transcendent objects cannot be had (nyāyyo, *lit.* inferred) by them; therefore has it been said that "it is difficult to determine (the existence of transcendent) objects by means of inference".' This shows the existence of a school of Materialists who admitted perception and empirical inference but discarded metaphysical inference on the grounds that what was in principle unperceivable was unknowable. For a valid inference to be possible, it is necessary to establish the truth of a universal proposition (vyāpti), which reveals a concomitance between a hetu and an anumeya (=sādhya-, cp. laukikahetūnām anumeyāvagame) and this is not possible unless both are in principle observables. It is difficult to say whether this school asserted that there was a necessary connection between cause and effect or merely held that the concomitance or sequence was only probable and therefore the inference was only probable. It is worth noting that one of the objections against inference brought out by group (1) was that

[1] *Op. cit.*, Vol. III, p. 536, fn. 2.

[2] 'Thus since in the supposed supra-sensuous transcendent world no case of hetu agreeing with the presence of its sādhya can be observed, no inductive generalization or law of concomitance can be made relating to that sphere.'

there was no necessity in the concomitance, despite our repeated observation of several instances. As Jayanta says in elucidating the theories of the Materialists, 'universality (vyāpti) is not established even by the observation of several instances (bhūyodarśanagamyā'pi) since there is the possibility of error even after observing a thousand instances: though we come to the conclusion that smoke and fire are concomitant (sahacāri, *lit.* go together) by observing several instances we cannot know that there is no smoke in the absence of fire despite this repeated observation'.[1] But whether they made this latter qualification (which, incidentally, is the same as the objection that Hume raised against causation and inference[2]) or not, it is clear that in limiting the inferable to the sphere of the verifiable, they were tacitly assuming the truth of the Verification Principle[3] and it is therefore this group rather than group (3) (*v. supra*, 89) which deserves to be called a positivist[4] school of thought. Purandara's statement that it is well known (lokaprasiddham, *lit.* known the world over) that the materialists accepted inference does not make sense unless they or the majority of them had in fact accepted the validity of both perception and inference in the above sense up to that time. That the reference to this school is not confined to Purandara's statements and their exposition is evident from the reference made to it by the Jain commentator Guṇaratna who in his Tarkarahasyadīpikā commenting on the phrase, mānam tvakṣajameva hi, in verse 83 of the Ṣaddarśanasamuccaya says that 'the particle "hi" in this phrase is added to denote a distinction, the distinction being that at times (kvacana) the Cārvākas welcome inferences such as "smoke" (implies fire) which are limited to stating what is within the reach of the world but not transcendent inferences (alaukikamanumānam) which (claim to) establish (the existence of) heaven, what is

[1] bhūyodarśanagamyā'pi na vyāptir avakalpate sahasraśo'pi taddṛṣṭe vyabhicārāvadhāranāt bhūyo dṛṣṭvā ca dhūmo'gnisahacāritigamyatām anagnau tu sa nāstīti na bhūyodarśanādgatiḥ, Nyāyamañjarī, p. 109.

[2] *A Treatise of Human Nature*, Vol. I, Part III, Section XIV. Cp. p. 169. 'If we define a cause to be an object precedent and contiguous to one another and where all the objects resembling the former are placed in a like relation of priority and contiguity to those objects that resemble the latter; we may easily conceive that there is no absolute nor metaphysical necessity, that every beginning of existence should be attended with such an object.'

[3] Warnock, *English Philosophy since 1900*, pp. 44 ff.

[4] Basham speaks of 'the positivism of Ajita' (*op. cit.*, p. 271) but he does not clarify his usage. Warder (*v. infra*, 97) uses the term of group (3) but as we have shown this is quite unjustifiable.

unseen (adṛṣṭa), etc.'[1] The fact that Vādideva Sūri and Guṇaratna are Jains and the other reference was in a Buddhist work shows that at least the Buddhist and Jain tradition was well aware of the existence of this school. When we consider this in the light of what we know of the Materialists from the Early Buddhist and Jain sources it seems probable that these early Materialists or at least one school among them believed in the validity of *both* perception and inference while giving priority to perception and restricting inference within the limits of the verifiable.

(95) The third group of Materialists, as classified according to their epistemological theories, is represented by Jayarāśi Bhaṭṭa's Tattvopaplavasiṃha, which is the only extant authentic text of the Materialists (lokāyata). Although this work was published in 1940, very few scholars seem to have taken note of it. Ruben (1954),[2] Jadunath Sinha (1956)[3] and Sharma (1960)[4] make no reference to it in discussing the philosophy of the Materialists and Chattopādhyāya (1959), who professes to make a specialized study of lokāyata-,[5] begins his book by lamenting the lack of any treatise of this school.

(96) The Tattvopaplavasiṃha refers to another work of the same school, the Lakṣaṇasāra (p. 20) or the 'Essence of Definition(?)', which may be his own work since after criticizing two of the characteristics of perception (avyabhicāri, vyavasāyātmakam) according to the Nyāya definition (N.S. 1.1.4) he refers the reader to the above work for the criticism of the other characteristic (avyapadeśyam). As the editors have pointed out (pp. iii, iv), the reference in Śrī Harṣa's Khaṇḍanakhaṇḍakhādya to a school of the Lokāyatas, which like the Mādhyamika school of Buddhism and the school of Śaṅkara is said to have denied the validity of all means of knowledge (pramānas) is most probably a reference to this school.

[1] P. 306, hi śabdo'tra viśeṣanārtho vartate, viśeṣaḥ punas Cārvākairlokayātrānirvahanapravaṇam dhūmādyanumānam iṣyate kvacana, na punaḥ svargādṛṣṭādiprasādhakam alaukikam anumānam iti.

[2] *Op. cit.*; however, he has more recently written an article on this subject entitled, 'Uber den Tattvopaplavasiṃha des Jayarāśi Bhaṭṭa eine Agnostizistische Erkenntniskritik' appearing in, 'Wiener Zeitschrift für die Kunde Süd-und Ostasiens und Archiv für indische Philosophie, Band II', 1958, pp. 140–53.

[3] *Op. cit.*

[4] C. D. Sharma, *A Critical Survey of Indian Philosophy*, London, 1960.

[5] *Op. cit.*, p. 6, '. . . in the ocean of uncertainty concerning the lost Lokāyata the only piece of definite information is that we are left with no original work on it'.

(97) The interest of this school for us lies in the fact that it seems to throw some light on a school of thought mentioned in the Nikāyas, which represented a standpoint of absolute nihilism or logical scepticism in rejecting all views but which at the same time has been called an 'annihilationist' (ucchedavāda-) or Materialist school (*v. infra*, 335). It also appears to explain a certain usage (*v. infra*, 116) of a phrase attributed to the early Materialists which would otherwise be inexplicable. Warder has seen in this branch of Lokāyata philosophers 'not materialists but positivists according to modern ideas' (*op. cit.*, p. 52) and says that 'we may perhaps connect Jayarāśi Bhaṭṭa's theory with Sañjaya Belaṭṭhiputta in the Sāmaññaphala Sutta, which, however, is stated as merely agnostic or sceptic without positivist content' (*ibid.*, p. 53). He calls Jayarāśi Bhaṭṭa 'a positivist' (*ibid.*) and this branch of Lokāyata as 'the positivist branch' (*ibid.*) which rejected perception whereas the 'ordinary Lokāyata as described in the Tattvasaṃgraha and elsewhere allows perception as the only means of cognition' (*ibid.*). He adds that this 'positivist trend may have been a later development in the Lokāyata-Cārvāka school rather than an early rival branch of Bārhaspatya' (*ibid.*). The editors of this text have also expressed the view that this work 'carries to its logical end the sceptical tendency of the Cārvāka school' (p. i) and have raised the question as to whether the author of this work is a mere sophist who has no views of his own, although they themselves do not think so (p. xiii).

(98) We may state at the outset that we do not agree with Warder's assessment of this philosophy as positivism and our objection is not that he is, as he says at the end of his paper, applying 'modern philosophical terms' to 'ancient doctrines' (*v. op. cit.*, p. 62). Nor can we see much of a connection between this philosophy and the views expressed by the sceptic Sañjaya. And since this early school of absolute nihilists or logical sceptics, who have also been called materialists, seems to contain the basic concepts of this philosophy we are more inclined to entertain the possibility that the germinal ideas or the roots of this school go back to the period of the Pāli Nikāyas and that this school was possibly an early rival branch of the other school which at that time accepted at least the validity of perception if not of inference as well.

(99) Since this work has been untranslated[1] and largely ignored since its publication it seems desirable to give a brief account of its nature

[1] Except for a brief extract of the criticism of anumāna in the Nyāya school, given in Radhakrishnan and Moore (*op. cit.*, pp. 236–46).

and contents before we form any conclusions about it. The work claims to be, as the editors have shown (pp. xi, xii) a text of the Lokāyata school. The author quotes Bṛhaspati who is sometimes mentioned by name with great respect (pp. 45, 88) and is once called the Sūtrakāra- (p. 79). In the second paragraph of his work he cites the proposition 'earth, water, fire, air are the real elements (tattvāni); by their combination (arise) the body, the senses, objects and consciousness'[1] which Guṇaratna in his Tarkarahasyadīpikā quotes[2] as the statement of Vācaspati (=Bṛhaspati). He also quotes with approval the sayings 'the worldly path should be followed . . . fools and the wise are alike in the eyes of the world'[3] which he attributes to the wisest of men (paramārthavidbhiḥ).

(100) And now begins the problem. He speaks of the tattvas (four elements) of the Lokāyata, but shows that we have no grounds for affirming that they are real. He uses an epistemological argument: 'We can talk of a means of knowledge (māna) only if it is valid (sallakṣaṇanibandhanam mānavyavasthānam, *lit.* the determination of a means of knowledge depends on its having the characteristic of existence) and the proof of the (existence of the) objects of knowledge (meyasthitiḥ) depends on the means of knowledge but if there is no means of knowledge (tadabhāve) how can we speak of the real existence of both (objects as well as means of knowledge)'.[4] This is not claimed to be a disproof of Bṛhaspati's proposition (quoted above) for it is said that in asserting that earth, etc., were tattvas he was indirectly referring to (pratibimbanārtham, *lit.* reflecting) the fact that if even what is widely accepted as real does not bear critical examination (vicāryamānāni na vyatiṣṭhante), then what of other things (kiṃ punar anyāni). But this is surely a departure from the materialist thesis, for how can a person who does not believe in the objective existence

[1] pṛthivyāpastejovāyuriti tattvāni tatsamudāye śarīrendriyaviśayasaṃjñā, p. 1.

[2] Guṇaratna's quotation adds caitanya as a by-product of the rest, yaduvāca Vācaspatiḥ, pṛthivyāpastejovāyuriti tattvāni tatsamudāye śarīraviṣayendriyasaṃjñā, tebhyaścaitanyam, *op. cit.*, p. 307. It may also be noticed that viṣaya- is placed before indriya- in this. The addition of caitanya- strongly suggests that this was the view of the school which admitted an emergent ātman considered a by-product, which Śīlāṅka distinguishes from the other school (*v. infra*, 115).

[3] laukiko mārgo'nusarttavyaḥ . . . lokavyavahāramprati sadṛśau bālapaṇḍitau, p. 1.

[4] sallakṣaṇanibandhanam mānavyavasthānam, mānanibandhanā ca meyasthitiḥ, tadabhāve tayoḥ sadvyavahāraviṣayatvam katham . . . p. 1.

of the material elements be called a materialist? Jayarāśi, therefore, cannot be reckoned a materialist, as far as his theory of the external world is concerned. He seems to deny the real existence of both this world as well as the next, in denying the reality of all tattvas and his work as its name implies is intended to 'upset all principles' (tattva-upaplava-) epistemological as well as ontological, and he claims to have done so at the end of his work (tadevam upapluteṣu tattveṣu, p. 125).

(101) His epistemological argument (assuming that his disproof of the pramāṇas is valid) only goes to prove that we do not or cannot *know* that there are real objects of knowledge and not that such objects do not exist. In other words, his argument should have led him to scepticism and not to nihilism. But it is important to observe that nowhere in his work does he claim to be a sceptic or grant the possibility of the existence of things even if he cannot know them. On the contrary he even uses metaphysical arguments (*v. infra,* 104) to disprove the existence of the soul. He is therefore not a sceptic but an absolute nihilist in his metaphysics though he may be called a logical sceptic in so far as he is sceptical of (i.e. doubts or denies) the possibility of knowledge.

(102) Though he is not a materialist, we may perhaps concede that he shows a certain partiality for materialism in that he seems to imply that the material tattvas have a greater claim to reality by the common consent of the world (loke prasiddhāni, p. 1). On pragmatic grounds (vyavahāraḥ kriyate) he says that we should believe in the existence of the body, of physical objects (ghaṭādau) and of pleasure (sukha-) (p. 1) and recommends as a wise saying that the 'way of the world (laukiko margaḥ) should be followed'. As he thus seems to recommend the materialist way of life, we may call him a pragmatic but not a metaphysical materialist.

(103) Jayarāśi's work is almost exclusively devoted to epistemology, if not for a brief section in which he criticizes the ātman-theories of Nyāya (pp. 74–8), Jainism (pp. 78–9), Sāṅkhya (pp. 79–81), Vedānta (pp. 81–2) and Mīmāṃsā (pp. 82–3). We shall translate a section in which he criticizes a Vedānta theory (not that of Śaṅkara) of the ātman since this would throw some light on the nature of his reasoning and the question as to whether he is a positivist. He is criticizing the theory that the soul (or pure ego) is of a blissful nature (ānandarūpam) and is

absolute (kaivalyam). He proceeds as follows:[1] 'Those who posit the blissful nature and absoluteness of the soul do not speak with reason. Why? If the soul has a blissful nature and it is introspective (svasaṃvedyam), then this experience will be present (prasaktam) in its saṃsāric state, in which case the effort to attain salvation is futile. If on the other hand this is not experienced in the saṃsāric state, the soul would have the nature of being enveloped with primeval defilements. Just as a jar when concealed under a cloth is not recognized as a jar, the soul when smeared with defilements is not known as a soul but this (argument) is false, since there is no congruity (vaiṣamyāt) between the instance and the example. In the case of our not recognizing the jar when it is hidden beneath the cloth there is no contact of the jar with the organ of sense, owing to the cloth concealing it and in its absence the sense-cognition of the jar does not take place. But here in the case of what is covered with defilements, what is concealed? The concealment of the experiencer and the object of experience cannot take place for the experiencer (vedaka-) and the experienced (vedyam) are of the nature of the soul. As in the case of the consciousness (vijñānam) of the Buddhists (Bauddhānām), it is experienced in the presence or the absence of objects. Since introspectibility is of the nature of the soul, it is experienced in the presence or the absence of defilements, as owing to the inactivity (akiñcitkaratvāt) of the defilements the soul persists as a different object. But if the defilements are identical with the soul, then in saying "the defilements are removed", are you not saying that the soul is removed, in which case it can be objected that there is no salvation!'[2]

[1] Ye'pi ānandarūpam ātmanaḥ, kaivalyam abhidadhati te'pi yuktivādino na bhavanti. Katham? Yady ātmanaḥ ānandarūpaṃ svasaṃvedyañ ca, tadā saṃsārāvasthāyām api tat vedyaṃ prasaktaṃ; tataś ca mokṣārthaprayāso niṣphalaḥ. Atha saṃsārāvasthāyām na vedyate anādimalāvaguṇṭhitam ātmanaḥ svarūpam, yathā paṭāntarite ghaṭe ghaṭabuddhir na bhavati, evam malalipte ātmani ātmabuddhir na bhavati; tad etad ayuktam, dṛṣṭāntadārṣṭāntikayoḥ vaiṣamyāt—paṭāntarite ghaṭe paṭabuddhir na bhavati paṭāntardhāne sati indriyeṇa sākam sambandho nāsti tadbhāvād ghate nendriyajaṃ vijñānaṃ sampadyate. Iha tu punaḥ malāvaguṇṭhanena kasya vyavadhānam kriyate? na vedyavedakayor vyavadhānam kriyate. Vedyaṃ vedakañ ca ātmasvarūpam eva—yathā Bauddhānāṃ svasaṃvedyaṃ vijñānaṃ tac ca viṣayasadbhāve 'pi vedyate tadabhāve'pi vedyate, yathātmanaḥ, svasaṃvedyaṃ svarūpam malasadbhāve'pi vedyate tadasadbhāve'pi vedyate, malasyākiñcitkaratvād ātmano 'rthāntaratvenāvasthānāt. Atha tādātmyena sthitāni malāni; tadā'malāny apanīyante' kimuktaṃ bhavati? Atmā'panīyate, tataś ca mokṣābhāvaprasangaḥ, pp. 81, 82.

[2] For a similar argument, *v.* Sthiramati, Madhyāntavibhāgaṭīkā, Edition par Susumu Yamaguchi, Nagoya, 1934, pp. 60 ff.

(104) In all his criticisms of the ātman-theories, Jayarāśi is employing dialectical arguments to disprove his opponent's thesis. In the above instance, it would be seen that he takes up the proposition p (ātmā ānandarūpam), put forward by his opponent. He then says that p implies the truth either of q (ātmā anandarūpam svasaṃvedyam) or not-q (ātmā ānandarūpam avedyaṃ). Both lead to contradictions showing that p is false. q implies r (moksārthaprayāso niṣphalaḥ), which contradicts one of the propositions or assumptions of his opponent's system. Not-q is self-contradictory, since q is self-evident (cp. vedyaṃ vedyakañ ca ātmasvarūpam eva). Therefore, his opponent's thesis p, is false. They are not the arguments of a positivist,[1] who wishes to show that no meaning can be attached to the concept of an ātman (soul) and hence it should be dispensed with, but the kind of argument that any metaphysician would employ against (to use a phrase of F. H. Bradley)[2] his 'brother metaphysician'.

(105) The rest of Jayarāśi's work is devoted entirely to the discussion of epistemological topics. He criticizes theories of the validity of knowledge put forward by the Mīmāṃsā school (pp. 22–7) and the Buddhists (pp. 22–32). Almost half the work is concerned with the criticism of the validity of perception as upheld in the Nyāya (pp. 2–22), by the Buddhists (pp. 32–58), in the Mīmāṃsā (pp. 58–61) and the Sāṅkhya (pp. 61–4). It is followed by the criticism of the theory of inference (anumāna) in the Nyāya (pp. 64–74) and of the Buddhists (pp. 83–109). The concluding section is a criticism of knowledge based on authority (śabda-, āptokti-), where the apauruṣeya- theory (pp. 116–20) and the views of the grammarians (pp. 120–5) are discussed. A page or two is devoted to the criticism of the ārthāpatti (presumption)—theory of Mīmāṃsā, as well as upamāna (comparison) and abhāva (negation) as means of knowledge (pp. 109–13). Sambhava- (inclusion) and aitihya- (report) are dismissed in two sentences (p. 113), the former being subsumed under inference (anumāna) and the latter under scriptural tradition (āgama). The space devoted to each possibly reflects to some extent the importance attached to these theories at the period in which he wrote, but we cannot fail to observe that he begins his work with the criticism of perception and then only goes on to discuss the problems of the validity of knowledge in general. Considering also the space allotted to the criticisms of perception one gets the

[1] Cp. Wittgenstein, *Tractatus Logico-Philosophicus*, p. 151, Sections 5.631–3.

[2] *Appearance and Reality*, Second Edition, London, 1906, p.1, 'He is a brother metaphysician with a rival theory of first principles.'

impression that the author thought that if perception, which was universally accepted and that even by some of the Materialist schools, was demolished, it goes without saying that no means of knowledge could be valid.

(106) His technique of argument is throughout the same and his criticisms are almost invariably directed against some specific theory. We may illustrate this by taking a few passages. In criticizing the Buddhist theory of perception, he takes up the definition of perception in the Nyāyabindu (1.4), viz. 'perception is free of construction (kalpanā' poḍham) and is incorrigible (abhrāntam)'.[1] He argues as follows: 'One should not say this since the sense of "free" (apohā) in the phrase "free of construction" is not to be found. Then is kalpanā itself to be excluded (apohyā)? What is kalpanā? Is the consciousness that arises with qualifications of quality, motion, species, etc., kalpanā, or is kalpanā the consciousness that produces memory or is it of the nature of memory, or does it arise from memory, or is it a reflection of the contact with speech, or is it the apprehension of speech, or is it of an unclear nature, or has it the nature of apprehending unreal objects, or is it itself unreal or is it the seeing of objects accompanied by inference (trirūpālliṅga-[2] gato'rthadṛś), or is it a reflection of objects past or future?'[3]

[1] Pratyakṣam kalpanāpoḍham abhrāntam, p. 32.

[2] *Lit.* 'the middle term which has the three characteristics (of a valid syllogism)' viz. 'the existence (of the middle term) in the *probandum*, in what is like the *probandum* and its absence in what is not (like the *probandum*)' (anumeye'tha tattulye sadbhāvo nāstitāsati), *v.* Randle, *Indian Logic in the Early Schools*, pp. 181 ff.; cp. H. N. Randle, *Fragments from Diṅnāga*, London, 1926, pp. 22–5; also, Bochenski, *Formale Logik*, p. 503, 53.10 and 53.11. He gives the formal rules as

(1) M is present in S (the fire on the mountain)
(2) M is present in XP (there is smoke in the kitchen which has fire)
(3) M is not present in X-Not-P (there is no smoke in the lake which has no fire).

[3] Iti na vaktavyaṃ, kalpanāpoḍhapadasya apohyārthāsambhavāt. Nanu kalpanaiva apohyā? Ke'yaṃ kalpanā? Kiṃ guṇacalanajātyādiviśeṣanotpāditaṃ vijñānaṃ kalpanā, āho smṛtyutpādakaṃ vijñānaṃ kalpanā, smṛtirūpam vā, smṛtyutpādyaṃ vā, abhilāpasaṃsarganirbhāso vā, abhilāpavatī pratītir vā kalpanā, aspaṣṭākarā, vā, atāttvikārthagṛhītirūpā, vā, svayaṃ vā'tāttvikī, trirūpālliṅgagato' rthadṛgvā, atītānāgatārthanirbhāsā vā?

Tad yadi guṇacalanajātyādi viśeṣanotpāditaṃ vijñānam kalpanā; tat kiṃ avidyamānaguṇacalanajātyādiviśeṣanotpādyatvena kalpanā, uta vidyamānotpādyatvena? Tad yadi avidyamānaguṇacalanajātyādiviśeṣanotpādyatvena kalpanātvam tad ayuktam; avidyamānasya janakatvābhāvād eva akalpanātvam. Atha vidyamānaguṇacalanajātyādiviśeṣanotpādyatvena kaplanā, tat kiṃ saviṣayaṃ

'Now if kalpanā is the consciousness that arises with the qualifications of quality, motion, species, etc., does it arise from unmanifest qualifications of quality motion, species, etc., or from manifest (qualifications)? If it is from unmanifest qualifications, it will not do, as there would be no kalpanā since it cannot be produced by what is unmanifest. But if kalpanā arises from manifest qualifications of quality, motion, species, etc., does the knowledge of kalpanā (kalpanājñānam) have an object or have no object? If the knowledge of kalpanā has an object, it will not do, for even when it produces quality, motion, species, etc., it will not be kalpanā, owing to the incongruity of the presence of an appropriate object. If kalpanā has no object, then the absence of an object being itself the cause of kalpanā, there would not arise the qualifications of quality, motion, species, etc. If it is without an object, then there would be no knowledge of kalpanā, nor knowledge of no kalpanā (akalpanājñānam) but pure knowledge. If kalpanā has the nature of knowledge, all knowledge would be knowledge of kalpanā.'

'Now if kalpanā is the knowledge that produces memory, it will not do, for memory arises even from the seeing of forms, etc., and that is not kalpanā.'

(107) It will be noticed from the above that Jayarāśi's method of attack consists in taking the concept of kalpanā, suggesting various alternative definitions, showing that some of these definitions (e.g. smṛtyutpādakaṃ jñānaṃ kalpanā) do not apply, while others (e.g. guṇacalanajātyādiviśeṣaṇotpāditaṃ vijñānaṃ kalpanā) lead to contradictions. The concept of kalpanā is therefore presumed to be self-contradictory and a definition which contains this concept is untenable. Since the best definitions of perception are all untenable, it is assumed that no true account of perception is possible and therefore perception as a means of knowledge is invalid.

(108) The criticism of the Nyāya account of perception proceeds on similar lines. The author takes up the definition of perception as given

kalpanājñānam, nirviṣayaṃ vā? Tad yadi saviṣayaṃ sat kalpanājñānam, tad ayuktam, guṇacalanajātyādijanyatve'pi na kalpanātvam arthasāmarthyasamudbhavatvasyānativṛtteḥ. Atha nirviṣayaṃ sat kalpanā tadā nirviṣayatvam eva kalpanātve kāraṇaṃ na guṇacalanajātyādiviśeṣanajanyatvam; yadi ca tan nirviṣayam, tadā na kalpanājñānam, nāpyakalpanājñānam, jñānamātratā syāt, jñānātmatayā ca kalpanātve sarvaṃ jñānaṃ, kalpanājñānaṃ syāt.

Atha smṛtyutpādakaṃ jñānaṃ kalpanā, tad ayuktam, rūpādidarśanād api smṛtir utpadyate, na ca kalpanātvam. *Op. cit.*, pp. 32-3.

in the Nyāyasūtra (1.1.4), viz. 'Perception arises from contact between sense-organ and object, is determinate (avyapadeśyam), non-erroneous (avyabhicāri) and non-erratic (vyavasāyātmakam)'.[1] Jayarāśi argues as follows:[2] 'It is non-erroneous (avyabhicāri) . . . (the text is here defective and words have been omitted) . . . Does its non-erroneousness consist in its arising from an abundance of non-defective causes or in the absence of obstacles or in the efficiency of the process or in any other way? If its non-erroneousness arises from an abundance of non-defective causes, in what way is the non-defective nature of the causes known? It is not from perception, since the proficiency of the eye, etc., is beyond the grasp of the senses. Nor is it from inference, since one does not apprehend a basis for inference (liṅgāntara-). Is not (then) this very knowledge the basis, which gives rise to the knowledge of its excellence? If so, the mutual dependence results in a difficulty. And what is it? A suspicion of defect in a cognition which arises in dependence on the virtues and defects of the senses, is not dispelled as in the case of a consciousness of sound produced by the effort of a person'.

(109) Jayarāśi seems to have picked out the characteristic of avyabhicāri despite the fact that avyapadeśya- occurs earlier in the definition in order to spotlight the fact that since perception cannot be shown to be non-erroneous it must be erroneous. This he demonstrates by suggesting different senses of avyabhicāri and arguing that the truth of none of them can be established.

(110) We may now draw our conclusions. The term 'positivism' has been applied to characterize the philosophy of Comte and his successors because of their anxiety to rid philosophy of speculative elements and have its basis in the data and methods of the natural sciences.[3] Empiricists like Hume and Mach have been called positivists because of their forthright rejection of metaphysics and attempt to confine philosophy

[1] indriyārthasannikarṣotpannaṃ jñānamavyapadeśyamavyabhicāri vyavasāyātmakaṃ pratyakṣam, p. 2.

[2] Tac cāvyabhicāri . . . kim aduṣṭakārakasandohotpādyatvena, āhosvid bādhārahitatvena, pravṛttisāmarthyena, anyathā vā? Tad yady aduṣṭakārakasandohotpādyatvena avyabhicāritvam, saiva karaṇānām aduṣṭatā kenāvagamyate? Na pratyakṣena, nayanakuśalāder atīndriyatvāt; nāpyanumānena liṅgāntarānavagateḥ. Nanu idam eva jñānaṃ liṅgaṃ taduttham tasya viśiṣṭatām gamayati; yady evam itaretarāśrayatvam duruttaram āpanīpadyate. Kiñca indriyāṇāṃ guṇadoṣāśrayatve tadutthe vijñāne doṣāśaṅkā nātivartate puṃvyāpārotpāditaśabdavijñāna iva, *op. cit.*, p. 2.

[3] Baldwin, *Dictionary of Philosophy and Psychology*, *s.v.* Positivism.

to the results of observation. More recently, the term has been used of the philosophy of the Logical Positivists[1] (the Vienna Circle, Wittgenstein of the *Tractatus Logico-Philosophicus*, Ayer of *Language, Truth and Logic*) who while rejecting metaphysics have broken away from the narrow empiricism and psychological atomism of positivists like Mach and Hume and have endeavoured to base their positivism on logical foundations.[2] The term is also sometimes loosely employed to refer to the modern Analytical Philosophers, who are really the successors of Russell and Moore. None of these positivisits have attempted to disprove the validity of perception and inference by metaphysical arguments as Jayarāśi does. On the contrary, they have been anxious to preserve the validity of perception and inference as recognized methods of knowing in the natural sciences, although they have tried to rid these concepts of speculative assumptions and linguistic confusions. The only point of comparison that we can see is that like Jayarāśi the modern positivist will also say that there are no ultimate 'tattvas' in a metaphysical sense, but the latter would not try to deny or disprove their existence and would merely hold that assertions about such super-sensuous realities are strictly meaningless. We cannot therefore agree with Warder's description of Jayarāśi's school as 'positivists according to modern ideas'.

(111) The anxiety on the part of the positivist to save science and eliminate metaphysics led him to formulate the Verification Principle, the acceptance of which almost became some time ago the hallmark of a positivist. When we observe that the second group of Materialists (group (2)) did almost the same for similar reasons in trying to distinguish between empirical or verifiable inference and unverifiable or metaphysical inference (*supra*, 94), it is this school which best deserves to be called the positivist school in Indian thought.

(112) Nor can we see the connection that Warder sees between Jayarāśi's theory and the thought of Sañjaya. The most we can say is that if Jayarāśi's denial of knowledge led him to scepticism rather than to nihilism, as it ought to have, then we may have argued that it was possibly similar to the grounds on which Sañjaya accepted scepticism, though we have no evidence whatsoever as regards the basis of the latter's Scepticism. All that we do know was that Sañjaya was a Sceptic,

[1] *v.* Warnock, *English Philosophy since* 1900, Ch. IV Warnock uses the term 'positivist' of the Logical Positivist (*v.* pp. 56, 58, 60).

[2] *v.* Ayer, *Language, Truth and Logic*, pp. 136 ff.

who granted the possibility of transcendent truths (e.g. hoti Tathāgato parammaraṇā, etc., *v. infra,* 176) without denying them outright and this is a sufficient ground for us to distinguish between the philosophies of the two.

(113) The suggestion made by the editors of this text and by Warder that this school of thought represents a later trend which carried to its logical end the sceptical tendency of the Lokāyata school cannot entirely be put aside. Once the validity of inference was denied, as it was, at some time, in the main branch of this school, it is evident that perception could not stand for long on its own feet. Besides, it is clear that Jayarāśi is criticizing the views prevalent during his time and from these criticisms alone we cannot deduce that there was a primitive core of beliefs in this school, which go back to earlier times. But when we find a reference in the Pāli Nikāyas to the existence of a school of Lokāyatikas, who were absolute nihilists and who probably denied the truth of all views, it raises a strong presumption as to whether we should not trace the origins of the school of Jayarāśi to an early rival branch of the other realist school or schools of Materialism.

(114) As we have already seen (*v. supra,* 57, 58), in the Saṃyutta Nikāya there is a mention of two brahmins, called lokāyatikā, who interview the Buddha. One of the views that they hold is that 'nothing exists', which according to the Comy. was a Materialist view[1] (*v. supra,* 59).

(114A) The view that 'nothing exists' is in fact occasionally mentioned elsewhere in the Nikāyas in contrast to its opposite, namely that 'everything exists' (sabbaṃ atthi), both of which are said to be two extreme views, which the Buddha following the middle way avoids.[2] In a similar manner is juxtaposed the 'view of personal immortality' (bhavadiṭṭhi) and the 'annihilationist view' (vibhavadiṭṭhi).[3] It therefore seems reasonable to suppose that the view that 'nothing exists' is also a *vibhava*ditthi. Now this latter term seems to denote the Materialist philosophies mentioned at D. I.34, 5, all of which are said to 'posit the cutting off (ucchedaṃ), the destruction (vināsaṃ) and the annihilation (*vibhavaṃ*) of the person'[4]. This means that it is very probable that the

[1] Sabbaṃ n'atthi sabbam puthuttan ti, imā dve *uccheda diṭṭhiyo* ti veditabbā, SA. II.76. [2] sabbaṃ atthīti eko anto sabbaṃ natthīti dutiyo anto, S. II.76.

[3] Dve'mā diṭṭhiyo bhavadiṭṭhi ca vibhavadiṭṭhi ca. Ye . . . bhavadiṭṭhim allīnā . . . vibhavadiṭṭhiyā te paṭiviruddhā. Ye vibhavadiṭṭhim allīnā . . . bhavadiṭṭhiyā te paṭiviruddhā, M. I. p. 65.

[4] sattassa ucchedaṃ vināsaṃ vibhavaṃ paññapenti, D. I.34.

theory that 'nothing exists' was either one of or was closely associated with the Materialist theories at the time of the Pāli Nikāyas.

(115) If so, what could these two lokāyata-materialist[1] views, one holding that 'nothing exists' and the other that 'everything is a plurality', be? We may identify the second with that school of Materialists who upheld the reality of the elements, which is represented by Ajita Kesakambali in the Nikāyas who speaks of the existence of at least the four elements, earth, water, fire and air (D. I.55) and which appears to be similar to if not identical with the first school of materialists[2] propounding a theory called 'the-soul-is-the-same-as-the-body' theory (tajjīvataccharīra-) in the Sūtrakṛtāṅga (2.1.9=2.1.19, SBE., Vol. 45, p. 342). According to Śīlāṅka's interpretation (*v. supra,* 85) there is another school of Materialists mentioned in the Sūtrakṛtāṅga at 2.1.10 (=2.1.21, 22, SBE., *ibid.*) which speaks of five elements, including ether (ākāśa). If Śīlāṅka's identification is correct, this latter theory clearly brings out the plurality and the reality of elements, which are described as uncreated (animmiyā, akaḍā), eternal (sāsatā) and independent substances (animmavitā, no kittimā, avañjhā). If the identity of the pluralist school with one of these schools is correct, then the other lokāyata theory, which denied the reality of all things looks very much similar to the absolute nihilism of Jayarāśi.

(116) Haribhadra in his Ṣaddarśanasamuccaya speaks of the lokāyatas[3] (lokāyatāḥ) being of the opinion that 'this world extends only as far as what is amenable to sense-perception'.[4] From this one may argue that 'lokāyata-' means 'what pertains to this world' or the 'philosophy of this-worldliness or materialism' as Chattopadhyaya has done.[5] We cannot agree that this was the original meaning of the word (*v. supra,* 65, 66) but there is no reason to doubt that at least one of the schools of the Materialists believed in the reality of this world and it is significant that the Materialist theory referred to in the Kaṭha Upaniṣad (1.2.6) speaks of the existence of this world and the denial of the next, ayaṃ loko, nāsti para iti, which is translated by Hume as 'This is the world! There is no other!' (*op. cit.,* p. 346) and by Radhakrishnan as

[1] lokāyata- is used in other senses and lokāyatika- for non-materialist views as well in the Nikāyas, *v. supra,* 59.

[2] I.e. on the basis of the language used to describe them, *v. infra.*

[3] *Op. cit.,* verse 80, lokāyatā vadantyevam . . ., p. 301.

[4] etāvāneva loko' yaṃ yāvānindriyagocaraḥ, *op. cit.,* verse 81, p. 301.

[5] *Op. cit.,* p. 3, 'Thus Lokāyata meant not only the philosophy of the people but also the philosophy of this worldliness or materialism.'

'this world exists, there is no other' (PU., p. 610). Now Medhātithi defining haitukāḥ at Manu. IV.30 (*op. cit.*, Vol. I, p. 342) asserts that the nāstikas upheld the doctrines of 'nāsti paraloko, nāsti dattam, nāsti hutam iti', i.e. 'there is no next world, no (value in) giving, no (value in) sacrifice'. But the theory of the Materialists as defined in the Pāli Nikāyas is somewhat different. Whilst mentioning 'natthi dinnaṃ natthi hutaṃ' (=Skr. nāsti dattaṃ, nāsti hutam), it also has the phrase, '*natthi ayaṃ loko,* natthi paro loko' (D. I.55, M. III.71). Prof. Rhys Davids has translated this phrase as 'there is no such thing as this world or the next' but the phrase as it stands literally means 'this world does not exist, the next world does not exist'. This has always presented a problem for while it is well known that the lokāyata-materialists denied the existence of the next world, it appears to be strange that they should be spoken of as denying the existence of this world as well, particularly when they were elsewhere supposed to affirm positively the existence of this world. It is the discovery of the philosophy of Jayarāśi which makes it possible for the first time to see that there was a lokāyata-materialist school which denied the existence of this world as well.

(117) We have, however, to face the problem as to how this theory, which denies the existence of this world as well as the next, comes to be associated with Ajita, who is represented as believing in the reality of the four elements. Was Ajita also a pragmatic Materialist like Jayarāśi? The more probable explanation seems to be that the Buddhists identified all the known materialist views with Ajita, who symbolizes the philosophy of Materialism, inconsistently putting together the tenets of mutually opposed schools since they both (or all) happened to be in some sense (metaphysical or pragmatic) materialists. This is also possibly the reason why Ajita, while propounding the theory of the four elements (catummahābhūtiko'yam puriso) like the first school of Materialists, mentioned in the Brahmajāla Sutta (D. I.34, ayam attā rūpī cātummahābhūtiko . . .) also inconsistently speaks of the existence of ākāśa (akāśaṃ indriyāṇi saṃkamanti).

(118) The above evidence seems to point to the existence of at least two schools of lokāyata-materialists, the pluralist school of metaphysical materialists, who believed in the reality of the elements and denied only the existence of a next world and the nihilist school of pragmatic materialists, who denied the reality of this world as well as the next. Since the materialist philosophies (in India) as a whole and

Jayarāśi's lokāyata in particular seem to be based on epistemological foundations, it seems not unlikely that this early nihilist school of lokāyata was a product of an epistemological nihilism, which denied even the validity of perception and paved the way for the birth of philosophical Scepticism, which almost immediately succeeds it. There is good reason to believe that the early lokāyata speculations were closely associated with the study of reasoning or the cultivation of the tarka-śāstra and lokāyata-materialism seems to have been an offshoot of lokāyata speculations in general, which were a branch of brāhmaṇical studies at one time (*v. supra,* 65). It is therefore very probable that it was this same school of nihilist lokāyata, which is represented as a school of logical sceptics in the Dīghanakha Sutta (M. I.497–501), which denied the truth of all views, since a representative of this school is called a materialist (ucchedavādo, *v. infra,* 121) in the commentary (MA. III.204) and as we have shown there is textual evidence to confirm this view (*v. infra,* 334). In the light of the evidence we have cited, it is difficult to resist the conclusion that this early lokāyata school of absolute nihilists, logical sceptics and pragmatic materialists were the precursors of the philosophy of Jayarāśi and were in time at least contemporaneous with the existence of the Pāli Nikāyas.

(119) Dr Warder says that 'another materialist school seems to have appeared among the kings themselves and especially their ministers, including perhaps the celebrated Vassakāra of Magadha, who in the Aṅguttara Nikāya, Vol. II, p. 172, expresses a realist view in conformity with Arthaśāstra Lokāyata' (*op. cit.,* p. 55). But the context hardly warrants such a grandiose conclusion. Here Vassakāra says that he holds the following view: 'If he who speaks of what he has seen as "thus I have seen", there is nothing wrong in it . . . of what he has heard as "thus I have heard" . . . of what he has sensed as "thus I have sensed" . . . of what he has understood as "thus I have understood", there is nothing wrong in it'. The Buddha does not wholly agree with this point of view and says that one should not assert even what one has seen, heard, sensed or known, if it is likely to be morally undesirable. The Buddha makes the same point elsewhere (M. I.395) where he says that one's speech should not only be true but also morally useful (atthasaṃhitaṃ) and not morally harmful (anatthasaṃhitaṃ). Vassakāra on the other hand seems to be satisfied if someone states and confines himself to the bare truth, as he has experienced it, irrespective of its moral consequences. This is not the doctrine of the Arthaśāstra,

which recommends the utterance even of untruths for the sake of political expediency but appears to be his own personal view. The context is ethical and one can hardly draw epistemological or philosophical conclusions from it, especially since Vassakara's statement is compatible with any philosophical standpoint, idealist, phenomenalist or realist. The fact that Vassakāra as an important Magadhan official may have studied the Arthaśāstra and the Arthaśāstra gives a naïve realistic account of the world has, in our opinion, little to do with the view expressed here.

(120) Whatever differences existed among the Materialists on epistemological matters they seem to have all agreed in criticizing the authority of the Vedas and the argument from authority. This probably goes back to the earliest times. In fact, the original stimulus in the genesis of the Materialist philosophy may have been provided by the dissatisfaction with the Vedic tradition at a time when those who would not still break with tradition found they could no longer agree with the old traditional knowledge and sought to replace acceptance of tradition and revelation with metaphysical inquiry. The statement attributed to the Materialists in the Sarvadarśanasaṃgraha that 'the impostors, who call themselves Vedic pundits are mutually destructive, as the authority of the jñānakāṇḍa (section on knowledge) is overthrown by those who maintain the authority of the karmakāṇḍa (section on ritual), while those, who maintain the authority of the jñānakāṇḍa reject that of the karmakāṇḍa',[1] may have a history that goes back to the earliest phase of Materialism, though this particular criticism itself would not have been possible at least before the termination of the Early Upaniṣadic period for it was probably at this time that the original Vedas as well the traditional lore including the Upaniṣads (*v.* Bṛh. 2.4.10, 4.5.11) are said to have been breathed forth by the Supreme Being.

(121) According to the Sarvadarśanasaṃgraha, the Materialists criticized the śruti or the revelational tradition as a valid means of knowledge on the grounds that the Veda is 'invalidated by the defects of falsity, contradiction and repetition' (anṛtavyāghātapunaruktadoṣairdūṣitatayā, p. 4). When therefore the Nyāya Sūtra very much earlier says that '(according to some the Veda) is unreliable since it has the defects of falsity, contradiction and repetition' (tadapramāṇyamanṛtavyāghātapunaruktadoṣebhyaḥ, 2.1.58) using identical language it is

[1] *The Sarvadarśanasaṃgrahaḥ*, Trans. E. B. Cowell, London, 1882, p. 4.

probably trying to meet the criticisms of the Materialists in particular, although this view was shared by the other heterodox schools as well. At the time of the Pāli Nikāyas we find the statement attributed to Ajita, the Materialist, who says that 'those who uphold the atthikavāda are making a false and baseless lament'.[1] Here the criticism is limited to the defect of falsity, probably because the term atthikavāda, is, in this context, used in a wide sense to denote not only the traditional philosophy of the Vedas but the philosophies of those heterodox sects as well, which believed in the concepts of soul, survival, moral responsibility or salvation. The common factor of these heterodox schools barring the Materialists was the belief in survival;[2] so the absence of a belief in survival is taken to be the defining characteristic of a Materialist, who is as a consequence called one who subscribes to the natthikavāda in the Pāli Nikāyas. This is clear from the use of the term natthikavāda in the Appaṇṇaka Sutta (M. I.403), where it is employed to denote the theory that 'there is no next world' (natthi paro loko, M. I.403) and we observe the following polarities of usage:

micchādiṭṭhi natthikavādo, M. I.403
„ akiriyavādo, M. I.406
„ ahetuvādo, M. I.408
sammādiṭṭhi atthikavādo, M. I.404
„ kiriyavādo, M. I.407
„ hetuvādo, M. I.409

When therefore these terms are employed together, e.g. ahetuvādā, akiriyavādā, natthikavādā (M. III.78, A. II.31), they are not to be treated as synonyms but as variants of micchādiṭṭhi.[3] Atthikavāda-, therefore, as used by Ajita has a wide connotation and we cannot presume that his criticism is limited to the Vedas though it certainly would have included it.

(122) Let us now examine the kind of argument that the Materialist during the time of the Pāli Nikāyas used in defending or proving his own beliefs and in criticizing the theories of others. We have for this

[1] Tesam tuccham musā vilāpo, ye keci atthikavādam vadanti, M. I.515.

[2] Even the Sceptics seem to have believed in survival in a pragmatic sense (*v. infra*, 163).

[3] The definition of natthika- as a 'sceptic, nihilist', of natthikadiṭṭhi- as 'scepticism, nihilistic view, heresy' and natthikavāda- as 'one who professes a nihilistic doctrine' in the PTS. Dictionary (*s.v.*) is inacurate and misleading, in the context of the Pāli Canon.

purpose to rely mainly on the account given of the Materialist schools in the Sūtrakṛtāṅga, since the Pāli Nikāyas (and their commentaries) which briefly state the doctrines of the Materialist schools but not the reasoning behind them, are not very informative on this subject.

(123) As for the nihilist school of lokāyata-materialists, we have no more information than what we have stated elsewhere (*v. supra,* 112; *infra,* 333, 334). As we have said they appear to have been logical sceptics, who denied the truth of all views, probably on epistemological grounds since there was no means of knowing anything, as even the validity of perception could not be relied on. The school on which we have the most information seems to be the positivist school (*v.* group (2), *supra,* 111), which upheld the priority of perception without denying empirical or verifiable inference. But before we deal with them it is necessary to dispose of another school of Materialists, which, if Śīlāṅka's interpretation is correct, relied on metaphysical or *a priori* arguments to construct their thesis of Materialism.

(124) The second book of the Sūtrakṛtāṅga speaks of four kinds of people representing four types of philosophies. Of these 'the first kind of man is the person, who asserts that the-soul-is-the-same-as-the-body' (paḍhame purisajāë tajjīvataccharīraëtti, Sū. 2.1.9),[1] i.e. the Materialists who identified the soul with the body. This seems to be the same as the first of the seven schools of Materialists mentioned in the Brahmajāla Sutta, which asserts that the 'soul is of the form of the body and is composed of the four great elements' (attā rūpī cātummahābhūtiko, D. I.34). It was also probably the philosophy attributed to Ajita, who speaks of the 'four elements composing the person' (cātummahābhūtiko ayam puriso, D. I.55) and much of whose language is in common with the account of the Sūtrakṛtāṅga,[2] though as we have suggested, doctrines attributed to him seem to be of a composite character (*v. supra,* 117). It also appears to be the minimum doctrine accepted on pragmatic grounds by the nihilist school of materialists as well.[3]

[1] The reference in Jacobi's translation is different (SBE., Vol. 45). It will be mentioned where relevant.

[2] Cp. Ard. Mag. kavotavannāṇi aṭṭhīṇi bhavanti with P. kāpotakāni aṭṭhīni bhavanti and Ard. Mag. āsandīpañcamā purisā gāmaṃ paccāgacchanti with P. āsandipañcamā purisā matam ādāya gacchanti.

[3] *v.* Jayarāśi's quotation, pṛthivyāpastejoyvāyuriti tattvāni (*op. cit.,* p. 1) and the Buddha's statement to Dīghanakha the materialist and logical sceptic, ayaṃ . . . kāyo rūpi *cātummahābhūtiko,* M. I.500.

(125) Now, it is said that 'the second kind of person is one who asserts the existence of the five great elements' (docce purisajāë pañcamahabbhūtiëtti, Sū. 2.1.10). This would appear to be a second school of Materialists, asserting the reality of the five elements including ākāśa (ākāse pañcame mahabbhūte, *loc. cit.*) if not for a qualification made towards the middle of this passage and the fact that we were led from the context to expect a different kind of philosophy. The Ardhamāgadhi text reads as follows: puḍhavī ege mahabbhūte, āü ducce mahabbhūte . . . iccete pañcamahabbhūyā aṇimmiyā . . . satantā sāsatā ayacchaṭṭhā, puna ege evam āhu- sato ṇatthi viṇāso asato ṇatthi sambhavo (*loc. cit.*). The presence of the word āyacchaṭṭha- seems to mean that the person who held the reality of the five elements also believed in the reality of the ātman as a sixth element, in which case this is not a Materialist philosophy at all and the passage may be translated as follows: 'Earth is the first element, water the second element . . . thus these five elements are uncreated . . . independent and eternal with ātman as the sixth (element); further, some say that, "there is no destruction of that which is and no origination of that which is not". Jacobi translates differently following Śīlāṅka[1] taking "puṇa ege evam āhu" with the previous sentence as follows: 'Earth is the first element, water the second element . . . These five elements are not created . . . are independent of directing cause or everything else, they are eternal. Some say, however, that there is a self besides the five elements. What is, does not perish; from nothing, nothing comes' (SBE., Vol. 45, p. 343). This translation is permissible though it deviates from the form in which the text is printed, but it does not solve the problem for it means that this passage is introducing not one but two theories, one a Materialist theory and the other a Realist theory which asserts the substantial existence of the soul as well. Śīlāṅka, as we pointed out (*v. supra*, 85), interprets the two theories as the Lokāyata (lokāyatamata-) and the Sāṅkhya respectively. He distinguishes this lokāyata from the former which he calls Tajjīvataccharīravāda[2] following the Sūtrakṛtāṅga though however he still considers this a species of lokāyata.[3]

[1] Tadevambhūtāni pañcamahabhūtānyātmaṣaṣṭāni punareke evamāhuḥ, *op. cit.*, Vol. II, fol. 18 on Sū. 2.1.10.

[2] Ayañca prathamo puruṣastajjīvataccharīravādī, *op. cit.*, Vol. II, fol. 17 on Sū. 2.1.9.

[3] *v.* Te caivamvidhastajjīvataccharīravādino lokāyatikāḥ, *op. cit.*, Vol. II, fol. 16 on Sū. 2.1.9.

(126) If we accept this dualist interpretation and that one of the theories spoken of is Materialism, it is necessary to reconcile ourselves to the fact that it seems to be different from that of the nihilist and the empiricist schools in that it is a product of pure reasoning. The belief in the plurality of the elements is probably grounded on some such premiss as 'what is distinguishable is separable in reality'.[1] Since we can distinguish between the qualities of earth, fire, etc., they have a separate reality. Now each of the real elements being real must have the characteristics of Being. That which is real cannot be destroyed since 'there is no destruction of Being' (sato ṇatthi viṇāso, *loc. cit.*); so each of the elements is indestructible and hence eternal (sāsatā) and without end (aṇihaṇā=Skr. anidhanāḥ). Likewise since 'nothing can come from Non-Being' (asato ṇatthi sambhavo), they must have had the quality of Being for all time; so that these elements could not have been created directly or indirectly (aṇimmiyā animmāvitā akaḍā ṇo kittimā ṇo kaḍagā, *loc. cit.*) and hence have no beginning (anāīyā, apurohitā). Again, each of these elements cannot affect the other elements for in such a case there would be loss of their Being and hence they are independent (satantā= Skr. svatantrāḥ) substances (avañjhā, i.e. not void, being plenums and not vacuums like the atoms of Democritus). This rational Atomistic Materialist school seems therefore to have made considerable use of Uddālaka's *a priori* premiss (*v. supra*, 25) that 'Being cannot come out of Non-being' much in the same way in which Empedocles and the Greek Atomists, Leucippus and Democritus, made use of Parmenides' *a priori* reasoning about Being in the history of Greek thought.[2] The only reference to this school outside Śīlāṅka[3] that we have been able to find is by Guṇaratna, who after describing the nāstikas who 'spoke of the world being composed of the four elements' (caturbhūtātmakaṃ jagadācakṣate, *op. cit.*, p. 300) says: 'But some who are somewhat like the Cārvākas (Cārvākaikadeśīyāḥ) think that ākāśa is the fifth element and speak of the world as being composed

[1] Hume makes good use of this premiss or principle (as he calls it) in a different connection, *v. op. cit.*, p. 35. What consists of parts is distinguishable into them and what is distinguishable is separable. Cp. p. 32.

[2] *v.* J. Burnet, *Greek Philosophy*, London, 1943, pp. 69, 95, 197.

[3] Śīlāṅka mentions a school of Materialists who believed in ākāśa as the fifth element even when he is commenting on the first school as follows: kesāñcillokāyatikānāmākāśasyāpi bhūtattvenābhyupagamādbhūtapañcako'panyāso na doṣāyeti, since some Materialists consider ether as an element the reference to five elements is not wrong, *op. cit.*, Vol. II, fol. 16 on Sū. 2.1.9.

of five elements'.[1] But whether they grew out of the deductive rational basis of their doctrines and fell in line with the epistemological outlook of the other schools, we cannot say in the absence of any evidence and we have therefore not included this school in our classification of Materialist theories according to their epistemological doctrines, particularly since Śīlānka's interpretation of the passage in the Sūtrakṛtāṅga itself is doubtful.

(127) The other Positivist school of Materialists appears to have been the more vigorous and the better known, since it seems to have made a strong impact on the epistemological theories of Early Buddhism. Most of the later accounts of this school take it for granted that its Materialist beliefs are a product of its epistemology. We have already quoted the views of Śīlāṅka, who was of the opinion that since the Materialists held perception to be the only source of knowledge they disbelieved in the existence of a soul (*v. supra,* 91). Guṇaratna says the same: 'therefore, the soul, good and evil and their fruits, heaven and hell, etc., which others speak of, do not exist *since they are not perceived* (apratyakṣatvāt)'.[2]

(128) The beliefs attributed to Ajita Kesakambali are precisely these and we may presume that they were arrived at by this principle of empirical reasoning, which as stated in the Nikāyas was of the form, aham etaṃ na jānāmi, aham etaṃ na passāmi, tasmā taṃ natthi, 'I do not know and see this, therefore it does not exist'. Ajita's beliefs are as follows:

(i) *There is no soul.* 'A person is composed of the four elements' (catummahābhūtiko ayam puriso).

(ii) *There is no value in morals or religious practices.* 'There is (no value) in sacrifice or prayer (natthi yiṭṭham, natthi hutam)', 'there is (no value) in giving (natthi dinnam)'; 'there are no good and evil actions, which bear fruit' (natthi sukaṭadukkaṭānaṃ kammānaṃ phalaṃ vipāko); 'there are no (obligations to) one's parents' (natthi mātā, natthi pitā).

(129) In holding sense-perception to be the ultimate basis of knowledge they seem to have criticized not only the claims to the authority

[1] Kecittu Cārvākaikadeśīyā ākāśam pañcamahābhūtam abhimanyamānāḥ, pañcabhūtātmakaṃ jagaditi nigadanti, *op. cit.*, p. 300.

[2] Tato yatpare jīvam punyapäpe tatphalam svarganarakādikaṃ ca prāhuḥ, tannāsti, apratyakṣatvāt, *op. cit.*, p. 302.

of the Vedic scriptures (*v. supra*, 121) but the claims to extrasensory perception or higher intuition (abhiññā) on the part of some of the religious teachers of their times. This seems to be the significance of Ajita's remark that 'there are no well behaved recluses and brahmins of good conduct, who can claim to know the existence of this world as well as the next by realizing this themselves with their higher intuition' (natthi loke samaṇabrāhmaṇā sammaggatā sammāpaṭipannā ye imañ ca lokaṃ parañ ca lokaṃ sayaṃ abhiññā sacchikatvā pavedenti, *loc. cit.*).

(130) That empiricism was the keynote of their arguments is evident, when we examine the few arguments of the first school of the Materialists recorded in the Sūtrakṛtāṅga. One of the arguments is that you cannot observe a soul separate from the body and therefore there is no soul apart from the body. The inference is directly drawn from observation and is inductive: 'As a man draws a sword from the scabbard (*kosīö asiṃ abhinivvaṭṭittā*) and shows it saying, "this is the sword and that is the scabbard" (ayam . . . asī ayaṃ kosī), so nobody can draw (the soul from the body) and show (it saying), "friend, this is the soul and that is the body" (ayam . . . āyā iyam sarīraṃ). As a man draws a fibre from the stalk of muñja grass (*muñjāö isiyaṃ*) and shows it saying, "this is the stalk and that is the fibre" (*ayam . . . munje iyam isiyaṃ*) . . .'.[1] We have underlined these examples given to illustrate the fact that the argument may have been suggested by what their opponents who held that 'the soul was different from the body'[2] were claiming. For, in the Kaṭha Upaniṣad (2.3.17) it is stated that 'one should draw up from one's own body the inner-ātman (antarātman) like a fibre from a stalk of muñja grass'[3] (antarātmā . . . taṃ svāccharīrāt *pravṛhen muñjād iveṣīkam*). This was possibly the subjective experience of a Yogin. The Buddhists while not committing themselves on this question as to whether the body was identical with the soul or was different from it since it is one of 'the things on which no definite view was expressed'

[1] Se jahāṇāmaë keī purise kosīö asiṃ abhinivvaṭṭittāṇaṃ uvadaṃsejjā ayamāüso asī ayaṃ kosī, evaṁ eva ṇatthi keī purise abhinivvaṭṭittāṇaṃ uvadaṃsettāro, ayamāüso āyā iyaṃ sarīram. Se jahāṇāmaë keī purise muñjāö isiyaṃ abhinivvaṭṭittā ṇaṃ uvadaṃsejjā, ayamāüso muñje iyaṃ isiyaṃ . . . Sū. 2.1.9, Vol. 2, fol. 11.

[2] anno jīvo annaṃ sarīraṃ, *ibid.* Cp. aññaṃ jīvaṃ aññaṃ sarīraṃ, Ud. 67, where it is a theory put forward and debated by some recluses and brahmins.

[3] Radhakrishnan has mistranslated the phrase muñjādiveṣīkam as 'the wind from the reed' (PU., p. 647).

(mayā anekaṃsikā dhammā desitā, D. I.191), themselves claimed that in certain jhānic states one could 'create psychic selves out of this body' (imamhā kāyā aññaṃ kāyaṃ abhinimmināti . . . manomayaṃ, D. I.77; cp. the attapaṭilābhas[1] or 'the attainment of selves', D. I.195), where this 'self' (kāya-, attapaṭilābha-) appears to be different from the body in the same way in which 'the stalk of muñja grass is separate from the fibre, the stalk being the one thing and the fibre another, although the fibre is pulled out of the stalk' (*ayam muñjo ayaṃ iṣīkā, añño muñjo* aññā isīkā, *muñjamhā tveva isīkā pavāḷhā*) (D. I.77) or in the same way in which 'a sword is different from the scabbard, the sword being one thing and the scabbard another, although the sword is drawn from the scabbard' (*ayaṃ asi ayaṃ kosi,* añño asi añño kosi, *kosiyā tv'eva asi pavāḷho, loc. cit.*). When, therefore, we consider the context of this argument it would appear that the Materialists were questioning and contesting the objective validity of these claims on the ground that one could not demonstrate for all to see that such a soul or 'self' was different from the body, since such claims could not be verified from sense-experience.

(131) The importance that the Materialists attached to verification in the light of sense-experience is brought out in these arguments. The point of the above argument seems to be that no meaning can be attached to the concept of 'different from' unless it was possible to observe a soul as separate from the body in this verifiable sense of 'difference'. In the other argument the importance of verifiability is more explicitly brought out. One cannot speak of the existence of the soul unless the soul is verifiable by sense-experience and since no such soul is perceived, it is those who say that it does not exist (asante) or it is not evident (asaṃvijjamāne) who would be making the 'right statement' (suyakkhāyaṃ=Skr. svakhyātam) about it. This argument seems to have had its repercussions in Buddhism, where the Buddha appears to be making a similar criticism of the concept of Brahmā, (*v. infra,* 550, 552) and we may state it fully following Jacobi's translation: 'Those who maintain that the soul is something different from the body cannot tell whether the soul (as separated from the body) is long or small, whether globular or circular or triangular or square or hexagonal or octagonal, whether black or blue or red or yellow or white, whether of sweet smell or of bad smell, whether bitter or pungent or astringent or sour or sweet, whether hard or soft or heavy or light or

[1] *v. infra,* 528–535.

cold or hot or smooth or rough. Those therefore who believe that there is and exists no soul speak the truth'.[1] The argument is that the soul cannot be seen since it has no visible form (long, globular) or colour (blue); likewise, it cannot be smelt (sweet smell), tasted (bitter) or known by touch (heavy, cold). Hence it cannot be perceived and one cannot speak of that which is not perceivable as existing. The Materialists seem to have adopted Berkeley's empiricist principle of, esse est percipi, and argued that, non percipi est non esse.

(132) It is, however, necessary to observe that even this argument is not an abstract one, entirely evolved by the Materialists, but seems to have been suggested by and specifically directed against their opponent's theories about the ātman or jīva. It would be seen that the ātman has shape and size according to some Upaniṣadic conceptions. At Kaṭha 2.3.17, the ātman is 'of the size of a thumb' (aṅguṣṭamātraḥ) and at Chāndogya 3.14.3, it is said to be 'smaller than a grain of rice' (aṇīyān vrīheḥ). Likewise the Jains held that the soul (jīva) took the shape of each body. Some of the Ājīvakas seem to have believed that the 'soul was octagonal or globular and five hundred yojanas in extent'[2] (jīvo aṭṭhaṃso gūḷaparimaṇḍalo, yojanāni satā pañca, Pv. 57, verse 29). As Basham has shown, according to late Ājīvika sources the soul was blue in colour.[3] The abhijāti doctrine[4] may possibly have been based on beliefs about the colour of the soul and it may be noticed that the colours mentioned here are also the colours of the abhijātis and are stated in the same order though the distinction between the white (sukka) and the pure white (paramasukka) is not made. These conceptions may have been suggested by experiences in trance-

[1] Anno bhavati jīve annam sarīram, tamhā te evaṃ no vipaḍivedenti, ayamāüso, āyā dīheti vā hasseti vā parimaṇḍaleti vā vaṭṭeti vā taṃseti vā caüraṃseti vā āyateti vā chalaṃsiëti vā aṭṭaṃseti vā kiṇheti vā ṇīleti vā lohiyahālidde sukkileti vā subbhigandheti vā dubbhigandheti vā titteti vā kaṭuëti vā kasāëti vā ambileti vā mahureti vā kakkhaḍeti vā maüëti vā guruëti vā lahuëti vā siëti vā usiṇeti vā niddheti vā lukkheti vā evaṃ asante asaṃvijjamāṇe jesiṃ taṃ suyakkhāyaṃ bhavati, Sū. 2.1.9. Vol. 2, fol. 11.

[2] The commentary (Paramatthadīpani, III.253) says that 'the soul is sometimes octagonal and sometimes globular' (jīvo kadāci aṭṭhaṃso kadāci gūlaparimaṇḍalo).

[3] *Op. cit.*, p. 270; 'Jīva . . . was the colour of a palai fruit', which is blue.

[4] Other explanations are, however, possible; *v.* G. P. Malalasekera and K. N. Jayatilleke, *Buddhism and the Race Question*, pp. 38–9 and p. 39, fn. 1.

states as Buddhaghosa has suggested.[1] Even the Buddhists while dispensing with the concept of a substantial soul, speaks of the experience in jhānic states of a 'consciousness (viññāṇaṃ) as being attached to (ettha sitaṃ, ettha paṭibaddhaṃ) though separate from the body of the four elements . . . like a blue, orange, red, white, or yellow string running through a diamond, bright, of the purest water, octagonal in shape (aṭṭhaṃsa-), well-cut, clear, translucent, flawless and perfect in every way'.[2] The Materialist criticism was, therefore, probably directed against the objectivity of these claims in view of the fact that they could not be demonstrated as verifiable in the light of sense-experience.

(133) That the positivism of these early Materialists was perhaps not entirely based on this psychological empiricism is suggested by an argument against the concept of the ātman based on an elementary linguistic analysis. This argument occurs as late as the verses quoted in the Sarvadarśanasaṃgraha but there is some reason to suppose that these verses preserve some of the primitive views of the Materialists. Besides, the argument has its counterpart in the early Buddhist texts, where the Buddha says that one should not be misled by language in talking about an ātman (*v. infra*, 533). The question as to whether the Buddhists borrowed the argument from the Materialists (or vice versa) or whether they both used it more or less contemporaneously for a common purpose depends on the methodological criteria that we adopt[3] but there is no gainsaying the fact that both the Materialists as well as the early Buddhists appear to have used this argument against the ātman-theorists, whether they were influenced by each other or not. The argument is, however, more explicitly stated by the Materialists and seems to be a criticism of one of the earliest conceptions of the

[1] He says (DA. I.119) that those who consider that the soul has material or visible form (rūpī attāti) do so on the grounds that the colour of their meditational device (kasiṇarūpam) is the soul, taking the consciousness that prevails in relation to it as his own; he, however, distinguishes the Ājīvikas and others who arrive at similar conclusions on purely logical grounds. Rūpī attā'ti ādisu kasiṇarūpaṃ attāti tattha pavattasaññaṃ c'assa saññā ti gahetvā va Ājīvakā'dayo viya takkamatten'eva vā.

[2] Ayaṃ kho me kāyo . . . cātumahābhūtiko . . . idañca pana me viññāṇaṃ ettha sitaṃ ettha paṭibaddhan'ti. Seyyathā pi . . . maṇi veḷuriyo subho jātimā aṭṭhamso suparikammakato accho vippasanno anāvilo sabbākārasampanno, tatra suttam āvutaṃ nīlam vā pītaṃ vā lohitaṃ vā odātaṃ vā paṇḍusuttaṃ vā, D. I.76.

[3] I.e. if we go strictly by the principle that whatever occurs in a later text is in fact later in origin, we would have to say that the Buddhists were the first to use this argument but this need not necessarily be true.

meaning of words, namely that the meaning of word is an object. The word for 'meaning' and 'object' in Indian thought is the same word 'artha' and the orthodox conception as noted by Kālidāsa is that 'the word and the object are closely allied'.[1] According to the Pūrva Mīmāṃsā, the relation between the word and its meaning is natural, necessary and eternal.[2] This means that the word 'I' must have an object which must be the substantial ego. Arguing from logic to reality one may hold that 'I'—statements must have as their subject a substantial pure ego, which is the ontological subject of the predicates. The Materialists contested this belief or argument urging that the subject of statements such as 'I am fat', etc., is the body which alone has the observable attribute of fatness,[3] while phrases such as 'my body' have only a metaphorical significance[4] and would mean 'the body that is I' just as when we speak of 'the head of Rāhu' we mean 'the head that is Rāhu'.[5] The Materialist thus seems to have pointed out on the basis of an elementary linguistic analysis that it is false to conclude that every proper or common name or grammatical subject entails the existence of a specific ontological entity, to which it refers.

(134) The other arguments recorded of the Materialists are all of the nature of destructive hypothetical syllogisms of the form modus tollendo tollens,[6] where the implicate is a proposition which is observably false or absurd entailing the falsity of the implicans. This seems to have been a favourite type of argument employed by disputants against their opponents during the time of the Pāli Nikāyas and the Buddhists also use arguments of this same kind against their opponent's theories (*v. infra*, 693–710). It consists in taking an assumption or proposition of your opponent's system (say, p) and showing that it implies a proposition q, which is observably false (or absurd),[7] thus implying that the original assumption or proposition is false and untenable, viz.

if p, then q
  not q
Therefore, not p

[1] Vāgarthāvivasampṛktau, i.e. united like the word and its object, Raghuvaṃsa, 1. 1.

[2] *v.* Hiriyanna, *Outlines of Indian Philosophy*, pp. 309 ff.

[3] *ahaṃ sthūlaḥ* kṛśo'smī ti sāmānādhikaraṇyataḥ, *dehaḥ sthaulyādiyogāc ca sa evātmā na cāparaḥ*, Sarvadarśanasaṃgraha, by Sāyana-Mādhava, Ed. V. S. Abhyankara, Second Edition, Poona, 1951, p. 7.

[4] Mamadeho'yam ityuktiḥ sambhaved aupacārikī, *op. cit.*, p. 7.

[5] Mama śarīram iti vyavahāro rāhoḥ śira ityādivad aupacārikaḥ, *op. cit.*, p. 6.

[6] Stebbing, *op. cit.*, p. 105.

[7] This is popularly known as *reductio ad absurdum*.

In Indian logic this would fall under tarka (*v.* Nyāya Sūtra, 1.1.40) i.e. indirect proof or confutation. Here again the evidence is from the Sarvadarśanasaṃgraha but the subject-matter appears to be early. The arguments are sometimes stated in the form of rhetorical questions but they can be easily converted into propositional form. We may illustrate this by stating the arguments in propositional form and comparing them with the actual form in which they are stated. Most of the arguments are against the validity of the sacrifice:

(i) If 'beings in heaven are gratified by our offering the śrāddha here' (p), then 'food given below should gratify those standing on the housetop'[1] (q), but q is observably false and absurd, implying the falsity of p. The implicate (i.e. q) is however stated in the form of the rhetorical question, 'then why not give the food below . . .'.

(ii) If 'the śrāddha produces gratification to those who are dead'[1] (p), then '(offerings in their home should) produce gratification to travellers' (q). But q is observably false and absurd. Here the implicate is stated in the form of the proposition 'here, too, in the case of travellers when they start, it is needless to give provisions for the journey'.[1] This is really an implicate of the implicate but the logic of the argument remains the same.

(135) There is a similar argument implying the falsity of the belief in survival:

(iii) If 'he who departs from the body goes to another world' (p) then 'he would come back for love of his kindred'[1](q). But p is observably false implying the falsity of p.

(136) This last (i.e. iii) is among the propositions which Pāyāsi puts to the test by devising experiments to test its validity instead of being merely satisfied with anecdotal or common-sense observations. Pāyāsi, who also appears to belong to the Positivist branch of the Materialists, deserves to be mentioned separately since he adopts the Materialist philosophy of life on the basis of empirical arguments and experimental evidence.[2] The dialogue between Pāyāsi and Kassapa, which is recorded in the Pāyāsi Sutta (D. II.316 ff.) is said to have taken place some time after the death of the Buddha.[3] It shows that at least by this

[1] Cowell's Translation, SDS., p. 10. We have not quoted the Sanskrit text here since it does not affect the form of the argument.

[2] *v.* Ruben, *op. cit.*, p. 109; Payasi machte noch ein anderes königliches Experiment.

[3] *v.* Prof. Rhys Davids, *Dialogues of the Buddha*, SBB., Vol. III, p. 347.

time, if not earlier,[1] some people had thought of consciously devising experiments to test the validity of a theory, however ill-conceived and ill-devised the experiments may have been, and either accepted or rejected the theory on the basis of the results obtained.

(137) Pāyāsi recounts a series of such experiments that he has performed with negative results in order to test the validity of the belief in survival. He approaches those who have led an immoral life when they are grievously ill and about to die and enjoins them to return to him if they survive in an unhappy state and inform him about their condition (D. II.320). He likewise approaches those who have led a moral life and instructs them accordingly (D.II. 323, 326). These experiments, he says, had negative results since none of the subjects came back after surviving death to tell him about their plight.

(138) The next set of experiments he mentions are designed to test whether a soul escapes from the body at death. However crude his experiments are, he seems to have taken great care in arranging them. He puts a man (a thief) alive into a jar, closes its mouth securely, covers it over with wet leather, puts over that a thick cement of moist clay, places the jar on a furnace and kindles a fire. When he believes that the man is dead, he takes down the jar, unbinds and opens its mouth and quickly observes it with the idea of seeing whether his soul issues out (D. III.332, 333). His failure to observe such a soul is taken as evidence that there is no soul. Another experiment that he performs is that of weighing (tulāya tulayitvā) a man's body before and after death. It is presumably assumed that if the weight is less after death, then something has left the body, namely his soul, but Pāyāsi finds to his consternation that after death the body was heavier (garutara-) so that it was evident to him that no soul had left the body (D. III.334). In yet another of his gruesome experiments he kills a man by stripping off cuticle, skin, flesh, sinews, bones and marrow, turning him around when he is almost dead to see whether any soul escapes from his body (D. II.336). Again, he flays a man alive cutting off his integument, flesh, nerves, bones and marrow to see whether at any stage he could observe a soul. This is probably based on the conception of the souls at Taittirīya Upaniṣad 2.1–5, which speaks of five souls[2], the one encased in the other. All these experiments assume that the soul is either an observable or material substance, possessed of weight, located in the body and passing out of it at death.

[1] *v.* Uddālaka's experiment, *supra*, 28.

[2] The pañcakośa theory.

(139) Whether the problem of man's survival can be studied experimentally, as some modern psychical researchers believe, or not, it is clear that Pāyāsi's experiments were misguided and ill-conceived and no results could be expected of them. But the fact that he devised and carried them out in order to test a theory shows that he had a fundamentally unbiased and scientific outlook to the study of a problem.

(140) We have suggested that some of the arguments of the Materialists implied a criticism of the objectivity of the claims of the mystics (*v. supra*, 130) in that what was objectively verifiable was limited to what was based on sense-experience. If the account given of the Materialist schools in the Brahmajāla Sutta is to be trusted, there seems to have been a class of Materialists who, while valuing the attainment of yogic states from a purely pragmatic point of view, denied the epistemic claims made on their behalf.

(141) Of the seven schools we identified the first with the first school of the Sūtrakṛtāṅga (*v. supra*, 115) which asserted that the soul was not different from the body. The second school which speaks of a 'higher[1] soul' (attā dibbo) still assuming the shape of the body (rūpī) is probably the same as the school referred to in Guṇaratna's quotations from Vacāspati (*v. supra*, 99) which spoke of a Materialist school holding that caitanya or consciousness was a distinguishable by-product of the material entities. The description of the third to the seventh schools are similar to the accounts given of jhānic states. Take the third school. It is said to posit the existence of a 'higher soul' (attā dibbo) which is described in the following phrase, *rūpī manomayo sabbaṅgapaccaṅgī ahīnindriyo* (*loc. cit.*). The description is identical with the self which is said to be created by the mind in jhāna, viz., so imimhā kāyā aññam kāyaṃ abhinimmināti *rūpiṃ manomayaṃ sabbaṅgapaccaṅgiṃ ahīnindriyaṃ* (D. I.77); it is the same as the 'mental self' (manomayo attapaṭilābho) attained in jhāna, viz. *rūpī manomayo sabbaṅgapaccaṅgī ahīnindriyo*, ayammanomayo attapaṭilābho (D. I.195). The souls posited in the remaining four schools are identical in description with the states of the four arūpajhānas. As Materialists, they are said to hold that all these emergent souls are destroyed with the destruction of the body. But the identity of the description of the souls with the jhānic states makes the very existence of these Materialist schools suspect. The possibility that they are hypothetical schools concocted by the

[1] For this sense of 'dibba-' *v.* O. H. de A. Wijesekera, 'Upanishadic Terms for Sense Functions', UCR., Vol. II, pp. 23, 24.

author of the Sutta who was anxious to present sixty-two theories in this Sutta cannot be ruled out especially since there seems to have been a belief at this time that there were 'sixty-two ways of life' (dvaṭṭhi paṭipadā,[1] D. I.54) which means that there would have to be sixty-two theories on which these were based. On the other hand, since the majority of the views stated here are, in our opinion, traceable to non-Buddhist sources we need not be too sceptical even of this list.[2] Even if five schools, each according to the state of jhāna mentioned, did not exist, we need not doubt the existence of at least one school of Materialists who claimed to attain jhānic or yogic states, while denying the ontological or epistemological claims made about them, especially since we seem to find some hints about the existence of such a school from other sources. Guṇaratna says that there were some yogis (yoginaḥ) who were nāstikas, where the context shows beyond doubt that he is using the term nāstika- to refer to the Materialist schools. His statement reads as follows: kāpālikā bhasmoddhūlanaparā *yogino* brāhmaṇādyantyajātāśca kecana *nāstikā* bhavanti, te . . . caturbhūtātmakaṃ jagadācakṣate (*op. cit.*, p. 300); here whether we take yoginaḥ as qualifying kāpālikāḥ or as a class by themselves it is clear that some yogis were Materialists. In the Taittirīya Upaniṣad, we find the cryptic statement, asadeva sa bhavati asadbrahme'ti veda cet (2.6.1.), which is translated by Radhakrishnan as 'non-existent, verily, does one become, if he knows Brahman as non-being'. If the statement that 'Brahman is non-being' was made by a person who had attained the yogic state described as the 'attainment of Brahman' (brahmaprāpta-, Kaṭha, 2.3.18), he would be a Materialist as defined above.

(142) Now if there was a class of Materialists who had attained one of the arūpajhānas, we can make some interesting deductions about their beliefs. For it is stated that when the fourth jhāna is attained immediately prior to entering the arūpajhānas (formless mystical states) the mind is 'clear and cleansed' (parisuddha-, pariyodāta-, D. I.75–6) and

[1] This is one of the Ājīvika doctrines propounded by Makkhali Gosāla (*v.* Basham, *op. cit.*, p. 242). Basham takes it to mean 'religious systems of conduct, of which the *majjhimā paṭipadā* of Buddhism was one' but has apparently not noticed the correspondence of the number sixty-two with the sixty-two theories frequently mentioned in the Buddhist texts.

[2] N. Dutt following Thomas does not think that the list of views in the Brahmajāla represents actual views current at the time; *v. Early Monastic Buddhism*, 2nd Edn., Calcutta, 1960, p. 36; cp. E. J. Thomas, *The Life of the Buddha*, New York, 1927, p. 199.

that when the mind is clear and cleansed, it acquires certain extrasensory faculties whereby it is possible to have a vision of one's past births (pubbenivāsānussatiñāṇa-, D. I.82) as well as the 'decease and survival of beings' (satte cavamāne upapajjamāne, D. I.82–3). If these Materialists acquired these 'extrasensory faculties' which ostensibly gave alleged evidence of survival, why is it that they believed in the annihilation of the soul at death? Did they like some moderns hold that these mystic states and the visions had in them, though real as experiences were nevertheless hallucinatory, delusive and non-veridical. The commentary seems to offer an explanation though it does not appear to be satisfactory. It says that 'there were two types of Materialists (*lit.* annihilationists), those who have attained jhāna (lābhī) and those who have not (alābhī). Those who have attained it observe the decease (of beings) but not their survival (cutiṃ disvā upapattiṃ apassanto-) with the clairvoyant vision of the worthy ones; he who is thus successful in observing only the decease but not the survival of beings accepts the annihilationist theory'.[1] The explanation is logically sound but it does not appear very plausible. It would be more likely that this school of Materialists asserted the possibility of attaining these mystical states but denied any claims regarding the validity of extrasensory perception in that they were private experiences which gave us no objective information.

[1] Tattha dve janā ucchedadiṭṭhiṃ gaṇhanti lābhī ca alābhī ca. Lābhī arahato dibbena cakkhunā cutiṃ disvā upapattiṃ apassanto, yo vā cutimattam eva daṭṭhuṃ sakkoti na upapattiṃ so ucchedadiṭṭhiṃ gaṇhāti, DA. I.120.

CHAPTER III

THE HISTORICAL BACKGROUND III—NON-VEDIC II—SCEPTICS, ĀJĪVIKAS AND JAINS

(143) In this chpater we propose to make a detailed study of the doctrines of the Sceptics, which are mentioned in the Pāli Nikāyas. They have influenced Early Buddhism (*v. infra*, 739, 813) and directly concern us. We shall also briefly examine the epistemological and logical doctrines of the Ājīvikas and Jains, which seem to have a bearing on the thought of the Canon.

(144) Traces of scepticism and agnosticism we find from the time of the Ṛgveda onwards (*v. supra*, 7). These instances are sporadic and there is no evidence of any widespread scepticism. Radhakrishnan says that the hymn to faith (śraddhā, R.V. 10.151) 'is not possible in a time of unshaken faith'[1] but there is nothing in the hymn itself to indicate the presence of scepticism at the time. This scepticism, as we said, found its latest expression in the *Nāsadīya* hymn (*v. supra*, 8–10), where it was extended to the very possibility of arriving at a final solution to a specific problem. This Ṛgvedic scepticism did not develop any further but we found certain undercurrents of doubt (vicikitsā) in the Brāhmaṇas (*v. supra*, 15). The doubt with regard to survival was first mooted in the Brāhmaṇas and appears in the Early Upaniṣads, where it was asked whether man can survive death, when nothing is left over to germinate in a next life (*v. supra*, 15). On the other hand, we found in the Upaniṣads a rational agnosticism approaching Kantian agnosticism, where Yājñavalkya rationally demonstrated the impossibility of knowing the ultimate reality or the ātman (*v. supra*, 43). Nevertheless, it was not an agnosticism proper in that it differed from Kantian agnosticism in one significant respect. For, although it was not

[1] Radhakrishnan and Moore, *op. cit.*, p. 34.

possible to apprehend ultimate reality conceptually it was still considered possible to have some sort of direct acquaintance with it in deep sleep, in the next life or in a mystical state.

(145) These sceptical hints of the earlier Vedic thought and the agnostic trends of the Upaniṣads could have paved the way for the growth of sceptical schools of thought, but the impetus and the occasion for their arising seem to have been provided by the presence of diverse, conflicting and irreconcilable theories, pertaining to moral, metaphysical, and religious beliefs. When there is a welter of contending views, people naturally become curious as to which view is true and in the absence of a safe criterion of truth become suspicious as to whether any view at all could be true.

(146) When a school of thought strongly urged the belief in survival and another vehemently denied it and both were able to adduce on the face of it equally strong arguments for their respective points of view, one becomes doubtful as to which view if at all could be true. When the Kaṭha said, 'this doubt (*vicikitsā*) there is with regard to a man deceased; "he exists" say some, "he exists not" say others' (1.1.20), it is probably echoing at least the uncertainties with regard to the problem of survival entertained by the intellectuals at that time in the presence of a school of Materialists, who strongly denied survival.

(147) That the intellectual confusion resulting from the presence of a diversity of views seems to have been the main motive for the birth of scepticism is apparent from the sayings and opinions ascribed to the Sceptics (ajñānikāḥ, ajñāninaḥ) by Śīlāṅka commenting on the Sūtrakṛtāṅga. One has, however, to be cautious in picking out the sayings ascribed to the Sceptics from those attributed to the ajñānikāḥ or ajñāninaḥ in general, since Śīlāṅka uses these terms in at least three senses. Sometimes he employs the word to denote 'the ignorant' religious teachers[1] following the usage of the Sūtrakṛtāṅga which uses the term in this sense at times (*v.* annāṇiyā, 1.1.2.16). He also uses the term of the Buddhists who, he says, are 'more or less ajñānikas since they consider that karma done out of ignorance (he probably means "unintentionally") does not result in bondage'.[2] Most often, however,

[1] samyagjñānavirahitā śramaṇā brāhmaṇāḥ, Vol. I, fol. 35 on Sū. 1.1.2.16.

[2] Śākyā api prāyaśo' jñānikā avijñopacitaṃ karma bandhaṃ na yātītyevaṃ yatas te 'bhyupagamayanti, Vol. I, fol. 217 on Sū. 1.12.2.

ajñānikāḥ, or ajñāninaḥ is used as a technical term to denote the Sceptics following the usage of the Sūtrakṛtāṅga (e.g. 1.1.2.27, 1.12.2) and in this sense the word is defined either as 'those who claim that scepticism is best' (ajñānam eva śreya ityevaṃvādinām, Vol. I, fol. 35 on Sū. 1.1.2.17) or as 'those in whom no knowledge, i.e. scepticism, is evident' (na jñānamajñānam tadvidyate yeṣāṃ te'jñāninaḥ, *loc. cit.*; cp. ajñānam vidyate yeṣām, Vol. I, fol. 215 on Sū. 1.12.2). The term is also sarcastically defined as 'those who move in ignorance or those who show themselves off to the extent of being extraordinarily wise' (ājñānikāḥ) (ajñānena vā carantītyajñānikāḥ; ājñānikā vā tāvat pradarśayante, Vol. I, fol. 215 on Sū 1.12.2). When, however, Śīlāṅka makes the statement that, Ājīvikādayo Gośālamatānusārino'jñānavādapravṛttāḥ, i.e. 'the Ājīvikas and the others who are the followers of Gośāla's doctrines are a product of ajñānavāda',[1] (*op. cit.*, Vol. I, fol. 36), one is at a loss whether to translate ajñānavāda here as 'ignorance' or as 'scepticism' in the general or special senses. Since Śīlāṅka elsewhere identifies the 'followers of Gośāla's doctrines' as the Vainayikas,[2] (moralists) which Professor Basham finds a 'puzzling reference',[3] it is unlikely that he thought of them as an offshoot of the Sceptics (ajñānavāda-) since he distinguishes the Vainayikas from the Ajñānikas.

(148) Despite these variant uses of the terms ajñānikāḥ and ajñāninaḥ on the part of Śīlāṅka, it is not difficult on the whole to pick out the references to the genuine Sceptics from the context. In one of these contexts he ascribes a statement which, if true, leaves us in no doubt that the conflict of theories and the consequent difficulty of discovering the truth was the *raison d'être* of scepticism. Barua has translated a part of this passage, leaving out the latter part (which is somewhat obscure) and has concluded from it that the Sceptics were stressing the moral dangers of subscribing to conflicting views as the reason for their scepticism.[4] He has mistranslated the phrase, bahutaradoṣasambhavāt, after reducing it to 'bahu dosāḥ' on his own and rendering it as 'many

[1] Professor Basham has not mentioned this statement where he has made a study of similar statements, *v. op. cit.*, pp. 174–7.

[2] *Op. cit.*, Vol. I, Fol. 151 on Sū. 1.6.27.

[3] *Op. cit.*, p. 177. Basham's attempt to explain the Vainayikas as a later schismatic sect of the Ājīvikas(?) is unsatisfactory since the Vainayikas are known as early as the Pāli Nikāyas (cp. venayiko, M. I.140; cp. D. I.174, santi eke samaṇabrāhmaṇā sīlavādā).

[4] Barua, *op. cit.*, p. 330.

moral injuries', whereas the context would have made it clear, had he translated the whole passage that bahutaradoṣa- here means 'the multitude of (intellectual) confusions' or the 'magnitude of mistakes (arising from claims to knowledge)'. We may render this passage as follows: 'For they (i.e. the Sceptics) say that those who claim knowledge (jñāninaḥ) cannot be stating actual facts since their statements are mutually contradictory, for even with regard to the category of the soul, some assert that the soul is omnipresent (*sarvagatam*) and others that it is not omnipresent (*asarvagatam*), some (say) it is of the size of a digit (*aṅguṣṭaparvamātram*) others that it is of the size of a kernel of a grain of millet (*śyāmākataṇḍulamātram*) some say it both has form and is formless (*mūrtamamūrtam*), some that it resides in the heart (*hṛdayamadhyavartinam*) and (others) that it is located in the forehead (*lalāṭavyavasthitam*), etc.—in respect of every category there is no uniformity in their assertions; there is no one with an outstanding intellect whose statements may be regarded as authoritative; even if such a person existed, he cannot be discovered by one with a limited vision according to the maxim that "one who is not omniscient does not know everything" for it is said "how can one desiring to know that a certain person is omniscient at a certain time do so if he is devoid of that person's intellect, his knowledge and his consciousness"; owing to the absence of the knowledge of the means, it cannot properly be accomplished; it cannot be accomplished because of the mutual dependence (of the two); for it is said "without a super-knowledge (viśiṣṭaparijñāna-) the knowledge of the means is not attained and as a result there is no attainment of the super-knowledge of the object"; knowledge cannot completely comprehend the nature of the object of knowledge, for it is said, "whatever is apprehended should have the parts, near, middle and outer but here only the near part is apprehended and not the others since it is determined by it (i.e. the nature of the object)"; as for exhausting the atom (paramāṇu-paryavasānatā?) with the (knowledge of) the near portion, considering the unrepresented parts out of the three parts, it is not possible to apprehend the atom by those with a limited vision owing to the excellence of its nature; therefore, since there is no omniscient person and since one who is not omniscient cannot comprehend the nature of an object as it is constituted, since all the theorists (sarvavādinām) have conceived of the nature of the categories in a mutually contradictory manner and those who have claimed super-knowledge (uttaraparijñāninām) are at fault (pramādavatām) Scepticism is best owing to the magnitude of the mistakes that arise (from claims to knowledge) (bahutaradoṣasambhavāt)'.[1]

(149) Even if Śīlāṅka, writing in the ninth century, has rightly represented the views of the Sceptics, we have no right to assume that in the day of the Pāli Nikāyas they also held the same view. The sophisticated argument based on certain conceptions about the nature of knowledge in order to disprove the possibility of omniscience certainly appears *prima facie* to be late but the general thesis of the Sceptics, that the possibility of knowledge is doubtful since the claims to knowledge were mutually contradictory, may well go back to the period of the earliest Sceptics. Śīlāṅka often quotes this idea sometimes as a maxim of the Sceptics as, for instance, when it is said that 'they posit the theory that since those who claim knowledge make mutually contradictory assertions, they cannot be stating the truth'[2] and sometimes without specific reference to the Sceptic as for instance when he says that 'since the various theories claiming knowledge (jñānaṃ) have arisen in contradiction to one another, they are not true; therefore, Scepticism is best of all.'[3] Śīlāṇka speaks of the kind of investigation (mīmāṃsā-) and reflection (vimarśa-) which leads to Scepticism as follows: 'Is this theory claiming knowledge (kimetad-jñānaṃ) true or false? Scepticism

[1] Tathāhi te ūcuḥ -ya ete jñāninas te parasparaviruddhavāditayā na yathārthavādino bhavanti, tathāhi-eke sarvagatamātmānaṃ vadanti, tathā'nye asarvagatam, apare aṅguṣṭaparvamātram, kecana śyāmākataṇḍulamātram, anye mūrtamamūrtaṃ hṛdayamadhyavartinaṃ lalāṭavyavasthitamityādyātmapadārtha eva sarvapadārthapuraḥsare teṣām naikavākyatā, na cātiśayajñānī kaścidasti yadvākyam pramāṇīkriyeta, na cāsau vidyamāno' py upalakṣyate'rvāgdarśinā, 'na sarvajñaḥ sarvaṃ jānātī'ti vacanāt, tathā c'oktam-' sarvajño'sāviti hyetattatkāle'pi bubhutsubhiḥ tajjñānajneyavijñānaśūnyairvijñāyate katham?'; na ca tasya samyak tadupāyaparijñānābhāvāt sambhavaḥ, sambhavābhāvaścetaretarāśrayatvāt, tathāhi —viśiṣṭaparijñānamṛte tadavāptyupāyaparijñānam upāyamantareṇa ca nopeyasya viśiṣṭaparijñānasyāvaptir iti, na ca jñānaṃ jneyasyasvarūpam paricchetum alam, tathāhi -yatkimupalabhyate tasyārvāgmadhyaparabhāgairnetarayoḥ, tenaiva vyavahitatvāt, arvāgbhāgasyā'pi bhāgatrayakalpanāt tatsarvārātīyabhāgaparikalpanayā paramāṇuparyavasānatā, paramāṇośca svabhāvaviprakṛṣṭatvādarvāgdarśaninām nopalabdhir iti, tadevaṃ sarvajñasyābhāvādasarvajñasya ca yathāvasthitavastusvarūpāparicchedāt sarvavādināṃ ca parasparavirodhena padārthasvarūpābhyupagamāt yathottaraparijñānināṃ pramādavatām bahutaradoṣasambhavād ajñānameva śreyaḥ, *op. cit.*, Vol. I, fol. 215, 6 on Sū. 1.12.2.

[2] Tairabhihitaṃ jñānavādinaḥ parasparaviruddhārthavāditayā na yathārthavadinaḥ, *op. cit.*, Vol. I, fol. 216 on Sū. 1.12.2.

[3] Na ca tāni jñānāni parasparavirodhena pravṛttatvāt satyāni tasmādajñānameva śreyaḥ, *op. cit.*, Vol. I, fol. 34 on Sū. 1.1.2.14.

is best since with an excess of knowledge, there is an increase of mistakes (doṣātireka-)'.[1]

(150) Even the reference to the conflicting theories about the ātman may be attributed to the early Sceptic, since each one of the theories stated were current by the time of the Pāli Nikāyas and all of them could be traced to the period of the Early Upaniṣads. Thus the pantheistic ātman, which is 'made of everything' (sarvamayaḥ, idammayaḥ adomayaḥ, Bṛh. 4.4.5) would be omnipresent (sarvagatam) while the transcendent ātman defined negatively (neti neti, Bṛh. 3.9.26) would not be so. Again at Kaṭha 2.3.17, the ātman is of 'the size of a digit' (*aṅguṣṭamātraḥ*), while at Chāndogya 3.14.3, the ātman is 'smaller than a kernel of a grain of millet'[2] (atmā aṇīyān *śyāmākataṇḍulāt*). Again at Bṛhadāraṇyaka 2.3.1, Brahman which is identical with the ātman is said 'both to have form and also be formless' (mūrtaṃ caivāmurtañ ca). Likewise at Kaṭha 2.3.17 the ātman 'resides in the heart' (hṛdaye sanniviṣṭaḥ) while at Aitareya Āraṇyaka 2.1.4.6 it (i.e. brahman=ātman) is located in the head (śiro'śrayata). It is not at all surprising that the Sceptics would have been quick to see these contradictions in the Upaniṣads in an age when the Vedāntic interpretation (or for that matter, the interpretations of Deussen or Radhakrishnan) which tries to synthesize all these contradictions, was not known.

(151) The sophisticated argument against the concept of omniscience appears to be too involved or complicated to belong to the early Sceptics but here again we need not doubt that they would have questioned the possibility of omniscience in an age when there was more than one claimant to omniscience. The leader of the Jains claimed omniscience according to the evidence of both the Buddhist as well as the Jain texts (*v. infra,* 311) and so did Pūraṇa Kassapa (*v. infra,* 196). Omniscience is claimed for Makkhali Gośāla in the later Tamil texts Civañānacittiyār and Nīlakēci as Prof. Basham has shown (*op. cit.,* p. 276), though there is no evidence that he himself claimed omniscience. It is not unlikely that since the Buddha argued against the claims to

[1] Kimetadjñānaṃ satyamutāsatyamiti? Yathā ajñānameva śreyo yathā yathā ca jñānātiśayastathā tathāca doṣātireka iti, *op. cit.,* Vol. I, fol. 35 on Sū. 1.1.2.17.

[2] Here the Upaniṣad is itself possibly trying to explain the contradictions in previous theories by turning them into paradoxes since it also says that the ātman 'is greater than the earth', etc.

omniscience on the part of religious teachers (*v. infra*, 311), the Sceptics would likewise have done so. The sayings which state that with a limited knowledge no one can know that any person is omniscient, e.g. 'nāsarvajñaḥ sarvajñaṃ jānāti'; 'sarvajño' sāviti hyetattatkāle pi bubhutsubhiḥ tajjñānajñeyavijñānarahitair gamyate katham' are also quoted elsewhere[1] and may possibly have been old sayings of the Sceptics. Another saying bearing on this topic specifically attributed to the Sceptics and criticized, reads as follows: 'All teachings are like the utterances of barbarians since they have no (epistemic) basis' (chinnamūlatvāt mlecchānubhāṣaṇavat sarvam upadeśādikam, *op. cit.*, Vol. I, fol. 35 on Sū. 1.1.2.17). This was possibly directed mainly against those who claimed to speak with authority on the presumption of their omniscience. On the basis of these sayings we may perhaps surmise that they argued that since the human intellect was limited no one could claim to know everything with such a limited intellect. They may have even extended this argument to arrive at their Scepticism. None of the metaphysical theories claiming to be true, which are the products of such a limited intellect, can be known to be true, since they are mutually contradictory. Now, no new theory can also be true since it is bound to contradict one or more of the existing theories. Therefore nothing can be known to be true. Thus the contradictions of metaphysics and the impossibility of omniscience may have led them to accept Scepticism. One thing we need not doubt and that is that these Sceptics more than any other thinkers of their age appear to have been struck by the fact that the conflicting theories not of one tradition but of all schools seemed to cancel each other out. And in this respect the Sceptics were really the children of the age in which they lived.

(151A) That the period immediately preceding the rise of Buddhism was one in which there was an interminable variety of views on matters pertaining to metaphysics, morality and religion is clear from the references to them in the Buddhist and Jain texts. The Brahmajāla Sutta (D. I.12–38) refers to fifty-eight schools of thought other than the four schools or types of Sceptics referred to. It is not improbable that some of these are only possible schools not current at the time (*v. supra*, 141) but there are good grounds to think that many of them were actually existing schools in view of the independent literary sources which refer to them. Similarly, the Sūtrakṛtāṅga mentions three hundred and sixty-three schools. This list is artificially made up mainly

[1] *v. op. cit.*, Vol. I, fol. 35 on Sū. 1.1.2.16.

but not solely on the basis of the categories of Jainism itself[1] but there would be little reason to deny the existence of the four main schools of Kriyāvāda, Akriyāvāda, Ajñānikavāda and Vainayikavāda and probably several subgroups among them. A brief account of the doctrines of some of these schools is given in several contexts of the Sūtrakṛtāṅga (1.1.1.8–18, 1.2.1–28, 1.6.27, 1.12.2–11, 2.1.14–30, 2.2.79) and these accounts do not appear to be in the least artificial.

(152) When we consider this historical background, it is only to be expected that the Sceptics should appear at this time. In the Sūtrakṛtāṅga, they are called the 'aṇṇāṇiyā' (Skr. ajñānikāḥ), i.e. the 'ignorant ones' or 'sceptics' or 'those who deny knowledge' (*v. supra*, 147), translated as 'agnostics' by Jacobi (SBE., Vol. 45, pp. 241, 315). They are mentioned in a few places (Sū. 1.1.2.17, 1.6.27, 1.21.1–2, 2.2.79) and are considered one of the four important schools of thought. But the information given about them in the texts themselves is meagre. It is said that 'the speculations (vīmaṃsā) of the Sceptics do not land them in ignorance (as they ought to); when they cannot instruct themselves in the truth (param), how can they instruct others' (aṇṇāṇiyāṇaṃ vīmaṃsā aṇṇāṇe ṇa viniyacchaī, appaṇo ya paraṃ nālaṃ, kuto annāṇusasiūṃ), Sū. 1.1.2.17). Jacobi translates aṇṇāṇe ṇa viniyacchaī, as 'cannot lead to knowledge' (*op. cit.*, p. 241) but this is not supported by the text or the commentary. Even if we translate, na vi-niyacchaī (Skr. na vi-niyacchati) as 'cannot lead to', aṇṇāṇe (Skr.

[1] Śīlāṅka makes up the list of 363 'schools' as follows (*v. op. cit.*, Vol. I, fol. 212, 3):

(i) Kriyāvādins	180	(kriyāvadināmasītyadhikṃ śatama bhavati)
(ii) Akriyāvadins	84	(akriyāvadinām . . . caturasīti)
(iii) Ajñānikas	67	(ajñānikānām . . . saptaṣaṣṭiḥ)
(iv) Vainayikas	32	(vainayikānām . . . dvātriṃśat)
	363	Total

(i) The 180 Kriyāvadins are as follows: the variables are—the *nine* categories of Jainism such as *jīva-*, etc., the *two* principles of *svataḥ* and *parataḥ*, the *two* attributes of *nitya-* and *anitya-*, the *five* concepts of *kāla,- sāvabhāva-*, *niyati-*, *īsvara-* and *ātman-*. This gives 9×2×2×5=180.

(ii) The variables are—the 7 categories of *jīva-*, etc., taken negatively, the *two* principles of *svataḥ* and *parataḥ*, the *six* concepts (note the difference of these concepts from those enumerated in (i)), viz. *kāla-*, *yadṛcchā-*, *niyati-*, *svabhāva-*, *īsvara-*, *ātma-*. This gives 7×2×6=84.

(iii) For Ajñānikas, *v.* infra, 157.

(iv) The variables are the *four* duties (of *manas-*, *vāk-*, *kāya-*, and *dāna-*) towards *seven* types of people; 7×4=28.

ajñāne) is not 'knowledge' but the opposite of it; the commentary explains the phrase as follows: 'Ajñāne' ajñānaviṣaye 'na niyacchati' na niścayena yacchati, nāvatarati (*op. cit.*, Vol. I, fol. 35), which means, the '(speculations) do not definitely take them or place them in the realm of ignorance'. What is meant is that their scepticism should lead them logically to the conclusion that they know nothing whatsoever, but in fact their 'reflections have the features of knowledge' (paryālocanasya jñānarūpatvāt, *loc. cit.*) and 'one cannot understand' (na budhyate, *loc. cit.*) how they claim to know such propositions as 'ignorance is best' (ajñānameva śreyaḥ, *loc. cit.*), etc. So when they claim that they are Sceptics they are (according to this Jain criticism) in fact claiming to have some knowledge as revealed by their *dicta* and thereby they are contradicting themselves. The other context in which something informative is asserted about the Sceptics states that 'these Sceptics being "experts" are uncommitted' (asaṃṭhuyā=asambaddhāḥ) (commentary, *op. cit.*, Vol I, fol. 215); Jacobi translates as "reason incoherently" (*op. cit.*, p. 316) but they have not overcome doubt; unskilled they teach the unskilled and utter falsehood without discrimination' (aṇṇāṇiyā tā kusalāvi santā, asanthuyā ṇo vitigicchatinnā, akoviyā āhu akoviyehiṃ, aṇāṇuvīttu musaṃ vayanti, Sū. 1.12.2).

(153) Though the Sūtrakṛtāṅga itself tells us little, Śīlāṅka's commentary, as we have already seen, is more informative. The main difference that we notice between Śīlāṅka's account and that in the Pāli Nikāyas is that the former stresses the intellectual grounds for their scepticism, while the emphasis in the latter is on the practical value or the pragmatic reasons for Scepticism. While the general argument for scepticism appears to have been the one we outlined above (*v. supra*, 148), an often quoted saying of the Sceptic throws a little more light on the rational basis of their scepticism. It is said that the Sceptics hold that 'scepticism is the best since it is difficult to gauge the thought processes of another' (paracetovṛttīnāṃ duranvayatvādajñānameva śreyaḥ, *op. cit.*, Vol. I, fol. 35 on Sū. 1.1.2.17; cp. paracetovṛttīnāṃ duranvayatvāt, *op. cit.*, Vol. I, fol. 216 on Sū. 1.12.1). The difficulty of knowing another's mind seems to be one of the reasons why the Sceptics held to their other dictum that 'all teachings are like the utterances of barbarians since they have no (epistemic) basic' (*v. supra*, 151). Śīlāṅka himself following the Sūtrakṛtāṅga makes use of this idea in another connection and observes that 'owing to the difficulty of knowing another's mind, they do not grasp what is intended by the words

of their teacher and thus repeat the other's words like a barbarian without understanding the real meaning'.[1] This idea seems to be borrowed from the Sceptics. The fact that Śīlāṅka himself does not as a Jain believe that one cannot know another's mind is clear from his criticism of this sceptical view. He says it is false (asat), because the Sceptics themselves cannot believe this. For they put forward views such as 'scepticism is best' (ajñānameva śreyaḥ, *v. supra*, 147) intended to instruct others. He quotes in his favour a non-sceptical view which says that 'the inner mind of another can be apprehended by his external features, gestures, movements, gait, speech and the changes in his eyes and face'.[2]

(154) Here again, we do not know on what grounds the Sceptic held the view that one cannot know another's mind but it is evident that this theory itself could have led him to scepticism. If one cannot know another's mind, communication is impossible and knowledge no longer becomes objective. We may profitably compare this view with that of the Greek sophist, who believed in the incommunicability of what we claim to know. In Gorgias' book[3] on 'Nature or the Non-existent', he sets forth three propositions, viz. (1) that nothing exists, (2) that if anything exists it cannot be known, and (3) that if it can be known, the knowledge cannot be communicated. The Ajñāṇikas seem to have agreed with propositions (2) and (3) but not (1) since quite consistently with their scepticism they could not categorically hold that 'nothing exists' but only that 'nothing could be known to exist'. This is the same as proposition (2), thus granting the possibility of existence. Now Gorgias proves proposition (2) by showing that knowledge is identical with sense-perception and that since sense-impressions differ with different people, no two people can have the same sense-impressions with regard to an object. Therefore knowledge, which must necessarily be objective, is not possible because of this subjectivity. For the same reason this knowledge being identical with sensation, cannot be communicated. The Indian Sceptics may possibly have reasoned on similar lines, though one cannot be quite certain about this, due to the lack of any definite evidence. The argument against the possibility of complete knowledge (*v. supra*, 148) seems to give a faint

[1] Evaṃ paracetovṛttīnāṃ duranvayatvādupadeṣṭurapi yathāvasthitavivakṣayā grahaṇāsambhavānniścayārthamajānānā mlecchavadaparoktam anubhāṣanta eva, *op. cit.*, Vol. I, fol. 35 on Sū. 1.1.2.16.

[2] ākārairiṅgitairgatyā ceṣṭayā bhāṣitena ca netravaktravikāraiśca gṛhyate 'ntargatam manaḥ, op. *cit.*, Vol. I, fol. 35 on Sū. 1.1.2.17.

[3] W. T. Stace, *A Critical History of Greek Philosophy*, pp. 116–7.

indication of this. Here it was said that whatever we apprehend has the three parts, near (arvāk-), middle (madhya-), and outer (para-) and that we in fact apprehend only the near part (tasyārvāgbhāgasyevopalabdhiḥ, *loc. cit.*). Now this is certainly true of visual perception and in a sense of sense-perception in general. We see only the near side (the side facing us) of objects, so that what each person sees of the object would be different according to the individual perspective. So if we are arvāg-darśinaḥ (a term which is frequently used in the sayings of Sceptics) or 'near-side-seers', our knowledge at least of physical objects, being dependent on our individual perspectives, would be subjective since these perspectives would be different with different individuals. In the absence of objectivity, there is no knowledge at all and the private experiences or impressions of the different individuals would be incommunicable. Whether the early Sceptics would have employed such reasoning or not it is difficult to say but they certainly seem to have held that one could not know another's mind and this seems to have been one of the grounds of their Scepticism.

(155) As we have seen, Śīlāṅka's account stresses the intellectual basis of their scepticism rather than the pragmatic or moral reasons for it, but the fact that they were also present is evident from some of his observations about the Sceptics. According to Śīlāṅka 'the Sceptics... conceive that even if there was knowledge it is useless (niṣphalam) since it has many disadvantages (bahudoṣavat)' (Ajñānikānām . . . jñānaṃ tu sadapi niṣphalam bahudoṣavaccetyevaṃabhyupagamavatām, *op. cit.*, Vol. I, fol. 215). This shows that they not only considered knowledge to be impossible but that it was useless. In enumerating the sixty-seven 'types' of Sceptics, Śīlāṅka puts the question of the Sceptic in two forms, viz. 'Who knows that the soul exists? Of what use is this knowledge? Who knows that the soul does not exist? Of what use is this knowledge? etc.' (san jīvaḥ ko vetti? kiṃ vā tena jñānena? asan jīvaḥ ko vetti? kiṃ vā tena jñānena? *op. cit.*, Vol. I, fol. 36 on Sū. 1.1.2.20; also Vol. I, fol. 212). The second of these forms is clearly meant to imply that they adopted Scepticism on pragmatic considerations as well.

(156) Sīlāṅka does not shed any more light on what the Sceptics considered as the defects or disadvantages (doṣa-) of knowledge but as we shall see the accounts in the Pāli Nikāyas pay a good deal of attention to this aspect of their scepticism. But since we shall be dealing with each school of Sceptics mentioned in the Brahmajāla Sutta

separately, we may briefly state here what the Sceptics seem to have considered to be the defects or disadvantages of knowledge. The sense in which the term doṣa- is used by Śīlāṅka in elucidating the views of the Sceptics is not very clear. In the passage in which knowledge was condemned ((*v. supra*, 148) as giving rise to a multitude of doṣa- (bahutaradoṣasambhavāt), it was apparent from the context that the word meant 'intellectual confusions' and not 'moral injuries' as suggested by Barua (*v. supra*, 148), who was probably influenced by the picture of the Sceptic as drawn in the Buddhist texts. The other uses (e.g. 'the greater the knowledge the greater the doṣa', yathā yáthā ca jñānātiśayas tathā tathā ca doṣātireka-, *op. cit.*, Vol. I, fol. 35 on Sū. 1.1.2.17) were less clear and doṣa- could here have meant (ambiguously) 'moral disadvantages'. In the Brahmajāla Sutta, however, we find that the first two schools of Sceptics held that there were undesirable psychological and moral consequences of claiming knowledge under conditions, when it was impossible to know the facts for certain. According to the first school (*v. infra*, 159), we have a liking or bias for (chando, rāgo) a proposition and a dislike or a bias against its contradictory (doso, paṭigho), when we come to accept it as true without valid grounds. Since this is grounded on one's prejudices for and against, the proposition itself is said to be false and its acceptance wrong or mistaken (musā). Now, uttering a falsehood or doing a wrong thing is a source of remorse (vighāto) and is a moral danger (antarāyo). According to the second school (*v. infra*, 166), the bias for or against is an entanglement (upādānam) which is again a moral danger (antarāyo). The third school (*v. infra*, 167) seems to have been impressed by the psychologically and morally disastrous consequences of debating their theories, on the part of those who claimed to know and believe in them. We must not forget that during this period not only were there a variety of theories but a good many of them were being hotly debated (*v. infra*, Ch. V), resulting in one party having to undergo the miseries of defeat. Sometimes these debates seem to have given rise to bickering and quarrels among the contending parties. This third school of Sceptics, if not the first and second as well, seem to have concluded that all this self-imposed unhappiness was due to baseless claims to knowledge and that Scepticism was superior to making such claims. It is probable that these were among the defects or disadvantages (doṣa-) of knowledge spoken of in some of Śīlāṅka's quotations from the Sceptics. If so it would be seen that there were both pragmatic as well as intellectual grounds for their scepticism.

(157) As we have mentioned (*v. supra*, 151) Śilāṅka speaks of sixty-seven 'types' of Sceptics in order to make up the figure three hundred and sixty-three, the number of schools of thought, mentioned in the Sūtrakṛtāṅga. But they are neither schools nor types and the list is artificially made up mainly but not solely out of the concepts of Jainism itself. He takes the nine categories (navapadārtha-) of Jainism, each according to the seven forms of predication (saptabhaṅgakāḥ). This gives sixty three (i.e. 9×7) forms of sceptical questions, which are considered to represent sixty three 'types' of Sceptics asking these questions. The last four 'types' are more interesting and possibly represent a kind of question, which the Sceptics themselves asked. They are as follows:

(i) Sati bhāvotpattiḥ ko vetti? Who knows whether there is an arising of psychological states?

(ii) Asati bhāvotpattiḥ ko vetti? Who knows whether there is no arising of psychological states?

(iii) Sadasati bhāvotpattiḥ ko vetti? Who knows whether there is and is no arising of psychological states?

(iv) Avaktavyo bhāvotpattiḥ ko vetti? Who knows whether the arising of psychological states is impredicable? Śilāṅka comments that the 'other three possibilities of predication do not apply in the case of the arising of psychological states'[1]. The question of 'the arising of consciousness' (saññuppāda-) is one on which there seems to have been a good deal of speculation during the period of the Pāli Nikāyas and four different theories on this subject are mentioned in the Poṭṭhapāda Sutta (D. I.180). This could have easily provoked these sceptical questions, but what is interesting is the fourfold mode of predication adopted. It is possible that Śilānka did this merely to complete the figure of sixty-seven and his explanation that this subject does not admit of the other forms of predication is too puerile to be taken seriously. But it is also not unlikely that the Sceptics in fact adopted a fourfold scheme of predication as we have suggested (*v. infra*, 184) in discussing the evidence from the Pāli texts

(158) The Pāli term used to refer to the Sceptics, namely, *Amarāvikkhepikā*, seems to be a nickname and has probably been correctly translated as 'eel-wrigglers' (Prof. Rhys Davids, SBB., Vol. II, pp. 37 ff.). It is however a word whose meaning is obscure and the

[1] Uttaram bhaṅgatrayam . . . bhāvotpattau na sambhavatīti, *op. cit.*, Vol. I, fol. 213.

commentary offers two explanations of it. It is said that it may mean 'those who are confused by their endless beliefs and words'.[1] The alternative explanation is that amarā stands for a species of fish, who are in the habit of running about in the water, constantly emerging and diving down so that it is difficult to get hold of them and that similarly this theory (Scepticism) runs hither and thither without arriving at a definite conclusion.[2] The fact that the commentator gives two alternative explanations of the word shows that he himself was uncertain about its meaning. The latter is probably to be preferred since amarā as meaning endless (pariyantarahita-) is far-fetched. Vācāvikkhepa- is used as a synonym of amarāvikkhepa-,[3] and probably means 'verbal jugglery' in view of the fact that these thinkers would have appeared in the eyes of their opponents to evade committing themselves with regard to the truth or falsity of a proposition. When Ajātasattu refers to the theory as just vikkhepaṃ he probably means the same, i.e. 'jugglery' or 'confusion'.

(159) The Buddhist texts refer to and briefly define the views of different schools of Sceptics. They are spoken of collectively as 'some recluses and brahmins who wriggle like eels. For when a question is put to them on this or that matter they resort to verbal jugglery and eel-wriggling on four grounds'.[4] The first of these schools is described as follows: 'Herein a certain recluse or brahmin does not understand, as it really is, that this is good or this is evil. And it occurs to him: I do not understand what is good or evil as it really is. Not understanding what is good or evil, as it really is, if I were to assert that this is good and this is evil, that will be due to my likes, desires, aversions or resentments. If it were due to my likes, desires, aversions or resentments, it would be wrong. And if I were wrong, it would cause me worry (vighāto) and worry would be a moral danger to me (antarāyo). Thus, through fear of being wrong (musāvādabhayā) and the abhorrence of being wrong, he does not assert anything to be good or evil and on questions being put to him on this or that matter he resorts to verbal jugglery and eel-wriggling, saying: I do not say so, I do not

[1] Amarāya diṭṭhiyā vācāya vikkhepo ti amarāvikkhepo. DA. I.115.

[2] Aparo nayo. Amarā nāma macchajāti, sā ummujjana-nimujjanādivasena udake sandhāvamānā gahetuṃ na sakkoti. Evam eva ayam pi vādo ito c'ito ca sandhāvati gāhaṃ na upagacchatī ti amarāvikkhepo vuccati, *loc. cit.*

[3] . . . vācāvikkhepaṃ āpajjati amarāvikkhepaṃ, D. I.27.

[4] Santi . . . eke samaṇabrāhmaṇā amarāvikkhepikā, tattha tattha pañham puṭṭhā samānā vācāvikkhepaṃ āpajjanti amarāvikkhepaṃ catūhi vatthūhi, D. I.24.

say thus, I do not say otherwise, I do not say no, I deny the denials (*lit.* I do not say, "no, no")'.[1]

(160) This description as it stands obviously admits of more than one interpretation. On a very literal interpretation of it, it need not represent the point of view of a Sceptic at all, unless we mean by a Sceptic a person who suspends his judgment on the truth or falsity of a proposition, in the absence of adequate evidence or grounds for believing in its truth or falsity. If this class of thinkers merely refused to assert that something was positively good or evil, unless they had objective grounds for doing so, without being misled by subjective bias due to their likes and dislikes, they would not be Sceptics but critical thinkers recommending the outlook of science or intelligent commonsense. The only difference from scientific scepticism, which advocates the suspension of judgment in the absence of good evidence or valid grounds for asserting the truth or falsity of a proposition, would be that these thinkers did not merely consider that it was intellectually unsatisfactory not to suspend judgment under such circumstances, but that it was a moral danger (antarāyo) as well not to do so.

(161) Such an evaluation, however, is *prima facie* improbable. For if they suspended judgment only until knowledge was possible without ruling out the possibility of knowledge altogether, they would not have been known to their opponents as having persistently refused to commit themselves by asserting or denying all the logically possible alternatives at least in respect of ethical propositions. It is, therefore, very probable that they not merely denied knowledge of ethical propositions but claimed that such propositions were, in principle, unknowable, and that if we held that such propositions were either true or false, as the case may be, we would be guided by our prejudices.

[1] Idha . . . ekacco samaṇo vā brāhmaṇo vā idaṃ kusalan ti yathābhūtaṃ na ppajānāti, idaṃ akusalan ti yathābhūtaṃ nappajānāti. Tassa evam hoti: Ahaṃ kho idaṃ kusalan ti yathābhūtaṃ nappajānāmi, idaṃ akusalanti yathābhūtaṃ nappajānāmi. Ahañ c'eva kho pana idaṃ kusalan ti yathābhūtam appajānanto, idaṃ akusalan ti yathābhūtam appajānanto idaṃ kusalan ti vā vyākareyyaṃ, idam akusalan ti vā vyākareyyaṃ, tattha me assa chando vā rāgo vā doso vā paṭigho vā tam mam'assa musā. Yam mam'assa musā so mam'assa vighāto. Yo mam'assa vighāto so mam'assaa ntarāyo ti. Iti so musāvādabhayā musāvādaparijegucchā n'ev'idaṃ kusalan ti vyākaroti na pana idaṃ akusalan ti vyākaroti, tattha tattha pañham puṭṭho samāno vācāvikkhepaṃ āpajjati amarāvikkhepaṃ: Evam pi me no. Tathā ti pi me no. Aññathā ti pi me no. No ti pi me no. No no ti pi me no ti. D. I.24–5.

Hence it would be wrong on our part to make these assertions or these assertions (or denials) would be false. Although their scepticism, with regard to ethical propositions (what was good and evil) is specifically referred to, it is not unlikely that their scepticism extended to all propositions and that they denied the possibility of any knowledge whatsoever in view of the fact that they are said to have given sceptical answers 'when questioned on this or that matter' (tattha tattha pañhaṃ puṭṭho, *loc. cit.*).

(162) This school of Sceptics is differentiated from the others on the grounds that they adopted scepticism 'through fear or aversion to asserting what was false (musā-vādabhāyā musāvādaparijegucchā)', since what was asserted (or denied) would be false if the assertion was due merely to one's likes or dislikes. Strictly speaking, however, an assertion made out of subjective bias need not necessarily be false, although it would be wrong to make the assertion unless there were good grounds for doing so. Therefore what is probably meant in this context is that in the absence of objective criteria for judging what was good or evil (or for asserting any proposition) we are led to hold some view or another out of subjective bias and that this is wrong. Whatever the explanation may be, it was the fear of believing in a proposition out of prejudice in the absence of certain knowledge that made them Sceptics. Their Scepticism is therefore due primarily to intellectual reasons but from the account given of it a moral reason was also present in that they hold that doing the wrong thing or uttering a falsehood could cause worry or remorse (vighāto) and be a moral danger (antarāyo) as well.

(163) This shows that despite their scepticism with regard to the objectivity or the knowability of moral judgments, they held certain subjective traits to be desirable. The commentary explains antarāya- as 'a hindrance to heaven or salvation'.[1] If this comment is relevant then this class of thinkers were not purely intellectual Sceptics but seem to have adopted scepticism on the grounds that knowledge was not only impossible but was a danger to moral development and salvation, a view which may have influenced Buddhism in regard to its attitude to the 'indeterminate questions' (avyākatas) (*v. infra*, 813). In the Sūtrakṛtāṅga, it is said that the Sceptics (Ajñānikavādāḥ) along with the other three main philosophical schools (Kriyāvāda, Akriyāvāda, Vainayikavāda) 'teach final beatitude and final deliverance' (2.2.79,

[1] Saggassa c'eva maggassa ca antarāyo, DA. I.155.

SBE., Vol. 45, p. 385). As Jacobi points out, in the commentary on the Uttarādhyayana Sūtra (18.23), it is said that the Sceptics (Ajñānavādinaḥ) 'contend that knowledge is not necessary for salvation but *tapas*'[1] is, and Jacobi commenting on this says that 'this seems identical with the karmapatha'.[1]

(164) The sacrificial brahmins of the Brāhmaṇas proper, who continued in the Upaniṣadic period recommending the path of action (karmamārga-), were undoubtedly against the claims to metaphysical and intuitive knowledge on the part of the Upaniṣadic thinkers. However, there is no reason to think that they were sceptics or agnostics in the matter of knowledge. They certainly claimed the veracity of certain ethical propositions. The modified theory of the path of action (karmamārga- or karmapatha-) to be found in the Īśā Upaniṣad and later in the Bhagavadgītā is less averse to knowledge. The Īśā, while condemning those who delight in knowledge as being in greater darkness than those who are ignorant,[2] nevertheless speaks of some kind of knowledge with which immortality is obtained (vidyayāmṛtam aśnute, *op. cit.*, 11). Barua calls the thinkers of the Kena Upaniṣad, viz. the Keniyas, 'sceptics' (*op. cit.*, pp. 261, 319). However, they were properly agnostics, who denied the possibility of conceptual or sensory knowledge of reality[3] while not denying that reality 'was known by an awakening' (pratibodhaviditam[4]). Likewise, faith (śraddhā) in the Upaniṣads was never divorced from knowledge and there is no evidence of a faith movement in the Upaniṣads, which decried knowledge. It is those who have both knowledge and faith[5] who attain immortality. Moreover, faith (śraddhā) is said to accompany both tapas and knowledge.[6]

(165) It is not intrinsically impossible that there were a set of thinkers in the Vedic tradition who, because they believed in the efficacy of

[1] SBE., Vol. 15, p. 83, fn. 2.

[2] Tato bhūya iva te tamo ya u vidyāyāṃ ratāḥ, 9.

[3] Na tatra cakṣur gacchati na vāg gacchati na manaḥ na vidmo na vijānīmo yathaitad anuśiṣyāt, 3; cp. 7; 2.2.3.

[4] 2.4. Radhakrishnan translates the phrase as 'when it is known through every state of cognition' and quotes in support a cryptic comment of Śaṅkara (bodham bodham prati viditam) but this surely contradicts what is stated one verse earlier, namely that 'it is not understood by those who understand it' (avijñātaṃ vijānatām, 2.3).

[5] Bṛh. 6.2.15, te ya evam etad *viduḥ*, ye cāmī araṇye *śraddhāṃ satyam* upāsate, . . .

[6] Muṇḍ. 1.2.11, *tapah śraddhe* ye hy upavasanty araṇye śāntā *vidvāṃso* . . .

rituals and the value of faith, pronounced that knowledge, whether empirical, metaphysical, or intuitive was a hindrance to moral progress and salvation. But their existence is not testified in the literature itself and it would be methodologically unsound to believe in their existence since we would have to depend on an *argumentum e silentio*. Even if they existed without leaving a trace of their doctrines in the Vedic literature, they cannot be identified with the first school of Sceptics as we know them from the passage under discussion. For in that case they should not declare the impossibility of knowledge but merely denounce it as morally dangerous. As we have shown (*v. supra*, 148–150) it is unlikely that this first school of Sceptics would have come into being before the air was polluted (or rather enriched) with a multitude of contending theories. Thus people came to feel on the one hand that knowledge was uncertain and on the other that claims to knowledge were morally dangerous in that one might believe in what was in fact untrue and/or lead a factious and contentious life engaged in dispute and debate in defending one's beliefs. It is in such circumstances that we can expect to find an intellectual scepticism at the theoretical level coupled with the practice of the good life as it was traditionally known or best understood at the time.

(166) The description of the second school of Sceptics is almost identical with that of the first except for the difference that according to these thinkers, to be led to believe in a proposition by one's likes, desires, aversions and resentments would be an entanglement (upādānam, D. I.25–6). Such entanglement would be a source of worry (vighāto) and as such a moral danger (antarāyo). Upādāna- literally means 'grasping' or 'clinging' (PTS. Dictionary, *s.v.* sense 2) but since these words express a pro-attitude[1] in that we grasp what we like or desire but not what we hate or are averse to, it would be better to translate the word as 'entanglement' or 'act of involvement'. For it is obviously intended to include the objects that we like as well as dislike. Prof. Rhys Davids translates the word as 'grasping condition of the heart which causes rebirth' (*op. cit.*, p. 38) but this, as standing for a concept of the Sceptics, need not, and indeed cannot, from the context have the same technical significance as it has in Buddhism. In the Buddhist context the word commonly means 'the entanglement or involvement that leads to becoming or survival in the next life'

[1] On the use of this word see P. H. Nowell-Smith, *Ethics*, Penguin Books, pp. 112–21.

(upādānapaccayābhavo, D. II.57) but there is no need to believe that these Sceptics, would have had such a definite belief in survival or rebirth, though they would not have dismissed the possibility. If as was said in the Sūtrakṛtāṅga, the Sceptics too entertained beliefs about heaven and salvation (*v. supra*, 613) it is possible that they held them on pragmatic grounds without claiming actual knowledge. For, if Śīlāṅka's observations are correct, a favourite dictum of theirs was 'Of what use is this knowledge' (kiṃ vā tena jñānena? *v. supra*, 155) as they did not believe that claims to knowledge had any pragmatic value. However, based on what is implied from the context, the more probable explanation is that this school of Sceptics merely considered it undesirable to be involved in beliefs based on one's likes or dislikes. They held this view not on the grounds that such involvement would lead to rebirth or survival but rather because such beliefs would be a source of worry and mental disquietude (vighāta-). In any case, it is clear that this school of thinkers, unlike the first, adopted Scepticism primarily out of moral considerations rather than for intellectual reasons although the latter were not absent.

(167) The next school of sceptical thinkers is said to argue as follows: 'I do not know, as it really is, what is good and what is evil and not knowing, if I were to pronounce that this is good or this is evil, then I would have to join issue, argue and debate with recluses and brahmins, learned, subtle, hair-splitters, skilled in controversy, who go about debunking with their intellect the theories of others. If I were to join issue, argue and debate with them, I would not be able to explain to them. If I were unable to explain to them, that would cause me worry (vighāta-) and be moral danger (antarāyo).' Thus because he fears and detests interrogation (anuyoga-)[1] he does not 'pronounce this to be good nor that to be evil'.[2]

[1] This is a technical term associated with the debate defined in the Caraka Saṃhitā, *v.* infra, 322.

[2] Ahaṃ kho idaṃ kusalan ti yathābhūtaṃ nappajānāmi, idaṃ akusalan ti yathābhūtaṃ nappajānāmi. Ahañ c'eva kho pana idaṃ kusalan ti yathābhūtam appajānanto, idaṃ akusalan ti yathābhūtam appajānanto idaṃ kusalan ti vā vyākareyyaṃ—santi hi kho pana samanabrāhmaṇā paṇḍitā nipunā kataparappavādā valavedhirūpā vobhindantā mañne caranti paññāgatena diṭṭhigatāni -te maṃ tattha samanuyuñjeyyuṃ samanugāheyyuṃ samanubhāseyyuṃ. Ye maṃ tattha samanuyunjeyyuṃ samanugāheyyuṃ, tesāhaṃ na sampāyeyyam. Yesāhaṃ na sampāyeyyaṃ so mam'assa vighāto so mam'assa antarāyo ti. Iti so anuyogabhayā anuyogaparijegucchā n'ev'idaṃ kusalan ti vyākaroti, na pan'idaṃ akusalan ti vyākaroti . . ., D. I.26.

(168) This passage is again obscure. As it stands it merely states that there were a set of thinkers, who, because of their ignorance of the truth or falsity of moral propositions, did not desire to engage in debate with skilled dialecticians. For they would not be able to convince them of their scepticism and this would be a source of worry and a moral danger to them.

(169) What is not clear from the above account is whether they wished to avoid debate because they were Sceptics or whether they adopted Scepticism because they wanted to avoid debate. The passage seems to be suggesting or saying both at once. On the one hand it seems to be saying that these thinkers 'do not know' that something is definitely good or evil and that their scepticism leads them to avoid debate, while on the other hand it seems to be saying that they do not want to 'pronounce that this is good or this is evil' because they feared debate. In the former case, as Sceptics, they would probably have found that they partially agreed with any or every thesis that their opponents put forward except of course the thesis that 'there is knowledge'. They had no particular thesis of their own that their opponents could disprove unless it be their scepticism itself. Thus it would have been difficult to convince their opponents of their scepticism inasmuch as according to the current rules of debate it was required that one party put forward a definite proposition to be proved (*v. infra,* 344). In the latter case, they would have adopted scepticism either because they saw the futility of debate where skilled dialecticians could apparently prove thesis as well as anti-thesis and/or because they saw the moral dangers of debate since debates resulted in the defeat of one party or the other and frayed tempers as well. They would have seen that there was no point or purpose in debate since one was nowhere nearer the truth at the end of it and at the same time feared debate because it could result in loss of their mental equanimity which they valued. This seems to be the more probable explanation judging from what we learned about these sceptics from Śīlāṅka's account.

(170) We have hitherto spoken of three schools of Sceptical thinkers, namely those who adopted scepticism primarily through fear of falsehood (musāvādabhayā), through fear of involvement (upādānabhayā) or fear of interrogation in debate (anuyogabhayā). All three schools considered the consequences of falsehood, involvement and interrogation psychologically undesirable in that they cause remorse or worry (vighāta-), which was a (moral) danger or hindrance (antarāya-). It

seems to be clear from this that there was much in common between these three schools or types of Sceptics and that they valued mental stability if not the cultivation of some sort of ideal state of mind.

(171) Apart from the few hints that we get about these Sceptics from Buddhist and Jain sources, we have not been able to trace any positive reference to them elsewhere in Indian thought. But the account given of the scepticism of Pyrrho, who is said to have been influenced by Indian thought,[1] bears a remarkable similarity to the point of view of these Sceptics. The quotation preserved by Aristocles from one of Timon's prose works and which is supposed to represent the views of Timon's teacher, Pyrrho, reads as follows: 'He himself (Pyrrho) has left nothing in writing but his disciple Timon says that the man who is to be happy must look to these three things: (1) what is the nature of things, (2) what attitude should we take to them, and (3) what those who take this attitude will gain by it. He says that he declared that things were in an equal degree indifferent and unstable and incapable of being tested. For this reason neither our senses nor our opinions are true or false. So we must not put our trust in them but be free from beliefs and inclinations and unshaken, saying of each thing in turn that it no more is than it is not or that it both is and is not or that it neither is nor is not. And those who take this attitude, Timon says will first gain speechlessness (ἀφασία) and then imperturbability (αταραξια)'.[2]

(172) One difference that we seem to observe on the surface is that Pyrrho's scepticism appears to be all-embracing while the scepticism of the three schools outlined above seems to have been more or less confined to moral propositions. But this appearance is deceptive. With regard to all three of these schools, it is stated, that they gave sceptical answers 'when questioned on each and every matter' (tattha tattha pañham puṭṭho, D.I., pp. 24, 25, 26). The reason for high-lighting the ethical examples was probably due to the Buddhists themselves being mainly concerned with this aspect of their teachings just as much as the account given by Śīlāṅka of the different 'types' of Sceptics (*v. supra*, 157) gave one the impression that the Sceptics were mainly interested in the concepts and categories of Jainism.

(173) If we compare the doctrines of the above three schools of Sceptics with the account given above of the scepticism of Pyrrho, it

[1] ERE., Vol. 11, p. 228, *v.* 'Sceptics'; he is said to have 'studied philosophy under Indian Gymnosophists and Chaldean Magi'.

[2] *Loc. cit.*, p. 229.

would be interesting to observe that both hold that (1) there were no beliefs or opinions which were true or false and therefore (2) we should give no positive answer to any of the logical alternatives. It would also be seen that (3) the four logical alternatives mentioned in Timon's account (i.e. is, is not, both is and is not, neither is nor is not) are identical with that of Sañjaya, the Buddhists and perhaps also of the three schools of Sceptics as we have shown below (*v. infra,* 184). Lastly (4) the value of the sceptical attitude is said by Pyrrho to lie in the fact that it promotes speechlessness (aphasia) and mental imperturbability (ataraxia), which seem to be the states of mind regarded as ideal by the above schools of Sceptics since they held that anything that caused mental instability was a hindrance. Because of Pyrrho's love of quietism, Burnet[1] thinks that Pyrrho is more of a quietist than a sceptic and is inclined to regard him as being nearer the Buddhist ideal: 'We see that those who knew Pyrrho well described him as a sort of Buddhist *arhat* and that is doubtless how we should regard him. He is not so much a sceptic as an ascetic and a quietist'. But when we see that Pyrrho's scepticism as well as his quietism are shared by the above schools of Sceptics, it would be more appropriate to regard him as having a closer kinship with them rather than with the Buddhists, who were opposed to their scepticism.

(174) Barua compares the school of Pyrrho with that of Sañjaya (*op. cit.,* p. 32) but as indicated below (*v. infra,* 180) it is not said of the school of Sañjaya, unlike in the case of the previous three schools, that it held non-scepticism to be a source of vexation or a hindrance. We therefore have no evidence that the school of Sañjaya valued mental equanimity. In the circumstances we would have to hold that Pyrrhonean scepticism would be nearer the three schools mentioned above than the school of Sañjaya, which in our opinion does not seem to have valued mental quietude at all.

(175) The fourth school of Sceptics is described in language identical with that used to define the philosophy of Sañjaya so that we may presume that Sañjaya was one of the foremost representatives if not the leader of this school. Sañjaya is described along with the other five teachers, who were contemporaries of the Buddha as being a well-known (ñāto), celebrated (yasassī) teacher and a leader of a sect (titthakaro) who was held in high esteem by the common folk (sādhusammato bahujanassa); he is also said to have a following (saṅghī

[1] *Loc. cit.,* p. 229.

gaṇī). This description occurs in a stereotyped sentence,[1] which is used of all the six heretical teachers several times in the Nikāyas (D. I.150, M. I.4, S. I.68, J. I.509). But since it is complimentary we need not doubt that it contained a good deal of truth. He may have been Sariputta's teacher prior to the latter's conversion to Buddhism.[2] Barua doubts this. He says that 'one may reasonably object to the identification of Sañjaya the Sceptic, who is designated in the Sāmaññaphala Sutta as Sañjaya Belaṭṭhaputta (or Belaṭṭhiputta) with Sañjaya described in the Vinaya Mahāvagga and the Dhammapada commentary as a Paribbājaka' (*op. cit.*, p. 325). However, if the commentarial tradition that Suppiya Paribbājaka was a disciple of Sañjaya[3] is correct, we need not doubt that Sañjaya himself was a Paribbājaka and was sometimes known as such.

(176) The sceptical philosophy of this school is defined as follows: 'Herein a certain recluse or brahmin is dull, stupid. And by reason of his dullness and stupidity, when questioned on this or that matter, he resorts to verbal jugglery or eel-wriggling: "If you ask me whether there is a next world, then if it were to occur to me (iti ce me assa) that there is a next world, I would pronounce that there is a next world. Yet, I do not say so, I do not say thus, I do not say otherwise, I do not say no, I deny the denials. Similarly with regard to the propositions, "there is no next world", "there is and is not a next world", "there neither is nor is not a next world", "there are beings who survive (death)", "there are no beings who survive", "there are and are no beings who survive", "there neither are nor are there no beings who survive", "there is a result and a consequence of good and evil actions", "there is no result or consequence of good or evil actions", "there is and is no result or consequence of good or evil actions", "the Perfect One (Tathāgato) exists after death", "the Perfect One does not exist after death", "the Perfect One both exists and does not exist after death", "the Perfect One neither exists nor does not exist after death"'.[4]

[1] saṅghino gaṇino gaṇācariyā ñātā yasassino titthakarā sādhusammatā ca bahujanassa, *loc. cit.*

[2] *v.* Malalasekera, DPPN., *s.v.* Sañjaya Belaṭṭhiputta.

[3] Paribbājako ti Sañjayassa antevāsi, DA. I.35.

[4] Idha . . . ekacco samaṇo vā brāhmaṇo vā mando hoti momūho. So mandattā momūhattā tattha tattha pañham puṭṭho samāno vācāvikkhepaṃ āpajjati amarāvikkhepaṃ: 'Atthi paro loko?' ti iti ce maṃ pucchasi, 'Atthi paro loko' ti ce me assa, "atthi paro loko" 'ti iti te naṃ vyākareyyaṃ. Evam pi me no. Tathā pi me no. Aññathā pi me no. No ti pi me no. No no ti pi me no. "Natthi paro loko?" ti . . . pe . . .' Atthi ca natthi ca paro loko? N'ev'atthi na n'atthi paro loko? Atthi sattā

(177) Professor Basham, dissenting from Barua's view that the passage mentioned above represents a doctrine that was held in good faith by a school of Pyrrhonists, thinks that the passage is 'probably satirical, a tilt at agnostic teachers who were unwilling to give a definite answer to any metaphysical question put to them' (*op. cit.*, p. 17). He adds that 'its agnosticism was never a part of the Ājīvika creed, and it may be omitted from further consideration' (*loc. cit.*).

(178) This seems to be unclear. For it may be asked whether (1) there was at least one school of Sceptics, (2) Sañjaya was a Sceptic, and (3) if Sañjaya was a Sceptic, he was an Ājīvika. If (2) and (3) are denied there is a contradiction inasmuch as elsewhere Professor Basham ascribes the 'sceptical philosophy' outlined in the Sandaka Sutta to Sañjaya (*op. cit.*, p. 19). Moreover, he states (*v. infra*, 195) that 'the *Sandaka Sutta* seems to embrace all six of the heretical teachers . . . in the category of Ājīvikas' (*op. cit.*, p. 96). From this it may be inferred that he considers 'agnosticism' or 'scepticism' (*v. op. cit.*, p. 19—both words are used indiscriminately) as part of the Ājīvika creed(s) in Barua's second sense of the term Ājīvika,[1] with which Basham agrees.[2] Nevertheless, at the beginning of his work he states the very opposite. Moreover, Professor Basham omits to discuss Śīlāṅka's statement to the effect that 'the Ājīvikas and others, who are followers of Gośāla's doctrines are a product of ajñānavāda' (*supra*, 147), whatever ajñānavāda may mean here.

(179) We are not anxious to prove that scepticism is part of the Ājīvika doctrines or not, though we would like to be clear about the use of the term Ājīvika, so as to avoid confusion (*v. infra*, 196). But if Prof. Basham is saying that there was no school (or schools) of Sceptics, but only 'agnostic teachers' who were sceptics only with regard to metaphysical questions, it is necessary to urge that, as we have shown above, the independent evidence and testimony of both the Buddhist as well as the Jain texts seem to point in the opposite direction. But

opapātikā? N'atthi sattā opapātikā? Atthi ca natthi ca sattā opapātikā? N'ev'atthi na natthi sattā opapātikā. Atthi sukaṭadukkaṭānaṃ kammānam phalaṃ vipāko? Natthi sukaṭadukkaṭānaṃ kammānaṃ phalaṃ vipāko? Atthi ca natthi ca sukaṭadukkaṭānaṃ kammānam phalaṃ vipāko? N'ev'atthi na n'atthi sukaṭadukkaṭānaṃ kammānam phalaṃ vipāko? Hoti Tathāgato parammaraṇā? Na hoti Tathāgato parammaraṇa? Hoti ca na hoti ca Tathāgato parammaraṇā? N'eva hoti na na hoti Tathāgato parammaraṇā? . . . D. I.27.

[1] 'Ājīvika—what it means', ABORI., Vol. 8, 1927, p. 183.

[2] *Op. cit.*, pp. 96, 97. 'We have seen that the second usage is very common in early Buddhist literature' (p. 98).

Sañjaya's scepticism may very well have been confined to metaphysical questions, as we ourselves consider to be a possibility following the suggestion of Jacobi (*v. infra,* 181).

(180) We are inclined to agree with Basham when he says that the above passage is 'satirical' but only in the sense that it seems to give a rather inexact version of the philosophy of Sañjaya, to whom the Buddhists seem to have been somewhat antipathetic. In fact, the account given gives the impression that Sañjaya was a naïve Sceptic, who adopted Scepticism out of sheer stupidity, either because he did not know the answers to the questions put to him or the fact that one of the logical alternatives must be true. Both the Brahmajāla Sutta and the Sāmaññaphala Sutta (D. I.58–9) versions emphasize the dullness and stupidity of this thinker as a result of which scepticism is the outcome. In the Brahmajāla Sutta, out of the sixtytwo philosophical schools, whose views are stated, this is the only one that is picked out as being 'a product of sheer stupidity' (mandattā momūhattā, *loc. cit.*). In the Sāmaññaphala Sutta, it is stated as the impression of Ajātasattu that Sañjaya 'was the most foolish and stupid'[1] of all the recluses and brahmins. If Sāriputta, who is lauded for his intelligence, could have been at one time the disciple of Sañjaya,[2] Sañjaya could not have been as stupid as he is made out to be and besides he would not have attracted such a large following. What then could be the motive for singling out this particular school of Scepticism as a product of folly? One difference that we notice is that in the former three schools of Sceptics there seems to be some conception of the good life, whether they believed in salvation or not, and the sceptical attitude seems at least to have been regarded as psychologically desirable in promoting one's peace of mind. Sañjaya on the other hand may have been a more thorough-going sceptic, who made no pretence about the desirability of scepticism as a way of life. He would thus have been much more outspoken and critical of the views of his opponents. As a result the Buddhists may have regarded him as being more deluded than the other Sceptics who in spite of their theoretical scepticism had the good sense to cultivate the tranquillity of mind, which was highly valued in Buddhism as well.

(181) Sañjaya's scepticism may have extended to the whole field of knowledge for he too is supposed to have given sceptical answers to

[1] Ayañ ca imesaṃ samaṇabrāhmanānaṃ *sabbabālo sabbamūḷho,* D. I.59.
[2] *v.* DPPN., *s.v.* Sāriputta.

all questions put to him. But if we examine the actual list of propositions mentioned (and here a whole list is given unlike in the case of the previous schools), it would be seen that they pertain to metaphysics (the next world, survival, transcendent existence) and morals (the consequences of good and evil). It is therefore not improbable that his scepticism was directed only to those questions, the answers to which were unverifiable and therefore unknowable or as Jacobi says 'transcendent or beyond human experience' (*op. cit.*, p. xxvii). In this respect the philosophy of Sañjaya may be compared with that of the positivist branch of the Lokāyata (i.e. group (2), *v. supra*, 89, 94), the difference being that these positivists seem to have denied the truth of these propositions or suggested that they do not make sense[1] while Sañjaya seems to grant the possibility of their truth, though denying that we have any means of knowing this, If so Sañjaya seems to have examined the truth-value of propositions in the light of relevant evidence. His philosophy, therefore, is as Ui sums it up 'a scepticism on the one hand and a primitive step of criticism of knowledge on the other hand, like the sophists[2] in the Greek philosophy'.[3]

(182) Another fact to be noted in the account given of Sañjaya's philosophy is that the propositions are arranged in a four-fold order of expression and the logical alternatives are not confined to simple assertions and denials. For instance, we find not only the expressions 'there is (atthi) a next world' and 'there is no (natthi) next world' but also the forms 'there is and is not (atthi ca natthi ca) a next world' and 'there neither is nor is there no (n'ev'atthi na n'atthi) next world'. This four-fold mode of expression, as we have shown later (*v. infra*, 581) appears to have been adopted in the Pāli Nikāyas alongside the usual two-fold mode. Keith gives the credit to Sañjaya for initiating this new four-fold logic: 'he seems as an agnostic to have been the first to formulate the four possibilities of existence, non-existence, both and neither . . .'[4]

(183) This is certainly a possibility that cannot be ruled out. His very scepticism may have led him to include the modes of expression 'both is and is not' and 'neither is nor is not', both of which are expressions sometimes used in common speech in addition to the ordinary

[1] The closest that the early Materialists came to saying this is their statement recorded in the Sūtrakṛtāṅga (*v.* supra, Ch. II, p. 46), viz. 'it is those who say that the (soul) does not exist or is not evident, who would be making the right statement about it'.

[2] *v.* infra, 326.

[3] The Vaiśeṣika Philosophy, p. 23.

[4] Buddhist Philosophy, p. 303.

assertions and denials, so as to make his scepticism and his scruples for truth appear more comprehensive. On the other hand there are two other alternatives worth considering, which appear to be more plausible than the one suggested.

(184) One of the alternatives is that the four-fold schema was not the innovation of Sañjaya but was held in common by all the schools of the Sceptics; in such a case Buddhism would have either borrowed this classification from the Sceptics or shared it with them. The other alternative is that the innovation was on the part of the Buddhists and that the Sceptics themselves including Sañjaya were not concerned with such problems.

(185) Let us consider the first alternative. We have already seen how Śilāṅka arranged the only example he seems to have taken from the Sceptics themselves in a four-fold schema (*v. supra*, 157). He may have done this merely to complete his figure of sixty seven 'categories' of Sceptics: but the fact that the example he took was not based on Jain concepts and his own admission that this particular example did not admit of more than a four-fold order of predications are possibly pointers to the fact that he was borrowing not only the example but the four-fold formula itself from the Sceptics. The adoption of such different schemas was perhaps characteristic of this period and was probably necessitated by the variety of doctrines, which had to be considered apart (*v. infra*, 573). Dr Basham has some evidence to show that the Ājīvikas under Makkhali Gosāla and the schismatic Jain sect of the Trairāśikas adopted a scheme of classifying propositions into three logical 'heaps' (rāśi) or categories (*v. infra*, 217–20). Now there is no known school of Indian thinkers apart from the Buddhist (barring Sañjaya who is known only through the references in Buddhist literature) who adopted a four-fold schema, but the five-fold formula of denial, which according to the accounts given, is common to all the schools of Sceptics, seems to be based on the acceptance of a four-fold form of predication. Let us examine this formula:

1. Evampi me no—I do not say so.
2. Tathā pi me no—I do not say thus.
3. Aññathā pi me no—I do not say otherwise.
4. No ti pi me no—I do not say no.
5. No no ti pi me no—*lit.* I do not say 'no, no.'

The commentary offers two explanations[1] of the meaning of this

[1] DA. I.115–6.

formula. According to the first explanation, proposition (1) is an indefinite rejection or denial (aniyāmitavikkhepo. DA. I.115). Proposition (2) is the denial of a specific proposition, e.g. the denial of the eternity view (sassatavāda-) when asked whether the world and the soul are eternal. Proposition (3) is the denial of a variant of (2), e.g. the rejection of the semi-eternal theory (ekaccasassataṃ), which is said to be somewhat different from (aññathā) from the eternity theory. Proposition (4) is the denial of the contrary of (2), e.g. the denial of the annihilationist theory (ucchedaṃ) when asked whether a being (tathāgato) does not exist after death. Proposition (5) is the rejection of the dialectician's view (takkivādam)[1] of a double denial, e.g. denying the position if asked whether a being neither exists nor does not exist after death.

(186) If we adopt the notations p. notp,[2] p.notp, not (p.notp) to represent the usual four-fold propositional formula of predication in Buddhism (i.e. corresponding to, is, is not, is and is not, neither is nor is not), we may represent the above commentarial explanation in symbolic form as follows, using the notation p= for an indefinite proposition; and—to express denial:

1. —(p=)
2. —(p)
3. —(p.notp)
4. —(notp)
5. —(not(p.notp))

It will be seen from the above that 2, 4, 3 and 5 (in this order) are the denials of the usual four propositional types in the order in which we stated them. The identifications of the commentator has some basis in the wording. He has seen that there was a double 'na' (two 'nots') in 5 (*no no* ti pi . . .) and identified it as a denial of a proposition of the form *na* eva . . . *na* (na) . . . Where he saw a single 'na' in 4 (*no* ti pi . . .) he identified it as a denial of a proposition of the form 'na . . .'. He then identified 2 (tathā pi . . .) as the denial of a simple assertion. In 4 (aññathā pi . . .) he saw a slight variation of 2 and identified it as a denial of a partial assertion. But what is most unsatisfactory is the

[1] This is called takki-vādam, i.e. the thesis of the sophist (vitaṇḍavādin) since he rejects or argues against both thesis as well as anti-thesis; he neither asserts p nor not-p.

[2] We are not using the negation sign (~p) or the form 'not p' since 'notp' is not the contradictory of p (*v.* infra, 575).

identification of 1. What does Buddhaghosa mean by an aniyāmita-vikkhepo? He can only mean the rejection of any one of the logical alternatives (which he has exhausted in 2, 4, 3 and 5) without specification, but the language (evampi me no) hardly suggests this.

(187) According to the second explanation, proposition (1) is the denial of an assertion e.g. if asked whether this is good, he denies it. Proposition (2) is the denial of a simple negation, e.g. if asked whether this is not good, denies it. Proposition (3) is a denial that what you are stating is different from both (1) and (2), e.g. if asked whether his position is different from both (1) and (2) (ubhayato aññathā), denies it. Proposition (4) is a denial that you are stating a point of view different from the above, e.g. if asked whether his thesis (laddhi) is different from the three earlier points of view (tividhenā'pi na hoti), denies it. Proposition (5) is a denial of the denials, e.g. if asked whether his thesis is to deny everything (no no te laddhī ti) he denies it. Thus he does not take his stand (na tiṭṭhati) on any of the logical alternatives (ekasmiṃ pi pakkhe). We may represent this explanation using symbols as explained above, as follows:

1. —(p)
2. —(notp)
3. —(—(1, 2))
4. —(—(1, 2, 3))
5. —(1, 2, 3, 4)

We have used the numerals as well, as equivalent to the formula that follows for otherwise the notation would appear too complicated and the point of adopting it would be lost. Thus, 3 means that 'you deny that your thesis is different from both your previous denial of the assertion and the denial of the negation'. The purpose of the commentator in both his explanations has been to show that the Sceptic does not take his stand on any of the logical alternatives. But this second explanation is less satisfactory than the first, since the explanations of propositions 3 and 4 appear to be very arbitrary and hardly related to the language used.

(188) We would like to suggest a third alternative explanation, which has the merit of being the simplest and the one having the closest affinities to the language used. Buddhaghosa's second explanation made the suggestion that the last proposition (no no ti pi me no) is a denial of the rejection of all the possible logical alternatives. This appears to be plausible since the statement literally means 'I do not

say "no, no"'. If so the others constitute the rejection of the usual four-fold logical alternatives. We may take them in the usual order and when we do so it would be noticed that on the whole they correspond with the language used. We may state this explanation in symbolic form, as follows:

1. —(p)
2. —(notp)
3. —(p.notp)
4. —(not(p.notp))
5. —(1, 2, 3, 4)

(189) If this five-fold formula of denial implies or is based on the four-fold modes of predication of logical alternatives, then in the light of the independent evidence from Śīlānka as well (*v. supra,* 157), the credit for adopting this schema should not go to Sañjaya alone, but should be shared by all these Sceptical schools of thought.

(190) It also appears to be equally plausible that it were the Buddhists who were the first to innovate and adopt this four-fold schema. We noticed that when Śīlāṇka tried to explain the existence of sixty-seven 'categories' of Sceptics, he did so by making them ask questions according to the seven-fold mode of predication (saptabhaṅgī) adopted by the Jains. From this we cannot argue that the Sceptics were the first to adopt the saptabhaṅgī formula, as Keith has done in the case of Sañjaya on precisely the same kind of evidence. In order to explain their sceptical attitude it was necessary for their opponents to represent them as not committing themselves on any one of the logical alternatives and it is natural for them to do this by showing them as dismissing the logical alternatives as they themselves understood them. It is therefore not surprising that the Jains should represent them as dismissing a proposition in all the seven modes of predication known to them, while the Buddhists picture them as discarding the four. Both these alternatives are more plausible than the one that Keith has offered in that they have some independent evidence to confirm them. We cannot therefore agree with Keith, when he dogmatically gives the credit to Sañjaya for being the 'first to formulate the four possibilities' (*loc. cit.*), when we know nothing about Sañjaya apart from the accounts we get of him in the Buddhist texts.

(191) Jacobi thinks that 'in opposition to the Agnosticism of Sañjaya, Mahāvīra has established the *syādvāda*' (*op. cit.*, p. xxvii). Superficially,

there seems to be some truth in this observation. The Jain syādvāda appears to be the opposite reaction to that of the Sceptics when faced with the same epistemological problem. The Sceptic doubts or denies all the logical possibilities, whereas the Jain asserts that they are all true in some sense or another. But this appearance of a radical contrast is deceptive and in fact although the two have to be distinguished, it would be quite wrong to consider them as being poles apart.

(192) The Buddhist in depicting the Sceptic as denying all the logical possibilities and denying these denials as well, has not given an accurate account of the point of view of the Sceptic in his anxiety to show that the latter is making self-contradictory assertions. It would appear that in denying the denials (no no ti pi me no, *loc. cit.*) the Sceptic was contradicting himself, but in fact he does not seem to have denied the possibilities outright. He would most probably have merely stated that he does not agree that p is the case quite categorically (as his opponent would have liked him to), since p may be true or p may be false and one cannot know this. This is different from a categorical denial of the possibilities. The position of the Sceptic would in fact be disclosed as follows:

1. p may (or may not) be the case
2. Notp ,,
3. p.notp ,,
4. Not(p.notp) ,,

(193) We may compare this with the standpoints of the Jains, which we may state as follows, confining ourselves to the first four possibilities only for the sake of the comparison:

1. p may be the case		syādasti
2. Notp	,,	syānnāsti
3. p.notp	,,	syādastināsti
4. (p. is inexpressible)	,,	syādavaktavyaḥ

(194) It would now appear as if, far from being poles apart, it is difficult to distinguish the two points of view. The difference is no doubt there for, by say, syādasti, the Jains do not mean that 'p may be the case' in the sceptical sense but that 'p is in fact the case from a certain point of view (naya)' (*v. infra,* 236–8). Instead of one developing in opposition to the other as Jacobi has suggested the two seem to have a common origin, though they part company at a certain point. When both were faced with the problem of diverse theories (which

could be stated as logical alternatives), both wondered whether any of them could be true. But while the Sceptic seems to have concluded that none of them could be known to be true, the Jain appears to have formed the conclusion that each one may be true (*v. infra,* 236). In the eyes of their opponents, both would have appeared to contradict themselves, the former by violating the Law of Excluded Middle (or rather the Law of Exclusion, since there were more than two logical alternatives, *v. infra,* 582) and the latter the Law of Contradiction (*v. infra,* 582).

(195) Another influential class of religious teachers who made their own contribution to the development of logical and epistemological thought were the Ājīvikas, who are distinguished from the Jains (nigaṇṭhas) in the Suttanipāta (*v. infra,* 375). Although the word, Ājivikāḥ, was used primarily of the followers of Makkhali Gosāla and secondarily in a loose sense, as shown by Barua[1] and Basham,[2] there is no evidence that the term was used of the Jains at least at the time of the Pāli Nikāyas. Dr Basham's deduction that 'the *Sandaka Sutta* seems to embrace all six of the heretical teachers, including the great leader of the *nigaṇṭhas,* Nigaṇṭha Nātaputta or Mahāvīra, in the general category of Ājīvikas' (*op. cit.,* p. 96) seems to be based on a misinterpretation. Since we have inferred that some of the doctrines criticized in the Sandaka Sutta are those of the Brāhmaṇic tradition (*v. infra,* 196) and Basham's assumption that 'the propagators of all the objectionable teachings (i.e. in the Sandaka Sutta) are classed together under the broad title of ājīvikas' (*op. cit.,* 20) would adversely affect some of our own conclusions, it seems necessary to point out why and where we differ from Professor Basham.

(196) The Sandaka Sutta criticizes four types of religions which are false (abrahmacariyavāsā) and four which are unsatisfactory (anassāsikaṃ brahmacariyaṃ) but not necessarily false. Nowhere in the Sutta are these teachings associated with the names of individuals. It is Basham who identifies these teachings with those of certain teachers on the basis of the wording (*op. cit.,* p. 19). He seems to have identified 'the teacher claiming omniscience' (*loc. cit.*) with Mahāvīra, for otherwise he would not have come to the above conclusion. This identification is arbitrary for the Sutta itself as we have said, mentions the omniscient teacher as a *type* and the Pāli Nikāyas themselves refer to

[1] B. M. Barua, 'Ājīvika-What it means', ABORI., Vol. 8, 1927, p. 183.
[2] *Op. cit.,* p. 97 ff.

both Pūraṇa Kassapa (*v. infra*, 383) as well as Nigaṇṭha Nātaputta as claiming omniscience. Secondly, Basham has refrained from identifying the traditionalist (anussavika-) as well as the rationalist (takkī vīmaṃsī). Had he done so he would have found that the traditionalists were mainly though not solely the Vedic brahmins as defined at M. II.211—santi, Bhāradvāja, eke samaṇa-brāhmaṇā anussavikā . . . seyyathā'pi brahmaṇā Tevijjā. The 'rationalists' as we have shown, were both brahmins as well as Samaṇas (*v. infra*, 375). Now Basham says that 'the conclusion of the Sutta is surprising' (*op. cit.*, p. 19) but had he made the above identification, to make his list complete, he would have found that his own conclusion would have been still more surprising, namely that even the Vedic brahmins would have to be called Ājīvikas according to this Sutta. Thirdly, Dr Basham seems to have assumed without justification that the 'Ājīvikā' in the quotation on which his entire conclusion is based, viz. Ime pan' *Ājīvikā* puttamatāya puttā, attānañ c'eva ukkaṃsenti pare ca vambhenti, tayo c'eva niyyātāro paññapenti, seyyath'īdaṃ Nandaṃ Vacchaṃ, Kisaṃ Saṅkiccaṃ, Makkhali Gosālan ti (*loc. cit.*, fn. 7) are identical with the religious teachers with whom he has associated the teachings mentioned in it. But the context of this quotation seems to tell a different story. It occurs in a digression at the end of the Sutta, when Sandaka Paribbājaka asks Ānanda a few questions, the last of which is, Kīva bahukā . . . imasmiṃ dhammavinaye *niyyātāro*? How many saints[1] are there in this religion? This question seems to have little to do with the earlier sermon of Ānanda on the different types of religions or religious teachers. Ānanda replies that there are over five hundred, to which Sandaka Paribbājaka, who is probably an Ājīvika in the loose sense of the term, says that as for the Ājīvikas 'they (can) claim only three saints' (tayo c'eva niyyātāro paññapenti). Lastly, Professor Basham quotes Chalmers's translation, which is inaccurate: 'yet they have only produced three shining lights'; even if we retain 'shining lights' as a free rendering of niyyātāro, which means 'those who have attained salvation' (*v. fn.* below), paññapenti (=Skr. prajñāpayanti, from pra+√jñā+causative suffix and not from pra+√jan) can only mean

[1] Formed from nis +√yā+tṛ, it is the intransitive sense that is evident in the usage; e.g. niyyanti dhīrā lokamhā, the wise go out of the world, S.V.6—in this sense *niyyātāro* would be 'those who have gone out', i.e. 'the saved', 'the saints'; cp. so niyyāti . . . sammā dukkhakkhayāya M. I.68. If as the PTS. Dictionary suggests (*s.v.*) the word is formed from nis +√yam we should have niyyanta-, niyyantāro on the analogy of ganta- from √gam. It cannot therefore mean 'guide, leader'.

'proclaim' or 'claim' (*lit.* make known). Thus the interpretation of 'the omniscient teacher' as a personal reference to the Jain leader irrespective of the other claimants, the failure to see the references to the Vedic religion and the Brāhmaṇic tradition, the failure to note the strict context of the quotation and perhaps even the mistranslation seem to have led Dr Basham to the above conclusion, with which we cannot agree for the reasons stated.

(197) In the general sense of the term Ājīvika-, even the Sceptics, whom Śīlāṅka seems to have associated with them were Ājīvikas. However, since it is necessary to consider the doctrines of the Sceptics separately we shall confine our usage of Ājīvikas to denote those Samaṇas, who were neither Jains, Materialists or Sceptics.

(198) To turn to our main problem, the Ājīvikas seem to have been influenced both by the rational tradition of the Early Upaniṣads as well as by the claims to intuitive knowledge on the part of the Middle and Late Upaniṣadic thinkers. One of their main metaphysical interests seems to have been the problems of time and change. Basham does not believe that Ājīvikism 'derived from Vedic or Brahmanical sources' (*op. cit.*, p. 98) but the hymns to Kāla in the Atharvaveda (19. 53, 54) seem to contain the germs of the determinist thesis, if determinism (niyati-) was one of the main doctrines of the Ājīvikas. In these hymns, Time (Kāla-) conceived as an hypostatized entity having everything under its control and 'beyond which there is no other greater force',[1] is said to have 'produced both the past and the future'[2] while it is itself eternally existent.[3]

(199) Now the main argument for niyati seems to have been based on the same *a priori* premiss of Uddālaka (*v. supra*, 25), which led to Metaphysical Materialism on the one hand (*v. supra*, 85, 115) and to the proto-Vaiśeṣika Realism of another Ājīvika thinker, Pakudha Kaccāyana (*v. infra*, 428). As Dr Basham has shown, the Jain commentators Śīlāṅka, Jñānavimala and Abhayadeva quote a verse ascribed to the niyativādins, which has the significant statement 'na "bhavyaṃ bhavati na bhāvino" sti nāśaḥ' (*op. cit.*, p. 221, fn.1) which means 'that which is not to be will not be, nor does that which is to be perish'. This is very similar to the *a priori* premiss, sato ṇatthi viṇāso asato

[1] Tasmād vai nā'nyatparamasti tejaḥ, 53.4.

[2] Kālo ha bhūtaṃ bhavyañ ca . . . ajanayat, 19.54.3.

[3] Kāla- is said to be 'eternal' (ajaraḥ, 19.53.1) and 'its axle is immortality' (amṛtaṃ nyakṣaḥ, 19.53.2).

ṇatthi sambhavo (*v. supra*, 85), the only difference being that what is conceived to be *Being* is not 'what is' but 'what will be' and what is *Non-being* is not 'what is not' but 'that which is not to be'. Now Being cannot be destroyed nor Non-Being come to be. Therefore 'what will be' cannot be destroyed, i.e. cannot be otherwise and 'that which is not to be' cannot come into being, i.e. will not be. The apparent self-evidence of the proposition that 'what will be cannot be otherwise' is based on the misconception that the future event which actually comes to pass in the course of time, 'exists' or has Being. Once this is accepted, the determinist conclusion follows; the same argument can be used to show that the past could not have been different from what in fact it was. So everything, past, present and future is unalterable and fixed. It is probably this very argument of the niyativādin, which provoked the Buddha to draw attention to the past, present and future usages of the verb 'to be' (ahosi, atthi, bhavissati) and enjoin the desirability of keeping 'these three linguistic conventions' (tayo'me niruttipathā) apart without confusing them, so that one may see that one cannot argue that 'what will be' (bhavissati) has existence (atthi) for the future that has not come into being and manifested itself has to be reckoned as 'what will be' (bhavissati) and cannot be reckoned as 'what is' (atthi)[1]. It is significant that it is said at the end of this section that even 'the ahetuvādins, the akiriyavādins and the natthikavādins cannot afford to condemn or reject these three linguistic conventions for otherwise they would be liable to censure'.[2] Here the akiriyavādin is a reference to Pūraṇa Kassapa, whose doctrine is called akiriyaṃ at D. I.53, while a doctrine stated in identical language is called akiriya-vāda- at M. I.404–5 (*v. supra*, 121). He seems to have been an outright niyativādin as his later reputation[3] shows. Ahetuvādin on the other hand is probably a reference to Makkhali Gosāla, but his doctrine is called saṃsāra-suddhi (salvation by transmigration) at D. I.53 though at M. II.408, the same stated in identical language minus the cosmology is called ahetuvāda-. His ahetuvāda- is evident from his language in

[1] S. III.71, Tayo 'me niruttipathā adhivacanapathā paññattipathā asaṃkiṇṇā asaṃkiṇṇapubbā na saṃkīyanti na saṃkıyissanti appaṭikuṭṭhā samaṇehi brāhmaṇehi viññūhi. Katame tayo. Yam rūpaṃ . . . vedanā . . . saññā . . . saṅkhārā . . . viññāṇaṃ atītaṃ ahosīti tassa saṅkhā, na tassa saṅkhā atthīti na tassa saṅkhā bhavissatīti. Yam rūpaṃ . . . pe . . . viññānaṃ, ajātaṃ apātubhūtam bhavissatīti tassa saṅkhā na tassa saṅkhā atthī ti na tassa saṅkhā ahosī ti . . . (*v.* infra, 527).

[2] *v. infra*, 527.

[3] According to Guṇaratna, Pūraṇa holds the view that the world is a product of niyati; Pūraṇo *niyati*-janitam, *op. cit.*, p. 20.

that he denied a cause (hetu) for moral degeneration or salvation[1] but at the same time it may be noted that it was Pūraṇa who was called a ahetu-vādin in the Mahābodhi Jātaka (J. V., pp. 237, 246; cp. Basham, *op. cit.*, p. 18). Makkhali seems to have been a syncretist thinker whose doctrine was highly eclectic in character. He appears to have believed in *niyati*- as well as *svabhāva* (=*bhāva*) and *yadṛcchā* (=saṅgati) and possibly even in *pariṇāma*. This is probably the reason why these central concepts of different schools are welded together in his doctrines. According to him all beings (sabbe sattā . . . bhūtā . . . jīvā) undergo development (*pariṇāma*). This culminates in the course of *time* (saṃsārasuddhi) in final salvation to which all beings are destined under the impact of the factors of *niyati*, *bhāva* and *saṅgati* (niyati-saṅgati-bhāva-pariṇatā). It is probably this eclecticism which helped him to bring together the scattered forces of the Ājīvikas differing among themselves and earn their leadership.[2] It was probably this same eclecticism which made it difficult for others to specify exactly what his doctrine was. Hence he has been called (in addition to ahetuvādin) a Vainayikavādin (*v.* Basham, *op. cit.*, p. 176) and an Ajñānavādin (*v. supra*, 147) by Śīlāṅka, while the Mahābodhi Jātaka calls him a Theist (Issarakāraṇavādin, *v.* Basham, *op. cit.*, p. 18). His belief in 'sixty two ways of life'[3] to be lived out in saṃsāra shows that he believed that all doctrines had their part to play in man's development, though man himself had no contribution to make.

(200) This differs from Dr Basham's assessment of Makkhali's doctrine and depends on what interpretation is given to the phrase niyati-saṅgati-bhāva-pariṇata-. We cannot discuss this problem in detail since it does not directly concern us. Professor Basham himself translates the above phrase following Buddhaghosa as 'developed by Destiny (niyati), change (saṅgati) and nature (bhāva)' (*op. cit.*, p. 225) and affirms that he prefers 'to follow Buddhaghosa and to take the three first elements of the compound as in *dvandva* relationship, translating the phrase as above' (*loc. cit.*). Two pages later, however, he says '*saṅgati* and *bhāva*, the manifestations of *niyati* in individuals, were only apparent and illusory modifications of the one principle, and did not in fact introduce new causal factors into the universal process' (*op. cit.*, p. 227). We differ from Dr Basham in following Buddhaghosa's interpretation consistently (since it is supported by

[1] Natthi hetu natthi paccayo sattānaṃ saṃkilesāya . . . visuddhiyā, D. I.53.
[2] *v.* Basham, *op. cit.*, p. 34.
[3] Dvaṭṭhi paṭipadā, D. I.54.

other evidence) without giving an exaggerated importance to the concept of niyati-. According to this interpretation Makkhali does not become a Strict Determinist since the opposite category of 'chance' or Indeterminism plays a significant part in his system. He therefore subscribed to niyativāda- only in the sense that he thought that *some* future events like salvation for all (*v.* saṃsārasuddhi sabbesaṃ, J. VI, p. 229) were strictly determined. In holding thus that some events of the future had Being he would also have shared in the above *a priori* argument. But this does not mean that he thought that human effort had anything to do with shaping the future since he denies this altogether.[1]

(201) We cannot also entirely agree with Professor Basham's theory that 'for the niyativādin causation was illusory' (*op. cit.*, p. 227). Since the causal conceptions of the niyativādin may be, in our opinion, important for understanding the Buddhist concept of causation we may pursue this problem here. Basham is led to this opinion on the basis that if Time was illusory, then motion and change are illusory and causation which is intimately bound up with these concepts must be illusory too (*v. op. cit.*, p. 236). He thinks, however, that this was a later development[2] influenced by 'the new doctrine of avicalita-nityatvam or a completely static universe' (*op. cit.*, p. 236). This assumption appears to be incorrect for, on the contrary, there is evidence to show that this doctrine of *avicalita-nityatvam* or the concept of a universe, motionless and permanent, was known in the time of the Pāli Nikāyas (*v. infra*, 402–8). As Dr Basham himself has suggested this doctrine was probably the result of the same kind of *a priori* reasoning as found in Parmenides (*loc. cit.*). Whether a niyativādin like Pūraṇa would also have shared this concept, it is difficult to say. It is certainly one of the logical implications of the doctrine of the unreality of Time, which seems to have been either a corollary of or the basis of the determinist thesis. If it was held by the niyativādin, then the doctrine of a double standard of truth (*v.* Basham, *op. cit.*, p. 230) could have been utilized to resolve the contradiction, which is probably what Parmenides himself does in speaking of a 'Way of Truth' and 'Way of Opinion'. This would mean that deterministic causation had a relative reality and not that it was entirely illusory.

[1] *v.* natthi attakāre . . . purisakāre, D. I.53.

[2] *v.* 'The universe seems to have been thought of as a continuous process, which was recognized by some later Ājīvikas to be on the ultimate analysis illusory', *op. cit.*, p. 227.

(202) Whether for the niyativādin, causation in the ultimate analysis was unreal or not, the fact of causation seems to have been accepted by him at least at the level of conventional truth. That even the later Ājīvika rigidly believed in causation in a strictly determinist sense is evident from the argument for niyati in Gunaratna's (14th C.) work, according to which it is necessary to posit the existence of the force of niyati in order to account for causes and effects (kāryakāraṇa). Professor Basham has given the gist of this argument but has failed to quote the sentence, which seems to imply a belief in causation on the part of the niyati-vādin. We may translate the argument as stated by Guṇaratna as follows: 'Whatever happens at any time, anywhere, is to be conceived as happening in the form of niyati only. Otherwise there would be no *definite sequence of causes and effects* (*kārya-kāraṇa-vyavasthā*) or a fixed pattern of anything, owing to the absence of a controlling agent'.[1]

(203) When we consider the arguments of the niyativādin as stated by Śīlāṅka (9th C.) we find that arguments based on the two principles of causal determination play a fundamental rôle. As Mill stated in his 'A System of Logic', the methods of discovering a causal connection are 'two in number' (*op. cit.*, 253) of which 'one is, by comparing together different instances in which the phenomenon occurs. The other is, by comparing instances in which the phenomenon does occur, with instances in other respects similar in which it does not. These two methods may be respectively denominated the Method of Agreement and the Method of Difference' (*loc. cit.*). These two principles known in Indian logic as the *anvaya-vyatireka-rīti* first appear in a concrete form in the causal formula of the Pāli Nikāyas. But this notion is constantly made use of by the niyativādin in arguing against his opponent. One of the arguments of the believer in karma, is that there is a causal connection between good karma and pleasant consequences and evil karma and unpleasant consequences. The niyativādin shows by applying the two principles of causal determination to what is observable in this world, that there is no such causal connection. Good is not always followed by happiness nor evil by grief, nor is the absence of good followed by the absence of happiness and the absence of evil by the absence of grief. The argument is actually stated as

[1] Yadyadā yato bhavati tattadā tata eva niyaten'aiva rūpeṇa bhavad upalabhyate. Anyathā kāryakāraṇavyavasthā *pratiniyatarūpavyavasthā ca na bhavet, niyāmakābhāvāt*, *op. cit.*, p. 12. Dr Basham in his quotation (*op. cit.*, p. 235, fn. 2) has omitted the phrase *underlined*.

follows: 'In this world, grief does not arise for a man even though he delights in evil courses, while for another person who does good, it does'.[1] It is thus concluded that there is no causal connection between evil and grief or good and happiness.

(204) The argument against the causal connection said to hold between human exertion and its fruits is again shown to be false by appeal to observation based on the two principles. If there was a causal connection then we should have the following sequences:

Presence of human exertion	Presence of its fruits
Absence of „ „	Absence of „ „

But what we observe is as follows:

Presence of human exertion	Absence of fruits
(Puruṣa-kāre sati)	(phalā'prāptiḥ)
Absence of human exertion	Presence of fruits
(Vyāpārā'bhave)	(viśiṣṭaphalā'vāptiḥ)

Thus it is argued that 'nothing is achieved by human effort'.[2] If we examine this argument we find that it is based on the assumption that 'equal effort (samāne puruṣakāre sati) must be followed by equal results',[3] which is based on the principle that variations in the cause are correlated with variations in the effect. This is explicitly stated in the argument that 'Time is not a causal factor, for since Time is uniform, its effects in the world could not be multiform. *There are variations in the effect only when there are variations in the cause* (Kāraṇa-bhede hi kārya-bhedo bhavati, n'ābhede)'.[4] This is similar to Mill's 'Fifth Canon',[5] an extension of the two original principles.

(205) These subtleties probably developed later, but there is some reason to believe that the basic argument based on the belief in the

[1] Atr'aikasy āsadanuṣṭhānaratasy 'āpi na dukkham utpadyate, parasya tu sadanuṣṭhāyino tad bhavati, Śīlāṅka, *op. cit.*, Vol. II, fol. 26, on Sū. 2.1.12; quoted by Basham, *op. cit.*, p. 234, fn. 3.

[2] Yadi puruṣakārakṛtaṃ sukhādyanubhūyeta tataḥ sevakavanikkarṣakādīnām samāne puruṣakāre sati phalaprāptivaiśadṛśyam phalā'praptiśca na bhavet. Kasya cittu sevādivyāparā'bhāve 'pi viśiṣṭaphalā'vāptir dṛśyata iti. Ato na puruṣakārāt kiñcid āsadyate. Śīlāṅka, *op. cit.*, Vol. I, fol. 30 on Sū. 1.1.2.2.

[3] The phrase, samāne puruṣakāre sati, implies samāna-phalaprāptiḥ as the expected consequence.

[4] Nā'pi kālaḥ kartā, tasy'aikarūpatvāj jagati phalavaicitryā 'nupapatteḥ. Kāraṇabhede hi kāryabhedo bhavati, nā'bhede, Śīlāṅka, *loc. cit.*

[5] 'Whatever phenomenon varies in any manner whenever another varies in some particular manner, is either a cause or an effect of that phenomenon, or is connected with it through some fact of causation', *op. cit.*, p. 263.

two principles of causal determination went back to the earliest times, since we seem to find a reference to it in the Sūtrakṛtāṅga itself.

(206) In introducing the 'fourth type of person' (caütthe purisajāë), who is a niyativādin (niyativaïëtti), the Sūtrakṛtāṅga (2.1.12) places the causal argument in the mouth of the Determinist as follows: iha khalu duve purisā bhavanti—ege purise kiriyamāïkkhaï, ege purise nokiriyamāïkkhaï, je ya purise kiriyamāïkkhaï je ya purise nokiriyamāïkkhaï, dovi te purisa tullā egaṭṭhā, kāraṇam avannā, i.e. here are two persons, one person maintains (the efficacy of) action while the other person denies (the efficacy of) action, but both of them are (ultimately) equal and alike on account of the cause (being niyati)'. Here the crucial phrase kāraṇamāvaṇṇā seems to have presented a difficulty to the translator. Jacobi renders kāraṇamāvaṇṇā as 'they are actuated by the same force' (*op. cit.*, p. 317) but in a footnote (fn. 2) he says that 'this is the interpretation of the commentators. But to the phrase kāraṇamāpannā they give here a meaning different from that in the following paragraphs. I therefore propose the following translation of the end of the paragraph: "are equally (wrong), (err) alike as regards the cause (of actions)" '. Dr Basham follows Jacobi's first translation, viz. 'Both equally and alike are affected by (a single) cause' (*op. cit.*, p. 233). We have closely followed Śīlāṅka who says, ata ekārthāvekakāraṇāpannatvāditi niyati-vaśen'aiva tau niyativādam aniyativādaṃ cāśritāviti bhāvaḥ,[1] i.e. thus (both are) alike since they are affected by the same cause, the sense being that by the force of niyati alone they have followed the niyativāda and the aniyativāda. Jacobi's second translation cannot be accepted since it is too much of a periphrasis which introduces concepts like 'wrong' and 'err' which are not found in or suggested by the context. But whether we translate kāraṇamāvaṇṇā as 'on account of the (same) cause' or 'as regards the cause' the significance that kāraṇa- had for the person using this term is clear from the example cited. He takes the case of two persons alike in other respects except for the fact that one is a kiriyavādin and the other an akiriyavādin and finds that latterly they are both still alike. This is the application of Mill's Method of Difference with negative results and may be represented symbolically[2] thus:

ABC—b c
BC—b c

where A=belief in niyativāda. From observing the two sequences one

[1] *Op. cit.*, Vol. II, fol. 25 on Sū. 2.2.12.

[2] Stebbing, *op. cit.*, p. 334.

may draw the conclusion that A is not a causal factor; so is not-A not a causal factor for the absence of A has made no difference to the result. So both those who claim that kiriya (the act) is a cause or that akiriya (the non-act) is a cause are equally wrong as regards the cause—this is in fact supported by Jacobi's second translation, though it is not supported by the actual wording of the argument. Although this negative conclusion—that belief in kiriya or akiriya cannot be the cause—seems to be implied, the actual conclusion that is drawn is a positive one, namely that niyati must be the causal factor. But this is an assumption, since niyati is a metaphysical factor, which is unobservable and cannot be discovered experimentally. Yet what is most significant is that the niyativādin seems to have been convinced in some sense of the fact of causation and made use of the causal argument, based on a belief in the principles of causal determination to show that his opponent was wrong. The problem is whether these concepts were borrowed from another school or were intrinsic to his own system.

(207) According to the argument of the niyativādin as stated by Guṇaratna (*v. supra*, 202), the niyativādin believed in a 'fixed pattern of causes and effects' (kārya-kāraṇavyavasthā) but we saw at the same time that Pūraṇa, the niyativādin, was called an upholder of the 'doctrine of causelessness'[1] (ahetuvāda-). The reason for these contradictory evaluations would be clear if we can comprehend the niyativādin's concept of causation. He denied whatever was held as the causes of events natural or metaphysical, by his opponents (e.g. puruṣakāra-, karma-, kāla-, īśvara-). This would have made him appear in the eyes of his opponents as one who denied all causes, internal or external, of events. But all his criticisms imply a belief in causation, which in the ultimate analysis turns out to be a belief in niyati conceived as the first and the efficient cause of all phenomena. Nature to him was a single rigidly deterministic system, in which no individual or separate causal lines[2] or processes were discoverable or distinguishable. All events and processes were caused but caused by the all-embracing metaphysical principle of niyati. For such a rigid determinist individual causal processes could not be conceived in isolation from the entire system. This would have appeared to be the very denial of causation as understood by some of their opponents and it is difficult to believe

[1] *v. supra*, 199. The term may also have been employed in the Nikāya period to denote yadṛcchā-vāda or 'Indeterminism' (=saṅgati) and Makkhali was probably an ahetukavādin in both these senses.

[2] On the use of the term 'causal lines', *v.* Russell, *Human Knowledge*, p. 333 ff.

that the conception of the principles of causal determination could have arisen in such a system. On the other hand if niyati was only a metaphysical controlling force which guaranteed the operation of the laws of cause and effect, as Guṇaratna's argument of the niyativādin would make us understand, we would have to say that he believed in causation with the difference that for him the supreme Cause of causes and causal processes was the factor of niyati. In such a case he would be an ahetukavādin only in the sense of denying the metaphysical validity of what his opponents conceived to be the hetu-s of things.

(208) Whatever the answer to this question, it seems probable that it was people who made use of the causal arguments of the kind employed by the niyativādins, who were called the 'causal argumentationists' (kāraṇa-vādā)[1] in the Mahāniddesa (*v. infra*, 367). This work comments on and defines the different types of 'expert debaters' (kusalā) referred to in the Suttanipāta, among whom the niyativādins have undoubtedly to be reckoned.

(209) The other arguments of the niyativādin as given by Śīlāṅka have been translated by Basham (*op. cit.*, pp. 231–4) and if we study them it would be seen that almost all of them are dialectical arguments having the following form: If p is true, then either q or not-q is true, but q implies r and not-q implies s, each of which (i.e. s, r) contradicts one of the assumptions or propositions posited by his opponent.

(210) We may illustrate this with an example.[2] Thus the theory that happiness and grief come about through the agency of God (Īśvara-) is criticized by showing that the concept of God's existence leads to contradictions, as follows: ' "If God exists" (p), then either "God has form" (q, Īśvaro mūrtaḥ) or "God has no form" (not-q, Īśvaro' mūrtaḥ). If q, then "he, like an ordinary person, is not omnipotent" (r, prākṛtapuruṣasy'eva sarvakartṛtvābhāvaḥ); and if not-q, then "his inactivity is greater than space" (s, ākāśasy'eva sutarāṃ niṣkriyatvam). Now both r and s contradict the definition of God, that he is omnipotent and all-active.

(211) This is one of the standard dialectical metaphysical arguments employed in later times and one may well doubt whether they were those of the early niyativādin, but we need not doubt that the early

[1] Kāraṇa-vādā can also mean 'those who debated about the first cause'; cp. Kiṃ kāraṇaṃ? Brahma?, Śvet. 1.1.

[2] *v.* Basham, *op. cit.*, p. 231, where the full text and the translation is given.

niyativādin did argue against his opponents and that his opponents were these same protagonists as mentioned by Śīlāṅka. Śīlāṅka states the fact that the niyativādin argued against those who claimed that the effort of the person (puruṣakāra-), Time (kāla-), God (īśvara-), Intrinsic Nature (svabhāva-) and Karma were respectively the causes of 'pleasurable and painful experience' (*sukhadukkha-*). The Śvetāśvarara Upaniṣad mentions that one of the questions debated by the brahmavādins is as follows: adhiṣṭhitāḥ kena sukhetareṣu vartām..he, where Śaṅkara explains sukhetareṣu as *sukhadukkheṣu*[1] and the sentence may be translated as 'governed by whom (or what) do we live in pleasure and pain'. Now, it is recorded in the Pāli Nikāyas not only that this was one of the topics that was hotly debated at the time (*v. infra,* 395) but that the parties to these debates were these same theorists. The opponents of the niyativādin according to Śīlāṅka are the following:

1. Yadi *puruṣakāra*kṛtaṃ sukhadukkhādyanubhūyeta . . . *v.* Basham, *op. cit.*, p. 230, fn. 1.
2. N'āpi *kālaḥ* kartā . . . *ibid.*, p. 231, fn. 1.
3. *Īśvarakartṛ*ke'pi sukhadukkhe na bhavataḥ . . . *ibid.*, fn. 2.
4. *Svabhāvasy*'āpi sukhadukkhādikartṛtva . . . *ibid.*, p. 232, fn. 1.
5. *Karmaṇaḥ*, sukhadukkham prati kartṛtvam . . ., *ibid.*, fn. 2.

Now it would be noted that four of these theories are specifically mentioned in connection with this very problem in the Devadaha Sutta (M. II.222). We may state them under the numbers corresponding to Śīlāṅka's list:

1. Diṭṭhadhamma-*upakkama*[2]-hetu sukhadukkhaṃ paṭisaṃvedenti.
3. *Issaranimmāṇa*hetu sukhadukkhaṃ paṭisaṃvedenti.
4. Saṅgati-*bhāva*[3]-hetu sukhadukkhaṃ paṭisaṃvedenti.
5. *Pubbekata-*[4]hetu sukhadukkhaṃ paṭisaṃvedenti.

(212) We may conclude from what we have said above that some of the Ājīvikas were rationalists who not only constructed their theories by reasoning but also defended them against their opponents by

[1] Adhiṣṭhitā niyamitāḥ kena sukhetareṣu *sukhaduḥkheṣu* vartāmahe, Ānanda Āśrama Series, No. 17, p. 18 on Śvet. 1.1.

[2] This is probably the same as purisa-*parakkama-*, A. IV.190, which is a synonym of purisa-thāma- and purisa-viriya-.

[3] bhāva-= sabhāva-, *v.* Basham, *op. cit.*, p. 226.

[4] Cp. the theory of purātana-karma-kṛtam, mentioned by Guṇaratna, *op. cit.*, p. 20.

employing reason to demolish their theories. But there is also some reason to think that these theories were not merely constructed *a priori* but had some basis in claims to paranormal perception or superhuman insight as well.

(213) Basham says that both 'Nigaṇṭha Nātaputta and Makkhali Gosāla certainly seemed to have laid claim to full enlightenment' (*op. cit.*, p. 92). In the case of Nigaṇṭha Nātaputta we have sufficient evidence to believe that he claimed omniscience. But in the case of the latter, although omniscience is claimed for him in later times (*v. supra*, 151), there is no evidence that he himself claimed omniscience. Yet as Basham has pointed out, he is said to have practised penance in order 'to acquire magic power and superhuman insight' (*op. cit.*, p. 50). Dr Basham goes to the extent of saying that on the evidence of the Buddhist and Jain texts 'it appears that he was capable, either honestly or by fraud, of producing psychic phenomena' (*op. cit.*, p. 51). The belief in prophecy, it would appear, should be the natural outcome of their determinist theory; if the future was wholly or partly determined, it should be possible to know this in some way or another, because the future exists in the same sense in which the present exists (*v. supra*, 199), which was the niyativādin's assumption. But it is also possible that for the niyativādin part of the reasons for believing in his determinist thesis were actuated by his belief in prophecy as the story of 'Gosāla and the Sesamum Plant' (*op. cit.*, pp. 47–9) seems to suggest. Basham does not exclude 'the possibility that the story has some basis in fact' (p. 49). One of the central features of the story was that it was possible to have precognitive experiences about at least some events in the future by means of one's intuitive knowledge. In fact it is said that it was for the purpose of acquiring this kind of intuitive knowledge that Gosāla practised meditation and penance (*op. cit.*, p. 50). On the evidence alleged, the possibility cannot be altogether excluded that these ascetics may have had or seem to have believed that they had a few precognitive experiences of the future, which either led them to or reinforced their determinist thesis. Nothing is knowable unless it is a fact; if the future is knowable it is a fact and this is not possible unless the future exists in some sense in or like the present—which is the determinist thesis.

(214) It is probable that some of the Ājīvika beliefs about the size and colour of the soul (*v. supra*, 132) are an externalization of experiences had in trance-states. It is, however, curious that Buddhaghosa says

quite the opposite. In explaining the epistemic origin of the beliefs in the soul having size and form after death, he says that these are the result of meditative experiences.[1] As an alternative, he suggests that it is the result '*purely of reasoning* as in the case of the Ājīvikas and others' (ājīvikādayo viya *takkamatten'*eva vā, DA. I.119). The historical truth behind this assertion is probably that Buddhaghosa was greatly impressed by the rational tradition of the Ājīvikas. While he was also aware that claims with regard to the size and colour of the soul were made on the basis of trance experiences, he did not identify these with the Ājīvikas because he thought that they were mere dialecticians (takkī-), which they probably were at the time at which he wrote.

(215) While there is no evidence to show that Makkhali Gosāla claimed omniscience, there is good evidence that Pūraṇa Kassapa, the pure Determinist, did so. Two brahmins meet the Buddha and tell him about Pūraṇa's claim to omniscience and what he claims to know in the following words: 'Pūraṇa Kassapa claims to be omniscient and all-seeing and to be possessed of an infinite knowledge and insight such that whenever he walks or stands, sleeps or keeps awake, his knowledge and insight is constantly present continuously at all times. This is what he says, "I abide knowing and seeing a finite world with my infinite knowledge" '.[2] As a determinist he probably claimed to know fully not only the past and the present but the future as well. The theory that 'the world was finite' (antavā loko) was one of those, which was debated at this time (*v. infra*, 382, 383). It is likely that arguments were evolved to 'prove' the validity of theories believed in on the basis of mystic experiences.

(216) While the doctrines of the Ājīvikas appear to have been held mainly on the basis of reasoning and perhaps of personal claims to supernormal insights as well, we cannot entirely discount the belief in tradition on the part of even the early Ājīvikas. According to a statement of Śīlāṅka, quoted by Basham (*op. cit.*, p. 175, fn. 3) they seem to

[1] DA. I.119. Rupī attā'ti ādisu kasiṇarūpam attā ti tattha pavattasaññañ c'assa saññā ti gahetvā . . . (They hold that) the soul has form (after death), etc., thinking that the soul has the form (colour) of the meditational device and taking its after-image as their own consciousness.

[2] A. IV.428. Pūraṇo . . . Kassapo sabbaññū sabbadassāvi aparisesañāṇadassaṇam paṭijānāti carato ca me tiṭṭhato ca suttassa ca jāgarassa ca satataṃ samitaṃ ñāṇadassaṇam paccupaṭṭhitan ti. So evam āha 'ahaṃ anantena ñāṇena antavantaṃ lokaṃ jānaṃ passaṃ viharāmī 'ti.

have had their own traditional scriptures: 'the Trairāśikas, who follow the doctrine of Gosāla, and who have twenty-one sūtras, arranged according to the order of the Trairāśika *sūtras* in the *Pūrvas*'. Now, the Suttanipāta makes a reference to 'the Vedas of the Samaṇas as well as those of the brahmins'.[1] Since the Samanas were classified in the Suttanipāta as the Ājīvikas and the Nigaṇṭhas (*v. infra*, 375), it is likely that these collections of scriptures of the Ājīvikas are among the 'Vedas of the Samaṇas' referred to. It shows that at least some of the Ājīvikas had a sacred scripture as early as the period of the Pāli Nikāyas, a fact which is confirmed by the quotations or adaptations from them, found in the early Buddhist and Jain texts.[2]

(217) The reference to the 'followers of Gosāla' (Gośālamatā'nusāriṇo), elsewhere called the Ājīvikas, as the Trairāśikas in the above statement of Śīlāṅka, is significant and points to the contribution made by them to epistemology and logic. While the Sceptics and the Buddhists evolved or adopted a four-fold logic, the Ājīvikas who were the followers of Makkhali Gosāla appear to have classified propositions into three mutually exclusive categories and had a theory of three-fold standpoints (naya-). Haribhadra in his *Vṛtti* on the Nandī-Sūtra identifies the Trairāśikas with the Ājīvikas: Trairāśikāśc Ājīvikā ev'ocyante.[3] As Basham has shown[4] Abhayadeva states in the commentary to the Samavayāṅga-Sūtra that 'these Ājīvikas were called Trairāśikas'.[5] On the basis of Śīlāṅka's statements Hoernle[6] had identified these Trairāśikas with the schismatic Jain sect of Trairāśikas, which came into existence over five centuries after Mahāvīra, but we agree with Dr Basham's contention[7] that the two have to be distinguished.

(218) Dr Basham says that 'the distinctive characteristic of the Ājīvika system of epistemology . . . was the division of propositions into three categories' (*op. cit.*, p. 274); but in fact there is another distinctive feature, namely the adoption of three standpoints (nayas) instead of the seven (or the two?) of Jainism. The passage quoted by

[1] Vedāni viceyya kevalāni, Samaṇānaṃ yāni p'atthi Brāhmaṇānaṃ, Sn. 529.
[2] Basham, *op. cit.*, p. 214 ff., 216 ff.
[3] Nandī Sūtra, by Devavācaka (Devarddhi Gaṇi). With the *Cūrṇi* (gloss) of Jinadāsa Gaṇi and the *Vṛtti* (commentary) of Haribhadra. Ed. Vijayadāna Sūri, 1931, Fol. 114.
[4] *Op. cit.*, p. 179, fn. 3.
[5] Ta eva c'Ājīvikās Trairāśikā bhaṇitāh, fol. 120 on Sam. 147.
[6] ERE., Vol. I, p. 262.
[7] *Op. cit.*, p. 178.

Basham from the Nandī commentary, fol. 113 (*v. op. cit.*, p. 274, fn. 5) does not in fact appear in the edition of the commentary, that we have used (i.e. Nandī Sūtra, with the comms. of Jinadāsa and Haribhadra, ed. Vijayadāna Sūri, Indore, 1931). In this edition, there are two passages more or less identical, which explain these aspects of the epistemology and logic of the Ājīvikas: one is by Jinadāsa Gaṇi in his *Cūrṇi* appearing on fol. 110 and the other is in the *Vṛtti* by Haribhadra in another form of Prakrit appearing on fols. 113, 114. The difference is merely dialectical, e.g. the *Cūrṇi* has 'te c'eva Ājīvikā terāsiyā bhaṇitā', etc., while the *Vṛtti* reads, 'te c'eva Ajiviyā terāsiyā bhaṇiyā'. These passages differ in a significant respect (*v. infra*) from the passage cited by Basham.

(219) We may take the Sanskrit version in Abhayadeva's commentary on the Samavayāṅga-Sūtra, which reads as follows: 'These Ājīvikas are called Trairāśikas. Why? The reason is that they entertain (icchanti) everything to be of a triple nature, viz. soul, non-soul, soul and non-soul; world, non-world, world and non-world; being, non-being, being and non-being, etc. *Even in* (api) considering standpoints they entertain a three-fold standpoint such as the substantial, the modal and the dual'.[1] Thus according to Abhayadeva, they are called Trairāśikas for two reasons, in having a three-fold mode of predication and a three-fold set of standpoints.

(220) The Prakrit versions are almost identically similar to this, the only difference being that instead of sarvaṃ tryātmakam icchanti they have, savvaṃ jagaṃ tryātmakam icchanti, which makes no material difference. But the passage quoted by Basham has significant variations. It defines Trairāśikāḥ in an additional sentence as follows: Tatas tribhī rāśibhiścarantīti Trairāśikāḥ, i.e. thus, since they work with three heaps they are (called) Trairāśikas. Since this definition occurs immediately after mentioning their three-fold standpoints (naya), the 'heaps' (rāśi) seem to refer to the different types of predication as well as the standpoints. The notable difference in this passage is that it speaks of the three nayas as 'dravy'āstikam paryāyāstikam ubhayāstikañ ca', whereas Abhayadeva has (*v. fn. supra*) 'dravyārthikaḥ paryāyārthikaḥ

[1] Ta eva c'ājīvikās Trairasikā bhaṇitāḥ. Kasmād?—ucyate, yasmātte sarvaṃ tryātmakam icchanti yathā jīvo'ajīvo jīvājīvaḥ, loko'loko lokālokah, sad asat sadasat ityevam adi, nayacintāyām api te trividham nayam icchanti tadyathā dravyārthikaḥ paryāyārthikaḥ ubhayārthikaḥ, Samavāyāṅgasūtram, with Abhayadeva's commentary, Ed. Nāginadāsa Nemachanda, 1938, fol. 120 on Sam. 147.

ubhayārthikaḥ' corresponding to the Prakrit 'davvaṭṭhiko pajjavaṭṭhiko ubhayaṭṭhiko ya' (Nandī Sūtra) (fol. 110). Are we to regard the latter as preserving a more faithful tradition, since the two fundamental nayas of the Jains are called the *dravyārthika*naya- and *paryāyārthika*naya-[1] and the Prakrit versions of the Nandī commentaries agree with the Sanskrit version of the Samavayāṅga commentary?

(221) According to Dr Basham, 'the Ājīvikas . . . seem to have accepted the basic principle of Jaina epistemology, without going to the over-refined extreme of *sapta-bhaṅgi,* as in the orthodox Jaina *syādvāda* and *Nayavāda*' (*op. cit.*, p. 275). This implies that the Ājīvikas were aware of the seven-fold formulae of the Jains and simplified them. But judged by the fact that the three-fold schema of predication is simpler than the four-fold schema of the Sceptics and Buddhists and the corresponding seven-fold schema of the Jains, it would appear to be earlier than both the Buddhist and the Jain schemas, with which the Ājīvikas could not have been acquainted when they evolved theirs.

(222) In fact, it can be shown that in the earliest Buddhist and Jain texts the very doctrine of the Trairāśikas, which seems to have necessitated the three-fold schema, is mentioned, *thus making it highly probable that it was at least earlier than the Jain schema.* For while the earliest stratum of the Pāli Nikāyas knows of the four-fold schema, one of the earliest books of the Jain Canon, the Sūtrakṛtāṅga, which makes an independent reference to this Trairāśika doctrine, does not mention the seven-fold schema, although it is aware of the basic principle of syādvāda (*v. infra,* 233).

(223) The Brahmajāla Sutta mentions a class of religious teachers, who were semi-eternalists (samaṇa-brāhmaṇā . . . ekacca-sassatikā ekacca-asassatikā, D. I.19), who hold that the world and the soul were partly eternal and partly not (ekaccaṃ sassataṃ ekaccaṃ asassataṃ attānañ ca lokañ ca paññapenti, *loc. cit.*). It is probably this same theory that is elsewhere referred to as the view that holds that the soul and the world are *both eternal and not eternal* (sassato ca asassato ca attā ca loko ca, M. II.233, Ud. 69). Four varieties of these semi-eternalists are mentioned in the Sutta, of which the second believes in the existence of an ethereal group of *Khiḍḍā-padosika* gods (santi . . . Khiḍḍāpadosikā nāma devā, *loc. cit.*). Now it is said that those who over-

[1] *v.* Guerinot, *La Religion Djaina*, pp. 130–1.

indulge in sporting in this Heaven[1] lose their memory, fall from this state and are reborn on earth (tamhā kāyā cavitvā itthattham āgacchati, *loc. cit.*). Such a person leaves the household life (anagāriyaṃ pabbajati), practises meditation and attains a jhānic state (ātappam anvāya . . . ceto-samādhim phusati, *loc. cit.*), whereby he sees this past life of his and realizes that in that world there are beings who do not over-indulge, and who are eternal (ye . . . na ativelaṃ hassa-khiḍḍā-rati-dhamma-samāpannā viharanti . . . te . . . na cavanti, niccā dhuvā sassatā avipariṇāmadhammā sassati-samaṃ tath'eva ṭhassanti, *loc. cit.*), while the others are liable to fall. The account given of this school may perhaps have undergone some distortion, but we can gather from what is stated that according to this school, there are three types of beings:

1. the *eternal* beings (sassatā) who live for ever in that state (sassati-samaṃ tath'eva ṭhassanti, *loc. cit.*).
2. the *temporal* beings who live in this world.
3. the *partly eternal and partly temporal* beings (ekaccaṃ sassataṃ ekaccaṃ asassataṃ) who fall from the eternal state and perhaps go back again after a lif(of restraint and meditation.

(224) We can see here more than the rudiments of the doctrine of *maṇḍala-mokṣa* or cyclic salvation (*v.* Basham, *op. cit.*, 257–61). The eternal beings would correspond to the *cempotakars* of the Civañāna-cittiyār, while those who fall would be the *maṇṭalars* (*v. op. cit.*, p. 260), the main difference being that a different reason is given here as to why the *maṇṭalars* return from that state. Now, Dr Basham says that this doctrine of cyclic salvation 'appears to have emerged some time after the death of Gosāla' (*v. op. cit.*, p. 259). He does not explain why it was necessary to await the death of Gosāla for the doctrine to emerge, but he has seen that it is mentioned as early as the Sūtrakṛtāṅga. However, it is not correct to say that 'it is *first* mentioned in the Sūtrakṛtāṅga' (*loc. cit.*). We may quote the original version in the Sūtrakṛtāṅga since the identity in language with the Pāli version is significant:

Suddhe apāvae āyā ihaṃ egesiṃ āhiyaṃ
Puṇo *kiḍḍā-padoseṇaṃ* so tattha avarajjhaī
Iha saṃvuḍe muṇī jāe pacchā hoī apāvae
Viyaḍambu jahā bhujjo nīrayaṃ sarayaṃ tahā.

Sū. 1.1.3.11–2.

[1] We have used capital H for 'Heaven' here to denote that in the opinion of this school it was an eternal state.

We may translate this as follows: 'It is said by some that the soul is pure and sinless, but again it sins (avarajjhaī) in that state owing to *kiḍḍā-padosa-* (pleasure and hatred? corruption through pleasure?); born here, he later (pacchā) becomes sinless as a restrained ascetic. As pure water free from pollution becomes again polluted (so does he again become sinful).' This stanza appears in fact to summarize what was stated in the Pāli version. The Pāli version explicitly stated that some beings were eternal although all the beings were called *Khiḍḍā-padosikā devā* and *Khiḍḍā- padosa-* (Ard. Mag. *kiḍḍā-padosa-*) was the cause of the fall according to both the Buddhist and the Jain accounts.

(225) Now, as Dr Basham has pointed out, Śīlāṅka identifies this doctrine of the Sūtrakṛtāṅga with that of the Trairāśika followers of Gosāla (*loc. cit.*). But interpreting this verse Śīlāṅka gives a different explanation of *kiḍḍā-padosa-* from that suggested in the Pāli texts, which tries to make out that the cause is excessive debauchery (ativelaṃ hassa-khiḍḍā-rati-dhamma-samāpannā, *loc. cit.*). Śīlāṅka gives a more sublime reason for their fall, which was probably the reason that the Trairāśikas themselves would have given, namely that the eternal soul has feelings about the true religion and 'is *elated* when his religion is revered (on earth) and other religions are looked down upon and is *angry* when his own religion is despised'[1] explaining kiḍḍā- and padosa- as this joy and anger respectively. It is possible that when the Buddha warned his disciples not to be elated when people praise his religion and not to be angry when people condemn it (Brahmajāla Sutta, D. I.3, *v. infra,* 739) he was influenced by what he believed to be the plight of the Ājīvika as a result of his elation and anger about his own religion. At the same time the Buddhist criticism that falling a prey to temptation was the cause of their fall may have had some basis in the Ājīvika beliefs themselves, since one of the greatest fears of the Ājīvika ascetic was that he may succumb to the caresses of 'the gods Puṇṇabhadda and Maṇibhadda' who tempt him on the verge of death (*v.* Basham, *op. cit.,* p. 257 ff.).

(226) Basham does not mention this Pāli parallel to the verse in the Sūtrakṛtāṅga, which was the reason why he thought that this doctrine,

[1] *Op. cit.,* Vol. I, fol. 45 on Sū. 1.1.3.11.2. Svaśāsanapūjam upalabhyā'nyaśāsana-parābhavaṃ c'opalabhya . . . pramodaḥ sañjāyate, svaśāsananyakkāradarśanāc ca dveśaḥ.

was not so important for the early Ājīvika.[1] But unless it was one of the cardinal doctrines both the Jains as well as the Buddhists would not have stated it in summarizing their views.

(227) This Trairāśika doctrine which found it necessary to posit three kinds of souls and perhaps three kinds of worlds corresponding to them as well as three kinds of being, appears therefore to be quite early. The evidence points to its having its origin in a sect of Ājīvikas (in the loose sense) independently of Gosāla, though it may have accepted Gosāla's leadership or merged with the followers of Gosāla later on. It is to this doctrine that Basham traces the necessity for the Trairāśika to posit a third possibility: 'The Ājīvika postulate of a third possibility, neither being nor non-being, must have formed a convenient logical basis for the unusual doctrine that some souls were compelled to return even from *nirvāṇa*. These would be classified in the third category, sadasat—emancipated from *saṃsāra* and yet not emancipated' (*op. cit.*, p. 275). We agree with this conclusion though not in the form in which Dr Basham states it, since the third possibility is not 'neither being nor non-being' but 'both being and non-being' (sadasat), which has to be distinguished from the former since the distinction was drawn in the time of the Pāli Nikāyas. The thesis of this school is, as we said, stated in the Pāli Nikāyas as '*sassato ca asassato ca attā ca loko ca*' which would probably have been equivalent to '*sanasanjīvaśca lokaśca*' in the terminology of the Trairāśika. This, it may be observed, is not a logical proposition which is contradictory as would appear from its form (since it seems to violate the Law of Excluded Middle) but an empirical proposition which is contingent (*v. infra*, 579). Thus, for this school the three logical alternatives would be: (1) p, (2) notp, (3) p.notp and not the usual two (1.p, 2.not-p) according to the Aristotelian schema.

(228) We are on less certain ground with regard to its doctrine of nayas in respect of its antiquity and significance. Dr Basham assumes that it is a simpler version of the seven-fold nayas of Jainism (*op. cit.*, p. 275). But there is another possibility.

One has to compare these three nayas considering the terminology with the two fundamental nayas of Jainism:

[1] *v.* his remark, 'This doctrine is not elsewhere mentioned in the Pāli or Jaina Prakrit texts, and seems not to have loomed large in the minds of the earlier Ājīvikas' (*op. cit.*, p. 259).

Ājīvika	*Jainism*	
1. Dravyārthika- (Substantial)	Dravyārthika-	(3) naigama-, saṃgraha-, vyavahāra-.
2. Paryāyārthika- (Modal)	Paryāyārthika-	(4) ṛjusūtra-, śabda-, samabhirūḍha-, evambhūta-.
3. Ubhayārthika- (Dual)	—	

It will be seen that the Ājīvika is more complex if we consider the fact that Jainism has nothing corresponding to the ubhayārthikanaya-, but on the other hand the Ājīvika has not subdivided (as far as our knowledge goes) the first two nayas. The fact that the first two nayas are held in common, points to a common origin, though later the Jains made further elaborations of these while the Ājīvikas added the third.

(229) One suspects a close connection between the *three* forms of predication and the *three* nayas. Are we to say that each of the forms of predication was possible *only* from one of the nayas, viz.

(1) Sat—according to the dravyārthikanaya-
(2) Asat—according to the paryāyārthikanaya-
(3) Sadasat—according to the ubhayārthikanaya-

e.g.

(1) A chariot exists as a substance, i.e. from a substantial point of view.
(2) A chariot does not exist as a collection of attributes, i.e. from the modal point of view (cp. the chariot simile in the Nikāyas (S. I.134) and the Milinda Pañha, 27).
(3) A chariot does and does not exist as a substance and as a collection of attributes, i.e. from the substantial-cum-modal or dual points of view.

(230) We find this usage substantiated in the Jain Canonical texts, which sometimes speak of something having the characteristic q from one standpoint, the characteristic not-q from another and the characteristics q and not-q from both standpoints. The Trairāśika usage was, therefore, probably not different from this. It also shows that though the Jains did not actually posit a separate dual standpoint they made

use of the substantial-cum-modal standpoint in principle. We may illustrate this by an example in the Bhagavatī Sūtra,[1] where the question is asked of Mahāvīra, 'Are souls . . . eternal or non-eternal?' (Jivā . . . kiṃ sāsayā asāsayā?) and it is replied that 'souls would be both eternal and non-eternal' (jivā siya sāsayā, siya asāsayā) and this is further explained by saying that 'they are eternal in respect of their substance and non-eternal in respect of their states' (davvaṭṭhayāë sāsayā, bhāvaṭṭhayāë asāsayā).

(231) Jainism is undoubtedly another well-known pre-Buddhistic school of thought which seems to have influenced Early Buddhism. But the Jain Canonical texts, as we have them, are on the whole later than the Pāli Nikāyas so that we cannot be at all certain of the degree to which and the direction in which this influence was felt by a study of their contents. Whatever the influence of Jain epistemological and logical theories on Buddhism and vice versa, both schools seem to have profited by the critical outlook of the Materialists and the Sceptics as well as the logical experiments of the Sceptics and the Ājīvikas. Since the Jain theory of knowledge is fairly well known[2] we would confine ourselves to stating those elements of the theory with which Early Buddhism, in our opinion, is likely to have been acquainted with.

(232) Barua was of the opinion that 'there is nowhere to be found in the older texts any systematic exposition of Mahāvīra's theory of knowledge' (*op. cit.*, p. 403) but Tatia assumes on the basis of some evidence that he adduces that 'the theory of knowledge of the Āgamas is very old and perhaps originated in the pre-Mahāvīra period' (*op. cit.*, p. 27). Since this evidence is drawn solely from the Jain texts one cannot accept this conclusion. However, when we consider the historical background and the metaphysics of Jainism it would seem reasonable to suppose that at least the basic notions of its theory of knowledge formed an integral part of that stratum of Jain thought with which early Buddhism was acquainted.

[1] Bhagavatī Sūtra, with Abhayadeva's commentary, 1939, Vol. I, fol. 545, 7, 2, 273.

[2] Guerinot, *op. cit.*, devotes a Chapter to the 'Théorie de la Connaisance et Logique' (pp. 120–33), where he mentions the main concepts in bare outline. Nathmal Tatia, *Studies in Jaina Philosophy*, Banaras, 1951, makes a detailed comparative study, but with a poor historical sense. *v.* also Das Gupta, *op. cit.*, Vol. I, pp. 165–8; Umesha Mishra, *History of Indian Philosophy*, Allahabad, 1957, Vol. I, 279–304; Jadunath Sinha, *op. cit.*, Vol. II, pp. 183–208; C. Sharma, *op. cit.*, pp. 48–62.

(233) Jainism recommends a cautious critical attitude to the problem of truth. This is reflected in its non-categorical theory of truth (anekāntavāda), which has given rise to the use of conditional propositions. It is said that 'the wise man should not joke or explain without (recourse to) conditional propositions' (ṇa yā vi panne parihāsakujjā, ṇa *yā' siyāvāya*[1] viyāgarejjā, Sū. 1.14.19). He should 'expound the analytical theory (*vibhajjavāyaṃ* ca viyāgarejjā) and use the two (permitted) kinds of speech, living among virtuous men, impartial and wise'.[2] Since the Buddha himself claims to be a vibhajja-vādin (*v. infra*, 446) we may here pause to consider Śīlāṅka's comment on this term.

(234) Śīlāṅka first explains the phrase, vibajjavāyaṃ (ca vibyāgarejjā), saying that it means 'one should expound the theory which unravels separate meanings' (pṛthagarthanirṇayavādam vyāgṛṇīyāt, *op. cit.*, Vol. I, fol. 256) and then goes on to suggest two alternative meanings for the term vibhajjavāda-: 'Either vibhajya-vāda- is *syādvāda*, which he should expound as it is nowhere at fault, is comprehensive since it is not contradicted by conventional usage, and is validated by one's own experience; or he should analyse, i.e. distinguish the senses properly (samyagarthān . . . pṛthakkṛtvā) and make his statement, viz. he should speak of permanence from the substantial standpoint and of impermanence from the modal standpoint; likewise (he may say that) all things exist from the point of view of their own substance, place, time and states and do not exist from the point of view of other substances, etc.; thus has it been said "he who would not entertain everything as existing from the four points of view of its form, etc., and as not existing from the opposite points of view, cannot take any stand"—he should resort to analytical statements of this sort.'[3] This explanation is largely based on Jain epistemological beliefs; but the general sense of vibhajja-vāda that Śīlāṅka speaks of was probably the original sense. It shows that the early Jains like the Buddhists who were

[1] Śīlāṅka, however, explains the phrase differently, taking it to mean, nā'pi c'āśīrvadam . . . vyāgṛṇīyat, nor should he utter blessings; *op. cit.*, fol. 255.

[2] Saṃkejja yā'saṃkitabhāva bhikkhū, vibhajjavāyaṃ ca viyāgarejjā, bhāsāduyaṃ dhamma-samuṭṭhitehiṃ, viyāgarejjā samayā supanne, Sū. 1.14.22.

[3] Tathā vibhajjavādam pṛthagarthanirṇayavādaṃ vyāgṛṇīyāt, yadi vā vibhajyavādaḥ, syādvādastaṃ sarvatrāskhalitaṃ lokavyavahāravisaṃvāditayā sarvavyāpinaṃ svānubhavasiddhaṃ vadet, athavā samyagarthān vibhajya, pṛthakkṛtvā tadvādaṃ vadet, tadyathā, nityavādaṃ, tathā svadravyakṣetrakālabhāvaiḥ sarve'pi padārthāḥ santi, paradravyādibhis tu na santi, tathā c'oktaṃ, 'sadeva sarvaṃ ko n'ecchetsvarūpādicatuṣṭayāt, asadeva viparyāsānna cenna vyavatiṣṭhate' ityādikaṃ vibhajya-vādaṃ vadet iti, *op. cit.*, Vol. I, fol. 256 on Sū. 1.14.22.

to follow them made use of analysis in understanding the meanings of statements (*v. infra,* 446 ff.).

(235) It would be seen that Sū. 1.14.22, quoted above, mentions 'two (permitted) kinds of speech' (bhāsāduyaṃ). This is a subject on which the early Jains as well as the Buddhists placed restrictions, necessitating classifications of propositions (speech) according to their truth-value, though these classifications are different in each case (*v. infra,* 594). According to the Jainism, 'there are four kinds of speech; the first is truth, the second is untruth, the third is truth mixed with untruth; what is neither truth, nor untruth, nor truth mixed with untruth, that is the fourth kind of speech: neither truth nor untruth'.[1] What is not permitted are the second and the third. The third kind—the half-truth or the mixed truth—is specially condemned (tatthimā taīyā bhāsā, jaṃ vadittā'ṇutappati, jaṃ channaṃ taṃ na vattavvaṃ, esā āṇā ṇiyaṇṭhiyā, Sū. 1.9.26).

(236) The attitude of relativism or non-categorical assertion (anekāntavāda-) is in a sense the opposite reaction to that of the Sceptic, when faced with the same problem (*v. supra,* 191). When the Sceptic was faced with a variety of conflicting theories, he came to the conclusion that none of them can be known to be true since all may be false and there was no criterion of deciding as to which was true. The Jain attitude seems to have been that each of these conflicting theories may contain an element of truth and as such be partly true and partly false or true from one point of view and false from another.

(237) This attitude is reflected in Mahāvīra's solution to at least some metaphysical problems. For instance, at this time the Materialists on the one hand held that the body and the soul were identical or that there was no soul apart from the body (*v. supra,* 130); on the other hand the eternalists held that the soul was different from the body (*v. infra,* 384–7). It is said that when Mahāvīra was asked whether 'the body was (identical with) the soul or different from it' (āyā, bhante, kāye anne kāye? Bhagavatī Sūtra, 13.7.495, *op. cit.,* fol. 1141), he is said to have replied that 'the body is (identical with) the soul as well as different from it' (āyā vi kāye anne vi kāye, *loc. cit.*). The same kind of reply is given in this context to the questions as to whether the body

[1] Cattāri bhāsājāyāīṃ, taṃ jahā: saccaṃ egaṃ paḍhamaṃ bhāsājāyaṃ bīyaṃ mosaṃ taīyaṃ saccāmosaṃ jaṃ n'eva saccaṃ n'eva mosaṃ n'eva saccāmosaṃ asaccāmosaṃ taṃ caütthaṃ bhāsājātaṃ, Āyāraṃga Sutta, 2.4.1.4.

has form (rūviṃ) or has no form (arūviṃ), is conscious (sacitte) or is not conscious (acitte), is a 'jīva or is an ajīva' (jīve vi kāye ajīve vi kāye, *loc. cit.*). These would appear to be self-contradictory propositions to assert, but Mahāvīra would have resolved the contradiction by saying that the soul is identical with the body from one point of view and different from the body in another point of view (naya-). It is only when 'one understands the true nature of all substance by all the standard means of knowledge (pramāṇa) and all the points of view (naya) that one's knowledge is comprehensive'.[1]

(238) These nayas are classified as seven in number ranging from the most general (naigama[2]) to the most specific (evambhūta). But there seems to have been a school, which believed only in four nayas, called the Catuṣkanayikas. Dr Basham is of the opinion that this is a 'small sub-sect of the Jainas with a somewhat unorthodox epistemology' (*op. cit.*, 327). Abhayadeva says in considering their origin that this school 'in considering standpoints believes that naigama is two-fold, being both general and specific, and that the general falls into the general and the specific into the specific—thus there are the general (saṃgraha-), the specific (vyavahāra-) and the existential (ṛjusūtra) standpoints; the verbal standpoints are all the same and thus there are four standpoints'.[3] This seems to suggest that the Catuṣkanayikas simplified the Jain schema, but it is by no means conclusive that this simplicity is due to the simplication of the complex rather than to the priority (in time) of the simpler. The passage that Weber[4] has quoted from a Nandī commentary contrasts the Ājīvikas, the Catuṣkanayikas and the Trairāśikas from each other as well as from the Jains, viz. 'Cha . . . *sasamaīyāni,* satta *ājīviyāṇi,* cha *caūkkanaīyāṇi* satta *terāsiyāni*'. They are all considered alien to 'one's own religion' (sva-samaya-, *v.* sasamaīyāni) so that the Catuṣkanayikas could not strictly have been a sub-sect tolerated by the Jains.

[1] Davvāṇa savvabhāvā savva-pamāṇehi jassa uvaladdhā, savvāhi nayavihīhiṃ vitthārarui tti nāyavvo, Uttarādhyayanasūtram, 28.24.

[2] There are, however, two explanations of this term (*v.* Jadunath Sinha, *op. cit.*, Vol. II, pp. 200–1).

[3] Nayacintā, tatra naigamo dvividhaḥ, sāṃgrāhiko 'sāṃgrāhikaśca tatra sāṃgrāhikaḥ saṃgrahaṃ, praviṣṭo' sāṃgrāhikaśca vyavahāram, tasmāt saṃgraho vyavahāro ṛjusūtraḥ śabdādayaścaika ev'etyevaṃ catvāro nayāḥ, Samavayāṅgasūtram, with Abhayadeva's commentary, Ed. Nāginadāsa Nemachanda, 1938, fol. 120 on Sam. 147.

[4] A. Weber, *Indische Studien*, Beiträge für die Kunde des indischen Alterthums, Band 16, Leipzig, 1883, p. 364.

(239) The attitude of mind that favoured this kind of relativism was also suspicious of the possibility of the truth lying in extreme points of view. We already found this in the compromise solutions of Mahāvīra who uses the expressions 'both . . . and' (syādastināsti) like the Trairāśikas with their sadasat to express the fact that two opposing points of view are both right and wrong and that their falsity consists in taking each extreme point of view to be the sole truth. At times Mahāvīra expressly states the truth is not to be found in extremes. It is said: 'He should not believe that (this world) is without beginning or without end, eternal or not eternal, according to the argumentation (of the heretics). From these alternatives you cannot arrive at truth; from these alternatives you are led to error' (Jacobi's Translation, SBE., Vol. 45, pp. 405, 406). The text reads: aṇādīyaṃ parinnāyā aṇavadaggeti vā guṇo, sāsayamasāsaë vā iti diṭṭhiṃ na dhāraë, *eëhiṃ dohiṃ ṭhāṇehiṃ* vavahāro na vijjaï. *eëhiṃ dohiṃṭhāṇehiṃ* aṇāyāraṃ tu jāṇaë (Sū. 2.5.2, 3). This point of view is in a sense a corollary of Jain relativism but, as would be seen, it plays a central rôle in Buddhism (*v. infra*, 607–9).

(240) When we examine the Jain sūtras we find classifications of various types of knowledge. These formal classifications may be late and belong to the post-Buddhistic era but there is little reason to doubt that the kinds of knowledge referred to were known in the pre-Buddhistic phase of Jain thought. Thus in the Sthānāṅga and the Nandī Sūtras, as pointed out by Vidyābhūṣana (*op. cit.*, p. 161, fn. 5), jñāna, which is the general term for knowledge is classified as follows:

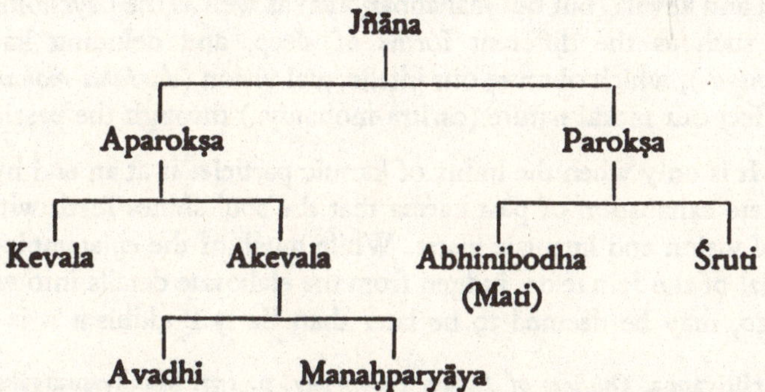

(241) We find here a classification that is peculiarly Jain, based as it is on the metaphysics of Jainism. Only extrasensory perception is denoted by aparokṣa or direct knowledge, while normal perception

would be classified under indirect knowledge (parokṣa) as mati or opinion which includes both normal perception as well as inference. Scripture or tradition also has a secondary place as indirect knowledge in strong contrast to the early Vedic valuation. Direct knowledge (aparokṣa) covers both absolute knowledge (kevala) which is infallible and is omniscience itself as well as the non-absolutist forms of direct knowledge, which are liable to error. These latter are avadhi or the direct perception of things extended in time or space without the mediation of the sense-organs and manaḥparyāya or telepathy. In fact direct knowledge is called direct perception (mukhya-pratyakṣa-[1]) in contrast to normal or common perception (samvyavahārika-pratyakṣa-[1]).

(242) This theory is a product of the Jain conception of the soul (jīva-), which is intrinsically omniscient. As it is cluttered up in the body with material karmic particles clouding its vision and as it has to see through the openings of the senses, normal perceptual vision can only be indirect. In fact all knowledge before the actual attainment of omniscience including kevala- itself, which is intrinsically present in every soul, are affected by these subtle karmic particles. There are eight varieties of them[2] but only three of them are epistemologically interesting, viz. (1) knowledge-obscuring karmas (*jñānāvaraṇīya-*), which affect the entirety of knowledge in all its forms (i.e. kevala, avadhi, manaḥparyāya, mati and śruti), (2) perception-obscuring karmas (*darśanāvaraṇīya-*), which affect normal perception, both visual (cakṣus) and non-visual (acakṣus), paranormal perception such as avadhi and kevala (but not manaḥparyāya) as well as the psychological states such as the different forms of sleep, and deluding karmas (*mohanīya-*), which obscure our intellectual vision (*darśana-mohanīya*) and affect our moral nature (cāritra-mohanīya) through the passions.

(243) It is only when the influx of karmic particles is at an end by the complete exhaustion of past karma that the soul shines forth with its natural vision and intrinsic lustre. While much of the epistemological material of the Jain texts, judged from the elaborate details into which they go, may be deemed to be later than Early Buddhism it is very

[1] *v.* Hiriyanna, *Outlines of Indian Philosophy*, p. 159. Mukhyapratyakṣa- is also called pāramārthika-pratyakṣa-, subdivided into the complete (sakala- i.e. kevala) and the incomplete (vikala-, i.e. avadhi and manaḥparyāya), *v.* Jadunath Sinha, *op. cit.*, Vol. II, p. 189.

[2] *v.* Jadunath Sinha, *op. cit.*, p. 224.

likely that the main elements of the theory and the different kinds of knowledge mentioned were known at a time at least coeval if not prior to Early Buddhism. If we consider the ways of knowing recorded in the Jain scriptures as shown above, without the valuation or interpretation given to them in accordance with Jain metaphysics we would have to say that the following means of knowledge are acknowledged in them namely, (1) perception, sensory and para-normal, (2) inference, (3) scripture or tradition. Paranormal or extrasensory perception would include (i) absolute knowledge or omniscience (kevala), (ii) clairvoyance and clairaudience (avadhi), and (iii) telepathy (manaḥparyāya). The Sūtras, however, regard *upamā* or comparison (analogy) as a means of knowledge different from inference. We have seen that the word *pramāṇa* was used in the sense of a 'means of knowledge' in the above quotation from the Uttarādhyayana Sūtra (*v. supra*, 237), but since the word appears to have come into currency in its technical sense during the time of Early Buddhism or at least not very much later (*v. supra*, 77), we cannot say how early or late its use in the Jain scriptures is. The earlier Jain word for a means of knowledge appears to have been not pramāṇa but *hetu*. We may see this in the classification of hetu-s in the sense of pramāṇas in the Bhagavatī and Sthānāṅga Sūtras as shown by Vidyābhūṣana (*op. cit.*, p. 162): athavā *heū* cauvvihe paṇṇatte taṃ jahā, *paccakkhe anumāne uvame āgame*, i.e. the means of knowledge have been declared to be four-fold, viz. perception, inference, analogy and tradition. This is confirmed by the definition of the term in the Caraka Saṃhitā, which as we have shown appears to have preserved an earlier logical terminology current at the time of the Pāli Nikāyas (*v. infra*, 323). This definition reads as follows: Hetur nāmopalabdhikāraṇaṃ tatpratyakṣam anumānam aitihyam aupamyam ity ebhir hetubhir yad upalabhyate tat tattvam (3.8.6.25), i.e. Hetu stands for the means of apprehension, viz. perception, inference, tradition and analogy; what is apprehended by means of these hetu-s is truth. We may note that of the hetu-s *pratyakṣa-* and *anumāna-* correspond to paccakkhe and anumāne of the Jain list, while *aitihyam* corresponds to āgame and *aupamyam* to uvame (=Skr. upamā). It is difficult, however, to say whether the Jains were the first to use the word in this sense. The Materialists are often called the 'haitukas',[1] probably because they used epistemological arguments or arguments based on hetu- in the sense of 'means of knowledge' to prove their

[1] *v.* Das Gupta, *A History of Indian Philosophy*, Vol. III, pp. 517–19.

theories or disprove their opponents (*v. supra,* 91). They may very well have been the first to use the term in this sense. The fact that the Jains did not use the term exclusively in the epistemological sense is clear from the rest of the quotation of Vidyābhūṣana from the Bhagavatī and the Sthānāṅga Sūtra, where *heū* is used in the sense of 'reason' in a formula bearing a close resemblance to the general causal formula appearing in the Pāli Nikāyas (*v. infra,* 771): athavā heū cauvvihe paṇṇatte taṃ jahā, atthi taṃ atthi so heū, atthi taṃ natthi so heū, natthi taṃ atthi so heū, natthi taṃ natthi so heū, i.e. the reasons (heū) are declared to be four-fold, the reason why something exists because something else exists, the reason why something exists because something else does not exist, the reason why something does not exist because something else exists, the reason why something does not exist because something else does not exist. As the examples given by Vidyābhūṣana would show (*loc. cit.*), they are four kinds of possible correlations between causally connected events or things. Thus, if x (fire) and y (smoke) are causally connected we can say that x is present because y is present, y being the reason (hetu) why we say that x is present. We may represent the four instances thus:

1. It is (atthi taṃ)	because (heū)	that is (atthi)
2. ,,	,,	that is not (natthi)
3. It is not (natthi taṃ)	,,	that is (atthi)
4. ,,	,,	that is not (natthi)

It may be observed that the causal formula of Buddhism states 1 and 4 (*v. infra,* 771). The similarity is obvious but the nature of the historical connection, if any, is difficult to determine.

CHAPTER IV

THE ATTITUDE TO AUTHORITY

(244) When we tried to classify the thinkers of the pre-Buddhistic era in accordance with their epistemological outlook and approach to problems, we found in Chapter I that the Vedic thinkers up to the time of Buddhism seemed to fall into three groups. Firstly, there were the traditionalists coming down from the period of the Brāhmaṇas who considered the sacred scriptures to be the most valuable source of knowledge. Secondly, there were the thinkers of the Āraṇyakas and Early Upaniṣads, who, while not entirely discarding scripture, thought that knowledge of reality was possible by reasoning and metaphysical speculation. While this second school of thinkers would have continued independently to evolve their own speculative theories there arose thirdly, the contemplatives of the Middle and Late Upaniṣads, who while relegating scripture to the realm of lower knowledge (aparā vidyā) and discarding reason (tarka) as an adequate means of obtaining knowledge of reality claimed that the only means of knowing reality was by having a personal and direct acquaintance or experience of it, by practising meditative techniques (yoga) and depending on the grace of God for the final vision or revelation.

(245) A study of the ways of knowing of the non-Vedic thinkers shows that they can be classified along with the second and third groups of the Vedic thinkers. There is little doubt that the Materialists made use of reason both in evolving as well as in propagating their views though reason for them was on the whole subservient to perception. The Sceptics likewise seemed to have reasoned their way into scepticism though with the exception of the school of Sañjaya, they made little use of it since they kept aloof from controversy. The Ājīvakas were a mixed lot; they were primarily rational metaphysicians and dialecticians though some of them seem to have claimed personal intuitional insights. Similarly the Jains or at least their leader claimed

personal and direct knowledge of things, while making use of reason in debate.

(246) If therefore we take the pre-Buddhistic background of thought as a whole these thinkers fall into three classes according to the stress they laid on a particular way of knowing, viz.

(1) The Traditionalists, who derived their knowledge wholly from a scriptural tradition and interpretations based on it. Prominent in this class were the brahmins who upheld the sacred authority of the Vedas.
(2) The Rationalists, who derived their knowledge from reasoning and speculation without any claims to extrasensory perception. The metaphysicians of the Early Upaniṣads, the Sceptics, the Materialists and most of the Ājīvakas fell into this class.
(3) The 'Experientialists', who depended on direct personal knowledge and experience, including extrasensory perception on the basis of which their theories were founded. Many of the thinkers of the Middle and Late Upaniṣads, some of the Ājīvakas and Jains are classifiable in this group. The Materialists, as empiricists, would also fall under this category if not for the fact that they denied the validity of claims to extrasensory perception.

(247) This classification, however, should not be too rigidly interpreted so as to consider these groups as mutually exclusive. Such was not the case, for the Traditionalists did not deny or fail to give a place to perception and reason. The Rationalists of the Early Upaniṣads likewise did not entirely do away with scripture, although the Materialists did. The Ājīvakas and later the Jains also had their scriptures which they held in great respect. The Experientialists of the Middle and Late Upaniṣads in like manner give a very limited place to scripture though they discard reason altogether. So what we can claim for this grouping is that when we consider the epistemological standpoints of these groups as a whole, the essential or final knowledge claimed by them is said to be derived mainly if not wholly from each of the sources of knowledge emphasized by each group.

(248) In examining the ways of knowledge recognized or accepted in Buddhism it would be pertinent to ask whether the Buddha or Early Buddhism can be classified under any of the above groups or to see what attitude Buddhism adopted towards them in respect of its own epistemological standpoint.

(249) There is a passage in the Saṅgārava Sutta which throws a good deal of light on this problem. Here the Buddha is talking with a brahmin student versed in the Vedas and Vedic lore, who asks him the following question: 'There are ... some recluses and brahmins who profess the basis of a religion (ādibrahmacariyakaṃ) after finding a final and ultimate insight (diṭṭhadhammābhiññāvosānapāramippattā) in this life. Now where does the venerable Gotama stand among them?'[1] The Buddha replies as follows: 'I say that there is a difference among those who profess the basis of a religion after finding a final and ultimate insight in this life. There are ... some recluses and brahmins who are Traditionalists (anussavikā), who profess the basis of a religion after finding a final and ultimate insight in this life, such as the brahmins of the Three Vedas (Tevijjā). There are also ... some recluses and brahmins who profess the basis of a religion after finding a final and ultimate insight in this life on mere belief alone (kevalaṃ saddhāmattakena) such as the Reasoners (takkī) and Metaphysicians (vīmaṃsī, *lit.* speculators). There are other recluses and brahmins who profess the basis of a religion after finding a final and ultimate insight in this life by gaining a higher knowledge personally (sāmaṃ yeva) of a doctrine (dhammaṃ) among doctrines not traditionally heard of before. Now ... I am one of those who profess the basis of a religion after finding a final and ultimate insight in this life by gaining a higher knowledge personally of a doctrine among doctrines not traditionally heard of before.'[2]

(250) We find here the Buddha classifying his predecessors and contemporaries in respect of their ways of knowing into three classes,

[1] Santi . . . eke samaṇabrāhmaṇā diṭṭhadhammābhiññāvosānapāramippattā ādibrahmacariyakam paṭijānanti. Tatra bho Gotama ye te samaṇabrāhmaṇā diṭṭhadhammābhiññāvosānapāramippattā ādibrahmacariyakam paṭijananti, tesam bhavaṃ Gotamo katamo ti? M.II.211.

[2] Diṭṭhadhammābhiññāvosānapāramippattānaṃ ādibrahmacariyaṃ paṭijānantānam pi kho ... vemattataṃ vadāmi. Santi ... eke samaṇabrāhmaṇā anussavikā, te anussavena diṭṭhadhammābhiññāvosānapāramippattā ādibrahmacariyaṃ paṭijānanti, seyyathāpi brāhmaṇā Tevijjā. Santi pana . . . eke samaṇabrāhmaṇā kevalaṃ saddhāmattakena diṭṭhadhammābhiññāvosānaparamippattā ādibrahmacariyaṃ paṭijānanti, seyyathāpi Takkī Vīmaṃsī. Santi eke samaṇabrāhmaṇā pubbe ananussutesu dhammesu sāmaṃ yeva dhammaṃ abhiññāya diṭṭhadhammābhiññāvosānapāramippattā ādibrahmacariyaṃ paṭijānanti. Tatra ye te samaṇabrāhmaṇā pubbe ananussutesu dhammesu sāmaṃ yeva dhammaṃ abhiññāya diṭṭhadhammābhiññāvosānapāramippattāādibrahmacariyaṃ paṭijānanti, tesāham asmi. M. II.211.

viz. (1) the Traditionalists (Anussavikā), (2) Rationalists and Metaphysicians (Takkī Vīmaṃsī), and (3) the 'Experientialists' who had a personal higher knowledge of the truth of their doctrines. He also identifies himself with members of this third group. These groups appear *prima facie* to be the same as the groups we found after a historical analysis of the background of Early Buddhist thought.

(251) Let us start with the criticism of the anussavikā. Now we find that anussava- is only one of many alleged means of knowledge criticized in the Pāli Nikāyas. It heads a list of ten possible ways of claiming knowledge which are condemned as unsatisfactory by the Buddha in addressing the Kālāmas (A. I.189) and on another occasion in a discourse to Bhaddiya Licchavi (A. II.191–3). On examining this list it will be noticed (*v. infra*, 259) that six of the items have reference to knowledge which is claimed on the basis of some sort of authority. It would therefore be better to consider the authoritative criterion of knowledge as a whole and inquire into the Buddhist attitude to it.

(252) The argument from authority may take many forms. If we confine ourselves to the Indian context, we find that many different types of knowledge from authority were accepted as valid by Indian thinkers. A brief résumé of these different types as recognized in post-Buddhist thought would not only help us to see the Early Buddhist criticism of authority in a better light, but also enable us to distinguish between the earlier pre-Buddhistic claims to knowledge based on authority, from the later forms.

(253) That the argument from authority was accepted by the orthodox schools is evident from the fact that śabda was accorded the dignity of a pramāṇa (i.e. a valid means of knowledge) by all of them excepting the Vaiśeṣika. The Pūrva-Mīmāṃsā preserves the earliest and the most orthodox view of śabda and uses the term to denote the authority of the Vedas alone. Even among Vedic assertions priority is claimed for the injunctive statements, i.e. commands (vidhi) and prohibitions (niṣedha) while explanatory assertions (arthavāda) are given a secondary status (M.S. 1.2.1) inasmuch as they are said to be dependent on the former. We see here reflected the attitude of the earliest ritualistic brahmins who valued the karmakāṇḍa alone above all else and upheld the absolute authority of the Vedas (*v.* our first group of Vedic thinkers).

(254) In contrast to this attitude is that of the Naiyāyikas for whom śabda means verbal testimony in general without specific reference to

the Vedic scriptures and stands for the testimony of experts. Vedic statements are included only as a special case of such testimony and are authoritative because God is all-knowing and presumably trustworthy (N.S. 2.1.68), the existence of God being independently proved by a metaphysical analogical argument (sāmānyatodṛṣṭa).

(255) The testimony of people who may be of any class, 'ṛsīs, āryas or mlecchas'[1] relate to empirical facts (dṛṣṭārtha) while that of the Vedas relates to non-empirical facts (adṛṣṭārtha). Even if the early Nyāya was atheistic,[2] it is not likely that the Vedas were rejected altogether for it seems to have been argued that the human authors of the Vedas, namely the ṛsīs, were āptas or reliable persons whose statements even with regard to non-empirical facts may be accepted (N.B. 1.1.8, 2.1.68). But what is significant is that the Mīmāṃsā claim to an absolute authoritativeness of the Vedas is criticized (N.S. 2.2.13–40) and that its authority is considered derivative from the general authority of reliable testimony, in this school which specialized in the study of logic. The Vaiśeṣika school, which became closely attached to the Nyāya, not only criticizes the absolute claim to authority of the Vedas (V.S. 2.2.21–37, 6.1.1. ff.) but does not treat śabda as a separate pramāṇa at all. It nevertheless subsumes both tradition (aitihya) as well as verbal testimony (śabda) under inference[3] and treats scriptural statements as śabda or testimony acceptable on the reliability of the seers. We thus see logicians of the Nyāya school treating the scriptural statements of the Vedas as a sub-class of verbal testimony and the metaphysicians of the Vaiśeṣika school treating them as a sub-class of inferential propositions. This attitude to the Vedas seems to bear some affinity to that of our second group of Vedic thinkers (*v. supra*, 244).

(256) The other schools represent a point of view midway between that of the Mīmāṃsā and the Nyāya-Vaiśeṣika. The Sāṅkhya as a metaphysical system accepts reliable assertions (āptavacana) as an independent source of knowledge (S.K. 4). Unlike the Naiyāyikas, it admits its non-personal authorship (S.P.S. 5.46) and independent

[1] ṛṣy-ārya-mecchānāṃ samānaṃ lakṣaṇam, N.B. 1.1.7. *v.* Ānanda Āśrama Series No. 91, p. 25.

[2] *v.* Garbe, *Philosophy of Ancient India*, p. 23; cp. Muir, *Original Sanskrit Texts*, Vol. 3, p. 133.

[3] *v.* Radhakrishnan, *Indian Philosophy*, Vol. 2, p. 182.

validity (S.P.S. 5.51) but it makes the Vedas superfluous by saying that the saved do not need it and the unsaved cannot grasp it (S.P.S. 5.47). Furthermore, it undermines its foundations by relying on reason alone in deducing its metaphysics. The Yoga likewise, while nominally accepting scripture as a separate source of knowledge (Y.S. 1.7), treats it as being of secondary utility in developing the highest yogic intuition (Y.B. 1.48). The Advaita Vedānta of Śaṅkara treats Vedic statements as falling within the scope of śabda, which for him is an independent pramāṇa. However, unlike the Prabhākara school of Mīmāṃsā, and like the others, it regards assertive statements as being of the same status as injunctive statements; but here again knowledge through the pramāṇas is sublated in the highest intuition. Incidentally it will be noticed that all these schools of Sāṅkhya, Yoga and Advaita Vedānta, while utilizing and upholding reason and granting the validity of scripture, claim the possibility of an ultimate personal knowledge which relegates both inference and scripture to a lower status. The Sāṅkhya comes closest to upholding reason but since it finds that its metaphysics leads to the conclusion that all empirical and rational knowledge is the result of a confusion between puruṣa and buddhi, it has to rely on yoga to resolve this confusion.

There is another important distinction made with regard to the authority of the Vedas, which has to be briefly examined before we investigate the fact and/or nature of the Early Buddhist criticism of the authoritarian claims of the Vedic thinkers. We find in post-Buddhistic times a controversy in the orthodox schools as to whether the Vedas derived their authority from a personal authorship, human or divine (pauruṣeya), or from the lack of personal authorship (apauruṣeya). The Naiyāyikas deduced the reliability of the Veda from the omniscience and trustworthiness of a personal Being (Īśvara) who revealed it or from the reliability of the seers who uttered the Vedic statements. On the other hand the Mīmāṃsakas asserted the reliability of the Vedas on the grounds of their eternity and argued that it had no human authors or divine founders and hence it was not affected by the defects of an instrument of knowledge (kāraṇadoṣa). Since it dealt with matters which were unverifiable it could not be contradicted. The Advaita Vedānta agrees with the Mīmāṃsā in this matter though it affects a compromise with the personal (pauruṣeya) view in claiming that God resuscitates the Vedas at the beginning of each epoch. It would be pertinent to investigate whether the Buddhist criticisms have any bearing on this problem.

(258) The different senses of śabda and the different forms of authoritative knowledge claimed in the post-Buddhistic philosophical tradition make it possible for us to see that the argument from authority took the following forms at least in this tradition:

(1) The authority of Vedic scripture (a) as being eternal, flawless and irrefutable in that it has no personal author or authors, human or divine; (b) as being revealed by an omniscient and perfect Being; (c) as statements of reliable (wise and good) persons.
(2) The authority of tradition, strictly non-scriptural but associated with the Vedic tradition (smṛti, aitihya).
(3) The authority of non-Vedic traditions.
(4) The authority of any reliable person.

(259) We stated that of ten possible ways of claiming knowledge criticized by the Buddha (*v. supra*, 251) six had reference to the acceptance of authority. These six in their order of appearance are as follows: (1) anussavena, (2) paramparāya, (3) itikirāya, (4) piṭakasampadāya, (5) bhavyarūpatāya, (6) samaṇo no garu. The mention of anussava in the top of the list and the singling out of the anussavikā as the first class of thinkers, who found a religion on anussava, possibly betrays the importance which was attached to anussava as a source of knowledge at this time. When we find that anussava is used in reference to the Vedic tradition we are led to believe that according to Early Buddhism this tradition was accepted on anussava.

(260) If we make a preliminary classification of what the words appear to mean in terms of the forms of authoritative knowledge they have reference to, we may group them as follows for purposes of discussion: The authority of

(1) the Vedic tradition as accepted on anussava though this term is not restricted to this sense.
(2) tradition in general, not necessarily Vedic (paramparā-)
(3) scripture in general as a collection of sacred sayings or *dicta theologica* of a religious group (piṭaka-sampadā-)
(4) testimony of experts (bhavyarūpatā-, samaṇo no garu)
(5) report or hearsay (itikirā-)

Let us examine the respective claims and criticisms made.

(261) Anussava has been translated by Woodward as 'report' (G.S. II.200) and Miss Horner uses the same word very often in her translations of the term (M.L.S. II.199, 360, 400) but renders it on two

occasions by 'tradition' (M.L.S. III.6, 20). What is puzzling is that she has rendered the term as 'report' even where the Vedic tradition is clearly indicated by the word (M.L.S. II.360, 400). Now the word is certainly used in the sense of 'hearsay' or 'report' in certain popular contexts (J. IV.441) and this sense has even been given semi-technical recognition where it is said that Kāli is the 'chiefest among laywomen who believe on hearsay' (aggam upāsikānaṃ anussavappasannānaṃ, A. I.26) for she is said to have overheard a conversation that took place between two people about the excellence of the Buddha and his teaching and attained the rank of sotāpanna thereby (DPPN., 1.587).

(262) But this sense looks very odd and unsatisfactory when the reference is clearly to the Vedic tradition. The Vedic brahmins certainly did not accept the Vedic scriptures on the basis of report. When it was said that the anussavikā profess a religion on anussava and the brahmins of the Three Vedas are said to be doing this, it is surely not the case that they were propounding a religion on just hearsay but on the unquestioned authority of their religious texts traditionally handed down. The translation of anussava as 'tradition' seems to suit this context better than 'report'. But even 'tradition' does not seem to convey fully the meaning of the term as may be evident from examining another context (M. II.170).

(263) Here (Caṅkī Sutta) the Buddha is conversing with a brahmin student who has 'mastered the Vedic scriptures' (tevijjake pāvacane kataṃ). The latter wishes to know the Buddha's views on the claims of the brahmins 'who came absolutely to the conclusion that this alone is true and all else is false' (ekaṃsena niṭṭhaṃ gacchanti: idam eva saccam mogham aññaṃ, *loc. cit.*) in respect of that which is a 'scriptural statement or hymn' (mantapadaṃ, *loc. cit.*) of the ancient brahmins. The Buddha replies that neither the present brahmins nor their teachers nor their teachers' teachers up to several generations nor even the 'original seers who composed and uttered the hymns' (pubbakā isayo mantānaṃ kattāro mantānaṃ pavattāro, *loc. cit.*) claimed direct personal knowledge of the truth of their statements saying 'I know this, I see this: this alone is true, all else is false' (aham etaṃ jānāmi, aham etam passāmi idam eva saccam mogham aññaṃ, *loc. cit.*). In such circumstances, it was a 'blind tradition' (andhaveṇi, *loc. cit.*) and the faith (saddhā) of the brahmins in the categorical truth of these statements was 'baseless' (amūlikā). To this it is replied that 'the brahmins do not merely go by faith in this matter, they also go by

anussava' (na kho 'ttha ... brāhmaṇā saddhāya yeva payirupāsanti anussavā p'ettha payirupāsanti, *loc. cit.*). The significance of this reply is lost if anussava is translated by 'report' as Miss Horner does. It would seem from this context that the brahmins were claiming the absolute authority and validity of Vedic scripture not merely out of faith in a tradition but out of faith in a sacred, holy or revelational tradition. The brahmin's reply has the effect of saying that the brahmins revere (payirupāsanti) the Vedas not out of faith alone, but on the grounds of revelation as well.

(264) We may inquire whether anussava has such a meaning in the Vedic tradition. There is no doubt that in the Upaniṣads what was heard as Vedic teaching was considered divine (daivam) or holy (Bṛh. 1.4.17). But there is no attested instance of anu + √śru used in reference to the Vedas in the Vedas, Brāhmaṇas or the classical Upaniṣads. In early Vedic usage anu + √śru is used merely in the sense of 'hearing about' (anusuśrāva kaścana, A.V. 11.4.25d) but in an Upaniṣadic use the significance of the prefix anu is felt where it is said that 'one hears again' in one's dreams what one has heard in waking life (śrutam anuśṛṇoti, Praśna 4.5). By the time of the Yoga Sūtra of Patañjali 'anuśravika-' is however used in the sense in which śruta was used in the Upaniṣads to denote 'Vedic teaching' (*dṛṣṭānuśravika*viṣayavitṛṣṇasya vaśīkārasaṃjñā vairāgyam, Y.S. 1.15; *v.* Comy. gurumukhād anuśrūyata ityanuśravo vedaḥ) and after that anu + √śru has the connotation of 'hearing from the Vedic tradition'.[1] Monier Williams gives the following meanings for anu + √śru (*s.v.* Sanskrit-English Dictionary), 'to hear repeatedly, especially from a sacred authority; anu-śrava, Vedic tradition (acquired by repeated hearing); anu-śruta, handed down by Vedic tradition'.

(265) This shows that sometime before the Y.S. and probably during the time of Early Buddhism anussava had come to mean the 'sacred Vedic tradition'. The word was better fitted to convey the idea than just śruta- because of the force of the prefix anu- implying a repeated systematic handing down of a tradition (cp. gītam pavuttaṃ samihitaṃ tad *anu*gāyanti tad *anu*bhāsanti bhāsitam *anu*bhāsanti vācitam *anu*vācenti, D. I.241; M. II.169, 170). Now in what did the sacredness or authority of the Veda depend on for these pre-Buddhistic Vedic

[1] Cp. ṛco yajūṃsi sāmāni nirame yajñasiddhaye ... sādhyās tair ayajan devān ityevaṃ *anusuśruma*, Harivaṃsa, 1.1.38–40; *v.* Śrīmān Mahābhāratam Harivaṃsaparvan, Ed. E. Kinjawadekar, Poona, 1936, p. 6.

thinkers. Was it on 'the continuity (unbrokenness) of the tradition and the absence of a known personal author' (sampradāyāvicchede sati asmaryamānakartṛkatvāt) as the Mīmāṃsā contends according to the Naiyāyikas.[1] Certainly the continuity of the tradition had weight but it is unlikely that at this time the conception of the non-personal authorship of the Vedas was at all seriously entertained.

(266) The Vedas were undoubtedly considered to have been handed down by an unbroken succession of teachers right down to historical times and this continuity of the tradition is tacitly assumed or in part asserted in the Buddhist criticisms as well. If they were considered to be divine in character it was because they were derived from God Himself according to the Vedic thinkers of these times.

(267) According to the earliest account of the divine origin of the Vedas[2] they are produced by the sacrifice of the Cosmic Person (Puruṣa, RV. 10.90). At a time when monistic principles of explanation were current, the Vedas were produced from them. Thus the Vedas as well as even the original ṛṣis (ṛṣayaḥ prathamajāḥ) at times are derived from Skambha, the Ontological Framework (AV. 10.7.14) or Kāla, Time (AV. 19.54.3) or Vāk (vāgakṣaram ... vedānām mātā, Tait. Br. 2.8.8.5). But before long the origin of the Vedas is ascribed to a personal divine being, possibly due to the influence of the Puruṣa-sūkta; Prajāpati is very often credited with the task of creating it. Thus, Prajāpatiḥ Somaṃ rājānam asṛjata, taṃ trayo vedā anvasṛjyanta (Tait. Br. 2.3.10.1); Prājāpatyo vedaḥ (Tait. Br. 3.3.2.1). In the Ś.Br., too, it is he who creates the Veda (6.1.1.8). It is significant that Prajāpati is identified with Brahmā in the Brāhmaṇas: Prājāpatyo Brahmā (Tait. 3.3.8.3), Prājāpatyo vai Brahmā (Gopatha Uttarabhāga 3.18). It should also be noted that in the Brāhmaṇas, Brahmā is very intimately associated with the Three Vedas (yenevāmuṃ trayyai vidyāyai tejo rasam prāvṛhat tena Brahmā Brahmā bhavati, Kauś. Br. 6.11; atha kena brahmatvaṃ kriyata iti traiyyā vidyayeti bruyāt, Ait. Br. 5.33; atha kena brahmatvam (kriyate) ityanayā traiyyā vidyayeti ha brūyāt, Ś.Br. 11.5.8.7).

(268) When we come to the earliest phase of the Upaniṣads we find Prajāpati continuing in his rôle as creator of the Vedas (Ch. 4.17.1–2).

[1] Sarvadarśanasaṃgraha, Ed. V. S. Abhyankar, Poona, 1951, pp. 270–71.

[2] At RV. 7.66.11, however, the ṛc (ṛcam) is created (dadhuḥ) by the kings Varuṇa, Mitra and Āryaman.

He is also a teacher of religious students (Bṛh. 5.2.1, Ch. 8.7–12). This rôle is soon taken over by Brahmā who is represented as the creator as well as the first teacher of the Vedas. A fact that needs to be taken account of is that while the conceptions of Brahman (neut.) as well as Brahmā (masc.) are found in the Brāhmaṇas,[1] the essential identity of the two is shown in the Brāhmaṇas by the formula that 'Brahman became Brahmā on his own' (Brahma brahmābhavat svayam, Tait. Br. 3.12.9.3). This identity is important in observing the close affinity that subsists between the two especially in the early Upaniṣads. This identity has again possibly been influenced by the Puruṣa-sūkta. Thus it is said at Bṛh. 1.4.1 that in the beginning this world was Ātman alone in the form of a Person (puruṣavidhaḥ) and soon after (Bṛh. 1.4.10) that in the beginning the world was Brahman which knew Himself (with the thought) 'I am Brahmā'.

(269) It is this reality sometimes referred to as Brahman (neut.) and more often as Brahmā (masc.) who is the first teacher of the Vedas. We see in the list of successive teachers at Bṛh. 2.6.1–3 and again at Bṛh. 4.6.1. and 6.5.1–4 that the line is traced right up to Brahman (neut.) which is translated by Radhakrishnan, inconsistently with the grammar and consistently with the meaning as Brahmā (PU. p. 210). The Upaniṣads themselves are not consistent in this usage.[2] At Ch. 8.15 we find it expressly stated that Vedic knowledge comes from Brahmā (masc.) who discloses it to Prajāpati who in turn tells Manu who tells human beings (taddhaitad brahmā prājāpatye uvāca . . .). Even when in the Middle and Late Upaniṣads the personal conception of Brahmā (masc.) came to be sharply distinguished from Brahman (neut.), the importance of this personal conception of Brahmā as the first deliverer of the Vedas and the creator of the world was so great that the earlier idea was still retained. At Muṇḍaka 1.1.1 all knowledge is traced to Brahmā (masc.) the first born of the gods and the maker of the universe (brahmā devānām prathamaḥ sambabhūva viśvasya kartā . . .). Similarly at Śvet. 6.18 the ultimate source of all knowledge (i.e. Brahman (neut.)) (cp. Śvet. 1.7) creates Brahmā

[1] Keith, Ṛgveda Brāhmaṇas Translated, HOS., Vol. 25, p. 27.

[2] At Bṛh. 2.4.10 where the Vedas and Vedic literature are said to have been breathed forth by the Great Being (mahadbhūtam) and at Bṛh. 4.5.11 where the entire world is thus breathed forth the impersonal conception dominates but this is probably due to the agnostic non-dualistic metaphysical theory propounded here.

(masc.) and delivers the Vedas to him. We may, therefore, conclude from this that at some time after the period of the AV. and before the Middle Upaniṣads there was a strong belief that the Vedas were created or taught by an omniscient personal Being, who came to be identified with Brahmā; at this time the Vedas were considered to be a sacred tradition and its sanctity lay primarily in the fact that it was ultimately heard from and handed down by Brahmā (or Prajāpati who is identified with Brahmā) in an unbroken tradition. When anussava is thus used by the brahmins versed in the Vedas as represented in the Buddhist texts to refer to the ground on which the Vedic scriptures were accepted, it seems to signify that the authority and veracity of the scriptures lay in the fact that they have been systematically heard (anu-śruta) by each generation of teachers going right back to the teacher, namely the omniscient Brahmā himself (cp. sarvavid brahmā, Gopatha Br. Pūrvabhāga, 2.18).

(270) That the brahmins who upheld the Vedic and the Brāhmaṇic tradition did so on the grounds that the knowledge contained therein was derived from a superhuman source seems to be implied, though it is not actually stated as such, in a criticism that brahmins are supposed to have directed against the class of religious teachers to which the Buddha belonged. Subha, the brahmin student, is upholding the superiority of householders' (gahaṭṭha) life to that of the recluse (pabbajita) (M. II.197); this point of view is reminiscent of the earlier Pūrvamīmāṣsā thinkers who valued the three aims of life (trivarga) namely dharma, the practice of the ceremonial religion, artha the pursuit of wealth and kāma the pursuit of worldly pleasure and decried mokṣa or salvation as unattainable in this life. He speaks of five virtues which the brahmins are expected to cultivate, namely truth (saccaṃ), austerity (tapaṃ), religious practice (brahmacariyaṃ),[1] study (ajjhenaṃ) and generosity (cāgaṃ)—virtues which are all emphasized at Tait. Upaniṣad 1.9–11. The Buddha criticizes these ethical recommendations on the grounds that neither the brahmins nor their teachers up to several generations nor even the original seers claimed to know the consequences of practising these virtues after realizing the fact with their higher knowledge (abhiññā sacchikatvā)

[1] It is clear from the general context that brahmacariya- here means the practice of the ceremonial religion and not 'celibacy', cp. the Tait. Upaniṣad 1.9–11, where the importance of offspring (prajā), begetting (prajananaḥ) and procreation (prajātiḥ) and also the necessity of 'not cutting off the line of progeny' (prajātantum mā vyavacchetsīḥ) is stressed.

although the Buddha himself could do so. Subha is enraged at this and says that one of the senior brahmins, Pokkharasāti, was of the opinion that these recluses and brahmins who claim 'an adequate spiritual kind of knowledge and vision' (alamariyañāṇadassaṇavisesaṃ) which is superhuman (uttarimanussadhammā) are making an assertion that is ridiculous (hassakaṃ), worthless, empty and vain. For how can a *mere human* (manussabhūto) have such a kind of knowledge (M. II.200, 201). This statement that superhuman knowledge is not possible (netaṃ ṭhānaṃ vijjati, *loc. cit.*) for a mere human being and that the claim to such knowledge was ridiculous seems to imply or suggest by contrast that the knowledge of the Vedic and Brāhmaṇic tradition was not based on personal human claims to knowledge but on the fact that the tradition itself is inspired, revealed or was of a superhuman origin. If this interpretation is correct, we may conclude that the early Buddhists were aware of the brahmins' claim that at least the knowledge pertaining to matters of morality and religion in the Vedic tradition was of a superhuman or divine origin.

(271) The late word for 'revelation' in the Indian tradition namely śruti (P. suti) is found in one of the earliest books of the Pāli Canon, the Suttanipāta, but its usage is obscure and it does not seem to have a clear-cut sense of 'divine revelation' as opposed to 'human tradition' as defined later in the Mānavadharmaśāstra 2.10 (śrutis tu vedo vijñeyo dharmaśāstraṃ tu vai smṛtiḥ). The PTS. Dictionary gives the following meanings of the term as occurring at Sn. 839, 1078 (na diṭṭhiyā, na sutiyā, na ñāṇena): 'hearing, tradition, inspiration, knowledge of the Vedas' (*s.v.* suti) and at another place (*s.v.* ñāṇa), translates 'diṭṭhi, *suti*, ñāṇa' as 'doctrine, *revelation*, personal knowledge'. There is a pun on the word when we examine the context, which makes it possible for the word to be interpreted to mean 'the Buddhist tradition'. The commentarial explanation (Mahāniddesa, I.188) at least of the word in the negative form (assutiyā) certainly does not favour the meaning of 'revelation' or 'Vedic tradition'. It explains suti- as 'what is heard or learnt' and says that such hearing or learning is desirable (savanaṃ pi icchitabbaṃ) and is of two sorts, the hearing from other sources or traditions (parato ghoso) and the hearing of Buddhist texts (suttaṃ, geyyaṃ . . .). In the classical Upaniṣads the word śruti- occurs three times merely in the sense of the 'hearing of the ear' (Bṛh. 3.4.2; 4.3.27) or the 'hearing of the sound of the soul when one's ears are closed with one's hands' (Ch. 3.13.8). It cannot

therefore be argued that the word 'suti' means 'revelation' in the later sense of the term, though the meaning of 'Vedic tradition' cannot be ruled out entirely in translating the term at Sn. 839 and 1078 at least in the positive occurrence 'sutiyā'. The sense of 'Vedic tradition' or even 'revelation' may be attributed to suti- in certain contexts of the Suttanipāta, which are very much reminiscent of the use of the term to denote 'what was learnt from the Vedic tradition' in the Upaniṣadic uses. For instance, when it is said that "some claim salvation (suddhiṃ, *lit.* purification) by *suta*-" (sutenāpi vadanti suddhiṃ, Sn. 1079) the reference can very well be to 'the acceptance of the Vedic revelation' though it may also be interpreted as the (literal) hearing of the ātman as at Ch. 3.13.8 (*v. supra*, 71).

(272) One logical difference between the use of suta- or suti- on the one hand and of anussava- on the other is that the latter denotes fairly clearly a definite means of knowledge whereas in the uses of suta- (Skr. śruta-) and suti- (Skr. śruti-) in both the Upaniṣadic and Early Buddhist contexts, the distinction between śabda (= śruta) as a prameya or 'object of knowledge' and of śabda as a pramāṇa or a 'means of knowledge' can only be determined by studying these contexts.

(272A) Let us now advert our attention to the criticism of anussava as a means of knowledge in the Buddhist texts. We found three possible senses in which the word is used: (1) as used of the Vedic tradition the word could mean 'divine revelation', systematically handed down; (2) it could also have meant 'authoritative tradition' the source of its authority being not clearly perceived or defined—in this sense it could have meant any tradition including or other than the Vedic; (3) lastly, it could have meant a 'report' come from mouth to mouth (cp. J. I.158, which comments on the particle 'kira' used in statements conveying information received from 'hearsay', as anussavatthe nipāto, i.e. a particle in the sense of 'hearsay').

(273) In the Buddhist texts we find an indirect criticism of the claim that the Vedas constitute a divine revelation and a direct criticism that the Vedic tradition was authoritative.

(274) The indirect[1] crticism of the claim to revelation is met with in the Tevijja Sutta. Here it is said that none of the teachers of the Vedic

[1] The Buddha is here not primarily concerned with criticizing the authority of the Vedic tradition but the claims made about the nature of Brahmā and the way of fellowship with him.

tradition, not even the original seers have had a direct knowledge or vision of Brahmā. They have not claimed to have 'seen Brahmā face to face' (Brahmā sakkhidiṭṭho, D. I.238) and they did not say, 'we know this, we see this (namely) where, in which direction and in which place Brahmā is' (mayaṃ etaṃ jānama mayaṃ etaṃ passāma yattha va brahmā yena va brahmā yahiṃ va brahmā ti, D. I.239).

(275) Radhakrishnan concludes from examining this Sutta that the 'Buddha does not like the idea of basing the reality of Brahman on Vedic authority, for when once we admit the evidence of revelation there is no end to it' (IP. I. p. 467). This conclusion appears to be strictly unwarranted by the context, which makes it clear that the Buddha is merely denying that the knowledge of/or about Brahmā in the Vedic tradition is not based on a direct vision or revelation of Brahmā at all, whatever the views the Buddha may have had on the validity of revelation itself. The Buddha does not *prima facie* appear to be averse to the 'idea of basing the reality of Brahman on Vedic authority' provided a valid claim to a real, personal knowledge of Brahmā was made by at least one of the teachers, on whom this tradition was based. The criticism made here is that the Vedic tradition as such is not, and cannot claim to be, a revelation. It is not a denial of the possibility of revelation altogether, though of course, the admission of such a possibility would be incompatible with the non-theistic character of Buddhism.

(276) We have already referred to the direct criticism of the Caṅkī Sutta (*v. supra*, 263) where the Buddha criticizes the claims of the brahmins to the absolute and exclusive authority and validity of scripture (mantapadaṃ) on the grounds that none of the seers claimed direct personal knowledge of its truth. This is in fact an express denial that the Vedic seers or their successors were experts whose testimony could be trusted in regard to what they said, by virtue of the fact that they themselves did not claim expert personal knowledge of the validity of what they asserted. This denial of any special insight to the seers was tantamount to a denial that they were competent persons (āpta-) whose testimony could be accepted.

(277) That the brahmins whom the Buddha converses with, are not the most orthodox brahmins of the Vedic tradition, has been the contention of Thomas[1] partly following Oldenberg.[2] We, on the

[1] *History of Buddhist Thought*, pp. 82–91.

[2] *Die Lehre der Upanishaden und die Anfänge des Buddhismus*, pp. 283 ff.

contrary, are maintaining that Early Buddhism was acquainted with the most orthodox Brāhmaṇic literature of the main Vedic schools (caraṇas)[1] in criticizing one of its most treasured conceptions, namely the sacred authority of the Vedic tradition. Since it would strictly fall outside the scope of our inquiry to examine the evidence that would go to prove the acquaintance that Buddhism shows of the main stream of the Vedic and Brāhmaṇic tradition and since this criticism affects our main contention in this Chapter, we have briefly indicated in an Appendix (*v.* Appendix I) how we differ from Thomas in his evaluation of the Tevijja Sutta made in the light of his presuppositions.

(278) The general criticism of anussava as a valid means of knowledge is such that it could apply to any of the three meanings, which we ascribed to the term, namely divine revelation, authoritative tradition and report. The Buddha says: 'There are five things which have a twofold result in this life. What five? (Belief based on) faith, likes, *anussava*, superficial reflection and approval of a theory thought about . . .; even if I hear something on the profoundest revelation (tradition or report) (svānussutaṃ) that may be empty, hollow and false, while what I do not hear on the profoundest revelation (tradition or report) may be factual (bhūtam), true and not otherwise. It is not proper (na alaṃ) for an intelligent person, safeguarding the truth to come categorically (ekaṃsena) to the conclusion in this matter that this alone is true and whatever else is false'.[2] At this, his interlocutor asks: 'To what extent, Gotama, is there safeguarding of the truth. To what extent does one safeguard the truth, we question Gotama on the safeguarding of truth?'[3] The Buddha replies: 'If a person has heard (from a revelation, tradition or report) then in saying "this is what I have heard" (from a revelation, tradition or report), he safeguards the

[1] *v.* Wijesekera, 'A Pali Reference to Brāhmaṇa-Caraṇa-s' in *Adyar Library Bulletin*, Vol. 20, Parts 3–4, pp. 294–309.

[2] Pañca kho ime . . . dhammā diṭṭhe va dhamme dvidhā vipākā. Katame pañca? Saddhā, ruci, anussavo, ākāraparivitakho, diṭṭhinijjhānakkhanti . . . Api ca svānussutaṃ yeva hoti tañca hoti rittaṃ tuccham musā; no ce pi svānussutam, tañca hoti bhūtaṃ tucchaṃ anaññathā . . . Saccam anurakkhatā . . . viññunā purisena nālam ettha ekaṃsena niṭṭhaṃ gantum: idam eva saccaṃ mogham aññan ti. M. II.170, 1.

[3] Kittāvatā pana, bho Gotama, saccānurakkhanā hoti? Kittāvatā saccaṃ anurakkhati? Saccānurakkhanaṃ mayam bhavantaṃ Gotamaṃ pucchāmā ti. *Loc. cit.*

truth, so long as he does not as yet come categorically to the conclusion that it alone is true and whatever else is false.'[1]

(279) We find here the Buddha asserting that a belief based on anussava can have the twofold result of turning out to be either true or false. Even if the assertion be from the most reliable revelation, tradition or report (anussava), there is no guarantee that it is true and it may very well be false. The right attitude to take is to suspend judgment regarding the truth of the assertion or proposition thus heard and say that 'I have heard p from anussava- but I do not claim to know p since p may be false!' This is clearly a rejection of revelation, tradition or report as a pramāṇa or a valid means of knowledge. For the truth or falsity of such a statement is to be judged by factors other than that of its claim to be the most reliable or authoritative revelation, tradition or report (svānussutam). The criticism also seems to presuppose that it is possible to determine the veracity of all the assertions by other means than that of revelation, etc., in so far as it is stated that what is accepted as reliable may prove to be in fact true or false. At the same time it should be noted that there is no rejection of revelation, tradition or report as being necessarily false since the possibility of truth is not ruled out. The attitude recommended towards these propositions bears some similarity to that of the Sceptics (amarāvikkhepikā) who likewise suspended judgment when faced with propositions, which may be true or false but differs radically from it, in view of the possibility, positively entertained, of knowing whether these propositions were in fact true or false *in this life itself* (note *diṭṭheva dhamme* dvidhā vipākā).

(280) In the Sandaka Sutta there is a criticism of religion based on anussava which throws a little more light as to why anussava was regarded as unsatisfactory as a means of knowledge. Here the speaker is Ānanda but he is supposed to be reporting[2] what the Buddha himself has declared (tena bhagavatā . . . akkhātā, M. I.518, 521). The second of the religions which are unsatisfactory but not necessarily false is said to be one based on anussava. It is said: 'Herein a certain religious teacher is a Traditionalist (anussaviko) who holds to the truth of

[1] Anussavo ce pi . . . purisassa hoti, evam me anussavo ti vadaṃ saccaṃ anurakkhati, na tveva tāva ekaṃsena niṭṭhaṃ gacchati: idameva saccaṃ mogham aññan ti. *Loc. cit.*

[2] Not in the sense that he is alleged to be reporting every Sutta which begins with the words, evaṃ me sutaṃ.

anussava (anussava-sacco) and preaches a doctrine according to anussava, according to what is traditionally handed down (itihaitihaparamparāya), according to the authority of scripture (piṭaka sampadāya). Now a teacher who is a Traditionalist and holds to the truth of anussava would have well-remembered it (sussataṃ pi hoti) or ill-remembered it (dussataṃ) and it would be true (tathā pi hoti) and it would be false (aññathā). On this an intelligent person reflects thus—this venerable teacher is a Traditionalist . . . so seeing that his religion is unsatisfactory (anassāsikaṃ) he loses interest and leaves it'.[1]

(281) We find here a good reason why an assertion that was handed down as a revelation, tradition or report was held to be untrustworthy. For even assuming that its origins were reliable it may be well-remembered (sussutam = Skr. su-smṛtam) or ill-remembered and the lapses of memory on the part of people transmitting a revelational or authoritative tradition or report can seriously affect the content of it so that what was originally a true proposition may in the course of time be so badly distorted as to make it false or unreliable.

(282) It is not so clear as to what is meant by 'tathāpi hoti aññathāpi hoti'. Miss Horner's translation 'he is both right and wrong' (M.L.S. II.200) is grammatically unjustifiable for satthuno (genitive case) cannot obviously be the subject of hoti. The subject of hoti is that which is sussatam and dussatam, namely the tradition (understood). Now aññathā (*lit.* otherwise) is an adverbial usage and its opposite anaññathā functions adjectivally and means 'true', e.g. taṃ ca hoti bhūtaṃ tacchaṃ *anaññathā* (M. II.170). Aññathā therefore may be presumed to mean 'false' while tathā would appear to mean the opposite from the context, namely 'true'. This usage is found elsewhere as well; taṃ tatheva hoti no aññathā, i.e. all of it would certainly be true and not false, D. III.135. So in this context the sentence would mean that 'the tradition (anussava) would be true as well as false'. But it would be self-contradictory to say that a tradition is true or false in the same sense at the same time. Although there may be a conception of partial truth (paccekasacca, *v. infra.* 599–601) in the Buddhist texts, it is unlikely that what is being said, is that every

[1] . . . idh' ekacco satthā anussaviko hoti anussavasacco, so anussavena itihaitihaparamparāya piṭakasampadāya dhammaṃ deseti. Anussavikassa kho pana . . . satthuno anussavasaccassa sussatampi hoti dussatampi hoti, tathā pi hoti aññathā pi hoti. Tatra viññū puriso iti paṭisañcikkhati: Ayaṃ kho bhavaṃ satthā anussaviko . . . So anassāsikam idaṃ brahmacariyan ti iti viditvā tasmā brahmacariyā nibbijja pakkamati. M. I.520.

tradition is partially true or has some truth in it, and is partially false and has some falsity in it as well. On this interpretation all traditions and reports would have some truth in them. It seems even to tally with the explanation as to why a religion based on anussava is criticized only as being 'unsatisfactory' (anassāsikaṃ) and not a 'false religion' (abrahmacariyakaṃ) since there is an element of truth in it.

(283) But this explanation does not seem to be probable since it contradicts what was already said in the Caṅkī Sutta (*v. supra*, 278) where it was pointed out that even the profoundest tradition (revelation or report) may turn out to be entirely false. The statement can be interpreted to mean either '(a tradition) is (partly) true and (partly) false' or '(a tradition) is (sometimes) true and (sometimes) false'. The first of these two interpretations is not different in meaning from the above. The second is to be preferred since it confirms what was already said in the Caṅkī Sutta. On this interpretation a revelation, tradition or report though 'well-remembered' may be false and though 'ill-remembered' may be true since there are four alternative possibilities.

1. sussataṃ tathā
2. sussataṃ aññathā
3. dussataṃtathā
4. dussataṃ aññathā

So what is probably meant is that a tradition (revelation or report) may be well-remembered or ill-remembered, and even if well-remembered, it may be true or false, for the reliability in the transmission of a tradition is no guarantee of its intrinsic truth.

(284) Still, a fact to be considered is that in this Sutta a religion based on anussava is criticized as being unsatisfactory rather than as being false. The reason for this would become clear if we note the fact that the 'religions' that are condemned as false are (1) Materialism (M. I.515), (2) a religion denying moral values (i.e. that there is no puñña or pāpa, M. I.516), (3) a religion denying moral responsibility (i.e. there is no cause—hetu—for moral degeneration, regeneration or salvation (M. I.517), and (4) a religion denying freewill (akiriyāvāda, M. I.517-8), It would seem that the four religions deemed to be unsatisfactory and not necessarily false would not have the defects of the four false religions. This means that in this context anussava could not have referred to the traditions of the Materialists or of any of the other three false religions. Therefore judging from the context the religion based on anussava here would have been one which, in

some sense, asserted survival, the reality of moral values, moral responsibility and freewill. On the other hand it is clear that when anussava was used in reference to a specific tradition it was almost invariably the Vedic tradition (M. II.170, 211). Now quite independently of the Buddhist texts we know that the Vedic and Brāhmaṇic religion at this time sponsored a belief in survival, had a code of ethics and a conception of moral reward and retribution. Although the Buddha criticizes the ancient seers (pubbakā isayo) for their lack of knowledge, he has the highest regard for them as virtuous men (isayo pubbakā āsuṃ saññatattā tapassino, i.e. the ancient seers were restrained ascetics, Sn. 284 ff.). The brahmins are likewise in the Buddhist texts represented as saying of the Buddha that he upholds kamma and freewill and does not desire evil for the brahmin race (samaṇo Gotamo kammavādī kiriyavādī apāpapurekkhāro brahmaññāya pajāya D. I.115, M. II.167). There is no bitterness or open antagonism towards the Vedic tradition nor a downright condemnation of it.[1] The evidence points to the fact that the Buddhists were more opposed to the Materialists than to the Vedic tradition and that the Buddhist criticism of the Vedic tradition is of a different character from that of the Materialists.

(285) The Materialist condemnation of the Vedic tradition, as we have shown above, was absolute. According to them the authors of the Vedas were both utterly ignorant as well as vicious; they are called 'buffoons, knaves and demons'[2] (*v. supra*, 121) but the Buddhists held that the original seers who were the authors of the Vedas merely lacked a special insight (abhiññā) but did not doubt their honesty or virtue (sīlaṃ ca ajjavaṃ . . . avaṇṇayuṃ, i.e. they praised virtue and rectitude, Sn. 292). The Materialists categorically repudiated the Vedas as false (anṛta), self-contradictory (vyāghāta) and repetitious (punarukta). Among the false beliefs taught in the Vedic tradition the Materialists would point to the belief in sacrifices, in a soul, in survival, in moral values and in moral retribution. The Buddhists on the other hand seemed to have held that the traditional beliefs of the Vedas were not wholly false. They criticized the Vedic conception of the sacrifice and denied the concept of a soul but agreed with the Vedas in asserting survival, moral values and moral retribution which are among the

[1] *v.* Oldenberg, *Buddha*, Tr. Hoey, London, 1882, pp. 170 ff.

[2] Trayo vedasya kartāro *bhaṇḍa-dhūrta-niśācarāḥ*, Sarvadarśanasaṃgraha, p. 14.

beliefs which formed part of the right philosophy of life (sammādiṭṭhi) as defined at M. III.72.[1]

(286) Even the Buddhist criticism of the institution of the sacrifice is not on the same level with that of the Materialists. The Materialists saw nothing but deception and fraud in the brahmanical conception of the sacrifice and would eschew the word yajña from their vocabulary altogether. The Buddhists while condemning the elaborate brahman sacrifices of the time as wasteful and immoral in that they involved a waste of effort and of valuable resources as well as the killing of animals (D. I.141), was not averse to the simple sacrificial offerings of the earliest brahmins who killed no animals for the occasion (Sn. 245) and made their offerings in good faith (dhammena). It was probably such sacrifices where there was no slaughter of animals that the Arahants could approach (nirārambhaṃ yaññam upasankamanti arahanto, i.e. the Arahants attend sacrifices in which there is no slaughter, A. II.43, S. I.76). We find Buddhism interpreting yañña at its best to be the highest religious life as advocated in Buddhism (Katamo yañño ... mahapphalataro ca mahānisaṃsataro ca ...? D. I.147 ff.) just as much as the Upaniṣads attempt to reinterpret yajña as the religious life (atha yad yajña ity ācakṣate brahmacaryaṃ eva tat, i.e. now what people call the sacrifice is just this religious life, Ch. 8.5.1). The significant difference, apart from the difference in the conception of the religious life, is that the Upaniṣads as part of the Vedic tradition generally did not directly attack yajña and are careful even when advocating ahiṃsā to make the single exception of the sacrifice (ahiṃsan sarvabhūtānyanyatra tīrthebhyaḥ, i.e. showing compassion to all creatures except at the sacrificial grounds, Ch. 8.15.1). The reason for this exception is obvious. To deny the sacrifice was to deny the authority of the injunctive assertions of the Veda and to deny the sacred authority of the Vedic tradition itself. This the Buddha did but the Upaniṣads never dared to do; however much of their speculations may have been at variance with orthodoxy.

(287) Just as much as the Materialists show the Veda to be contradictory the Buddhist texts too tend to show up the contradictions of the Brahmanical literature, placing the statements in the mouths of the

[1] 'There is (value in) alms, sacrifice and prayer, there is consequence and result of good and evil actions, etc.' (atthi dinnaṃ, atthi yiṭṭaṃ, atthi hutaṃ, atthi sukaṭadukkaṭānaṃ kammānam phalaṃ vipāko ...).

brahmins themselves (e.g. brāhmaṇā nānāmagge paññapenti, i.e. the brahmins propose diverse paths—to salvation, D. I.237). But sometimes when this is done, the Buddha agrees with one of the points of view expressed by the brahmins. Two brahmin students, both of whom have mastered the Vedas came to the Buddha and confess that there is a dispute (vivāda) between them as to whether one is a brahmin by birth (jātiyā brāhmaṇo hoti Bhāradvājo iti bhāsati, Sn. 596) or by virtue of one's duties (ahaṃ ca kammaṇā brūmi, *loc. cit.*). The Buddha agrees with the latter point of view (kammaṇā brāhmaṇo hoti, Sn. 650). Whether it was part of the intention of these citations to expose the contradictions of the Brahmanical literature, is not clear but there is not much reason to doubt that they were genuine contradictions actually found in the Brāhmaṇical literature. For example in the Vajrasūcikā Upaniṣad of the Sāma Veda where it is debated as to what makes a brahmin, two of the points of view put forward, both of which are criticized, are the very ones put forward by the two brahmin students above (tarhi jātir brāhmaṇa iti cet tan na, 5 and tarhi karma brāhmaṇa iti cet tan na, 7).

(288) We thus see that while the Materialists proclaimed the utter falsity and self-contradictory nature of the Vedic literature the Buddhist criticism of the Vedic tradition was different. Buddhism undoubtedly undermined the authority of Vedic scriptures in denouncing the institution of the sacrifice, thus questioning the authority of the Vedic injunctions. It also found on epistemological grounds that the statements of any tradition may be true or false and cannot be accepted on the authority of the tradition, however sacred it may be, but it actually found on examination that some of the Vedic teachings were in fact true and acceptable unlike the Materialists, who condemned them all.

(289) Let us look at the Buddhist criticisms of the Vedic tradition in the light of the later claims which we have outlined above (*v. supra*, 253–257), made on behalf of this tradition by the orthodox schools. The main Buddhist criticism was that the authors of the Vedas or their successors did not have any special insight nor did they admit seeing directly the truth of their assertions and claim infallibility for them. The denial that the seers had a direct vision and knowledge of Brahmā was also tantamount to a denial that the Vedic tradition could claim to have been derived from Brahmā. Now both these criticisms are of a pauruṣeya-theory, which was advocated later by the Nyāya-Vaiśeṣika only out of all the orthodox schools. We have already

stated the evidence which seemed to indicate how in the Brāhmaṇic and Early Upaniṣadic tradition, Vedic knowledge was deemed to be derived directly from a divine omniscient being, namely Prajāpati or Brahmā. At the same time there seems to have arisen about this time the belief that the original seers had a special intuitive knowledge of the Vedic dharma. This is apparent from Yāska's statement: sākṣātkṛtadharmānaḥ ṛṣayo babhūvuḥ, i.e. the seers had a direct personal knowledge of dharma, Nirukta, 1.20. It is this notion which the Nyāya utilizes to define the competency of the seers when it bases Vedic authority on the testimony of experts (āptāḥ): kim punar āptānāṃ prāmāṇyam, sākṣātkṛtadharmatā bhūtadayā yathābhūtārtha-chikyāpayiṣā iti,[1] i.e. wherein lies the validity of experts—(it lies in) the fact that they have a direct knowledge of dharma, compassion for beings and a desire to speak the truth. It seems to have been this very notion which was the main target of the criticism of the Buddhists who granted the honesty and trustworthiness of the seers but denied any special knowledge to them.

(290) It is very likely that in the pre-Buddhistic and pre-Materialistic phase of the Vedic tradition there was no clearly formulated theory of the basis of Vedic authority although belief in Vedic authority was undoubtedly present and it is natural that clear-cut theories should begin to emerge only after this authority was questioned, as it was, by the heterodox schools. Judging from the material, the pauruṣeya theory would seem to have had strong potentialities at this time. But it is retained only by a school or schools, which may be considered the least orthodox and the least concerned about knowledge based on authority because of its preoccupation with logic and its emphasis on reason. There seems to be more than one reason for this but one of the factors, why the pauruṣeya-theory was not generally favoured, may be the criticisms of this theory on the part of the Buddhists.

(291) The Pūrva-Mīmāṃsā which represents the views of the most orthodox brahmins who pre-eminently valued Vedic dharma gives up the pauruṣeya-theory altogether (M.S. 1.8.27) and bases the authority of the Vedas on the novel theory of the eternity of words (M.S. 1.7 ff.) and the very absence of a personal author. The theory that the truth or falsity of Vedic injunctions cannot be verified by any

[1] Vātsyāyana, Nyāyabhāṣyam, Ānanda Āśrama Series No. 91, p. 145 on N.S. 2.1.68 (2.1.69, SBH. Edition).

of the other means of knowledge available to humans (M.S. 1.4) also appears to meet an objection implied in the Buddhist criticism that the assertion of a tradition may be true or false. The Buddhist point of view assumes and entails the possibility that the assertions of a tradition or revelation can be verified by other means of knowledge available to us. For otherwise they cannot turn out to be true or false. The Pūrva-Mīmāṃsā appears to meet this objection when it safeguards Vedic propositions against the possibility of error at the cost of making them unverifiable.

(292) Whether the Pūrva-Mīmāṃsā is actually trying to meet the criticisms of Buddhism, it is in fact difficult to say with any degree of certitude. We cannot also fully agree with Radhakrishnan when he says that the Mīmāṃsā Sūtra 'may belong to the period immediately after the rise of Buddhism' (IP., II, p. 376, fn. 1) merely because Kumārila's interpretation of M.S. 1.3.5 and 6 constitutes a criticism of the authoritativeness of the statements of the Buddha. Nevertheless the apparent attempt to meet the Buddhist criticisms by propounding quite a novel theory cannot be entirely ignored, especially when taken in the light of Kumārila's observations. While the Nyāya and Vaiśeṣika, if they were originally atheistic, would have propounded the pauruṣeya-theory in the sense of the competency of the human Vedic seers, Bādarāyaṇa the author of the Brahmasūtra has been credited with the perpetuation of the other form of the pauruṣeya-theory that the Vedas sprang from the personal Brahmā at the beginning of creation (*v.* Muir, *op. cit.*, p. 208). Since Jaimini was acquainted with Bādarāyaṇa, whom he refers to by name in no less than five places[1] in the M.S. (1.1.5; 5.2.19; 6.1.8; 10.8.44; 11.1.63) and with whose views he generally agrees, there is little reason to think that he was ill-acquainted with the worth of the pauruṣeya-theory when he decided to reject it, owing to its vulnerability.

(293) There is one criticism however which does not seem to have been met by any of the apologists on behalf of the infallibility of the Vedas. From the time of the Brāhmaṇas it was generally assumed that the seers were not the authors or composers of the Vedas, which they saw by some supernatural insight or vision (*v. supra*, 13). The Buddhists not only denied any higher insight (abhiññā, the term for extrasensory perception in Buddhism) on the part of the seers but

[1] *v.* Radhakrishnan, *Indian Philosophy*, Vol. II, p. 376, fn. 1.

quite emphatically stated that the hymns were *composed* by them. The original seers (pubbakā isayo) are constantly described as 'the makers and the utterers of the hymns' (mantānaṃ kattāro mantānaṃ pavattāro, D. I.242, M. II.169) even though it is seemingly admitted that they practised tapas (isayo pubbakā . . . tapassino, Sn. 284). With the emergence of the conception of the eternity of the Vedas, it could not possibly have been held that the seers composed them, for even if they were *de facto* composing them, they were giving utterance to something that was eternal (*v.* the argument that a word is the same even if it is uttered several times or by several persons, M.S. 1.6.19.20). The brahmin interlocutors concur with the Buddha in regard to the criticisms made. This is undoubtedly due partly to the fact that what is reported is not a live discussion with real brahmin opponents but a Buddhist version of it. But it is of significance that, as Muir has shown, after a careful sifting of the evidence that 'the Vedic ṛṣis themselves . . . do not seem to have had any idea, either of their hymns being uncreated or derived from the eternal Brahmā or of their being infallible' (*op. cit.*, III, p. 283). The Vedic seers claim to make (√kṛ), compose (√takṣ), produce (√jan) (*op. cit.*, p. 232 ff.) and we may add utter (*avadan*nṛtāni . . . RV. 1.179.2; cp. P. pavattāro) the hymns but do not claim to see them, although Radhakrishnan says with no historical justification 'that the ṛṣi of the Vedic hymns calls himself not so much the composer of the hymns as the seer of them' (IP. I. p. 128). Even the Vedic Anukramaṇi-s speak of the ṛṣis as the authors of the hymns (yasya vākyaṃ sa ṛṣiḥ) as Muir (*op. cit.*, p. 85), following Colebrooke[1] had already pointed out. It is only later that it is urged that they 'see the Veda by means of an extrasensory perception' (atīndriyārthadraṣṭāraḥ ṛṣayaḥ . . ., Vedārthaprakāśa on Taittiriya Saṃhitā, quoted *ibid.*). The Buddhist criticisms therefore appear to be realistic in so far as they were made in the light of the objective facts as they saw them.

(294) As we saw above, the term anussavikā (Traditionalists) was not exclusively used in reference to the teachers of the Vedic tradition, although when it came to a matter of criticizing a specific tradition it was more often than not the Vedic tradition that was being assailed. This shows that despite the presence of other traditions the Vedic tradition was the most influential and all attention is focused on questioning its authority. Two of the other terms used in the criticism

[1] *Miscellaneous Essays*, Vol. I, p. 12.

G

of the various forms of traditional authority, namely paramparā- and piṭakasampadā- are also actually used in close association with the Vedic tradition (brāhmaṇānaṃ purāṇam mantapadaṃ itihaitiha-*paraṃparāya piṭakasampadāya*, M. II.169; anussavena itihaitiha-paramparāya dhammaṃ deseti, M. I.520[1]). The word paramparā- means a 'series or a succession' (*s.v.* PTS. Dictionary) and the Buddha compares the generations of Vedic teachers to a string of blind men (andhaveṇi)[2] clinging to one behind the other in succession (paramparāsattā, D. I.239, M. II.170). Paramparā can also denote the 'unbroken succession of the teaching' rather than of the teachers, an interpretation which would fit in better with the meaning of itihaitihaparamparāya (i.e. according to the successively handed down teaching) which would be equivalent to Skr. aitihyapāramparyayā (*v.* Vṛtti on Pāṇini 5.4.23, upadesapāramparye aitihyam, Böhtlinck, Pāṇini's acht Bücher Grammatischer Regeln, Band I, p. 342). There is, however, no basic difference in the two meanings and paramparā- as denoting the 'unbroken succession of the teaching or teachers' is undoubtedly one of the important factors which counted for the authoritativeness of the tradition as is always recognized (cp. sampradāyāvicchede sati . . . i.e. in the absence of a break in the tradition, S.D.S., p. 127).

(295) Though paramparā thus occurs in connection with the Vedic tradition, the fact that it is used in distinction to that of anussava as a means of knowledge, quite apart from the meaning of the word itself which has no intrinsic connection with the Vedas, is a sufficient indication that what is criticized at A. I.189 and A. II.191 (mā anussavena, mā paramparāya . . .) is the acceptance of a tradition in general on the grounds that it has been successively handed down or the belief in a teacher on the grounds that he belongs to a successive line of teachers, handing down a tradition (cp. Comy., paramparākathāya mā gaṇhittha, do not accept on the grounds of a traditional teaching, AA. II.305). In this connection it is important to remember that Buddhism refers

[1] Here there is no verbal mention of the Vedic tradition but as we have shown by an analysis of this context, it is the Vedic tradition that the author of the text had primarily in mind.

[2] There is some confusion as to whether the second word of this compound is veṇi=string or veṇu=bamboo. Andhaveṇūpamam (D. I.239) or andhavenūpamaṃ (v.l). can be decompounded as either veṇi+upamam or venu+upamam but the v. l. andhaveṇumaññe (M. II, 170, fn. 3) can only be veṇu=bamboo, succession=Skr. vaṃsaḥ, used of the line of teachers at Bṛh. 2.6.1; 4.6.1; 6.5.1.

to 'the Vedas of the Samaṇas as much as to the Vedas of the Brāhmaṇas'.[1]

(296) Today, it may appear strange as to why anyone should accept an assertion merely because it is in a tradition. But in the context of Ancient India, we must not forget that the antiquity of a continuous tradition was itself a criterion in favour of its acceptance. This was probably the reason why the Jains and later even the Buddhists vied with each other in claiming the antiquity of their respective traditions over all others.

(297) The next kind of knowledge based on authority which is criticized is said to be due to 'itikirā(f)' (itikirāya, Nd. I.360, 400, 482, Nd. II.108) which has been translated as 'hearsay' (Woodward, G.S. II.200; *s.v.* PTS. Dictionary). There is a variant reading 'itikiriyāya' which is sometimes preferred by the editors (Poussin and Thomas) to 'itikirāya' (Nd. I.400, ed. Poussin and Thomas; cp. Nd. II.108, ed. Stede). The Niddesa represents a later stratum within the Canon itself, as it is a commentary on two sections of the Suttanipāta and the form itikiriyāya is either due to an attempt to 'correct' itikirāya on the misunderstanding that the nominal base is itikiriyā- or is the result of an attempt to form an abstract noun, viz. *itikirya-> itikiriya- which by contamination with kiriyā gives itikiriyāya for the instrumental case. The earlier form itikirāya is certainly to be preferred as the more authentic reading. Now there seems to be some correspondence in usage between itikira- and itihaitiha- (cp. mā paramparāya mā itikirāya mā piṭakasampadāya, A. I.189 with itihītiha (v. l. itihitiha) paramparāya piṭakasampadāya, M. I.520, II.169). The latter is formed by the base (particle) iti with the addition of the particles -ha and -kira both of which are used in introducing anecdotal material. Itiha also occurs in the texts in introducing a supposedly historical fact (D. I.1, M. I.151) or a legendary circumstance (M. I.331). But this usage is not consistent, for it often occurs as a connective translated as 'in this way' (M. I.168). The negative anītiha (*v.* l. anitiha) is in fact semantically the negative not of itiha but of itihītiha and is used to denote 'what is not based on hearsay or tradition'. Thus the Buddha is said to have preached 'a religion not based on itiha' (brahmacariyaṃ anītihaṃ ... adesayi so Bhagavā, A. II.26). An elder is said to have attained and realized 'the dhamma which is not based on itiha' (dhammo anītiho, Th. I.331). Again, the Buddha is said to proclaim 'a dhamma

[1] *Vedāni* viceyya kevalāni, *samaṇānaṃ yāni-p'atthi brāhmaṇānaṃ*, Sn. 529.

which is not based on itiha, knowing which in this life itself ...' (kittayissāmi dhammaṃ diṭṭhe dhamme anītihaṃ yaṃ viditvā ... Sn. 1053) one would transcend the world.

(298) In contrast to this is the use of itihaitiha always in reference to the Vedic religion (Sn. 1084, M. I.520, II.169, S. I.154). At Sn. 1053, a brahmin student tells the Buddha that what was taught him 'outside the religion of Gotama' (huraṃ Gotamasāsanā) was of the form '"so it has been" "so it will be", all of which is based on itiha and all of which increases speculation' (iccāsi iti bhavissati sabbaṃ taṃ itihītihaṃ sabbaṃ taṃ takkavaḍḍhanam). The contrast is between the means of knowledge in the Buddha's religion and the means of knowledge in the Brahmanical religion. The Buddha's religion is personally verifiable in this life (sacchikato sayaṃ, Th. I.331; diṭṭhe dhamme viditvā, Sn. 1053) and is not based on itiha while the Brahmanical religion is presumably not so, is based on itiha and is speculative.

(299) What is itiha? From the above analysis it would appear that it included the speculative material in the Brāhmaṇic religion pertaining to the religious life. Now we saw above that the Tait. Ār. distinguished between two kinds of material in tradition namely scripture (smṛti) and traditional instruction (aitihya) (*v. supra*, 67). The very use of smṛti rather than śruti to denote the main textual tradition is perhaps an indication of the antiquity of this usage[1] and shows that √smṛ and √śru were indiscriminately employed in reference to scripture at this time. (Note a similar confusion in the Pāli texts—dussataṃ = du-smṛtaṃ and sussataṃ = su-smṛtaṃ of anussavikā = anu-śrav-ika-, √śru at M. I.520.) That part of the tradition which was not classifiable under smṛti seems to have been listed under aitihya. Now aitihya is an abstract noun, formed from itiha- according to Pāṇini's rule 5.4.2 (ananta-āvasatha-itiha-bheṣajaññyaḥ) and the fact that he thought the function of the word was worth explaining is perhaps an index to the antiquity of the conception of aitihya, which is defined in the Vṛtti as 'ityeṣa nipātasamudāye upadeśapāramparye aitihyam' (*v. supra*, 294). So aitihya is the basis for the belief in the validity of 'traditional instruction' which may have comprehended all the ancillary sciences of the Vedas including the legendary lore and the speculative theories of the Brahmanical tradition. When the Suttanipāta (Sn. 1053) spoke

[1] Mishra, *History of Indian Philosophy*, I, p. 88, translates smṛti as 'memory' but it is unlikely that memory was distinguished from pratyakṣa at this time.

of itihītiha as constituting speculative theories of the form 'so it has been' (iccāsi = iti āsi) and 'so it will be' (iti bhavissati) the reference is probably to the cosmological and eschatological theories of the Brāhmaṇas and the Early Upaniṣads.

(300) Aitihya would have almost certainly included 'the legendary and historical lore' (itihāsa-purāṇam) part of which formed the material of the later Purāṇas. Itihāsa and purāṇam are mentioned as separate items at Bṛh. 2.4.10 but as a single item at Ch. 3.4.1, 2 (itihāsapurāṇaṃ). Later they are mentioned together as the fifth item of Vedic study (ātharvanaṃ caturthaṃ itihāsapurāṇam pañcamaṃ, Ch. 7.1.2, 4; 7.2.1; 7.7.1; itihāsaḥ is the fifth item though not specifically called the fifth even at Bṛh. 2.4.10). The Buddhist texts, too, always speak of itihāsa as the fifth item of Vedic studies (itihāsapañcamaṃ, D. I.88, A. I.163, III.223). It may be noticed that itihāsa is the first item after the three Vedas and the Ātharvanam and we may perhaps conjecture that all the Vedic branches of study from itihāsa[1] onwards were originally classified under aitihya, derived from itiha- used in introducing a legendary tale (*v. iti ha* āsa). With the expansion of the concept of śruti and the definition of the validity of smṛti in terms of śruti, aitihya would have shrunk in meaning until it came to denote a rumour of uncertain origin generally introduced with the words 'iti ha ūcuḥ'.[2] This is the sense in which the Nyāya knows of aitihya as a means of knowledge and which in the Nyāya Sūtra is not rejected but subsumed under anumāna or 'inference' (N.S. 2.2.1). For the Paurāṇikas, it was too precious a term and concept to be rejected as the validity of their literature depended on it. Thus they of all the schools regard aitihya as a separate source of knowledge.

(301) The Carakasaṃhitā on the other hand preserves the earlier wider meaning of aitihya. In fact it goes so far as to include the whole of scripture as a source of knowledge under aitihya alone, the sources of knowledge being perception (pratyakṣa) inference (anumāna),

[1] Śankara comments on itihāsapurānaṃ as bhāratapañcamānaṃ at Ch. 7.1.2, but on Bṛh. 2.4.10 he speaks of itihāsa as ūrvaśīpurūravaśoḥ samvādādir 'ūrvaśī hāpsarā ityādi brāhmaṇam eva (cp. Ś.Br. 11.5.1.1) and of purāṇam as asad vā idam agra āsid ityādi (cp. Ś.Br. 6.1.1.1). The difference reveals the bias in Śaṅkara's comments; on this *v.* B. Faddegon, 'The Catalogue of Sciences in the Chāndogya Upaniṣad' in Acta Orientalia, IV, 42–54.

[2] 'iti hocuḥ' ityanirdiṣṭapravaktṛkam pravādapāramparyam (Vātsyāyana Nyāyasūtrabhāsya, p. 93). Other definitions similar to this from Nyāya literature, *v.* B. Jhalakīkar, Nyāyakośa, *s.v.*

scripture (aitihya) and comparison (aupamya).[1] Aitihya is defined as 'consisting of reliable assertions of the Veda, etc.' (aitihyaṃnāma āptopadeśa vedādi, 3.8.6.33). The Epics distinguish aitihya and scripture (āgama) though it is difficult to see what exactly is meant by aitihya here.[2] It seems clear, therefore, that when the Buddhist texts spoke of Vedic theories and speculations being based on itihaitiha as contrasted with Buddhist theories which are anītiha, it was using the word in the earlier wider sense, according to which aitihya would have embraced all the Vedic learning other than the bare textual scriptural tradition.

(302) The Niddesa defines anītiham as 'na itihītihaṃ, na itikirāya, na paramparāya, na piṭakasampadāya, na takkahetu, na nayahetu, na ākāraparivitakkena, na diṭṭhinijjhānakkhantiyā, sāmaṃ sayaṃ abhiññātaṃ attapaccakkhaṃ dhammaṃ' (II.49). Likewise the positive form itihītiham is defined in identical language (itikiriyāya- *v.* l. itikirāya-paramparāya . . . na attapaccakkhaṃ dhammaṃ, Nd. II.108). The essence and point of this definition is that what is not itihītiham or in other words knowledge in Buddhism, is not derived from any of the authoritative criteria or from any kind of logical reflection or speculation, while it is claimed that Vedic knowledge is so derived. The criticism seems to be directed at the validity of the legendary and historical material as well as the speculative theories of the Brāhmaṇas, Āraṇyakas and possibly the Early Upaniṣads, all of which were probably classified under aitihya in the Brāhmaṇical tradition at this time.

(303) Although we find a certain correspondence in the usages of itikirā and itihaitiha it may be noticed that the Niddesa definitions do not identify the two. According to this definition itikirā as a means of knowledge is a sub-class of itihītiha. The latter denotes any kind of authoritative or reflective knowledge while the former refers to one specific kind of authoritative knowledge. On this analysis itikirā may at least mean 'hearsay or rumour' as a source of knowledge. This is the later sense of aitihya as found in the Nyāya or at most 'legendary history' as a source of knowledge, which was probably the sense in which the Paurāṇikas used the term. The particle kira- according to

[1] *v.* Carakasaṃhitā, 3.8.6.31–34.

[2] *v.* aitihyam anumānañ ca pratyakṣamapi cāgamaṃ, Rām. 5.87.23 (reference as given in the St Petersburg Dictionary, *s.v.* aitihyam); also in the Mahābhārata, *v.* Prasad, *History of Indian Epistemology*, p. 84.

the earlier and the later commentarial tradition is used to convey a 'report by hearsay' (kirasaddo anussavatthe, J. I.158, kirā ti anussavatthe nipāto, J. II.430, kirasaddo anussavane, PvA. 103; in all these instances anussava is used in the later sense of 'report'). But since the Niddesa as being a commentary within the Canon represents a later stratum within the Canon itself, it is difficult to say whether itikirā has the same meaning[1] in its possibly earlier context in the Aṅguttara Nikāya (it does not occur elsewhere in the Canon other than in the Niddesa). It remains a problem as to why itihītiha is not mentioned as a source of knowledge in the Aṅguttara list especially when the concept is often referred to and is known early (cp. Sn. 1053, 1084, etc.) in the Canon. Was it because at this time it was conceived to be identical with itikirā? Was it just an omission on the part of the author of this text or is it that he has analysed the subcategories within itihītiha as set forth in the Niddesa definition? Another curious fact is the omission of anussava in the Niddesa definitions. Was it because itikirā was identical with anussava at that time (*v. supra* definitions of kira at J. I.158 and II.430). The evidence is too meagre and it is futile to speculate.

(304) The next source of authoritative knowledge criticized is piṭakasampadā. This term appears to present no difficulty and it seems to mean the acceptance 'on the authority of the scriptural texts', presumably on the principle that whatever propositions agree with these texts are true and whatever disagree are false. But there seems to be a difference of opinion between the translator, the commentator and the PTS. Dictionary on the rendering of this term. The PTS. Dictionary knows of only two meanings of piṭaka (*s.v.*) namely (1) basket and (2) (fig.) a technical term for the three main divisions of the Pāli Canon and piṭakasampadā is rendered as 'according to the Piṭaka tradition or on the grounds of the authority of the Piṭaka' (*s.v.* sampadā, PTS. Dictionary). This means that the statement has reference only to the concept of authority within Buddhism since by piṭaka is to be understood only one of the Piṭakas or the three main collections of texts of the Theravāda and other Buddhists. Since, as we have seen, the word (piṭaka) is used in reference to the Vedic tradition (M. I.520, II.169), this interpretation is not correct as the word is employed to denote the collections of texts of other schools. The Buddhist texts are aware of the hymns (manta-) having been put

[1] The Comy. (AA. II.305) is not very helpful. It merely says acceptance on the grounds that 'it is so' (evaṃ kira etan ti).

together or collected (samihitaṃ, D. I.238; cp. Skr. saṃhitā) and refer to the Vedas of the Samaṇas as well (*v. supra*, 295); by piṭaka they seem to have meant such a collection of texts. This general sense of piṭaka in Buddhism should, therefore, be treated as prior to its later exclusive use of the term.

(305) Now, Woodward translates the term as 'on the proficiency of the collections' (G.S. II.200) but the commentary would favour 'according to the conformity with the texts' since it explains the term as acceptance 'on the ground that it agrees with the statements of our text' (amhākaṃ piṭakatantiyā saddhiṃ sametī ti, AA. II.305). Woodward's translation is admissible since sampadā can mean 'proficiency' (e.g. sīlasampadā, paññāsampadā) but the word may perhaps denote a characteristic of piṭaka (piṭakassa sampadā) and mean *lit.* 'the worth of the piṭaka' and therefore 'the authority of the piṭaka'. It is not unlikely that the Vedic brahmins and even the other schools at this time were in the habit of weighing the truth or falsity of propositions in the light of their conformity with their respective scriptures. In fact it is this same principle which is later recognized as a formal criterion for judging the value (i.e. the truth-value) of a statement in a traditional text (smṛti), namely by its conformity or disagreement with the śruti or revealed scripture.

(306) The other two forms of acceptance or authority in our interpretation fall under the category of the testimony of reliable persons or what was later accepted as āptopadeśa in the Nyāya school (*v.* āptopadeśaḥ śabdaḥ, N.S. I.1.7). It is said that one should not accept a proposition as true on the grounds of bhavyarūpatā- translated as 'because it fits becoming'[1] (G.S. II.200). This translation is obscure and the translator appears to have been trying to give an over literal rendering of bhavya- (from √bhū to be, become) and rūpa (having the nature of, fitting) but even so it is not strictly correct for bhavya- means 'ought to be or become' rather than 'becoming'. A strictly literal translation would be 'because of its having the nature of what ought to be'. A free rendering of this same sense would be 'because of its propriety or fittingness'. It would mean the acceptance of a proposition on the grounds of its being specifically *fitting* or appropriate to a context or situation. Ethical theorists have sometimes advocated

[1] Mrs Rhys Davids too quotes this approvingly, *v. Wayfarer's Words*, Vol. III, p. 1104.

'fittingness' as a criterion for the rightness of an action.[1] According to them, an action would be right if it is the appropriate or proper action in the situation. It is a notion that could be extended to the field of truth. This interpretation of bhavyarūpatā though possible is unlikely, for it is too abstract a conception for the sixth century BC and for Indian thought in general, which loves the concrete rather than the abstract. An alternative interpretation would be to regard bhavyarūpatā (propriety) as referring to the person from whom a proposition is accepted rather than to the proposition itself. In fact, quite often bhabba- (= bhavya-) in the sense of 'suitable or capable' qualifies persons rather than non-persons (e.g. bhabbā te antakiriyāya, It. 106; bhabbo dhammaṃ viññātuṃ, Ud. 49 but see bhabbarūpo, Ud. 79). This interpretation would also have the merit of being supported by the commentary (ayaṃ bhikkhu bhabbarūpo imassa kathaṃ gahetuṃ yuttaṃ, i.e. this monk is a capable person, one ought to accept his statement, AA. II.305). We may then translate the phrase as 'on the ground of the competence (or reliability) of the person'. This would be in effect the same as verbal testimony (āptopadeśa, āptavacana) as a means of knowledge, as recognized in the late Indian philosophical tradition.

(307) The next kind of authoritative knowledge is also of the same character. Woodward translates, samaṇo no garu, as 'out of respect for a recluse' (G.S. II.200). But the phrase as it stands admits of three slightly different renderings. We may translate it as 'our (no) recluse (samaṇo) is a respected teacher (garu)' or 'our recluse is esteemed[2] (garu)' or '(this) recluse is respected by us (no)'. The first two senses were probably not strictly distinguished from the last for elsewhere we find the statement: satthā no garu, satthugāravena ca mayaṃ vadema, i.e. our teacher is respected, we speak out of respect for the teacher, M. I.265. On the whole it would have meant the acceptance of a statement on the prestige-value of the person uttering it. The former (bhabbarūpatā) takes account of the intrinsic qualities or worth of the person, while the latter his prestige, which is quite a different thing. The distinction it may be noted is drawn in the Pāli texts. Thus it is urged that one may have a reputation as a good preacher of the dhamma (dhammakathika-) even though one may not be capable, when the audience happens to be foolish, while a capable preacher may

[1] P. H. Nowell Smith, *Ethics*, Penguin, 1954, pp. 120–1, 186–7.

[2] The word can mean 'teacher' or 'respected'.

not have the reputation of being a good preacher with the same audience (A. II.138).

(308) We have now discussed the several forms of knowledge based on authority mentioned in the list given in the Aṅguttara Nikāya. With the exception of anussava, which came in for detailed criticism as the form of authoritative knowledge *par excellence*, no reasons are given here or elsewhere as to why the other forms of knowledge based on authority were unsatisfactory or unacceptable. Perhaps we have to assume that the same reasons for which anussava was unsatisfactory apply to the rest, namely, that such assertions may turn out to be true or false and therefore there is no guarantee that they are true on the grounds on which they are accepted. Another reason is suggested by the Niddesa when it is said that the knowledge based on the various forms of authority and reasoning (*v. supra*, 259; *infra*, 314) is not 'personally realized and directly verified by oneself' (sāmaṃ sayaṃ abhiññātam attapaccakkhadhammaṃ, *loc. cit.*). Thus even if a belief based on authority is true, it is not the same as knowledge as defined and accepted in Buddhism and therefore it is not to be regarded as knowledge (*v. infra*, 714, 783).

(309) The Aṅguttara Nikāya list, which we have discussed cannot also be assumed to be exhaustive. We have already noticed that it appeared to omit itihītiha- unless (1) this was considered to be identical with itikirā, or (2) the list from itikirā to diṭṭhinijjhānakkhanti constituted an analysis of the categories within itihītiha as the Niddesa definition would seem to imply. There is a general antagonism to the acceptance of knowledge based on any kind of authority in the Pāli Nikāyas, especially external non-Buddhist sources of knowledge and this finds expression occasionally against other forms than those we have discussed. Thus when Saccaka in debate with the Buddha invokes the opinion of the majority (mahatī janatā, M. I.230) in favour of the truth of a belief that he holds, he is quietly rebuked with the remark that the belief of the majority has nothing to do with the truth of the thesis in question (kiṃ hi te . . . mahatī janatā karissati, iṅgha tvaṃ sakaṃ yeva vādaṃ nibbeṭhehi, i.e. what has the opinion of the majority to do here . . . try to extricate your own thesis, M. I.230).

(310) Another form which the criticism of the acceptance of authority has taken in Buddhism is perhaps the denial of omniscience. One of the religions criticized as unsatisfactory is that which is claimed to be based on the omniscience of the teacher. The claim to omniscience is defined

as follows: 'Herein a certain teacher claims infinite knowledge and vision as being omniscient and all-seeing (saying that) when he walks or stands still, when he is asleep or awake there is knowledge and vision present to him constantly and continually'[1] (M. I.519). This is criticized on the assumption that no person can be omniscient in this sense. The assumption is not that of the Theist, who would argue that God alone is omniscient but not any created being, since omniscience is denied of Brahmā as well. Brahmā is not omniscient (aññadatthudaso) despite what he and those who revere him believe, since there are some things that he does not know, which are known to the Buddha (D. I.17, 18, M. I.326–9). In fact even if the Ṛgvedic seers claimed a direct revelation from Brahmā, this lack of perfect knowledge on his part according to Buddhism would have constituted the Buddhist criticism of the complete veracity of this revelation. As for human omniscience, the criticism is not that there are certain things that a human teacher claiming omniscience does not know but that 'there is no recluse or brahmin who would know or see everything *all at once* . . . for such a thing is impossible' (natthi so samaṇo vā brāhmaṇo vā yo *sakideva* sabbañ ñassati sabbaṃ dakkhiti . . . n'etan ṭhānāṃ vijjati, M. II.127). It is said that the Buddha makes this observation with good reason (heturūpam . . . āha, saheturūpam . . . āha, *loc. cit.*) but the reason is not given anywhere in the Pāli texts, and far from it being expressly denied, the possibility is in fact indirectly granted that with the above qualification there can be a person, who can claim to be omniscient (Ye te . . . evam āhaṃsu: samaṇo Gotamo evam āha: natthi so samaṇo vā brāhmaṇo vā yo sabbaññū sabbadassāvī aparisesaṃ ñāṇadassanam paṭijānissati, n'etaṃ ṭhānan vijjatī ti na me te vuttavādino abbhācikkhanti ca pana mamṃ te asatā abhūtenā ti, i.e. those who say that the recluse Gotama denies that there can be a recluse or brahmin who would claim to be omniscient, all-seeing and having an infinite knowledge and vision, for such a thing is impossible, are not reporting me accurately and are accusing me of saying what is untrue and false, *loc. cit.*).

(311) The teacher who claims to be omniscient constantly and continually at all times whether asleep or awake is criticized on the grounds that his lack of omniscience would be evident from his actions. For instance he enters an empty house and receives no alms, a dog bites

[1] Idha . . . ekacco satthā sabbaññū sabbadassāvī aparisesaṃ ñāṇadassanaṃ paṭijānāti: carato ca me tiṭṭhato ca suttassa ca jāgarassa ca satataṃ samitaṃ ñāṇadassanaṃ paccupaṭṭhitaṃ.

him, he meets a fierce elephant, horse or bull, has to ask for the names of people, of villages or hamlets or to find his way. The text is aware that these criticisms can be met by the rejoinder (and this was probably the case) that all these eventualities were inevitable but foreseen (cp. suññam me agāraṃ pavisitabbaṃ ahosi, tena pāvisiṃ . . . i.e. I had to enter an empty house, therefore I entered, M. I.519). One of the religions thus criticized is undoubtedly Jainism; we are often told that the Nigaṇṭha Nātaputta claimed omniscience (M. II.31, A. III.74) and this, we know, was 'one of the fundamental dogmas of the Jainas' (*v.* Jacobi, Jaina Sūtras, Part II, SBE., Vol. 15, p. xvi). But as we have shown there were other claimants to omniscience at this time (*v. supra,* 196) and the above criticism is levelled against a type of religion rather than a specific one. What could have been the reason (hetu) that the author of the text (M. I.127) was thinking of when he denied the possibility of omniscience in the above sense but left the possibility open for someone to be omniscient in the tautological sense of having the potentiality of knowing anything but not knowing everything all at once (sakideva)? We can understand why the continuity of omniscience in all the states of the individual is not considered possible—no one would think that one can have knowledge when one is asleep (sutta-). But why is this further qualification made that one cannot know everything all at once? Buddhism makes much of the principle that the infinite cannot be grasped by a finite measure. It is said that 'there is no measure of the person who has attained the goal (i.e. Nirvāṇa)' (atthaṃ gatassa na pamāṇam atthi, Sn. 1076). A calculator (gaṇaka), accountant (muddikā) or 'statistician' (saṅkhāyaka) cannot measure the amount of the grains of sand in the Ganges or the water of the ocean, presumably considered infinite (S. IV.376). If omniscience was reckoned to consist in knowing an infinite set of propositions all at once, then this was not possible for a finite mind. And, perhaps, no objection was seen in principle to the possibility of a finite mind knowing any finite set of such propositions at any particular time. In any case a claim to omniscience in any sense was not to be accepted without examining the validity of such a claim, at least, negatively by the simple tests of common sense.

(312) We have dealt here with the Buddhist criticism of the argument from authority as found in traditions which Buddhism criticizes. We are still left with the problem of the rôle of authority within Buddhism, which we have considered in a later chapter (*v.* Ch. VIII).

CHAPTER V

THE ATTITUDE TO REASON

(313) In this Chapter we propose to examine the Buddhist attitude to reason, as employed by their opponents. This involves an investigation into the grounds on which the takkī (?) were criticized and this entails the inquiry as to who the takkī (D. I.16, etc.) or takkikā (Ud. 73) were. Were they a class of sophists who employed fallacious reasoning for destructive purposes merely to outwit their opponents in debate, without having any theories of their own? Or were they thinkers, who made a rational defence of their theories or even rational metaphysicians, who founded speculative theories on the basis of reason? Or is the word takkī (or takkikā) used in a wider sense to include and refer to both these classes of people? We shall be concerned primarily with the examination of the conception of takka- and the Buddhist criticism of it.

(314) In the list from the Aṅguttara Nikāya, claims to knowledge made on ten grounds in all are criticized as unsatisfactory (*v. supra*, 251). Six had reference to claims to knowledge on the basis of some kind of authority and these we dealt with in the previous chapter. The remaining four are claims to knowledge on the basis of some kind of reasoning or reflection. This appears to be in agreement with the Buddha's contention that he does not belong to the class of teachers who are reasoners (takkī) and speculators (vīmaṃsī), who base their knowledge on reasoning and speculation. The four grounds of knowledge condemned were:

(1) takka-hetu
(2) naya-hetu
(3) ākāra-parivitakkena
(4) diṭṭhi-nijjhāna-kkhantiyā

(315) Just as anussava played a predominant rôle in the list of six, takka- seems to be the keyword here. The commentary explains takka-hetu as 'takka-gāheṇa' (AA. II.305), which may be translated as either 'by comprehending reasons' or 'by adhering to logic'. But

gāheṇa is not the semantical equivalent of hetu and a more literal translation would be 'on the grounds of takka' since hetu means (1) cause, reason, condition or (2) suitability (*s.v.* PTS. Dictionary) in the Pāli Canon and in this context it would probably mean 'reason' or 'ground'. This is in fact the earlier meaning[1] of the term in the Upaniṣads, e.g. etasya *hetor* vyānam evodgītham upāsīta, i.e. for this reason one should meditate on the diffused breath as Udgītha (Ch. 1.3.5). But in this context it could mean not just 'ground' but even 'epistemological ground' (pramāṇa), a sense which is found in the Jain Canonical scriptures (*v. supra,* 243) and is retained in the Carakasaṃhitā which defines the word as follows: hetur nāmopalabdhikāraṇam tatpratyakṣamanumānamaitihyam aupamyam ity ebhir hetubhir yad upalabhyate tattattvam, i.e. hetu is the cause of apprehension, viz. perception, inference, tradition and comparison and what is apprehended by these means is true, 3.8.6.25.

(316) As for takka (which we have provisionally rendered as 'reason' or 'logic') it does not make much sense however the word may be translated, unless we know who the takkī and takkikā were and what kind of takka they employed. We can do this by examining the specific theories associated with them with a view to determining the nature of their reasoning. In the Nyāya Sūtra, tarka- is an 'indirect proof' used to demolish the opponents' theory (N.S. 1.2.1) and this use has resulted in tarka- being regarded on the whole as 'mere destructive criticism'. However, it would be our endeavour to show that it had a positive connotation in the Nikāya usage, where it is used primarily to denote the reasoning that was employed to construct and defend metaphysical theories and perhaps meant the reasoning of sophists and dialecticians only in a secondary sense. Needless to say this goes against the assumptions of almost all scholars (*v. infra*) although it is necessary to add that Schayer had noticed a more positive use of tarka- in the scholastic period: 'In der Epoche der scholastischen Synthese wurde diese Typ des mittelbaren Beweises als *tarka* bezeichnet mit ausdrücklicher Hervorhebung, dass die Aufgabe des *tarka* nicht bloss die negative Kritik (*vitaṇḍā, dūṣanā*) des Gegners, sondern die positive Begrundung der eigenen These ist.'[2]

[1] The later uses recorded exclusively denote the sense of 'cause' (Śvet. 5.12; 6.5, 16, 17; Mait. 6.30).

[2] 'Altindishe Antizipationen der Aussagenlogik, Studien zur indischen Logik II' in *Extrait du Bulletin de l'Academie Polonaise des Sciences et des Lettres, Cracovic* 1933, p. 93.

(317) Scholars have often referred to the takkī as 'sophists' even using the word 'sceptics' interchangeably with it (*v. infra*, 319). It was probably Oldenberg who set the tone for using the word 'sophist' in this loose sense. He speaks of a 'species of Indian sophistic' (eine Art indischer Sophistik[1]) and compares it with the Greek sophistic movements, as though the two were exactly parallel developments: 'Certain phenomena which developed themselves in the busy bustle of the ascetic and philosophizing circles, may be described as a species of Indian sophistic; wherever a Socrates appears, sophists cannot fail to follow. The conditions under which this sophistic arose were quite similar to those which gave birth to their Greek counterpart . . . there followed Gorgiases and Protagorases and a whole host of ingenious, species, somewhat frivolous virtuosi, dealers in dialectic and rhetoric. In exactly the same way there came after the earnest thinkers of the masculine classical period of Brahmanical speculation a younger generation of dialecticians.'[2] When he goes on to enumerate these 'dialecticians' he seems to include almost all those thinkers mentioned in the Pāli Canon, who did not belong to the Vedic tradition, leaving out the Jains. The list is as follows, though we have to infer on the basis of his remarks whom probably Oldenberg had in mind when his references are not quite specific:

(a) '. . . the professed controversialists with an overweening materialist or sceptical air, who were not deficient in either the readiness or the vitality to show up all sides of the ideas of their great predecessors, to modify them, to turn them into their opposites' (*op. cit.*, p. 69). Is this a reference to the amarāvikkhepikā (Sceptics) who looked at all sides of a question without committing themselves to any point of view, though they were certainly not Materialists?

(b) Those who discussed about the 'eternity or transitoriness . . . infiniteness or finiteness of the world' (*loc. cit.*). This seems to be a reference to the diverse schools of religions which held these mutually opposed views referred to at Ud. 66–70, etc., although the list is far from complete.

(c) Then spring up the beginnings of a logical scepticism, the two doctrines, of which the fundamental propositions run, 'everything appears to me true' and 'everything appears to me untrue" (*loc. cit.*). This appears to be a reference not to 'the two doctrines', but to the

[1] *Buddha, Sein, Leben, Seine Lehre, Seine Gemeinde,* 13 Anflage, Stuttgart, 1959, p. 79.

[2] *Buddha,* Tr. W. Hoey, London, 1882, pp. 68-9.

three doctrines attributed to three schools or religious teachers who opposed each other, the third doctrine being 'some views appear to me true and some false' (ekaccaṃ me khamati ekaccaṃ me na khamati, M. I.498), which was opposed to both the above.

(d) 'Men wrangle over the existence of a world beyond, over the continuance after death'. This is either a reference to Ajita Kesakambali (D. I.55), the Materialist or to the Materialists in general (D. I.34, 35) or to certain mutually opposed theories such as 'taṃ jīvaṃ taṃ sarīraṃ' (the soul is the same as the body, D. I.160) and its opposite or 'hoti tathāgato parammaraṇā' (the soul exists after death, D. I.188) and the other three possibilities, interpreted on the assumption that 'tathāgato' here means 'soul' (DA. I.118).

(e) Makkhali Gosāla, who denies 'freewill' (D. I.53).

(f) Pūraṇa Kassapa, who denies 'moral government' (*loc. cit.*) (*v.* D. I.52).

(g) Saccaka, who boasts about his dialectical invincibility (M. I.227 ff).

(318) It is curious that although Oldenberg speaks of the above 'sophists' as 'dialecticians' and probably has the takkī in mind, not one of the above persons or classes of thinkers have expressly been called takkī in any specific context in the Pāli Canon. Besides, it could be seen that the word 'sophists' is used in a very wide and loose sense to include the moral sceptics (amarāvikkhepikā), the logical sceptics (c) dialecticians like Saccaka (g), Materialists (d) and others who held positive theories about the nature of man, morals or the universe (b and d). This loose use of the word 'sophist' is perpetuated by Mrs Rhys Davids, who also uses the word 'sceptic' almost as synonym of 'sophistical'. She says: 'There appears to have been parallel with the Absolutist beliefs, a good deal of scepticism current when Buddhism arose. . . . The most important of the sceptic schools was that of the Ājīvakas'.[1] She then goes on to speak of 'another sophistical school headed by Ajita of the Hair-garment' (*ibid.*, p. 86). In a later work she speaks of 'Sañjaya the sophist' and of Sariputta as being 'fed up with Sañjaya's sceptical sophisms'.[2]

(319) Vidyabhusana was one of the first to suggest not only that the term takkī in the Pāli Canon refers to sophists, but that they may have belonged to the Buddhist, Jain or the Brāhmaṇical communities: 'It is

[1] *Buddhism*, undated, Williams and Norgate, p. 85.
[2] *Śākya or Buddhist Origins*, p. 136.

not known whether these men were Buddhists, Jainas or Brahmaṇas, perhaps they were recruited from all communities. They were not logicians in the proper sense of the term but they appear to me to have been sophists, who indulged in quibble and casuistry.[1]' He speaks of the takkī as 'sophists' and 'argumentationists' and of the vīmaṃsī as 'casuists'. Keith quotes Vidyabhusana and apparently accepts his interpretation of takkī: 'The old Pāli texts ignore the names Nyāya or Vaiśeṣika: in the Brahmajāla Sutta we hear in lieu of them only of takkī, sophists and vīmaṃsī, casuists, and in the Udāna takkikas appear as in the Epic and Purāṇas.'[2]

(320) It seems desirable, therefore, that we have a clear idea of the meaning of the term 'sophist' before we apply it in the Indian context to refer to any of the thinkers mentioned in the Pāli Canon. Its meaning derives from its usage in reference to the itinerant teachers of Athens in the fifth century BC. These 'Gorgiases and Protagorases' as Oldenberg calls them were first and foremost sceptics who denied the objectivity of knowledge and therefore the possibility of knowledge. They were also the first to found schools for the study of rhetoric and reasoning. But since they did not believe that reasoning led to valid knowledge, they cultivated and taught for a fee the art of using fallacious reasoning merely for the sake of victory in debate or discussion.[3] Thus the Concise Oxford Dictionary defines a 'sophist' as an 'ancient Greek paid teacher of philosophy and rhetoric; captious or fallacious reasoner, quibbler' (*s.v.*) and 'sophism' as a 'false argument intended to deceive' (*s.v.*).

(321) The Greek sceptics were sophists, but how correct is it to say that the Indian sceptics, if we mean by the latter the amarāvikkhepikā of the Buddhist texts and the aṇṇāṇiā of the Jain texts, were also sophists? It is possible that they arrived at their scepticism by some kind of reasoning (*v. supra*, 151, 154). But what matters for the definition of 'sophist' and the use of the term to apply to them is whether they employed a fallacious reasoning merely for the sake of victory in debate without any scruples for truth.

(322) Now most of these sceptics shunned debate and we can be quite certain that the third school of sceptics did so (*v. supra*, 169) either because of their scepticism, which induced them to believe no

[1] *History of Indian Logic*, p. 227. [2] *Indian Logic and Atomism*, p. 13.
[3] Russell, *A History of Western Philosophy*, p. 94 ff.

particular thesis could be known to be either true or false or because they adopted scepticism out of intellectual cowardice with the intention of avoiding debate. The key term or phrase in this passage stated that their scepticism was due to 'fear or disgust at anuyoga' (anuyogabhayā anuyogaparijegucchā, D. I.26). Now anuyoga is a technical term in logic but as a technical term it is found in the combined form, niranuyojyānuyogaḥ (censuring the non-censurable), which is one of the occasions for rebuke (nigrahasthāna, N.S. 5.2.1) and is defined as consisting of rebuking a person who does not deserve rebuke (anigrahasthāne nigrahasthānābhiyogo, N.S. 5.2.23). This gives the possible meaning of 'censure' for anuyoga but the general word for censure would be niggaha (Skr. nigraha-) which is also found in the same stratum (cp. niggahito 'si, D. I.8) in at least a semi-technical sense. We should therefore have expected the author of this passage to have said niggaha-bhayā if he had the idea of censure in mind. There is another reason why the meaning of 'censure' would not suit this context. Niggaha- can only occur towards the end of a debate, but these sceptics were afraid of the very idea of joining issue in a debate and Prof. Rhys Davids considering the context translates the above phrase as 'fearing and abhorring the joinder of issue' (SBB., II, p. 39). This is in fact nearer the original etymology as well, as being formed from anu + √ yuj to join. The PTS. Dictionary does not record this unusual semi-technical use of anuyoga- but gives 'invitation, appeal, question' (*s.v.*) as possible meanings of the term. Now the verb anuyuñjati is used in the sense of 'asking a question, call to account, take to task' (Vin. II.79; *s.v.* PTS. Dictionary). This raises the question as to whether anuyoga could mean 'interrogation' by skilled dialecticians as the context demands. And this is precisely the sense in which the term is defined as a technical term of logic in the Caraka Saṃhitā, where it was said that 'anuyoga is an inquiry made about the substance or text of some science or other by a person versed in them, for the purpose of testing someone's knowledge, understanding or replies or (the inquiry) 'what is the cause' when one's opponent proposes (the thesis) 'the soul is eternal'': anuyogo nāma yattadvidyānāṃ tadvidyair eva sārdham tantre tantraikadeśe vā praśnaikadeśo vā jñānavijñānavacanaprativacanaparikṣārtham ādiśyate, yathā nityaḥ puruṣa iti pratijñāte yatparaḥ ko hetur ityāha so'nuyogaḥ 3.8.6.44. This is just what these sceptics feared, namely interrogation on the part of skilled dialecticians (paṇḍitā nipuṇā kataparappavādā vāḷavedhirūpā, D. I.26). The alternative definition gives a possible reason why they did not wish to make positive assertions, for it is when something is posited or a positive assertion is made (pratijñāte) that the others could then question them whereas if there were no truths that they could uphold, they were quite immune to the attacks of able controversialists owing to their very scepticism.

(323) Incidentally, we have already noticed two logical terms preserved in the Caraka Saṃhitā in older senses attested by the Jain or the Buddhist texts. One was 'hetu' in the sense of 'pramāṇa' (*v. supra*, 315) and the other is anuyoga. Keith has expressed the view that the variations in the meanings of logical terms in the Caraka Saṃhitā from that of the Nyāya Sūtra were due to the ignorance of the author of Caraka Saṃhitā of the standard terminology.[1] This is an unwarranted assumption for if this terminology is independently supported by the usages of the Buddhist or Jain texts, it shows not that the author of the Caraka Saṃhitā was ignorant of the meanings of these terms, but that these terms are from an earlier logical tradition not made use of by the author of the Nyāyasūtra, though the latter may have been aware of them and consciously rejected them.

(324) If, thus, the third school of sceptics clearly shunned debate altogether, the picture they present would be the very opposite of that of the Greek sceptic, who welcomed debate in order to prove the worth of his scepticism by disproving each and every thesis that came in his way. There is also no reason to think, as we have said, that the first two schools of Sceptics were in principle different from the third in this respect. The fact that the first school was said to be 'afraid of falsehood' (musāvādabhayā, D. I.25) showed that they had certain scruples for truth and they would therefore not try to denounce every theory that was put forward in debate merely because they did not believe in it. Besides these first three schools regarded the moral consequences of non-scepticism, for different reasons, to be a source of worry or vexation (vighāta-) and since they may have realized that 'vexation could result from debate' (vivāde sati vighāto, M. I.499) it is unlikely that they would have debated their scepticism at all. There is, however, one respect in which the outlook of these three schools of Scepticism may be compared with that of Protagoras, though not of

[1] 'Nor can any stress be laid on the variations from the Nyāya school; an unscientific exposition of this kind need reflect nothing more than the lack of knowledge of its author and sheds no light on the early history of the school', *op. cit.*, p. 13.

the later Greek Sceptics. We have shown that despite their moral scepticism at the intellectual level, they probably subscribed to the traditionally or conventionally accepted moral and religious practices. Now it is said that Protagoras in spite of his disbelief in objective truth 'was led to a defence of law and convention and traditional morality. While as we saw, he did not know whether the gods existed, he was sure they ought to be worshipped'.[1] The significant difference however was that the Indian Sceptic even regarded non-scepticism as a moral danger.

(325) We have tried to show that if takkī means 'sophist' then at least the three schools of Sceptics we spoke of above were not sophists and much of the confusion in calling them sophists seems to have sprung from the assumption that since the Greek sceptics were sophists, the Indian sceptics were probably the same.

(326) The case is, however, different with the school of Sañjaya who, we suggested, did engage in debate in defence of his scepticism (*v. supra*, 180). Among the propositions which he refused to declare were either true or false, was, hoti Tathāgato parammaraṇā (the Tathāgata exists after death) and its other three alternatives (D. I.27). These are among the very propositions the truth of which was said to have been hotly debated by various religious theorists at this time (*v.* Ud. 67). Could Sañjaya have been criticizing one of these theses at one time and an opposing thesis at another? Did he do so because he felt that the arguments against each of these alternatives were equally strong, though he did not discard the possibility that any one of them could be true? Or did he merely criticize these theories to display his dialectical skill, regardless of the cause of truth because he felt that truth was impossible in these matters? The context seems to favour on the whole the former interpretation. On both interpretations Sañjaya would have been using takka (tarka) merely to disprove his opponent's thesis—the sense in which the word is used in the Nyāya Sūtra (*v. supra*, 316). But if the latter interpretation was true he would come close to being the Indian counterpart of the Greek sceptic-sophist, with the difference that while the Greek scepticism was all embracing in scope Sañjaya's was probably limited to the range of transcendent propositions. Apart from the tentative character of this identification there is no reason to think that Sañjaya represented a

[1] Russell, *op. cit.*, p. 97.

widespread movement in Indian thought at this time. Even if our identification is correct, he seems to be the exception rather than the rule in the Indian context.

(327) Let us now examine the theories which Oldenberg thought constituted 'the beginnings of a logical scepticism', to see what their logical and epistemological foundations were. The reference is evidently to the three kinds of theories about 'views' (diṭṭhi) mentioned in the Dīghanakha Sutta and which are as follows:

(1) sabbam me khamati—I agree with every (view)

(2) sabbam me na khamati—I agree with no (view)

(3) ekaccam me khamati, ekaccam me na khamati—I agree with some (views) and disagree with other (views).

(328) It is said that 'those who firmly hold and dogmatically assert that any one of these theories is alone true and the others false' (imaṃ diṭṭhiṃ thāmasā parāmassa abhinivissa vohareyyaṃ: idameva saccaṃ mogham aññan ti (M. I.498) is likely to engage in contentious debate with their other two opponents (dvīhi assa viggaho, *loc. cit.*) resulting in 'dispute, vexation and worry' (viggahe sati vivādo, vivāde sati vighāto, vighāte sati vihesā, *loc. cit.*). The Buddha speaks well of the second point of view (i.e. 2) as tending towards dispassion (asarāgāya santike, *loc. cit.*) and lack of attachment, excitement, dogmatism and involvement (asaṃyogāya . . . anabhinandanāya . . . anajjhosānāya . . . anupādānāya santike, *loc. cit.*), whereas the first and the third views have the opposite qualities. Dīghanakha, his interlocutor, is exceedingly pleased at this, since it was his own view but the Buddha goes on to explain that holding the second view dogmatically and clinging to it is as bad as holding the other views.[1]

(329) A distinction appears to be drawn between two ways of holding view (2). The first is to hold dogmatically to this view with the readiness to defend it against its contrary and contradictory. This involves 'not giving it up as a view and the possibility of changing it for another' (tañ ca diṭṭhiṃ nappajahanti aññañ ca diṭṭhiṃ upādiyanti, M. I.398). The other way of holding (2) is to hold it non-dogmatically and disinterestedly 'giving it up as a view and with no possibility of changing it for another' (tañ c'eva diṭṭhiṃ pajahanti aññañ ca diṭṭhiṃ

[1] Yā ca kho me ayam diṭṭhi: sabbam me na khamatī ti, imañ ce ahaṃ diṭṭhiṃ . . . abhinivissa vohareyyaṃ . . . dvīhi me assa viggaho, i.e. if one dogmatically clings to this theory namely 'I do not agree with any view' he would be at loggerheads with two parties, M. I.499.

na upādiyanti, *loc. cit.*) as a result of which he does not enter into debate to defend any view (since he is disinterested in all views) and does not suffer the consequences of debate.

(330) If we call the former way of subscribing to view (2), 2(a) and the latter way 2(b) it would appear from the context that Dīghanakha is holding 2(a). This is evident from the introductory dialogue:

Dīghanakha: I hold the view that I disagree with every view (ahaṃ . . . evaṃdiṭṭhi: sabbaṃ me na khamatī ti, M. I.397).

Buddha: Do you agree with the view that you hold, namely that you disagree with every view (Yā . . . esā . . . diṭṭhi: sabbaṃ me na khamatīti, esā pi te diṭṭhi na khamatī ti, *loc. cit.*).

Dīghanakha: Even if I agree with this view, it is all the same (Esā ce me diṭṭhī . . . diṭṭhi khameyya, tam p'assa tādisameva, tam p'assa tādisam eva, *loc. cit.*).

(331) The purpose of Buddha's question, judging from the rest of the context, seems to be to elicit this information, although it gives the appearance of a dialectical trap in a paradox situation. Asserting 'I do not agree with any view' is a paradox situation of the same logical type as saying 'everything I say is false', which appears to be false if true and true if false. For if I agree with the view that 'I do not agree with any view' than I am agreeing with some view and my statement is false, whereas if I do not agree with the view that 'I do not agree with any view', then I am contradicting myself. Dīghanakha's reply, in fact, amounts to saying that even if he agrees with this view it still remains a fact that he does not agree with all other views. Since this is not followed up by an attempt to show that Dīghanakha is thereby making a false statement or is contradicting himself, the Buddha's rejoinder is not meant to be a criticism of Dīghanakha's point of view, but is apparently intended to elicit the information as to whether he is dogmatically holding to this theory, as he appears to be from the subsequent discussion. 2(b) on the other hand is the view that the Buddha speaks well of and which he ascribes to 'certain recluses and brahmins' (eke samaṇabrāhmaṇā, M. I.398).

(332) Who could these 'recluses and brahmins' be who subscribed to the view 'sabbam me na khamati', which among other things is said to be 'anupādānāya santike' (tending to the absence of involvement, M. I.498)? It is very probable that they were no others than those Sceptics (amarāvikkhepikā), who valued mental tranquillity, avoided debate and anything that causes vexation (vighāta, cp. D. I.25, 26)

and among whom at least one school (the second) is said to have regarded non-scepticism as an upādāna (involvement) of which they were afraid and with which they were disgusted (cp. *upādāna*-bhayā *upādāna*-parijegucchā, D. I.26 and an*upādānāya* santike, M. I.498). That the Buddhist attitude to the amarāvikkhepikā was on the whole a favourable one is also apparent from the place they receive in the Sandaka Sutta (M. I.520, 521), where the religion of these Sceptics was classified as one of the four unsatisfactory but not totally false religions. It also tends to confirm our supposition that the Sceptics, despite their intellectual scepticism had a conception of the moral and religious life.

(333) We said that 2(a) seems to be the theory that Dīghanakha himself held. Now, according to the commentary not only is Dīghanakha said to be a Materialist (uccheda-vādo = *lit.* annihilationist, but synonymous with 'Materialist' at this time) but 'sabbam me na khamati' is interpreted differently. 'Sabbam' is said to be 'all rebirths and conceptions, which do not please him' (sabbā me uppattiyo . . . paṭisandhiyo na khamanti, MA. III.204). Miss Horner disagreeing with this comment, says that 'Gotama, however, takes "all" in its literal sense' (M.L.S. II.176, fn. 6) but does not clarify what this literal sense was. She translates 'sabbam me na khamati' as 'all is not pleasing to me' (*loc. cit.*) but if we interpret 'all' here to mean just 'everything in the universe' or even as 'sense-data and thoughts' according to the definition of sabba- at S. IV.15, it is difficult to see the reason for conflict and debate between three people who held the views 'everything pleases me', 'nothing pleases me' and 'some things please me'. The context makes it evident that diṭṭhī (views) form the content of sabbaṃ for when Dīghanakha says 'sabbaṃ me na khamati', the Buddha asks 'esā pi te *diṭṭhi* na khamati' (*loc. cit.*) and it is replied 'esā me . . . *diṭṭhi* khameyya' (*loc. cit.*). From this we may presume that sabbaṃ here means 'all (diṭṭhi-s)'. The fact that the radical form of khamati is closely associated in usage with diṭṭhi (e.g. *diṭṭhi*-nijjhāna-*kkhan*ti, S. II.115; IV.139; A. I.189; II.191; M. II.170) lends support to our view. We may therefore translate the statement, sabbaṃ me na khamati, as we have done, as 'I approve of or agree with no (view)' and it is evident that Oldenberg himself took it in this sense, for otherwise he would not have seen here the 'beginnings of a logical scepticism'.

(334) It is a problem as to which school of thought Dīghanakha belonged. As a nihilist who disagreed with and denied every thesis that

was put forward by his opponents in debate, Dīghanakha, the paribbājaka,[1] (Dīghanakho paribbājako M. I.497) may have belonged to Sañjaya's school of paribbājakas, the only school of debating sceptics. The only historical connection that we can see, is that Dīghanakha was a nephew of Sāriputta (DPPN., *s.v.* Dīghanakha) and Sāriputta is presumed to have been an adherent of Sañjaya before he joined the Buddha. But this does not explain how tradition came to associate him with the Materialists and identify him as a member of that group. This commentarial identification of him as a Materialist is in fact confirmed by the text as well. In the course of the dialogue the Buddha tells Dīghanakha that he should regard 'the body which has form, is composed of the four primary elements and arises from father and mother (kāyo rūpī cātummahābhūtiko mātapettika-sambhavo, M. I.500) as not a soul (anattato samanupassitabbo, *loc. cit.*)'. The wording is unusual,[2] occurs rarely and is identical with the phraseology used to describe the first school of the Materialists (viz. attā rūpī cātummahābhūtiko mātāpettikasambhavo, D. I.34). It appears as if the Buddha was making a specific criticism of the Materialist theory. There is therefore reason to think that Dīghanakha was in fact a Materialist. As a nihilist Materialist, he may be identified with the school of nihilist Lokāyata, which denied the truth of every thesis (*v. supra*, 113). We do not know what kind of arguments they employed but if they were called takkī (and we have no evidence that they were) they would have employed takka for purely destructive criticism in order to pull down their opponents' theories.

(335) The opposite of Dīghanakha's view 'sabbaṃ me khamati' (I agree with every view) is also said to be held by a school of recluses and brahmins (eke samaṇabrāhmaṇā, *loc. cit.*). This point of view resembles, if it is not identical with the anekāntavāda of the Jains. According to this theory every view is true from some standpoint (naya) or other and in general[3] no view can be categorically false. The proposition 'S is P' (syādasti) as well as 'S is not P' (syānnāsti) can both be true according to different standpoints (*v. infra*, 589). This logic would entail the truth in some sense of all views. The doctrine of naya is mentioned in some of the early Jain sūtras (*v. supra*, 237) and it is not impossible that it was known, when the Pāli Nikāyas

[1] I.e. a wandering ascetic.

[2] The normal formula would have been rūpaṃ attato na samanupassitabbaṃ, vedanā . . . saññā, etc.

[3] The Jains did, however, have a conception of falsity (*v. infra* 589).

came to be composed. It seems to have also been a doctrine of the Trairāśika Ājīvikas (*v. supra*, 227). While the Sceptics (amarāvikkhepikā) disagree with every view, anekāntavāda represents the opposite point of view of agreeing with every view for some reason or other denying the Law of Contradiction or giving it a new meaning altogether (*v. infra*, 589, 590). Since there is good evidence for the existence of the Sceptics there is little reason to doubt the more or less contemporaneous existence of the opposing theory on the evidence of the Jain scriptures. The commentary is not helpful in identifying this view since it makes no direct comment on it, but it seems indirectly to suggest or assume that 'Sabbaṃ me khamati' is the eternalist view being the opposite of Dīghanakha's Materialist position while 'ekaccaṃ me khamati . . .' (I agree with some views) is said to be the semi-eternalist view. But this explanation is far-fetched and therefore inadmissible for had the compiler of this sutta been thinking of the eternalist or semi-eternalist views there is no reason why he should not have employed more direct and less ambiguous language and said 'sassataṃ (or sassata-diṭṭhi) me khamati' instead of 'sabbaṃ me khamati' and 'ekaccasassataṃ (or ekaccasassata-diṭṭhi) me khamati' instead of 'ekaccaṃ me khamati ekaccaṃ me na khamatī'.

(336) This relativism of the Jain would have been opposed in debate to the scepticism of Sañjaya, the nihilism of that branch of Lokāyata and the 'particularism'[1] of the others but their reasoning can hardly be called sophistical. With the possible but doubtful exception of Sañjaya, we do not find in Indian soil the Greek counterpart of the sceptic-sophist. The nihilist Lokāyatika, judging by the example of Jayarāśi, would have been too forthright in his condemnation of all theses to be adjudged a sceptic and in any case we know very little about the reasoning of this early school of nihilist Lokāyata for us to come to any positive conclusions.

(337) On the other hand there is a constant reference in Indian thought to vitaṇḍa and the vitaṇḍavādin. The vitaṇḍavādin is neither a sceptic nor a sophist though this latter term is often mistakenly employed in translating the term. He has no views of his own but merely indulges in eristic (*s.v.* Runes, Dictionary of Philosophy) for the purpose of securing victory in argument. The Nyāyasūtra defines vitaṇḍa as 'the

[1] I am using this word to denote those who held that some views were true (i.e. agreed with some views).

criticism of the proofs of the opposite side' (svapratipakṣasthāpanāhīno vitaṇḍā, 1.2.3) but the word has a derogatory connotation. In the Carakasaṃhitā it is defined as 'merely imputing faults to one's opponents' theory' (parapakṣe doṣavacanamātram eva, 3.8.6.20). It is a form of wrangling which is closely associated with, though strictly distinguished from, jalpa, defined in the N.S. as 'the defence (*lit.* proof) or attack of a proposition in the aforesaid manner by quibbles (chala), analogues (jāti) and other processes which deserve censure'.[1] The Carakasaṃhitā, on the other hand, defines jalpa as 'proving ones own thesis by one's own reasons and thereby discrediting the opposing thesis'.[2] The difference in the definitions probably show that there was no standard usage of these terms, but it can be seen that both texts use vitaṇḍā to denote mere attacks on the opposite side for the purpose of gaining victory in debate. Both jalpa and vitaṇḍā, which are unscrupulous and fallacious forms of reasoning, are recommended in the N.S. in dealing with opponents 'for safeguarding the interests of truth, just as fences of thorny boughs are used to protect the growth of seeds'[3] but this represents a late view after the Nyaya was accepted by orthodoxy.

(338) One of the earliest occurrences of the word vitaṇḍa, is in Pāṇini's Aṣṭādhyāyī (4.4.102). The word does not occur in the Pāli Nikāyas, but Buddhaghosa comments on lokāyata (D. I.88), lokāyatika- (S. II.77) and lokakkhāyika- (D. I.8) as *vitaṇḍa-* (*v. supra,* 57). But what was 'the art of casuistry' (vitaṇḍasattha, vitaṇḍavādasattha-) for Buddhaghosa, it must be remembered was 'the art of reasoning' (tarkaśāstra-) for Śaṅkara (*v. supra,* 54) and we cannot conclude from this that the brahmins were cultivating the art of casuistry at this time for any special reason. While Buddhaghosa associates this vitaṇḍasattha- with the brahmins, the Saddanīti associates it with the titthiyas (lokāyataṃ nāma ... titthiyasatthaṃ)[4] a word which has a wider connotation and at least includes the Samaṇas (*v.* nānātitthiyā samaṇabrāhmaṇā ... i.e. various recluses and brahmins who were heretics, Ud. 66). The examples given both by Buddhaghosa and Aggavaṃsa

[1] Yathoktopapannaś chalajātinigrahasthānasādhanopālambho jalpaḥ 1.2.2.

[2] Svapakṣam svahetubhiḥ sthāpayataḥ tatparapakṣamudbhāvayataḥ eṣa jalpaḥ, 3.8.6.20.

[3] Tattvādhyavasāyasaṃrakṣanārtham jalpavitaṇḍe vījaprarohasaṃrakṣanārtham kaṇṭakaśākhāvaraṇavat, 4.2.50.

[4] *v.* Saddanīti, *La Grammaire Palie D'Aggavaṃsa,* Ed. Helmer Smith, London, 1928, p. 361.

(*v.* SBB., II. p. 167 f.) are similar but it would be noticed that an argument pertaining to the creation of the world is placed on the same footing as an argument that the crow is white or the crane is black. We cannot on this evidence argue that there were vitaṇḍavādins at this time, but if we have reason to believe that the art of reason had been cultivated from the time of the early Upaniṣads, we have no reason to disbelieve that vitaṇḍavādins or casuists may have existed both among the Samaṇas and the brahmins at this time, if there is any independent evidence for their existence.

(339) We may therefore inquire whether there was a class of people, who may be called vitaṇḍavādins or casuists in as much as they were primarily interested in displaying their dialectical skill and defeating their opponents, regardless of the nature of the arguments used. Saccaka (*v.* (g), *supra,* 317) to some extent answers to this description. He is described as 'one who indulged in debate, a learned controversialist, who was held in high esteem by the common people' (bhassappavādako paṇḍitavādo sādhu sammato bahujanassa, M. I.227, 237). There is no reason to doubt that he was one 'who excelled in debate' (bhassappavādako, *s.v.* PTS. Dictionary, where it is explained as 'one who proposes disputation, one who is fond of debate and discussions') for otherwise his opponents would not have given him the credit for this. He is said to have held debates (vādena vādaṃ samārabhitā, M. I.250) with the six famous teachers Pūraṇa Kassapa, Makhali Gosāla, etc. The list includes Nigaṇṭha Nātaputta, although he is described as a follower of Nigaṇṭha (nigaṇṭha-putto, M. I.227, 237). It is implied that he defeated them in debate, Saccaka is made to say that when he joined them in debate, they evaded in one way or another (aññena aññaṃ paṭicari, M. I.250), shifted the topic of discussion (bahiddhā kathaṃ apanesi, *loc. cit.*) and showed signs of irritation, anger and displeasure. These are among the recognized 'occasions for censure' (nigrahasthāna, *v. infra*, 372) and their mention here implies that Saccaka was victorious in these debates. Saccaka boasts (or is represented as boasting) about his dialectical skill in magniloquent language.[1] This exaggerated picture of his dialectical attainments is however not justified by his actual performance, at least as reported by his opponents in the Cūla-Saccaka Sutta (M. L.227 ff.) for he falls a victim to a simple dialectical argument of the Buddha. Even if we call him a casuist because of his eagerness merely to display his dialectical skill, according

[1] M. I.227 *v.* Oldenberg, *Buddha,* Tr. Hoey, p. 70.

to the picture drawn of him, it is clear even from the presented version of the debate, that Saccaka had his own private convictions and tried to defend them with his own reasons. He holds the theory that the individual (purisapuggalo) is composed of five selves, the bodily self (rūpattā-Skr. rūpātmā, M. I.230), the hedonic self (vedanattā), the mental self (saññattā), the active self (saṅkhārattā) and the cognitive self (viññāṇattā) on the grounds that all activities including the possibility of moral behaviour depend on their substantial existence (*loc. cit.*). This theory bears some resemblance to the theory that the person (puruṣaḥ) is composed of five selves (ātmā) as propounded in the Taittirīya Upaniṣad (2.2.5). The concepts of the selves and their order is not identical, but the two theories are sufficiently similar to bear comparison as may be seen from the following:

Saccaka	*Taittirīya Upaniṣad*
rūpattā (has bodily form as the soul)	annarasamaya (-ātma)[1] (the soul consisting of the essence of food)
saṅkhārattā (has dispositions as the soul)	ātmā prāṇamayaḥ[2] (the soul consisting of organic activities)
saññattā (has ideation as the soul)	ātmā manomayaḥ (the soul consisting of the mind)
viññāṇattā (has cognition as the soul)	ātmā vijñānamayaḥ (the soul consisting of cognition)
vedanattā (has feeling as the soul)	ātmā ānandamayaḥ (the soul consisting of bliss)

Even the argument that the first ātman is composed of the essence of food since all life that dwells on the earth (prajāḥ . . . yāḥ kāś ca pṛthivīṃ śritāḥ, 2.3.1) depend on food (annād jāyante . . . annena vardhante, *loc. cit.*) is similar to Saccaka's argument that man has his body as ātman (rūpattā) because among other things all organic and sentient life (bījagāmabhūtagāma, M. I.230) grows to maturity in dependence on the earth (paṭhaviṃ nissāya, *loc. cit.*). If this Upaniṣadic teaching was not the source of Saccaka's inspiration and he was in fact a strict adherent of Nigaṇṭha's doctrine (*v.* DPPN., Vol. 2, *s.v.* Saccaka),

[1] Note that rūpa (bodily form) is described as 'formed of the four great elements and *thriving on gross food*' (cātummahābhūtiko *kabaliṅkārāhārabhakkho*, D. I.186), i.e. annamaya (formed of food).

[2] The saṅkhāra-s include 'in and out breathing' (assāsapassāsā . . . kāyasaṅkhāro, M. I.301), which is equivalent to prāṇa in the Upaniṣads (*v.* Bṛh. 3.9.26; Kaṭha, 2.2.5.).

then the closest teaching to the one that he propounds would be the theory of the five asti-kāyas (jīva, ākāśa, dharma, adharma, pudgala) all of which have a substantial existence, being dravyas,[1] although in that case only two of the astikāyas (i.e. jīva and pudgala) would in any way correspond with his five selves (i.e. with viññāṇa and rūpa respectively).[2] Whatever the origin of Saccaka's theory he seems anxious to defend it and therefore he cannot be called a casuist (vitaṇḍavādi-), who was merely interested in outwitting others in debate in order to display his dialectical skill.

(340) Another set of thinkers who appear *prima facie* to be vitaṇḍa-vādins are the recluses and brahmins, whom the third school of Sceptics (*v. supra*, 167) feared would engage them in debate. They were described as 'learned (paṇḍitā), subtle (nipuṇā), hairsplitters (vālavedhirūpā), who have mastered the doctrines of others (kata-parappavādā)[3] and who go about shattering (vobhindantā) with their intelligence (paññāgatena) the theories put forward (diṭṭhigatāni)' (D. I.26). The fact that they were called 'hairsplitters' who make it their business to study the theories of others in order to controvert them strongly suggests that they were a class of vitaṇḍavādins primarily interested in exhibiting their dialectical skill by defeating their opponents in debate.

(341) There seems to be an eye-witness's account of these 'recluses and brahmins' (samaṇabrāhmaṇā) in action at S.V.73, where Kuṇḍaliya tells the Buddha that he rests in parks (ārāmanisādi) and frequents assemblies (parisāvacaro) and that it is a habit of his to wander in the afternoon from park to park and from pleasaunce to pleasaunce where he sees (passāmi) certain recluses and brahmins (eke samaṇa-brāhmaṇe) holding debates (kathaṃ kathente), merely for the merit of defending their own theories (itivādapamokkhānisaṃsam eva) and of censuring (their opponents' theories) (upārambhānisaṃsaṃ).

(342) The only other place in the Nikāyas, where the two terms occur together is in the Alagaddūpama Sutta where it is said, te (i.e. ekacce moghapurisā) upārambhānisaṃsā c'eva dhammaṃ pariyāpunanti

[1] Hiriyanna, *Outlines of Indian Philosophy*, p. 161.

[2] Cp. Sakkāyadiṭṭhi (Sakkāya=sat kāya?=astikāya? *v.* Franke, *Dighanikayo*, p. 45; Geiger, *Pali Grammar*, para. 24; Kern, Toev. II 52; JRAS., 1894, p. 324.

[3] Prof. Rhys Davids has 'experienced in controversy' (SBB., II.38). The Comy. on M. I.176 gives both meanings, kataparappavāde te viññāta-parappavāde c'eva parehi saddhiṃ katavādaparicaye (MA. II.197).

itivādapamokkhānisaṃsā, which Miss Horner translates 'they master this dhamma simply for the advantage of reproaching others and for the advantage of gossiping' (M.L.S. I.171). Itivādapamokkhānisaṃsatthaṃ (A. II.26) has likewise been rendered by Woodward as 'concerned with a flood of gossip' (G.S. II.28). This sense is favoured by the PTS. Dictionary as well, which explains itivāda- (*s.v.*) as 'speaking so and so, talk, gossip' and itivādappamokkha- (*s.v.* pamokkha-) as 'pouring out gossip'. But this is a sense which does not at all suit the translation of the term vādapamokkhāya in the sentence, 'cara vādapamokkhāya' (D. I.8) where Prof. Rhys Davids following the Comy. and the demands of the context has translated the phrase as 'set to work to clear your views' (SBB., II.15) although in a footnote (fn. 3) he has suggested Gogerly's alternative rendering '(depart) that you may be freed from this disputation' on the grounds that the parallel passage at M. I.133 seems to support such a meaning. Prof. Rhys Davids calls this 'the only parallel passage' (*loc. cit.*) but in fact the word vādapamokkha- occurs elsewhere (A. II.9, S. V.73) and Gogerly's rendering certainly would not suit S. V.73, for these 'recluses and brahmins' could surely not have been discussing or debating (kathaṃ kathenti) 'for the advantage of being freed from discussion'.

(343) We would favour the commentarial explanation which is supported by the etymology of the word, the several contexts as well as by independent evidence. Commenting on itivādappamokkhānisaṃsā (M. I.133), it is said that it means 'for the advantage of (ānisaṃsā) defending (*lit.* freeing) one's theory (vādapamokkha-) in this manner (evaṃ)'.[1] This is further explained as 'when one's opponents (pare) raise objections (*lit.* impute defects, dose āropite) to one's own theory (sakavāde), then we shall remove those objections (*lit.* free it from that defect, taṃ dosaṃ mocessāma) in such and such a manner'.[2] Upārambhānisaṃsā is likewise explained as 'for the advantage of finding fault (*lit.* imputing defects, dosāropanānisaṃsā) with a theory of one's opponents (paresaṃ vāde)'.[3] So what is meant according to this explanation is that some people learn the Dhamma either for the mere sake of defending it against others' criticisms or for the sake of criticizing with its help the theories of others. And this is condemned,

[1] Evaṃ vādappamokkhānisaṃsā, MA. II.107.

[2] Parehi sakavāde dose āropite taṃ dosaṃ evañ ca evañ ca mocessāmā ti iminā ca kāraṇena pariyāpuṇantī ti attho, MA. II.107.

[3] Paresaṃ vāde dosāropanānisaṃsā, MA. II.106, 107.

for the Dhamma according to this Sutta is to be regarded as a plan of action and not as a theory to be clung to and pitted against other theories in debate either for the purposes of defending it or criticizing with its aid opposing theories. The moral that the Dhamma should not be studied purely out of a dialectical interest in it possibly reflects the intellectual climate of these times, when theories were being defended and attacked largely for the sake of displaying one's dialectical skill. It confirms the picture that we get from the statement of Kuṇḍaliya who reported that he saw recluses and brahmins in parks defending and attacking theories merely for the advantage of (ānisaṃsam eva) of such defence (itivādappamokkha-) and attack (upārambha-).

(344) According to the Nyāyasūtra (1.2.1) a debate (vāda) comprises 'defence and attack' (sādhana-upālambha), the defence of one's own theory by means of the genuine criteria of knowledge (pramāṇa) and the criticism of one's opponent's theory by means of indirect arguments (tarka). But when defence and attack become an end in itself merely for the sake of victory in debate and any means are employed for the purpose it is called jalpa (yathoktopapannaś chalajātinigrahasthāna-*sādhanopālambho* jalpaḥ, N.S. 1.2.3). The usage of this term in the Caraka Saṃhitā, as we saw above (*v. supra*, 337), was somewhat different. Here jalpa- and vitaṇḍā were not used in a derogatory sense and jalpa- was defined as proving one's own theory on its own grounds and vitaṇḍā as 'merely imputing faults to one's opponent's theory' (*parapakṣe doṣavacanam*ātram eva). One may compare this definition of vitaṇḍā with the Pāli commentarial definition of upārambha as *paresaṃ vāde doṣāropanam*, i.e. imputing defects to the theory of one's opponents. Now upālambha also occurs in the Caraka Saṃhitā as a technical term and is defined as 'the imputation of defect to the reason adduced' (upālambho nāma hetor doṣavacanam, 3.8.6.51) and this in the context of the debate would be very similar to vitaṇḍā as understood in both the Caraka Saṃhitā and the Nyāya Sūtra.

(345) From the above, we cannot fail to observe the identity in word and meaning between upārambha- as used in the Pāli passages in the context of the debate and upālambha as used in the Nyāyasūtra and as defined in the Caraka Saṃhitā (Skr. upālambha- > P. upārambha-, *v.* Geiger, Pali Literatur und Sprache, p. 60, section 45). It is also in sense not strictly distinguishable from vitaṇḍā as defined both in the Caraka Saṃhitā and the N.S. One can also observe a certain similarity in meaning between sādhana as employed in the N.S., jalpa as used in

the Caraka Saṃhitā and itivāda-ppamokkha- as used in the Pāli Nikāyas and as explained in the Comy. The difference is that while sādhana and jalpa are used in the positive sense of proving one's own thesis, itivādapamokkha- has a negative connotation of defending one's own theory against the defects imputed to it by one's opponents.

(346) Since these ardent dialecticians are said to have been primarily motivated by the advantage of (anisaṃsā) of successful defence or attack, it is not unlikely that at least some of them were vitaṇḍavādins in the later sense of the term but in the absence of any authentic samples of these debates and in our ignorance of the kind of reasoning employed by them we cannot adjudicate on this problem with any degree of certitude.

(347) The use of jalpa and vitaṇḍa in a non-derogatory sense in the Caraka Saṃhitā is, however, not without significance, since it probably harks back to a time when the dialectical devices of these debaters were not still recognized as casuistry and the distinction between good and bad reasoning was either not drawn or was very thin. Victory and defeat depended largely on the whims of the audience (pariṣad) and the decision would have varied greatly with the nature of the audience for some audiences are said to be learned (jñānavatī pariṣad, C.S. 3.8.6.13) and others foolish (mūḍhapariṣad, C.S., *loc. cit.*). The Caraka Saṃhitā speaks of the expedient of not debating further with a person who is anxious to continue a debate once the audience has shouted him down as having been vanquished.[1] It is obvious that the prejudices and beliefs of the audience played a large part in the decisions they gave. This at least appears to be the view of the Buddha, who recounts the following situations in which the decisions of the audience (parisā) need not be objective when it is acclaimed that someone is learned and victorious:

'A certain person

(1) suppresses an unrighteous theory (adhammikaṃ vādam) with an unrighteous theory (adhammikena vādena). This pleases an unrighteous audience (adhammikaṃ parisam rañjeti) which, with a loud uproar, acclaims him learned (uccāsaddā mahāsaddā hoti paṇḍito vata bho paṇḍito vata bho ti).

[1] Cp. sakṛd apihi parikṣepikaṃ nihitaṃ nihitaṃ āhur iti n'āsya yogaḥ kartavyaḥ, i.e. one should not endeavour (to continue to debate with) one who has been rejected even once on the grounds that he has been vanquished, C.S. 3.8.6.13.

(2) suppresses a righteous theory with an unrighteous theory. This pleases an unrighteous audience, which acclaims him learned.

(3) suppresses a partly righteous and partly unrighteous theory (dhammikañ ca vādaṃ adhammikañ ca vādaṃ) with an unrighteous theory. This pleases an unrighteous audience which acclaims him learned' (A. V.230).

(348) When victory depended on the decisions of a fickle audience, it would be natural that the reasoning would have been largely directed at winning it over by any dialectical device at the command of the debater rather than be aimed at unravelling the nature of truth. But with critical audiences and a growing knowledge of the nature of sophisms (chala, jāti, ahetu, vākyadoṣa, etc.) perhaps among this very class of people who cultivated this art, a time would have come when it was possible to distinguish good reasoning from fallacious reasoning. This time seems to be coeval with the composition of some of the Suttas since the Sandaka Sutta recognizes a difference between what is 'well-reasoned' (su-takkitaṃ) and 'ill-reasoned' (du-ttakkitaṃ) (M. I.520).

(349) This class of dialecticians called 'hairsplitters' (vāḷavedhirūpā) is restricted to the class of 'recluses and brahmins' (samaṇa-brāhmaṇā) in the first book of the Dīgha Nikāya (*v.* D. I.26, 162) but elsewhere the same description is used of a wider class of people (*v.* M. I.176; M. II.122, 123). In these contexts, it is said that there are 'certain learned *kṣatriyas, brahmins, householders* and *recluses*', subtle hair-splitters who go about shattering with their intelligence the theories (of others) (... ekacce khattiyapaṇḍite ... brāhmaṇapaṇḍite ... gahapatipaṇḍite ... samaṇapaṇḍite ... nipuṇe kataparappavāde vāḷavedhirūpe, vobhindantā[1] maññe caranti paññāgatena diṭṭhigatāni). These 'learned men' (paṇḍitā) of these four classes are referred to in other places as well (*v.* M. I.396; S. III.6) and the four kinds of 'debating assemblies' (parisā) are formed of these four classes of people, if we leave out the celestial beings (khattiyaparisā, brāhmaṇaparisā, gahapatiparisā, samaṇaparisā ... D. III.260; M. I.72; A. IV.307).

(350) These controversialists, who had made a study of the theories of others and who were anxious to display their dialectical skill are said to 'frame questions' (pañhaṃ abhisaṅkharonti) when they hear that the recluse Gotama is about the place, with the intention of

[1] At M. II.123 bhindantā occurs in place of vobhindantā.

questioning him (M. I.176, II.122, 123; cp. M. I.396; S. III.6). It is said that they frame questions in such a manner that 'if they questioned thus and he answers thus, we shall join issue with him thus and if questioned thus he answers thus we shall join issue with him thus' (evañ ce no puṭṭho evaṃ byākarissati, evam pi'ssa mayaṃ vādaṃ aropessama, evañ ce pi no puṭṭho evaṃ byākarissati, evam pi'ssa mayaṃ vādam āropessāmā ti, M. I.176, II.122). This description seems to suggest that the favourite questions that they devised were in the form of dilemmas.[1] There are two examples of such dilemmas or 'two-pronged questions' (ubhatokoṭikam pañhaṃ, M. I.393, S. IV.323), which are known in Indian logic in general as 'questions with a double noose' (ubhayataḥpāśā, *v.* Bagchi, Inductive Reasoning, pp. 182, 183). Both these questions are asked by kṣatriyas and they are said to be instigated by Nigaṇṭha Nātaputta. One is by Prince Abhaya (Abhayarā jakumāra) and the other by the headman (gāmaṇi) Asibandhakaputta. From the concluding section of the Abhayarājakumāra Sutta, it is evident that this question is to be reckoned among the class of questions framed and asked by these controversialist learned men (M. I.395, 396). They are the earliest dilemmas to be recorded in the history of Indian thought.

(351) The dilemma is 'a form of argument, the purpose of which is to show that from either of two alternatives, an unwelcome conclusion follows'.[2] This fact is exhibited in the form in which the argument is stated at M. I.392, 393. The propositions constituting the argument may be stated as follows:

p—bhāseyya nu kho ... Tathāgato taṃ vācaṃ, yā sā vācā paresaṃ appiyā amanāpā, i.e. would the Tathāgata make statements which are displeasing and unpleasant to others.

q—atha kiñcarahi ... puthujjanena nānākaraṇaṃ, puthujjano pi hi tam vācaṃ bhāseyya, yā sā vācā paresaṃ appiyā amanāpā, i.e. then how is he different from the ordinary individual, who also makes statements which are displeasing and unpleasant to others.

r—(= not-p) -na ... Tathāgato taṃ vācaṃ bhāsati yā sā vācā paresaṃ appiyā amanāpā, i.e. the Tathāgata would not make statements which are displeasing and unpleasant to others.

[1] In addition to dilemmas (dupadaṃ pañhaṃ), the Comy. mentions trilemmas (tipadaṃ pañhaṃ) and quadrilemmas (catuppadaṃ pañhaṃ) as well (MA. II. 197), but I have not found any examples of trilemmas or quadrilemmas in the Pāli Canon.

[2] Stebbing, *A Modern Introduction to Logic*, p. 107.

n—atha kiñcarahi ... Devadatto byākato: āpāyiko Devadatto atekiccho Devadatto, i.e. then why has he pronounced about Devadatta that he is doomed to hell ... that he is incorrigible?

(352) The argument is stated in a form adapted to the needs of conversation, but if we restate p, q, r, and n in the indicative mood in the light of what is meant, the form of the argument is as follows:

If p, then not q; and if r (= not-p), then not-n,
But either p or r (= not-p)
(Law of Excluded Middle);
Therefore, either not-q or not-n.

(353) It will be seen that this is a complex constructive dilemma (*v.* Stebbing, *op. cit.*, p. 108). The Buddha is faced with the prospect of either admitting that 'he is not different from the ordinary individual who also makes statements which are displeasing and unpleasant to others' (not-q) or of admitting that 'he has not pronounced about Devadatta that he is doomed to hell ... that he is incorrigible' (not-n). The latter admission would be evidently false and the former damaging to his reputation. In fact we have here a subsidiary argument of the form *modus tollendo ponens*:[1]

Either not-q or not-n (conclusion of the above),
Not (not-n) (since not-n is evidently false),
Therefore not-q.

(354) The Buddha escapes from this dilemma by admitting p in a qualified sense (na ... ekaṃsena, i.e. not categorically, M. I.393) which does not imply not-q and is therefore not led to accept not-q. There is no reason to suppose that the person who framed this question was aware of the logical form of the arguments as we have represented them but there is no doubt that the question as stated in this Sutta embodies a valid dilemma.

(355) Asibandhakaputta's question (S. IV.323 ff.) which has also been called an '*ubhatokoṭikaṃ* pañham' is not so explicitly stated as the one above. Besides, it contains a conception of consistency which formal logic does not take account of. This is the sense in which one's actions may be said to be consistent or inconsistent with the views that one claims to hold (*v. infra*, 598 for the definition of this concept of consistency). In addition, the second prong of the dilemma is not

[1] *v.* Stebbing, *op. cit.*, p. 105.

stated but merely implied and it is only the fact that it is called a dilemma (ubhatokoṭikaṃ pañhaṃ) that justifies our reconstruction of it. The statements that constitute the argument are as follows:

p (= B asserts t)—Bhagavā anekapariyāyena kulānaṃ anuddayaṃ vaṇṇeti.[1]

q (= B acts as if he does not believe t)—Bhagavā dubbhikkhe ... mahatā bhikkhusaṅghena saddhiṃ cārikaṃ carati, ucchedāya Bhagavā kulānaṃ paṭipanno.[2]

We have to assume that the second half of the dilemma is made up of the following implicative premiss:

If not-p; then r, where not-p = 'B does not assert t' and r = 'B is not different from an ordinary person'. We may now state the dilemma as follows:

If p (B asserts t) then not-q (B acts as if he does believe t) and if not-p (B does not assert t) than r (B is not different from an ordinary person).

But, either p or not-p (Law of Excluded Middle).

Therefore, either not-q or r.

(356) This again would be a complex constructive dilemma, although we are less certain of its form owing to the qualifications that had to be made.

(357) Even if these kṣatriyas did cultivate the elements of reasoning, as appears to be evident from the questions that they have framed, there is no reason to believe judging from these questions that they were casuists (vitaṇḍavādins) for the questions are about what may have appeared to intelligent people at this time as the contradictions of the Buddha. They are quite straightforward and there is no quibbling in them. In fact, the attitude that the Buddha himself had towards this intelligentsia provides ample proof that this class of people as a whole cannot be classified as quibblers and casuists. The Buddha himself says that he agrees with them on certain matters and disagrees with them on other matters (*v.* santi eke samaṇabrāhmaṇā paṇḍitā nipuṇā kataparappávādā vāḷavedhirūpā vobhindantā maññe caranti paññā-

[1] The Exalted One in various ways speaks well of showing compassion to people.

[2] The Exalted One during a famine . . . goes about (for alms) with a large concourse of monks and (thus) behaves in a way detrimental (to the interests of) people.

gatena diṭṭhigatāni. Tehi pi me saddhiṃ ekaccesu ṭhānesu sameti, ekaccesu ṭhānesu na sameti, D. I.162). It is said that what they assert to be good (sādhu) and bad (na sādhu) at times, the Buddha too pronounces to be good and bad and vice versa (*loc. cit.*) but at times what they assert to be good, the Buddha asserts to be bad and vice versa (*loc. cit.*). This clearly shows that these 'learned men' (paṇḍitā) were not all dialecticians or casuists but were intelligent critics, who made a rational assessment of the views they studied. The Buddha claims to have made many converts from among them, even without the necessity of answering their questions or engaging them in debate (na ... pañhaṃ pucchanti kuto vādaṃ āropessanti, aññadatthu Bhagavato savākā sampajjanti, M. I.176, II.123). In fact, the questions that they ask are not always intended to display their dialectical skill but are critical and fact-finding, if we may judge from the sample of questions, the answers to which are taught to a monk who intends to go to the Pacchābhūma country, where it is said that there are many such 'learned khattiyas, brahmins, householders and recluses' (khattiya-paṇḍitā pi brāhmaṇa-paṇḍitā pi gahapati-paṇḍitā pi samaṇa-paṇḍitā pi, S. III.6–8), who are 'investigators' (*vīmaṃsakā*), who will ask him such questions (pañhaṃ pucchitāro, *loc. cit.*).

(358) The Buddha goes on to say that they more often than not praise him, after making a comparative study of the doctrines and lives of different religious teachers (amhe va tattha yebhuyyena pasaṃseyyuṃ, D. I.163). They seem to have been no other than the intelligentsia of the age, who made a critical study of the various theories prevalent at the time and cultivated what knowledge they could lay their hands on. The Buddha calls them 'the intelligent or rational ones' (viññū, D. I.163–5) and he seems primarily to have addressed this class of people and put his theories to the test at their hands. This is probably the reason why a good person (sappo so) is defined as one who is blameless in the eyes of the *viññū* (ananuvajjo viññūnaṃ, A. II.228), while the entire teaching of the Buddha (i.e. the Dhamma) was described as one 'which was to be realized individually by the *viññū*' (dhammo ... paccattaṃ veditabbo viññūhi, A. II.56). The viññū represented for the Buddha the impartial critic at the level of intelligent common sense and the Buddha and his disciples sometimes introduce the 'viññū puriso' or the hypothetical rational critic when it seems necessary to make an impartial and intelligent assessment of the relative worth of conflicting theories

(*v.* M. I.403ff., 515ff.). There is no evidence that this class of people were called takkī in the sense of 'reasoners' or 'rationalists', although *vīmaṃsakā* 'investigators' is used as an epithet on one occasion to describe them (S. III.6) and it may be noted that *vīmaṃsī* (investigator) is a term used conjointly with takkī very often (cp. takkī vimaṃsī, D. I.16, 21, 23, 29; M. II.211).

(359) From our investigations so far we found that with the possible exception of Sañjaya's school there was little evidence for the existence of sophists in the Greek sense of the term. It is however not unlikely that there were quite a few vitaṇḍavādins among the dialecticians (kataparappavādā ... vobhindantā caranti) but as we have shown there is no reason to believe that the majority of them belonged to this class. There is no evidence in Pāli literature that either of these two classes were called takkī, although the word takka (tarka) was later employed in the Nyāyasūtra to denote an indirect argument used to disprove one's opponent's thesis.

(360) We are now in a position to consider classes (b), (d), (e) and (f) of our list (*v. supra*, 317). All of them represent definite theories about the nature of man, his destiny or the universe and some of them were attributed to well-known teachers at this time. All these theories mentioned by Oldenberg constitute only a sample of the many theories, which on the evidence of the texts can be shown to have been debated during this period. It can be shown that some of these theories were constructed by takka and presumably all of them were defended by takka against the attacks of their opponents. The word is clearly employed to denote the kind of reasoning on which these debated theories were being defended or criticized in the course of discussion. It is said in the context of the debate that 'people say the two things "true" and "false" employing takka on views' (takkañ ca diṭṭhīsu pakappayitvā 'saccaṃ, musā' ti dvayadhammam āhu, Sn. 886). In the light of the evidence that we have, these debaters have to be distinguished on the whole from the sophists, casuists (vitaṇḍavādi) and dialecticians, discussed above. There is no sense in calling these theorists sophists for they were not sceptic-sophists in the Greek sense of the term, nor were they vitaṇḍavādins for despite their anxiety to score a victory in debate, there is little doubt that they cherished the truth of their own theories. Whether and to what extent they used, consciously or unconsciously, fallacious forms of reasoning

in the rational defence of theories and in the criticism of their opponents, it is difficult to determine in the absence of positive evidence. But a study of the institution of the debate as it was conducted at this time gives some glimpses of what could have been meant by the word 'takka' as employed to denote the procedure of reasoning used in these discussions.

(361) We have shown in a previous Chapter that the debate was a flourishing institution before the rise of Buddhism (*v. supra*, 50). When, therefore, the Suttanipāta says that 'these debates have arisen among the Samaṇas' (ete vivādā samaṇesu jātā, Sn. 828), it almost seems to imply that it was a practice which existed earlier but which has caught on among this class of people. The use of the term kathojjaṃ (Sn. 925, 828) to denote the 'debate' among the Samaṇas seems to bear indirect testimony to this fact. Kathojjaṃ is explained in the Comy. as a 'quarrel or debate' (kathojjaṃ vuccati kalaho . . . vivādo, Nd. I.163). It is translated in the PTS. Dictionary as 'dispute, quarrel' (*s.v.*) but it seems to be a technical term for the debate (e.g. virame kathojjaṃ, one should desist from the debate, Sn. 838) and is obviously derived from kathā + udya giving *kathodya > P. kathojja- and seems to be a word coined on the analogy of *brahmodya*, which was the early Brāhmaṇic term for this institution (*v. supra*, 46). The kathojja- seems to have taken the place among the Samaṇas of the *brahmodya* among the brahmins.

(362) Frequent reference is made to the debate in the Duṭṭhaṭṭhaka-, Pasūra-, Cūlaviyūha-and the Mahāviyūha Suttas of the Aṭṭhakavagga of the Sutta Nipāta, one of the earliest sections of the Pāli Canon. It is called the vāda (vādañ ca jātaṃ muni no upeti, Sn. 780; cp. Sn. 825, 859). The term vivāda is also used (Sn. 796, 862, 863, 828, 896, 912). So is kathā (yutto *kath*āyaṃ parisāya majjhe, Sn. 825). These words have later become the commonly accepted terms for the debate and have been given formal definitions by writers of textbooks on logic. But we have no right to assume that any of these formal definitions are applicable to the debate as understood and conducted at this time. The definition in the Nyāya Sūtra (1.2.1) is already elaborate. It not merely mentions the adoption of a thesis and anti-thesis (pakṣa-pratipakṣa-parigraho) but speaks of the employment of the five-membered syllogism (pañcāvayavopapannaḥ) but it is interesting as it states, as we have already seen, that tarka (indirect proofs) is used to demolish the opponent's theory. The simplest definition is again in the

Caraka Saṃhitā (vādo nāma yatparasparena saha śāstrapūrvakam vigṛhya kathayati, i.e. a debate is that in which there is mutual contentious discussion based on texts, 3.8.6.20) and this seems to apply to the debate as we find it pictured in the Pāli Canon (*v. infra*, 368).

(363) The Caraka Saṃhitā speaks of two kinds of debate, the friendly debate (sandhāya-sambhāṣā, 3.8.6.10) and the hostile debate (vigṛhya-sambhāṣā, *loc. cit.*) and we seem to find this distinction already in the Sutta Nipāta where in the context of the vāda (debate) it is said that 'some hold controversy (vadanti) in a hostile spirit (duṭṭhamanā) while others do so in a spirit of truth (saccamanā)' (Sn. 780). In the Nikāyas the words saṃvadati and vivadati respectively, seem to be used to indicate this distinction as for example at M. I.500, na kena ci saṃvadati, na kena ci vivadati, where the Comy. draws the distinction by saying that when an 'Eternalist' (sassáta-vādi) argues with an 'Eternalist' it is saṃvadati but when an 'Eternalist' argues with a 'Semi-Eternalist' (ekacca-sassata-vādi) it is vivadati (MA. III.208). But the fact that the Caraka Saṃhitā used vigṛhya kathayati for the definition of vāda (*v. supra*, 362) probably indicates that this was the commonest type of debate. This seems to be the case even in the Suttanipāta where the expressions viggayha vadanti (Sn. 878, Skr. vigṛhya vadanti) and viggayha vivādiyanti (Sn. 879, 883, 904) are the commonest and a viggayhavāda is defined as one in which a person claims his own theory to be the 'real truth' (saccaṃ tathiyaṃ, Sn. 883), while condemning his opponent's theory as 'utterly false' (tucchaṃ musā, *loc. cit.*) or claims 'completeness' (paripuṇṇaṃ, Sn. 904) for his own theory (sakaṃ dhammaṃ, *loc. cit.*) while condemning his opponent's theory as 'inferior' (hīnaṃ, *loc. cit.*). It is not only the theory that is condemned but the person. It is said: 'Diverse "experts" hold hostile debates, clinging to their own theories (saying) "he who knows thus, knows the truth, while he who criticizes this, is ignorant". They call their opponent an inexpert fool—thus do they hold hostile debate'.[1] 'The criterion with which he dubs the other a fool is the one with which he claims to be an expert; himself claiming himself to be an expert (kusalo)—so does he speak.'[2] The term kusala-, it may be observed, is the same as that employed in the Caraka Saṃhitā

[1] Sakaṃ sakaṃ diṭṭhi paribbasānā, viggayha nānā kusalā vadanti: 'yo evaṃ jānāti sa vedi dhammaṃ, idaṃ paṭikkosaṃ akevalī so'. Evam pi viggayha vivādiyanti, 'bālo paro akusalo' ti cāhu, Sn. 878, 879, cp. 882.

[2] Yen'eva bālo ti paraṃ dahāti, tenātumānaṃ kusalo ti cāha, sayam attanā so kusalo vadāno, aññaṃ vimāneti tath'eva pāvā, Sn. 888.

to denote one who has expert knowledge of the debate (e.g. . . . praśaṃsanti kuśalāḥ, 3.8.6.13). This use of impolite language may have easily led to frayed tempers giving the impression of, if not actually resulting in, quarrels. The C.S. says that contentious language (vigṛhyabhāṣā, 3.8.6.15) may arouse keen hatred in some and there is nothing that such an infuriated person is incapable of doing or saying, but experts (kuśalāḥ) who speak aptly condemn quarrelling (kalahaṃ, *loc. cit.*) among good people. This seems to be the reason why in the Pāli Nikāyas, the words for 'quarrel' and 'debate' are sometimes used synonymously.[1]

(364) This does not mean that there was no formal procedure in such a debate, for this seems to be implied in the following observation (to quote Woodward's translation): 'If this person on being asked a question does not abide by the conclusions, whether right or wrong, does not abide by an assumption, does not abide by recognized arguments, does not abide by usual procedure—in such a case this person is incompetent to discuss' (G.S. I.179). Woodward has translated ṭhānāṭhāne as 'conclusions whether right or wrong' but the Comy. explains this term as meaning 'reasons and non-reasons' (ṭhānāṭhāne na saṇṭhātī ti *kāraṇākāraṇe* na saṇṭhātī, AA. II.309). He has likewise translated akaccho as 'incompetent to discuss' but it literally means 'not to be debated with' (= Skr. akathyaḥ). It shows that debates or discussions were to be held only with persons who abided by the set procedure (paṭipadā, A. I.197) and not with those who violated it, implying that there was a recognized procedure in debates.

(365) The Pāli Nikāyas, as well as the Caraka Saṃhitā, call the debate viggāhika-kathā (cp. vādo . . . vigṛhya kathayati, *v. supra*, 362) and speak of a class of recluses and brahmins (eke samaṇa-brāhmaṇā), who are 'addicted to the debate' (viggāhikakathaṃ anuyuttā, D. I.8), which Prof. Rhys Davids renders as 'addicted to the use of wrangling phrases' (SBB. II.14). There is a stereotyped passage here which is repeated elsewhere in the Nikāyas (M. II.243; S. III.11) and which is introduced by the sentence, kathaṃ viggayha kattā hoti, i.e. how is one a contentious debater (at S. II.11); this shows that Prof. Rhys Davids' translation is strictly incorrect. It is intended to be a brief account of

[1] Kuto pasūtā *kalahā* vivādā, Sn. 862; diṭṭhi-*kalahāni*, diṭṭhi-bhaṇḍanāni, diṭṭhi-viggahāni diṭṭhi-vivādāni, diṭṭhi-medhagāni, Nd. I.103; bhaṇḍanajātā *kalaha*jātā vivādāpannā describing nānātitthiyā samaṇabrāhmaṇā paribbājakā, holding different theories, Ud. 66; *kalaha*viggaha-vivāda-, D. I.59.

the language used in the debate and meagre as it is, it gives us a glimpse of what took place. We may pick out those statements that seem to have a bearing on the kind of reasoning that was employed in these debates, viz.

(1) Sahitaṃ me, asahitaṃ te, i.e. the text is on my side, there is no text on your side.

(2) Pure vacanīyaṃ pacchā avaca, i.e. you state later what ought to be stated earlier.

(3) Pacchā vacanīyaṃ pure avaca, i.e. you state earlier what ought to be stated later.

(4) Āropito te vādo, niggahīto 'si, i.e. you put forward the thesis, (now) you are censured.

(366) These statements tend to make it very probable that there was a conception of valid and invalid reasoning at this time.

(367) We have differed in our translation of, sahitaṃ me, from Prof. Rhys Davids who renders it as 'I am speaking to the point' and from the Comy. which explains the phrase as 'my language is apt (siliṭṭhaṃ), meaningful (atthayuttaṃ) and accompanied by reasons (kāraṇayuttaṃ)' (DA. I.91). This commentarial explanation cannot, however, be entirely set aside as it may be preserving a genuine tradition. Our language would be meaningful and substantial if it lacks the defects of speech (vākyadoṣa), of which the C.S. enumerates five types[1] (3.8.6.46) namely (i) saying too little (nyūnam), which occurs when there is an omission of the reason (hetu), the example (udāharaṇa-) the application (upanaya) and the conclusion (nigamana), (ii) saying too much (ādhikyam) consisting of irrelevancy or repetition, (iii) meaninglessness (anarthakam), where there is a mere collection of words, (iv) incoherence (apārthakam), where there is a disparateness of categories (parasparena ayujyamānārthakam, *loc. cit.*) and, lastly, (v) contradiction (viruddha), consisting of opposition to the example (dṛṣṭānta), established tenet (siddhānta), or context (samaya). The concepts are too elaborate and developed to belong to the period of the Pāli Nikāyas. The technical uses of udāharaṇa (= āharaṇa), upanaya and nigamana (= niggamana) are not earlier than the Kathāvatthu,[2] which is one of the latest books of the Pāli Canon.[3] But the two basic

[1] *v.* Vidyabhusana, *History of Indian Logic*, p. 34.

[2] Aung and Rhys Davids, *Points of Controversy*, pp. xxix ff.

[3] *v.* Winternitz, *A History of Indian Literature*, Vol. II, University of Calcutta, 1933, p. 171; cp. *Geschichte der indischen Litteratur*, Vol. II, 1, 137; Aung and Rhys Davids, *Points of Controversy*, p. 1.

concepts in this definition of sahitaṃ, namely that such language is *meaningful* and *accompanied by reasons* are not foreign to the earliest books of the Pāli Nikāyas (*v. infra*, 543). Besides, kusalā (experts), which was used both in the Suttanipāta and the C.S. to denote those who were 'experts' at debating, is defined in the Mahāniddesa, a commentary on the Aṭṭhakavagga incorporated in the Nikāyas (Khuddaka Nikāya) as 'hetuvādā, lakkhaṇavādā, kāraṇavādā, ṭhānavādā sakāya laddhiyā', i.e. those who spoke with reasons (hetu-kāraṇavada) spoke exactly (lakkhaṇavādā, i.e. *lit.* spoke with definitions), and spoke aptly in accordance with each one's theory (ṭhānavādā), (Nd.I 294). Ṭhānavāda would literally mean 'those who speak according to the occasion' and who would thereby escape the defect of speech (vākyadoṣa) called viruddha (*v. supra*), which would arise if the language would not conform to the context (samaya). We have therefore enough evidence within the Nikāyas to support the meaning that the Comy. gives to sahitam but the usage óf this word is obscure. It may etymologically mean 'what is well put together' (sam + past passive participle of $\sqrt{}$dhā, to place) and come to mean language that is so constructed but such a word is not attested elsewhere.

(368) On the other hand, samihitaṃ (= saṃhitaṃ, cp. saṃhitā) in the sense of 'a collection of texts' is found in the Nikāyas (*v. supra*, 304). This explanation is supported by the Sanna (sub-commentary) which is quoted by Prof. Rḥys Davids (SBB. II.14, fn. 6). It also appears to be confirmed by the definition of vāda in the C.S. where it said that the discussion was 'based on scriptural texts' (śāstrapūrvakaṃ, *v. supra*, 362). If this explanation is correct, it shows that the argument from authority played an important part in the reasoning. Where the two parties to a debate subscribed to two different scriptural traditions there would appear to be not much scope for such arguments. But even then the scriptures held sacred by the other side could always be quoted against them.[1]

(369) The statement, pure vacanīyam pacchā avaca (2) looks very much like criticizing one's opponent with employing the fallacy of atītakāla- or kālātīta-. Kālātīta- is defined in the N.S. (1.2.9.) as the 'reason which is adduced when the time is past, when it might hold good' (kālātyayāpadiṣṭaḥ kālātītaḥ) and atīta-kāla is reckoned among one of the five fallacies of reason (hetvābhāsaḥ, N.S. 1.2.4). The definition of

[1] It is likely that the Materialist cited the text Bṛh. 2.4.12 against their Vedic opponents since they appear to have quoted this in support of their own doctrines.

atītakāla- in the C.S. (3.8.6.50) leaves us in no doubt that our identification is correct. It is said, atītakālaṃ nāma yat *pūrvaṃ vācyaṃ tat paścād ucyate*, (i.e. atītakāla- occurs when what ought to be stated earlier is stated later), which is the same as, *pure vacanīyaṃ pacchā avaca*. According to this definition the fallacy of atītakāla 'occurs when that which ought to be stated earlier is asserted later and then it is untenable owing to the lapse in time or it occurs when one censures later instead of censuring when the time for censure (nigraha) has arisen and then owing to the lapse in time, the censure is ineffective'.[1]

(370) If the above identification is correct then statement (3) is a likely reference to the opposite fallacy of *petitio principii*, namely of stating or assuming earlier in the premisses what ought to follow later in the conclusion. The N.S. knows of two kinds of *petitio principii*, prakaraṇasama 'equal to the question' ('begging the question') and sādhyasama 'equal to what is to be proved' both of which are classed as fallacies (1.2.4). Prakaraṇasama is defined as 'the reason which provokes the very question for the solution of which it was employed'[2] in the N.S. In the C.S. prakaraṇasama is said to be a kind of fallacy or non-reason (ahetu) for 'that which is the thesis (pakṣah) cannot be the reason'.[3] An example is given. In order to prove, anyad śarīrād ātmā nityaḥ, the soul is different from the body and is eternal, you proceed as follows: 'The soul is different from the body, therefore it is eternal. The body is not eternal, therefore the soul must be different from it'.[4] Here the thesis that is to be proved is the compound proposition 'the soul is different from the body and is eternal'. If in the proof one assumes the truth of one of its constituents, as the example suggests, one is committing the fallacy of prakaraṇasama or 'begging the question'. Incidentally, it may be observed that the two propositions in the example adduced are among the very theories the truth of which is said to be hotly debated during the time of the Pāli Nikāyas. 'Śarīrād anya ātmā' or 'anyaḥ śarīrād ātmā' is the theory that the 'soul is different from the body' and is the same as Pāli 'aññaṃ

[1] . . . yatpūrvaṃ vācyaṃ, tat paścād ucyate, tatkālātītatvād agrāhyam bhavatī ti pūrvaṃ vā nigrahaprāptam anigṛhya pakṣāntaritam paścānnigṛhīte tattasyātītakālatvān nigrahavacanam asamartham bhavatī ti, *loc. cit.*

[2] Yasmāt prakaraṇacintā sa nirṇayārtham apadiṣṭaḥ prakaraṇasamaḥ, 1.2.7.

[3] nahi ya eva pakṣaḥ, sa eva hetuḥ, 3.8.6.49.

[4] anyaḥ śarirād ātmā nitya iti pakṣe brūyāt yasmād anyaḥ śarīrād ātmā, tasmānnityaḥ, śarīraṃ hyanityam ato vidharminā c'ātmanā bhavitavyam ityeṣa c'āhetuḥ, 3.8.6.49.

jīvaṃ aññaṃ sarīraṃ' to which was opposed the theory 'taṃ jīvaṃ taṃ sarīraṃ', i.e. the 'soul is identical with the body' (Ud. 67, *v. infra*, 379, 384, 387). Ātmā nityaḥ, 'the soul is eternal' is the same as sassato attā (M. II.233) to which was opposed the theory asassato attā (M. II.233). Sādhyasama is defined in the N.S. as 'that which is indistinguishable from what has to be proved, since it has to be proved'[1] (1.2.8). The C.S. knows of two kinds of *petitio principii*, namely the saṃśayasama and varṇyasama. Samśayasama is said to occur 'when that which is the cause of doubt is regarded as dispelling the doubt',[2] and varṇyasama 'when the reason is not different from the subject'.[3] We cannot assume that all these various forms of the fallacy of *petitio principii* were known during the time of the composition of the Pāli Nikāyas, but we are merely making the minimum inference that statement (3) seems to betray some awareness of the fallacy of *petitio principii*, however this might have been understood at the time.

(371) Statement (4) contains one of the key terms of the debate (*niggahīto*'si), which was used when there arose an 'occasion for censure' (nigrahasthānam), which according to the N.S. occurred when 'there was misunderstanding or lack of understanding'[4] on the part of one's opponent. The N.S. enumerates no less than twenty-four such occasions for censure (5.2.1). The C.S. also gives a strict definition of the term although it does not enumerate the different occasions for censure as such. According to the C.S. it results in defeat (parājaya-prāptiḥ) and occurs 'when the disputant either fails to understand what the audience understands, when repeated thrice or when one censures that which is not censurable or refrains from censuring that which is censurable'.[5]

(372) One of the nigrahasthānas is fallacies (hetvābhāsāḥ) (N.S. 5.2.1) and there is no reason to suspect that the fallacies indicated by statements (2) and (3) were not regarded as such. There is no direct mention of individual nigrahasthanas in the Pāli Nikāyas but a few indirect references are made to them. Where the Buddha engages the

[1] sādhyāviśiṣṭas sādhyatvāt sādhyasamaḥ, 1.2.8.

[2] ya eva saṃśaya-hetuḥ sa eva saṃśaya-ccheda-hetuḥ, 3.8.6.49.

[3] yo heturvarṇyāviśiṣṭaḥ, *ibid.*

[4] vipratipattir apratipattiś ca nigrahasthānam, 1.2.19.

[5] trirabhihitasya vākyasyāparijñānam pariṣadi vijñānavatyāṃ yad vā ananuyojyasyānuyogo'nuyojyasya c'ānanuyogaḥ, 3.8.6.57.

Nigaṇṭha Nātaputta in debate on questions 'relating to the prior end' (pubbantam ārabbha, M. II.31) and Saccaka is said to have engaged the famous six teachers in debate (M. I.251, *v. supra*, 339) their opponents are said to have 'shifted the topic of conversation' (bahiddhā kathaṃ apanesi), which is an indirect way of saying that they were defeated as is implied by the context, since this is identical with the nigrahasthāna of arthāntaram or 'shifting the topic' (N.S. 5.2.1). In the account of the Buddha's debate with Ambaṭṭha on the problem of caste, there are again a few indirect references to nigrahasthānas. Here it is said that when the Buddha questions someone up to a third time (yāva tatiyakaṃ, D. I.95) according to the rules and the latter fails to answer then 'his head would split into seven pieces'.[1] This is a picturesque way of saying that his opponent would suffer ignominious defeat in such circumstances, for as we can see from the definition of nigrahasthāna in the C.S. (*v. supra*), when a question was asked in debate three times and the opponent failed to answer, then it was an occasion for nigraha- or defeat. Now this Sutta enumerates the occasions on which the opponent would incur this defeat and mentions them as (a) na vyākarissasi; (b) aññena vā aññaṃ paṭicarissasi; (c) tuṇhī va bhavissasi and (d) pakkamissasi. Of these (c) which means remaining silent is easily identifiable with the nigrahasthāna of ananubhāṣanam or 'silence' (N.S. 5.2.1), (d) which means 'going away' is most probably the same as vikṣepah, *lit.* 'throwing off, postponing' (N.S. 5.2.1), which is defined by Gotama as 'stopping a debate on the pretext of some duty',[2] and by Vātsyāyana in the Gotamasūtrabhāṣyam as 'when one interrupts a debate on the pretext of some duty (saying) "I find I have this business to attend to; when that is over I shall resume the debate" (then) there is the nigrahasthāna called vikṣepa';[3] (a), which means 'not explaining clearly' has to be distinguished from (c), which means remaining silent or not answering. Prof. Rhys Davids has translated it as 'if you do not give a *clear* reply' (*op. cit.*, 116). If this is correct, it may imply the forms of meaningless and incoherent speech which have been reckoned among the nigrahasthānas such as nirarthakam (meaningless), avijñātārthakam

[1] Cp. Ś. Br. 11.4.19 (*v.* SBE., Vol. 44, p. 53, fn. 2) asya puruṣasya mūrdhā vipatet, 'the head of this person will fall apart' (said in the context of the debate).

[2] Kāryavyāsaṅgāt kathāvicchedo vikṣepaḥ, 5.2.20.

[3] Yatra kartavyaṃ vyāsajya kathāṃ vyavacchinatti'idam me karaṇīyaṃ vidyate tasminnavasite kathayiṣyāmi' ti vikṣepo nāma nigrahasthānam, Bhāṣya on N.S. 5.2.20.

(unintelligible), apārthakam (incoherent) and aprāptakālam (inopportune) (N.S. 5.2.1). We are left with the phrase, aññena vā aññaṃ paṭicarissasi (b), which is translated by Prof. Rhys Davids as 'go off upon another issue' (*op. cit.*, p. 116). It is, explained in the Comy. as 'covering up or concealing' (ajjhottharati paṭicchādeti, DA. I.264). The literal rendering of this sentence as 'if you will evade in one way or another' seems to give the best sense and refers most probably to some of the many ways of evasion such as 'shifting the proposition' (pratijñāntaram), 'renouncing the proposition' (pratijñānyāsaḥ), 'shifting the reason' (hetvāntaram), etc. (N.S. 5.2.1), which are mentioned among the nigrahasthānas, although it is difficult to determine which of them could have been intended owing to our ignorance of the extent of the knowledge of nigrahasthānas at this time. The paribbājaka Ajita tells the Buddha that a friend of his called Paṇḍita has thought of (cintitāni) about five hundred thought-situations (pañcamattāni cittaṭṭhāna-satāni) in which other religious teachers (aññatitthiyā), when censured (upāraddhā) would realize that they were censured (A.V. 230). The context is that of the debate and although the number five hundred is undoubtedly an exaggeration, one wonders whether the reference could in any way be to the nigrahasthānas; but the statement is altogether too vague and obscure for us to make any surmises on the basis of it.

(373) However, it seems to be justifiable to infer from this brief account of the debate that reasons were being adduced in proof of the theories put forward by various proponents at this time and that the validity of this reasoning was being questioned by their opponents. There seems to have been, therefore, a conception of valid and invalid reasoning (cp. sutakkitam pi . . . duttakkitam pi hoti, M. I.520) at this time. This reasoning is called takka (Sn. 885, 886) and as we have seen, it is said that 'people say the two things "true" and "false" by employing takka on views' (Sn. 886). What is probably meant is that in the process of debating people utilize reason to prove that certain theories are true and others false. The Comy. (Nd.I 295), however, gives a somewhat different explanation. It says, 'by reasoning, thinking and reflection they construct, create and evolve theories and then assert and declare that mine is true and yours false'.[1] According to this

[1] takkayitvā vitakkayitvā saṃkappayitvā diṭṭhigatāni janenti sañjanenti nibbattenti . . . diṭṭhigatāni janetvā sañjanetvā nibbattetvā . . . mayhaṃ saccaṃ, tuyhaṃ musā ti evam āhaṃsu, evaṃ kathenti, evaṃ bhananti . . .

explanation it is the theory that is constructed by takka, but this cannot account for the syntax unless we change the wording to, takkena diṭṭhim pakappayitvā (having fashioned a view by takka). As it is, takkaṃ ca diṭṭhīsu pakappayitvā, can be construed in one of two ways, consistently with the grammar and syntax, viz. (1) 'thinking about (many) views, having constructed (pakappayitvā) (one) . . .', taking takkaṃ as the present participle or (ii) 'employing reason on the views', taking takka- as the object of pakappayitvā. We would prefer (ii) as it does not involve a periphrasis. The commentator would not be averse to the meaning we suggest, since he suggests both alternatives in commenting on udāhu te takkaṃ anussaranti (Sn. 885), where he says that 'they (i.e. these debaters) are led by and carried away by their reasoning, thinking and imagination or they declare and assert what is beaten out by logic and speculative inquiry and is self-evident to them'.[1] The problem is whether these theories were both constructed by takka- as well as defended by takka-. There is no doubt that all these theories that were debated were defended or criticized by takka, but it is doubtful whether all of them were also constructed by takka, although no doubt a good many of them probably were (*v. infra*, 435).

(374) Of the sixty two theories mentioned in the Brahmajāla Sutta only four (D. I.16, 21, 23, 29) are specifically associated with the takkī and are said to be 'constructed by takka' takka-pariyāhataṃ, *loc. cit.* As for the others it is implied that some (e.g. the three 'Eternalist' (sassatavāda) and the three 'Semi-Eternalist' (ekacca-sassata-vāda) theories (other than the two attributed to takka), are at least not wholly due to takka (*v. infra*, 416) but to jhānic perception, while it is not specified whether the others (e.g. the Materialist and Survivalist theories) are due to takka or not. Now the Suttanipāta speaks of 'sixty three (theories) associated with the debates of the Samaṇas' (yāni ca tīṇi yāni ca saṭṭhi, samaṇa'ppavādasitāni, Sn. 538). Assuming that these 'sixty three' theories included at least many of the sixty two theories of the Brahmajāla Sutta, the possibility is left open as to whether some of the theories which were not constructed by takka were still debated and defended by takka. The Mahāniddesa, which we must not forget is a book belonging to the Nikāyas, speaks of the 'sixty two theories' (dvāsaṭṭhi-diṭṭhigatāni), presumably of the Brahmajāla

[1] takkena vitakkena saṃkappena yāyanti niyyanti vuyhanti . . . athavā takka-pariyāhataṃ vīmaṃsānucaritaṃ sayaṃpaṭibhānaṃ vadanti kathenti . . ., Nd. I.294.

Sutta as being 'fashioned' (pakappitāni) in the sense of being 'thought out (kappita), constructed by the mind (abhisaṅkhata) and put together (saṇṭhapita)' (p. 186), but this does not mean fashioned or constructed by takka- in the sense of takka-pariyāhata. So when the Suttanipāta says that these 'doctrines are fashioned and constructed' (pakkappitā saṅkhatā vassa dhammā, Sn. 783), there is no reason to assume that they were rationally constructed, though being debated they were probably rationally defended and attacked.

(375) At D. I.8 it was said that the people who were addicted to debating were 'samaṇas and brāhmaṇas' (*v. supra*, 365). In the Suttanipāta more often than not, it is the saṃanas who are mentioned in connection with these debates (Sn. 828, 883, 884, 890). It may be that the word Samaṇa[1] is being used at least at times in a loose sense to include the brahmins as well, since among the sixty three theories associated with them, would have been many of the sixty two theories attributed conjointly to the 'samaṇas and brāhmaṇas' (samaṇa-brāhmaṇā, D. I.12 ff.) in the Brahmajāla Sutta. Sometimes the theories are associated with the tithyā (Sn. 891, 892) and sometimes called 'the opinions of individuals' (sammutiyo puthujjā, Sn. 897, 911). The titthiyā, who habitually debate (vādasīlā) are classified as the Ājīvikas (ājīvikā) and the Nigaṇṭhas (nigaṇṭhā) (Sn. 381). There is, however, no doubt that the debates of the brahmins were also known, since in the same context there is a mention of 'those brahmins who habitually debate and (among whom) there are some old brahmins' (Ye . . . brāhmaṇā vādasīlā, vuddhā cā'pi brāhmaṇā santi keci, Sn. 382). The classification of the debaters, as mentioned in the Suttanipāta, would therefore be as follows:

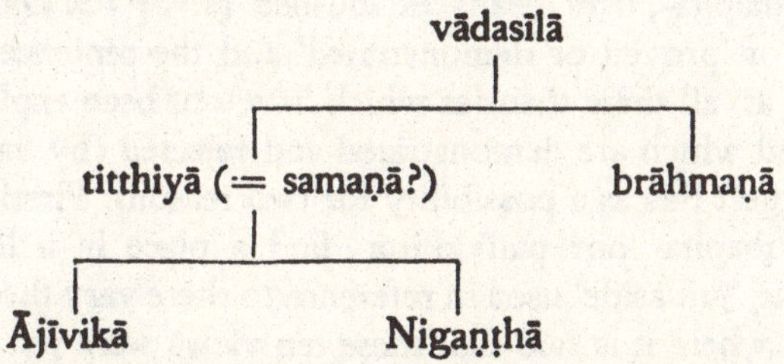

The picture that we get elsewhere in the Nikāyas of these debaters is very much the same, except that there is a mention of paribbājakas as

[1] Bṛh. 4.3.22 mentions śramaṇa- and tāpasa- as religious sects presumably other than the brahmins.

well, as for example at Ud. 66–9, where there is a reference to nānātitthiyā samaṇabrāhmaṇā paribbājakā,[1] who are said to be 'debating and making verbal thrusts at each other' (vivādāpannā aññamaññaṃ mukhasattīhi vitudantā viharanti, Ud. 67).

(367) The evidence that we have adduced shows that there were theories backed by reasoning, which were being debated at this time, both by the brahmins as well as the samaṇas. When therefore the Pāli Nikāyas give lists of such theories, which are said to be debated, we need not doubt their authenticity. Since the word takka was employed to denote the kind of reasoning that was employed in these debates, takkī may very well have meant the '*reasoners*' or debaters who participated in these debates.

(377) One of the earliest lists of topics said to be vigorously debated by 'many and various heretical teachers, recluses, brahmins and paribbājakas' (sambahulā nānātitthiyā samaṇabrāhmaṇā paribbājaka, Ud. 66) contains the ten theses on which the Buddha refused to express an opinion, namely the *avyākatas*. Each of these theses is said to be held by a school of recluses and brahmins (santi eke samaṇabrāhmaṇā evaṃvādino evaṃ-diṭṭhino, *loc. cit.*) who were at loggerheads with each other in maintaining the truth of its own thesis (vivādāpannā . . . vitudantā viharanti, ediso dhammo, n'ediso dhammo, n'ediso dhammo ediso dhammo, *loc. cit.*). At M. I.426 where this same list of ten is mentioned, it is introduced as follows: yān'imāni diṭṭhigatāni Bhagavatā avyākatāni *ṭhapitāni paṭikkhittāni*. This is translated by Miss Horner as 'those (speculative) views that are not explained, set aside and ignored by the Lord' (M.L.S. II.97). Here ṭhapitāni can certainly mean 'set aside' and we do not disagree with this translation, but it is also possible that ṭhapita-, here means 'established' (*s.v.* PTS. Dictionary) in the sense of 'proved or demonstrated' and the sentence may then be translated as 'all these theories which have not been explained by the Buddha and which are demonstrated and rejected (by various schools)'. We suggest this as a possibility for two reasons. Firstly, we find that neither ṭhapita- nor paṭikkhitta- find a place in a list of synonyms, meaning 'put aside' used in reference to these very theories. Thus, at A. II.41, where it is said that these ten views were put aside by the Buddha, the language used is as follows: sabbāni 'ssa tāni nuṇṇāni honti cattāni vantāni muttāni pahīnāni paṭinissaṭṭhāni. The

[1] The Jābāla Upaniṣad mentions how a brahmin may become a paribbājaka, *v.* 5.

same sentence occurs again in the same Nikāya with the addition of panuṇṇāni after honti (V.31: this is a v.l. even at II.41) but both ṭhapitāni and paṭikkhittāni are conspicuous by their absence, which is very unusual for the normal Pāli idiom. Secondly, we find that sthāpanā (from √ sthā) is a technical term, used in the sense of formally demonstrating the truth of a theory in the C.S. and is defined as 'the proof of the proposition by means of reasons, examples, applications and conclusions' (tasya eva pratijñāyā hetubhir dṛṣṭāntopanayanigamaiḥ sthāpanā, 3.8.6.23). It is also significant that the proposition taken to illustrate the process of sthāpanā is nityaḥ puruṣaḥ, i.e. 'the soul is eternal' and which is the same as the proposition 'sassato attā' given in a longer list of propositions said to be debated at this time (*v.* Ud. 69).

(378) It is worth trying to identify the schools which put forward each of these theses to see what kind of arguments were adduced in support of them. The theses are as follows:

(1) sassato loko, the world is eternal.
(2) asassato loko, the world is not eternal.
(3) antavā loko, the world is finite.
(4) anantavā loko, the world is infinite.
(5) taṃ jīvaṃ taṃ sarīraṃ, the soul is identical with the body.
(6) aññaṃ jīvaṃ aññaṃ sarīraṃ, the soul is different from the body.
(7) hoti tathāgato param maraṇā, the saint exists after death.
(8) na hoti tathāgato param maraṇā, the saint does not exist after death.
(9) hoti ca na ca hoti tathāgato param maraṇā, the saint does and does not exist after death.
(10) n'eva hoti na na hoti tathāgato param maraṇā, the saint neither exists nor does not exist after death.

(379) The easiest to identify is (5), which is evidently the main thesis of the Tajjīvataccharīravāda school of Materialists (*v. supra*, 124). In a general sense, however, the thesis was maintained by all the Materialist schools.[1] It was based on the epistemological argument

[1] Buddhaghosa identifies the thesis as that of the Materialists (tena vo vādo ucchedavādo hotī ti, DA. I.319 on D. I.159, 160). Dhammapāla (UdA. 340), however, identifies this view with the Ājīvikas: jīvaṃ ca sarīrañ ca advayaṃ samanupassati, etena Ājīvakānāṃ viya rūpī attā, ayaṃ vādo dassito hoti, i.e. he sees the soul and the body as non-dual; by this is indicated the theory of the Ājīvikas, who hold that the soul has form. But this is unlikely, since the Ājīvikas believed in survival and therefore distinguished the soul from the body; see, however, the theory of re-animation (Basham, *op. cit.*, pp. 28, 31–3, 49).

that there was no observable soul, apart from the body and only the observable exists (*v. supra*, 91). The Materialists also probably held (8), and perhaps (3) and (2) as well.

(380) (8) is interpreted to mean in the Comy. that 'the soul does not exist after death'; hoti tathāgato ti ādisu, satto tathāgato ti adhippeto, i.e. in the statements, hoti tathāgato, etc., by tathāgata- is meant the 'soul', DA. I.118; cp. tathāgato ti attā, the tathāgata is the 'soul', UdA. 340. But the contemporary evidence of the Nikāyas themselves shows beyond doubt that the word 'tathāgato' was used to denote the 'perfect person' or the 'saint' as understood in each religion. It is said that religious teachers used to 'declare about the state of survival of their best and highest disciples, who had attained the highest attainment, after they were dead and gone'[1] (yo pi'ssa sāvako *uttamapuriso paramapuriso paramapattipatto* taṃ pi sāvakaṃ abbhatītaṃ kālakataṃ upapattīsu vyākaroti, S. IV.398) and elsewhere we find that the phrase, uttamapuriso paramapuriso paramappattipatto used as a synonym of tathāgato, viz. yo pi so avuso tathāgato *uttamapuriso paramapuriso paramapattipatto* taṃ tathāgataṃ imesu catusu ṭhānesu paññapayamāno paññapeti: hoti tathāgato param maraṇā ti vā. Na hoti . . ., S. IV.380. The Materialist would, of course, not have a conception of the perfect person, but he would have certainly denied the truth of this statement even in this sense.[2]

(381) The epistemological arguments of the Materialists may have been extended to show that the world was finite in space (3) and time (2) but we have no definite evidence that they did so. Since the observable world is finite in space and time, they may have argued that the world was in fact finite in space and time and we find Dhammapāla commenting on thesis (2) identifying it as the view of the Materialists (asassato ti satta pi ucchedavādā dassitā, i.e. (by the thesis), 'the world is not eternal' was indicated the seven Materialist schools, UdA. 344).

(382) Thesis (3) was certainly put forward by the school of Finitists, mentioned in the Brahmajāla Sutta of the Buddhists and the Sthānāṅga Sūtra of the Jains. In the latter work, eight classes of Akiriyavādins are mentioned, of whom the third is called *mitavādī* (Finitists).

[1] Ajita, the Materialist, is included among the religious leaders who make these pronouncements, but this is obviously a mistake which would have occurred in the course of the oral transmission of the texts.

[2] Cp. 'the fool and the wise man are utterly annihilated at the destruction of the body and does not exist after death' (bāle ca paṇḍite ca kāyassa bhedā ucchijjanti na honti param maraṇā, D. I.55).

According to the commentary, they are called by this name because they held that the souls were limited in size and number and the world was finite in extent. It is said that 'they hold that the world is finite since it comprises the seven continents and the ocean' (atha mitam saptadvīpasamudrātmakatayā lokaṃ vadanti, Sthānāṅga Sūtra, ed. Venicandra Suracandra, Bombay 1920, Vol. II, fol. 425). These Mitavādins are contrasted with the Annihilationists (Ard. Mag. samuccheda-vātī, *loc. cit.*) and with the Deniers-of-the-next-world (na-santi-paraloka-vātī, *loc. cit.*). [This last class is clearly identifiable with the Materialists, according to their description in the commentary where it is said that they argue 'that there is no soul, since it is not cognizable by perception or any other means of knowledge and in its absence there can be no karma having the characteristics of good or evil or a next world or salvation'.[1]] From this it is clear that among those who held this thesis (3) were non-Materialists. It is an argument based on a popular belief and this kind of argument has been called anussutika-takka[2] by Buddhaghosa (*v. infra*, 416). The Mitavādins have been included in the class of Antānantikā (i.e. Finitists and Infinitists) in the Brahmajāla Sutta but here the thesis that the world is finite (antavā ayaṃ loko parivaṭumo, the world is finite and spherical, D. I.22) is not based on reasoning, but yogic perception.

(383) This latter theory (in the Brahmajāla Sutta) is similar if not the same as that of Pūraṇa Kassapa, who says that 'with his infinite intelligence he has a direct knowledge of a world that is finite' (aham anantena ñāṇena *antavantaṃ lokaṃ* jānaṃ passaṃ viharamīti, A. IV.428). The Comy. to the Brahmajāla Sutta tries to make out that this is an erroneous inference, on the basis of a yogic experience. It says: '... without developing the corresponding image to the limits of the world-sphere, he takes it as the world and abides in the awareness that the world is finite' (... paṭibhāganimittaṃ cakkavāḷapariyantaṃ avaḍḍhetvā taṃ loko ti gahetvā anta-saññī lokasmiṃ viharati, DA. I.115). The person whose reasoning is based on yogic perception is called by Buddhaghosa a lābhitakkī (*v. supra*, 146). If Pūraṇa's claim to omniscience was equivalent to the Jain claim to kevala-jñāna

[1] nāstyātmā pratyakṣādipramāṇāviṣayatvāt ... tadabhāvān na puṇyapāpalakṣaṇam karma, tadabhāvān na paraloko nāpi mokṣa iti, Sthānāṅga Sūtra, Vol. II, fol. 426.

[2] Buddhaghosa says that 'reasoners are of four types' (catubbidho takkī, DA. I.106) and enumerates the *anussutika-* as the first.

(*v. supra,* 242) he would have denied this altogether, since there was no possibility of such knowledge being erroneous. We do not know what reasoning Pūraṇa employed in debating this theory if he did so, although we know that the Ājīvikas, who used reason, also claimed yogic perception (*v. supra,* 212–15).

(384) Thesis (6) is again identifiable with more than one school. It would have been a tenet of the school of Pakudha (*v. infra,* 428) who maintained the integral existence of a soul, distinct from the body, probably on the basis of *a priori* reasoning (*v. infra,* 428). It was undoubtedly held also in the first three 'schools' of Eternalists mentioned in the Brahmajāla Sutta (D. I.13–16), which maintained 'the eternity of the soul and the world' (*sassatañ attānañ* ca *lokañ* ca, *loc. cit.*). Since these three 'schools' differed only in regard to the difference in the degree of their claims to retrocognition (*v.* pubbenivāsaṃ anussarati, D. I.13 ff.) we may treat them as one school. The argument seems to have been that since pre-existence, as perceived by jhāna or yoga (*v.* ātappamanvāya . . . anuyogamanvāya . . . ceto samādhiṃ phusati, *loc. cit.*), was a fact, it was necessary to posit the existence of an eternal soul to account for it. Buddhaghosa describes this argument as follows: 'Remembering two or three (previous) births, if he argues "I myself existed in such and such a place in the past, therefore the soul is eternal", then he is one who reasons on the basis of remembering his past births' (dve tisso jātiyo saritvā 'aham eva pubbe asukasmiṃ nāma ahosiṃ, tasmā sassato attā' ti takkayanto *jatissaratakkī* nāma, DA. I.107). In arguing that the soul was eternal they probably inferred that the soul was different from the body, which was evidently not eternal.

(385) It is possible to identify this school with some degree of probability with one of the Upaniṣadic schools of thought. In the Sutrakṛtāṅga, where the Materialists (Tajjīvataccharīravādins) criticized the thesis that the 'soul is different from the body' (anno jīvo annaṃ sarīraṃ, 2.1.9, *op. cit.,* Vol. II, fol. 11 = P. aññaṃ jīvaṃ aññaṃ sarīraṃ), they argued that their opponents could not point to the soul as a separate entity from the body, just as one may remove 'a fibre from a muñja stalk' (muñjāo isiyaṃ, *loc. cit.*) and show it separately. Now this example, as we have shown (*v. supra,* 130), is found in the Kaṭha Upaniṣad and known in the Pāli Nikāyas. The use of this simile signifies the practice of jhāna or yoga since it was said that 'one should draw out (the ātman) from one's own body, like an arrow-shaft

from a reed'.[1] In fact it is even specifically stated that 'the soul shines not forth but is *seen* by subtle seers with superior and subtle awakened intellect' (ātmā na prakāśate, dṛśyate tvagryayā buddhyā sūkṣmayā sūkṣmadarśibhiḥ, Kaṭha 1.3.12) in a context which enjoins the practice of yoga (*op. cit.*, 1.3.13). Now in this Upaniṣad, it is stated that 'the ātman is constant and eternal ... and is not slain when the body is slain' (nityaḥ *śaśvato'* yaṃ ... na hanyate *hanyamāne śarīre*, 1.2.18). According to the Upaniṣad the ātman is claimed to be *seen* by these yogis as distinct from the body as a result of the practice of yoga, against which the Materialists argued (*v. supra*, 131) that this could not be objectively demonstrated. This is a somewhat different argument from the one stated in the Brahmajāla Sutta but both these schools seem to be very similar in their outlook.

(386) Even the schools of the Semi-eternalists mentioned in the Brahmajāla Sutta (D. I.17–22) in so far as they believed in the integrity of the soul, may be deemed to have subscribed to the theory that 'the soul was different from the body'. The fourth school is said to have argued (*v.* takkī, D. I.21) that 'the soul as consciousness, mind, or intelligence is eternal' (cittaṃ ti vā mano ti vā viññāṇan ti vā ayaṃ *attā* nicco dhuvo *sassato*, *loc. cit.*) while the soul consisting of the sense-organs is not eternal (cakkhun ti sotan ti ... ayaṃ *attā asassato*). This implies that consciousness regarded as the soul is eternal and different from the body. The theory results from metaphysical arguments based on empirical premisses (*v. infra*, 430).

(387) The Caraka Saṃhitā too records an argument of the same type of a school which held the thesis that 'the soul is different from the body'. It reads as follows: 'Since when the eternal soul is present in the body, the signs of life are cognizable and (they) are not cognizable at the departure (of the soul), the eternal soul is different from the body' (yathā nityamātmani śarīrasthe jīvaliṅgānyupalabhyante tasya cāpagamānnopalabhyante tasmād anyaḥ śarīrād *ātmā nityaśc*'eti, 3.8.6.52). It is difficult to identify the school which put forward this argument but one may compare the phrase *ātmā nityaḥ* in this passage with *attānicco* in the Pāli version in the previous paragraph. This argument is also a metaphysical (causal) argument based on empirical premisses; when the soul is present, the signs of life are present and when the soul is absent, the signs of life are absent. Therefore the soul is the cause of the signs of life and not the body, which must be

[1] *v.* Hume, *The Thirteen Principal Upaniṣads*, p. 361.

different from it. The argument is metaphysical since the soul is an unverifiable.

(388) Thesis (1) seems to have been held in the same schools, which asserted the eternity of the soul, since later we find the view presented in the form sassato attā ca loko ca (*v. infra,* 395). We do not find anywhere in the literature of this period a view which combined the eternity of the soul with the non-eternity of the world and vice versa. The probable reason for this is that there was a logical connection between the concepts of attā and loka- at this time. We saw that the Mitavādins (*v. supra,* 382) held that the soul *as well as* the world was finite (mita-) in size. This intimate relation between ātman and loka-, goes back to the Brāhmaṇic analogy between the microcosm and the macrocosm, which weighed heavily in the minds of thinkers even at this time. It finds explicit expression in the Upaniṣads where it is said that 'one should regard the ātman as his loka-' (ātmānam eva lokam upāsīta, Bṛh. 1.4.16). As such the arguments for the eternity of the soul would have been considered as *ipso facto* arguments for the eternity of the world as well. We may notice that even in Buddhism the end of the world is where one's experiences cease to be (*v.* Nāham ... sandhāvanikāya lokassa antam ñātayyaṃ ... ti vadāmi. Na c'āham ... appatvā' va lokassa antaṃ dukkhass' antakiriyaṃ vadāmi, A. IV.430).

(389) Thesis (7) would have been held in any school which believed in the eternity of the soul in a personal sense. Among them probably were some of the Early Upaniṣadic schools for we find it said both in the Bṛhadāraṇyaka and the Chāndogya Upaniṣads that those who practised religion in the highest sense of the word, live for ever in the Brahma worlds. There is no impersonal conception in these contexts of a union with Brahman. At Bṛh. 6.2.15 it is said that 'those who meditate on the truth with faith in the forest' (araṇye śraddhām satyam upāsate) are after death conducted to 'the Brahma worlds where they dwell for ever and in their case there is no return' (te teṣu brahmalokeṣu parāḥ parāvato vasanti, teṣāṃ na punar āvṛttiḥ). The use of brahmalokeṣu (in the plural) and the fact that they are conducted to them by a 'divine spirit' (puruṣo mānasaḥ, Bṛh. 6.2.15 = puruṣo'mānavaḥ, Ch. 4.15.5) is indicative of the pluralist and personal conception. We have no evidence regarding the possible reasons that were adduced in support of this belief, in the eternal existence of the perfect person. We can only make a suggestion. There was a widespread belief at this time in the *a priori* premiss that 'what exists cannot cease to exist'.

We find it in the Jain Sūtras (*sato* ṇatthi *vināso*, *v. supra*, 126) and we find the Buddha accusing the Materialists of asserting the 'destruction of an existent being' (*sato* sattassa . . . *vināsam*, D. I.34). It is possible that this same premiss was made use of to argue that the perfect person who had the quality of 'existence' (sat) could not cease to be and therefore lived eternally in this state.

(390) Thesis (9) was held by the Trairāśika Ājīvikas, who posited the state of *sadasat* (being and non-being) primarily for this reason, though it is difficult to see how this theory was defended (*v. supra*, 227).

(391) Many theories can be adduced in regard to the school in which thesis (10) was probably held. The Commentator Dhammapāla identifies it with the Sceptics: 'one should understand that the Sceptics are indicated by (the thesis) "the tathāgata neither exists nor does not exist after death" ' (n'eva hoti na na hoti tathāgato param maraṇā ti iminā pana amarāvikkhepavādā dassitā hontī ti veditabbaṃ, UdA. 340). This is an ingenious suggestion. The Sceptic, for Dhammapāla is apparently the casuist (vitaṇḍavādin) who denies the truth of both thesis as well as anti-thesis and holds that 'neither p nor not-p' is the case. But this is not supported by the texts for not only was there no evidence that the Sceptics were vitaṇḍavādins, but it was quite clear on the evidence of the texts that Sañjaya, the amarāvikkhepika, rejected this latter alternative as well. If we accept Dhammapāla's suggestion we would have to make a drastic revision of the texts, which is too radical an undertaking.

(392) Both Mrs Rhys Davids and Barua have suggested that this type of expression is employed to denote that no real attributes can be asserted or denied of unreal objects (*v. infra*, 573) but there is no evidence that even the Materialists did in fact regard 'tathāgata' as an unreal concept. It is more likely that this particular theory was held in a school or schools, which claimed that neither existence nor non-existence can be predicated of the saint after death, since personal epithets cannot be predicated of impersonal being. We find two such schools of thought in the Upaniṣads, (i) the rational impersonalism of Yājñavalkya, who asserted that 'after death' (pretya), there was 'neither consciousness' (na saṃjñā), 'nor a state of blankness' (na moha-)[1]—which is equivalent to saying, he neither exists in our sense

[1] *v. supra*, 44.

of existence nor does not, since a living person who exists (hoti) is said to be 'possessed of consciousness' (saviññāṇaka, A. I.132) and a dead body which has ceased to exist is called 'devoid of consciousness' (apetaviññāṇa, Dh. 41); and (ii) the mystic impersonalism of the Middle and Late Upaniṣads. The Śvetāśvatara Upaniṣad speaks of 'a third stage after death which is a product of meditation' (tasyābhidhānād tṛtīyaṃ dehabhede, 1.11), presumably a stage which is describable as neither existence nor non-existence and in the late Māṇḍūkya this 'double na' form of expression is used to describe a 'fourth stage' (caturthaṃ), which is described as 'neither cognition nor non-cognition' (na prājñam nāprajñam, 7) and is said to be strictly 'indescribable' (avyapadeśyam, *loc. cit.*). We do not, however, know on what grounds these theories were defended, if they were debated.

(393) Lastly, thesis (4) is probably that of the Jains. The theory is ascribed to Nigaṇṭha Nātaputta, who, it is said, claims omniscience and says that 'with his infinite intelligence he has a direct knowledge of a world that is infinite' (aham anantena ñāṇena anantaṃ lokaṃ jānaṃ passaṃ viharāmi, A. IV.429). We have changed the reading in the PTS. text from, antavantena ñāṇena antavantam lokam, to, anantena ñāṇena anantaṃ lokaṃ, on the basis of the *variae lectiones*. The reason for doing so is that as the translator Hare has observed,[1] if both Pūraṇa Kassapa and Nigaṇṭha Nātaputta, who are mentioned here, are said to be omniscient, then their knowledge (ñāṇa-) must be infinite. As for loka-, it is obvious from the fact that both are said to be 'in direct contradiction with each other' (aññamaññaṃ ujuvipaccanīkavādānaṃ, *loc. cit.*) that one held that the world is finite and the other that it was infinite. The variant readings offer both possibilities for each, but we have ascribed to Pūraṇa the view that the world is finite and therefore it is necessary to emend the reading from antavantam to anantam in the case of Nigaṇṭha Nātaputta. The Jain texts are not very helpful in solving this problem for, according to the Jain theory, space is classified as 'mundane' (lokākāśa) and 'supramundane' (alokākāśa).[2] If the former was intended by loka- in the Buddhist context, then it is finite since it is contained within alokākāśa, but the latter is infinite (ananta-) and is said to be 'perceivable by omniscience' (sarvajñadṛṣṭigocara).[3] In the Brahmajāla Sutta, this theory is said to

[1] G.S. IV. 288, fn. 2.
[2] *v.* Jadunath Sinha, *A History of Indian Philosophy*, Vol. II, p. 233.
[3] *Ibid.*

be a product of developing yoga and attaining with regard to the world the consciousness that it is infinite (ananta-saññī lokasmiṃ, D. I.27) as a result of which one holds that 'the world is infinite and unbounded' (ananto ayaṃ loko apariyanto, *loc. cit.*). The Comy. explains saying that 'one who has developed one's meditational device beyond the limits of the world-sphere becomes conscious of its infinitude' (cakkavāḷa-pariyantaṃ katvā vaḍḍhitakasino pano anantasaññī hoti, DA. I.115). Such a person is said to oppose the falsity of the theory that the world is finite and spherical ('antavā ayaṃ loko parivaṭumo' ti tesaṃ musā, D. I.23), but it is difficult to see how two theories, both based on mystical experiences, could have been opposed in debate unless they were defended or criticized on rational grounds as well. The Upaniṣads too support the mystical basis of this view, where space (ākaśa) identified with one's soul presumably in a yogic mystical experience, is said to be infinite (ananto) and unbounded (aparimito) in all directions. 'Verily in the beginning this world was Brahman, the infinite one—infinite to the east, infinite to the south, infinite to the west, infinite to the north, above and below, infinite in every direction . . . unbounded . . . the soul that is space.'[1]

(394) The commentator of the Udāna identifies this theory with that of Kapila (i.e. Sāṅkhya) and Kaṇāda (i.e. Vaiśeṣika) though not exclusively: etena KapilaKaṇādādi vādā dassitā honti, by this the theories of Kapila and Kaṇāda, etc., are specified, UdA. 339. Now Sāṅkhya certainly considers space as infinite.[2] So does Vaiśeṣika consider ākāśa or space to be all-pervading.[3] But there is no evidence that these theories in any developed form existed at the time of the Pāli Nikāyas.[4]

[1] Brahma ha vā idam agra āsit, eko'nantaḥ, prāg ananto dakṣinato'nantaḥ, pratīcyananta udīcy ananta ūrdhvañ c'avāñ ca sarvato'nantaḥ . . . aparimito . . . ākāśātmā, Mait. 6. 17.

[2] Sāṅkhyapravacanabhāṣya, 2.12.

[3] *v.* Radhakrishnan, *Indian Philosophy*, II, p. 189.

[4] Jacobi believed in an extensive influence of Sāṅkhya on Buddhism; *v.* 'Der Ursprung des Buddhismus aus dem sāṅkhyayoga', *Nachrichten von der Königliche Geselschaft der Wissenschaften zu Göttingen*, philosophisch-historisch Klasse, 1896. Pischel agreed with him; *v. Leben und Lehre des Buddha*, p. 61. So did Schayer; *v. Vorarbeiten zur Geschichte der Mahayanistischen Erlösungslehren*, München, 1921, p. 235. But these speculations are groundless as shown by Oldenberg (*v. Die Lehre der Upanishaden und die Anfänge des Buddhismus*, p. 357) and Thomas, *History of Buddhist Thought*, pp. 77–81.

(395) In addition to the above ten theses, which are said to be debated by rival groups 'deeply attached to their respective theories which they cherish' (nānādiṭṭhi-nissaya-nissitā, Ud. 67), there is another list of sixteen theories in this same context, which are said to be similarly debated. They may be classified under four groups according to the topics discussed:

I. The *duration* of the soul and the world:

(a) sassato attā ca loko ca, the soul and the world are eternal.
(b) asassato attā ca loko ca, the soul and the world are not eternal.
(c) sassato asassato ca, the soul and the world are both eternal and not eternal.
(d) n'eva sassato n'āsassato, the soul and the world are neither eternal nor not eternal.

II. The *cause* of the soul and the world:

(a) sayaṃkato attā ca loko ca, the soul and the world are self-caused.
(b) paraṃkato attā ca loko ca, the soul and the world are caused by external agency.
(c) sayaṃkato ca paraṃkato ca attā ca loko ca, the soul and the world are both self-caused as well as caused by external agency.
(d) asayaṃkāro ca aparaṃkāro ca adhicca-samuppanno, the soul and the world have neither self nor external agency as a causal factor and are uncaused.

III. The *duration* of the experiences of pleasure and pain as well as of the soul and the world:

(a) sassataṃ sukhadukkhaṃ attā ca loko ca, the experiences of pleasure and pain, the soul and the world are eternal.
(b) asassataṃ sukhadukkhaṃ attā ca loko ca, the experiences of pleasure and pain, the soul and the world are not eternal.
(c) sassatañ ca asassatañ ca . . . loko ca, the experiences of pleasure and pain, the soul and the world are both eternal and not eternal.
(d) n'eva sassatañ ca n'asassatañ ca . . . loko ca, the experiences of pleasure and pain, the soul and the world are neither eternal nor not eternal.

IV. The *cause* of the experiences of pleasure and pain, the soul and the world:

(a) sayaṃkataṃ sukhadukkhaṃ attā ca loko ca, the experiences of pleasure and pain, the soul and the world are self-caused.

(b) paraṃkataṃ sukhadukkhaṃ attā ca loko ca, the experiences of pleasure and pain, the soul and the world are caused by external agency.

(c) sayaṃkatañ ca paramkatañ ca . . . loko ca, the experiences of pleasure and pain, the soul and the world are both self-caused as well as caused by external agency.

(d) asayaṃkāraṃ aparaṃkāraṃ adhiccasamuppannaṃ ca . . . loko ca, the experiences of pleasure and pain, the soul and the world have neither self nor external agency as a causal factor and are uncaused.

(396) *Prima facie* this looks an artificial list, but it is not difficult to show that it contains a summary of views which were probably debated at this time. It will be seen, however, from scrutinizing the list that the views set forth under I and II are contained in the corresponding groups under III and IV respectively. The reason for distinguishing them is due either to the fact that the topics under I and II used to be discussed separately or the author of this passage tried to magnify the list by separating them. We may therefore ignore I and II and consider III and IV.

(397) The views listed under III appear to be mere extensions of the avyākata-theses, sassato loko (*v.l. supra*, 378) and asassato loko (*v.* 2, *supra*, 378). As we have shown, there is a logical connection between the concepts of attā (soul) and loka- (world) (*v. supra*, 388) so that the school which held the view sassato loko would also have subscribed to the view sassato attā, such that, sassato attā ca loko ca, would be in fact the thesis of one and the same school.[1] There seems to be a similar connection between the presence of the ātman (attā) and its experiences (sukhadukkha) such that if the ātman was eternal, its experiences (sukhadukkha) will also be eternal. We may therefore conclude that (i) sassato loko, (ii) sassato attā ca loko ca, (ii) sassataṃ sukhadukkhaṃ attā ca loko ca, are substantially one and the same view, since (i) implies (ii) and (iii). By a similar train of reasoning it may be shown that III (b) is implied by the thesis asassato loko, which we identified with the Materialist school of thought (*v. supra*, 379).

(398) III (c) and (d) are the other two logical alternatives according to the fourfold scheme. The problem is whether they were merely

[1] It may be observed that there is no school which combined the eternity of the soul with the non-eternity of the world and vice versa.

hypothetical possibilities or actual schools of thought existing at this time.

(399) The Comy. identifies III (c) with the doctrines of the four schools 'which maintain that the soul and the world are partly eternal and partly not eternal' (ekaccaṃ *sassataṃ* ekaccaṃ *asassataṃ attānañ ca lokañ* ca, D. I.17) in the Brahmajāla Sutta. The second of these schools, as we observed, was that of the Trairāśika Ājīvikas, which posited the new category of sadasat (*v. supra*, 227). There is nothing intrinsically objectionable in this identification.

(400) It is difficult exactly to identify III (d), but we can suggest two plausible hypotheses. It will be seen that if the highest reality was conceived as Timeless, it is natural that it should be thought that temporal epithets having a durational significance cannot be predicated of it. Now both sassata- (eternal) and asassata- (non-eternal) in their normal use have a durational connotation and if ātman and the loka- were conceived as Timeless, then the attributes sassata- and asassata- cannot be predicated of it and these concepts would be describable as 'neither sassata nor asassata' (n'eva sassato na asassato). In the Mait. Upaniṣad it is said that 'there are two forms of Brahman, time and the timeless (akālaḥ); that which is prior to the sun is the timeless, without parts, but that which begins with the sun is time, which has parts' (dve vāva brahmaṇo rūpe kālaś cākālaś cātha yaḥ prāg ādityāt so'kālo'kalo' tha ya adityād yaḥ sa kālaḥ, sakalaḥ . . . 6.15). Later this Brahman is called 'the *ātman* of the sun' (adityātmā brahma, *loc. cit.*). While all things are subject to time, time itself is under the control of the timeless as explained in the verse:

kālaḥ pacati bhutāni sarvāṇy eva mahātmani
yasmin tu pacyate kālo yas taṃ veda sa vedavit,
(Mait. 6.14.)

i.e. time cooks all things in the great *ātman*; he who knows in what time is cooked, knows the Veda, *loc. cit.*. . .; a similar verse is quoted in the Jātakas:

kālo ghasati bhūtāni sabbān'eva sahattanā
yo ca kālaghaso bhūto so bhūtapacanim paci,
(J. II.260.)

i.e. time consumes all beings including one's self; the being who consumes time cooks the cooker of beings.

(401) This shows that the Buddhist texts were aware of the concept of the timeless, since the concept of what 'consumes time' is the same as 'that in which time is consumed (*lit.* cooked)' (yasmin tu pacyate kālaḥ). It is therefore possible that it was this theory that was alluded to by III (d). The only problem is that in such a case it is difficult to see how sukhadukkha- the 'experience of pleasure and pain' could be timeless! A possible explanation is that the author of this passage included this in order to preserve the symmetry of his classifications.

(402) A more plausible hypothesis would be to identify III (d) with an Ājīvika doctrine which denied the reality of time altogether and seems to have been a product of *a priori* reasoning. According to this theory time was illusory in a static universe in which there was no multiplicity or motion. It is the doctrine of *avicalita-nityatvam* (*lit.* motionless permanence), which Basham mistakenly believed was a *later* development of the Ājīvika school (*op. cit.*, p. 236) since he failed to see the evidence for the existence of this doctrine in both the Buddhist as well as the Jain texts. The version of the doctrine given in the Sūtrakṛtāṅga misled even Śīlāṅka, who erroneously identified it with the Śūnyavāda school of Buddhism and this in turn misled Jacobi (*v. infra*). The Sūtrakṛtāṅga (1.12, 6, 7) associates the doctrine with a school of akiriyavādins and states it as follows: 'Te evam akkhanti abujjhamānā virūva-rūvāni akiriyavāī . . . nāicco uēī na atthameti, na candimā vaḍḍhati hāyati vā salilā na sandanti na vanti vāyā vanjho niyato kasine hu loē', i.e. those Akiriyavādins, who have no understanding propose diverse (theories) . . . the sun does not rise or set, the moon does not wax or wane, rivers do not flow and winds do not blow; the whole world is deemed (niyato = niścitaḥ, Comy.) to be unreal (vañjho = Skr. vandhyaḥ, *lit.* void). This is a doctrine which denies the reality of multiplicity and motion and asserts that the world of appearance is unreal. Now Jacobi translating the above passage says in a footnote quoting Śīlāṅka that 'this is the opinion of the Śūnyavādins' (SBE., Vol. 45, p. 317, fn. 1) meaning by the Śūnyavādins the Buddhist school of Śūnyavāda and in his Introduction (*op. cit.*, p. xxv) Jacobi himself considers this identification as correct. Now, in the first place, Jacobi's footnote is misleading and inaccurate, since Śīlāṅka identifies this theory with both the Buddhists as well as the Materialists. Commenting on te evam akkhanti, he says 'te CārvākaBauddhādayo 'kriyāvādino evam ācakṣate', i.e. those Materialists, Buddhists and others, who are akriyāvādins say so, *op. cit.*,

Vol. I, fol. 220 on Sū. 1.12.6). The ascription of this theory to the Materialists would have been strange if not for the fact that we now know that there was a school of nihilist Lokāyata which denied the reality of this world as well. Śīlāṅka's comments show beyond doubt that he had in mind this nihilist school to which Jayarāśi belonged, since he criticizes with the help of a quotation the main epistemological argument on which the whole thesis of this school, as we have shown (*v. supra,* 100), was based, viz. Lokāyatikānāṃ sarvaśūnyatve pratipādyatvena pramāṇam asti, tathā c'oktam *tattvānyupaplutānī* ti yuktyabhāve na siddhyate sā'sti cet saiva nastattvam tatsiddhau sarvam astu sat, *loc. cit.,* i.e. the Lokāyatikas do have a means of knowledge in putting forward the theory that nothing exists for it has been said, 'that all principles have been upset' is not proved in the absence of reason, but if reason exists, then that is a principle for us and when that is proven, everything should exist'. As an alternative Śīlāṅka considers this doctrine as a corollary of the kṣaṇikavāda of the Buddhists, viz. Bauddhānām apyatyantakṣanikatvena vastutvābhavaḥ prasajati, *loc. cit.,* i.e. owing to the (doctrine of) excessive momentariness the Buddhists deny the real existence of things. In this it can be shown that both Śīlāṅka and Jacobi who followed him are mistaken, since this identical doctrine is mentioned in one context in the Pāli Canon as a heretical teaching (diṭṭhi): Na vātā vāyanti, na najjo sandanti, na gabbhiniyo vijāyanti, na candimasuriyā udenti vā apenti vā esikaṭṭhāyiṭṭhitā (S. III.202), i.e. winds do not blow, rivers do not flow, women with child do not give birth, the sun and the moon does not rise or set, (they all) stand firm as pillars'.

(403) We may therefore safely rule out the contention of Śīlāṅka and Jacobi that this is a view of the Buddhists. It is not so easy to rule out the possibility that this view was held in the nihilist school of Lokāyata, particularly since there was some evidence for the early existence of this school (*v. supra,* 334) but nothing that is contained in the passage suggests that it could belong to this school and it is clear that Śīlāṅka was himself merely suggesting plausible hypotheses. Besides, it is unlikely that the nihilist Materialists would have made a detailed denial of the reality of motion since they merely denied the existence of the world as such on epistemological grounds, because there were no valid means of knowing it.

(404) Barua had noticed this passage in the Sūtrakṛtāṅga, though not its Pāli parallel, and boldly identifies it with certain doctrines in the

Upaniṣads. He says: 'Referring obviously to the Muṇḍakas, the Gautamakas, the Katyāyanas and others Sudharman adds: They declare that the sun does not rise there (in the Brahma-world), nor does it set . . .' (*op. cit.*, p. 197). By adding the words 'in the Brahma-world' in his translation, unsupported by the original, he has distorted its meaning since the original says that the sun does not rise, etc., *in this world* (implied by the examples given). If the Brahma-world was meant by the passage, it is surely absurd to say according to this passage that the Brahma-world was 'barren' (vañjho). Barua is evidently thinking of the stanza which occurs at Kaṭha 2.2.15 = Muṇḍ. 2.2.11 = Śvet. 6.14; viz. *na tatra sūryo* bhāti *na candratārakam* n'emā vidyuto bhānti kuto'yam agniḥ, i.e. the sun shines not there, nor the moon nor stars, these lightnings shine not, much less this fire. Now the counterpart of this Upaniṣadic verse is found in the Udāna as Barua himself was the first to point out (*op. cit.*, p. 424) and reads as follows: *na tattha* sukkā jotanti *ādicco nappakāsati, na tattha candimā bhāti* tamo tattha na vijjati, Ud. 9. It appears from the context that this is a description of the Buddhist state of Nibbāna. Since Barua was ignorant of the Pāli parallel to the Sūtrakṛtāṅga passage, he failed to observe that his identification, dependent on the slender basis of the mere similarity of a sentence, did not hold water, since the Buddhists could not have been criticizing their own views, which would be the case if Barua's identification was correct. We cannot therefore agree with Barua's attempt to see in this passage this particular Upaniṣadic doctrine.

(405) If we compare the Jain and the Buddhist versions we observe that according to the former account the world is unreal or void (vañjha) and according to the latter account everything is firm (esikaṭṭhāyiṭṭhitā). Now, these two epithets occur together in the description of the doctrine of Pakudha Kaccāyana, viz. vañjhā kūṭaṭṭhā esikaṭṭhāyiṭṭhitā, a phrase which recurs in the description of the soul (attā) and the world (loko) in each of the eternalist theories (D. I.14, 15, 16). At the same time it may be noticed that, as Basham has observed, the doctrine of immobility was part of Pakudha Kaccāyana's theory.[1] This was the reason why he surmised that the 'new doctrine of Avicalita-nityatvam' was 'imported into the Ājīvika

[1] He speaks of Pakudha's 'Parmenidean doctrine of immobility' (*op. cit.*, p. 17) and says that he 'maintained that elementary categories were as firm as mountains, neither moving . . .' (*op. cit.*, p. 236).

system by the school of Pakudha' (*op. cit.*, p. 236). It would therefore appear most plausible to suggest that here was the original doctrine of avicalita-nityatvam, which was part and parcel of Pakudha's theories from their very inception. Plausible as this may appear, there is a serious difficulty which makes it necessary to distinguish between the two theories, which seem to us to have had an independent origin, though they have fused together in later Ājīvikism.

(406) Pakudha, it may be observed, was a realist (*v. infra*, 427). His categories were real and in this sense they were 'firm as pillars' (esi-kaṭṭhāyiṭṭhitā). But the Sūtrakṛtāṅga version of the other passage speaks of 'the whole world' (kasine loë = Skr. kṛtsnaḥ lokaḥ) as being 'unreal or void' (vañjho = Skr. vandhyaḥ = artha-śūnyaḥ, devoid of objects, Śīlāṅka, *loc. cit.*). This passage does not speak of separate categories as in the case of Pakudha's theory but says of the entire world that it is unreal, while for Pakudha at least his elemental categories were real. If so, it may be asked why Pakudha's categories are also called vañjha (= Skr. vandhyaḥ). In fact, as we have shown (*v. infra*, 426) Pakudha's categories should have been called not vañjha but avañjha as in fact they are called in the Sūtrakṛtāṅga parallel passage to Pakudha's doctrines (*v. infra*, 425), which neither Rhys Davids nor Basham seem to have compared with the Pāli version. But vañjha- is ambiguous and Buddhaghosa explains the word as meaning 'barren' (*v. infra*, 426) in the sense that these categories being substances could not *affect* or *produce* other substances. Vañjha- in the sense of 'unreal' does not fit the context of Sū. 1.12.6, where quite clearly the world of appearance as opposed to reality is considered unreal. We therefore have to distinguish the two doctrines. Pakudha was a realist who believed in the reality of the elements and denied the reality of motion but not of multiplicity, while the unknown author of the other doctrine was probably an idealist who believed in the unreality of the empirical world and denied the reality of motion and of multiplicity as well.

(407) To return to the problem we were discussing, we find according to this theory that motion or change and hence time was considered unreal. If so, temporal epithets like sassata- (eternal) and asassata- (non-eternal) could not be predicated of a world in which time was unreal. Hence they put forward the theory III (d).

(408) The theory appears to be a product of reasoning rather than of imagination or mystic experience. Dr Basham has suggested that the

doctrine of *avicalita-nityatvam* is a corollary of the niyativādin's thesis that time is unreal, from which it follows that motion and change are unreal; he has seen a similarity with 'the system of Parmenides' (*op. cit.*, p. 236). We agree with this last observation, but we think that the simplest explanation is to regard it as a corollary of the most widely accepted premiss at this time, namely that 'being was real'. From this it follows that being is changeless and therefore what appears to change or move must be unreal. The world of appearance, which is a world of motion and change is therefore unreal, so that from the ultimate point of view nothing moves or changes.

(409) The commentator Dhammapāla gives a different explanation of III (d): 'The proposition "neva sassato nāsassato ..." represents the theory of the Sceptic. They see the defects in the theory of the Eternalists and the Non-eternalists and adopt this sceptical view' (n'eva sassato n'āsassato ti iminā amarāvikkhepavādo dassito. Te hi sassatavāde ca asassatavāde ca dosaṃ disvā 'n'eva sassato nāsassato attā ca loko cā'ti vikkhepaṃ karontā vicaranti, UdA. 344). We have already seen why this kind of explanation of the Sceptic's point of view is unsatisfactory (*v. supra*, 391).

(410) The fact that the propositions constituting IV (a)–(d) concerning the *cause* of the experience of pleasure and pain, the soul and the world were vexed questions which were being debated at this time, finds independent confirmation from the Upaniṣads and the Jain texts. The Śvetāśvatara Upaniṣad represents the brahmavādins (brahmavādinaḥ, 1.1), presumably in the brahmodyas (*v. supra*, 46) holding disputes with regard to the following questions, (i) kiṃ kāraṇam, what is the cause, (ii) kutaḥ sma jātāḥ, whence are we born, (iii) jīvāma kena, whereby do we live, (iv) kva ca sampratiṣṭhāḥ, on what are we established, (v) adhiṣṭhitāḥ kena *sukhetareṣu* vartāmahe, ruled by what do we dwell in pleasure and pain (sukhetareṣu = sukhadukkheṣu, Śaṅkara). It may be noted that problems (i)–(iv) concern the ultimate *cause* of things, i.e. of the world and the soul, and (v) the cause of the experiences of pleasure and pain. The confirmation from the Jain texts has already been noticed (*v. surpa*, 211) and would be evident from the sequel.

(411) We do not propose to make a detailed study of the numerous theories mentioned in the Buddhist and Jain texts, which have to be

included under IV, since considerations of space forbid us from doing so. We shall confine ourselves to making a few observations.

(412) Proposition IV (b), for instance, is identified with various schools by the commentator as follows: 'It means that the soul and the world are made or created by another, i.e. by Īśvara, Puruṣa, Prajāpati, Time or Prakṛti' (atthato parena Issareṇa vā Puriseṇa vā Pajāpatinā vā kālena vā pakatiyā vā attā ca loko ca nimmito ti attho, UdA. 345). Let us confine ourselves only to the first theory.

(413) Issara- in the sense of God as the creator is known in the Nikāyas. At D. III.28, the theory that the origin of the universe is to be traced to creation by Issara is mentioned as a theory put forward by one of the current schools of thought (santi eke sāmaṇabrāhmaṇā Issarakuttaṃ ... aggaññaṃ paññapenti, i.e. there are some recluses and brahmins who propose the theory that the origin of the world is (to be traced to) creation on the part of Issara). Elsewhere, we find that 'pleasure and pain may be due to creation by Issara (= Skr. Īśvara)' stated as one of the current theories (sattā Issaranimmāṇahetu sukhadukkhaṃ paṭisaṃvedenti, M. II.222, A. I.273). In the Śvetāśvatara Upaniṣad we find that Īśvara, who is the 'highest God of the gods' (īśvarānāṃ paramam maheśvaram, 6.7) is considered the ultimate 'cause' (kāraṇam, 6.9). In the Jain texts, the theory that Īśvara is the cause of the world (loë), souls (jīva-) as well as of pleasure and pain (suhadukkha-) is expressly stated; Īsarena kaḍe loë ... jīvājīvasamaütte suhadukkha samanniē, i.e. the world has been created by Īśvara ... endowed with souls and non-souls, pleasure and pain, Sū. 1.1.3.6). Here Śīlāṅka mentions the argument from design as the argument put forward by the Theists. The argument as stated by Śīlāṅka takes as its major premiss the proposition that 'whatever is characterized by design is seen to be preceded by an intelligent cause' (yadyatsaṃsthānaviśeṣavattattadbuddhimatkāra(ṇa)pūrvakam, *op. cit.*, Vol. I, fol. 42 on Sū. 1.1.3.6); the things in the world, it is said, are characterized by design and (considering the nature of the design) 'the author of the whole universe cannot be an ordinary person but must be Īśvara himself' (yaśca samastasyāsya jagataḥ kartā sa sāmānyapuruṣo na bhavatītyasāvīśvara iti, *loc. cit.*). It is an inductive argument with a metaphysical conclusion, an argument from empirical facts to transcendent reality which, the positivist school of Materialists argued, does not come within the sphere of inference proper (*v. supra*, 94). There is no direct evidence that the argument was known

to the Pāli Nikāyas, but the argument from evil against the possibility of a creator (*v. infra*, 698), which is an extension of the argument from design, showing that if God exists evil must be part of the design, may have been intended to counter an argument of the above sort.

(414) Proposition IV (c) is explained in the Comy. as the theory that holds that both God as well as oneself are causal factors in the genesis of the experiences of pleasure and pain: 'It is the belief of some that God, etc., in creating the soul and the world do not create entirely of their own accord but take into consideration the good and evil of each being (considered as) a co-operative cause and thus the soul and the world is self-caused and caused by another' (yasmā attānañ ca lokañ ca nimminantā Issarādayo na kevalaṃ sayam eva nimminanti, atha kho tesaṃ tesaṃ sattānaṃ dhamm'ādhammānaṃ sahakārikāraṇaṃ labhitvā'va tasmā sayaṃ kato ca parakato ca attā ca loko cā ti ekaccānaṃ laddhi, UdA. 345). We find traces of this theory in the Śvetāśvatara Upaniṣad although Īśvara here is in general the one primary and sole cause of all things. While God remains the creator, each person assumes various forms according to his deeds (karmānugāny anukrameṇa dehī sthāneṣu rūpāṇy abhi samprapadyate, 5.11). Thus karma- is also a causal factor in addition to Īśvara.

(415) It is necessary to understand what is meant by adhiccasamuppannaṃ in proposition IV (d), if we are to identify any of the schools which put forward this thesis. As we have shown (*v. infra*, 763) it seemed to have been originally coined to denote the concept of yadṛcchā which means 'chance' or 'fortuitous circumstance' in sense equivalent to saṅgati or 'what happens to come together'. Thus, it denoted a casual occurrence as opposed to a causal occurrence. But before long it seemed to have been extended to denote any non-causal occurrence, which was non-causal in the sense of being opposed to a causal occurrence (paṭicca-samuppanna-) as understood in Buddhism. In this latter sense it was apparently equated with ahetu-appaccayā (A. I.173). Thus, in this sense it came to denote both the niyativāda-, which is a Strict Determinism as well as yadṛcchā-vāda-, which is its opposite or Indeterminism. While the usage within the Nikāyas supports this explanation, it also has the sanction of the commentator Dhammapāla who says: 'Adhiccasamuppanna- means "arisen by chance"; it is called the theory of fortuitous origination as

(events) arise without any cause. Therefore (tena) even the ahetuka-vāda- is to be included in it' (adhicca-samuppano ti *yadicchāya* samuppanno, kena ci kāraṇena vinā uppanno ti adhiccasamuppannavādo dassito. Tena ahetukavādo pi saṅgahīto hoti, UdA. 345). We have discussed some of these theories and the kind of reasoning they employed in the second chapter (*v. supra*, 198–210).

(416) We have discussed above the theories which were said to have been actually debated at this time. We may observe that they represent a wider variety of schools than envisaged by classes (b), (d), (e) and (f) of our list (*v. supra*, 317). We have been able to identify many of the schools in which these theories were held, but it would have been noticed that the kinds of reasoning employed by these theorists were many and various. It is necessary to distinguish between (a) the kind of consideration which led to the construction of the theory from (b) the reasons employed in the defence of the theory against their opponents' criticisms. In so far as reason played a part in (a), we may observe that some theories (*v. supra*, 379, 387, 389, 408, 413, 415) were the product of pure reasoning, while in the case of others reasoning played only a minor rôle. These latter are classifiable into those in which reasoning is employed on the alleged data of extrasensory perception (*v. supra*, 383, 384, 393) and those in which reasoning is based on premisses derived from report (*v. supra*, 382). In fact, Buddhaghosa's list of different kinds of '*reasoners*' (takkī) proves useful in classifying the above theorists. This is what he says: 'There are four types of *reasoners*, one who reasons on a premiss based on tradition (or report), one who reasons on a premiss based on retrocognition, one who reasons on a premiss based on jhānic experience and the pure reasoner. In this connection, he who hears such a statement as "there was a king named Vessantara" and argues on the basis of it that "if Vessantara is identical with the Exalted One, then the soul is eternal" and accepts this theory is one who reasons on a premiss based on tradition (*anussutiko*). One who remembers one or two (prior) births and argues that since it was he who existed in the past in such and such a place, therefore the soul is eternal, is one who reasons on a premiss based on retrocognition (*jatissara-takkī*). He who, because of his jhānic experience, argues that since his soul is happy in the present, it must have been so in the past and it will be so in the future and accepts the theory (that the soul is eternal) is an intuitionist reasoner (*lābhī takkiko*). But a pure reasoner (*suddhatakkiko*)

is one who accepts this theory on pure reasoning of the form if p is true, q is true or if p is true, q is not true'.[1]

(417) While we do not meet with any instance of the use of the word takkika- to mean 'sophists' or 'casuists' (vitaṇḍavādi) in the Pāli Canon, there is some reason to suggest that the word is used in the above sense of 'reasoners'. We have to draw our conclusions from the suggested meaning of the word takkika- in its only occurrence at Ud. 73: evam obhāsitam eva titthiyānaṃ yāva sammāsambuddhā loke n'uppajjanti, na *takkikā* sujjhanti na c'āpi sāvakā, duddiṭṭhī na dukkhā pamuccare ti, i.e. so long as the perfectly enlightened ones do not arise in the world, neither the takkikas nor the disciples would attain salvation; holding false theories (dud*diṭṭhī*), they would not be released from suffering. This passage occurs in the general context of debates and controversies which are the subject of discussion continuously from pp. 66–72 and in which all the debated theories that we discussed are mentioned (pp. 66–70). The other clue that the passage gives is the obvious reference of takkika- to the *titthiyas* (*v.* titthiyānāṃ) and in the general context of the passage we note that titthiyā is used in reference to 'the recluses, brahmins and/or wandering ascetics', who held the various philosophical theories and debated them: sambahulā nānā*titthiyā* samaṇabrāhmaṇā paribbājakā ... nānā*diṭṭhikā*, Ud., 66.7.

(418) It may be argued that takkika- here means 'quibbler' on the ground that the suffix -ka has a derogatory connotation (cp. samana*ka*, D. I.90; pandita*ka*, bahussuta*ka*, tevijja*ka*, D. I.107). But it may be noted that this same suffix is often added with hardly any change of meaning (cp. kaṇṭa- = thorn, Miln. 351 and kaṇṭaka, Sn. 845; mañca, Sn. 401 and mañca*ka*, S. I.121). The fact that it was necessary to add the affix ku- in front to give a really derogatory meaning to the word (kutārkika-, *s.v.* Monier-Williams, Sanskrit English Dictionary) in Sanskrit, shows that the word by itself did not necessarily have such a meaning. We may also note that takkikā in the above passage are

[1] Tattha *catubbidho takkī*, anussutiko jātissaro lābhī suddhatakkiko ti. Tattha yo 'Vessantaro nāma rājā ahosī' ti ādīni sutvā, tena hi 'yadi Vessantaro' va Bhagavā sassato attā ti takkayanto diṭṭhiṃ gaṇhāti, ayaṃ *anussutiko* nāma. Dve tisso jātiyo saritvā, 'aham eva pubbe asukasmiṃ nāma ahosiṃ, tasmā sassato attā' ti takkayanto *jatissara-takkī* nāma. Yo pana lābhitāya, 'yathā me idāni attā sukhito atīte evam āsi, anāgate pi evaṃ bhavissatī 'ti takkayitvā diṭṭhiṃ gaṇhāti, ayaṃ *labhī takkiko* nāma. 'Evaṃ sati idaṃ hoti, evaṃ sati idaṃ na hotī 'ti takkamatten' eva pana gaṇhanto *suddha-takkiko* nāma, DA. I.106, 107.

discussed on a level with the sāvakā 'the disciples of the Buddha' and that the attitude to the takkī in the Sandaka Sutta (*v.* M. I.520) is a comparatively favourable one, since they are classified not among the upholders of false religions but of religions which are unsatisfactory or unconsoling. In the light of the above evidence it seems reasonable to suggest, as against Vidyabhusana and Keith, *et al.*, that takkikā is used here to mean 'reasoners' or 'debaters' in general and not for a narrow class of quibblers or sophists.

(419) Whatever the meaning of takkika- in the above context, the term takkī is quite clearly used of a 'rationalist' in the sense of a 'pure reasoner' (suddha-takkika) who constructed a metaphysical theory on the basis of reasoning. In this sense takkī and vīmaṃsī (investigator, speculator) go together. There are four such theories mentioned in the Brahmajāla Sutta, as being the product of such rational speculation. We may examine them to see the kind of reasoning on which they are based.

(420) The first is described as follows: 'Herein a certain recluse or brahmin is a reasoner and speculator. By the exercise of reason and speculative inquiry, he arrives at the following self-evident (conclusion): the soul and the world are eternal, independent, steadfast as mountain peaks and as firm as pillars—these beings transmigrate and fare on, die and are reborn and exist for ever and for ever.'[1]

(421) Oldenberg saw in this passage the Sāṅkhya dualism of the eternal puruṣa and prakṛti and noting the fact that puruṣa is called kūṭastha in Sāṅkhya held that this was an inexact description of Sāṅkhya. Thomas, half-heartedly following Oldenberg, says, adverting to the inaccuracy of the description that this passage (along with another of the same type) 'speak(s) of doctrines that were rejected even without being understood'.[2] Since Sāṅkhya applies the epithet kūṭastha only to the puruṣa[3] it is admitted that this is not an exact account of the essentials of Sāṅkhya thought. We would conclude from this as against Oldenberg and Thomas that this is not a reference to Sāṅkhya philosophy at all.

[1] Idha . . . ekacco samaṇo vā brāhmaṇo vā takkī hoti vīmaṃsī. So takka-pariyāhataṃ vīmaṃsānucaritaṃ sayaṃ-paṭibhānam evam āha: Sassato attā ca loko ca vañjho kūṭaṭṭho esikaṭṭhāyiṭṭhito, te ca sattā sandhāvanti saṃsaranti cavanti upapajjanti, atthi tveva sassati-saman ti, D. I.16.

[2] *History of Buddhist Thought*, p. 77.   [3] *Ibid.*

(422) The description exactly fits the account given of Pakudha's philosophy at D. I.56. The epithets *vañjha-*, *kūṭaṭṭha-* and *esikaṭṭhāyiṭṭhita-* qualify the soul (attā-) and the world (loko) in the accounts given of the other three Eternalist theories as well (*v.* D. I.14, 15, 16) but the only theory which we know independently to be a product of reasoning and in which the soul (jīve = attā) as well as the categories that comprise the world are described with the same set of epithets, is that of Pakudha Kaccāyana.

(423) Now, Jacobi had observed the parallel to Pakudha Kaccāyana's philosophy in the āyacchaṭṭhavāda (= Skr. ātma-śaṣṭha-vāda) mentioned in the Sūtrakṛtāṅga. Of this, he says: 'This seems to have been a primitive or a popular form of the philosophy which we now know under the name of Vaiseshika. To this school of philosophy we must perhaps assign Pakudha Kaccāyana of Buddhist record' (SBE., Vol. 45, p. xxiv). Jacobi does not give any reasons for these identifications but judging from what he says he seems to have been struck by the pluralistic realism, which is a feature common of the philosophies of Vaiśeṣika, Pakudha Kaccāyana and the Ātmasaṣṭhavāda.

(424) The Ātmaśaṣṭhavāda asserts the reality of the five material elements and the soul, each regarded as a permanent substance: santi panca-maha-bbhūyā, ihamegesi ahiyā āyacchaṭṭho puṇo āhu, āyā loge ya sāsaë (Sū. 1.1.1.15), i.e. herein it is asserted by some that there are five great elements; further they say that the soul is the sixth (substance) and that the soul and the world are eternal. The statement, āyā loge ya sāsaë (= Skr. ātmā lokaśca śāśvataḥ) which is equivalent to Pāli, attā loko ca sassato (cp. sassato attā ca loko ca, D. I.16) makes it quite evident that this was one of the theories, which held that the soul and the world were eternal.

(425) The other passage from the Sūtrakṛtāṅga which we have already quoted (*v. supra,* 126) in discussing the theory of metaphysical materialism, which is also promulgated in it, tells us one of the premisses on which the reasoning of this school was based. That it is identical with the theory described at Sū. 1.1.1.15 cannot be doubted when we note the identity of the description: iccete *pañcamahabbhūyā* aṇimmiyā aṇimmāvitā akaḍā ṇo kittimā ṇo kaḍagā aṇāīyā aṇihaṇā avanjhā apurohitā satantā *sāsatā āyacchaṭṭhā*, puṇa ege evam āhu—sato ṇatthi viṇāso asato ṇatthi sambhavo.

(426) Superficially there is a difference between this theory and that of Pakudha Kaccāyana, since the latter speaks of the 'soul as the

seventh (substance)' (jīva-sattame, D. I.56) whereas the former speaks of the 'soul as the sixth (substance)' (atma-śaṣṭha-). The difference is due to the fact that the Buddhist version does not mention ākāśa- (corresponding to āgāse pañcame mahabbhūte, Sū. 2.1.10 = SBB., 2.1.22) though it mentions the other four elements in the same order as the Jain version; at the same time it mentions sukha- and dukkha- as substances (kāya-), which are omitted in the Jain account probably because they play a different rôle to that of the other substances (*v. infra*) and are therefore not on the same footing. But these differences do not touch the core of the doctrine. The close similarity or identity of the two theories is seen from the identity of the descriptions of the material elements and the soul in the two accounts: Pakudha Kaccāyana's substances (kāyā) are described with the epithets *akaṭā* (not made), *animmitā* (not created) and *animmātā* (not caused to be created,[1] i.e. not indirectly created). The same epithets qualify the material elements and the soul in the Jain version; viz. *akaḍā* (= P. akaṭā), *animmiyā* (= P. animmitā), *animmāvitā* (= P. animmāpitā). There is however an apparent difference which we have already discussed (*v. supra,* 406), when the Buddhist version says that the substances were *vañjha-* whereas the Jain version says that that they were *avañjha-*, but there is no contradiction since *vañjha-* is here used in the sense of 'barren'[2] meaning 'unproductive' or 'independent' corresponding to satantā (= Skr. sva-tantrāḥ) in the Jain account whereas *avañjha-* in the latter means 'not void' or 'real'; the Buddhist account too makes it quite clear that the elements were real and permament substances.

(427) The metaphysics of Vaiśeṣika bears a general similarity to the philosophical outlook of the above theory. The atomistic pluralism of Vaiśeṣika posits the real and independent existence of the soul (ātman) as well as the five elements, all of which are regarded as substances[3] as in the above theory. Obvious differences no doubt exist, such as the fact that the Vaiśeṣika is a Kriyāvāda philosophy,[4]

[1] The Jain parallel (animmāvitā) and the Comy. (animmātā ti animmāpitā, DA. I.167) support this translation.

[2] i.e. unproductive; Dr Basham says following the Comy., 'they are barren (vañjhā), which must imply that they do not multiply as do living beings' (*op. cit.*, p. 262). What is meant by that they do not produce or affect anything else being independent substances.

[3] *v.* Hiriyanna, *Outlines of Indian Philosophy*, p. 229.

[4] Jacobi points this out, *v.* SBE., Vol. 45, p. xxv.

which posits the existence of more substances and categories than are envisaged in the above theory. It is therefore difficult to say whether this was a proto-Vaiśeṣika theory or the nucleus from which the later Vaiśeṣika theory emerged, but it is necessary to observe that the similarity seems to extend to another important feature of the two philosophies. The Caraka Saṃhitā, which as we have seen, appears to have preserved an earlier logical terminology than that of the Nyāya tradition (*v. supra*, 323), seems also to have preserved an earlier definition of two central concepts in the philosophy of Vaiśeṣika, sāmānya- and viśeṣa-:[1]

sarvadā sarvabhāvānāṃ sāmānyaṃ vṛddhikāraṇam
hrāsahetur viśeṣaśca pravṛttir ubhayasya tu,

i.e. *sāmānya* is the cause of the increase and *viśeṣa* the cause of decline of all events at all times and there is a continuity of both. This is certainly different from the meanings of 'universals' and 'particularity' attached to these concepts in orthodox Vaiśeṣika and shows at least what changes this philosophy underwent before assuming its present shape. Now Keith had noticed a correspondence between the six elements of Pakudha Kaccāyana and the six factors of Empedocles,[2] which means that sukha- (pleasure) and dukkha- (pain) are comparable to Empedocles' principles of Harmony and Strife. Whether they played a similar rôle in the philosophy of Pakudha Kaccāyana, it is difficult to say in the absence of positive evidence, but the fact that they were not mentioned in the Sūtrakṛtāṅga account nor in some of the later Ājīvika accounts[3] which were aware of them, possibly indicates that they played a different rôle in his theory from that of the other elements, perhaps, analogous to the rôle of sāmānya and viśeṣa in the proto-Vaiśeṣika philosophy, as found in the Caraka Saṃhitā.

(428) The philosophy of Pakudha Kaccāyana seems to be a perfect product of *a priori* reasoning and we have already shown the steps of this reasoning in discussing the genesis of this philosophy, without the concept of the soul (*v. supra*, 126). The presence of the concept of the soul makes no difference to the argument and we need not repeat this here. It is important to reiterate that two premisses seem to have been accepted as self-evident, (i) that what is distinguishable has

[1] *v.* 1.1.43; Prasad, *History of Indian Epistemology*, p. 123, where the reference is wrongly given as *Śarīra*, I.43, whereas the verse occurs in Sūtrasthāna, 1.43.

[2] Keith, *Religion and Philosophy of the Vedas*, HOS., Vol. 32, p. 611.

[3] Basham, *op. cit.*, p. 91.

a separate reality—a basic assumption or premiss of the Vaiśeṣika philosophy,[1] and (ii) that being cannot be destroyed nor come from non-being. This latter premiss is actually stated at Sū. 2.1.9 (= SBE., 2.1.22), which gives an account of this philosophy and Pakudha seems to have made use of it in the same way in which Empedocles makes use of this same premiss, which he derived from Parmenides.[2] From these premisses it follows in a few self-evident steps that there must be discrete independent substances (the material substances and the soul), uncreated and indestructible. Being independent (Ard. Mag. satantā, P. vañjhā) substances, they do not affect each other (na aññamaññaṃ vyābādhenti, *lit.* do not obstruct each other, *loc. cit.*) and Keith is certainly mistaken in talking about their 'interaction' (*loc. cit.*).

(429) This theory which is said to be a 'product of (rational) thinking and (metaphysical) speculation' (takka-pariyāhataṃ vīmaṃsānucaritaṃ, *loc. cit.*) is also said to be *sayaṃ-paṭibhānam*, which we have rendered as 'self-evident' and which has been translated by Prof. Rhys Davids as 'conclusion of his own' (SBB., Vol. II, 29). The Comy. explains this as 'what has become merely evident to him' (attanā paṭibhānamattasañjātaṃ, DA. I.106). Paṭi-bhāti (Skr. prati + √ bhā, to appear)[3] means 'to appear, to be evident, to be before one's mind, to occur to one, to be clear' (*s.v.* PTS. Dictionary) and sayaṃ-paṭibhānam would therefore mean 'what appears clearly and distinctly before oneself', which is the same as 'self-evident'. This, coupled with the fact that 'sato ṇatthi vināso, asato ṇatthi sambhavo' is an *a priori* premiss and the conclusion was evidently reached by *a priori* reasoning, 'self-evident' here almost has the connotation of 'known *a priori*'. There is however no evidence that the distinction between *a priori* reasoning and empirical reasoning was recognized in the Nikāyas, although there appears to be a distinction between takka- and anumāna- which roughly corresponds to a distinction between logical reasoning and empirical reasoning (*v. infra*, 757 f.). We may therefore conclude that sayaṃ-patibhānam here has at least a psychological connotation of 'self-evident', if not a logical connotation.

[1] The very word Vaiśeṣika is formed from viśeṣa- which means 'difference', the central concept of Vaiśeṣika philosophy.

[2] Stace, *A Critical History of Greek Philosophy*, p. 82; 'Parmenides . . . had taught that whatever is, remains always the same, no change or transformation being possible. Empedocles here too follows Parmenides. . . .'

[3] Cp. *Points of Controversy*, pp. 378 ff.

(430) The thesis of the second theory which is said to be a product of reason and speculation and which is introduced in identical language to that of the first, is as follows: 'That which is called the eye, the ear, smell, taste and touch is a self which is impermanent, unstable, not eternal and subject to change. But that which is called thought, mind or consciousness is a soul which is permanent, steadfast, eternal and not subject to change, it abides for ever and ever'.[1] Thomas following Oldenberg considers this passage too as an account of Sāṅkhya. But he considers it an inexact account, since according to Sāṅkhya 'not only the five senses but also the group to which mind belongs, stands on the side of material nature' (*op. cit.*, p. 77). The Comy. says that it is the argument of one who holds that the sense-organs are destructible but that the mind is indestructible: 'He sees the dissolution of the eye, etc. But since thoughts cease no sooner the antecedent states have given rise to the consequent states, he fails to observe the more rapid dissolution of the mind. Not seeing that, he believes that just as much as birds leave one tree and hide in another, so when this personality breaks up, the mind goes elsewhere'.[2]

(431) We may dismiss the identification with the Sāṅkhya theory altogether for there is no similarity or point of comparison between the two at all. The theory can be partly traced to one of the many Upaniṣadic theories about the ātman. At Bṛh. 5.6.1, the person consisting of the mind is said to be the supreme reality: *manomayo 'yaṃ puruṣaḥ* . . . sa eṣa sarvasyeśvaraḥ, i.e. this person consisting of the mind . . . is the lord of all. In the same section, it is said that when a person departs from this world at death he goes to a world where he dwells (as a person) eternally: yadā vai puruṣo 'smāllokātpraiti . . . sa lokaṃ āgacchaty aśokaṃ ahimaṃ, *tasmiṃ vasati śāśvatīḥ samāḥ*, i.e. when this person departs from this world . . . he goes to a world where there is no heat or cold and there abides for ever, 5.10.1. We may compare the use here of *śāśvatīḥ samāḥ* with *sassati-samaṃ* in the

[1] Yaṃ kho idaṃ vuccati cakkhun ti pi sotan ti pi ghānan ti pi jivhā ti pi kāyo ti pi ayaṃ attā anicco addhuvo asassato vipariṇāmadhammo. Yañ ca kho idaṃ vuccati cittan ti vā mano ti vā viññāṇan ti vā ayaṃ attā nicco dhuvo sassato avipariṇāmadhammo sassatisamaṃ tath'eva ṭhassatī ti, D. I.21.

[2] Ayaṃ cakkhādīnaṃ bhedaṃ passati. Cittaṃ pana yasmā purimaṃ purimaṃ pacchimassa pacchimassa paccayaṃ datvā' va nirujjhati, tasmā cakkhādīnaṃ bhedato balavataram pi cittassa bhedaṃ na passati. So tam apassanto yathā nāma sakuṇā evaṃ rukkhaṃ jahitvā aññasmiṃ nilīyante, evam eva imasmiṃ attabhāve bhinne cittaṃ aññattha gacchatī ti . . ., DA. I.114.

Pāli version. Unfortunately, we are not given the reasoning behind this view, which is often the case with Upaniṣadic theories. Buddhaghosa's analogy of the bird (compared to the soul) and the tree is found in the Upaniṣads (Praśna 4.7; Śvet. 4.6) but not in the context that he suggests. The argument based on observation that the person can exist without the sense-organs but not without prāṇa or the life-breath (identified with the 'intelligential self' in the Kauśītaki Upaniṣad[1]) is often mentioned (Bṛh. 1.3.1–7, 1.7–13) but in these contexts, manas (mind) is treated as one of the sense-organs. We have not been successful in tracing the argument in pre-Buddhistic thought. The argument possibly was that sense-organs being material were destructible while the mind being immaterial was indestructible and that what was indestructible was immortal, but this is pure surmise.

(432) The next thesis based on reasoning and speculation and introduced in identical language as the first reads as follows: 'This world is neither finite nor infinite. Those recluses and brahmins who say that the world is finite and spherical are wrong. Those recluses and brahmins who say the world is infinite and without limit are also wrong. And so are the recluses and brahmins who say that the world is both finite and infinite'.[2] The Comy. is unhelpful and it is difficult to see what the reasoning of this school could have been. We would tentatively suggest that it could be the view of the school which held the doctrine of *avicalitanityatvam* (*v. supra*, 402–8) and which, probably on the basis of *a priori* arguments, proved the unreality of multiplicity, motion and of the world. According to this theory if the world was unreal (vañjha), then space was unreal and therefore the spatial epithets 'finite' or 'infinite' could not be predicated of it. So the world is 'neither finite nor infinite' and the three other logical alternatives based on the conception that space was real are proved to be false.

(433) The next rational thesis is: 'The soul and the world are noncausal in origin' (adhicca-samuppanno attā ca loko ca, D. I.29). Prof. Rhys Davids translates the phrase as 'fortuitous in origin' but as we

[1] This is the main theme of this Upaniṣad; *v.* . . . prāṇo'smi prajñātmā, 3.2, 'I am the breathing spirit, the intelligential self' (Hume, *The Thirteen Principal Upanishads*, p. 321).

[2] N'evāyaṃ loko antavā na panānanto. Ye te samaṇa-brāhmanā evam āhaṃsu: 'Antavā ayaṃ loko parivaṭumo' ti tesaṃ musā. Ye pi te samaṇa-brāhmanā evam āhaṃsu: 'Ananto ayaṃ loko apariyanto' ti tesaṃ pi musā. Ye pi te samaṇa-brāhmaṇā evam āhaṃsu: 'Antavā ca ayaṃ loko ananto cā 'ti tesaṃ pi musā . . . D. I.23, 24.

have shown (*v. supra,* 415; *v. infra,* 763) whatever the original etymological meaning of the word, we find that in usage it referred to either (a) a purely Deterministic theory or (b) a purely Indeterministic theory. If it was the former, it could be identified with the niyativādin's thesis, which as we have shown (*v. supra,* 199) was a product of *a priori* reasoning; the Comy. explains adhiccasamuppanna- as 'noncausal in origin' (akāraṇa-samuppannaṃ, DA. I.118) and this may very well imply the niyativāda-, which has been called the *ahetuka-vāda* (the non-causal theory, *v. supra,* 415) in the Nikāyas.

(434) The above four theories are the only four which are stated in the Nikāyas to be exclusively the product of *takka-* (cp. takkapariyāhataṃ) and according to the Comy. those who constructed these theories would have to be classified as suddha-takkikā or 'pure reasoners'. There are, however, a few theories mentioned in the Pañcattaya Sutta of the Majjhima Nikāya, which according to the commentary are a product of various kinds of reasoning (*v. supra,* 416) including pure reasoning. Thus the theory that 'the soul and the world were extremely happy' (ekanta-sukhī attā ca loko ca, M. II.233) in our pre-existent state[1] is said to be a theory that can have one of three epistemic origins: 'This theory may arise as that of the mystic (who reasons on the data of his experiences), the person who remembers his past births (and reasons on this basis) and the (pure) reasoner. In the case of the mystic, the theory arises as a result of his recalling by means of his retrocognitive knowledge his (past) life in a kṣatriya family as extremely happy; similarly in the case of the person remembering his prior births, who experiences happiness in this life and recalls that his soul was in the same state in the previous seven lives. In the case of the (pure) reasoner, it arises as a result of his experiencing happiness in this life and arguing that he was identically the same in the past'.[2]

(435) We are now in a position to see that the term takka- meant in the Pāli Nikāyas either (i) the kind of reasoning with which the theories, which were debated at this time, were defended or criticized, even if they may not have been in origin products of reasoning at all, or

[1] Note that this theory is a pubbantānudiṭṭhi, 'a theory relating to the prior end (i.e. pre-existence)', M. I.233.

[2] Ayam diṭṭhi lābhi-jātissara-takkīnaṃ vasena uppajjati: lābhino hi pubbenivāsañāṇena khattiyakule ekantasukham eva attano jātim anussarantassa evaṃ diṭṭhi uppajjati, tathā jātissarassa paccuppannaṃ sukham anubhavato atītāsu sattasu jātisu tadisam eva attabhāvaṃ anussarantassa, *takkissa* pana idha sukhasamaṅgino atīte p'āham evam eva ahosin ti *takken'eva* uppajjati, MA. IV.24.

(ii) the kind of reasoning with which the speculative, rational metaphysical theories were constructed and which the commentator has called 'pure reasoning'. We found that these latter appear to have been constructed on the basis of *a priori* reasoning, but the instances were too few and their identity too uncertain for us to be quite sure about this. So when it was enjoined that 'one should not accept (a theory) on the grounds of takka-' (mā takka-hetu, *v. supra,* 314), it meant that 'reasoning' of the type (i) or (ii) should not be considered as giving knowledge of the truth of these theories.

(436) This is further clarified in the Sandaka Sutta, where it is said that one of the four types of religions which are said to be unsatisfactory but not necessarily false is that based on 'reason and speculation'. It says: 'Herein . . . a certain teacher is a reasoner and investigator; he teaches a doctrine which is self-evident and is a product of reasoning and the pursuit of speculation. But in the case of a person who reasons and speculates, his reasoning may be good or bad, true or false'.[1] In this passage too we have the same problem that we met with in the passage referring to the anussavikā- (*v. supra,* 282). The text reads: takkissa . . . satthuno . . . sutakkitam pi hoti duttakkitam pi hoti, tathā pi hoti aññathā pi hoti, which is translated by Miss Horner as, 'If a teacher is a reasoner . . . part is well-reasoned and part is badly reasoned and is both right and wrong' (M.L.S. II.200). For the same reasons, which we urged against a similar translation of the previous passage (*v. supra,* 282, 283), we would prefer to translate this (literally) as 'It is (sometimes) well-reasoned and (sometimes) ill-reasoned by a teacher who is a reasoner and it is (sometimes) true and (sometimes) false'. This would give the four possibilities:

1. sutakkitaṃ tathā, i.e. well-reasoned true
2. sutakkitaṃ aññathā, i.e. well-reasoned false
3. duttakkitaṃ tathā, i.e. ill-reasoned true
4. duttakkitaṃ aññathā, i.e. ill-reasoned false.

If this explanation is correct, it means that the truth or falsity of a theory in relation to fact cannot be judged by the consistency of its reasoning, for even a well-reasoned theory may be false in the light of contingent facts and an ill-reasoned theory true. The soundness of

[1] Idh'ekacco satthā takkī hoti vīmaṃsī, so takkapariyāhataṃ, vīmaṃsānucaritaṃ sayam paṭibhānaṃ dhammaṃ deseti. Takkissa kho pana . . . satthuno vīmaṃsissa sutakkitam pi hoti duttakkitam pi hoti, tathā pi hoti aññathā pi hoti, M. I.520.

the reasoning is no guarantee of truth in the same way in which (as it was said) what was accepted on the best authority may be false (*v. supra*, 279).

(437) The next ground for accepting a proposition which is said to be unsatisfactory is *nayahetu* (*v. supra*, 314). There are two senses of naya- with an epistemological import, which were probably current at this time. One is the sense of 'standpoint' as found in the school of the Trairāśika Ājīvikas and the Jains (*v. supra*, 218, 228), while the other was the sense of 'inference'. The former sense is not met with elsewhere in the Canon, while the latter is viewed with favour. Thus at S. II.58 and Vbh. 329 (*v. infra*, 758) it is not all considered illegitimate or unsatisfactory in any way to infer from an observed present causal occurrence that it would have held true in the past and would hold true in the future. In one place in the Jātakas (IV.241) naya- is used for 'right inference' (nayaṃ nayati medhāvi, i.e. the wise man draws a right inference) as opposed to anaya- for 'wrong inference'[1] (anayaṃ nayati dummedho, i.e. the fool draws a wrong inference). One therefore wonders whether it is not preferable to render naya- here as 'standpoint' or 'point of view' and translate nayahetu as 'because it is a standpoint or a point of view', which is appropriate to the context. There is, however, a context in the same stratum as the passage under discussion in which 'nayena nayati' is used for 'infers in this manner' where it is not clear whether the inference is legitimate or not. It is said that the brahmin Todeyya 'infers in this manner' (iminā nayena neti, A. II.180). Here the inference seems to be that from the premisses p and q (*v. infra*) he infers r:

p—paṇḍito rājā Eleyyo, the king Eleyya is wise.
q—(yasmā) . . . samaṇo Rāmaputto rañño Eleyyassa paṇḍitena paṇḍitataro, (since) . . . the recluse Ramaputta is wiser than the wise king Eleyya.
r—tasmā, rājā Eleyyo samaṇe Rāmaputte abhippasanno, therefore the king Eleyya is exceedingly pleased with the recluse Rāmaputta.

This instance is given to illustrate the general principle that 'it is impossible . . . for an evil person to recognize an evil person' (aṭṭhānaṃ . . . yaṃ asappuriso asappurisaṃ jāneyya, *loc. cit.*) and it seems

[1] *The Comy.* (*loc. cit.*) explains anayaṃ neti as akāraṇaṃ kāraṇan ti gaṇhāti, i.e. takes as a reason what is not a reason.

as if the above inference is considered illegitimate.[1] The context is obscure and although the verb neti is used in the sense of 'infers', naya- is not used in the sense of 'inference' but of 'method' or 'manner of inference' which was probably the origin of the secondary meaning of 'inference', which the term has acquired.

(438) The next ground on which it is said that one should not accept a proposition as true is that of ākāra-parivitakka-, translated by Woodward as 'after considering reasons' (G.S. II.200), following the commentary which has 'thinking that this is a good reason after reflecting over reasons in this manner' (sundaraṃ idaṃ kāraṇan ti evam kāraṇa-parivitakkena, AA. II.305).

(439) The sense is attested in the PTS. Dictionary (*s.v.*) which gives 'reason, ground, account' as the fifth meaning of ākāra- and gives D. I.138, 139 as the instances in the Canon. But the term does *not* occur in the sense of 'reason' in this context. The text reads: dasah' ākārehi paṭiggāhakesu vippatisāram paṭivinodetum, which has been correctly rendered by Prof. Rhys Davids as 'in order to prevent any compunction that might afterwards in ten *ways* arise...' (SBB., II.179). The term, however, *does* occur in the sense of 'reason' at M. I.320. This context throws much light on the exact use of ākāra- in this sense. Here it is said that if others were to question a monk as to 'what were the *reasons* (*ākārā*) or the grounds (anvayā) on which he says that "the Exalted One is perfectly enlightened"' (ke ... *ākārā* ke *anvayā*[2] yen'āyasmā evam vadesi: sammāsambuddho Bhagavā ... *loc. cit.*), he should be in a position to reply that he has studied the dhamma and 'had come to realize by his own personal higher knowledge the truth of part of the dhamma and has come to the conclusion (on this basis) that "the Exalted One was perfectly enlightened"' (tathā thatā 'haṃ tasmiṃ dhamme abhiññāya idh'ekaccaṃ dhammaṃ dhammesu niṭṭhaṃ agamaṃ ... sammāsambuddho Bhagavā ..., *loc. cit.*). Such a belief based on reasons is said to be 'a belief based on *reasons* and grounded in personal experience' (*ākārā*-vatī saddhā dassana-mūlikā, *loc. cit.*). This ākāra- is here used to denote the 'reasons' which are adequate for one to have a rational belief (saddhā) not amounting to knowledge (ñāṇa, *v. infra*, 666). When, therefore, it is said that 'one

[1] As an exercise in logic it is clear that one cannot infer r from p and q, unless one assumes an extra premiss.

[2] Cp. anvaye ñāṇaṃ (*v. supra*, 758) for 'inductive knowledge'; probably in origin, *lit.* 'knowledge of causes'.

should not accept (anything as true) after reflecting on reasons' what is meant is reflecting on reasons, not quite adequate for one to claim knowledge.

(440) The next ground is that of diṭṭhi-nijjhāna-kkhanti translated as 'reflection on and approval of some theory' (G.S. II.200). The Comy. suggests 'because it agrees with our theory accepted after consideration and after being convinced of it' (amhākaṃ nijjhāyitvā khamitvā gahita-diṭṭhiyā saddhiṃ sameti, AA. II.305). We have seen that khamati occurs with diṭṭhi in the sense of 'approving of' or 'agreeing with' some theory (e.g. sabbaṃ me khamati, M. I.497, *v. supra*, 333). But nijjhānaṃ khamati occurs as a single phrase to describe the conviction that dawns after thinking about a theory (or the dhamma) and intelligently examining its meaning, viz. te taṃ dhammaṃ pariyāpunitvā tesaṃ dhammānaṃ paññāya atthaṃ na upaparikkhanti, tesaṃ te dhammānaṃ paññāya atthaṃ anupaparikkhataṃ na *nijjhānaṃ khamanti* . . ., i.e. they learn a doctrine but do not intelligently examine its meaning, and not intelligently examining its meaning they do not become convinced of it, M. I.133. The positive use is also found: sutvā dhammaṃ dhāreti, dhatānaṃ dhammānaṃ attham upaparikkhati, attham upaparikkhato dhammā *nijjhānaṃ khamanti* dhammā nijjhānakkhantiyā sati chando jāyati, i.e. having heard the doctrine he bears it in mind, and examines the meaning of doctrines borne in mind; in examining the meaning he becomes convinced of the doctrines borne in mind and being convinced of its meaning there arises the desire (to live up to it). We may observe from these passages that nijjhānakkhanti occurs after intelligent consideration of a theory is followed by the desire to act in accordance with it (cp. chando jāyati . . . ussahati, *loc. cit.*). This implies that nijjhānakkhanti means the 'conviction that results from thinking about a theory' (nijjhāna- = ni + √dhyā, to think, cp. ātmā . . . *ni-didhyā*sitavyaḥ, Bṛh. 2.4.5, 4.5.6). So the phrase diṭṭhi-nijjhāna-kkhantiyā would mean 'because one is convinced of some theory'. This would favour the meaning suggested by the Comy. rather than the translator, e.g. one accepts that p is true because it agrees with a theory that one is convinced of.

(441) The Pancattaya Sutta records sixteen theories, which are said to be accepted on subjective considerations (saddhāya, out of faith; ruciyā, out of one's likes, authority (anussava-, *v. supra*, 261–93) as well as the kind of rational reflection defined above as ākāra-parivitakka and diṭṭhi-nijjhāna-kkhanti). After enumerating the theories it

says: 'It is impossible that one should have a perfect and clear personal knowledge of these (theories) apart from believing in them out of faith, likes, authority, consideration of some reasons (ākāra-parivitakka-) or conviction based on reflecting on them (diṭṭhi-nijjhāna-kkhanti). In the absence of a perfect and clear personal knowledge, even if these recluses and brahmins acquire a partial knowledge (*lit.* clarify only a part of their knowledge) of them, it would be an entanglement (upādāna-) of theirs' (... tesaṃ vata aññatr eva saddhāya aññatra ruciyā aññatra anussavā aññatra *ākāraparivitakkā* aññatra *diṭṭhinijjhānakkhantiyā* paccattaṃ yeva ñāṇaṃ bhavissati parisuddhaṃ pariyodātan ti n'etaṃ ṭhānaṃ vijjati. Paccattaṃ kho pana ñāṇe asati parisuddhe pariyodāte, yad api te bhonto samaṇabrāhmaṇā tattha ñāṇabhāgamattam eva pariyodapenti, tad api tesaṃ bhavataṃ samaṇabrāhmaṇānaṃ upādānaṃ akkhāyati, M. I.234).

(442) It will be seen that one cannot hope to have perfect knowledge (ñāṇa) of a proposition or theory by the consideration of some reasons for it (ākāra-parivitakka-) or by the conviction that dawns by merely reflecting on it (diṭṭhi-nijjhāna-kkhanti). Belief on the basis of these two kinds of rational reflection, is placed on the same footing on epistemological grounds as faith (saddhā), authority (anussava-) or purely subjective considerations like likes or dislikes (ruci). We have already observed that in the Caṅkī Sutta it was said that these five grounds of acceptance of a theory or proposition (viz. saddhā, ruci, anussava-, ākāraparivitakka-, diṭṭhinijjhānakkhanti-) were said to have a 'twofold result in this life itself' (diṭṭhe'va dhamme dvidhā vipākā, M. I.170, *v. supra*, 278, 279) namely of turning out to be either true or false for 'even that which is well reflected upon (suparivitakkitaṃ, M. I.171) or well thought out (sunijjhāyitaṃ, *loc. cit.*) is liable to be baseless, unfounded and false, while that which is not well reflected upon or not well thought may turn out to be true, factual and not false' (api ca ... suparivitakkitaṃ yeva hoti ... sunijjhāyitaṃ yeva hoti, tañ ca hoti rittaṃ tucchaṃ musā; no ce pi suparivitakkitaṃ hoti, no ce pi sunijjhāyitaṃ hoti, tañ ca hoti bhūtaṃ tucchaṃ anaññathā, *loc. cit.*). The moral was that 'an intelligent person safeguarding the truth should come absolutely to the conclusion that p is true and not-p false' (viññunā purisena nālaṃ ettha ekaṃsena niṭṭhaṃ gantum: idam eva saccaṃ, mogham aññan ti, *loc. cit.*) on any of the above grounds.

CHAPTER VI

ANALYSIS AND MEANING

(443) In this Chapter we propose to examine the nature of the analytical outlook, which is one of the features of the thought of the Pāli Canon. It is to this outlook that we have to trace the tendency towards classification, definition and the delimitation of the meaning of terms, which becomes very marked in the Abhidhamma Piṭaka. Earlier in the Nikāyas the analytical approach, combined with an empiricism, results in certain important insights and observations with regard to the meaning of propositions.

(444) The cautious critical and analytical approach towards the study of the nature of things is undoubtedly an inheritance of Buddhism from the mood of the age in which it takes its rise. The Materialists had discarded all that was hitherto taken on faith or trust in the most hallowed of traditions and contrasted baseless belief with the knowledge of what can be directly perceived and proved on the basis of perception. The Sceptics went a step further and denied the possibility of knowledge altogether, in the face of a medly of conflicting theories and probably doubted the evidence of the senses as well (*v. supra*, 154). All this could not but have an impact on the elite of the age, the ***viññū purisā***, perhaps typified by a person like Pāyāsi (*v. supra*, 136 ff.), who tried to salvage what he could of the old beliefs with the new methodology and critical outlook though with negative results.

(445) Since Buddhism tried to appeal to this intelligentsia (*v. supra*, 358), it could not afford to establish itself by dogmatic appeals, but had to rely on rational persuasion based on a critical outlook. The appeal to reason seems to have been quite common at this time, judging by the fact that both the orthodox as well as their opponents resorted to it. The Buddhist and Jain works, as we have seen (*v. supra*, 378 ff.), mention many metaphysical theories belonging to

diverse schools of thought, orthodox and heterodox, which were rationally constructed if not rationally defended against each other. The Maitrī Upaniṣad reinforces and confirms what we learn from the heterodox literature (*v. supra*, 77). It stresses the importance of basing our claims to knowledge on valid means of knowledge. At the same time it presents a picture of the atmosphere of confusion and controversy which was a product of the rational temper of the age. It mentions the 'hindrances to knowledge' (jñānopasargāḥ, 7.8) present at this time when there were those 'who love to distract the believers in the Veda by the jugglery of false arguments, comparisons and paralogisms' (ye ... vṛthā tarka-dṛṣṭānta-kuhakendrajālair vaidikeṣu pariṣṭhātum icchanti, *loc. sit.*). It warns Vedic students not to associate with them (taiḥ saha na saṃvaset, *loc. cit.*) and laments that 'the world disturbed by false reasoning (*lit.* false comparisons and proofs) does not discern the difference between the wisdom of the Vedas and the rest of knowledge' (... mithyā-dṛṣṭānta-hetubhiḥ bhrāmyan loko na jānāti veda-vidyāntarantu yat, *loc. cit.*).

(446) In the face of a critical audience, those who wished to propagate their doctrines, had to be critical themselves. It is not surprising therefore that the leader of the Jains recommends the importance of 'analysis' or 'vibhajyavāda' (*v. supra*, 233) in the exposition of doctrines and the Buddha himself claims to be 'an analyst and not (a dogmatist), who makes categorical assertions' (vibhajjavādo ... ahaṃ ... nāhaṃ ... ekaṃsavādo, M. II.197).

(447) What is meant by this claim is clear from the context. The Buddha is asked for his opinion as to the truth of the two propositions: 'The householder succeeds in attaining what is right, just and good' (gahaṭṭho ārādhako hoti ñāyaṃ dhammaṃ kusalaṃ, *loc. cit.*); 'the monk does not succeed in attaining what is right, just and good' (na pabbajito ārādhako hoti ñāyaṃ dhammaṃ kusalaṃ, *loc. cit.*). The Buddha says that one cannot make a categorical assertion (na ... ekaṃsavādo) as to the truth or falsity of propositions of this sort.[1] In the case of the first of the above propositions, if the subject had the characteristic, micchā-paṭipanna- (of bad conduct), then the proposition is false, but if the subject had the opposite characteristic (i.e. sammā-paṭipanna-, 'of good conduct'), the proposition would be true (*loc. cit.*). It is implied that there are certain propositions of which

[1] More examples are given in this Sutta.

it is not possible to say whether they are true or false, without clearing up ambiguities and making certain qualifications and the Buddha is an analyst in so far as he analyses such propositions and makes the requisite qualifications without asserting that they are categorically true or false.

(448) This is similar to though not identical with the Jain point of view, which advocates the attitude of non-absolutism or anekāntavāda with regard to the truth-value of propositions. Propositions according to Jainism are true or false only in respect of certain standpoints or nayas (*v. supra*, 228) and not in any absolute or categorical sense. This means that certain qualifications have to be made or the naya (standpoint) in respect of which the proposition is asserted has to be specified before we can ascertain its truth or falsity.

(449) While in the case of Jainism no proposition could in theory be asserted to be categorically true or false, irrespective of the standpoint from which it was made, in Buddhism such categorical assertions were considered possible in the case of some propositions. But the fact that the Buddha did not make a categorical assertion as to the truth-value of some propositions (e.g. the avyākata-s or unanswered questions),[1] the truth of which was being hotly debated at this time (*v. supra*, 378) seemed to have earned him the reputation in certain circles of being one who did not make any categorical assertions at all. The wandering ascetic Poṭṭhapāda says 'we do not know of any categorical doctrine preached by the recluse Gotama' (na kho pana mayaṃ kiñci samaṇassa Gotamassa ekaṃsikaṃ dhammaṃ desitaṃ ājānāma, D. I.189) supporting this statement of his, by referring to the fact that the Buddha has not categorically declared that any of the avyākata-theses were either true or false. The Buddha in reply says, 'I have taught and laid down doctrines (of which it is possible to make) categorical (assertions) and I have taught and laid down doctrines (of which it is not possible to make) categorical (assertions)' (ekaṃsikā pi . . . mayā dhammā desitā paññattā, anekaṃsikā pi . . . mayā dhammā desitā paññattā, D. I.191). The former are illustrated by the example of the four noble truths[2] and the latter by the avyākata-theses.[3]

[1] We are using this word to denote the ten unanswered questions considered as propositions in the indicative form (*v. supra*, 378).

[2] Katame . . . ekaṃsikā dhammā desitā . . .? 'Idaṃ dukkhan ti, etc.', D. I.191.

[3] Katame . . . anekaṃsikā dhammā desitā . . .? 'Sassato loko' ti vā . . ., etc., *loc. cit.*

Prof. Rhys Davids translates ekaṃsika- here as 'certain' (SBB., Vol. II, p. 256) and anekaṃsika- as 'uncertain' (*loc. cit.*) but this is a strictly incorrect rendering of ekaṃsika- and anekaṃsika-. The PTS. Dictionary also supports this translation; it explains ekaṃsika- as 'certain' and anekaṃsika- as 'uncertain, indefinite' in referring to this context (*s.v.* ekamsika-). Indefinite is certainly better than 'uncertain' in bringing out the epistemological import of the word, if it could mean a proposition of which 'one cannot definitely say that it is true or false' not because of any uncertainty on the part of the knowing subject but on the very nature of the proposition itself (*v. infra*, 477). In the contexts of ekaṃsa- (M. I.393) and ekaṃsa-vāda- (M. II.197, A. V. 190) the word clearly means a categorical assertion as opposed to a conditional assertion (vibhajja-vāda-). Here a conditional assertion (vibhajja-vāda-) would be an anekaṃsa- (or anekaṃsika-) vāda. In Jainism the two classes coincided. For according to the anekāntavāda, only conditional assertions (note, vibhajjavāyaṃ ca viyāgarejjā, *v. supra*, 233) were possible. The obvious similarity of the etymology and meaning of the two words, anekaṃsika- and anekānta- may also be noted. Anekaṃsika = an + ek(a) + *aṃs(a)* + ika and anekānta- = an + ek(a) + *anta* and while aṃsa means 'part, corner or edge' (*s.v.* aṃsa, PTS. Dictionary) anta means 'end or edge'.

(450) But in Buddhism it is necessary to note that while not all propositions were anekaṃsika; those which were, fell into at least two categories, (1) those which after analysis (vibhajja-) could be known to be true or false (*v. supa*, 447), and (2) those like the avyākata-theses, which could not be thus known. Besides, in the Pāli Canon there was nothing strictly corresponding to the naya-doctrine of the Ājīvakas and the Jains, although the theory of double truth (*v. infra*, 615, 618) functions in a way essentially like the naya-theory. In Jainism all statements would be relative (anaikāntika-) because of the relativity of the standpoints. In Buddhism one could not say of all non-categorical statements (anekaṃsika-) that they were true or false from some standpoint or another. In a sense we may say this of the propositions, which it was considered necessary to analyse further before determining their truth or falsity. Thus we could say that the proposition, 'gahaṭṭho āradhako hoti ñāyaṃ dhammaṃ kusalaṃ' (*v. supra*, 447) is true from one point of view, namely if 'gahaṭṭho' is qualified by 'sammā-paṭipanno' but is false from another point of view namely if 'gahaṭṭho' is qualified by 'micchā-paṭipanno'. But in the case of the

avyākata-theses it was not possible to determine their truth or falsehood even after analysis or from any point of view (however, *v. infra*, 814).

(451) So while the analytic approach appears to be partly inspired by the Jain example, it takes a different turn in Buddhism, when we consider the epistemology of the two systems.

(452) The division of statements according to their truth-value into the categorical and the non-categorical and the latter into the analysable and the non-analysable which seems to be implied by the contexts referred to above, is reflected in the analysis of questions which are said to be of four types. It is said that 'a person is not a fit person to debate (or discuss with) if he, when asked a question does not categorically explain a question which ought to be categorically explained, does not analytically explain a question which ought to be explained analytically, does not explain with a counter-question a question which ought to be explained with a counter-question and does not set aside a question which ought to be set aside'.[1] In the same context a person who does the opposite is said to be a 'fit person to debate with' (kaccho hoti, *loc. cit.*). More generally it stated elsewhere that 'there are these four kinds of explanations of questions' (cattar'imāni ... pañha-vyākaraṇāni, A. II.46). The four are as follows:

(1) pañho *ekaṃsa-vyākaraṇīyo*, i.e. a question which ought to be explained categorically.
(2) pañho *paṭipucchā-vyākaraṇīyo*, i.e. a question which ought to be replied with a counter-question.
(3) pañho *ṭhapanīyo*, i.e. a question that should be set aside.
(4) pañho *vibhajja-vyākaraṇīyo*, i.e. a question which ought to be explained analytically.

(453) It may be noticed that the order in which these questions are mentioned is different from that of the previous passage, but a verse that follows, which may possibly be earlier than the prose passage, preserves the order at A. I.197:

ekaṃsa-vacanaṃ ekaṃ *vibhajja-vacanaṃ* paraṃ
tatiyaṃ *paṭipuccheyya* catutthaṃ pana *ṭhāpaye*,
loc. cit.

[1] Sacāyaṃ ... puggalo pañhaṃ puṭṭho samāno ekaṃsa-vyākaraṇīyaṃ pañhaṃ na ekaṃsena vyākaroti, vibhajja-vyākaraṇīyaṃ pañhaṃ na vibhajja vyākaroti, paṭipucchā-vyākaraṇīyaṃ pañhaṃ na paṭipucchā vyākaroti, ṭhapanīyaṃ pañhaṃ na ṭhapeti, evaṃ santāyaṃ ... puggalo akaccho hoti, A. I.197.

(454) It is possible that the earliest division was into (1) ekaṃsa-vyākaraṇīya-pañha- and (2) anekaṃsa-vyākara-ṇīyapañha- corresponding to the two kinds of statements (ekaṃsikā dhammā and anekaṃsikā dhammā) mentioned at D. I.191. Later, the latter class would have been subdivided into the (a) vibhajja-vyākaraṇīya- and the (b) ṭhapanīya-, corresponding to the two classes of statements that were not ekaṃsika- (*v. supra*, 450). Paṭipucchā-vyākaraṇīya is, in fact, a sub-class of vibhajja-vyākaraṇīya, as will be seen below.

(455) Although this classification of questions is found in the Nikāyas, nowhere in the Pāli Canon is there an attempt to explain and illustrate what is meant by these four kinds of questions. We have to seek these explanations in the Comy. to the Aṅguttara Nikāya (AA. II.308, 309), the Milindapañha (pp. 144, 145), the Abhidharmakośa,[1] the Sphuṭārthābhidharmakośavyākhyā[2] and Poussin's account of the Abhidharmakośa commentaries.[3]

(456) The Mahāvyutpatti (83, p. 29) records the four kinds of explanations (of questions) in the order in which they are stated in the Aṅguttara verse (*v. supra*, 453) and the prose passage at A. I.197 (*v. supra*, 452): ekaṃsa-vyākaraṇam, vibhajya-, paripṛcchā-, *sthāpanīya-vyākaraṇaṃ*. The only innovation it makes is to add vyākaraṇam after sthāpanīya- whereas the Pāli account (A. II.46) merely says ṭhapanīya-, while mentioning vyākaraṇa- along with the other three types. We cannot deduce from this that ṭhapanīya- 'setting aside' was not really considered an explanation of the question since there is the mention of, *cattāri* .... pañhavyākaraṇāni (*loc. cit.*).

(457) While the Pāli Abhidhamma is strangely silent about these questions, the Abhidharmakośa records a verse mentioning not only the four types of questions but four examples illustrating them as well, viz.

> ekāṃśena vibhāgena pṛcchātaḥ sthāpanīyataḥ
> vyākṛtam maraṇotpattiviśiṣṭātmānyatādivat,
> *loc. cit.*

(458) These examples, as will be observed, are different from those we meet with in the Pāli tradition and we cannot assume that the original division in the Nikāyas was intended to be illustrated by examples of the sort adduced, especially when we find that there was

[1] 5.22, Ed. R. Sankṛtyāyana, Benares, 1955, p. 137.
[2] Yasomitra, Ed. U. Wogihara, Tokyo, 1932–6, pp. 465–7.
[3] *v.* L'Abhidharmakośa, Poussin, Vol. 5, sections 21, 22.

no agreement in this regard within the non-Pāli traditions themselves. This does not mean that we can trust the Pāli tradition as giving a wholly correct account of the four types of questions and it is necessary to examine the illustrations in the light of what we can glean from the Nikāyas themselves as to the meaning of these questions.

(459) There is little doubt about the kind of question to which a categorical reply is due, although there is no attempt to demarcate its exact logical boundaries. The Milindapañha gives the example of the impermanence of the skandhas (i.e. the constituent factors of one's personality) and puts the question in the form 'rūpaṃ aniccan ti? vedanā . . . saññā . . . saṅkhārā . . . viññāṇaṃ aniccan ti?' (i.e. Is form impermanent? Feelings . . . ideas . . . conative dispositions . . . cognition impermanent? p. 145). The Ābhidharmikas,[1] explained in the Vyākhyā as the ṣaṭpādābhidharmapāṭhin-s,[2] i.e. most probably the Sarvāstivāda school[3] give the same example among other examples.[4] So do the Mahāsaṅghikas.[5] Buddhaghosa gives the example of 'cakkhuṃ aniccaṃ?' (i.e. is the eye impermanent? AA. II.308)—to which we must answer categorically 'āma, aniccaṃ' (i.e. yes, it is impermanent). All the above examples are taken from the Nikāyas themselves.[6]

(460) The clearest example of a categorical question which the Nikāyas would have envisaged would be one based on the assertion that the ekaṃsikā dhammā were the four truths (*v. supra*, 449). The question would be of the form, 'Is the world full of suffering?' It is possibly an attempt to base their illustrations on these examples which led the Ābhidharmikas to mention the following questions as categorically answerable, viz. 'Le doleur est-elle bien définie . . . le chemin est-il bien défini?' (Poussin, *op. cit.*, p. 45).

(461) The example given by the Vaibhāṣikas in the Abhidharmakośakārikā is the question of the form, sarve mariṣyantī ti, i.e. does everyone die?[7] to which one should reply categorically, mariṣyanti, i.e. they die.

[1] Vibhāṣā 15.13; *v.* Poussin, *op. cit.*, Vol. V, p. 45, fn. 3. [2] *Ibid.*

[3] Cp. Jñānaprasthānaśāstra of Katyāyanīputra, Tr. and Ed. S. B. Śāstri, Vol. I, Śāntiniketan, 1955, Foreword, 'Of the seven Sarvāstivāda texts, the *Jñānaprasthānaśāstra* is the principal work and the other six which are called *pāda* are only supplements to it.' [4] Poussin, *op. cit.*, Vol. V, p. 45.

[5] Poussin, *op. cit.*, Vol. V, p. 47. [6] *v.* S. II.124 and S. II.244 ff.

[7] Poussin, *op. cit.*, Vol. V, p. 44.

(462) There is no agreement in the different traditions in the examples given to illustrate the nature of a question which ought to be answered after analysis. The Milindapañha gives the example, 'aniccaṃ pana rūpan ti?' (i.e. impermanent, it seems, is matter?) after giving 'rūpaṃ aniccan ti?' as an example of a categorically answerable question. Buddhaghosa, who seems to be following the model of the Milindapañha in framing his examples, has 'aniccaṃ nāma cakkhun ti?' (i.e. impermanent, it seems, is the eye?) as an example of this type of question (after giving cakkhuṃ aniccan ti? as an example of the first type). Both these examples do not seem to differ in principle from the examples given by them to illustrate the categorical question, since these examples admit of a categorical reply. Thus the answer one would normally expect to the question, 'aniccaṃ pana rūpan ti?' would be a straightforward 'yes' or 'āma, aniccaṃ rūpaṃ'. But both the Milindapañha as well as Buddhaghosa seem to find that this question has a certain ambiguity or obliqueness, which has to be cleared up analytically when answering it. Thus the suggested answer to aniccaṃ nāma cakkhun ti? is 'na cakkhum eva sotam pi aniccaṃ, ghānam pi aniccaṃ . . .' i.e. 'it is not the eye alone (that is impermanent), the ear and the organ of smell are impermanent as well'. Thus, this kind of answer is intended to clear up any ambiguities in the questions concerned.

(463) The Abhidharmakośakārikā illustrates this question with the example, 'sarve janiṣyantī ti?'[1] for which the suggested reply is sakleśā janiṣyanti na nikleśa', i.e. as Poussin translates, 'les êtres revêtus de passion naîtront; les êtres exempts de passion ne nâitront pas' (*loc. cit.*). At first sight it would seem that this question too admits of a categorical reply; one may answer the question by saying, na sarve janiṣyanti, i.e. all are not born. This is, in fact, the suggestion of Bhadanta Rāma who 'disent que la deuxième question appelle, comme la premiére, une réponse catégorique . . .' (Poussin, *op. cit.*, p. 45). But if the purpose of an answer is to clear up as far as possible the doubts of the question it is not served by this kind of reply. Na sarve janiṣyanti, may mean that 'no one is reborn' or that 'some are reborn'. If it means the second, one would still not be certain as to which types of persons would be reborn and which not. The suggested answer apparently clears up these doubts in the mind of the questioner by analytically examining

[1] *Ibid.*, i.e. 'Is everyone reborn?'

the doubts and ambiguities implicit in the question. So we cannot entirely agree with Bhadanta Rāma's dissent.

(464) The Ābhidharmikas give a much more elaborate example.[1] If a deceitful person desires instruction about the dharmas, he should make distinctions and say in reply that the dharmas are numerous, past, future and present and ask him about which dharmas he wants to know. If he replies that he wants to know about past dharmas, he should distinguish and say that past dharmas are many such as rūpa, saṃjñā, etc., and ask him about which past dharmas he wishes to know. If he asks about rūpa one should distinguish and say that there are three rūpas, good, bad and undefined. This is a very unsatisfactory example. To say, 'Je désire que le Vénérable me dise les *dharmas*'[2] is strictly not to ask a question. The question would strictly be, 'What are the dharmas?' to which it would be possible to answer categorically by enumerating all the dharmas and making in the process the necessary distinctions as well. Besides it is necessary to find out the intentions of the questioner before deciding upon the nature of the question and it is therefore not surprising that the Ābhidharmikas should say that 'le même question, posée par un homme perfide, est la question à laquelle il faut répondre par question' (Poussin, *op. cit.*, 46). Even without this complication the suggested answer contains a counter-question (e.g. les dharmas sont nombreux, passes, futures, presents. Lesquels désires-tu que je dise?) and it would therefore be difficult to distinguish it from the third type of question. We cannot therefore consider this as a valid example of a vibhajja-vyākaraṇīya question as understood in the Nikāyas.

(465) An example of such a question is mentioned in the Nikāyas in another context than that which we have already discussed (*v. supra*, 447). It is said that 'the foolish person Samiddhi gave a categorical reply to a question of the wandering ascetic Potaliputta, which ought to have been replied after analysis' (Samiddhinā moghapurisena Potaliputtassa paribbājakassa vibhajja-byākaraṇīyo pañho ekaṃsena byākato, M. III.208). The question referred to is, 'sañcetanikaṃ ... kammaṃ katvā kāyena vācāya manasā, kiṃ so vediyatī ti?' (i.e. having performed a volitional act with one's body, speech or mind, what does he experience?, M. III.207). Samiddhi replies this categorically saying, 'sañcetanikaṃ ... kammaṃ katvā kāyena vācāya manasā dukkhaṃ so vediyatī ti' (having performed a volitional act

[1] Poussin, *op. cit.*, p. 46. [2] *Ibid.*

with one's body, speech or mind one experiences suffering, *loc. cit.*). This reply is erroneous probably because the term sañcetanikaṃ kammaṃ (volitional act) is ambiguous and can mean (i) sañcetanikaṃ kusalaṃ kammaṃ (a good volitional act), (ii) sañcetanikaṃ akusalaṃ kammaṃ (an evil volitional act), or (iii) sañcetanikaṃ avyākataṃ kammaṃ (a neutral volitional act) and the reply will differ in each case. The Mahāsaṅghikas seem to have noticed this instance in the Nikāyas and give it as an example of this kind of question (Poussin, *op. cit.*, p. 47). The analysis (vibhajya) required in answering this kind of question consists therefore in clearing up the ambiguities implicit or even remotely implied in the terms or the form in which the question is put.

(466) The third kind of question, the paṭipucchāvyākaraṇīya-, appears in fact to be only a subdivision of the second type, since the necessity for the counter-question is again due to the ambiguities in the original question, which in fact can be cleared up by an analytical answer instead of putting the onus on the questioner by asking him what he means by this or that term. The Milindapañha in illustrating this type of question merely gives the example, 'cakkhunā sabbaṃ vijānatī ti?' (does one know everything with the eye? *loc. cit.*) but does not tell us what the counter-question should be. The counter-question probably would be a request to clear up the ambiguity of 'sabbaṃ' by asking, sabbaṃ rūpam udāhu sabbaṃ saddaṃ . . . ? (Is it every form or every sound or . . . ?). The question is therefore not logically different from a question of the second kind since it could be analytically answered as follows: cakkhunā sabbaṃ rūpaṃ vijānāti, api ca na sabbaṃ saddaṃ vijānāti . . ., i.e. one knows every form with the eye but one does not know any sound. . . . Buddhaghosa gives the example, yathā cakkhuṃ tathā sotaṃ, yathā sotaṃ tathā cakkhun ti?' (Is the eye the same as the ear and the ear the same as the eye? *loc. cit.*) It is said that one should counter-question the questioner and ask him in what sense he is using the word 'same'. If he answers that it is 'in the sense of seeing' (dassanaṭṭhena) one's reply should be 'no' and if it is 'in the sense of impermanence' (aniccaṭṭhena) one's reply should be 'yes'. It is clear that this ambiguity could have been dealt with, without the necessity for the counter-question.

(467) The Abhidharmakośakārikā gives the example, 'Is man superior or inferior?' (Poussin, *op. cit.*, p. 44). One should reply this with the question, 'In relation to whom?' (*loc. cit.*) and if he says, 'In relation

to the gods' (*loc. cit.*), he should reply 'he is inferior' (*loc. cit.*), but if he says, 'In relation to the beings of the lower worlds' (êtres des mauvaises destinées, *loc. cit.*), he should reply, 'he is superior' (*loc. cit.*). Here again the counter-question which is necessitated by the ambiguity of the terms 'viśiṣṭa-' (superior) and 'hīna' (inferior) may be cleared up in the very first answer by specifying the senses in which man is inferior and superior respectively. Bhadanta Rāma thought that this question was of the first type and one could reply it categorically as follows: 'L'homme, en effet, est en même temps supérior et inférieur d'après le point de comparaison' (Poussin, *op. cit.*, p. 45). But this is a mistake since in specifying, 'd'après le point de comparison' one is making an 'analysis'. The Ābhidharmikas, as we have already remarked, do not strictly distinguish this type of question from the second. It is the same question as the second, which becomes paṭipucchā-vyakaraṇīya and is intended to confuse and confound the questioner when he happens to be a deceitful person (śaṭha) (*v.* Poussin, *op. cit.*, p. 46).

(468) The Mahāsaṅghikas have the merit of picking on an example taken directly from the Nikāyas. When the Buddha is asked the question, saññā nu kho ... purisassa attā, udāhu aññā saññā añño attā, i.e. is consciousness a person's soul or is consciousness one thing and the soul another? D. I.185, he replies with the question, kiṃ pana tvaṃ ... attānam paccesi, i.e. what do take to be the soul?, *loc. cit.* The Mahāsaṅghikas give this same example.[1] In this context perhaps the counter-question may be justified for one of the words (attā, soul) used by the questioner admitted of such a variety of usages at this time that no one but the user could have known exactly the sense in which he was employing the term. But even here it may be noted that the reply is based on an analysis of the meaning of the term attā.

(469) The next kind of question mentioned, the ṭhapanīya-, is interesting in so far as it seems to have a modern parallel in the kind of question which the Positivist dismisses as meaningless and therefore unanswerable. The Milindapañha (p. 145), the Aṅguttara Comy.[2] (AA. II.309), the Mahāsaṅghikas (Poussin, *op. cit.*, p. 48), and even

[1] Poussin, *op. cit.*, p. 47, Poussin has mistakenly given the reference as Dīgha, i. 195 when it should be D. I.185.

[2] Here it is said, taṃ jīvaṃ taṃ sarīran ti *ādīni* puṭṭhena pana, 'avyākataṃ etaṃ Bhagavatā'ti ṭhapetabbo, i.e. when questioned whether the 'soul is the same as the body', etc., one should set it aside as unexplained by the Exalted One.

Ābhidharmikas (Poussin, *op. cit.*, p. 47) agree in giving the avyākata-theses in question form as examples of this kind of question. The Mahāsaṅghikas mention fourteen theses by extending the theses, antavā loko and sassato loko, into the four logical alternatives (*v. infra*, 571) instead of the two, but curiously enough this extension is not made in the Pāli Canon, which knows of only ten avyākata-theses.

(470) There is no doubt that these theses were regarded in the Nikāyas as those doctrines about which no categorical assertion was made (*v. supra*, 449). At M. I.426 it was said: yān'imāni diṭṭhigatāni Bhagavatā abyākatāni *ṭhapitāni* paṭikkhittāni—sassato loko iti pi asassato loko iti pi . . ., i.e. those metaphysical theories which have not been explained and *which have been set aside* and rejected by the Exalted One (*v. supra*, 377). This shows that the Nikāyas clearly recognized these questions as those which were to be set aside.

(471) The problem is why these questions were set aside. Buddhaghosa defines a ṭhapanīya pañha as 'a question which ought not to be explained and which ought to be set aside on the ground that it was not explained by the Exalted One' (avyākatam etaṃ Bhagavatā ti ṭhapetabbo, eso pañho na vattabbo, ayaṃ ṭhapanīyo pañho, AA. II.309). This is not very helpful, for he is virtually saying that these questions ought to be set aside because they have been set aside by the Buddha. But the problem really is why the Buddha considered these questions as 'those which ought to be set aside'.

(472) Did these questions have a certain property which made them unanswerable or were they in principle answerable categorically or analytically though set aside for a special reason. If the latter was the case, the questions do not belong to a logically different type whereas if the former is the case, they would fall into a class of their own. It is also possible that the questions which were classified as ṭhapanīya were a mixed lot, of which some were to be set aside for the former reason and others for the latter.

(473) We have discussed in a later Chapter what consideration lead us to conclude that these questions were 'to be set aside' (ṭhapanīya) on pragmatic grounds since belief in any of the possible answers was considered irrelevant and otiose for our purpose (*v. infra*, 814). It is possible to argue that these questions were regarded to be in principle answerable categorically though dismissed for pragmatic reasons but it is necessary to note that nowhere is it directly stated that these

beliefs were either categorically true or categorically false. They were only pacceka-saccas (individual or partial truths, *v. infra*, 599–601) and a product of wrong reflection.[1] When we consider all the evidence it is clear that at least some of these questions were considered to have such a logical nature that no answer or no categorical answer could be given to them.

(474) Four of the avyākata-questions concern the existence of the Tathāgata (*v. supra*, 378) after death. If a categorical asnwer to the question as to whether the Tathāgata exists or is born (upapajjati, *v. infra*, 477) after death was possible, it should be possible to say according to the laws of logic (*v. infra*, 582, 583) that one of the four alternatives must be true. Now we observe that the Buddha takes the four (logically) possible answers and shows that none of them 'fit the case' (upeti), or adequately describe the situation, viz. upapajjatī ti . . . na upeti na upapajjatī ti . . . na upeti, upapajjati ca na ca upapajjatī ti . . . na upeti, n'eva upapajjati na na upapajjatī ti . . . upeti, i.e. (to say) that he is born . . . does not fit the case, that he is not born . . . does not fit the case, that he is and is not born . . . does not fit the case, that he is neither born nor not born . . . does not fit the case, M. I.486. This means that no categorical answer to the question, vimutta-citto . . . kuhiṃ upapajjatī ti? (i.e. where is the one whose mind is emancipated . . . born? *loc. cit.*), which is in intent the same as the question, hoti Tathagato param maranā? i.e. does the Perfect One exist after death?

(475) Vaccha, the interlocutor in the above context, is confounded by this reply[2] of the Buddha apparently because he thought that *one* of the logical alternatives *must* be true and says that he has lost whatever faith he derived from the earlier part of the discourse. The Buddha then reassures Vaccha saying that there is no cause here for lack of discernment or confusion and goes on to illustrate with a simile why none of the possible answers 'fit the case'. Since this simile is important we shall reproduce it here:

Buddha: If this fire in front of you were to go out (*lit. blow out*), would you know 'this fire in front of me has gone out (*lit. blown out*)' (sace te . . . purato so aggi *nibbāyeyya* jāneyyasi tvaṃ: ayaṃ me purato aggi nibbuto ti, M. I.487).

[1] . . . Sassato loko . . . asassato loko . . . antavā loko . . . anantavā loko . . . ayaṃ . . . diṭṭhi. . . *ayonisomanasikārahetu* uppannā . . ., A. V.187.

[2] Cp. Etthāhaṃ bho Gotama aññāṇaṃ āpādiṃ, ettha sammohaṃ āpādiṃ . . ., M. I.487.

K

Vaccha: If the fire in front of me were to go out, I would know, 'this fire in front of me has gone out' (sace me . . . purato so aggi nibbāyeyya jāneyyāhaṃ: ayaṃ me purato aggi nibbuto ti, *loc. cit.*).

Buddha: Now if someone were to ask you, '*this fire in front of you, which has gone out, in which direction has it gone*, eastern, western, northern or southern', questioned thus, how would you reply? (sace pana taṃ . . . evaṃ puccheyya: yo te ayaṃ purato aggi nibbuto so aggi ito katamaṃ disaṃ gato puratthimaṃ vā pacchimaṃ vā uttaraṃ vā dakkhiṇaṃ vā ti, evaṃ puttho tvaṃ . . . kin ti byākareyyāsī ti?).

Vaccha: (I would say) It does not fit the case. The fire, which blazed on account of the fuel of grass and sticks, comes to be reckoned as (saṅkhaṃ gacchati) 'gone out', since it had consumed (the fuel) and was not fed with more (fuel) (na upeti . . . yaṃ hi so . . . aggi tiṇa-kaṭṭhupādānam paṭicca ajali, tassa ca pariyādānā aññassa ca anupāhārā nibbuto t'eva saṅkhaṃ gacchatī ti, *loc. cit.*).

(476) This simile clearly illustrates that the question, 'in which direction has the fire gone?' is one to which no categorical reply by means of any of the (logical) alternatives is possible by the very nature (logical) of the question. No categorical reply would aptly describe the situation. The question is grammatically correct in its form and appears to have meaning owing to the logic of 'go out'. This verb is used with person words and it makes sense in such usages to ask 'in what direction has he gone out?'. A categorical and meaningful answer specifying the direction is possible to this question. Now our symbolism or linguistic usage permits us to extend the use of 'go out' for such processes as fires or lights, but in such situations we would be committing a category mistake[1] if we assume that the going out takes place in a specific direction. It therefore makes no sense to ask 'in which direction has the fire gone?'[2] for we would be making a category mistake and thereby asking a nonsensical question, to which no meaningful answer is possible. In fact, Wittgenstein gives the same example to illustrate this kind of question which our symbolism apparently permits, though it is based on a confusion of the logic of

[1] *v.* Gilbert Ryle, 'Categories' in, *Logic and Language*, ed. A. G. N. Flew, Second Series, p. 75.

[2] We can ask, 'in which direction did the fire spread?' but this is different.

concepts,[1] 'Thus it can come about that we aren't able to rid ourselves of the implications of our symbolism, which seems to admit of a question like, "Where does the flame of a candle go to when it's *blown out*?" "Where does the light go to?" We have become obsessed with out symbolism.—We may say that we are led into puzzlement by an analogy which irresistibly drags us on.'[2]

(477) It is therefore clear that the author of this Sutta considered this question as a meaningless one and as falling into a type of questions which were by their very nature (logical) unanswerable and have therefore to be 'set aside'. This question is given as an example to illustrate the nature of the question, 'vimuttacitto ... kuhiṃ upapajjatī ti?' (*v. supra*, 474) which is also said to be one to which no categorical reply is possible and since this is in effect intended to be in intent the same question as, 'hoti Tathāgato param maraṇā?' we may presume that at least these questions were considered to be ṭhapanīya in the sense that 'they ought to be set aside as unanswerable' as, owing to the very form in which the quesion is put, it is strictly meaningless and no meaningful answer in any of the logical alternatives was therefore possible.

(478) The Abhidharmakośakārikā alone gives the following example to illustrate this kind of question: 'Les *skandhas* sont-ils la même chose que le *sattva* ou être-vivant, ou en sont-ils différents?' (Poussin, *op. cit.*, p. 44). The explanation given clearly classifies it as a meaningless question, that is a question whose logical character is such, as to make it impossible of being answered by a categorical reply. It is said that the term 'être-vivant' in the question does not refer to any entity and it is therefore like the question, 'Is the son of a barren woman white or black?' (*loc. cit.*). Here the descriptive phrase 'the son of a barren woman' does not refer to anything since it is logically impossible for a barren woman to have a son. Hence the question, which asks for the relationship between an existent thing (the *skandhas*) and a non-entity is literally meaningless and has to be set aside. This example does not occur in the Pāli Canon, although it is stated here that the Tathāgata is not to be identified with the skandhas nor considered separate from them (S. III.111; S. IV.383) and Buddhaghosa identifies Tathāgata- with satta- (= a being) though we think

[1] Cp. Ninian Smart, *A Dialogue of Religions*, London, 1960, p. 47, makes CB. (i.e. Ceylon Buddhist) say in reference to this assertion, 'The assertion has no clear meaning: a flame neither goes North nor in any other direction . . .'.

[2] Ludwig Wittgenstein, *The Blue and Brown Books*, Oxford, 1958, p. 108.

he is mistaken in this (*v. supra*, 380). The Sūtra-kṛtāṅga however refers to the Buddhist view as follows: 'Some fools say that there are five skandhas of momentary existence. They do not admit that (the soul) is different from nor identical with (the elements) . . .'[1]

(479) There are a number of questions regarded as 'inappropriate questions' (na kallo pañho, *v. infra*) which are set aside in the Nikāyas on the ground that they are literally meaningless. Thus the question 'What is decay and death and of whom is this decay and death?' is said to be 'a misleading question' (na kallo pañho) to ask. The reason is given: 'If one were to say "what is decay and death?" and "of whom is this decay and death?" or if one were to say decay and death is one thing and this decay and death belong to another, both these (questions) are the same (in meaning), only the wording is different.'[2] The question is supposed to assume and imply that the subject of the attributes is ontologically different from the atttributes themselves and is thus considered to give a misleading picture of the facts. In the context are mentioned the two avyākata-theses, 'taṃ jīvaṃ tam sarīraṃ, aññaṃ jīvaṃ aññaṃ sarīram' (S. II.61, *v. infra*, 814). Such questions which are suggested by the grammar of the language but which give or imply a false or distorted picture of the nature of reality were considered 'inappropriate' (na kallo) and were presumably set aside. A long list of such inappropriate questions of the same model or logical structure are mentioned (*v. loc. cit.*). Elsewhere, the question, 'Who feeds on the food of consciousness?' (ko nu kho . . . viññāṇāhāraṃ āhāreti?, S. II.13) is given as an example of an inappropriate question. Here too the question implies the existence of an agent of the action apart from the action itself. Similar questions mentioned in the context are: ko nu kho phusati . . . vediyati . . . tasati . . . upādiyati?, i.e. who indeed (is the agent who) touches . . . experiences . . . recoils . . . grasps? *loc. cit.*).

(480) Another example of a somewhat different character from the above is the question 'Is there anything else after complete detachment from and cessation of the six spheres of experiences?' (channaṃ . . . phassāyatanānaṃ asesavirāganirodhā atth'aññaṃ kiñcī ti? A.

[1] Pañca khandhe vayantege, bālā u khana-joīno aṇṇo aṇaṇṇo nevāhu, heūyaṃ, ca aheūyaṃ, *op. cit.*, Vol. I, fol. 25.

[2] katamaṃ jarāmaraṇaṃ kassa ca panidaṃ jarāmaraṇan ti iti vā . . . yo vadeyya, aññaṃ jarāmaraṇaṃ aññassa ca panidaṃ jarāmaraṇan ti vā . . . yo vadeyya, ubhayam etaṃ ekattaṃ vyañjanam eva nānaṃ, S. II.60, 61.

II.161). The question is put in its four logically alternative forms and dismissed with the answer 'do not (ask) thus' (mā h'evaṃ, *loc. cit.*). This means that the question is a ṭhapanīya-pañha. The reason given is that, 'in talking thus one ascribes phenomenal reality[1] to what is not phenomenally real' (iti vadaṃ appapañcam papañceti, *loc. cit.*). The realm of sensory and mind experience constitutes the realm of the phenomenally real (yāvatā channaṃ phassāyatanānaṃ gati, tāvatā papañcassa gati, yāvatā papañcassa gati, tāvatā channaṃ phassāyatanānaṃ gati, *loc. cit.*) and with the cessation of the former, the latter ceases to be for oneself (channaṃ ... asesāvirāganirodhā papañcavūpasamo, *loc. cit.*). The objection to the question seems to be that the question imputes to transcendent reality the characteristics of 'existence', 'non-existence', etc., which have a valid application only within the realm of experience.[2]

(481) There are questions mentioned, where all four of the logical alternatives may be false (*v. infra*, 585) but these questions are not to be treated as ṭhapanīya-pañha since the questions have been categorically answered. The Nikāyas distinguish between the two types by using the formula 'mā h'evam' (do not (say) so) for all the four alternatives of a ṭhapaṇīya-, while in the former case the usual negation, 'no h'idaṃ' (it is not so) is used for each of the four alternatives (*v.* A. II.163).

(482) The term vi + √bhaj- is found in another important sense in the Pāli Canon to denote 'a detailed classification, exposition or explanation' of a brief statement or title, e.g. ye c'ime bhotā Udenena cattāro puggalā *saṃkhittena vuttā* vitthāreṇa *avibhattā* sādhu me bhavaṃ Udeno ime cattāro puggalā *vitthārena vibhajatu* anukampaṃ upādāya, M. II.161. The brief statement is called an *uddesa* which has to be analysed and explained in detail: ko nu kho ... Bhagavatā saṃkhittena *uddesassa* uddiṭṭhassa vitthārena atthaṃ avibhattassa vitthārena atthaṃ vibhajeyya (M. III.193; cp. 198, 223). Such a detailed analysis and explanation is called a *vibhaṅga* as opposed to its *uddesa*; uddesañ ca *vibhaṇgañ* ca (M. III.187, 192). There are a number of Suttas, which are called *vibhaṅgas* in this sense, e.g. Cūlakamma-

[1] For a discussion and elucidation of this sense of *papañca*, *v.* Sarathchandra, *Buddhist Psychology of Perception*, The Ceylon University Press, Colombo, 1958, pp. 4–10.

[2] Cp. the condemnation of the question as to what the 'antithesis' (paṭibhāga) of Nirvāṇa was (M. I.304).

vibhaṅga, Mahākammavibhaṅga, Saḷāyatana*vibhaṅga*, Uddesa*vibhaṅga*, Araṇa*vibhaṅga*, Dhātu*vibhaṅga*, Sacca*vibhaṅga*, Dakkhiṇa*vibhaṅga* (M. III.202–257). It is also in this sense that the second book of the Abhidhammapiṭaka is called a 'Vibhaṅga', as is evident from the contents.

(483) Vibhaṅga in this sense involves both classification as well as definition. Mrs Rhys Davids speaking of the 'logical analysis of the skandhas' in the Vibhaṅga (and the Dhammasaṅgaṇi) says that 'it resembles our more modern logical procedure known as Determination or the conjunctive and disjunctive combination of terms far more than the older system of classification by way of genus, species and differentia. This latter method would of course, have been repugnant to Buddhists, as involving the philosophical principle of substance and co-inhering qualities. . . . For the Buddhist, things and ideas of things were not analysable into substance and qualities. They were aggregates—the interpretations by mano or viññāṇa of the various forms of impression or 'contact'—phassa. These were analysable into a number of relations and aspects making up the Buddhist view of life and the universe. And to understand any given term or name of an aggregate was to know it in all the relations under all the aspects that were recognized in their philosophy and ethics' (Vbh. p. xvii). Elsewhere, speaking of definition in the Abhidhamma she says, 'they consist very largely of enumerations of synonymous or partly synonymous terms of as it were overlapping circles'.[1] She expresses the same view in her article on 'Logiç (Buddhist)': 'hence their definitions consist in the laying together of mutually intercrossing, over-lapping or partially coinciding notions'.[2]

(484) These observations, while not being entirely beside the point, stand in need of qualification in many respects. It is probably true that for the Buddhist, things and ideas were not analysable into substance and qualities in the ontological sense. This is clear from the fact that, as we have seen (*v. supra*, 479), certain questions were dismissed as misleading by virtue of the fact that in the form in which they were put they seemed to imply a difference in an ontological sense between a subject and its attributes or appendages. But this does not mean that things were regarded in Buddhism as not having attributes but only relations. In the later Buddhist theory of definition as Mrs

[1] *Buddhist Psychology*, Second Edition, London, 1924, p. 139.
[2] ERE., Vol. 8, p. 133.

Rhys Davids herself has shown,[1] it was necessary in defining a concept to state its *lakkhaṇa* (essential characteristic), *rasa* (basic function), *paccupaṭṭhāna* (antecedent condition) and *padaṭṭhāna* (resultant condition). We note here that stating the *lakkhaṇa* or 'essential attribute' is of first and foremost importance and although this theory of definition in *its developed form* is met with for the first time only with the commentators Buddhaghosa and Buddhadatta,[2] its origin can be traced to the Nettippakaraṇa, which mentions not only *lakkhaṇa* and *padaṭṭhāna*, but *paccupaṭṭhāna* as well, although Mrs Rhys Davids incorrectly says that the Nettippakaraṇa 'gives the first and last of Buddhaghosa's four heads'.[3] The Nettippakaraṇa undoubtedly places great stress on the concepts of *lakkhaṇa* and *padaṭṭhāna* which it classifies among the 'sixteen guides (to salvation)' (soḷasa-hārā, p. 1), which are its main topics of investigation, but some of the definitions do mention the concept of *paccupaṭṭhāna* as well.

(485) In the section on padaṭṭhāna (pp. 27 ff.), a number of words are defined in terms of *lakkhaṇa* and *padaṭṭhāna*. We may then consider the following representative examples:

(i) 'Greed' has the characteristic of wanting, its resultant condition is stealing (patthanalakkhaṇo lobho, tassa adinnādānaṃ padaṭṭhānaṃ, 27).
(ii) 'Desire' has the characteristic of attachment; its resultant condition is (the interest in) what is attractive and pleasant (ajjhosānalakkhaṇo taṇhā, tassa piyarūpaṃ sātarūpaṃ padaṭṭhānaṃ, *loc. cit.*).
(iii) 'Absence of hatred' has the characteristic of not harming; its resultant condition is absence of killing (abyāpajjhalakkhaṇo adoso, tassa pāṇātipātā veramaṇī padaṭṭhānaṃ, *loc. cit.*).

Here *lakkhaṇa* is used to denote the 'basic characteristic' of a concept which distinguishes it from everything else, but in the section on lakkhaṇa, the term is used in the sense of a 'property' common to members of a class, e.g. all the six internal spheres (of sense) have a common property in the sense of being 'executioners' (sabbāni hi cha ajjhattikāni āyatanāni vadhakaṭṭhena ekalakkhaṇāni, 30). These two 'senses' are basically the same in that the essential characteristic of a

[1] *Buddhist Psychology*, Second Edition, 1924, p. 189; ERE., Vol. 8, p. 139; *Points of Controversy*, London, 1915, p. li.
[2] *v.* Atthasālinī, 109, 263 ff.; Abhidhammāvatāra, 2 ff.
[3] *v.* 'Logic (Buddhist)' in ERE., Vol. 8, p. 133 under *Literature*.

thing is a property common to members of the class to which it belongs. The word padaṭṭhāna is not used consistently. It is sometimes the 'antecedent causal condition' which is a predominant factor in bringing about an effect. Thus in the following sequences:

pāmujjaṃ pītiyā *padaṭṭhānaṃ*, i.e. exultation is the antecedent condition of joy
pīti passaddhiyā *padaṭṭhānaṃ*, i.e. joy is the antecedent condition of composure
passaddhi sukhassa *padaṭṭhānaṃ*, i.e. composure is the antecedent condition of happiness
sukhaṃ samādhissa *padaṭṭhānaṃ*, i.e. happiness is the antecedent condition of concentration and insight
samādhi yathābhūtañāṇadassanassa *padaṭṭhānaṃ*, i.e. concentration is the antecedent condition of true knowledge and insight, p. 29,

each preceding state is said to be the precedent or 'antecedent condition' (padaṭṭhāna-) of what follows. Its definition is given: 'whatever is a condition by way of decisive support and is a causal factor is a *padaṭṭhāna*' (yo ko ci upanissayo yo ko ci paccayo, sabbo so *padaṭṭhānaṃ*, 29). But when 'stealing' (adinnādānaṃ) was said to be the *padaṭṭhāna-* of 'greed' (*v. supra*), *padaṭṭhāna* is the resultant condition and not the antecedent cause. Its identification with upanissaya-, which is a phenomenon which 'will belong either to the past or the future'[1] according to the *Paṭṭhāna* implies this same ambiguity. The two senses seem to have been distinguished only after *paccupaṭṭhāna* came to be consistently employed to denote the 'antecedent condition' and *padaṭṭhāna* came to mean the 'resultant condition'. But *paccupaṭṭhāna* is a concept which is also employed in the Nettippakaraṇa, contrary to Mrs Rhys Davids' remark (*v. supra*, 484). Thus saddhā is defined in two ways, once with the concept of *paccupaṭṭhāna-* and again with *padaṭṭhāna-*:

(i) 'Faith' (saddhā) has the characteristic of submission and the antecedent condition of inclination (okappanalakkhaṇā saddhā adhimutti*paccupaṭṭhānā*, 28)
(ii) 'Faith' (saddhā) has the characteristic of aspiring towards; its resultant condition is unshakable conviction (abhipatthayanalakkhaṇo saddhā tassa aveccappasādo *padaṭṭhānaṃ*, *loc. cit.*).

[1] Nyanatiloka, *Guide Through the Abhidhamma Pitaka*, Second Edition, Colombo, 1957, p. 121.

So is pasāda defined in both ways:

(i) 'Faith' (pasādo) has the characteristic of placidity (*lit.* non-turbulence) and the antecedent condition of tranquillity (anāvila-lakkhaṇo pasādo sampasīdana*paccupaṭṭhāno*, *loc. cit.*)

(ii) 'Faith' (pasādo) has the characteristic of placidity and its resultant condition is belief (anāvilalakkhaṇo pasādo tassa saddhā *padaṭṭhā-naṃ*, *loc. cit.*).

(486) The fact that things have a certain basic characteristic or characteristics, which justify our use of certain terms to denote them is taken for granted in the Nikāyas as well. Thus it was assumed in the Upaniṣads that whatever was ātman must have the characteristics of intrinsic control, permanence and happiness, viz. the ātman is the 'inner controller' (antaryāmin, Bṛh. 3.7.1) is 'ageless' (vijaraḥ, Ch. 8.7.1) and 'free from sorrow' (*v. supra*, 33). These are assumed to be the attributes or characteristics of the ātman, where Saccaka argues with the Buddha and claims the truth of the proposition, 'my body is my ātman' (rupaṃ me attā, M. I.232). The Buddha points out that rūpa- has none of the characteristics of an ātman. It does not change according to one's will (*v.* vattati te tasmiṃ rūpe vaso: evaṃ me rūpaṃ hotu, evam me rūpaṃ mā ahosī ti—no h'idaṃ, i.e. do you have control of your body (such that you could determine): 'thus let my body be and thus let my body not be'—It is not the case, *loc. cit.*); it is 'impermanent and sorrowful' (aniccaṃ dukkhaṃ, *loc. cit.*). We thus see that both Saccaka and the Buddha assume that whatever is ātman must have these characteristics (lakkhaṇa-).

(487) Terms are formally defined sometimes in the Nikāyas and more often in the Abhidhammapiṭaka but no consistent pattern of definition is followed. This is perhaps due partly to the nature and importance of the terms defined and the influence of the Brāhmaṇic tradition as well, but it is also due to the absence of a clear conception of definition.

(488) While the Brāhmaṇas resorted to fanciful etymologies in defining the use of words[1] we find often in the Nikāyas an attempt to define the meaning of terms with wrong (i.e. historically incorrect) definitions. This was possibly done intentionally in order to suggest a new use of these terms. Thus it is said that a 'brāhmaṇa' (a brahmin) should be so called 'because he has cast out evil' (bāhitapāpo ti

[1] Keith, *Religion and Philosophy of the Vedas*, HOS., Vol. 32, p. 483.

brāhmaṇo, Dh. 388). 'Rūpa- is that by which one is afflicted with heat, cold, etc.' (ruppatī ti tasmā rūpan ti vuccati, kena ruppati? sītena, uṇhena . . ., S. III.86), although it is doubtful whether the etymology of rūpa is in any way connected with the verbal root of ruppati, to be hurt.

(489) The etymology is not always wrong, for there are many instances in which the correct verbal root is indicated, e.g. when saññā is defined by correctly relating it with the verbal form sañjānāti and by mentioning a few typical instances of saññā: sañjānātī ti . . . tasmā saññā ti vuccati, kiñca sañjānāti . . . nīlakam pi sañjānāti pītakam pi sañjānāti . . . lohitakam pi . . . odātam pi, i.e. it is called saññā, because one recognizes (with it), what does one recognize? One recognizes what is blue, yellow, red, white, M. I.293. This kind of definition in extension[1] is at times resorted to with greater exactness in the Abhidhammapiṭaka, though sometimes a definition in intention or even several such definitions are given along with it.

(490) Thus that rūpa which is denoted by the term 'rūpāyatanaṃ' (the field of visual phenomena) is defined as follows: 'whatever form, which is dependent on the four great elements, is possessed of hue, brightness and visual appearance, and causes impressions (such as) what is blue, yellow, red, white, black . . . long, short, shall, large, circular, globular, square, hexagonal . . . depth (ninna-thalaṃ) . . . shade, light, brightness, darkness, mist, cloud . . . the hue and brightness of the moon, the sun, the stars . . ., etc. (yaṃ vā pana aññam pi atthi rūpam . . .), which one has seen (passi), is seeing (passati), will see (passissati) or would see (passe) with the eye, which is itself unobservable, though possessed of impressions, is form, the field of visual phenomena and the sphere of form—this is the field of visual phenomena' (yaṃ rūpaṃ catunnaṃ mahābhūtānaṃ upādāya vaṇṇa-nibhā-sanidassanaṃ sappaṭighaṃ nīlam pītakaṃ lohitakaṃ odātaṃ kālakaṃ . . . dīghaṃ rassaṃ anuṃ thūlaṃ vaṭṭaṃ parimaṇḍalaṃ caturaṃsaṃ chaḷaṃsaṃ . . . ninna-thalaṃ chāyā ātapo āloko andhakāro abbhā mahikā . . . canda-maṇḍalassa vaṇṇa-nibhā suriya-maṇḍalassa vaṇṇa-nibhā tārakarūpānaṃ vaṇṇa-nibhā . . . yaṃ vā panaññam pi atthi rūpaṃ . . . yaṃ . . . cakkhunā anidassanena sappaṭighena passi vā passati vā passissati vā passe vā rūpam p'etaṃ rūpāyatanam p'etaṃ rūpa-dhātu p'esā—idaṃ taṃ rūpaṃ rūpāyatanaṃ, DhS., 617, p. 139.

[1] Stebbing, *op. cit.*, p. 422.

(491) Several ways of defining are combined in this complex definition of the term rūpāyatanaṃ. We notice a definition in extension enumerating typical instances of different kinds of visual phenomena such as hues (blue, yellow, etc.), shapes (long, short, square, etc.), depth, darkness, light, shade and degrees of brightness. Then there is a definition in intention by stating that they all have the property of being observable in an actual or hypothetical (*v.* passe, would see) sense by the eye. Then again one may possibly discern a definition by definite description,[1] when it is said that it is 'the form which is dependent on the four great elements, is possessed of hue, brightness and visual appearance and causes impressions'. Finally there is a substitution of partly synonymous verbal phrases, e.g. rūpam p'etaṃ . . . rūpadhātu p'esā, which Johnson calls 'biverbal definition'.[2]

(492) This is not all. More definitions of rūpāyatanaṃ follow, all given in intension and where the characteristics mentioned are, (i) that on which the eye focuses itself (*lit.* strikes) in an actual or hypothetical sense (yaṃ rūpaṃ . . . cakkhuṃ paṭihaññi vā paṭihaññati vā paṭihaññissati vā paṭihaññe vā, DhS., 618, p. 140), (ii) that which would cause an impression in an actual or hypothetical sense on the eye (yaṃ . . . cakkhumhi . . . paṭihaññi, etc., DhS., 619), (iii) that which in conjunction with the eye gives rise to a visual impression in an actual or hypothetical sense (yaṃ . . . cakkhuṃ nissāya cakkhu-samphasso uppajji vā, etc., DhS., 620), (iv) that which in conjunction with the eye gives rise to, in an actual or hypothetical sense, feeling, percepts, volitions and visual cognitions resulting from visual impressions (yaṃ . . . cakkhuṃ nissāya cakkhu-samphassajā vedanā . . . saññā . . . cetanā . . . cakkhuviññāṇaṃ uppajji vā uppajjati vā uppajjissati vā uppajje vā, DhS., 620).

(493) We do find many instances of bi-verbal definitions, where there is a mere substitution of verbal phrases and which as Mrs Rhys Davids pointed out were 'over-lapping or partially coinciding notions' (*v. supra*, 483). As a typical example we quote the definition of *jarā*: yā tesaṃ tesaṃ sattānaṃ tamhi tamhi sattanikāye jarā jīraṇatā khaṇḍiccaṃ pāliccaṃ valittacatā āyuno saṃhāṇi indriyānaṃ paripāko, Vbh., 99. We may compare this with the definition of *rūpassa jaratā*: yā rūpassa jarā jīraṇatā . . . indriyānaṃ paripāko, DhS., 644, p. 144—where the phrase, 'tesaṃ tesaṃ sattānaṃ tamhi tamhi sattanikāye' is

[1] Stebbing, *op. cit.*, p. 424. [2] W. E. Johnson, *Logic*, Part I, p. 103 ff.

omitted as the concept defined has a more restricted connotation than the concept jarā. This shows that there was an attempt to secure exactness within the framework of these definitions. Besides, the use of overlapping synonyms cannot by itself be considered a defect specially in view of the finding that words in use do not have an exact connotation and that general terms unite things by virtue of 'family resemblances' rather than by properties that all the members of the class referred to have in common.[1]

(494) Judged by traditional Western conceptions of definition we may say that the definiens is equivalent to (except where there is overlapping) and is not wider or narrower than the definiendum[2] but the rules concerned with the purpose of definition[3] are often violated. Expressions occurring in the definiendum recur in the definiens. Obscure terms less well known that the term defined occur in the definiens and negative expressions are used in the definition, even when the definiendum is not negative. Take the following examples:

(a) Katamaṃ taṃ rūpaṃ rūpassa lahutā?
Yā rupassa *lahutā lahu*-pariṇāmatā *adandhanatā avitthanatā*—idaṃ taṃ rūpaṃ rūpassa lahutā (DhS., 639, p. 144).

(b) Tattha katamaṃ sammā-ājīvo?
Idha ariya-sāvako *micchā-ājīvaṃ* pahāya *sammājivena* jīvitaṃ kappeti: ayam vuccati sammā-ājīvo (Vbh., 105).

(c) Tattha katamo samma-ājīvo?
Yā *micchā-ājivā* ārati virati paṭivirati veramaṇi akiriyā akaraṇaṃ anajjhāpatti veḷānatikkhamo setughāto *sammā-ājivo* maggaṅgam maggapariyāpannaṃ: ayaṃ vuccati sammā-ājīvo (Vbh., 107).

(495) It may be observed that in (a) lahutā and lahu recur in the definiens with negative expressions (adandhanatā, avitthanatā), which are at the same time more obscure,[4] than the definiendum. Likewise (b) and (c) are two alternative definitions of sammā-ājiva showing that even in the same stratum a single standard definition was not given.

[1] *v.* Wittgenstein, *Philosophical Investigations,* Vol. I, p. 31e; cp. G. J. Warnock, *English Philosophy Since 1900*, pp. 68 ff.

[2] Stebbing, *op. cit.*, p. 424.

[3] *Ibid.*, p. 425.

[4] This is, of course, to some extent arbitrary. The definition throws light on the use of lahutā to someone acquainted with the meaning of adandhanatā, vitthanatā but not acquainted with the meaning of lahutā.

Sammā-ājīva is repeated in the definiens, which seeks to define the expression negatively in terms of micchā-ājīva.

(496) Despite these obvious defects, the definitions occasionally give us an insight into the exact technical use of the term. This is especially so when the definition is by definite description. Take the following definition of *māyā* (deceit): Idh'ekacco kāyena duccaritaṃ caritvā vācāya duccaritaṃ caritvā manasā duccaritaṃ duccaritvā tassa paricchādanahetu pāpikaṃ icchaṃ paridahati: mā maṃ jaññā ti icchati, mā maṃ jaññā ti saṃkappeti, mā maṃ jaññā ti vācaṃ bhāsati, mā maṃ jaññā ti kāyena parakkamati: yā evarūpā māyā māyāvitā accasarā vañcaṇā ... pāpakiriyā-ayaṃ vuccati māyā, i.e. here a certain person commits a misdeed with body, speech or mind and in order to conceal it, forms evil resolve; he wishes that he be not found out, he hopes, ... he prays ... he endeavours by his behaviour that he be not found out—deceit of this sort, fraud, trickery, guile, ... evil-doing is called 'deceit' (*māyā*). Here we find a definition by definite description followed by a bi-verbal definition. At DhS., 646 (p. 144) kabaliṅkāro āhāro (gross food) is defined in extension followed by a definite description. Thus there is a good deal of variety in the definitions employed contrary to what Mrs Rhys Davids has led us to believe and it is necessary to judge each of them on its own merits, when we assess their value as definitions.

(497) Speaking of classification, which in fact goes hand in hand with definition, Mrs Rhys Davids says: 'The import of a number of terms is set out, usually in dichotomic division but sometimes in the distinctively Indian method of presenting the by-us so called Laws of Thought thus, Is *A B*? If not, is *A* not *B*? If not, is *A* both *B* and not *B*? If not, is *A* neither *B* nor not *B* (in other words is *A* a chimaera?)'[1] This statement too is misleading for it does not give an exact account of the kind of classification found in the Pāli Canon.

(498) If we take the term ñāṇa- (knowledge), for instance, as classified in the Vibhaṅga (*v.* Ñāṇa-vibhaṅga, pp. 306–334), we find that there is no attempt to give a single comprehensive classification of ñāṇa- by a process of dichotomous division. Instead, we find a number of different classifications separately listed. The only order followed is a numerical order. Firstly, we find mentioned the single characteristics

[1] ERE., Vol. 8, p. 133.

of ñāṇa- as used in various senses and contexts. Then follows a list of classifications where 'knowledge' (ñāṇa-) in some sense is two-fold, viz.

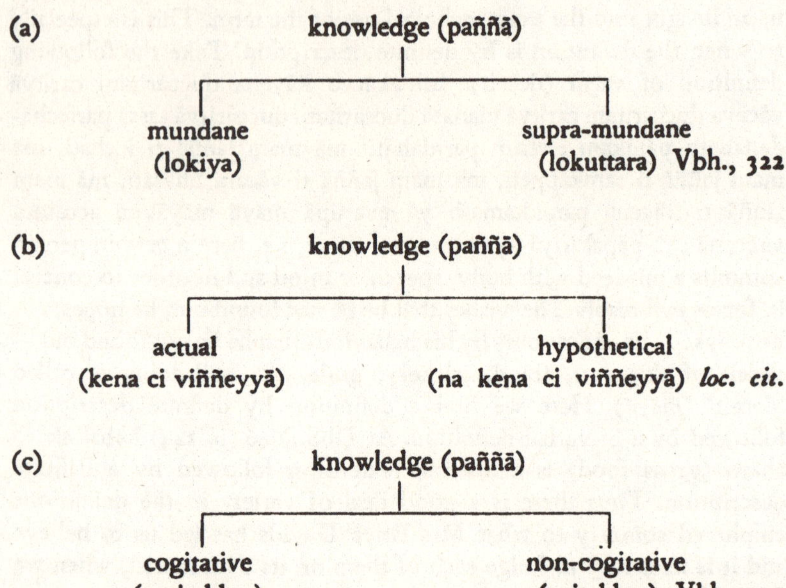

Each is a separate dichotomous division. This is followed by lists of three, viz.

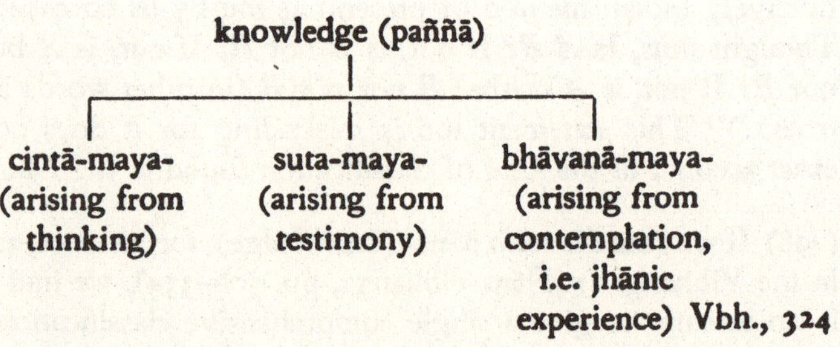

As the explanation makes clear, this classification is based on a strictly dichotomous division, which is implied rather than stated and this may be exhibited as follows:

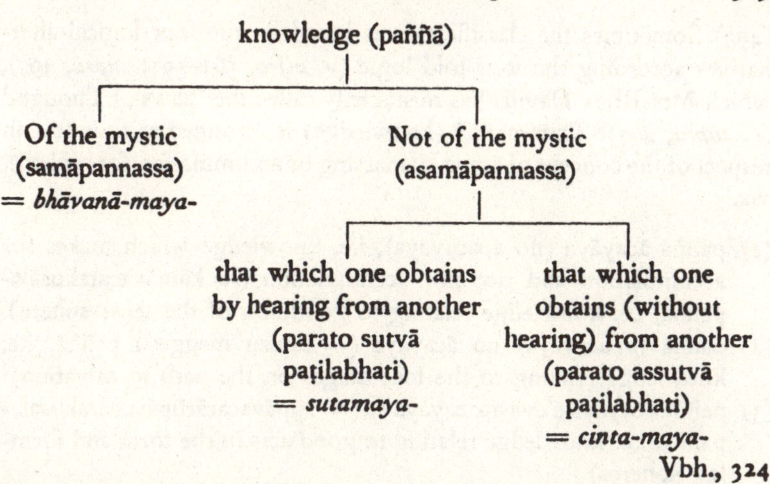

Then follow lists of three, four, etc., up to ten. An examination of these lists would show that the classes are mutually exclusive and the fallacy of cross-division or of over-lapping classes[1] is not met with. The division is exhaustive and the sum of the sub-classes equals the whole class that is divided or classified, but the successive steps of the division do not proceed by gradual stages and in this sense we do not have a strictly dichotomous division. Thus paññā (knowledge) is classified under four sub-classes as (1) kāmāvacara (of the sense-sphere), (2) rūpāvacara (of the form-sphere), (3) arūpāvacara (of the formless sphere), and (4) apariyāpanna (unbounded), but if the principle of dichotomous division was adopted we should have the following classification:

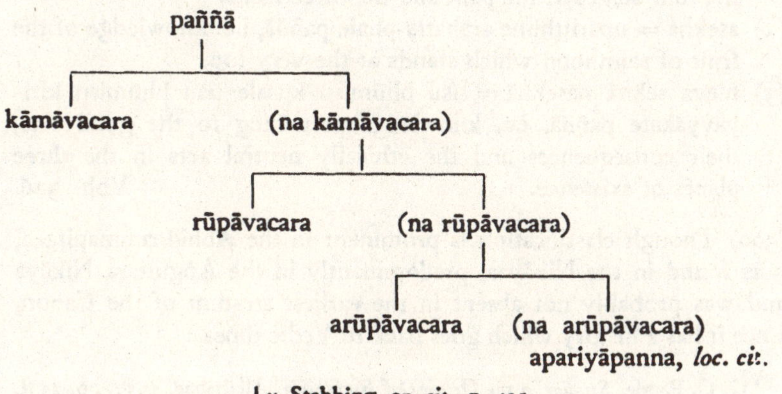

[1] *v.* Stebbing, *op. cit.*, p. 435.

(499) Sometimes the classification is based on the four logical alternatives according the four-fold logic (*v. infra*, 561–591; *supra*, 497), which Mrs Rhys Davids has mistakenly called the 'Laws of Thought' (*v. supra*, 497). Thus paññā (knowledge) is classified as four-fold in respect of the concept of ācaya- (amassing or accumulation for rebirth), viz.

(1) paññā ācayāya (no apacayāya), i.e. knowledge which makes for accumulation and not non-accumulation (= kāmāvacarakusala-paññā, i.e. knowledge relating to good acts of the sense-sphere).
(2) paññā (apacayāya) no ācayāya (= catusu maggesu paññā, i.e. knowledge relating to the four stages on the path to salvation)-
(3) paññā ācayāya c'eva apacayāya ca (= rūpāvacarārūpāvacarakusala-paññā, i.e. knowledge relating to good acts in the form and formless spheres)
(4) paññā n'eva ācayāya no apacayāya (= avasesā paññā, the rest of knowledge). Vbh., 330.

This kind of classification is frequently met with in the Nikāyas as well, e.g. the classification of individuals into the four types: (1) attantapo, i.e. one who torments himself, (2) parantapo, i.e. one who torments others, (3) attantapo ca parantapo ca, i.e. one who torments himself as well as others, and (4) n'evattantapo na parantapo ca, i.e. one who neither torments himself nor others, M. I.432–344. Where one of the alternatives presents a null class, only the other alternatives are mentioned, viz. the classification of paññā (knowledge) under:

(1) sekha = catusu maggesu tīsu phalesu paññā, i.e. knowledge of the four stages of the path and the three fruits.
(2) asekha = upariṭṭhime arahatta-phale paññā, i.e. knowledge of the fruit of sainthood which stands at the very top.
(3) n'eva sekhā nāsekhā = tīsu bhūmisu kusale tīsu bhūmisu kiriyāvyākate paññā, i.e. knowledge pertaining to the good acts, their consequences and the ethically neutral acts in the three planes of existence. Vbh., 326.

(500) Though classification is prominent in the Abhidhammapiṭaka, it is found in the Nikāyas, predominantly in the Aṅguttara Nikāya and was probably not absent in the earliest stratum of the Canon, since it has a history which goes back to Vedic times.[1]

[1] G. C. Pande, *Studies in the Origins of Buddhism*, Allahabad, 1957, pp. 25 ff.

(501) One of the epistemological problems connected with classification is posed in the Kathāvatthu. Classification appears to presuppose the necessity of general or abstract ideas, as opposed to particular ideas denoting particular things. The general term 'cow' refers to a class of cows as opposed to this or that particular cow. How can a single word signify a whole class of things? Berkeley argued against Locke's theory of abstract ideas though he did not deny that words can have a general as well as a particular connotation.[1] Some schools[2] seemed to have argued against the Theravādins on the ground that 'there do not exist any ideas which can be grouped together by other ideas' (n'atthi keci dhammā kehici dhammehi saṅgahitā, Kvu. 335). This is one of the earliest references to the problem of universals.

(502) These opponents of the Theravādins seem to have argued that one cannot group together ideas by means of other ideas 'in the same way as two bullocks may be grouped together by a rope or a yoke' (yathā dāmena vā yottena vā dve balivaddā saṅgahitā, Kvu. 336). This means that general ideas, which refer to a whole class of things, grouped together are considered impossible. It is difficult to see the reason for their opinion but they probably held that physical analogies could not be extended to the realm of ideas, which was probably the reason, why they also held the opinion that 'there are no mental states connected with other mental states (n'atthi keci dhammā kehici dhammehi sampayuttā, Kvu. 337), in the way that 'oil pervades sesamum or sugar pervades cane' (yathā tilamhi telaṃ anugataṃ anupaviṭṭhaṃ, ucchumhi raso anugato anupaviṭṭho, Kvu. 338). The argument probably was that ideas cannot be manipulated like physical objects. Therefore they cannot be grouped together by a general idea in the way one physically puts together material things. The Theravādin argues against them by making them admit that things can be conceived as a class or whole and that this implies the existence of general ideas: 'But you do not also deny that ideas may combine or be included with other ideas under a concept of totality or universality? e.g. pleasant, painful or neutral feelings are computed under the class of 'feeling' (Nanu atthi keci dhammā kehici dhammehi gaṇanaṃ gacchanti, uddesaṃ gacchanti, pariyāpannā ti? Sukhā vedanā ... dukkhā vedanā ... adukkhamasukhā vedanā katamaṃ khandhagaṇanaṃ gacchatī ti? Vedanākkhandhagaṇanaṃ gacchatī ti, Kvu. 335, 336).

[1] *v.* G. J. Warnock, *Berkeley*, Penguin Books, 1953, pp. 60–71.

[2] According to the Comy. the 'Rājagirikas and Siddhatthikas' (*v.* Points of Controversy, p. 195).

(503) The adoption of classification and definition betrays a desire to avoid ambiguity and achieve exactness in the use of terms for the sake of clarity of thought. This same motive seems to underlie the process of defining and delimiting the use of terms by means of pairs of statements[1] in the Yamaka. But the nature (logical) and significance of these statements seem to have been wholly misunderstood by Mrs Rhys Davids, who edited this text and Keith, who appears to have been influenced by her opinions.

(504) Mrs Rhys Davids expressed the view that 'the world probably contains no other such study in the applied logic of conversion as the Yamaka' (p. xvi). Since conversion is not possible without a knowledge of the distribution of terms, it was assumed that the author of the Yamaka was aware of the distribution of terms. And probably since this was not possible without a certain development in the study of logic, it was assumed that the Yamaka 'was compiled in order to develop a new growing logic or in order to apply such a logic, taught already in the abstract' (p. xviii). Keith who is normally very sceptical of such claims says that 'in the Yamaka . . . the distribution of terms is known and the process of conversion is elaborately illustrated, but without a trace of appreciation of logical theory'.[2] Thus Keith too admits a knowledge of conversion and the distribution of terms on the part of the Yamaka, though he is not prepared to grant a knowledge of the logical theory behind it.

(505) Let us first be clear about the use of the term 'conversion'. As Stebbing says, 'by the converse of a proposition we ordinarily mean another proposition in which the terms have been interchanged' (*op. cit.*, p. 63). Thus 'All *P* is *S*' would be the conversion in this sense of 'All *S* is *P*'. But this would violate the rules of distribution and therefore conversion in the legitimate logical sense is defined as 'a form of immediate inference in which from a given proposition another is inferred having for its subject the predicate of the given proposition' (*loc. cit.*). In this legitimate sense of the term, the conversion of 'All *S* is *P*' is not 'All *P* is *S*' but 'Some *P* is *S*'.

(506) Now assuming that the word 'conversion' was used by Mrs Rhys Davids and Keith in the proper technical sense of the term, it would follow that of the pairs of statements in the Yamaka (and the whole work consists of such statements), one was an immediate

[1] *v.* Yamaka (PTS. edition), p. xv.

[2] *Buddhist Philosophy*, p. 304.

inference from, being the conversion of the other. But an examination of these statements will reveal nothing of the sort.

(507) Let us examine a set of statements from the Khandha Yamaka (p. 16). We find sets of pairs in the form of question and answer. Take the first set.
It consists of a pair of questions and answers:

(i) Rūpaṃ rūpakkhando ti? Piyarūpaṃ sātarūpaṃ, na rūpakkhandho; rūpakkhandho rūpañ c'eva rūpakkhandho ca, i.e. Is (all) form (classifiable as) the aggregate of form. What is attractive-form (piyarūpa-) an pleasant-form (sātarupa-) is form, but not (classifiable as) the aggregate of form. The aggregate of form constitutes both form as well as the aggregate of form.

(ii) Rūpakkhandho rūpan ti? Āmantā, i.e. Is the aggregate form (classifiable as) form? Yes.

(508) These two statements[1] together tell us the exact logical boundaries of the use of the term rūpaṃ and rūpakkhandho and in the light of this information, we may diagrammatically represent the relationship as follows:

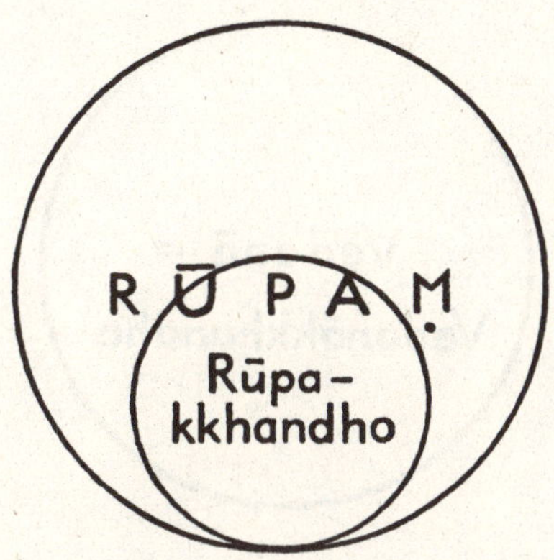

(509) We can see that not all rūpa is rūpakkhandha- for piyarūpa- and sātarūpa- are rūpa-, but not rūpakkhandha-. But as the next statement

[1] Cp. Wittgenstein, *op. cit.*, p. 10e: 'We might very well also write every statement in the form of a question followed by a "Yes"; for instance: 'Is it raining? Yes!" Would this show that every statement contained a question?'

tells us, all rūpakkhandha- is rūpa. We may restate the statements (i) and (ii) without the question form[1] as follows:

(i) Some rūpa- is rūpakkhandha-, i.e. Some *S* is *P* (*S*i*P*)
(ii) All rūpakkhandha- is rūpa, i.e. All *P* is *S* (*P*a*S*)

It is clear that (ii) is not the converse of (i),[2] though (i) could be regarded as the converse of (ii), but it is obvious that it could not have been the intention of the author to regard it as such, for if so he would have in the first place stated (ii) first.

(510) Let us consider the next pair:

(i) Vedanā vedanākkhandho ti? Āmantā, i.e. Is (all) feeling (classifiable as) the aggregate of feeling? Yes.
(ii) Vedanākkhandho vedanā ti? Āmantā, i.e. Is (all that belongs to) the aggregate of feeling (classifiable as) feeling? Yes.

(511) Here the two concepts coincide, for all that is vedanā is vedanākkhandha- and all that is vedanākkhandha- is vedanā and we may diagrammatically represent this as:

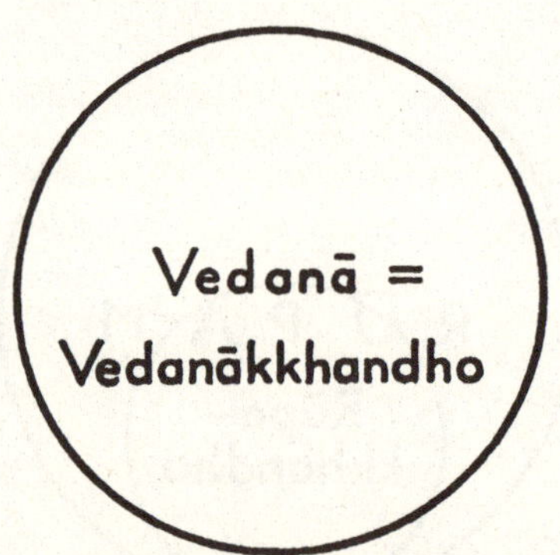

(512) We may eliminate the question (and answer) form and restate the propositions asserted as follows:

(i) All vedanā is vedanākkhandho, i.e. All *S* is *P* (*S*a*P*)
(ii) All vedanākkhandho is vedanā, i.e. All *P* is *S* (*P*a*S*)

[1] *v.* fn. 1, previous page. [2] *v.* Stebbing, *op. cit.*, p. 68.

Now any textbook on logic would tell us[1] that (ii) is not the converse of (i) nor (i) the converse of (ii). One is not an immediate inference from the other but they are independent statements giving us information about the relative use of the concepts contained in them. To regard (ii) as the converse of (i) would be to violate the rule of distribution, which states that 'no term may be distributed in an inferred proposition unless it is distributed in the original proposition'.[2] Now in a universal affirmative proposition (i.e. *S*a*P*), the subject is distributed and the predicate is undistributed.[3] If we convert it as *P*a*S*, an undistributed term in the original gets distributed and the rule is violated, resulting in an illegitimate conversion.

(513) Now are we going to say that the author of the Yamaka, in the light of the above evidence, was ignorant of the distribution of terms and the process of conversion. All this is absurd. The Yamaka does not consist of a set of logical exercises and is not a textbook on applied logic at all. The members of the pairs of statements do not stand to each other in the logical relation of one being an immediate inference of the other. To conceive them as such is wholly to misunderstand the purpose of the book, which is not an exercise in logical gymnastics, but is intended to convey to the reader the exact logical boundaries of important concepts in the light of their actual technical usage. The fact that some of these statements may in fact turn out to be the converse of the other is to be counted as purely accidental and is not due to any conscious intention on the part of the author to make an immediate inference from the one statement. As an example of this type we may state the following:

(i) Dukkhaṃ dukkhasaccan ti? Āmantā, i.e. Is suffering (classifiable as) the truth of suffering? Yes.

(ii) Dukkhasaccaṃ dukkhan ti? Kāyikaṃ dukkhaṃ cetasikaṃ dukkhaṃ ṭhapetvā avasesaṃ dukkhasaccaṃ dukkhasaccaṃ na dukkhaṃ, kāyikaṃ dukkhaṃ cetasikaṃ dukkhaṃ dukkhañ c'eva dukkhasaccañ ca, i.e. Is all that (is classifiable as) the truth of suffering, suffering? Excepting physical and mental suffering the rest of the truth of suffering is the truth of suffering: physical and mental suffering (is classifiable) both as suffering and as the truth of suffering. Yamaka, 174.

[1] J. Welton, *A Manual of Logic*, London, 1922, p. 257.

[2] Stebbing, *op. cit.*, p. 63.

[3] *Ibid.*, p. 49.

This may be diagrammatically represented as follows:

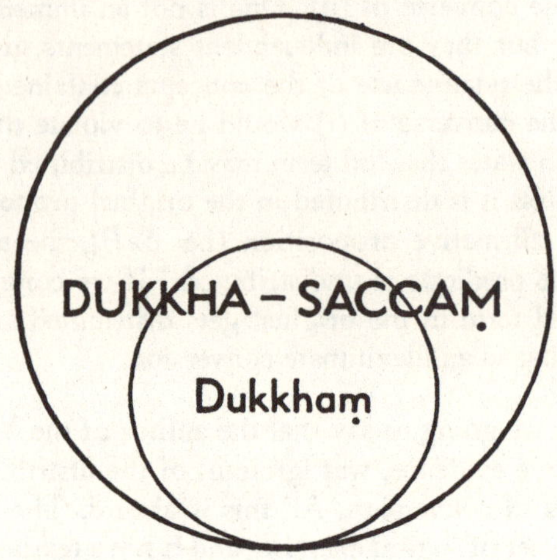

In propositional form we have:

(i) All dukkha- is dukkhasacca-, i.e. All *S* is *P* (*SaP*)
(ii) Some dukkhasacca- is dukkha-, i.e. Some *P* is *S* (*PiS*)

(514) Here (ii) is a valid conversion of (i) but it is evident from the context that it was not intended as a conversion. It merely happens to be so in view of the fact that the denotation of dukkha-sacca- includes members not included under dukkha-.

(515) Perhaps examples of this sort which are not infrequently found, led Mrs Rhys Davids and Keith to the mistaken theory that here we have (as Keith put it) 'the process of conversion elaborately illustrated', but it is even possible that Mrs Rhys Davids has misunderstood the process of conversion as known in logic for she, in fact, suggests the following illegitimate example of a conversion, 'e.g. "All *Y* is *M*"; now does this mean that all *M* is *Y*? *For unless it does* (italics mine), we cannot pass on to say, All *X* is *Y* just because all *X* happens to be also *M*' (Yamaka, p. xvii).

(516) The emphasis on 'analysis' in the Pāli Canon is reflected in the importance attached to the concept of catu-paṭisambhidā or the 'four branches of logical analysis' (*s.v.* PTS. Dictionary) corresponding to pratisaṃvidā of the Buddhist Sanskrit texts.[1] One who has mastered them is said 'to attain the imperturbable state before long' (na cirass

[1] *v.* Edgerton, BHS. Dictionary, *s.v.*

eva akuppaṃ paṭivijjhati, A. III.119) and 'to be held in great esteem' (garu ca bhāvanīyo ca, A. III.113) by one's co-religionists. Sāriputta, who is held up as an example unto others[1] is said to have mastered these techniques in a comparatively short time (A. II.160). One of the books of the Khuddaka Nikāya is called the Paṭisambhidāmagga and a chapter of the Vibhaṅga is called the Paṭisambhidāvibhaṅga (pp. 293–305). According to the explanation given of the four kinds of analysis[2] *atthapaṭisambhidā* stands for analysis of meanings 'in extension', *dhammapaṭisambhidā* for analysis of reasons, conditions or causal relations, *niruttipaṭisambhidā* for analysis of (meanings 'in intension' as given in) definitions and *paṭibhāṇasambhidā* for analysis of intellect to which things knowable by the foregoing processes are presented.

(517) Aung and Mrs Rhys Davids tell us that '"attha" does not refer to verbal meanings'[3] but this is quite unhistorical and incorrect. The Vibhaṅga (294) quite clearly says that one of the senses of attha in the compound attha-paṭisambhidā is 'the meaning of what is spoken', namely of words and sentences, viz. so tassa tass'eva bhāsitassa atthaṃ jānāti: ayaṃ imassa bhāsitassa attho ayaṃ imassa bhāsitassa attho ti: ayaṃ vuccati attha-paṭisambhidā, i.e. he comprehends the meaning of whatever is spoken (such as) 'this is the meaning of this sentence' 'that is the meaning of that sentence'—this is called the analysis of meaning. The monks apparently learned the dhamma by heart and then examined the meaning of what they learnt (cp. sutvā dhammaṃ dhāreti, dhāritānaṃ dhammānam atthaṃ upaparikkhati, i.e. hearing the dhamma they bear it in mind and then examine the meaning of what they have learnt by heart, M. II.173). This examination of meaning probably constituted part of attha-paṭisambhidā. The clearing of ambiguities by analysis and the giving of detailed exegeses of short titles learnt (i.e. the two meanings of vi + √bhaj) in all likelihood also constituted attha-paṭisambhidā for in mentioning the attainment of atthapaṭisambhidā by Sāriputta, it is said that he could 'reveal, *analyse* and clarify' (vivarāmi, *vibhajāmi* uttānīkaromi, A. II.160) and 'exegetically explain' questions put to him (*v.* so maṃ pañheṇa—ahaṃ veyyākaraṇena, *loc. cit.*). Attha- is also

[1] Cp. Esā tulā etaṃ pamāṇaṃ mama sāvakānaṃ bhikkhūnaṃ yadidam Sāriputta-Moggallānā ti, i.e. Sāriputta and Moggallāna represent the standard and the ideal for my disciples and monks, A. II.164.

[2] *v. Points of Controversy*, pp. 377–382; Comy. to the Paṭisambhidāmagga (PTS. edition), Vol. II, p. 147 f.

[3] *Points of Controversy*, p. 378.

used in this context in the Vibhaṅga for 'resultant phenomena' as Aung and Mrs Rhys Davids have shown (*op. cit.*, p. 379).

(518) In this latter sense atthapaṭisambhidā is distinguished in the Vibhaṅga from dhamma-paṭisambhidā or the analysis of antecedent phenomena or causes.[1] *Nirutti-paṭisambhidā* is nowhere clearly defined in the Canonical texts. Edgerton gives 'explanation not necessarily etymological of the meaning of a word or text' (*s.v.* nirukti- in BHS. Dictionary) on the basis of the Buddhist Sanskrit usages and it is defined in the Vibhaṅga as '-abhilāpe ñāṇam' (p. 294), i.e. 'knowledge of the utterance'. If it means what Aung and Mrs Rhys Davids tell us it means, all definitions would fall under it.

(519) *Paṭibhāṇā-sambhidā* is constantly defined in the Vibhaṅga as 'ñāṇesu ñāṇaṃ' (Vbh., 293 ff.) i.e. 'knowledge about knowledge'. As such all analyses of knowledge from a psycho-ethical or epistemological standpoint, as for instance in the Ñāṇa-vibhaṅga of the Vibhaṅga (pp. 306–334) or in the Ñāṇa-kathā of the Paṭisambhidāmagga (pp. 4–134) would fall under it.

(520) This analysis of language, meaning and knowledge combined with an empiricist outlook (*v. infra*, 536, 793) seems to have resulted in a few important insights about the nature of language, meaning and its relation to truth. This analytical approach to the study of language and meaning, it must be remembered, is not new to Buddhism but can be traced to the Brāhmaṇic period, when great advances were made in grammatical and linguistic studies as is evidenced by Yāska's Nirukta.[2] Yāska refers to two classes of scholars in linguistics, the Nairuktas or etymologists and the Vaiyākaraṇas or the grammarians[3] and the Nikāyas represent the orthodox brahmin as being a *padaka*[4] and a *veyyakāraṇa* (padako veyyākaraṇo, D. I.88). The first lessons in linguistic analysis would have been learnt in studying vyākaraṇa- for as Goldstücker says 'vyākaraṇa means "undoing", i.e. it *undoes* words and undoes sentences which consist of words ... and likewise unfolds all the linguistic phenomena, which are inseparable from the

[1] Cp. hetumhi ñāṇaṃ dhamma-paṭisambhidā, hetuphale ñāṇaṃ attha-paṭisambhidā, i.e. the knowledge of a cause is dhammapaṭisambhidā and the knowledge of the effect is atthapaṭisambhidā, Vbh., 293.

[2] Keith, HOS., Vol. 32, p. 488.

[3] *v.* T. Goldstücker, *Panini*, London, 1861, p. 171.

[4] *v.* L. Sarup, *The Nighaṇṭu and the Nirukta*, Oxford University Press, 1920, p. 57; Etymology (i.e. nirukti) is necessary for the analysis of the Saṅhitā text into the pada-pāṭha and of words into their component elements.

meeting of words'.[1] By the time of the Pāli Nikāyas this word (veyyākaraṇa) seems to have acquired an extra-grammatical connotation and come to mean any kind of 'analytical exposition'. It is probably in this sense that the Brahmajāla Sutta which contains an analysis and classification of current philosophical theories is called a 'veyyākaraṇa-' (D. I.46), though the word is also used in the more general sense of a 'reply' to a question (D. I.223, A. II.160).

(521) Let us examine what the Nikāyas have to say on the nature of the words and sentences in relation to meaning and knowledge.

(522) In Indian linguistic philosophy there were two schools of thought in regard to what was considered to be the fundamental units of expression. One held that the statement as a whole (vākya-) or the proposition was fundamental while the other held that the terms (pada-) were fundamental. As Śāstri says, 'there are primarily two schools of thought on the nature of the proposition. Of these two one believes in the indivisibility of the proposition, while the other admits its divisibility. The former is usually called the *vākya-vādin* while the latter is known as the *padavādin*'.[2] Now it is a curious fact, as Jaini has pointed out,[3] that in the Pāli Nikāyas and in fact in the Buddhist tradition as a whole, the word pada- is used to denote the whole statement and not just its words or terms. Whether this implies that the Buddhists considered the whole statement as the fundamental unit as against the Brahmins, who were analysing the statement into its component terms (cp. pada-pāṭha, paḍaka, *v. supra*, 520), it is difficult to say, but it is worthy of note that both in the Nikāyas (*v. infra*, 536) and in the Kathāvatthu (*v. infra*, 708), the meaning of a proposition is considered as a whole.

(523) In any case, with regard to the use of both words and sentences, we find that the Buddha is anxious to avoid disputes which are purely verbal in character and the confusions which arise when we transgress the limits of linguistic convention. He says that 'one should not cling to dialectical usage nor go beyond the limits of convention' (janapadaniruttiṃ nābhiniveseyya sāmaññaṃ nātidhāveyya, M. III.230, 234). The detailed explanation makes clear what is meant. 'And how does one cling to dialectical usage and go beyond convention? Here people

[1] *Op. cit.*, p. 196.

[2] G. Sastri, *The Philosophy of Word and Meaning*, Calcutta, 1959, p. 95.

[3] P. S. Jaini, 'The Vaibhāṣika Theory of Words,' BSOAS., Vol. XXII, Part I, 1959, pp. 98, 99.

recognize the same object in some parts of the country as a "vessel" (pāti), (in other parts) they recognize it as a "bowl" (pattaṃ) . . . a "cup" (vitthaṃ) . . . a "goblet" (sarāvaṃ) . . . In the circumstances, if one were to dogmatically accept and cling to each one of these (usages) in the different parts of the country, saying "this alone is the true (usage), the rest are false", then there would be a clinging to dialectical usage and a transgression of convention . . . If in the circumstances one were to use these terms as used in the different parts of the country saying "they use these (terms) to refer to this (object)" without dogmatically clinging to any one of them, then there would be no clinging to dialectical usage and no transgression of convention.'[1]

(524) This illustrates the kind of verbal dispute and confusion that can arise by transgressing the limits of convention. If someone says, 'this is a vessel' and someone else says, 'no, this is a bowl' referring to one and the same object, we have a purely verbal dispute which cannot be settled by having a closer look at the facts but only by discerning the limits of the conventional usages of the words 'vessel' and 'bowl'. These verbal disputes which can easily arise when people who speak the same language with dialectical differences come together. But differences of this sort were probably aggravated at this time by the acceptance of what was probably the orthodox theory of the meaning of words. Speaking of the relation of a word and its object the Pūrva Mīmāṃsā says 'autpattikas tu śabdasyārthena . . .' (1.1.5), which is rendered by Pandit Mohan Lal Sandal as 'certainly there is an eternal connection between the word and its meaning . . .'[2] and by Jha as 'on the other hand the relation of the word with its meaning is inborn (and eternal) . . .'.[3] The critics of this theory are said to argue, *inter alia*, from the evanescent nature of words. Words are caused because they are perceptible (karmaika tatra darśanāt, 1.1.6), they do not persist (asthānāt, 1.1.7), they are constructed (karoti śabdāt, 1.1.8) and have original and modified forms (prakṛtivikṛtyaś ca, 1.1.10). According to the Bṛhadāraṇyaka Upaniṣad, the world is composed of

[1] Kathañ ca janapadaniruttiyā ca abhiniveso hoti samaññāya ca atisāro? Idha tad ev'ekaccesu janapadesu 'pāti' ti sañjānanti 'pattan' ti sañjānanti, 'vitthaṃ' . . . 'sarāvaṃ' . . . Iti yathā yathā naṃ tesu tesu janapadesu sañjānanti, tathā tathā thāmasā parāmassa abhinivissa voharati: idam eva saccaṃ moghaṃ aññan ti. Evaṃ kho janapadaniruttiyā ca abhiniveso hoti samaññāya ca atisāro . . . Iti yathā yathā naṃ tesu tesu janapadesu sañjānanti: idaṃ kira 'me āyasmanto sandhāya voharantī ti, tathā tathā voharati aparāmasaṃ. Evaṃ kho janapadaniruttiyā ca anabhiniveso hoti samaññāya ca anatisāro, M. III.234–5.

[2] SBH., Vol. 27, Part I, p. 2.

[3] SBH., Vol. 10, p. 8.

a triad, each thing presumably having its specific name (nāma), form (rūpa) and function (karma) (1.6.1–3); name and form are real (nāmarūpa- satyam, *loc. cit.*). The world was created by Brahmā with each thing being given its own name and form (taṃ nāmarūpābhyām eva vyākriyate asau nāma, ayaṃ idaṃ rūpa iti, 1.4.7). Even if things perish, the name does not perish 'for the name is eternal' (anantaṃ vai nāma, 3.2.12). As against this, we find the Buddhists pointing to not only the dialectical variations in language but the changes in nomenclature that take place with time. Thus it is pointed out that 'the hill Vebhāra had a different name and designation' (Vebhārassa pabbatassa aññā va samaññā ahosi aññā paññatti, M. III.68) at different times. The name of the hill Vepula and the people resident in its environs differed from age to age (S. II.190–2).

(525) In the Nikāyas we often notice attempts to avoid ambiguity and vagueness by specifying whether expressions have the same meaning or not. Thus it is asked 'whether the expressions appamāṇā cetovimutti, ākiñcaññā cetovimutti, suññatā cetovimutti and animittā cetovimutti have different meanings, the words too being different or have the same meaning, (despite) the words being different' (nānaṭṭhā c'eva nānābyañjanā ca, udāhu ekaṭṭhā, byañjanam eva nānan ti, M. I.297, cp. S. IV.296). The answer is that 'there is a sense in which the meanings are different as well as the words and a sense in which the meanings are the same, the words alone being different'.[1] This shows that it was not a [illegible]med that a difference in language necessarily implies a difference in meaning, which judging from what Yaska says appears to have been the prevailing theory of meaning at the time.

(526) Yāska lays down his principle of the meaning of words as follows: tāni cet samānakarmā[illegible] samāna-nirvacanāni nānakarmāṇi cen nānā-nirvacanāni,[2] i.e. (as translated by Sarup[3]) 'if their meanings are the same, their etymologies should be the same; if their meanings are different their etymologies also should be different'. It may be noticed that the word used for 'meaning' is karmāṇi which literally means 'functions' or 'uses'.[4]

[1] Atthi kho . . . pariyāyo yaṃ pariyāyaṃ āgamma ime dhammā nānaṭṭhā c'eva nānābyañjanā ca atthi ca kho . . . pariyāyo yam pariyāyaṃ āgamma ime dhammā ekaṭṭhā, byañjanam eva nānaṃ, M. I.297.

[2] *The Nighaṇṭu and the Nirukta*, ed. L. Sarup, University of Punjab, 1927, p. 48.

[3] *The Nighaṇṭu and the Nirukta*, O.U.P., 1920, p. 58.

[4] Note Wittgenstein's theory that the meaning of a word is its 'use', *The Blue and Brown Books*, p. 67.

(527) Of greater epistemological significance is the importance attached to linguistic convention. We have already noticed the saying that 'one should not overstep the limits of conventional usage' (*v. supra*, 523). This is illustrated by the following passage: 'There are these three linguistic conventions or usages of words or terms which are distinct, have been distinct in the past, are distinct at present and will be distinct in the future and which are not ignored by the recluses and brahmins who are wise. Which three? Whatever material form there has been, which has ceased to be, which is past and has changed is called, reckoned and termed "has been" (ahosi), it is not reckoned as "it exists" (atthi) nor as "it will be" (bhavissati)[1] . . . (It is the same with) whatever feelings, percepts, dispositions, consciousness . . .; whatever material form is not arisen, nor come to be, is called, reckoned or termed "it will be" and it is not reckoned as "it exists" or "it has been" . . .; whatever material form has arisen and has manifested itself, is called, reckoned and termed "it exists" and it is not reckoned as "it has been" nor as "it will be" . . . Even the ahetukavādins, the akriyāvādins and the nāstikas should think that these three linguistic conventions, usages of terms or words should not be flouted and violated. And why is that? Because of the fear of being blamed, found fault with and censured.'[2] This, as we have shown (*v. supra*, 199), is probably a criticism of the *a priori* arguments of the Determinists (*v.* ahetukavāda-, akiriyavāda-) which presuppose a violation of these conventions. The mention of the nāstika-scan possibly be a reference to the school of Metaphysical Materialists, whose existence was doubtful but who made use of the *a priori* premiss of the reality of Being (*v. supra*, 126). The very concept of Being is not possible without a violation of this convention. If Being = what exists, then only the specious present has being, for the past and the future do

[1] For a discussion of puzzle questions arising from the problem of 'existence' in the time scale, *v.* Wittgenstein, *The Blue and Brown Books*, p. 109.

[2] Tayo me . . . nirutti-pathā adhivacana-pathā paññatti-pathā asaṃkiṇṇā asaṃkiṇṇapubbā na saṃkīyanti na saṃkīyissanti appaṭikuṭṭhā samaṇehi brāhmaṇehi viññūhi. Katame tayo? Yaṃ hi . . . rūpaṃ atītaṃ niruddhaṃ vipariṇataṃ ahosī ti tassa saṅkhā aḥosī ti tassa samaññā ahosī ti tassa paññatti. Na tassa saṅkhā atthī ti na tassa saṅkhā bhavissatī ti . . . vedanā . . . saññā . . . saṅkhārā . . . viññaṇaṃ. Yaṃ . . . rūpaṃ ajātaṃ apātubhūtaṃ bhavissatī ti tassa saṅkhā . . . tassa samaññā . . . tassa paññatti . . . yaṃ rūpaṃ jātaṃ pātubhūtaṃ atthī ti tassa saṅkhā . . . tassa samaññā . . . tassa paññatti. Na tassa saṅkhā ahosī ti na tassa saṅkhā bhavissatī ti . . . Ye pi . . . ahetuvādā akiriyavādā natthikavādā te pi'me tayo niruttipathā adhivacanapathā paññattipathā na garahitabbaṃ na paṭikkositabbaṃ amaññiṃsu. Taṃ kissa hetu? Nindābyārosanā-bhayā ti. S. III.70–73.

not exist at the present moment. But when we talk of the concept 'Being' without a time reference, we violate this convention and assume that the past as well as the future has existence in the sense in which the present has existence. On the other hand the philosophers of Non-Being, the nihilist Lokāyatikas (*v. supra*, 116) were also guilty of violating this convention for they deny that even the present has Being because it passes away. For them the past does not exist, the present does not exist and the future does not exist, for everything passes away, while the opposite is true for his opponent. As it is said, 'the world rests on the two doctrines Being (atthitam) and Non-Being (natthitam) but he who rightly sees the *arising* of the world as it really is, does not hold that there is Non-Being in the world and he who rightly sees the *cessation* of things, as it really is, does not hold that there is Being in the world ... that 'everything exists' is one extreme and that 'nothing exists' is the other extreme ... (Dvayanissito ... loko yebhuyyena atthitañ c'eva natthitañ ca. Lokasamudayaṃ ... yathābhūtaṃ sammappaññāya passato yā loke natthitā sā na hoti, lokanirodhaṃ ... yathābhūtaṃ sammappaññāya passato yā loke atthitā sā na hoti... sabbaṃ atthī ti kho ayaṃ eko anto, sabbaṃ natthī ti ayaṃ dutiyo anto, S. II.17). The importance attached to not transgressing the boundaries of linguistic convention thus appears to have been directed against certain metaphysical theories which resulted from it.

(528) While it was necessary to observe convention in order to avoid misleading forms of expression, certain conventions could by their very nature give rise to misunderstanding. So while observing convention it is necessary not to be led astray by it. 'The emancipated person' is said 'to make use of current forms of speech without being led astray by them' (vimuttacitto ... yañ ca loke vuttaṃ tena voharati aparāmasan[1] ti, M. I.500). The Poṭṭhapāda Sutta gives atta-paṭilābha as an example of an expression which may be misleading.

(529) In order to understand the significance of this criticism, it is necessary to compare the doctrine criticized in the Poṭṭhapāda Sutta with its corresponding Upaniṣadic doctrine. The *atta*-paṭilābhas or 'obtainments of selves' are said to be three in number:

(1) Rūpī cātummahābhūtiko kabaliṅkārāhārabhakkho = *oḷāriko* atta-paṭilābho, i.e. the obtainment of *the gross self*, which has form, is made of the four great elements and feeds on gross food.

[1] *lit.* without grasping at it.

(2) rūpī manomayo sabbaṅgapaccaṅgī ahīnindriyo = *manomayo* attapaṭilābho, i.e. the obtainment of *the mental self*, having form, mental, in perfect possession of its parts and not lacking in faculties.

(3) Arūpī saññāmayo = *arūpo* attapaṭilābho, i.e. the obtainment of *the formless self*, formless and possessed of consciousness.

D. I.195.[1]

(530) They are trance-states described as the 'selves' of a person and correspond to the conception of the selves as described in the Taittirīya Upaniṣad (2.2–5),[2] where it may be noted, five selves (the pañcakośa) are mentioned of which three seem to correspond to their counterparts above, viz.

(1) annarasamaya-ātman, i.e. the self formed of the essence of food, 2.1.1.

(2) manomaya- ātman, i.e. the mental self, 2.3.1.

(3) vijñānamaya-ātman,[3] the conscious cognitive self, 2.4.1.

(531) Now in the Poṭṭhapāda Sutta, we find the Buddha arguing against the theory that there were integral selves or entities, which constituted the person. It is argued that from the experiential point of view when self (1) is real (sacco), selves (2) and (3) are not real and when self (2) is real, selves (1) and (3) are not real, etc. (yasmiṃ samaye oḷāriko attapaṭilābho hoti, *mogh'*assa tasmiṃ samaye manomayo attapaṭilābho hoti, *mogho* arūpo attapaṭilābho hoti, oḷāriko assa attapaṭilābho tasmiṃ samaye *sacco* hoti. Yasmiṃ samaye manomayo attapaṭilābho hoti, *mogh'*assa tasmiṃ samaye oḷāriko attapaṭilābho hoti *mogho* arūpo attapaṭilābho hoti, manomayo assa attapaṭilābho tasmiṃ samaye *sacco* hoti . . ., D. I.199). Since these 'selves' were attained at different times, it does not make sense, it is said, to say that any one of them is real in an absolute sense but only that each is real at the time of attaining it while the others were not real *at that time* (yo me ahosi atīto attapaṭilābho sveva me attapaṭilābho *tasmiṃ samaye sacco* ahosi *mogho anāgato* attapaṭilābho, *mogho paccuppanno* . . ., D. I.201). This

[1] Cp. the doctrine of the two *kāyas* at D. I.76–7, where the (1) material self—described as, rupī cātummahābhūtiko odānakummāsūpacayo, and (2) the mental self—rupī manomayo sabbaṅgapaccaṅgī ahīnindriyo correspond to (1) and (2) above. *v.* also the 'selves' posited by the Materialists at D. I.34 (*v. supra*, 130).

[2] Cp. Kaṭha Upaniṣad 3.13, where there is a progressive emergence of the selves in the Yogic process; cp. Pañcattaya Sutta, M. II.237.

[3] Note that *viññāṇañcāyatana-* is one of the *arūpa* states.

is apparently directed against the metaphysical views held with regard to these selves by some of the Upaniṣadic thinkers, as for instance when it is urged at Tait. 2.2.1–5 that all these selves were real or at Kaṭha 2.3.17, where it is assumed that 'the person ... ever seated in the heart of creatures is the (real) inner self, which one should draw out from one's own body like a shaft from a reed[1] (puriso'ntar ātmā sadā janānāṃ hṛdaye sanniviṣṭaḥ taṃ svāc charīrāt pravṛhen muñjād iveṣīkaṃ . . .).

(532) The Buddha uses the term attapaṭilābha- to describe these states but does not assume that there is an entity or entities corresponding to the word 'atta-' within one's person or body. This is illustrated by the example of the milk which changes into cream, yoghurt, curd and butter (khīramhā dadhi dadhimhā navanītaṃ navanītamhā sappi sappimhā sappimaṇḍo, D. I.201). At the stage when milk has turned into any of these states it cannot be called by any other name than the name appropriate to describe each state (yasmiṃ samaye khīraṃ hoti, n'eva tasmiṃ samaye 'dadhī' ti saṅkhaṃ gacchati . . . *loc. cit.*). To this extent one cannot overstep convention. Nor should one assume that each of these names signifies an entity within the changing process.

(533) The fact that we use the word 'I' constantly to refer to ourselves seems to imply the existence of an ontological subject corresponding to the grammatical subject 'I' of the sentences we use. In many of the Upaniṣads where the identity between the individual soul and the ultimate world-ground was being taught there was little doubt that 'ahaṃ' in sentences like, eso *ahaṃ* asmi (this I am) (Ch. 8.11.1) meant the personal ego conceived as a substantial entity and generally considered to reside within the body (*v. supra*, 531). Against this the Materialists argued that the personal pronoun 'I' (also 'my') in 'I'-sentences referred to the body and not to a mental substance (*v. supra*, 133). The Buddhists appeared to have opposed both these schools of substantialists by contending that there was no permanent substantial entity that could be observed to correspond to the term or concept 'I' or 'soul' (cp. n'eso *aham* asmi, na m'eso *attā*, M. I.40) and that we should not be misled by the apparent implications of the use of language. Words like *atta*-paṭilābha- are 'expressions, turns of speech, designations in common use in the world which the Tathāgata

[1] Note that this very simile is mentioned where these selves are mentioned at D. I.77.

makes use of without being led astray by them' (Itimā ... loka-samaññā lokaniruttiyo lokavohārā lokapaññattiyo yāhi Tathāgato voharati aparāmasan ti, D. I.202). On the basis of this sentence, though perhaps with little knowledge of its specific context, Ogden and Richards[1] have observed that 'the rejection of misleading forms of language was carried still further by Buddhist writers in their rejection of the "soul"'.

(534) Jaini, referring to this passage in the Poṭṭhapāda Sutta, gives a different twist to it both in his comments as well as in the translation of the passage itself. He says: 'The term *paññatti* occurs several times in the Suttas, always referring to designations or concepts recognized as unreal in themselves nevertheless used in common parlance. In the *Phoṭṭhapāda-sutta*,[2] for instance, the Buddha, while speaking on various speculations on the nature of self, says that a word like *atta-paṭilābha* or expressions like past, present or future or milk, curds, butter, ghee, etc., are merely names, expressions, turns of speech, designations in common use in the world. The Tathāgata, although he makes use of these is not led astray by them (i.e. knows them as unreal').[3] In the first place, that *paññatti* is used in the Suttas (Jaini does not himself quote any instances) for 'concepts recognized as unreal in themselves' is incorrect as, for instance, the use of the term dukkha-*paññatti* (S. IV.39) clearly shows—we cannot say that according to the Suttas, dukkha- is unreal! On the other hand in the context of the Poṭṭhapāda Sutta, the Buddha quite explicitly approves of the statement to the effect that the empirical self *was* real in the past *is* real in the present and *will be* real in the future, viz. 'I *did exist* in the past, *not that I did not*; I *will exist* in the future, *not that I will not*, and *I do exist* in the present, *not that I do not*' (Ahos'āhaṃ atītam addhānaṃ nāhaṃ nāhosiṃ, bhavissām'āhaṃ anāgatam addhānaṃ nāhaṃ na bhavissāmi, atthāhaṃ etarahi nāhaṃ natthī ti, D. I.200). Besides, a careful study of the context will show that it was not the intention of the author to say that 'milk, curds, butter, ghee, etc.', are *mere* words which do not denote anything real (as Jaini says) but that in the first place we should not overstep convention by calling what comes to be called (saṅkham gacchati, D. I.201) 'curds' by the names 'milk', 'butter', etc., and secondly assume that 'milk' or 'butter'

[1] *The Meaning of Meaning*, London, 1923, pp. 53–4.
[2] This is probably a misprint for Poṭṭhapāda Sutta.
[3] The Vaibhāṣika Theory of Words and Meanings, BSOAS., Vol. 22, Part I, 1959, pp. 99, 100.

is in some mysterious way present as an entity in 'curds' so that each of these terms like the term 'ātman' (atta-) denotes an entity that persists in some mysterious fashion without being perceived. Lastly, Jaini's use of the term '*merely*' (in his translation) is without justification considering that the original has nothing corresponding to it and in no way suggests it. In this respect, Jaini is probably merely following Prof. Rhys Davids, who also had 'merely names' though he interprets the passage correctly (*v.* SBB., Vol. II, p. 263, fn. 1). Perhaps Prof. Rhys Davids was influenced by the use of the Upaniṣadic expression 'vācārambhaṇaṃ vikāro nāmadheyaṃ'[1] ('the modification is merely a verbal distinction, a name', Hume, *op. cit.*, p. 241) which is used to signify that what is perceived (e.g. fire) is only an appearance or modification (vikāraḥ) of the essences (the three forms, trīṇi rūpāṇi, Ch. 6.4.1) or of the ultimate reality Being (sat). But the Pāli passage constitutes the very denial of this idea.

(535) These observations, despite their antiquity do in fact foreshadow some of the criticisms made by the modern Analytical Philosophers. Russell says that 'substance in a word is a metaphysical mistake, due to the transference to the world-structure of the structure of sentences composed of a subject and predicate'[2] and Wittgenstein observes that 'the idea that the real "I" lives in my body is connected with the peculiar grammar of the word "I" and the misunderstandings that this grammar is liable to give rise to'.[3] The statements of the Pāli Nikāyas on this subject are perhaps less explicit but there is little doubt that they are on the same lines.

(536) Of greater significance is the concept of the 'meaningless statement', which probably resulted from this analysis of the nature and meaning of statements. The Buddha refers to statements (bhāsitaṃ) of a certain character as 'appāṭihīrakataṃ ... sampajjati' (D. I.193, 194, 195, 239, 241, 242, 243, 244, M. II.33, 41) and statements of the opposite character as 'sappāṭihīrakataṃ (bhāsitaṃ) sampajjati' (D. I.198[4]). Likewise the dhamma- (doctrine) as taught by the Buddha is said to be 'not appāṭihāriya-' (M. II.9) but 'sappāṭihāriya-' (D. II.104; III.125; M. II.9; A. I.276; S. V.260, 261; Ud. 63; Kvu. 561).

[1] Ch. 6.1.6. [2] *A History of Western Philosophy*, p. 225.

[3] *The Blue and Brown Books*, p. 66.

[4] The reference 'D. III.121' in the PTS. Dictionary (*s.v.* sappāṭihīrakata-) is erroneous.

(537) There are many problems associated with the meaning of these terms. Are the characteristics of bhāsitaṃ (a statement) described by the phrases 'appāṭihīrakataṃ sampajjati' and 'sappāṭihīrakataṃ sampajjati' equivalent to the characteristics 'appāṭihāriya-' and 'sappāṭihāriya-' respectively? What is this characteristic or in other words what do these phrases mean? Lastly, what is the etymology of these words?

(538) There seems to be a certain measure of unanimity with regard to the answer to the first question in that scholars seem to refer to the other usage as being synonymous.[1] The PTS. Dictionary even goes to the extent of confusing the one expression with the other.[2]

(539) We notice that 'appāṭihīrakata-' and 'sappāṭihīrakata-' occur in the first book of the Dīgha Nikāya and once in the Majjhima Nikāya, while 'appāṭihāriya' and 'sappāṭihāriya-' do not occur in the first book, although they are found in the second book and occur in all the Nikāyas in similar though not identical contexts. They seem to have replaced the more cumbersome earlier expressions with a simple adjectival phrase (appāṭihāriya-; sappāṭihāriya-).

(540) Scholars are divided as to the answer to the second question. The translations proffered are many and various. We wish to put forward the theory that statements (bhaṣitaṃ) characterized as 'appāṭihīrakataṃ sampajjati' or 'appāṭihāriyaṃ' are in some sense 'lacking in meaning'. An examination of the contexts of the kinds of statements which are so described shows that in an important sense they 'do not make sense' and are 'meaningless' (niratthakaṃ) as explained in one of the commentaries (MA. III.273, appāṭihīrakatan ti . . . *niratthakaṃ* sampajjati). The etymology of the word, however, is obscure but usage is the surer clue to the meaning of the term than its etymology.

(540A) The meanings suggested are quite a few and may be classified as follows:

I (a) *appāṭihīrakataṃ bhāsitaṃ*	(b) *sappāṭihīrakataṃ bhāsitaṃ*
1. Talk without ground (Prof. Rhys Davids, SBB., II, pp. 257, 259)	1. Talk well-grounded (Prof. Rhys Davids, SBB., II, p. 262).

[1] *v.* Prof. Rhys Davids who while commenting on appāṭihīrakata- and sappāṭihīrakata- refers to sappāṭihāriya as 'a closely allied expression', SBB., II, p. 257, fn. 3; cp. Horner, M.L.S. II.210, fn. 2.

[2] Thus it gives one of the references of sappāṭihāriya- (*s.v.*) as D. I.198, whereas the actual word found is sappāṭihīrakata-.

2. Witless talk; Foolish talk (Prof. Rhys Davids, SBB., II, pp. 258, 259, 307 ff.)
3. Not apposite (talk) (Prof. Rhys Davids, SBB., II, p. 257, fn. 3).
4. Incomprehensible talk (Horner, M.L.S. II.230)
   Gerede, das ohne Überlegung (Franke, Dīgha Nikāya, p. 155, fn. 3)
   Gerede, das ohne vorsichtige Zurückhaltung (*loc. cit.*)
5. Unüberlegtes Gerede (Franke, *op. cit.*, p. 155)
6. Indisputables (Franke, *op. cit.*, p. 155, fn. 3)
   Nicht erst noch zu Widerlegendes (*loc. cit.*)
7. Ungeniesbares Geshwätz (*loc. cit.*)

2. Apposite (talk) (Prof. Rhys Davids, SBB., II, p. 257, fn. 3).

II (a) *appāṭihāriya-*

1. unconvincing (talk) (Horner, M.L.S. II.210)
2. (talk) without arguments (Horner, M.L.S. II.210, fn. 2)
3. Witless (talk) (Horner, *loc. cit.*)
4. Unreliable talk (Horner, *loc. cit.*)
5. Without wonders (Woodward, G.S. I.254)
6. Incomprehensible[1] (Neumann, Majjhima Nikāyo, II, p. 318)

(b) *sappāṭihāriya-*

1. convincing (talk) (Horner, *loc. cit.*)
2. Accompanied by wonders (Woodward, G.S. I.254)
3. Intelligible[1] (Neumann, Majjhima Nikāyo, II, p. 318)
4. A thing of saving grace (Prof. Rhys Davids, SBB.)
   That brings salvation with it (Mrs Rhys Davids, K.S. V.232; *v.* fn. 2)

(541) Of the above, Franke's suggestions are based on various conjectural etymologies of the word, considering the context as well. The PTS. Dictionary is largely influenced by the belief that the term is derived from the word P. pāṭihāriya- > P. pāṭihera- (both attested in Pāli) meaning 'miracle' and regards the idea of 'substantiated' and

[1] *v.* PTS. Dictionary, *s.v.* pāṭihāriya; Neumann has '(nicht) unerfassbar'.

'well-founded' as derivative from it. Thus it explains sappāṭihīrakata- as 'made with wonders, substantiated by wonders, substantiated, well-founded', (*s.v.*) sappāṭihāriya- as 'accompanied by wonders' (*s.v.* pāṭihāriya-).

(542) Even if the word is etymologically the same as pāṭihīra = miracle, the meaning is not at all suggestive of the sense of 'wonder' or 'miracle' and all translations suggesting it are strictly unwarranted by the contexts. In fact, Prof. Rhys Davids had already noticed this when he said 'the Pāli word for miracle comes from the same root (prati + √har); but to render here "unmiraculous" would make nonsense of the passage and both my own and Windisch's rendering of the word in M.P.S. ("Buddhist Suttas", p. 43; Māra und Buddha, p. 71), must be also modified accordingly' (SBB., II., p. 257, fn. 3). Besides to translate sappāṭihāriya- as 'accompanied by miracles' goes against the grain of what is said about the preaching of the dhamma in the Nikāyas themselves. For instance, in the Kevaḍḍha Sutta the Buddha specifically says that he has asked his monks not to perform miracles before laymen for the purpose of conversion.[1] He speaks of the dangers of performing wonders[2] and of thought-reading in public,[3] while speaking in praise of 'the miracle of instruction' (anusāsanipāṭihāriyaṃ, D. I.214), which in fact was instruction without miracle. It is possible that there is here a pun on the word pāṭihāriya- which we are unable to appreciate, since we are unacquainted with the meaning of pāṭihāriya- in the above contexts where there is no sense of or association with 'miracle'.

(543) Most of the translations follow several suggestions of the commentaries, none of which incidentally support a direct or derivative meaning of 'miracle'. Thus the Comy. explains sappāṭihāriya- at M. II.9 as 'sakāraṇa-' (MA. III.241), i.e. 'with cause' on the basis of which scholars have suggested I (a) 1, I (b) 1, II (a) 1 and 2, and II (b) 1. But this translation does not suit all the contexts (e.g. M. II.41) nor even the context for which it is suggested. Here it is stated:

abhiññāya Samaṇo Gotamo dhammaṃ deseti, no anabhiññāya
sanidānaṃ Samaṇo Gotamo dhammaṃ deseti, no anidānaṃ
sappāṭihāriyaṃ Samaṇo Gotamo dhammaṃ deseti, no appāṭihāriyaṃ
(M. II.9).

[1] Na kho ahaṃ . . . evaṃ dhammaṃ desemi: etha tumhe . . . gihīnaṃ . . . iddhipāṭihāriyaṃ karotha, D. I.212. [2] iddhi-pāṭihāriyaṃ, *v.* D. I.212, 213.
[3] ādesanā-pāṭihāriyaṃ, V.D. I.213, 214.

It is obvious that abhiññāya and sanidānaṃ are not used synonymously and therefore we have no grounds for surmising that sappāṭihāriyaṃ is synonymous with sanidānaṃ, which clearly means 'with causes or reasons'.

(544) Similarly I (a) 2 and II (a) 3 have been suggested by the comment, patibhāna-virahitaṃ (DA. II.380, *v.* 1), i.e. void of intelligence. This sense is too wide for it is possible to conceive of instances when a statement could be 'unintelligent' but not describable as appāṭihīrakata- or appāṭihāriya-. Some of the suggestions of the commentaries are suitable for certain contexts, but their inaptness is seen by their inapplicability to others. Thus the comment on sappāṭihāriya- at A. I.226 (*v.* G.S. I.254, fn. 3) is, paccanīkapaṭiharaṇena sappāṭihāriyaṃ eva katvā kathema (AA. II.374) i.e. by striking a blow at my adversaries, I speak with striking effect. This suits several contexts where the following sentence occurs, viz. uppannam parappavādaṃ sahadhammena suniggahītaṃ niggahetvā sappāṭihāriyaṃ dhammaṃ desetuṃ (D. II.104, III.125, Ud. 63), i.e. to preach the doctrine with striking effect after righteously refuting a criticism that has arisen. But this meaning especially in its negative form 'without striking effect' would be totally unsuited for contexts like D. I.193 ff., 239 ff. and M. II.33. Another such suggestion is yāva niyyānikaṃ katvā, i.e. 'making it salutary or efficacious for salvation', which is the comment[1] on sappāṭihāriyaṃ at S. V.260, 261 and, aniyyānikaṃ sampajjati (MA. III.273), i.e. 'becomes not efficacious for salvation' which is the comment on appāṭihīrakata- at M. II.33. This has suggested II (b) 4, but it is a typically scholastic sentiment and hardly describes the statements of the brahmins as given at D. I.193 ff. and M. II.33.

(545) Prof. Rhys Davids' suggestion of 'apposite' and 'non-apposite' for sappāṭihīrakata- and appāṭihīrakata- respectively on the basis of Buddhaghosa's comment sappāṭiviharaṇaṃ[2] (DA. II.381; *v.* Prof. Rhys Davids, SBB., II, p. 257, fn. 3) seems to come very close to describing the character of these statements. So does Neumann's[3] 'intelligible' and 'incomprehensible'. Of the numerous commentarial explanations, the one that fits the contexts best is the comment, amūlakaṃ niratthakaṃ sampajjati (MA. III.273), i.e. 'becomes baseless and meaningless' and of the two suggestions 'baseless' and 'meaningless'

[1] *v.* K.S. V.223, fn. 2.
[2] This is only a *v.* 1, the reading being sappāṭiharaṇaṃ.
[3] *v.* PTS. Dictionary, *s.v.* pāṭihāriya-.

the latter is to be preferred but we can do so only after a careful study of the nature of these statements as they appear in their contexts.

(546) The standard example of an appāṭihīrakatam bhāsitam and one that is often repeated is the following: ahaṃ yā imasmiṃ janapade janapadakalyāṇī taṃ icchāmi taṃ kamemī ti (D. I.193, 241, M. II.33), i.e. I like and am in love with the beauty queen of this country. Now the expression 'the beauty queen of this country' is a definite description[1] and it is held that 'sentences containing definite or indefinite descriptions are logically inappropriate expressions';[2] but this does not mean that the statement is meaningless, in the sense in which this term is used by the Positivists.

(547) Wherein then lies the 'baselessness' (amūlakaṃ) or 'meaninglessness' (niratthakaṃ) of this statement. Before we examine the context in greater detail we may observe an ambiguity in the use of the definite description, 'the beauty queen of this country'. Such descriptions may be of three sorts, viz. (1) where what is described is existentially exemplified (i.e. there is an instance of it), e.g. 'the queen of England' where there is a person answering to the description, (2) where there is no instance although an instance is conceivable, e.g. 'the queen of France', and (3) where an instance is not even conceivable the situation being purely ideal, e.g. 'the queen of Utopia'. Now the expression 'the beauty queen of this country' is ambiguous in that it may belong to categories (1) or (2) and we are not sure which it is. In other words, there may or may not be instances of this definite description. Let us assume that there aren't. Let us assume that we are in a country in which no one has been given the title (officially or unofficially) 'the beauty queen of this country'. Then if someone in this country were to say, 'I love the beauty queen of this country' we would find this statement extremely odd, because the expression, 'the beauty queen of this country' does not stand for anything and 'expressions containing words "which do not stand for anything" ' would be meaningless statements.[3] This is, in fact, according to Ewing one 'of the conditions under which verbal expressions could be said to be meaningless'.[4]

(548) But supposing the definite description has an instance and there is a person answering to the description 'the beauty queen of this

[1] Stebbing, *op. cit.*, p. 149. [2] *Ibid.*, p. 151.

[3] *v.* K. N. Jayatilleke, 'Factual Meaning and Verification' in UCR., Vol. 13, pp. 6, 8. [4] A. C. Ewing, 'Meaninglessness' in *Mind*, 1937, p. 359.

country', could we still say that the statement, 'I love the beauty queen of this country' is meaningless? Modern Positivists would say that this statement is not meaningless at all, but according to the Pāli Nikāyas, it would seem that the *context* can render such a statement meaningless. From the account given, it is in fact the context which makes the above statement meaningless. The context is one in which the person who makes this statement confesses that he does not know whether this beauty queen whom he professes to love was 'a kṣatriya, a brahmin, a vaiśya or śūdra' (khattiyī vā brāhmaṇī vā vessī vā suddī vā, D. I.241), does not know 'what family or personal name she had' (evaṃ nāmā evaṃ gottā ti vā, *loc. cit.*), does not know 'whether she was tall, short, dark, brunette or golden in colour or in what village or town or city she dwells' (dīghā vā rassā vā kālī vā sāmā vā maṅguracchavī vā ti, amukasmiṃ gāme vā nigame vā nagare vā ti, *loc. cit.*). In other words he claims to like and love a person whom he has not 'seen or known' (na *jānāsi* na *passasi*, *loc. cit.*).

(549) According to this account it would appear that *X*'s statement 'I love *Y*' is meaningless since (i) one is not sure whether there is an instance of *Y*, and (ii) even if there is, it does not make sense for *X* to say that he loves *Y* unless he has some acquaintance direct or indirect with *Y*, such that he could specify at least one of the characteristics of *Y*. (ii) alone can give meaning to the use of the word 'love' which (in this context) must have a person as object and its use would otherwise be lacking in meaning. In other words, there is no verifiable content to the statement from the point of view of *X* who is making it.

(550) The similarity as well as the difference of this example from that of an argument that the Materialists used against the concept of the 'soul' (*v. supra*, 131) is worth noting. The Materialists argued that we could not speak of the existence of the soul unless we could specify whether the soul was 'long or small, globular, circular or triangular . . . black, blue . . . of sweet smell or of bad smell . . . was bitter or pungent . . . hard or soft, etc.' Since their opponents did not attach a verifiable content to the concept of soul (ātman), one could not talk of its existence. Here in the Nikāyas it is considered meaningless to make a statement unless the speaker could attach a verifiable content to each of its terms. In the Sūtrakṛtāṅga account it is not specifically said that a statement containing the word 'soul' is meaningless, since it is an empty concept with no verifiable content but the Pāli Nikāyas seem

to be saying that a statement in which no verification or meaning is attached to one of its terms (by the speaker) is in fact meaningless.

(551) The other example given is that of 'a person who makes a stairway in a public square to ascend a mansion' (puriso catummahāpathe nissenim kareyya pāsādassa ārohanāya, D. I.243) but when asked to describe the 'mansion' is unable to give any account whatsoever. He is unable to say where the mansion is situated 'whether in the eastern direction, southern, western, or northern' (puratthimāya disāya dakkhiṇāya disāya pacchimāya disāya uttarāya disāya, *loc. cit.*) and whether the mansion was 'high, low or of medium height' (ucco vā nīco vā majjho vā ti, *loc. cit.*). In other words, he claims to make a stairway to ascend a mansion which he has neither seen nor known. His statement is considered meaningless since he can attach no meaning or verification to the term 'mansion' which is one of the terms of his statement.

(552) Now the above are only examples intended to illustrate statements which are describable as appāṭihīrakataṃ ... sampajjati, i.e. become meaningless. Let us examine the original statements so considered. The following is such a statement attributed to the Vedic brahmins, viz. ayam eva ujumaggo, ayam añjasāyano niyyāniko niyyāti takkarassa Brahmasahavyatāya (D. I.241), i.e. this is the straight path, this is the direct way which makes for salvation and leads him who acts according to it to a state of companionship with Brahmā. This statement is considered meaningless, since no meaning or verification is attached by those who make it to the term 'Brahmā' (God). None of the brahmins or their several generations of teachers are said to have claimed 'a direct vision of Brahmā' (Brahmā sakkhidiṭṭho, *loc. cit.*); they 'do not claim to know where, whence or whither Brahmā is' (te ... na evaṃ āhaṃsu, mayaṃ etaṃ jānāma, mayaṃ etaṃ passāma yattha vā Brahmā yahiṃ vā Brahmā, *loc. cit.*) but 'they claim to teach a path to the companionship of Him, whom they have not seen or known' (te ... yaṃ na jānanti yaṃ na passanti tassa sahavyatāya maggaṃ desessanti, *loc. cit.*).

(553) Likewise a statement made by recluses and brahmins, namely that 'the soul is extremely happy and without defect after death' (ekantasukhī attā hoti arogo paraṃ maraṇā, D. I.192) is considered meaningless. This is because those who make it are considered unable to attach any meaning to the term 'ekantasukhī' (extremely happy)

not having experienced a feeling of extreme happiness themselves;[1] nor can they attach any meaning to the concept of 'an after-life in which one is extremely happy' (ekantasukhī attā ... param maraṇā, *loc. cit.*), since they cannot claim to have directly seen or known of the existence of such a world[2] nor indirectly acquired any information about such a world;[3] they have no knowledge of the path that leads to a direct vision of such a world.[4] In other words, they can attach no verifiable content to the statement or to the concepts in it.

(554) We meet with another example in the Cūḷasakuludāyi Sutta, which is of a slightly different character. As the context is important, we may translate the dialogue as we find it in the Pāli, as follows:

Buddha: What, Udāyi, is your teacher's teaching? (Kin ti pana te, Udāyi, sake ācariyake evaṃ hotī ti?, M. II.32)

Udāyi: Our teacher's teaching is that 'this is the highest colour, this is the highest colour' (amhākaṃ sake ācariyake evaṃ hoti: ayaṃ paramo vaṇṇo, ayaṃ paramo vaṇṇo ti, *loc. cit.*)

Buddha: What is that colour? (Katamo so paramo vaṇṇo ti? *loc. cit.*)

Udāyi: That colour than which there is no other colour which is higher or better, is the highest colour (yasmā vaṇṇā añño vaṇṇo uttaritaro vā paṇītataro vā natthi, so paramo vaṇṇo ti, *loc. cit.*)

Buddha: What is that colour than which there is no colour higher or better? (katamo pana so vaṇṇo yasmā vaṇṇā añño vaṇṇo uttaritaro vā paṇītataro vā natthī ti? *loc. cit.*)

Udāyi: *That colour than which there is no other colour which is higher or better, is the highest colour* (yasmā vaṇṇā añño vaṇṇo uttaritaro vā paṇītataro vā natthi, so paramo vaṇṇo ti, *loc. cit.*)

Buddha: You say that the 'highest colour' is that than which there is no other, which is higher or better. *But you do not specify that colour.* It is like a person saying, 'I like and am in love with the beauty

[1] Tyāhaṃ evaṃ vadāmi: Api pana tumhe ... ekaṃ vā rattiṃ ekaṃ vā divasaṃ upaḍḍhaṃ vā rattiṃ upaḍḍhaṃ vā diviasaṃ ekantasukhiṃ attānaṃ sañjānāthā ti (*loc. cit.*), i.e. I ask them whether they have experienced extreme happiness within themselves for one night or day or even for half a night or day and they reply that they have not.

[2] Tyāhaṃ evaṃ vadāmi: Api pana tumhe ... ekantasukhaṃ lokaṃ jānaṃ passaṃ viharathā ti? Iti puṭṭhā no ti vadanti, *loc. cit.*

[3] Api pana tumhe ... yā tā devatā ekantasukkhaṃ lokaṃ uppannā tāsaṃ bhāsamānānaṃ saddaṃ suṇātha ... Iti puṭṭhā no ti vadanti, *loc. cit.*

[4] Api pana tumhe jānātha: 'Ayaṃ maggo ayaṃ paṭipadā ekantasukhassa lokassa sacchikiriyāyā' ti? Iti puṭṭhā no ti vadanti, *loc. cit.*

queen of this country' ... (yasmā vaṇṇā añño vaṇṇo uttaritaro vā paṇītataro vā natthi, so paramo vaṇṇo ti vadasi; tañ ca vaṇṇaṃ na *paññapesi.* Seyyathā pi puriso evaṃ vadeyya: Ahaṃ yā imasmiṃ janapade janapadakalyāṇi, taṃ icchāmi taṃ kāmemī ti ... (*loc. cit.*)

(555) Here the statement, 'that colour than which there is no other colour which is higher or better is the highest colour' is said to be 'meaningless' (appāṭihīrakataṃ bhāsitaṃ, M. II.33) because what is meant by 'the highest colour' is not specified. No meaning by way of anything verifiable is attached to the phrase 'the highest colour' in this context. The statement is a tautology or a definition when the answer (to the question asked) should be in the form of a contingent proposition. It is like someone when asked 'what is the best beer?' replying 'that beer than which there is none better'. It lacks contextual propriety and this is another consideration, which may render it meaningless.[1]

(556) We thus observe that all the above statements have a certain characteristic in common, namely that no verifiable content is attached by the speaker to some of the symbols or words contained in them. On the other hand, the statement, which can be described as having the opposite characteristic namely, sappāṭihīrakataṃ bhāsitaṃ, is said to be the following: The Buddha is asked a question: 'What is the attainment of a formless self for the elimination of which you preach a doctrine, so that the corrupt states of those who follow it decline, the pure states increase and one realizes oneself with one's higher knowledge, attains to and abides in the perfection of wisdom and maturity'? (katamo pana so arūpo attapaṭilābho yassa tumhe pahānāya dhammaṃ desetha yathā paṭipannānaṃ vo saṃkilesikā dhammā pahīyissanti vodāniyā dhammā abhivaḍḍhissanti, paññāpāripūriṃ vepullatañ ca diṭṭhe va dhamme sayaṃ abhiññā sacchikatvā upasampajja viharissathā ti? D. I.198). The reply consists in demonstrating the means of attaining and abiding in the state described, viz. 'this is the attainment of the formless self ...' (ayaṃ vā so arūpo attapaṭilābho ..., *loc. cit.*). The example is given of a person who claims to be constructing a stairway to ascend a mansion but unlike in the previous case (*v. supra*, 551) is able to indicate or show what the mansion is and what it is like.[1] In other words, these statements have a meaning

[1] *v.* K. N. Jayatilleke, *op. cit.*, p. 12.

[1] So ce evaṃ vadeyya: Ayaṃ vā so ... pāsādo yassāham ārohanāya nisseṇiṃ karomi, tass' eva pāsādassa heṭṭhā ti, D. I.198, i.e. He would answer in this manner: 'This is the mansion beneath which I am constructing my stairway in order to ascend it'.

for the words constituting them, in that there is a method of verification for discovering what is meant, whether the statement be true or false.

(557) In a sense the statements which are called appāṭihīrakata- are baseless (amūlakam, *v. supra*, 545) in that the persons making them do not do so on the basis of any evidence or arguments which justify their assertion. But this seems to be incidental in that this explanation does not hold good for the example given at M. II.33 (*v. supra*, 554). We would, therefore, considering the above contexts prefer the meaning of 'meaningless' (niratthakam, *v. supra*, 540) for appāṭihīrakata- and appāṭihāriya-, a sense which, it may be observed, is attested by the Comy. as well.

(558) It is necessary, however, both to compare as well as to distinguish this sense of 'meaningless' from the sense in which Positivists have considered certain statements meaningless, when they did not conform to the Verification Principle. In the above contexts, the statements were not considered apart from the speaker and the context in which they were uttered, whereas the Positivists examine the meaningfulness of statements irrespective of the speakers or their contexts. For the Positivist, a statement to have meaning must be in principle verifiable but verification for him is solely in respect of sense-experience, whereas the Pāli Nikāyas would admit extrasensory experience as well (*v. infra*, 750 ff.). While therefore some statements that the Positivist considers to be meaningless would also be considered meaningless by the Buddhist, many statements which would be verifiable and meaningful for Early Buddhism would be unverifiable and meaningless for the Positivist. The statement 'God exists' would be meaningless for the Positivist for it is unverifiable in his sense of the term. We found similarly that statements about the existence of Brahmā (*v. supra*, 552) were considered appāṭihīrakata- but this is not because these statements were unverifiable and meaningless in principle, but because no meaning was attached to them by the people asserting them, though in principle it was possible to do so.[1] Likewise,

[1] This is apparent from the conclusion of the Tevijja Sutta (D. I.249 ff.) where the Buddha says that just as much as one born and bred in Manasākaṭa does not hesitate or falter in his reply if someone were to ask him for the road to Manasākaṭa-, the Buddha as having a direct knowledge and vision of Brahmā, can vouch for his existence (though not in the Theistic sense) and point out the way leading to survival in his world.

some statements that would be meaningless for Early Buddhism would be meaningful for the Positivist. Thus the statement 'I am constructing a stairway to ascend a mansion' would be quite meaningful for the Positivist but this same statement, as we have seen (*v. supra*, 551, 556) would be meaningless in one context and meaningful in another for the Buddhist.

(559) Franke said that, die ubersetzung von appāṭihīrakata- ist nicht sicher (*op. cit.*, p. 155, fn. 3) but it is not so much the translation but the etymology of the term that is not certain. Since there is no connection of pāṭihīra- in this context with the sense of 'wonder' it is doubtful whether its meaning could be derived from pāṭihīra = miracle. Franke himself suggests several etymologies inconclusively.[1] The closest that the commentary comes to offering an etymological explanation is, paṭiharaṇa-virahitaṃ (DA. II.380) for appāṭihīrakata-. Now, ud + ā + √hṛ, is used for 'utter' in this stratum (cp. dhammaṃ paṇītam taṃ *udāhareyya*, i.e. let him utter that excellent dhamma, Sn. 389), presupposing a hypothetical *udāharaṇa-* for 'utterance' though udāharaṇa- itself comes to mean before long an 'illustration or example' which throws light on an utterance (cp. udāharaṇam āharitva dassento, taking an example and showing, J. III.401). Could prati-haraṇa- have meant the 'sense' or 'basis' of the utterance or 'that on account of which (prati-) (there was an) utterance (haraṇa-)'? If so, is appāṭihīrakata- = paṭiharaṇa-virahita (*v. supra*) = sense-less, baseless. Pāṭihīra- is a contracted form of pāṭihāriya- (*v.* sappāṭihāriya- and appāṭihāriya-); by metathesis, pāṭihāriya- > *pāṭihīra- > pāṭihīra- (PTS. Dictionary, *s.v.* pāṭihīra-). We have to consider pāṭihāriya-, 'having sense' on the above hypothesis as an adjectival formation from paṭi-hara- with the above meaning of paṭiharaṇa-, but it is necessary to emphasize the fact that all this is very conjectural.

[1] (1) A participle of necessity from prati + √hṛ 'to throw back' which he says fits very well the meaning of sappāṭihāriyaṃ at D. II.104, but this would not suit other contexts; (2) prati + √hṛ, 'to take up, eat, enjoy' (cp. ā-hār-a = food) giving the meaning 'unenjoyable' 'indigestible' for appāṭihīra-. This is far-fetched; (3) absolutive from prati + √hṛ, in the sense of 'weighing carefully' or 'holding back' in the sense of not committing yourself immediately, but as Franke admits such a root does not exist; (4) prati + √hṛ also in the sense of 'hold back' but of roots ending in ṛ (short) no such absolutive, as Franke says, could be formed., *loc. cit.*

CHAPTER VII

LOGIC AND TRUTH

(560) In this chapter we propose to investigate what is meant by the four forms of predication or the four logical alternatives (*v. supra,* 182) as they appear in the Buddhist texts. This will be followed up by an inquiry into the nature of truth, as understood in the Buddhist texts.

(561) There seems to be considerable confusion among scholars as to what was meant by this four-fold schema. Poussin speaks of it as 'a four-branched dilemma' of Buddhist dialectic and believes that it violates the principle of Contradiction. He says, 'Indians do not make a clear distinction between facts and ideas, between ideas and words; they have never clearly recognized the principle of contradiction. Buddhist dialectic has a four-branched dilemma: Nirvāṇa is existence or non-existence or both existence and non-existence or neither existence nor non-existence. We are helpless'.[1] Mrs Rhys Davids in a passage that we have already quoted (*v. supra,* 497), suggested that they are 'Laws of Thought'. Later, referring to this same passage, she says, 'To revert to the Laws of Thought—the way in which Indian logic presented the second and third of these (Contradiction and Excluded Middle) has been mentioned'.[2] Barua too favours this interpretation and in fact calls them 'the four laws of thought':[3] '. . . the happy result of this mode of discussion or "wrangling" among the learned wanderers was that in the time of Buddha the four laws of thought were recognized as a matter of course. These are in their applications to propositions:

1. (If A is B), A is B.
2. A cannot be both B and not-B.
3. A is either B or not-B.
4. A is neither B nor not-B.' (*loc. cit.*)

[1] *The Way to Nirvana,* Cambridge University Press, 1917, p. 111.

[2] ERE., Vol. 8, p. 133, Article on 'Logic (Buddhist)'.

[3] *A History of Pre-Buddhistic Indian Philosophy,* University of Calcutta, p. 47, 1921.

He adds that 'these are implied in such interrogative propositions as are met with throughout the Buddhist canonical texts' (*loc. cit.*).

(562) Now neither Poussin's view that this logic is due to a failure to understand or respect the principle of Contradiction nor the views of Mrs Rhys Davids and Barua that they are laws of thought, bear critical examination. We find as early as Uddālaka an awareness in Indian thought of the importance of consistency and the principle of Contradiction, when it was held that it could not both be true that Being came out of Being and Non-Being (*v. supra*, 25). In the Nikāyas, consistency is regarded as a criterion of truth (*v. infra*, 597) and it is stated that 'truth is one and not two', ekaṃ hi saccaṃ na dutīyam atthi, Sn. 884; *v. infra*, 597. The dilemmas present two alternatives one of which is the contradiction of the other (M. I.392, *v. supra*, 351–6). In fact, in one place in the Saṃyutta Nikāya, we come very close to a formal statement of the principle of Non-Contradiction. Nigaṇṭha Nātaputta converses with Citta and in the course of the discussion, the former makes the following two observations about the latter:[1]

(i) passantu yāva ujuko c'āyaṃ Citto gahapati yāva asaṭho . . . amāyāvi (p), i.e. see how upright, honest and sincere Citta, the householder, is.

(ii) passantu yāva anujuko c'āyaṃ Citto gahapati yāva saṭho . . . māyāvi (~p), i.e. see how Citta, the householder, is not upright, honest or sincere.

Citta is anxious to show that Nigaṇṭha Nātaputta is contradicting himself and says, sace purimaṃ saccaṃ pacchimaṃ te micchā, sace pacchimaṃ saccaṃ purimaṃ te micchā, i.e. if your former statement (p) is true, your latter statement (~p) is false and if your latter statement (~p) is true, your former statement (p) is false. In other words, in the above situation when the statements are of the form p and ~p, it cannot be the case that both p and ~p are true (~(p. ~p)), which is the formal statement of the principle of Contradiction.[2] Barua has likewise drawn our attention to a passage in the Kathāvatthu[3] where it is pointed out that it is self-contradictory to assert that something 'exists' and 'does not exist' in the same sense at the same time.

(563) The contentions of Mrs Rhys Davids and Barua that they are laws of thought are equally fantastic. The 'four laws of thought' that

[1] S. IV.298, 299.
[2] Stebbing, *op. cit.*, p. 191.
[3] *Op. cit.*, p. 49; *v.* Kvu. 159.

Barua is speaking of are presumably the law of Identity (see below, 1), the law of Contradiction (see below, 2), the law of Excluded Middle (see below, 3) and 'the law of Double Negation'[1] (see below, 4). In the first place Barua's 'A is neither B nor not-B' is not the principle of Double Negation as understood in Western logic, where it is defined as equivalent to 'A is not not-A'.[2] 'A is neither B nor not-B' appears in fact to be a violation of the principle of Excluded Middle, which states that 'A is either B or not-B'. Secondly, a study of the four forms of predication, as they stand, is sufficient to show that they are not laws of thought. The four forms of predication are:

1. S is P, e.g. atthi paro loko (there is a next world).
2. S is not P, e.g. natthi paro loko (there is no next world).
3. S is and is not P, e.g. atthi ca natthi ca paro loko (there is and is no next world).
4. S neither is nor is not P, e.g. n'ev'atthi na natthi paro loko (there neither is nor is there no next world).

(564) It will be seen that (1) is not the law of Identity but a simple affirmative categorical assertion; (2) is not the law of Contradiction but a negative assertion or denial, it being a problem as to whether it is the contradictory or merely the contrary of (1); (3) and (4) are assertions not recognized in Aristotelian logic although statements of this form sometimes occur in everyday parlance even in Western languages.[3] Considered as laws of thought or in the light of their conformity to them (3) violates (i.e. is the negation of) the law of Contradiction and (4) violates the law of Excluded Middle. Judged by their form in the light of Aristotelian logic (3) and (4) are necessarily (logically) false propositions. No wonder Poussin said 'we are helpless!'

(565) Now what do these propositions really mean? We have already attempted to answer this question in an article entitled 'Some Problems of Translation and Interpretation II',[4] and we do not propose to repeat this here. We intend merely to summarize briefly the gist of what we have said and make some added observations.

(566) Since then there have been a few articles written around this subject but in none of them is there a serious attempt to clarify the problems involved. The first is that of P. T. Raju writing in the

[1] Barua, *ibid.* [2] Stebbing, *op. cit.*, p. 191.

[3] *v.* Article by C. Lewy on 'Calculuses of Logic and Arithmetic' in *Proceedings of the Aristotelian Society*, Supplementary Vol. 20, pp. 36, 37.

[4] UCR., Vol. 8, pp. 45–55, 1950.

'Review of Metaphysics' (Vol. 7, 1953–4, pp. 694–713) on 'The Principle of Four-Cornered Negation in Indian Philosophy'. Raju is mainly concerned in this article with Nāgārjuna's negations or denials of the truth of propositions, expressed according the above four-fold formula. He compares them with similar negations of Śaṅkara. However, it did not occur to him that before we can understand the nature of these negations, it was necessary to know exactly what he was negating or in other words the nature of these four types of assertions. He says that 'the principle seems to have been first used by Sañjaya' (*op. cit.*, p. 694) adding that 'those philosophers who gave a negative answer to all four questions were called "eel-wrigglers" by the Buddhists' (*loc. cit.*). Without giving an iota of evidence he goes on to say that 'Gautama the founder of the school of Nyāya . . . called such philosophers *vitaṇḍavādins*' (*op. cit.*, p. 695). He then gives an account of the seven forms of Jain predication, which is found in most textbooks on Jainism. Where he has tried to throw some light, in passing, on the four-fold formula of the Pāli Nikāyas, it is either not backed up with good evidence or it is plainly self-contradictory. Thus he seems to identify the Jain syād avaktavya (may be, it is unpredicable) with the Buddhist assertion of the form 'S is neither P nor not-P'. But all that he says on this subject is as follows: 'Now indescribability means that S is neither P nor not-P. P and not-P are opposites and therefore cannot be applied simultaneously to the same subject . . . It is the same as saying that 'S is neither P nor not-P' (*op. cit.*, p. 699). In trying further to explain the statement 'S is neither P nor not-P' he says that 'in mathematics "śūnya" means "zero" and in metaphysics it means "that which is neither positive nor negative" (*op. cit.*, p. 701), but one page later without further ado, he denies even this: "then zero becomes a quantity of which all the four alternatives are denied; it is neither positive, nor negative, nor both positive and negative *nor neither positive nor negative*" (*op. cit.*, p. 702; italics mine)'.

(567) The next article to appear on this subject is by Professor Archie J. Bahm on the intriguing subject of 'Does Seven-fold Predication Equal Four-Cornered Negation Reversed?'[1] But his attempt is disappointing, since as he admits and as is evident from the article itself, his knowledge of the subject is gleaned from 'reading Raju's article' (*op. cit.*, p. 130) and 'his conclusion did not result from a study of the sources' (*loc. cit.*). He says that 'this study purports to show that an

[1] *Philosophy East and West*, Vol. 7, Nos. 3 and 4, pp. 127–30.

attempt to reverse the principle of four-cornered negation, so that one may have a four (or more)—fold principle of affirmation, results naturally and logically in the seven-fold system of predication' (*op. cit.*, p. 128). Despite these obvious defects in Bahm's article, he does make a significant contribution towards solving the riddle (logical) of the four-fold assertions when he says, 'To affirm "is", "is not", "both is and is not" and "neither is nor is not" jointly when "is" and "is not" are interpreted as contradictories and "neither is nor is not" as involving[1] an excluded middle is to assert contradictorily. But if on the other hand, "is" and "is not" (or "a" and "non-a") are interpreted as opposites rather than as contradictories and "neither is nor is not" (or "neither a nor non-a") is interpreted not as involving an excluded middle but as presupposing that there is something which is neither the one nor the other (its opposite), then no contradiction is involved' (*op. cit.*, p. 128). According to this theory we do not fall into logical difficulties if we treat not-P (in the four assertions) as the contrary and not the contradictory of P. This is in principle the solution that we had offered in our own treatment of the subject and we shall further examine this solution below.

(568) The latest article to appear on this subject is by Shosun Miyamoto, entitled 'The Logic of Relativity as the Common Ground for the Development of the Middle Way'[2] Miyamoto takes (2) to (5) of the five-fold assertions (*v. supra*, 185) which he attributes to Sañjaya (but which in fact are either shared by all the Sceptics or were exclusively Buddhist, *v. supra*, 184–90) and says that four of them are equivalent to (I) to (IV)[3] of the four-fold formula, viz.

The four-fold formula		*Sañjaya's statements*
		1. I do not think of them in such a manner (evam pi me no).
I	=	2. I do not think of them as being identical (tathā ti pi me no).
II	=	3. I do not think of them as being different (aññathā ti pi me no).
III	=	4. I do not think of denying them (no ti pi me no).
IV	=	5. I do not think of not denying them (no no ti pi me no).

(*op. cit.*, p. 75).

[1] What he probably means is 'violating the principle of Excluded Middle'.
[2] Buddhism and Culture, ed. Susumu Yamaguchi, Kyoto, 1960, pp. 67–88.
[3] We shall use these roman numerals to refer to the four forms of predication.

(569) This is different from our identification of equivalence (*v. supra*, 188) but Miyamoto does not give any reasons for his identifications, nor is he consistent for he later equates (IV) with (1) (*op. cit.*, p. 81). He considers that Sañjaya's 'system is quite near to the Buddhist standpoint of indescribable or inexpressible' (avyākata-, avyākṛta-)' (*op. cit.*, p. 71) and holds that 'Sañjaya's thought is not far removed from the logic of *Śūnya* of the Mādhyamika' (*loc. cit.*). On the logic of the four-fold formula itself he sheds little light: 'This type of a logical view of nature could not entertain any preconceptions nor be compromising by maintaining one particular view only. It expresses a desire to view nature in her actual state, a logic in pursuit' (*op. cit.*, p. 75). This seems to stress the similarity of this logic with the anekāntavāda- of Jainism. But a few pages later he holds without offering any explanation that Jain syādvāda stands midway between the position of Sañjaya and the Buddhist point of view: 'The Jains maintained the indeterminate non-exclusive view of nature (anekāntavāda), a half-way position between the Sañjaya non-committal no-standpoint view and the Buddhist Middle Way view' (*op. cit.*, p. 79). A page later, however, he identifies the Jain scheme with the four membered logic of Buddhism as follows:

<table>
<tr><th>Jain schema</th><th></th><th>Buddhist schema</th></tr>
<tr><td>1. syād asti (may be, it is)</td><td>=</td><td>I</td></tr>
<tr><td>2. syān nāsti (may be, it is not)</td><td>=</td><td>II</td></tr>
<tr><td>3. syād asti nāsti (may be, it is and it is not)</td><td>=</td><td>III</td></tr>
<tr><td>4. syād avaktavya (may be, it is unpredicable)</td><td rowspan="4">=</td><td rowspan="4">IV</td></tr>
<tr><td>5. ayād asti avaktavya (may be, it is and it is unpredicable</td></tr>
<tr><td>6. syān nāsti avaktavya (may be, it is not and it is unpredicable</td></tr>
<tr><td>7. syād asti nāsti avaktavya (may be, it is and it is not, and is unpredicable</td></tr>
</table>

(570) He observes that since the term 'avaktavya-' (the inexpressible) occurs in (4) to (7) ' "It may be inexpressible" refers to member four of the Buddhist logic' and adds 'while at the same time it also refers to the first member of the Sañjaya logic', i.e. 'I do not understand them (questions) in such a manner' (*op. cit.*, p. 81), contradicting what he had said earlier (*v. supra*, 568). He sees a similarity between the systems of Sañjaya, Jainism and Buddhism, though he is not clear as to what he means: 'The crucial fact however about the three logical systems

compared above is that in each what corresponds to the fourth member expresses "neither is nor is not", "denial", "inexpressible" and the non-causal (ahetu) and that in these systems Sañjaya, Jaina and Buddhism firmly stand on the side against any form of nihilism' (*op. cit.*, p. 81).

(571) In determining what is meant by the four forms of predication, we cannot decide *a priori* what is meant by these particular forms of speech. We have to proceed empirically and examine what is meant in the light of historical and contextual considerations. The Nikāyas seem to regard them as 'the four possible positions' or logical alternatives[1] that a proposition can take. Thus, other religious teachers, it is said, in fixing the status of the Tathāgata or the perfect person (*v. supra*, 380) after death do so 'according to these four positions' (imesu catusu ṭhānesu, S. IV.380) and not 'outside these four positions' (aññatra imehi catuhi ṭhānehi, *loc. cit.*) meaning by the four positions statements of the form 'hoti Tathāgato param maraṇā', etc., in the four alternatives. The fact that it was thought that one could not posit the status of the Tathāgata outside these four positions is significant; it shows that these four positions were considered to be mutually exclusive and exhaustive or in other words to be the possible logical alternatives.

(572) Of the four alternatives, the first is a simple affirmative categorical assertion. The second appears to be the opposite of this, but whether it is the contrary or the contradictory is a problem that needs to be examined. Judged by Aristotelian standards, the third and fourth alternatives appear to be very problematic (*v. supra*, 564).

(573) We have seen that the third, which was a double-ca (and) type of assertion ('ca (and) . . . ca (and)') was introduced by the Trairāśika Ājīvikas (*v. supra*, 222–7) to denote a class of things which could not be described by propositions of the first or second type. We may also note the fact that the fourth or double-na (not) type of assertion comes down from the earliest times. It first appears in the Nāsadīya hymn (*v. na asad* āsīt *na* u *sad* āsīd tadānīm, RV. 10.129.1) and is made use of by Yājñavalkya (*nēti neti*, Bṛh. 4.5.15; *v. supra*, 44, 392) and the

[1] Mrs Rhys Davids, refers to them as 'logical alternatives' in one place notwithstanding her other pronouncements: '. . . the Indian mind playing about with its four logical alternatives, A is B, A is not B, A is both B and not B, A is neither B nor not B, *Buddhist Psychology*, Second Edition, London, 1924, p. 248; Keith comes near to this when he says they are 'the four possible modes of framing a proposition' (*Buddhist Philosophy*, p. 137).

Māṇḍūkya Upaniṣad (*v. supra*, 392). This kind of expression is used to denote the fact that conceptual epithets cannot be predicated of the non-conceptual (the ultimate reality, the highest mystical state, the impersonal state after death as conceived by Yājñavalkya). Both Mrs Rhys Davids[1] and Barua[2] have suggested that this kind of expression could be employed to denote that no real attributes could be ascribed to what was unreal, but they have not given any examples of such an usage in Indian thought. It is however a plausible suggestion and we have ourselves shown that what was meant by the expression, 'N'eva sassato na asassato . . . loko', i.e. 'the world . . . is neither eternal nor not eternal' was that temporal epithets (sassata, asassata) cannot be predicated of a world (loko) which is timeless (*v. supra*, 400) or unreal (*v. supra*, 407). As for the suggestion of the Comy. that the Sceptic holds that 'neither p nor not p' is the case in rejecting both thesis as well as anti-thesis, we found that it was not corroborated by the evidence of the texts (*v. supra*, 391).

(574) Now if we refer to the four forms of predication by the Roman numerals I, II, III, IV respectively, what we intended to show in our article (*v. supra*, 565) was that III and IV, despite their form, were *contingent* propositions, purporting to give us information about some alleged state of affairs. Let us take an example, where we are quite certain about the meaning of III and IV:

I Antavā ayaṃ loko (parivaṭumo), i.e. this world is finite (and bounded all round).

II Ananto ayaṃ loko (apariyanto), i.e. this world is infinite (and not bounded all round)

III Antavā ca ayaṃ loko ananto ca, i.e. this world is both finite and infinite.

IV N'evāyaṃ loko antavā na panānanto, i.e. this world is neither finite nor infinite.

D. I.22, 23.

Here (I) states that the world has the characteristic 'finite' *in all respects*; this is clear from the further qualification, parivaṭumo, 'bounded all round'. II states that the world has the opposite or the contrary characteristic of being 'infinite' *in all respects* (*v.* apariyanto).

[1] 'If not, is A neither B nor not-B (in other words is A a chimaera)', *v. supra*, 497.

[2] 'The fourth Law . . . is applicable to . . . the conception of something which is really nothing . . .', *op. cit.*, p. 49.

Now III *does not state* that the world is both finite in all respects (I) and infinite in all respects (II). This would be self-contradictory, if we mean by loka- the same thing in both cases. It states that the world is both finite *in some respect* and infinite *in another respect.* For it is said that those who hold this theory 'conceive the world to be finite in one dimension and infinite in another' (uddham adho antasaññī lokasmiṃ viharati tiriyaṃ anantasaññī, (D. I.23). IV is said to be the point of view of a 'reasoner' (takkī, *loc. cit.*), according to whom the epithets 'finite' and 'infinite' cannot be predicated of the world and hence it is said that he disagrees with I, II, and III (*loc. cit.*). This too, it may be noted, is not a contradictory statement but a different point of view quite distinct from I, II and III. It resembles the point of view of Kant who showed in his 'Critique of Pure Reason' that one could on the one hand argue that 'the world was finite (in space and time)' and also that 'the world was infinite'. However, since the conclusions contradict each other we are faced with an antinomy, the tṛuth being that spatial (and temporal) attributes (e.g. finite, infinite) are subjective.[1] It will be noticed that according to this four-fold logic, a person who denies that 'the world is finite' and asserts the contradictory, namely that 'it is not the case that the world is finite' may be one who holds II, III, or IV. The Aristotelian logic of two alternatives tends to obscure these finer distinctions while the above logic of four alternatives tends to highlight them, showing them as separate logical alternatives.

(575) It is, however, necessary for the purpose of this four-fold logic to interpret II, as Bahm pointed out (*v. supra*, 567), as the contrary or opposite and not as the contradictory of (I). For example, if we take the epithet *sukhī-* (experiencing pleasure, happy), we can have the assertion, I, so sukhī, 'he is happy'. Since 'na sukhī' is the contradictory and 'dukkhī' (unhappy) the contrary of sukhī-, i.e. II would be 'so dukkhī'. III would be 'so sukhī ca dukkhī ca' and IV 'so n'eva sukhī na dukkhī'. III and IV are here not self-contradictory statements. III describes the person, who experiences both pleasurable as well as painful sensations and IV the person whose experiences have a neutral hedonic tone, being neither pleasurable nor painful. We find in fact the following four-fold predication about the hedonic experiences of the

[1] Immanuel Kant's *Critique of Pure Reason*, Tr. by N. K. Smith, London, 1933; for the proofs that the world is finite and that it is infinite, *v.* pp. 396–402; space is an *a priori* form of intuition, not reality, pp. 71 ff., 77, 80–91, 123, 163, 244, 399–400, 440, 449.

soul, which are mutually exclusive and together exhaustive of all the possibilities:

I Ekanta-sukhī attā hoti, i.e. the soul is extremely happy.
II Ekanta-dukkhī attā hoti, i.e. the soul is extremely unhappy.
III Sukha-dukkhī attā hoti, i.e. the soul (has mixed feelings of) happiness and unhappiness.
IV Adukkhamasukhī attā hoti, i.e. the soul has no (feelings of) happiness or unhappiness.

D. I.31.

(576) We may cite numerous examples of this type from the Canon. To take an example which is often repeated:

I Puggalo attantapo . . ., i.e. the person, who torments himself (e.g. the ascetic).
II Puggalo parantapo . . ., i.e. the person, who torments others (e.g. the hunter).
III Puggalo attantapo parantapo ca . . ., i.e. the person who torments himself as well as others (e.g. the king who initiates and participates in a sacrifice causing the destruction of life with much discomfiture to himself).
IV Puggalo n'evattantapo na parantapo . . ., i.e. the person who neither torments himself nor others (e.g. the arhant).

M. 1.341 ff.; Pug. Pañ. 55 ff.

One of the reasons for adopting this logic seems to be the fact that this four-fold schema gave a better and finer classification of the empirical data (thus preventing much ambiguity in utterances) than that offered by the strictly dichotomous division.

(577) While the majority of the four forms of predication are explicable on the above basis, taking (II) as the contrary and not the contradictory of (I), there are some instances where we are faced with an apparent difficulty. This is where (II) appears by virtue of its form, to be the contradictory of (I):

e.g. I atthi paro loko, i.e. there is another world.
II natthi paro loko, i.e. there is no other world.
III atthi ca natthi ca paro loko, i.e. there is and is no other world.
IV n'ev'atthi na n'atthi paro loko, i.e. there neither is nor is there no other world.

D. I.27.

(578) Are we to regard, natthi paro loko, as the contradictory or the contrary of atthi paro loko? Going purely on the morphology or the word-form of the sentence it would appear to be the contradictory. But this is due to the ambiquity of language. As Stebbing says, 'A considerable amount of dispute turns up upon the fact that our words have ragged edges. We cannot always be sure whether the propositions we are concerned to maintain *contradicts* our opponent's assertion or is merely incompatible with it. If the two assertions are contradictory, then in disproving our opponent's assertion we thereby establish our own. But if they are *contraries*, the disproof of his assertions leaves our own still to be established' (*op. cit.*, p. 62). We maintain that, the proposition, natthi paro loko, should according to its context be treated as the contrary and not the contradictory of, atthi paro loko, despite the linguistic form. The reason for this would be clearer if we proceed from the unambiguous to the ambiguous cases. In the unambiguous case the difference between the contrary and the contradictory is reflected in the linguistic form, viz.

I so sukhī—so na sukhī (contradictory)	II so dukkhī (contrary) III so sukhadukkhī IV so adukkhamasukhī

The distinction is less clear, but still noticeable in:

I so rūpī—na so rūpī (contradictory)	II so arūpī (contrary) III so rūpī ca arupī ca IV so n'eva rūpī nārupī

The difference is not noticeable but nevertheless has to be maintained in the following, since the contradictory of (I) is ambiguous and could mean II, III or IV.

I atthi paro loko—na (atthi paro loko) (contradictory)	II natthi paro loko (contrary) III atthi ca natthi ca paro loko IV n'evatthi na natthi paro loko.

(579) The fact that propositions of the form, 'S is P' and 'S is not P' are not always mutually contradictory *in actual usage* is clear from the fact that together they do not always exhaust the possibilities as they

ought to according to the law of Excluded Middle. Lewy[1] in discussing this problem says that in the case of Mr Braithwaite we are inclined to say that 'Mr Braithwaite is neither bald nor not bald' without saying that either the proposition 'Mr Braithwaite is bald' or the proposition 'Mr Braithwaite is not bald' is true. Lewy suggests at the end of this article that one of the ways of avoiding this problem is 'to contract a logical calculus' in which the principle of Excluded Middle does not hold. But it is just this kind of logical calculus, as we have shown in our article (*v. supra*, 565), that is being used in the Pāli Canon, treating statements of the form, 'S is both P and notP' and 'S is neither P nor notP' (giving a different use for each of these two types) as contingent propositions which are empirically meaningful in certain situations in which, considering the facts, we are not justified in using the propositional forms, 'S is P' or 'S is not P'.[2]

(580) Sometimes in adopting this four-fold schema for purposes of classification only three of the possible four alternatives are mentioned, presumably when no instances are found for the other alternative. Thus, we have:

I. saññī-vādā, D. I.31.
II. asaññī-vādā, D. I.32.
IV. n'evasaññī-nāsaññī-vādā, D. I.33.

But there is no mention of saññāsaññī-vādā, presumably because there were no instances of theories which asserted that 'the soul was both conscious and unconscious' after death. This is added evidence that the list of theories in the Brahmajāla Sutta need not be considered a merely artificial list, giving mere logical possibilities (*v. supra*, 141).

(581) Whether the four-fold logical alternatives were adopted by the Buddhists from the Sceptics or not (*v. supra*, 190), the logic of it was the same. The difference lay in the different uses to which they put the schema. The Sceptics used it to show that each of the four alternatives may or may not be true and that the truth cannot be known. The Buddhists considered at least one of the alternatives to be true in any particular case and made use of it for purposes of logical classification, when they did not resort to dichotomous division (based on the two-fold logic, *v. supra*, 497 f.). They also rejected all four alternatives,

[1] *v.* C. Lewy, 'Calculuses of Logic and Arithmetic', pp. 36 ff. in PAS., Supplementary Vol. 20.
[2] For a full discussion of this problem, *v.* pp. 49–55 in our article.

when they considered the question meaningless (i.e. a ṭhapanīya pañha) and rarely negated all four alternatives when they considered the answer 'yes' to each of the alternatives as misleading (*v. supra*, 481).

(582) Let us illustrate all this. When we have four alternatives, then according to the Law of Non-Contradiction,[1] not more than one alternative can be true and according to the Law of Exclusion (for there is no Middle[2] since we are dealing with four possibilities) at least one alternative must be true. Now in the case of a two-fold logic or a logic with two alternatives (like the Aristotelian) we have four truth-possibilities since each of the possibilities p or not-p may be true or false. We may represent this by a truth-table as follows:

	1	2	3	4
p	T	F	T	F
not-p	F	T	T	F

Of the four possibilities (3) and (4) are excluded by the Laws (Non-Contradiction and Excluded Middle) of the system and we are left with (1) and (2) as the logical alternatives or the alternative possibilities. Likewise, in a four-fold logic or a logic of four alternatives, we are left with only four possibilities, the others being ruled out by the Laws (Non-Contradiction and Exclusion) governing the system. If we draw up a truth-table it will be seen that out of sixteen truth-possibilities, only four (*v.* 1–4, below) alternatives are permissible:

	1	2	3	4	5	6	7	etc., up to 16
I. p	(T)	F	F	F	T	F	T	
II. notp (contrary)	F	(T)	F	F	T	F	T	
III. both p and notp	F	F	(T)	F	T	F	T	
IV. neither p nor notp	F	F	F	(T)	T	F	F	

(583) Let us take an example from the Nikāyas that confirms this. Supposing I say '*I know* what has been seen, heard, sensed, thought, attained, sought and reflected upon by the class of recluses and brahmins, then *it would be false* for me to say, *I do not know* what has been seen, heard . . . *it would likewise be false* for me to say, *I know and*

[1] *v.* K. N. Jayatilleke, *op. cit.*, p. 52.

[2] We can still speak of the recognition of the Law of the Excluded Middle in the sense that no 'middle' between 'true' and 'false' is recognized but owing to the ambiguity of the phrase 'Excluded Middle' we have dropped it.

do not know what has been seen, heard . . . and *false* for me to say, *I neither know nor do not know* what has been seen, heard . . .'. Now this is a literal translation of a passage appearing at A. II.25, viz. yaṃ . . . sassamaṇa-brāhmaṇiyā pajāya . . . diṭṭhaṃ sutaṃ mutaṃ viññātaṃ pattaṃ pariyesitaṃ anuvicaritam manasā *taṃ ahaṃ jānāmi* . . . Yaṃ . . . diṭṭhaṃ sutaṃ . . . *taṃ ahaṃ na*[1] *jānāmī* ti vadeyyaṃ *taṃ* mama *assa musā, taṃ ahaṃ jānāmi na ca jānāmī* ti vadeyyaṃ *tam p'assa tādisam eva, tam ahaṃ n'eva jānāmi na na janāmī* ti vadeyyaṃ *taṃ* mama *assa kali.* This example illustrates the fact that when one alternative was taken as true, it was assumed that every one of the other alternatives were false. In this case when (I) is true, it is said that each of the alternatives (II), (III) and (IV) were false.

(584) When the four alternatives happened to be those of a ṭhapanīya pañha or a meaningless question all four alternatives were *rejected* rather than *negated* because the question in each of the alternatives was not considered to be a proper question (kallo pañho). Thus we have the four alternatives:

I. Channam phassāyatanānaṃ asesavirāganirodhā atth'aññaṃ kiñcī ti?
   i.e. is there anything else after complete detachment from and cessation of the six spheres of experience?
II. . . . natth'aññaṃ kiñcī ti?
III. . . . atthi ca n'atthi c'aññaṃ kiñcī ti?
IV. . . . n'ev'atthi no n'atth'aññaṃ kiñcī ti?

The replies to each of these questions is of the form 'mā h'evaṃ', i.e. do not say so (A. II.161). The response to the other avyākata-questions is also similar since these questions are 'not answered but set aside' (avyākatāni ṭhapitāni, M. I.426; *v. supra,* 481). In other words these questions were *not negated but rejected.* Raju (*v. supra,* 566) and Bahm (*v. supra,* 567) have therefore misdescribed their nature as far as the Pāli Canonical position is concerned by calling this doctrine that of 'four-cornered negation' when it ought properly to be called 'four-cornered rejection'.

(585) In fact, it is all the more necessary to distinguish the four-cornered rejection from four-cornered negation, which is also rarely

[1] This na has been erroneously omitted from the text.

met with in the Nikāyas. Consider the answers to the following four alternative forms of a question:

I. Kin nu kho . . . vijjāya antakaro hotī ti? Is it the case that one attains the goal by means of knowledge?
II. Kin nu kho . . . caraṇena antakaro hotī ti? Is it the case that one attains the goal by means of conduct?
III. Kin nu kho . . . vijjācaraṇena antakaro hotī ti? Is it the case that one attains the goal by means of both knowledge and conduct?
IV. Kin nu kho . . . aññatra vijjācaraṇena antakaro hotī ti? Is it the case that one attains the goal without knowledge and conduct?

Taking II as the contrary of (I), the question is in the form of the four logical alternatives. The answer to each of these four alternatives is of the form 'na h'idaṃ', i.e. it is not so (note the difference from the above), the reason being that while 'knowledge' and 'conduct' are necessary conditions for final salvation they are not sufficient conditions. This denial of all the four logical alternatives is in apparent violation of the Law of Exclusion (*v. supra*, 582), but this is not a peculiarity of this logic, since we meet with this paradoxical situation even with Aristotelian logic, e.g. when a non-smoker is confronted with the question 'have you given up smoking?'

(586) It is necessary to distinguish the above four-fold logic from the logic of the Jain *syādvāda*, which is radically different from it. We shall refer to the seven forms of predication of Jainism by the Indian numerals 1, 2, 3, 4, 5, 6, 7 and the four logical alternatives by the Roman numerals I, II, III and IV. Now it was the contention of Raju, Bahm and Miyamoto (*v. supra*, 566, 567, 569) that 4 (syādavaktavya-) was the same as IV (S is neither P nor notP), while Bahm and Miyamoto further identified (*v. supra*, 567, 569) 1, 2, 3 of Jainism with I, II, III of Buddhism respectively. This is mistaken and is due to a failure to understand the logic of each system, as a result of which they seem to have been misled by mere superficial similarities. It appears on the face of it that we could identify 1, 2, 3, 4 with I, II, III, IV respectively:

Jain	*Buddhist*
1. syād asti (may be, it is)	I. atthi (it is)
2. syād nāsti (maybe , it is not)	II. natthi (it is not)
3. syād asti nāsti (may be, it is and it is not)	III. atthi ca natthi ca (it is and it is not)
4. syād avaktavyaṃ (may be, it is unpredicable)	IV. n'ev'atthi na ca natthi (it neither is nor is not)

But if we examine the interpretation and usage of each we may observe the radical difference behind the superficial resemblance. The interpretation given of syād avaktavyam[1] is that it is logically impossible to assert 1 and 2 of an object *simultaneously* (3 asserts them *successively*). It is implied that the object has a mysterious character, which is impredicable. IV has no such implication and asserts on the contrary that there is an instance of S, such that it does not have the characteristic P or its contrary notP. For example, one of the four possible types of individuals is called 'n'ev'attahitāya paṭipanno na parahitāya' (i.e. he does not act in his own welfare nor for the welfare of others, A. II.95), which means that there is an individual S such that he does not have the characteristic 'attahitāya paṭipanno' (P) nor the characteristic 'parahitāya paṭipanno' (notP). It does not mean that S is indescribable in any way nor that there are no individuals, of whom the characteristics P and notP cannot be predicated simultaneously for in fact the person described as 'attahitāya ca paṭipanno parahitāya ca' (*loc. cit.*) has these characteristics simultaneously.

(587) Another significant difference is that I, II, III, and IV are logical alternatives in Buddhism, whereas this is not the case with the seven forms of predication in Jainism. In Buddhism, as in Aristotelian logic, only one alternative could be true, but in Jainism each of the seven alternate forms of description (or any disjunction of them) could be true. According to Buddhism an object correctly describable by I cannot at the same time be correctly described by II, III, or IV, whereas in Jainism an object correctly describable by 1 is also correctly describable by 2–7, which supplement 1 and do not exclude it.

(588) We may define the difference between the Jain logic and the Aristotelian (which is similar in this respect to the Buddhist, *v. supra*, 582, 587) by drawing up truth-tables to illustrate the possibilities that each allows for. For Aristotelian logic, as we have already shown, we have four truth-possibilities of which two, i.e. the cases in which p and not-p are both true and both false are ruled out by the laws of the system. But according to Jain logic, if we confine ourselves to the first two forms of predication only (to avoid complexity) all four truth-possibilities are permissible, viz.:

	1	2	3	4
p (syād asti)	T	F	T	F
not-p (syān nāsti)	F	T	T	F

[1] *v.* Radhakrishnan, *Indian Philosophy*, Vol. I, p. 303; cp. Raju, *op. cit.*, p. 700.

(589) It will be noticed that (3) and (4) are not ruled out, since p may be true from one standpoint and not-p from another; similarly p may be false from one standpoint while not-p is also false from another standpoint. It is necessary to remember that Jain logic admits of falsity (nayābhāsa). This happens when the particular assertion is not possible from the standpoint from which it is made. For instance, if I assert that a thing (which exists) does not exist (syād nāsti) from the point of view of its own form (svarūpa), substance (svadravya), place (svakṣetra) and time (svakāla), the statement would be false. So in drawing up our truth-table to represent the possibilities according to Jain logic, it is necessary to take account of another variable (in addition to the truth-value), namely the standpoint (naya). Let us for the sake of simplicity, take two alternative forms of predication (syād asti and syād nāsti) and two standpoints, x and y. This gives sixteen truth-possibilities in all, since there would be four possibilities for each of the four possibilities in the above table, viz.:

	1	2	3	4	5	6	7	8
(p) syād asti	Tx	Tx	Ty	Ty	Fx	Fx	Fy	Fy
(not-p) syān nāsti	Tx	Ty	Tx	Ty	Fx	Fy	Fx	Fy

	9	10	11	12	13	14	15	16
(p) syād asti	Tx	Tx	Ty	Ty	Fx	Fx	Fy	Fy
(not-p) syān nāsti	Fx	Fy	Fx	Fy	Tx	Ty	Tx	Ty

(590) Since it would be self-contradictory to assert jointly the truth or the falsity of both alternates from the same standpoint we can rule out possibilities 1, 4, 5 and 8 by this Law of Non-Contradiction, which holds good for this system. Then again, if we know that p can be true only from standpoint x and not-p only from standpoint y, then it would follow (logically) that p is false from standpoint y and not-p false from standpoint x. This means that p would have the truth-possibilities Tx and Fy only and not-p the truth-possibilities Ty and Fx only, all other possibiiities (i.e. 3, 6, 10, 11, 12, 13, 14 and 15 in addition to the above) being ruled out. This leaves us with four truth-possibilities as follows:

	1	2	3	4
p (syād asti)	Tx	Fy	Tx	Fy
not-p (syād nāsti)	Ty	Fx	Fx	Ty

(591) This shows the radical difference between the logic of *syādvāda* and of the *catuṣkoṭi*, i.e. the Buddhist logic of 'four alternatives'. The former represents seven forms of predication, which supplement each other, each of which may be true simultaneously with the others from its own standpoint. The latter represents four alternatives of which (as understood in the Canon)[1] only one could be true. In this respect, this logic resembles the Aristotelian, except for the fact that the latter is a two-valued logic of two alternatives while the former is a two-valued logic of four alternatives. Until recently it was believed in the Western world that Aristotelian logic was the only logic and that it reflected the structure of reality but, with the discovery of many-valued logics by Lucasiewicz and Lobochevsky, this view is no longer universally held. This means that our choice of a logical system is to some extent arbitrary and dependent on the needs and nature of our discussion. The Buddhist four-fold logic is in this respect no more true or false than the Aristotelian and its merits should be judged by its adequacy for the purposes for which it is used. It is not at all necessary to feel helpless before it (as Poussin did!), if its nature and significance is understood.

(592) Before we leave this topic, we may make some observations on an article by Robinson,[2] in which he makes a few comments on the *catuṣkoṭi*. He calls this the *Tetralemma* (*op. cit.*, p. 301), but since we have treated the four alternatives as propositional functions, following Schayer,[3] and since they are basic to a whole system of logic, we prefer to call this 'the four-fold logic'; we do not call Aristotelian logic 'the dilemma' because it is a logic of two alternatives. We agree with Robinson when he says that 'the four members' (i.e. the four alternatives) are 'in a relation of exclusive disjunction' ('one of but not more than one of "a", "b", "c", "d" is true') (*loc. cit.*); this we have actually shown to be the case (*v. supra,* 583). We cannot agree with his observation that 'the tetralemma resembles the four Aristotelian forms in some ways. Both sets comprise propositions constructed from two

[1] Nāgārjuna's position is different but this is beyond the scope of our study

[2] Richard H. Robinson, 'Some Logical Aspects of Nāgārjuna's System' in, *Philosophy East and West,* Vol. 6, No. 4, January 1957, pp. 291–308.

[3] 'Altindische Antizipationen der Aussagenlogik' in *Studien zur indischen Logik,* Extrait du Bulletin de l'Academie Polonaise des Sciences et des Lettres cracovic 1933, p. 93; Schayer represents the four alternatives as p, ∼p, (p.∼p), (∼p.∼(∼p)). We are, however not treating 'p' as the contradictory of 'p' and hence we have written 'notp' instead (*v. supra,* 186).

terms and the constants (functors) 'all', 'some', and 'not' '(*op. cit.*, p. 303). If we do so, we treat (I) as an universal affirmative proposition, which it is not (at least always) (*v. supra*, 574). For similar reasons, the explanation of II as corresponding to an Aristotelian E-type proposition, of III as 'the conjunction of I and O forms' (*loc. cit.*) and IV as the 'conjunction of E and A forms' (*loc. cit.*) is unsatisfactory. His proposal to interpret the fourth alternative as: 'No x is A and no x is not A' (*op. cit.*, p. 302), which is true 'when x is null' (*loc. cit.*) is contradicted by usage in the Pāli Nikāyas (*v. supra*, 576, IV).

(593) Let us examine the conception of truth as we find it in the Nikāyas. There is no direct inquiry into the nature of truth (in the epistemological sense) in them, but the value placed on truth (in the wider sense) was so great that some observations about the nature of truth (in the above sense) were, perhaps, inevitable.

(594) In the Abhayarājakumāra Sutta, we find statements classified according to their truth-value, utility (or disutility) and pleasantness (or unpleasantness). The intention of the classification is to tell us what kinds of propositions the Buddha asserts. If propositions could be true (bhūtaṃ, tacchaṃ) or false (abhūtaṃ, atacchaṃ), useful (atthasaṃhitaṃ) or useless (anatthasaṃhitaṃ), pleasant (paresaṃ piyā manāpā) or unpleasant (paresaṃ appiyā amanāpā), we get eight possibilities in all as follows:

1.	True	useful	pleasant
2.	,,	,,	unpleasant
3.	,,	useless	pleasant
4.	,,	,,	unpleasant
5.	False	useful	pleasant
6.	,,	,,	unpleasant
7.	,,	useless	pleasant
8.	,,	,,	unpleasant

The text reads as follows: 'The Tathāgata does not assert a statement which he knows to be untrue, false, useless, disagreeable and unpleasant to others (i.e 8). He does not assert a statement which he knows to be true, factual, useless, disagreeable and unpleasant to others (i.e. 4). He would assert at the proper time a statement which he knows to be true, factual, useful, disagreeable and unpleasant to others (i.e. 2). He would not assert a statement which he knows to be untrue, false, useless, agreeable and pleasant to others (i.e. 7). He would not assert a statement which he knows to be true, factual, useless, agreeable and pleasant to others (i.e. 3). He would assert at the proper time a statement which he knows to be true, factual, useful, agreeable and pleasant to others (i.e. 1)'.[1] We may observe that possibilities 5 and 6 are omitted (*v. infra*, 605).

(595) According to this passage the Buddha asserts propositions which are true, useful and are either pleasant or unpleasant at the right occasion. This appears to be a departure from the earlier statement in the Suttanipāta, where it is said that 'one should say only what is pleasant' (piyavācam eva bhāseyya, Sn. 452), unless we say that this apparent exception holds good only in the case of the Tathāgata. The reason given is that sometimes it is necessary to say what is unpleasant for the good of an individual, just as out of love for a child one has to cause a certain amount of pain in order to remove something that has got stuck in its throat (M. I.394, 395).

(596) But the interest of this passage for us, lies in its disclosing the relationships of truth to utility (and pleasantness). Let us first inquire as to what could be meant by 'true' in these contexts. The word used is 'bhūtaṃ, tacchaṃ' (cp. bhūtaṃ, tacchaṃ anaññathā, M. II.170). The use of bhūtaṃ in the sense of 'true' is significant for it literally means 'fact, i.e. what has become, taken place or happened'. Likewise yathābhūtam, which means 'in accordance with fact', is often used synonymously with truth. It is the object of knowledge—'one knows what is in accordance with fact' (yathābhūtam pajānāti, D. I.83, 84). This tacitly implies the acceptance of a correspondence theory of truth. In the Apaṇṇaka Sutta there is a conscious avowal of this theory. Falsity is here defined as the denial of fact or as what does not accord with fact. A false belief, a false conception and a false statement are defined as follows: 'When in fact there is a next world, the belief occurs to me that there is no next world, that would be a false belief. When in

[1] '. . . yaṃ Tathāgato vācaṃ jānāti abhūtaṃ atacchaṃ anatthasaṃhitaṃ, sā ca paresaṃ appiyā amanāpā, na taṃ Tathāgato vācaṃ bhāsati; yam pi vācaṃ jānāti bhūtaṃ tacchaṃ anatthasaṃhitaṃ, sā ca paresaṃ appiyā amanāpā, tam pi vācaṃ na bhāsati; yañ ca kho vācaṃ jānāti bhūtaṃ tacchaṃ atthasaṃhitaṃ, sā ca paresaṃ appiyā amanāpā, tatra kālaññū hoti tassa vācāya veyyākaraṇāya. Yaṃ vācaṃ jānāti abhūtaṃ atacchaṃ anatthasaṃhitaṃ, sā ca paresaṃ piyā manāpā, na taṃ vācaṃ bhāsati; yaṃ pi vācaṃ jānāti bhūtaṃ tacchaṃ anatthasaṃhitaṃ sā ca paresaṃ piyā manāpā, tam pi vācaṃ na bhāsati; yañ ca kho vācaṃ jānāti bhūtaṃ tacchaṃ atthasaṃhitaṃ, sā ca paresaṃ piyā manāpā, tatra kālaññū hoti tassa vācāya veyyākaraṇāya. M. I.395.

fact there is a next world, if one thinks that there is no next world, that would be a false conception. When in fact there is a next world, one asserts the statement that there is no next world, that would be a false statement' (Santaṃ yeva kho pana paraṃ lokaṃ; natthi paro loko ti'ssa diṭṭhi hoti, sā'ssa hoti micchādiṭṭhi. Santaṃ yeva kho pana paraṃ lokaṃ: natthi paro loko ti saṅkappeti, svāssa hoti micchāsaṅkappo. Santaṃ yeva kho pana paraṃ lokaṃ: natthi paro loko ti vācaṃ bhāsati, sā'ssa hoti micchāvācā, M. I.402). Thus, while false propositions entertained as beliefs or conceptions or expressed as statements are considered false, when they do not correspond with or deny facts, true beliefs, conceptions or statements are said to be those which reflect or correspond with fact. The words used for true beliefs, conceptions or statements are sammādiṭṭhi, sammāsaṅkappo and sammāvācā respectively, which literally mean '*right* belief, etc.', but here 'right' (sammā) being the opposite of 'micchā' (false) is synonymous with 'true': 'When in fact there is a next world, the belief occurs to me that there is a next world, that would be a true belief...' (Santaṃ yeva kho pana paraṃ lokaṃ: atthi paro loko ti'ssa diṭṭhi hoti, sā'ssa hoti sammā diṭṭhi, M. I.403).

(597) Though truth is defined in terms of correspondence with fact, consistency or coherence is also considered a criterion of truth. We have already cited an example from the Nikāyas, where it is clearly shown that, when two statements contradict each other, it cannot be the case that both statements are true for 'if p is true, not-p is false and if not-p is true, p is false' (*v. supra,* 562). In the Suttanipāta referring to numerous theses put forward by various theorists the question is asked 'Claiming to be experts, why do (they) put forward diverse theories—are truths many and various...?' (kasmā nu saccāni vadanti nānā... kusalā vadānā: saccāni su tāni bahūni nānā... Sn. 885) and answered: 'Truths, indeed, are not many and various' (na h'eva saccāni bahūni nānā... Sn. 886). It is in this context that the statement is made that 'truth is one without a second' (ekaṃ hi saccaṃ na dutīyam atthi, Sn. 884). The Buddha in arguing with his opponents appeals to this principle of consistency by showing that their theories are false because they are contradicting themselves. Thus, in the debate with Saccaka, the Buddha says at a certain stage in the discussion, referring to his opponent's statements that 'his later statement is not compatible with the former nor the former with the later' (na kho te sandhīyati purimeṇa vā pacchimaṃ, pacchimena vā purimaṃ, M. I.232).

Here the consistency called for is the coherence with the various statements and implications of a theory.

(598) But it is important to note that there is another sense of consistency recognized in the Nikāyas. This is the consistency between the behaviour of a person and his statements. In this sense, it is claimed that the Buddha 'practised what he preached and preached what he practised' (yathāvādī tathākārī, yathākārī tathāvādī, It. 122). One does not normally speak of this kind of consistency as *logical* consistency; but when Toynbee says that 'the Buddha was an *illogical* evangelist',[1] and speaks of his 'sublime inconsistency' (*op. cit.*, p. 64) or 'sublimely *illogical* practice' (*op. cit.*, p. 73) he is using 'illogical' in this novel sense. We have tried to state more precisely what is meant by 'illogical' here[2] and have found two senses, (1) when A asserts p and acts as if he believes p is false, and (2) where A asserts p and p is false (where p is a statement descriptive of A's behaviour, which is directly relevant to the truth-value of p).

(599) Despite this emphasis on consistency, which runs through the Nikāyas, we find an early reference to the concept of pacceka-sacca, i.e. individual (private) or partial truth (?). *Prima facie* this notion appears to run counter to the conception of truth as being consistent. This concept first appears in the Suttanipāta in reference to the diverse theories put forward by controversialist debaters. It is said that 'these individuals dogmatically cling to (*lit.* are immersed in) individual (or partial?) truths' (pacceka-saccesu puthū niviṭṭhā, Sn. 824). The term is also used to denote the avyākata-theories, which as we have shown were also debated (*v. supra*, 378). These theories are called 'the several *paccekasaccas* of the several recluses and brahmins' (puthusamaṇa-brāhmaṇānaṃ puthupaccekasaccāni, A. II.41; V.29). Now pacceka-literally means 'each one' (*s.v.* PTS. Dictionary) or 'individual' and the BHS. Dictionary suggests 'individual (alleged) truths' for pratyeka-satya (*s.v.*). What could be the significance of the use of this term? Could we interpret this to mean that each of these theories had an element of truth and were in fact 'partial truths'. This is very strongly suggested by the parable of the blind men and the elephant (Ud. 68). A number of men born blind (jaccandhā) are assembled by the king who instructs that they be shown (dassesi), i.e. made to touch an

[1] *An Historian's Approach to Religion*, p. 77.

[2] *v.* K. N. Jayatilleke, 'A Recent Criticism of Buddhism' in UCR., Vol. 15, Nos. 3 and 4, pp. 136 ff.

elephant. They touch various parts of the elephant such as the forehead, ears, tusks, etc. They are then asked to describe the elephant and each reports *mistaking the part for the whole* that the elephant was like that portion of the elephant which was felt by him. There are ten conflicting accounts in all corresponding in description to the ten parts touched and these are compared to the ten avyākata-theses put forward by the various recluses and brahmins. If we interpret the parable literally one would have to say that their theses too mistakenly describe the part for the whole and in so far as they constitute descriptions of their partial experience, they have an element of truth but are deluded in ascribing to the whole of reality what is true only of the part or in other words what is partially true. Since it were these very avyākata-theses that were called pacceka-saccas it would appear to be not without justification to translate this word as 'partial truths'. One may in fact even suggest, though with little historical justification, that these theses were 'indeterminate' (avyākata-) in the sense of being neither true nor false[1] analogous to the sense in which avyākata- is used to denote what is 'neutral' in moral contexts where 'what is indeterminate (avyākata-) are acts which are neither good nor evil . . .' (ye ca dhammā kiriyā n'eva kusalā na akusalā . . . ime dhamma avyākatā, DhS., 583, p. 124). If such an interpretation is to be justified, we would have to say that these avyākata-theses were a product of partial descriptions of reality, their error consisting in regarding these partial accounts as descriptions of the whole of reality. They would be the misdescribed experiences of different thinkers like the blind men's accounts of the elephant. In fact, it is almost suggested in the Brahmajāla Sutta that not merely the avyākata-theses but all the sixty two philosophical theories 'result from impressions' (phassapaccayā, D. I.42, 43; cp. te vata aññatra phassā paṭisaṃvedissantī ti n'etaṃ ṭhānaṃ vijjati, i.e. it is impossible that they would entertain (these theories) without the impressions they had, D. I.43, 44)—i.e. perceptive, sensory and extrasensory and cognitive experience—and that these theories were presumably only partial accounts of reality.

(600) But this conception of truth is not developed in the Nikāyas and if we hold the above account of pacceka-sacca as a 'partial truth' we

[1] This is in fact a sense in which 'indeterminate' is used in logic, e.g. '. . . if a three-valued logic is proposed in which the law of the excluded middle is replaced by the trichotomy every proposition is either true or false or *indeterminate* . . .' A. Pap, *Semantics and Necessary Truth*, Yale University Press, New Haven, 1958, p. 169.

would have to regard this conception as a remnant of early Jain influence on Buddhism. The conception of partial or relative truth was basically a Jain conception, for according to Jainism a number of apparently conflicting theories could each be true according to a standpoint (*v. supra,* 588–90). As such the parable of the blind men and the elephant is much more appropriate to the context of Jainism and it is probable that the Buddhists borrowed it from a Jain source, since as Radhakrishnan says 'the Jains are fond of quoting the old story of the six[1] blind men, who each laid hands on a different part of the elephant and tried to describe the whole animal'.[2]

(601) We feel, however, that the more probable explanation of the use of the term pacceka-sacca- is that it is sarcastic and means as Edgerton says 'individual (alleged) truth, applied to doctrines of heretical sects' (*s.v.* pratyeka-satya-, BHS. Dictionary). The reason for this is that the theory that truth is one (ekaṃ) and not two (dutīyam) or many (nānā) is promulgated in the very stratum in which the term paccekasacca occurs (*v. supra,* 597). But while denying the objective truth of several incompatible theories, the Buddhists do not seem to have doubted the reality of those experiences on the basis of which these theories were propounded. Sn. 886 says that 'there are not many and various permanent truths in the world apart from conscious experience' (na h'eva saccāni bahūni nānā, aññatra saññāya niccāni loke). This phrase 'apart from conscious experience' seems to make the same point as the parable of the elephant and the blind men and the statement in the Brahmajāla Sutta quoted above (*v. supra,* 599), that the sixty two views were based on our (subjective) impressions, which though real do not make the theories true.

(602) If truth is what corresponds with fact and is consistent within itself, what was the relation of truth to utility? Mrs Rhys Davids, arguing against the theory that the Buddha was a rationalist suggests that he be called an 'utilitarian' in the sense of being a pragmatist, for whom truth is what 'works'.[3] She says: ' "Utilitarian" might be urged with some weight. "Rationalistic" surely not. In the very Sutta chosen to illustrate the latter assertion, the Kālāma discourse, the rational grounds for testing a gospel are only cited to be put aside. . . . The one

[1] In the Buddhist (Udāna, 68) version there are at least ten blind men, though their number is not specified.

[2] *Indian Philosophy,* Vol. I, p. 301.

[3] *v.* Ewing, *The Fundamental Questions of Philosophy,* p. 56.

test to be used is "What effect will this teaching produce on my life"?'[1] Poussin too calls Early Buddhism 'pragmatic': 'nous avons defini l'ancienne dogmatique comme une doctrine essentiellement "pragmatique" . . .'[2]

(603) This pragmatism of Buddhism is also strongly suggested by the parable of the arrow (M. I.429) and the parable of the raft (M. I.134). The parable of the arrow occurs in reference to the avyākata-theses and the gist of it is that a man struck with a poisoned arrow should be concerned with removing the arrow and getting well rather than be interested in purely theoretical questions (about the nature of the arrow, who shot it, etc.), which have no practical utility. The moral is that man should only be interested in truths which have a practical bearing on his life. In the same context it was said that the avyākata-questions were not answered because 'it was not useful, not related to the fundamentals of religion, and not conducive to revulsion, dispassion, cessation, peace, higher knowledge, realization and Nirvāṇa' (na h'etaṃ atthasaṃhitaṃ n'ādibrahmacariyakaṃ, na nibbidāya na virāgāya na nirodhāya na upasamāya na abhiññāya na sambodhāya na nibbānāya saṃvattati, M. I.431). The parable of the raft has the same motive and is intended to indicate the utilitarian character of the teachings or the 'truth' of Buddhism. The truths are useful for salvation but even they should not be clung to however useful they may have been. It is said: 'I preach you a dhamma comparable to a raft for the sake of crossing over and not for the sake of clinging to it . . .' (Kullūpamaṃ vo . . . dhammaṃ desissāmi nittharaṇatthāya no gahaṇatthāya . . . M. I.134). A person intending to cross a river and get to the other bank, where it is safe and secure makes a raft and with its help safely reaches the other bank but however useful the raft may have been (bahukāro me ayaṃ kullo, *loc. cit.*), he would throw it aside[3] and go his way without carrying it on his shoulders; so it is said that 'those who realize the dhamma to be like a raft should discard the dhamma as well, not to speak of what is not dhamma' (kullūpamaṃ vo . . . ājānantehi dhammā pi vo pahātabbā, pag'eva adhammā, M. I.135). We cannot

[1] *Wayfarer's Words,* Vol. III, pp. 1103, 1104.

[2] *Bouddhisme,* Third Edition, Paris, 1925, p. 129.

[3] Cp. Wittgenstein, 'My statements are elucidatory in this way: he who understands me finally recognizes them as senseless, when he has climbed out through them, on them, over them. (He must so to speak throw away the ladder, after he has climbed up on it.)' Tractatus Logico-philosophicus, 6.54, p. 189. According to the Mādhyamika, even the 'right view' (sammadiṭṭhi) is a view although it has a pragmatic value and all views (diṭṭhi-s) are false.

interpret this to mean that the dhamma is true only by virtue of its utility and that it ceases to be true when it ceases to be useful. What is meant is that unlike the answers to the avyākata-questions (which were 'not useful' (na atthasaṃhitaṃ, *v. infra,* 811) for salvation, the dhamma was useful for salvation and its value (though not its truth-value) lay in its utility. It ceases to have value, though it does not cease to be true, when one has achieved one's purpose with its help by attaining salvation.

(604) We may conclude from this that the truths of Buddhism were also considered to be useful (atthasaṃhitaṃ) for each person until one attains salvation. This is confirmed by what is stated in the passage quoted above (*v. supra,* 594) where it was said that the Buddha speaks only what is true and useful, whether pleasant or unpleasant. We may sum this up by saying that the truths of Buddhism were considered to be pragmatic in the Buddhist sense of the term, but it does not mean that Early Buddhism believes in a pragmatist theory of truth.

(605) According to the pragmatist theory of truth 'a belief is true if it is useful and false, if it is not, or more widely . . . a belief is true if "it works"'.[1] Now in the passage quoted above (*v. supra,* 594), the possibility was granted that there could be statements which were true but useless. This means that a statement could be useless without being false, thus showing that utility (atthasaṃhitaṃ) was not considered to be a definition or an infallible criterion of truth. But on the other hand, it is curious that the list of possibilities mentioned in the passage are only six and as we have shown (*v. supra,* 594) there is a failure to mention statements which are both false as well as useful (pleasant or unpleasant). It is difficult to say whether this omission was accidental or intentional, for we have to depend on an *argumentum e silentio.* If it was intentional, we would have to say that it was not reckoned one of the possibilities either because it was considered self-contradictory to say of a statement that it was false but useful[2] or because such statements did not in fact exist. This (i.e. both these latter alternatives) seem likely not because of any pragmatist theory of truth but because of the peculiarly Buddhist use of the term 'useless' (na atthasaṃhitaṃ). Here attha- (*s.v.* PTS. Dictionary) is not just 'what is advantageous' in the

[1] A. D. Woozley, *The Theory of Knowledge,* p. 134.

[2] *v.* Woozley, *op. cit.,* p. 134; 'But that it is useful is surely not what is meant by saying that it is true. For if it were what is meant, then the proposition "that belief was false but it was useful" would be self-contradictory'.

broad utilitarian sense of the term, but what is morally good in the sense of being useful for the attainment of the goal of Nirvāṇa. Since falsehood or the assertion of a statement which is false (musāvāda) was considered a moral evil, it would have been held to be logically or causally impossible for what is false, i.e. what is morally evil to result in what was useful in the sense of being morally advantageous or good (atthasaṃhitaṃ).

(606) While truth is not defined in terms of utility it seems to have been held that the claims of a belief to be true were to be tested in the light of personally verifiable consequences. Mrs Rhys Davids says that according to the Kālāma Sutta 'the one test to be used is "what effect will this teaching produce on my life" ' (*v. supra*, 602). What the Sutta states is that 'you should reject those beliefs (as false) when you yourself realize that when they are accepted and lived up to they conduce to lack of welfare and unhappiness' (yadā ... tumhe attanā va jāneyyatha ... ime dhammā samattā samādinnā ahitāya dukkhāya saṃvattanti-atha ... tumhe pajaheyyātha, A. II.191). As we have shown in the light of other evidence (*v. infra*, 797) verifiability in the light of experience, sensory and extrasensory, is considered a characteristic of truth but what is thus claimed to be true is held to be true only by virtue of its 'correspondence with fact' (yathābhutam). Thus, verifiability is a test of truth but does not itself constitute truth.

(607) Many of the important truths in Buddhism are considered to lie midway between two extreme points of view. Extreme realism, which says that 'everything exists' (sabbaṃ atthī ti) is one extreme (eko anto) and extreme nihilism which asserts that 'nothing exists' (sabbaṃ natthī ti) is the other extreme (dutiyo anto)—the truth lies in the middle (S. II.76). Similar anti-theses which are false are the doctrines of eternalism (sassatadiṭṭhi) and annihilationism (ucchedadiṭṭhi) (S. II.20, III.98), the Materialist conception that the body and the soul are identical (taṃ jīvaṃ taṃ sarīram, S. II.60) and the dualist conception that they are different (aññaṃ jīvaṃ aññaṃ sarīraṃ, *loc. cit.*), the Determinist thesis (sabbaṃ pubbekatahetu, A. I.173) and the Indeterminist thesis (sabbaṃ ahetuappaccayā, *loc. cit.*), that we are entirely personally responsible for our unhappiness (so karoti so paṭisaṃvediyati, S. II.20) and that we are not at all responsible for our unhappiness (añño karoti añño paṭisaṃvediyati, *loc. cit.*), extreme hedonism (kāmasukhallikānuyogo, S. IV.330, V.421) and extreme asceticism (attakilamathānuyogo, *loc. cit.*). In all these instances it is said that the Buddha 'without falling

into these two extremes preaches the dhamma *in the middle*' (ete ubho ante anupagamma *majjhena* . . . dhammaṃ deseti). Thus the mean between two extreme views is held to be true. The 'middle way' (majjhimā paṭipadā) which is a mean both in the matter of belief[1] as well as of conduct is said to 'make for knowledge . . . and bring about intuition and realization' (ñāṇa-karaṇī. . . . abhiññāya sambodhāya . . . saṃvattati, M. I.15).

(608) Logically, there is no reason why the truth should lie in the middle rather than in one of the two extremes though most people would be inclined to think that a moderate view, which takes count of the elements of truth in all the extreme views with regard to a particular matter, is more likely to be true than any of the extreme views. The problem, however, is whether it was dogmatically assumed that the truth must lie in the middle or on the other hand whether it was considered that the truth in the above instances happened to lie between two extremes. The second appears to be the more plausible alternative in the light of the facts. When the Buddha held that neither the paths of over-indulgence nor of extreme asceticism makes for spiritual progress and happiness, this is considered to be a finding based on his experiences and experiments (*v. infra*, 794–7). Likewise the truth of the other syntheses or the middle views is claimed to be established independently.

(609) This attempt to reconcile opposing theses was not an entirely new venture in the history of Indian thought. We first met with it in Nāsadīya hymn, which tries to effect a synthesis between mutually contradictory theories (*v. supra*, 9). Even the idea of the fruitful mean appears to be foreshadowed in the Aitareya Āraṇyaka, where it is said that one should not be over-generous or miserly but avoiding both extremes should give at the proper time: '. . . if a man says om (yes) to everything then that which he gives away is wanting to him here. If he says om (yes) to everything then he would empty himself and would not be capable of any enjoyments . . . If a man says "no" to everything then his reputation would become evil and that would ruin him even here. Therefore let a man give at the proper time, not at the wrong time. Thus *he unites the true and the untrue and from the union of these two he grows and becomes greater and greater*' (Ait. Ār. 2.3.6.11–13;

[1] Cp. Sthiramati, Madhyāntavibhāgaṭikā, ed. S. Yamaguchi, Nagoya, 1934, v. Antadvayavarjane pratipattiḥ (the principle of the avoidance of the two extremes), pp. 233–251.

v. SBE., Vol. 1, pp. 230–1). We find here the idea of synthesis and the fruitful mean which makes for growth and development (*v. supra*, 607) and which may have suggested the idea of the mean in Buddhism, though, of course, the mean in Buddhism is not a synthesis between truth and untruth.

(610) The doctrine of the two kinds of knowledge, the higher and the lower, which made its appearance in the Middle and Late Upaniṣads (*v. supra*, 75) and the theory of standpoints adopted by the Trairāśika Ājīvikas (*v. supra*, 228, 229) and the Jains (*v. supra*, 228) has its counterpart in Buddhism in the doctrine of the two kinds of truth, conventional-truth (sammuti-sacca) and absolute truth (paramattha-sacca). There is, however, no clear-cut distinction between these two kinds of truth in the Pāli Canon. What we do find is a distinction between two types of Suttas (Discourses) which seems to have provided a basis for the later emergence of the doctrine of the two kinds of truth in medieval times; but even this latter theory, which appears in the commentaries, must be distinguished from the doctrine as understood by modern orthodoxy.[1]

(611) The two kinds of Suttas are the nītattha- ($\sqrt{}$nī, to infer+attha= meaning) or 'those of direct meaning' and the neyyattha- or 'those of indirect meaning'.[2] In one place in the Aṅguttara Nikāya the importance of distinguishing between these two types of Suttas is stressed and it is said that those who confuse the two misrepresent the Buddha: 'There are these two who misrepresent the Tathāgata. Which two? He who represents a Sutta of indirect meaning as a Sutta of direct meaning and he who represents a Sutta of direct meaning as a Sutta of indirect meaning'.[3] On the basis of this Edgerton has remarked that 'In Pāli neither is *ipso facto* preferred to the other; one errs only in interpreting one as if it were the other' (BHS. Dictionary, *s.v.* nītārtha-). On the other hand Edgerton says that 'in BHS. a nītārtha text . . . is recommended as a guide in preference to one that is neyārtha' (*loc. cit.*). This is certainly so.[4] But even in the Pāli the very fact that one is called

[1] *v.* Ledi Sadaw, 'Some Points in Buddhist Doctrine' in JPTS., 1914, pp. 115–163; cp. Nyanatiloka, *A Guide Through the Abhidhamma Piṭaka*, p. 2.

[2] *v.* Poussin, L'Abhidharmakośa, Vol. IX, p. 247; St Schayer, 'Pre-Canonical Buddhism' in *Archiv Orientalni*, Vol. 7, 1935, p. 121, has 'texts with literal meaning' for nītattha- and 'of symbolical (meaning)' for neyyattha-.

[3] Dve'me Tathāgataṃ abbhācikkhanti. Katame dve? Yo ca neyyatthaṃ suttantaṃ nītattho suttanto ti dīpeti; yo ca nītatthaṃ suttantaṃ neyyattho suttanto ti dīpeti, A. I.60.

[4] *v.* Poussin, *op. cit.*, Vol. IX, p. 246, fn. 2.

a nītattha Sutta, whose meaning is plain and direct and the other a neyyattha- in the sense that its meaning should be inferred in the light of the former, gives the former a definite precedence over the latter.

(612) No examples are given in the Canon of the two kinds of Suttas, referred to, and we have to seek this information in the commentaries. The commentary on the above passage tries to illustrate the difference: 'A Sutta of the form "there is one individual, O monks", "there are two individuals, O monks", "there are three individuals, O monks" . . . , etc., is a Sutta of indirect meaning. Here although the perfectly Enlightened One speaks of "there is one person, O monks", etc., its sense has to be inferred since there is no individual in the absolute sense (*paramatthato*). But a person because of his folly may take this as a Sutta of direct meaning and would argue that the Tathāgata would not have said "there is one individual, O monks", etc., unless a person existed in the absolute sense. Accepting the fact that since he has said so there must be a person in the absolute sense, he represents a Sutta of indirect meaning as a Sutta of direct meaning. One should speak of a Sutta of direct meaning (as of the form), "this is impermanent, sorrowful and devoid of substance (soul)". Here the sense is that what is permanent is at the same time sorrowful and lacking in substance. But because of his folly, this person takes this as a Sutta of indirect meaning and extracts its sense saying, "there is something which is eternal, happy and is the soul" and thus represents a Sutta of direct meaning as a Sutta of indirect meaning'.[1]

(613) This explanation seems to trace the distinction between these two kinds of discourse to the statement of the Buddha that there were 'expressions, turns of speech, designations in common use in the world which the Tathāgata makes use of without being led astray by them' *v. supra,* 533). For according to this statement, the Buddha is constrained to use language which has misleading implications and we have

[1] Ekapuggalo bhikkhave, dve'me bhikkhave puggalā, tayo'me bhikkhave puggalā . . . ti evarūpo suttanto neyyattho nāma. Ettha hi kiñcāpi sammāsambuddhena ekapuggalo bhikkhave ti ādi vuttaṃ, *paramatthato* pana puggalo nāma natthī ti evaṃ assa attho netabbo va hoti. Ayam pana attano bālataya nītattho ayaṃ suttanto: paramatthato hi puggale asati, na Tathāgato ekapuggalo bhikkhave ti ādīni vadeyya. Yasmā pana tena vuttaṃ, tasmā paramatthato atthi puggalo ti gaṇhanto taṃ neyyatthaṃ suttantaṃ nītattho suttanto ti dīpeti. *Nītatthan* ti aniccaṃ dukkhaṃ anattā ti evaṃ kathitattham. Ettha hi aniccam eva dukkham eva anattā yevā ti attho. Ayam pana attano bālataya neyyattho ayaṃ suttanto attham assa āharissamī ti niccaṃ nāma atthi, sukhaṃ nāma atthi, attā nama atthī ti gaṇhanto nītatthaṃ suttantaṃ neyyattho suttanto tī dīpeti nāma, AA. II.118.

to infer what he means, without these implications, if we are to understand him rightly. In other words when he is speaking about things or persons we should not presume that he is speaking about entities or substances; to this extent his meaning is to be inferred (neyyattha-). But when he is pointing out the misleading implications of speech or using language without these implications, his meaning is plain and direct and nothing is to be inferred (nītattha-). This is a valid distinction which certainly holds good for the Nikāyas at least, in the light of the above statement.

(614) When the commentaries distinguish these two kinds of discourse as absolute (paramattha-) and conventional (sammuti-), they are making this same distinction. We have already seen the use of the term 'absolute' (paramattha-) to imply the direct discourse (nītattha-) of the Buddha (*supra*, p. 629, fn. 1). We find this more explicitly stated at another place in the Aṅguttara Comy.: '"Individual" refers to conventional speech and not to absolute speech. Two-fold is the teaching of the Buddha, the Exalted One, viz. conventional teaching and absolute teaching. Here such (sayings as refer to) a person, a being . . . (constitutes) conventional teaching. Such (speech as refers to) the impermanent, the sorrowful, the soulless, constituents . . . (constitute) the absolute teaching . . .'.[1] The Comy. to the Kathāvatthu says the same.[2]

(615) But the commentaries go a step further. They characterize these two kinds of discourse, the direct (nītattha-) and the corrigible (neyyattha-) as two kinds of *truth*. A verse, which is quoted in the commentaries to the Aṅguttara and the Kathāvatthu in the same contexts as the above, reads as follows (with a slight variation in the fourth line):

Duve saccāni akkhāsi Sambuddho vadataṃ varo
sammutiṃ paramatthañ ca *tatiyaṃ n'ūpalabbhati*
sanketavacanaṃ saccaṃ lokasammutikāraṇaṃ
paramatthavacanaṃ saccaṃ—dhammānaṃ tathalakkhaṇaṃ
(KvuA., *op. cit.*, p. 34)
—dhammānaṃ bhūtalakkhaṇaṃ
(AA. I.95),

[1] Puggalo ti sammutikathā, na paramatthakathā. Buddhassa hi bhagavato duvidhā desanā: sammutidesanā paramatthadesanā cā ti. Tattha puggalo satto . . . ti evarupā sammutidesanā. Aniccaṃ dukkhaṃ anattā khandhā . . . ti evarūpā paramattha-desanā . . ., AA. I.94.

[2] Kathāvatthuppakaraṇa-Aṭṭhakathā, JPTS., 1889, p. 34.

i.e. 'The Perfectly Enlightened One, the best of teachers, spoke two truths, viz. conventional and absolute—one does not come across a third; a conventional statement is true because of convention and an absolute statement is true as (disclosing) the true characteristics of things'.

(616) This step is not taken in the Pāli Canon, where probably the impact of the statement of the Suttanipāta that 'truth was one without a second' (ekaṃ hi saccaṃ na dutīyam atthi, *v. supra,* 597) was strongly felt. This statement seems in fact to have had a wide currency for as Poussin points out we meet with the question in the Vibhāṣā, 'si les verites sont quatre, pourquoi Bhagavat dit-il qu'il y a une vérité?'[1] Even in the Bodhisattvabhūmi, where truth (satya-) is classified under one to ten divisions, the first is that 'truth is one in the sense of being non-contradictory' (avitathārthena tāvad ekam eva satyaṃ na dvitīyaṃ)[2] although the second says that 'truth is two-fold as *saṃvṛti* and *paramārtha*' (dvividhaṃ satyaṃ saṃvṛtisatyaṃ paramārthasatyañ ca). The saying that there is one truth but not a second contradicts this later saying (*v. supra,* 615) that there are two truths but not a third.

(617) But although the commentaries speak of these two kinds of truth, it is necessary to note that they do not imply that what is true in the one sense, is false in the other or even that the one kind of truth was superior to the other, notwithstanding the use of the term 'paramattha' (absolute) to denote one of them. The Comy. to the Aṅguttara says, 'the Exalted One preaches the conventional teaching to those who are capable of listening to this conventional teaching and penetrating the meaning, discarding ignorance and acquiring eminence. But to those who are capable of listening to his absolute teaching and penetrating the truth, discarding ignorance and attaining distinction, he preaches the absolute truth. There is this simile on this matter. Just as if there were a teacher, who explains the meaning of the Three Vedas and is versed in the regional languages; to those who would understand the meaning if he spoke in the Tamil language, he explains it in the Tamil language and to another who would understand (if he spoke in)

[1] 'Documents D'Abhidharma Les Deux, les Quatre, les Trois Vérités, Extraits de la Vibhāṣā et du Kośa de Saṃghabhadra' in *Mélanges Chinois et Bouddhiques,* Vol. 5, Bruxelles, 1937, p. 161.

[2] Ed. U. Wogihara, Tokyo, 1930–6, p. 292.

the Āndhra language, he speaks in that language'.[1] We note that the penetration of the truth is possible by either teaching, conventional or absolute; it is like using the language that a person readily understands and there is no implication that one language is superior to the other. The Comy. to the Kathāvatthu also emphatically says, 'But whether they use conventional speech or absolute speech, they speak what is true, what is factual and not false'.[2]

(618) But the view of modern orthodoxy differs from even that of the Comy. It is necessary to point this out, though it is strictly outside our scope, since frequent reference is made by scholars to the article of Ledi Sadaw[3] for enlightenment on this subject. Sadaw, speaking of 'two kinds of truth' goes on to say that a conventional truth is 'just an erroneous view' (*op. cit.*, p. 129). Ultimate truth for Sadaw 'is established by the nature of things (*sabhāvasiddham*), it is opposed to mere opinion' (*loc. cit.*). But this view is contradicted by the Comy. where it was said, te sammutikathaṃ kathentā pi saccam eva *sabhāvam* eva amusā'va kathenti (translated above). According to Sadaw, what is *true* according to conventional truth, i.e. 'a person exists' (to take his own example) is *false*[4] according to ultimate truth. This is a doctrine of standpoints, as in Jainism (*v. supra*, 228), where p is true from standpoint x and false from standpoint y. But this does not represent the position of the Nikāyas, where it would be true to say, 'a person exists in the present' (*v. supra*, 534) so long as one does not mean by 'person' a substance enduring in time. Convention requires that I use such words as 'I' or 'person' but so long as one is not misled by their

[1] . . . Bhagavā ye sammutivasena desanaṃ sutvā atthaṃ paṭivijjhitvā mohaṃ pahāya visesaṃ adigantuṃ samatthā tesaṃ sammutidesanaṃ deseti. Ye pana paramatthavasena desanaṃ sutvā atthaṃ paṭivijjhitvā mohaṃ pahāya visesaṃ adhigantuṃ samatthā tesaṃ paramatthadesanaṃ deseti. Tatrāyam upamā: yathā hi desabhāsakusalo tiṇṇaṃ vedānaṃ atthasaṃvaṇṇako ācariyo ye damilabhāsāya vutte atthaṃ jānanti tesaṃ damilabhāsāya ācikkhati, ye andhabhāsādisu aññatarāya tesaṃ tāya bhāsāya . . ., AA. I.94, 95.

[2] Te sammutikathaṃ kathentā pi saccaṃ eva sabhāvam eva amusā'va kathenti. Paramatthakathaṃ kathentā pi saccam eva sabhāvam eva amusā'va kathenti. KvuA., JPTS., 1889, p. 34.

[3] 'Some Points in Buddhist Doctrine' in JPTS., 1914, pp. 115–63; referred to in PTS. Dictionary, *s.v.* paramattha-; Points of Controversy, p. 180, fn. 1; Poussin, *op. cit.*, Vol. VI, p. 139, fn. 5.

[4] Cp. 'Nevertheless it is just an erroneous view. How so? Because a being who in reality (sabhāvato) does not exist, is spoken of as if he existed. According to ultimate truth, to say 'there is no personal entity' is neither untruthful nor mere opinion' (*loc. cit.*).

implications (of a perduring entity) the statement is true. Nyānātiloka's contention that 'in the Sutta the doctrines are more or less explained in the words of the philosophically incorrect "conventional" everyday language (vohāravacana) understood by anyone, whilst the Abhidhamma on the other hand makes use of purely philosophical terms true in the absolute sense (paramatthavacana)'[1] ignores in the first place the distinction between the direct (nītattha-) and the indirect (neyyattha-) Suttas within the Nikāyas; this is not suggested even by the commentarial tradition and is contradicted by the presence of the *Puggala-paññatti* within the Abhidhamma.

(619) The origin of this theory of double truth in Buddhism is, therefore, as we said, based on this distinction of the two types of discourse (*v. supra,* 614). This close connection between the two has been noticed by Oltramare who places vyavahāra and paramārtha, samvṛti and tattva side by side with neyārtha and nītārtha[2] and call them 'les deux vérités', although he does not trace the nature of the connection between the two. But the use of the words sammuti and paramattha in the Pāli Canon also has much to do with the later emergence of this theory.

(620) In its earliest use, sammuti denotes the 'commonly accepted (theories or beliefs)' of the various debating recluses and brahmins.[3] Close to the sense of 'conventional truth' is the use of sammuti at S. I.135, where it is said that 'just as much as the word "chariot" is used when the parts are put together, there is the use (*sammuti*) of the term "being" (satto) when the (psycho-physical) constituents are present' (yathā pi aṅgasambhārā hoti saddo ratho iti evaṃ khandhesu santesu hoti satto ti sammuti, Quoted Kvu. 66). Paramattha is used for 'the highest goal' in the earliest phase,[4] while in the latest phase in the Canon paramaṭṭhena[5] means 'in the absolute sense'. The two words, sammuti and paramattha- are nowhere contrasted in the Canon though

[1] *Guide Through the Abhidhamma Piṭaka*, p. 2.

[2] *L'Histoire des Idees Theosophiques dans L'inde-La Théosophie Bouddhique*, Paris, 1923, p. 300.

[3] Cp. Yā kā ci sammutiyo (=dvāsaṭṭhi-diṭṭhigatāni, No. 1, 308) puthujjā, Sn. 897; sakam sakaṃ sammutim āhu saccam, Sn. 904; ñatvā ca so sammutiyo puthujjā, Sn. 911; cp. yā kāś cana samvṛtayo hi loke, Bodhisattvabhūmi, 48.

[4] Cp. paramattha-pattiyā, Sn. 68; paramattha-dassiṃ, Sn. 219.

[5] Puggalo n'upalabbhati saccikaṭṭha-paramaṭṭhena, i.e. a person is not found in the real and absolute sense, Kvu. 1.

we meet with the term sammuti-sacca (conventional truth) on one occasion in the Kathāvatthu, without the term paramattha-sacca (*v. infra*, 621).

(621) We do, however, find sammuti-ñāṇa (conventional knowledge) though not its counterpart paramattha-ñāṇa just as much as we find paramaṭṭhena but not sammuti—aṭṭhena. The Saṅgīti Sutta says that 'there are four (forms of knowledge)—the (direct) knowledge of dhamma, the inductive knowledge (of dhamma, *v. infra*, 611), knowledge of the limits (of others' minds) and conventional knowledge' (cattāri ñāṇāni—dhamme ñāṇaṃ, anvaye ñāṇaṃ, paricchede ñāṇaṃ, sammutiñāṇaṃ, D. III.226). The list occurs in the Vibhaṅga, where they are explained in greater detail, but even here all that is said about conventional knowledge is that leaving out the first three kinds of knowledge, the rest of knowledge is conventional knowledge.[1] The Comy. on the Dīgha Nikāya says the same,[2] following the Vibhaṅga, and the only additional comment that the Comy. to the Vibhaṅga makes is that 'it is conventional knowledge because it is commonly believed to be knowledge'.[3] The Kathāvatthu reveals a difference of opinion as to whether 'conventional knowledge has only truth as its object and nothing else (sammutiñāṇaṃ saccārammanañ ñeva na aññārammanan ti, Kvu. 310). According to the Comy. 'this discourse is to purge the incorrect tenet held by the Andhakas,[4] that the word "truth" is to be applied without any distinction being drawn between popular and philosophical truth'.[5] If this comment is relevant, the distinction that is drawn by the orthodox Theravādin is that 'the knowledge pertaining to medical requisites on the part of a donor of them falls into the category of "conventional truth" ' (gilānapaccaya-bhesajjaparikkhāraṃ dadantassa atthi ñāṇaṃ, gilānapaccayabhesajja-parikkhāro ca sammutisaccamhi, Kvu. 311). Since the opponent is made to admit that 'with this (conventional) knowledge one does not comprehend sorrow, does not abandon its cause, does not realize its cessation and does not cultivate the path' (tena ñāṇena dukkhaṃ parijānāti, samudayam pajahati, nirodhaṃ sacchikaroti, maggaṃ

[1] Ṭhapetvā dhamme ñāṇam anvaye ñāṇam paricce ñāṇam avavesā paññā sammutiñāṇaṃ, Vbh. 330.

[2] Ṭhapetvā dhamme ñāṇaṃ, ṭhapetvā anvaye ñāṇam, ṭhapetvā paricce ñāṇaṃ avasesaṃ sammutiñāṇaṃ, DA. III.1020.

[3] ñāṇan ti sammatattā sammutiñāṇaṃ nāma hoti, VbhA., 417 (*Sammohavinodanī*, London, 1923).

[4] Bareau, *op. cit.*, pp. 92, 220.

[5] Aung and Mrs Rhys Davids, *Points of Controversy*, p. 180.

bhāvetī ti? Na h'evaṃ . . ., *loc. cit.*), we have to presume that this kind of knowledge is absolute knowledge (paramatthañāṇa) and comes within the realm of absolute truth (paramatthasacca), although neither of these words are used. This surmise is confirmed by the fact that the theories pertaining to the content of *paramārtha-satya* in the BHS. and the Chinese texts all revolve round the Four Noble Truths. Poussin has listed no less than five theories on this subject.[1] The first is that 'les deux dernieres vérités . . . sont *paramārthasatya*' (*op. cit.*, p. 163), the second that 'seul le *mārgasatya* est *paramārthasatya* . . .' (*loc. cit.*), the third that 'seul le principe: "Toutes choses sont vides et sans-soi" est *paramārthasatya*' (*op. cit.*, p. 164) and the fourth which is the view of P'ing-kia to the effect that 'les quatre vérités sont *samvṛti* et *paramārtha*' (*loc. cit.*). Poussin says that 'la Vibhāṣā ignore une cinquieme opinion: que la troisieme vérité . . . seule est *paramārtha*' (*op. cit.*, p. 165), but if our above deduction is correct, we would have to add a sixth opinion (of the Theravādins), namely that all four truths constitute the content of paramārtha-satya only. This is the closest that the Pāli Canon comes to distinguishing two aspects of truth—but the distinction here unlike in the Comy. and the article of Sadaw is a distinction of subject-matter and not a distinction of two kinds of truth in real or apparent contradiction with each other.

[1] 'Les Deux Vérités' in *Mélanges Chinois et Bouddhique*, Vol. 5, pp. 163–165.

CHAPTER VIII

AUTHORITY AND REASON WITHIN BUDDHISM

(622) In Chapters IV and V we discussed the attitude of Buddhism to authority and reason respectively. The general conclusion was that neither could be trusted as giving us certain truth. The general context of the discussion, however, seemed to show that by 'authority' here was meant mainly, if not solely, the authority of other religious traditions (and persons) than that of Buddhism. In this chapter, we propose to examine to what extent, if at all, this attitude to authority and reason is maintained within Buddhism.

(623) In this inquiry, we shall strictly confine ourselves to the Buddhism of the Pāli Canon, for we feel that much of what has been said on this subject[1] is vitiated by the fact that almost the entire field of Buddhism (the different schools, ancient and medieval) has been treated together, with little regard for historical perspective.

(624) We have to ask ourselves three questions in trying to elucidate the place of authority within Buddhism. First, does Buddhism or the Buddha uncritically accept any doctrines on authority from the prevalent traditions? Secondly, is the attitude recommended towards the authority of external traditions and persons the same as that expected towards the doctrines of Buddhism itself? Thirdly, irrespective of the answer to this second question, do the disciples of the Buddha accept any doctrines on the authority of the Buddha?

(625) The answer to the first question on the part of scholars has on the whole been in the affirmative. According to Oldenberg, 'it is certain that Buddhism has acquired as an inheritance from Brahmanism, not merely a series of its most important dogmas, but, what is not less

[1] *v.* Poussin, 'Faith and Reason in Buddhism' in *Transactions of the Third International Congress for the History of Religions*, Vol. II, 1908, pp. 32–43; Keith, *Buddhist Philosophy*, Ch. II.

significant to the historian, the bent of its religious thought and feeling, which is more easily comprehended than expressed in words'.[1] Prof. Rhys Davids says that 'Gautama was born and brought up and lived and died a Hindu ... There was not much in the metaphysics and principles of Gautama which cannot be found in one or other of the orthodox systems'[2] and again that 'Buddhism grew and flourished within the field of orthodox belief'.[3] Radhakrishnan is of the same opinion: 'Early Buddhism is not an absolutely original doctrine. It is no freak in the evolution of Indian thought.'[4]

(626) There is, however, a difference between a critical and uncritical acceptance of ideas, prevalent at the time, and the above statements do not make it very clear which was the case with Buddhism. But Thomas is much more specific, when speaking of Buddhism he says 'it started from special Indian beliefs, *which it took for granted.* The chief of these were the belief in transmigration and the doctrine of the retribution of action ... *they were already taken for granted* as a commonly accepted view of life by most Indian religions'[5] (italics mine).

(627) On the other hand, Keith going on the suggestions of (the earlier) Mrs Rhys Davids[6] that the Buddha could not disregard the ordinary terminology of his time[7] has suggested the purely hypothetical possibility, which he himself does not accept, that the Buddha did not accept the dogma of transmigration, since it contradicted his anattā doctrine, viz. 'Or more frankly, we may accept the view that the Buddha himself was a true rationalist and absolutely declined to accept the dogma of transmigration'.[8] This view is in fact seriously put forward by Jennings, who holds that the Buddha did not believe or even teach rebirth or karma[9] (in the sense of personal responsibility for our actions).

[1] *Buddha*, Tr. Hoey, London, 1882, p. 53.
[2] *Buddhism*, pp. 83–4.
[3] *Op. cit.*, p. 85.
[4] *Indian Philosophy*, Vol. I, p. 360.
[5] *v.* E. J. Thomas, 'Buddhism in Modern Times' in UCR., Vol. 9, p. 216.
[6] I.e. Mrs Rhys Davids, before she changed her views radically about the nature of the doctrines of Early Buddhism.
[7] *v. Buddhist Psychology*, p. 21; *Compendium of Philosophy*, p. 278. cp. Prof. Rhys Davids' view that there is much subtle irony in the discourses of the Buddha, SBB., Vol. II, pp. 33, 160, 163; cp. Poussin, JA., 1902, Vol. II, p. 250.
[8] *Buddhist Philosophy*, p. 14.
[9] J. G. Jennings, *The Vedantic Buddhism of the Buddha*, Oxford University Press, London, 1947, pp. xxii–xxvii, xxxvi–lv.

(628) This latter view is clearly in contradiction with the texts and we have to accept these statements in the texts, which speak of rebirth and karma, as genuine on methodological grounds, unless there are very strong considerations against such acceptance. That the concept of personal responsibility appears at first sight to be incompatible with the doctrine of anattā (soullessness) is no good ground for rejecting these doctrines since these texts themselves are conscious of this problem and do not think that there is a discrepancy. It is said that 'a certain monk entertained the thought that since body, feelings, ideas, dispositions, and consciousness is without self, what self, can deeds not done by a self, affect' (aññatarassa bhikkhuno evaṃ cetaso parivitakko udapādi: Iti kira, bho, rūpaṃ . . . vedanā . . . saññā . . . saṅkhārā . . . viññānaṃ anattā anattakatāni kammāni kam attānaṃ phusissatī ti, M. III.19). This is the same as saying that if there is no self, there can be no personal identity and no personal responsibility but this is dismissed as an unwarranted corollary of or as going beyond the teaching of the Buddha (cp. satthu-sāsanaṃ atidhāvitabbaṃ maññeyya, *loc. cit.*). The paen of joy said to have been uttered by the Buddha on attaining enlightenment stresses the fact of freedom from 'repeated birth' (jātipunappunaṃ, Dh. 154). The conception of ***salvation from***[1] is intimately connected in Buddhism with the belief in rebirth. It is therefore an integral part of Early Buddhist belief and much of Buddhism would be unintelligible without it.

(629) But this need not commit us to the view that rebirth (and karma) are uncritically or dogmatically accepted from the earlier or prevalent religious tradition. The only evidence adduced by those who put forward or suggest this view, is that rebirth is almost universally accepted in the Indian religious tradition. Since Buddhism too subscribes to this view, it is argued that Buddhism dogmatically accepted this theory from the prevalent tradition. From this it follows that the Buddha himself was violating the very injunction he was making, when he asked people not to accept a doctrine merely because it was found in a tradition, etc. (*v. supra*, 260).

(630) With all deference to scholarship, we wish to submit that this conclusion arises from both an unhistorical as well as an uncritical survey of the material. In fact, that a belief is found in a stratum *A* and in a chronologically successive stratum *B*, provides no conclusive evidence that the thinkers of stratum *B* uncritically and dogmatically

[1] *v.* N. Smart, *A Dialogue of Religions*, pp. 31 ff.

accept it from the thinkers of stratum *A*. If we say so, it would follow that even a good scientist uncritically or dogmatically accepts the theories of his predecessors with whom he happens to agree, merely on the grounds of this agreement!

(631) Let us examine the credentials of the above widely accepted theory. In the first place it is false to say that rebirth was universally accepted by the Indian religious tradition prior to the advent of Buddhism. There is no trace of a belief in rebirth in the Ṛgveda,[1] where we find only sporadic references to a belief in a life after death. The Atharvaveda, too, makes no reference to the doctrine. The Brāhmaṇas show a greater interest in the after-life and we meet with a variety of views on this subject but no conclusive reference to rebirth is found. The conception of a 'second death' (punar mṛtyu) is pregnant with the possibility of developing the idea of rebirth and all that can be said is that 'the Brāhmaṇas contain all the suggestions necessary for the development of the doctrine of rebirth'.[2]

(632) In the Early Upaniṣads, there is intense speculation on the subject of the after-life and rebirth is only one of the many theories that are mooted. At this time the very possibility of survival appears to have been questioned (*v. supra,* 86). In one place, rebirth is clearly ruled out as impossible. It is said: '. . . there are three worlds, the world of men, the world of the fathers and the world of the gods. The world of men is obtained through a son only, not by any other means . . .' (. . . trayo vāva lokāḥ manuṣyalokaḥ pitṛlokaḥ devaloka iti. So'yaṃ manuṣyalokaḥ putreṇaiva jayyaḥ nānyena karmaṇā . . ., Bṛh. 1.5.16). This means, in other words, that there is no possibility of a future life on earth for the person who dies.

(633) Speculation seems to have resulted in a number of one-life-after-death theories of survival at this time, some of them coming down from the Brāhmaṇic tradition. The belief in the possibility of a 'second death' (punar-mṛtyu) and in devices intended to avert this, is still strong in the earliest stage of the Upaniṣads (*v.* Bṛh. 1.2.7; 1.5.2; 3.3.2). But despite this conception, we do meet with a number of theories, which contemplate the possibility of a single after-life. We have already referred to the theories of Yājñavalkya (*v. supra,* 44), Prajāpati (*v. supra,* 40) and Uddālaka (*v. supra,* 40), which, as we have shown,

[1] *v.* Radhakrishnan, *op. cit.*, pp. 113–116; cp. Oldenberg, *op. cit.*, pp. 47 ff.; Mrs Rhys Davids, *Buddhist Psychology*, Ch. II, 'The Basic Doctrine of Rebirth', pp. 245 ff.

[2] Radhakrishnan, *op. cit.*, p. 135.

were probably known to the Buddhist texts. We may add to this list. We meet with the early pantheistic theory that 'the karma of he who reveres the soul as the world does not perish and out of this soul he creates whatever he likes (after death)' (*sa ya ātmānam eva lokam* upāste na hāsya karma kṣīyate asmādd hy eva ātmano yad yat kāmayate tat tat sṛjate, Bṛh. 1.4.15). Since his karma does not get exhausted, he would presumably live in this state for ever. This same theory of personal immortality is mentioned in the Nikāyas as the theory which states that 'the soul is my world, after death I shall be permanent, stable, eternal, not subject to change and I shall remain in that condition eternally' (*so loko so attā,* so pecca bhavissāmi nicco dhuvo sassato avipariṇāmadhammo sassatisamaṃ tath'eva ṭhassāmī ti . . ., M. I.135, 136). Another such theory holds that the person who is made of mind (manomayo'yaṃ puruṣaḥ, Bṛh. 5.6.1) after departing from this world goes to the wind, the sun, the moon and to the world that is without heat, without cold and lives there eternally—a theory which we have identified with one of the rational eternalist theories referred to in Buddhism (*v. supra,* 431). As we said, the Brāhmaṇic theories persist in a slightly different dress. Thus, the belief that we attain the company of the sun is found at Ch. 3.17.6, 7 and this is the theory which appears in the Kauśītaki Brāhmaṇa and is noted in the Nikāyas (*v. infra,* 820). In the Taittirīya Upaniṣad there is a theory that the person after death changes his states from one to another: '. . . asmāl lokāt pretya etam annamayam ātmānam upasaṅkrāmati . . . prāṇamayaṃ . . . manomayaṃ . . . vijñānamayaṃ . . . ānandamayaṃ' (i.e. after departing from this world proceeds to the (state of the) self consisting of food . . . consisting of the life-principle . . . consisting of mind . . . consisting of understanding . . . consisting of bliss, 3.10.5). Now these 'selves', as we have shown, partly correspond to the 'selves' mentioned in the Poṭṭhapāda Sutta (*v. supra,* 529) and here the first is said to be *rūpī,* i.e. 'has form'[1] and the last *arūpī,*[2] i.e. 'has no form'. It is likely that it was this theory of survival that was thought of when it was held in the Brahmajāla Sutta that 'the soul has form and does not have form (after death)' (attā rūpī ca arūpī ca . . ., D. I.31).

(634) The first clear reference to the theory of rebirth or the return to earth to become man or animal is found at Bṛh. 6.2.15–16, Ch. 5.10.1–8 and Kauś. 1.2. It is only in the Kaṭha Upaniṣad that for the first time

[1] *Rūpī* cātummahābhūtiko . . . ayaṃ olariko attapaṭilābho, D. I.195.
[2] *Arūp'* saññāmayo, ayaṃ arūpo attapaṭilābho, *loc. cit.*

the theory is generally accepted (1.2.6; 2.2.7) and thereafter we find its acceptance in the Muṇḍaka (1.2.10), Śvetāśvatara (5.12), Praśna (5.3–5) and Maitrī (3.1).

(635) If the rise of Buddhism is to be placed sometime after the Kaṭha Upaniṣad and before the Maitrī (*v. supra*, 80, 81), there is little ground for holding in the light of the above evidence, either that the acceptance of this belief was widespread or that the belief was of great antiquity.

(636) Besides these alternative theories of survival, which were current at that time, it should not be forgotten that there was an influential body of thinkers, according to the evidence of both the Buddhist and the Jain texts, who doubted the possibility of knowing the ultimate truth about survival (*v. supra*, Ch. III). There is little doubt that Buddhism was influenced by this sceptical movement (*v. infra*, 739).

(637) Lastly, we have to reckon with very influential Materialist schools of thought at this time (*v. supra*, Ch. II). The reference to seven Materialist schools of thought was possibly exaggerated (*v. supra*, 141) but the number probably reflects the impact of Materialist thinking at this time on the thought of Buddhism. This impact must have been very strong for when the Buddha comes to classify the thinkers of his day, he gives equal prominence to the Materialists as against the Eternalists. He says: 'There are these two theories—the theory of personal immortality and the annihilationist (Materialist) theory. Those recluses and brahmins who hold to, seek refuge in and cling to the theory of personal immortality are utterly opposed to the annihilationist theory and those recluses and brahmins who hold to, seek refuge in, and cling to the annihilationist theory are utterly opposed to the theory of personal immortality'.[1] Similarly juxtaposed with equal weight are the Eternalist theory (sassatavāda, sassatadiṭṭhi) and the Materialist theory (ucchedavāda, ucchedadiṭṭhi, *v.* S. II.20; S. III.98, 99). The doctrine of *anattā* in denying or discarding the concept of the soul, which was one of the central theses of the Eternalists seems to make the Buddha veer more towards the Materialists than the Eternalists. In fact, in his own time according to the evidence

[1] Dve'mā . . . diṭṭhiyo: bhavadiṭṭhi ca vibhavadiṭṭhi ca. Ye hi keci . . . samaṇā vā brāhmaṇā vā bhavadiṭṭhim allīnā bhavadiṭṭhim upagatā bhavadiṭṭhim ajjhositā, vibhavadiṭṭhiyā te paṭiviruddhā. Ye hi keci . . . samaṇā vā brāhmaṇā vā vibhavadiṭṭhim allīnā vibhavadiṭṭhim upagatā vibhavadiṭṭhim ajjhositā, bhavadiṭṭhiyā te paṭiviruddhā, M. I.65.

of the Nikāyas, we find his own contemporaries accusing him of being a Materialist and not an Eternalist. It is said that 'the recluse Gotama declares the cutting off, the destruction and the annihilation of a real being' (samaṇo Gotamo *sato sattassa ucchedaṃ vināsaṃ vibhavam paññapeti,* M. I.140); it is the same language that is used to describe the main thesis of Materialism, viz. itth'eke *sato sattassa ucchedaṃ vināsaṃ vibhavam paññapenti* (D. I.34, 35). Elsewhere it is stated much more specifically as a current belief that 'the recluse Gotama is a Materialist, who teaches a doctrine of Materialism and trains his disciples in it' (ucchedavādo samaṇo Gotamo ucchedāya dhammaṃ deseti tena ca sāvake vineti, A. IV.182 ff.). We have also shown that Buddhism appears to have been impressed by the epistemology of the Materialists and tried to adopt it in its own way (*v. infra*, 737). In the light of this it is very unlikely that the Buddha who would have been well-acquainted with the Materialist critique of the doctrine of survival, would have uncritically accepted the doctrines of rebirth and karma, unless he had at least believed he had good grounds for it.

(638) Besides the Materialists and the Sceptics there was the wider class of the *viññū* or the élite whom, as we have shown (*v. supra*, 358) the Buddha was particularly keen on addressing and converting. A man like Pāyāsi would probably fall into this class and he, as we have seen (*v. supra*, 136–139), showed a healthy interest in the problem of survival, going so far as to perform experiments in order to discover the truth about it. Even if we dismiss him as a Materialist, who was more interested in exposing the falsity of the belief, we find that the sermons addressed to the *viññū* do not, unlike many other sermons. assume the truth of rebirth or even of survival. Thus, in the Apaṇṇaka Sutta, where the Buddha appeals to the reflections of the 'rational person' or the viññū puriso (*v.* tatra . . . viññū puriso iti patisañcikkhati, M. I.404, 406, 408, 409, 410, 411) he does not assume the truth of the belief in survival or moral responsibility but uses a 'wager argument' (*v. infra*, 686) to show that it would be better in the long run to entertain such a belief and act accordingly, irrespective of the consequences. In the Sandaka Sutta, where again we find a similar appeal to the reflections of a 'viññū puriso' (M. I.515, 516, 517, 518), there is no assumption of the belief in survival and the appeal is purely to rationalist considerations.

(639) When we thus look at the problem historically, we find that there are no grounds for holding that the belief in rebirth was universal

or even widespread prior to the advent of Buddhism. There were Materialists, Sceptics and those who believed in survival without subscribing to the doctrine of rebirth. These theories were known and criticized in the Buddhist texts and there is no reason to believe that the criticisms of the theory of rebirth by the Materialists, Sceptics and others was not known to the Buddhists. The élite seem to have had an open-minded attitude on the subject and when the Buddhists did accept the theories of rebirth and karma, they seem to have done so on the ground that their truth was verifiable (*v. infra*, 754, 755) though we may doubt whether this kind of verification was sufficient or adequate to claim the veracity of these theories. But one thing is certain and that is that we have no grounds for saying that Buddhism took for granted dogmatically or uncritically accepted these doctrines from the prevalent tradition. That these doctrines were almost universally accepted in the post-Buddhistic Indian tradition is due largely to the fact that the Jains and the Buddhists, the most influential critics of the orthodox Vedic tradition, accepted them and the Materialists who came under fire from all these schools of thought, gradually faded out of the Indian philosophical scene. But the picture that we get at the time of the rise of Buddhism is somewhat different and it would be quite unhistorical to presume that it was the same as what it was in later times.

(640) Let us turn to the second question. Is the attitude recommended towards the authority of external traditions and persons the same as that expected towards the doctrines of Buddhism itself? The question is related to the alleged omniscience of the Buddha. Did the Buddha claim omniscience and expect his statements to be treated as the pronouncements of an omniscient being? If not, how authoritative were these statements?

(641) Scholars have made statements to the effect that the Buddha was omniscient without distinguishing the question as to whether this was a claim of his or of his disciples, immediate or of a later time. On this ground, they have argued that Early Buddhism was an authoritarian creed, meaning thereby that the Buddha's statements were in fact taken or intended to be taken on the authority of the omniscient Buddha. Both Poussin and Keith quote with approval the words of Kern, who said that 'Buddhism is professedly no rationalistic system, it being a superhuman (uttarimanussa) Law, founded upon the decrees

of an omniscient and infallible Master'.[1] Keith goes on to say that 'he (i.e. the Buddha) is omniscient and he himself claims to be completely free from fault, one in whom no blemish can be found' (*op. cit.*, p. 35). Keith refers in support of this statement of his to AN. IV.82 (*v.* fn. 6) but A. IV.82 does not support him. It is merely said here that 'the Tathāgata has four things he need not guard against ... perfect conduct of body ... perfect conduct of speech ... perfect conduct of mind ... and a perfect livelihood, whereby he need not be on his guard that someone would find him out'.[2] This text, as will be seen, merely claims the moral perfection of the Tathāgata and makes no mention of his omniscience or lack of it.

(642) Poussin starts by saying that 'la vielle doctrine bouddhique prétend et à juste titre, être un foi, mais elle admet le principe du libre examen'.[3] In stressing its claim to be a faith, he says: 'Que le Bouddhisme soit essentiallement une foi, l'adhésion à la parole de l'Omniscient ...'.[4] But the only text he quotes from the Pāli tradition for the omniscience of the Buddha is 'Milinda, p. 214' (*op. cit.*, p. 132, fn. 2.) where 'omniscient' is said to be an epithet of the Tathāgata.[5] This is better than Keith's citation but the Milinda is far removed in time from the Canon but, perhaps, Poussin is not talking here about 'la vielle doctrine bouddhique', though he does not make himself clear.

(643) Much earlier Poussin had expressed the same views, addressing the third international congress of religions. He is anxious to show in this paper that 'Buddhism is contradiction itself'[6] and that 'it has been no happier in making out a comprehensive theory of the relations between faith, reason and intuition' (*loc. cit.*). He says that 'Buddhism was at the same time a faith in revealed truths and a philosophical institution' (*op. cit.*, p. 33) and makes the following observations: 'documents and theories point to conflicting statements: the old Buddhism pretends and rightly to be a creed. But it admits the principle

[1] *Manual of Buddhism*, p. 50; quoted Poussin, *Bouddhisme*, Third Edition, 1925, p. 132, fn. 3; also Keith, *Buddhist Philosophy*, p. 33.

[2] Cattāri Tathāgatassa arakkheyyāni . . . parisuddhakāyasamācāro . . . parisuddhavacīsamācāro . . . parisuddhamanosamācāro . . . parisuddhājivo yaṃ . . . rakkheyya 'mā me idaṃ paro aññāsī'ti, *loc. cit.*

[3] *Bouddhisme*, Third Edition, p. 130.

[4] *Op. cit.*, p. 132; cp. by the same author, JRAS., 1902, pp. 363 ff. and JA., Vol. II, pp. 252 ff.

[5] Sabbaññu-vacanaṃ Tathāgatassa . . . vacanaṃ.

[6] 'Faith and Reason in Buddhism' in *Transactions of the Third International Congress for the History of Religions*, Vol. II, p. 42.

of 'libre examen'; still more it considers critical inquiry as the one key to the comprehension of truth ...' (*loc. cit.*). 'Buddhism is a faith and a creed, a respectful and close adhesion to the word of the one Omniscient' (*op. cit.*, p. 34). He adds, 'innumerable are the documents which establish this point' (*loc. cit.*) but not a single reference is given to the Pāli Canon where it is said or implied that the Buddha was omniscient. He does not make it clear whether on his view the Buddha both claimed omniscience and/or was acclaimed omniscient by his disciples, though he holds that the latter is true: 'according to his disciples the Buddha alone knows everything ...' (*loc. cit.*).

(644) Some Canonical texts are referred to in the sequel apparently intended to show that the Buddha claimed omniscience and/or was acclaimed omniscient. There is a reference to the Kevaḍḍha Sutta, where the Buddha claimed to know the answer to a question, which even Brahmā was ignorant of (D. I.223). The parable of the elephant and the blind men (*v. supra*, 599) is mentioned with the remark, 'human wisdom always falls short in some point. To be saved one must refer to the Omniscient' (*loc. cit.*). Lastly, there is a reference to a passage in the Aṅguttara Nikāya (presumably A. IV.163 ff.), where the Buddha is compared to a granary, whence men bring every good word, followed by the remark that 'they show beyond doubt that Buddhism is a faith and creed' (*loc. cit.*). Keith quotes these same passages to make the same point.[1]

(645) Now an examination of these passages will show that they do not establish the fact that the Buddha claimed omniscience or was believed to be omniscient by his disciples. The point of the Kevaḍḍha Sutta is to show that Brahmā did not know the answer to the question, 'where do these four great elements ... cease to be?' (kattha nu kho bhante ime cattāro mahābhūtā aparisesā nirujjhanti, D. I.223). The Buddha alters the question so as to preserve the naïve realistic theory of the external world, viz. 'where does water, earth, fire and air not penetrate ...?' (kattha āpo ca paṭhavī tejo vāyo na gādhati ... *loc. cit.*) and answers it. The fact that he answers it is not intended to imply that the Buddha was omniscient but only that Brahmā was ignorant as he is elsewhere said to be (cp. avijjāgato ... Brahmā, M. I.326) of matters pertaining to the transcendent reality or Nirvāṇa. The Buddha, where he disclaims omniscience, claims to have three kinds of knowledge, viz. (1) knowledge of his diverse past births, (2) clairvoyance,

[1] *Op. cit.*, p. 33.

and (3) the knowledge of the destruction of the 'intoxicants', i.e. the knowledge of the means to and the fact of Nirvāṇa (*v. infra*, 801). Brahmā, not having attained Nirvāṇa, lacks the third (i.e. 3). With regard to (1), Brahmā's knowledge is said to be limited;[1] the same is the case with (2), for the Buddha claims to know the existence of three groups of gods of whom Brahmā is ignorant.[2] So the Kevaḍḍha Sutta merely reinforces Buddha's claim to possess a 'three-fold knowledge'.

(646) The parable of the blind men and the elephant likewise does not seem to imply the omniscience of the Buddha. It merely tries to illustrate the fact that the other religious teachers had at best only a partial vision of reality[3] (*v. supra*, 599). By implication the Buddha had a total vision of reality, but this is not the same as a claim to omniscience, for in such a case we would have to say that every metaphysician who makes such a claim is claiming omniscience!

(647) We can again hardly draw the inference that omniscience is claimed for the Buddha when it is said in the Aṅguttara Nikāya that 'whatever is well-spoken is the word of the Exalted One' (yaṃ kiñci subhāsitaṃ, sabbaṃ taṃ tassa bhagavato vacanaṃ . . ., A. IV.164), if we take this statement in the context in which it is made. This is not a saying attributed to the Buddha, but to a little known monk Uttara who says this in a mythological context, addressing Śakra, the king of the gods. In its context, there is a simile accompanying the utterance: 'If there is a granary in the vicinity of a village or hamlet and people were to carry grain in pingoes, baskets, in their robes and hands . . . then if one were to ask the question 'from where are you carrying this grain', the proper reply would be to say that it was from this large granary. Even so, whatever is well-spoken is the word of the Exalted One'.[4] What it means in its context, is that those

[1] It is said that 'his memory is defective' (tassa . . . sā sati muṭṭhā, M. I.329) owing to his prolonged existence in that state.

[2] *v.* Atthi . . . aññā tayo kāyā tattha tvaṃ na jānāsi na passasi, tyāhaṃ jānāmi, passāmi, i.e. there are three other groups of which you have no direct knowledge, which I know and see, *loc. cit.*

[3] *v.* Aññatitthiyā . . . paribbājakā andhā acakkhukā, Ud. 70.

[4] Seyyathā pi gāmassa vā nigamassa vā avidūre mahādhaññarāsi, tato mahājanakāyo dhaññaṃ āhareyya kācehi pi piṭakehi pi ucchaṅgalehi pi añjalīhi pi . . . yo nu evaṃ puccheyya: kuto imaṃ dhaññam āharathā ti . . . amumhā mahāddhaññarāsimhā āharāmā ti kho sammā vyākaramāno vyākareyya. Evam eva . . . yaṃ kiñci subhāsitaṃ sabbaṃ taṃ tassa Bhagavato vacanaṃ . . ., A. IV.164.

'well-spoken' utterances made by the disciples of the Buddha at a time and place when the Buddha had appeared are the utterances of the Buddha. This appears to be the contextual significance of this remark, which is used to illustrate that an utterance of Uttara's was not really his, since he was merely echoing the words of his master (*v.* kiṃ pan'idaṃ bhante ayasmato Uttarassa sakaṃ paṭibhāṇaṃ udāhu tassa Bhagavato vacanaṃ . . .? i.e. is this a product of your own insight or is it an utterance of the Exalted One . . .? A. IV.163). It is strange that this statement should be torn out of its context, to make it say something that it does not even remotely suggest in its context.[1]

(648) Apart from the negative conclusions following from an examination of the above passages, we have the positive claim on the part of the Buddha that he should be regarded not as one who is omniscient all the time but as one who has 'a three-fold knowledge' (*v. infra*, 801), which even others can develop (*v. infra*, 752). This attitude of not claiming omniscience for the Buddha seems to have been maintained right up to the time when the Vibhaṅga was composed for this book gives the most elaborate account of the ten cognitive powers of the Buddha (*v. infra*, 805) with no mention of his alleged omniscience. In the Nikāyas, we find a list of ten verses, containing no less than a hundred epithets of the Buddha,[2] where the epithets sabbaññū (omniscient) or sabba-dassāvi (all-seeing) or any of its synonyms are conspicuous by their absence (*v.* M. I.386).

(649) But the Buddha appears to have been acclaimed omniscient in the Theravāda school sometime before the Pāli Canon was finally completed for we find such a claim made in the Paṭisambhidāmagga and the Kathāvatthu. The Paṭisambhidāmagga in its section called 'the discourse on knowledge' (ñāṇakathā) specifies 'what is meant by the omniscience of the Tathāgata' (katamaṃ Tathāgatassa *sabbaññutañāṃ*, 131). It begins by saying that his omniscience consists in 'knowing everything conditioned and unconditioned without remainder' (sabbaṃ saṅkhataṃ asaṅkhataṃ anavasesaṃ jānātī ti, *loc. cit.*) and in 'knowing everything in the past, present and future' (atītam . . . anāgatam . . . paccuppannaṃ sabbaṃ jānātī ti, *loc. cit.*). It then goes on to list a number of components of his omniscience, the last of which is

[1] Keith even confuses this statement with its illegitimate converse, 'whatever has been said by the Buddha is well-said,' occurring in the Bhabru Edict; *v. op. cit.*, p. 33.

[2] If we count 'Bhagavato' which is repeated ten times, there would be 101 epithets in all.

that 'he knows everything that has been seen, heard, sensed, thought, attained, sought and searched by the minds of those who inhabit the entire world of gods and men'.[1] This is followed by the inquiry as to the sense in which the Buddha is 'all-seeing' (kenaṭṭhena samanta-cakkhu, *op. cit.*, p. 133). This word (samanta-cakkhu) is used with a slightly different connotation from that of sabbaññū and curiously enough the 'omniscience of the Buddha' comes to be classified as one of the fourteen kinds of knowledge, which constitute the knowledge of the Buddha (cp. cuddasa Buddhañāṇāni ... sabbanññutanñāṇaṃ Buddhañāṇaṃ, *loc. cit.*). Whatever this may mean, it is clear from this section that omniscience is claimed for the Buddha by disciples far removed in time from the Buddha himself. Similarly, the Kathāvatthu urges as a matter of common belief that the Buddha is omniscient (sabbaññū) and all-seeing (sabba-dassāvi). These two epithets occur in a list of eight epithets (Tathāgato[2], Jino[3], Satthā[4], Sammā-sambuddho[5] *Sabbaññū Sabbadassāvi* Dhammassāmi[6] Dhammapaṭisaraṇo, Kvu. 228) five of which (see footnotes) are found in the Sutta Piṭaka as regular epithets of the Buddha. It may be concluded from the above that neither did the Buddha claim omniscience nor was omniscience claimed of the Buddha until the very latest stratum in the Pāli Canon and that is even after most of the books of the Abhidhamma had been completed.

(650) We cannot therefore hold that the Buddha claimed authority for his statements on the grounds that he was omniscient. Nor can we say that he received his knowledge from an omniscient divine source as seems to be implied in Poussin's statement that 'Buddhism... was a faith in *revealed* truths' (*op. cit.*, p. 33). The injunction on the part of Brahmā to the Buddha to preach his religion (*v.* desassu bhagavā dhammaṃ, M. I.169) does not imply that the Buddha gained his knowledge from Brahmā, especially when we see it said that Brahmā was ignorant of the deeper spiritual truths of Buddhism (*v. supra*, 645). Przyluski has also expressed the view that the Early Buddhist scriptures constitute a revelation. He says: 'In Buddhist thought the notion of *śruti* is far more important than generally believed. It explains the frequently used term of bahuśruta,—rendered literally in Chinese by to-wen 'who has heard much'. The initial formula of the sutra, *evam*

[1] Yāvatā sadevakassa lokassa . . . diṭṭhaṃ sutaṃ mutaṃ viññātaṃ pattaṃ pariyesitam anuvicaritam manasā sabbaṃ jānāti ti, *loc. cit.*

[2] Sn. 467, D. I.12. [3] Vin. I.8, Sn. 697. [4] Sn. 545, D. I.110.

[5] Dh. 187, Vin. I.5. [6] S. IV.94.

mayā śrutam not only alludes to the sacred texts by Ānanda, when the First Council was held, but also indicates that these texts were revealed and that the whole of them constitute the *śruti*. And just as *śruta-* is opposed to dṛṣṭa- or śruti- to pratyakṣa- the former term applied as compared to the latter, a knowledge of superior quality. It seems easier now to understand why Pāli diṭṭhi- 'view, opinion' is so frequently used deprecatingly with the meaning of 'ill-founded or false opinion'.[1] In a footnote commenting on *śruti* (*op. cit.*, p. 246, fn. 2) he says that 'it is true that for Buddhaghosa followed in this respect by European scholars (Kern, Manual of Buddhism, p. 2, quoted by Poussin, Opinions, p. 35) *evam mayā śrutam* means, sammukhā paṭiggahītaṃ (DA. I.31)'. But this interpretation he says is 'a later one' (*loc. cit.*). This view is surprising. It goes against everything that we know from and about the Pāli Canon. In the first place there is no reason to doubt the traditional explanation that 'evam me sutam' means 'thus have I heard', even if we doubt the rest of the tradition that they were the words of Ānanda. This phrase introduces a Sutta, which has been reported by someone who had learnt it in an oral tradition. It preserves the same non-dogmatic attitude recommended in the Caṅkī Sutta that when someone has heard something from a tradition (anussavo) he preserves the truth, if instead of dogmatically claiming that it was the case he says, 'this is what I have heard from the tradition' (*evam me* anussavo, M. I.171; *v. supra*, 278). If the Buddha himself introduced his statements with the words, 'evam me sutaṃ', we would have reason to believe that he was giving expression to something that he received from a human or divine source. Not only does he not say anything of this sort but claims on the contrary the following: 'I do not say this having heard it from another recluse or brahmin, but what I myself have seen and experienced, that I speak' (taṃ kho pana ahaṃ . . . nāññassa samaṇassa va brāhmaṇassa va *sutvā vadāmi*, api ca yad eva me sāmaṃ ñātaṃ sāmaṃ diṭṭhaṃ sāmaṃ viditaṃ—tam evāhaṃ vadāmī ti, It. 59, 60, 74; M. III.186). We see here the very opposite of what Przyluski was suggesting, namely the superior valuation of *diṭṭham* (what is seen) over *sutaṃ* (what is heard) (cp. *supra*. 69). Przyluski has also apparently confused diṭṭham with diṭṭhi (*v. infra*, 742).

(651) What attitude, then, was expected towards the statements of the Buddha? Is it the same as the attitude recommended towards all

[1] J. Przyluski, 'Dārṣṭāntika, Sautrāntika and Sarvāstivādin' in IHQ., Vol. 16, p. 246.

teachings in the Kālāma Sutta or is it different? There seems to be a considerable divergence of opinion among scholars on this subject. It relates to the problem of the rôle of saddhā (belief, faith) in Early Buddhism and scholars are divided in their opinions. As we have already said, Poussin sees in Buddhism 'a faith and creed' (*v. supra*, 644) and in its pretence to be a creed in which critical inquiry is held out as the one key to the comprehension of knowledge (*v. supra*, 543), he holds that the attitude of Buddhism is conflicting, if not self-contradictory. Faith says Poussin is 'the root of the correct view' (*loc. cit.*) in Buddhism. He quotes the statement 'the Law saves the believer and destroys the unbeliever' (*op. cit.*, p. 35) and even says 'Buddha's word is to be believed without inquiry' (*loc. cit.*). Keith is more or less of the same view. He says that faith in Buddhism is an 'indispensable preliminary' (*op. cit.*, p. 34) and it 'is the root of correct knowledge' (*loc. cit.*) and 'the means by which a man may ... cross to the safety of Nirvāna' (*op. cit.*, p. 35) and adds that 'the teaching of the Buddha saves him who has faith but destroys the faithless' (*loc. cit.*). He says, however, that 'there is some place for the operations of reason' (*loc. cit.*) and unlike Poussin (who thought that the critical outlook contradicted the emphasis on faith) believes that 'happily enough (there) is a bridge built between the final authority of the Buddha and the demand of the individual for respect to his intellectual independence' (*loc. cit.*), since 'Buddha's teaching ... appears as the occasion but not the cause of the knowledge' (*loc. cit.*) and the individual 'has another mode of testing the value of the Buddha's teaching' (*loc. cit.*) namely by personal verification. Both Poussin and Keith had based their observations on the contents of both the Pāli tradition and the BHS. works, but Mrs Rhys Davids too, whose observations are based almost solely on a study of the Pāli Canon stresses the importance of faith in Buddhism: 'Years of study in Buddhism has shown me that for it faith is no less important than it is for all religions worthy of the name.'[1]

(652) On the other hand, Dr Gyomroi-Ludowyk on the basis of a study of the Pāli Nikāyas has observed that 'wherever the word *saddhā* is met with in the early Pāli texts a noteworthy difference between its importance and that of faith in Christianity will be observed'.[2] According to her, ' "Faith" in the sense of trust, confidence

[1] *Wayfarers' Words*, Vol. III, p. 1124.

[2] 'The Valuation of Saddhā in the Early Buddhist Texts' in UCR., Vol. 5, p. 37.

in the teacher can be easily understood as an emotion insufficient for salvation but extremely important on the way to it' (*op. cit.*, p. 35) and goes on to say that 'that does not mean that he (i.e. the Buddha) expects them to accept everything without contradiction, he certainly does not prohibit criticism and judgment . . . Absolute *a priori* faith is never demanded' (*op. cit.*, p. 36). She tries to show that knowledge is valued above faith in this culture. It is not by chance that the ten powers of a Buddha (M. I.69, 70) are all intellectual and these ten powers are only the 'normal' human intellect developed (*op. cit.*, p. 37). The Buddha praises disciples not for their faith but for their wisdom (S. I.191). Sāriputta is lauded for his wisdom (A. I.23) while in the case of Vakkali, 'the highest of those who had faith' (A. I.24), it is requested that he should not be attached to his person but should concentrate on the dhamma (S. III.119 ff.). His excessive faith was a hindrance to salvation.[1] Faith likewise is not a characteristic of an Arahant.[2] It has no place in the Noble Eight-fold Path: 'if *saddhā* had been regarded as essential to the attaining of Nibbāna, it certainly would have found its place in the Noble Eight-fold Path' (*loc. cit.*). Lastly she points out that the person who is described as a 'saddhā-vimutta' which is rendered in the PTS. Dictionary (*s.v.*) as 'emancipated by faith' and whom Barua[3] classifies as an 'Arhat' is not emancipated at all while 'in the lowest rank is the Saddhānusāri, who develops the five faculties essential to *mukti* by way of blind faith in and through the law of the Buddha' (*loc. cit.*). She finds the translation of saddhā as 'faith' as strictly misleading and says: 'if in using the word "faith" for saddhā in translating, one restricts oneself to its meaning of "confidence, trust, belief" no objection can be raised to it',[4] though she also observes that 'as time went on the *bhakti* cult paved the way for a new and higher valuation of saddhā' (*op. cit.*, p. 48).

(653) When we approach the problem historically in the light of the evidence from the Pāli Canon, we are more inclined to agree with the theory of Dr Gyomroi-Ludowyk than that of Poussin and Keith. But it is necessary to distinguish at least two strata in the evaluation of saddhā within the Pāli Canon. In what was probably the earlier stratum the acceptance of saddhā was strictly consonant with the spirit of the Kālāma Sutta (*v.* Ch. IV and V) whereas in the next

[1] *Op. cit.*, p. 40. [2] *v.* S. III.82, 161, S. V.194, 205, 433; but *v.* S. V.202.
[3] 'Faith in Buddhism' in *Buddhist Studies*, ed. B. C. Law, Calcutta, 1931, pp. 345 ff. [4] *Op. cit.*, p. 49.

stratum it is not, although attempts are made to bring it in harmony with its outlook.

(654) Poussin's and Keith's treatment of the subject suffer from treating many different strata together. It is also necessary to point out a mistranslation on the part of both when the former says that 'the Law saves the believer and destroys the unbeliever' (*v. supra*, 651) and the latter that 'the teaching of the Buddha saves him who has faith but destroys the faithless' (*v. supra*, 651). The original reads as follows: '... sabbadevamanussānaṃ imasmiṃ dhamme *assaddhiyaṃ* vināseti, saddhāsampadaṃ uppādeti. Ten'etaṃ vuccati:

vināsayati assaddhaṃ saddhaṃ vaḍḍheti sāsane
evam me sutaṃ icc'evaṃ vadaṃ Gotamasāvako'

DA. I.31.

Both Poussin and Keith take 'saddhaṃ' in this stanza to denote the person, viz. 'the believer', 'him who has faith' and 'assaddhaṃ' to mean 'the unbeliever, the faithless' but the prose introduction and the context as a whole shows that this is incorrect. Assaddhiyaṃ always stands for 'disbelief' (*s.v.* PTS. Dictionary) and never for the 'disbeliever' (e.g. *assaddiyaṃ* kho pana Tathāgatappavedite dhammavinaye parihānam etaṃ, i.e. *lack of faith* is a sign of decline in the religion preached by the Buddha, A. V.158). Similarly it is obvious that 'saddhā-sampadaṃ' (the accusative of saddhā-sampadā) cannot mean 'the person who has the wealth of faith' but just 'the wealth of faith'. We may translate the prose and in its light the stanza as follows: 'It destroys the lack of faith of all gods and men in this doctrine and it generates the wealth of faith. Therefore has it been said: "It destroys lack of faith and promotes faith in the religion—in this vein have I heard a disciple of Gotama speaking".' This verse, therefore, does not offer a threat of destruction to those who would not believe, as is suggested by the inaccurate renderings of both Poussin and Keith.

(655) The usage of saddhā (faith, belief) in the Pāli Canon is such that the meanings of bhatti- (devotion = Skr. bhakti), pema- (filial affection) and pasāda- (mental appreciation) overlap with it, e.g. idha ... ekacco puggalo ittara*saddho* hoti, ittara*bhattī* ittara*pemo* ittara*pasādo*, i.e. here a person has very little faith, very little devotion, very little affection and very little appreciation, A. III.165. The Comy. to the Puggalapaññatti defines these uses as follows: 'Faith is devotion in the sense of continuous adoration. Affection is classifiable as the

affection of faith and filial affection. But appreciation and faith are identical' (punappunaṃ bhajanavasena saddhā va bhatti. Pemaṃ saddhā-pemaṃ gehasitapemaṃ ti vattati. Pasādo saddhā pasādo vā, 248). According to this appraisal saddhā is closest in meaning to pasāda—with which it is identified and we find this exemplified in the usages in the Nikāyas. The Jñānaprasthāna (1.19) defines śraddhā as 'cetasaḥ praśādaḥ'[1] (appreciation of mind) and we find 'cetaso pasāda-' in the Nikāyas where we can expect saddhā: yato yato imassa dhammapariyāyassa *paññāya* atthaṃ upaparikkheyya labheth' eva attamanataṃ labhetha *cetaso pasādaṃ*, i.e. inasmuch as he examines with his intellect the meaning of this doctrinal passage he obtains satisfaction and a mental appreciation (of it), M. I.114. We note here that cetaso pasāda- is 'mental appreciation' or the 'intellectual joy' resulting from intelligent study and a clarification of one's thoughts.[2] Lack of pasāda- is likewise correlated with lack of understanding, e.g. saddhammaṃ avijānato pariplavapasādassa paññā na paripūrati, i.e. the wisdom of a person who does not understand the good doctrine and whose pasāda- is fickle does not increase, Dh. 38. Similarly, *aveccappasāda-* in the Buddha, his Doctrine and his Order (Buddhe ... dhamme ... saṅghe aveccappasādena samannāgato hoti, M. I.37) seems to mean 'faith based on understanding' since avecca- seems to mean 'having understood', e.g. yo ariyasaccāni avecca passati, i.e. he who having understood sees the noble truths, Sn. 229. Here the Comy. has paññāya ajjhogāhetva, 'having comprehended with one's intelligence'. The Comy., however, has 'acala-' (unshaken) for the same word at D. I.217, but this is probably a secondary meaning since 'faith born of understandin^g' (aveccappasāda-) is similar to 'rational faith' (ākāravatī saddhā, M. I.320) which is said to be 'rooted, established, fixed and irremovable' (mūlajātā patiṭṭhitā ... daḷhā asaṃhāriyā, *loc. cit.*). We have to presume that avecca- (*s.v.* PTS. Dictionary) is formed from ava + present participle from √i, 'to go', meaning 'understand' (cp. avagata- from ava + √gam, 'to go' = understood, *s.v.* PTS. Dictionary). It is said that failure to investigate and understand results in lack of pasāda-, e.g. ananuvicca apariyogāhetvā pasādanīye ṭhāne appasādam upadaṃseti, i.e. one shows lack of faith in a situation in which one ought to have faith as a result of not

[1] *v.* Poussin, L'Abhidharmakośa, II, p. 106, fn. 3; Poussin translates 'cetaso praśādaḥ' as 'la clarification de la pensee' (*op. cit.*, II, p. 156).

[2] Poussin translates 'cetaso praśādaḥ' as 'la clarification de la pensee' (*op. cit.*, II, p. 156).

investigating and understanding.[1] Dr Gyomroi-Ludowyk in a 'Note on the Interpretation of Pasīdati'[2] has shown that pasāda- is different from 'faith' as understood in Western religions, where it means 'to believe in something which cannot be explained' culminating in the attitude of *credo quia absurdum*. She concludes that 'we can render pasīdati most appropriately as a mental attitude which unites deep feeling, intellectual appreciation and satisfaction, clarification of thought and attraction towards the teacher' (*op. cit.*, p. 82).

(656) It is necessary to observe that there could be many aspects to the study of the concept of faith in Buddhism. Faith has an affective, conative and a cognitive aspect. When Dutt says that saddhā 'carries two distinct meanings (1) one is faith (pasāda) producing pīti- (serene pleasure), and (2) the other is self-confidence producing viriya (energy)',[3] he is speaking of the affective and the conative aspects of saddhā respectively and not of two different uses of the word altogether. But when he says that (1) is an antidote to vicikicchā (doubt) and moha (delusion) he is confusing the affective with the cognitive aspect of faith as 'belief'. We shall be mainly concerned with this last aspect since it is the only aspect which has an epistemological significance.

(657) But the post-Canonical literature from the Milindapañha onwards speaks mainly about the first two aspects of faith and Dutt seems to have been led largely by the accounts they give. Thus, both in the Milindapañha (34) and the Atthasālini (section 304), saddhā is said to have the characteristics of appreciation (sampasādana-lakkhaṇa) and endeavour (sampakkhandana-lakkhaṇa). The first (sampasādana-lakkhaṇa-) represents the affective characteristic of faith. It corresponds to what was denoted by pasāda- in the Nikāyas. Now pema- (filial affection) and bhatti- (devotion) are also used synonymously with saddhā (in its affective aspect) in the Nikāyas, but while the affective trait of pasāda- was highly valued (*v. supra*, 655), pema- is less so and bhatti- hardly occurs. In its only use which approximates to the sense of saddhā (apart from the instance quoted, *v. supra*, 655), bhatti- denotes the 'allegiance' or 'devotion' which an evil person has towards another evil person (asappuriso asappurisa*bhatti* hoti, M. III.21) or a good person may have towards another good person (M. III.23).

[1] A. III.139; cp. purimena kathasallāpena ahu pasādamattā sā pi me etarahi antarahitā, i.e. the little faith that resulted from the previous conversation has now disappeared, M. I.487.
[2] UCR., Vol. 1, pp. 74–82.
[3] N. Dutt, 'Place of Faith in Buddhism' in IHQ., Vol. 16, p. 639.

There is no usage even remotely suggesting the impact of a bhakti cult.[1] Pema- is used synonymously with saddhā (M. I.142, 444, 479) and even pasāda- (niviṭṭhasaddho niviṭṭha*pemo* ... abhi*ppasanno*, A. III.326) and is considered to have limited value. Those 'who have mere faith and mere affection for the Buddha are destined to heaven' (yesaṃ mayi saddhāmattam pemamattaṃ, sabbe te saggaparāyaṇā, M. I.142). But it is a condition that can lapse (cp. ... yam pi'ssa taṃ saddhāmattakaṃ pemamattakaṃ tamhā pi parihāyi, i.e. he would decline from that state of mere faith or affection, M. I.444) and it is a sentiment that can generate undesirable emotions. Hatred can arise out of affection for a person (pemā doso jāyate, A. II.213); if a person whom one likes and holds dear is addressed in undesirable and foul language by another it arouses hatred towards him (yo kho myāyam puggalo iṭṭho kanto manāpo, tam pare aniṭṭhena akantena amanāpena samudācaranti ti so tesu dosaṃ janeti, *loc. cit.*). Attachment to a person is said to have five drawbacks (pañc'ime ... ādinavā puggalappasāde, A. III.270). As such, it is a hindrance to salvation in this life and even attachment to the Buddha is no exception in this respect (*v. supra*, 652).

(658) The Nettippakaraṇa draws attention to the cognitive aspect of saddhā, when it says *inter alia* that 'faith has the characteristic of trust and the proximate state of belief (inclination)' (okappana-lakkhaṇā saddhā adhimutti-paccupaṭṭhānā, 28). This was the sense which Dr Gyomroi-Ludowyk proposed for saddhā (*v. supra*, 652) and we find that this sense is supported by even the pre-Buddhistic use of the term. By a comparative study of the use of śraddhā and bhakti in the Vedic literature, Miss Das Gupta has shown that 'śraddhā in the Vedic texts, at least in the Vedic Saṃhitās must have conveyed a sense which was never akin to the mood of *bhakti* as a form of loving devotion to a personal deity but simply implied *confidence, trust or belief based on a knowledge of truth* (italics mine) ... and even in later literature śraddhā is not always used synonymously with *bhakti* ... The term *bhakti* in the technical religious sense is nowhere employed in the Vedic Saṃhitas'.[2] This sense of 'confidence, trust and belief' is quite prominent in certain contexts of the use of the term in the Canon. It is

[1] On the concept of *bhakti* in Indian thought, *v.* J. McKenzie, *Hindu Ethics*, Oxford University Press, 1922, Ch. V and pp. 124, 130 f., 136, 159 f.; cp. E. W. Hopkins, *Ethics of India*, New Haven, 1924, Ch. VII and pp. 200, 204, 214.

[2] Miss M. Das Gupta, 'Śraddhā and Bhakti in the Vedic Literature', in IHQ., Vol. 6, p. 322.

said of a person who comes to learn the art of mounting an elephant and using the elephant-driver's hook that if he lacks *saddhā* he would not be able to acquire that which can be acquired by *saddhā*;[1] here saddhā denotes the 'confidence, trust and belief' in the instructions of the teacher.

(659) The object of saddhā in the Nikāyas is most frequently the Buddha. The favourite phrase is 'having heard his doctrine he acquired faith in the Tathāgata' (taṃ dhammaṃ sutvā Tathāgate saddhaṃ paṭilabhati, M. I.179, 267, 344; M. III.33). If saddhā means 'belief', 'acquiring faith in the Buddha' is equivalent to saying 'believing in the Buddha' and what is meant by believing in the Buddha is that one believes that what the Buddha says is true. As Woozley points out, 'certainly we do talk of believing in a person but there we mean that we believe that what he says is true'.[2] The verb, pasīdati, 'to have faith in, appreciate' also has the person of the Buddha as the object (e.g. Satthari pasīdiṃ, M. I.320) but pasāda- in the compound aveccappasāda- (*v. supra,* 655) frequently has the Buddha, his teaching (Dhamma) and his Order (Saṅgha) as the objects.[3] Here 'faith' or belief in the Dhamma means the statements that constitute the Dhamma or the teachings of the Buddha. Likewise, believing in the Saṅgha implies believing in the truth of the utterances of the Saṅgha; since these were more or less derived from the Buddha,[4] it again ultimately implies a belief in the statements of the Buddha.

(660) It would appear from all this that the expected attitude towards the statements of the Buddha was one of belief rather than of neutralism or disbelief and this appears *prima facie* to go against the injunctions of the Kālāma Sutta, which says that one should not accept the truth of propositions on authoritative grounds (*v. supra,* 259).

(661) But a careful study of what is in fact said in the Kālāma Sutta with the concept of saddhā as it occurs in probably the earliest stratum of the Canon presents a very different picture. It tends to show, as we shall see in the sequel, that the attitude to authority recommended by the Buddha is not contradictory to and is in fact compatible with the attitude recommended by the Buddha towards his own statements.

[1] M. II.94. [2] *The Theory of Knowledge,* p. 26.
[3] M. I.37, II.51; A. I.222, II.56, III.212, 332, 451, IV.406, V.183.
[4] Cp. Bhagavammūlakā no . . . dhammā, i.e. our doctrines originate with the Exalted One, A. IV.158, 351.

(662) In order to see this it is imperative that we have a clear picture of what the sermons to Kālāma and Bhaddāli do and do not state. A careful scrutiny of the material we studied in Ch. IV would show that these sermons *do* state that no statements should be accepted on authority because it is possible that such statements may turn out to be either true or false (*v. supra*, 283, 308). They *do not* state that such statements should be rejected altogether, nor do they state that we should not test the opinions of others but should rely entirely on our own wits for the discovery of truth. In fact, in asserting that one should not accept *p* on authority because *p* may be true or false, it is also implied that one should not reject *p*, because *p* may be true. This is exemplified in the attitude of the disciple as represented in the Nikāyas, which should be one of neither acceptance nor rejection, when one is in doubt as to the truth of a statement. Where 'a fellow-monk claims the highest knowledge, one should neither accept what he says nor reject it but without acceptance or rejection should question him'[1] in order to test the veracity of his statement. It appears to be a common attitude at this time for we find a certain householder (aññataro gahapati) adopting it towards a statement of the Buddha (M. II.106) and the wandering ascetic Potaliputta having this same attitude towards a statement of the monk Samiddhi (M. III.207). The passage addressed to Kālāma (*v. supra*, 251, 259) ends on the note that one should reject (pajaheyyātha, A. II.191) opinions as false only after one has tested them in the light of one's own experience (attanā va jāneyyātha, *loc. cit.*) taking into account the views of the wise (cp. viññūgarahitā vā viññūpasatthā vā, *loc. cit.*). This means that statements claiming to be true on authority should be rejected as false only after one has discovered their falsity after personally verifying them. It does not rule out the possibility but on the contrary seems to imply that those statements claiming to be true should be tested before deciding to accept or reject them.

(663) This is just what the Buddha seems to demand from his hearers regarding his own statements. He does not want his own statements accepted on his authority nor rejected but seems to demand that they be tested and accepted if they are found to be true and presumably rejected if they are found to be false. This attitude is well-expressed in

[1] Idha . . . bhikkhu aññaṃ byākaroti . . . tassa bhikkhuno bhāsitaṃ n'eva abhinanditabbaṃ na paṭikkositabbaṃ anabhinanditvā appaṭikkositvā pañho pucchitabbo, M. III.29.

a late verse, which appears in the Tattvasaṃgraha (3588) and the Tibetan version of the Jñānasamuccayasāra.[1] It reads as follows: 'Just as wise men (test a claim to be gold) by burning, cutting and rubbing (on a touchstone), my statements, O monks, should be accepted after examination and not out of respect for me' (tapāc chedāc ca nikaṣāt suvarṇam iva paṇḍitaiḥ, parīkṣya bhikṣavo grāhyam madvaco na tu gauravāt). This verse is not found in the Nikāyas but it reflects the attitude of the Buddha as often represented in the Nikāyas. The Buddha is anxious to see that his statements are not accepted out of respect for his authority as the teacher—the very thing that he condemns in the Kālāma Sutta. On one occasion he asks, 'would you, O monks, knowing and seeing thus say, "our teacher is respected, we say so out of respect for our teacher" ' (Api nu tumhe, bhikkhave, evaṃ jānantā evam passantā evaṃ vadeyyātha: satthā no garu, satthugāravena ca mayaṃ vademā ti M. I.264). The monks submit that it is not so.

(664) Thus if we interpret the Kālāma Sutta as saying that one should not accept the statements of anyone on authority nor even seriously consider the views of others in order to test their veracity but rely entirely on one's own experiences in the quest and discovery of truth, then this would be contradictory to the concept of saddhā in the Pāli Nikāyas. But if, on the other hand, we interpret the Kālāma Sutta as saying that while we should not accept the statements of anyone as true on the grounds of authority, we should test the consequences of statements in the light of our own knowledge and experience in order to verify whether they are true or false, it would be an attitude which is compatible with saddhā as understood in at least one stratum of Pāli Canonical thought. As we have shown above (*v. supra*, 662, 663) we have reason to believe that this latter interpretation is the correct one.

(665) According to this interpretation we may provisionally accept a propostion for the purposes of verifying its truth so long as we do not commit ourselves to the view or claim that the proposition is true prior to verification. We find the stages of this process of verification stated in the Caṅkī Sutta. The first is that of the provisional acceptance of a proposition or doctrine for the purposes of verification. It is called the stage of 'safeguarding the truth' (saccānurakkhaṇā, M. II.171), which consists in a person who believes in *p*, safeguarding

[1] For the reference see the detailed note of V. Bhattacharya, *The Basic Conception of Buddhism*, Calcutta, 1934, p. 11, fn. 9.

the truth by professing that this is his belief without dogmatically coming to the conclusion that it is true (*v. supra*, 278). The actual provisional accèptance is made only after ensuring the honesty, unbiased nature and intelligence of the person from whom such a statement is accepted. It is said that he first 'examines the person in respect of three things' (tam enaṃ ... tīsu dhammesu samannesati, *loc. cit.*). He examines the person to make sure that 'his mind is not obsessed with those selfish motives that may make him say that one knows or sees when one does not, or make him convert others to his view so that it would for long work for their discomfort and woe'.[1] He likewise examines him to see whether 'his mind is obsessed with malevolent motives' (dosanīyehi dhammehi pariyạdinnacitto, M. I.172) or 'ignorance' (mohanīyehi dhammehi, *loc. cit.*). It is only after he has satisfied himself in this way that he believes in or professes faith in what he says (atha tamhi saddhaṃ niveseti, M. I.173).

(666) In the Vīmaṃsaka Sutta, the test is more stringent and it is only after partial but personal verification of the truth of a statement that there is a mention of faith or belief in the statement. Here it is said that 'an enquiring monk, who can read the thoughts of another, should examine the Tathāgata to determine whether he is enlightened or not' (vīmaṃsakena bhikkhunā parassa cetopariyāyam ājānantena Tathāgate samannesanā kātabba, sammāsambuddho vā no vā iti viññāṇāyā ti, M. I.317). It is said that 'the Tathāgata is to be examined in respect of two things, namely of what can be learned by observation and by hearing about him' (dvīsu dhammesu Tathāgato samannesitabbo cakkhusotaviññeyyesu dhammesu, M. I.318). One should observe that he does not have nor is reputed to have morally corrupt (saṅkiliṭṭhā) or mixed[2] (vītimissā) modes of conduct but only virtuous conduct.[3] One should ensure that this is so for a long period and not merely for a short term. We may see from this that doubt about the claims of the Tathāgata is not condemned, but in fact plays a central rôle in the process of inquiry which is considered to be essential,

[1] ... samannesati ...: atthi nu kho imassa āyasmato tathārupā lobhanīyā dhammā yathārūpehi lobhanīyehi dhammehi pariyādinnacitto ajānaṃ vā vadeyya jānāmī ti apassaṃ vā vadeyya passāmī ti, paraṃ vā tathattāya samādapeyya yaṃ paresaṃ assa dīgharattaṃ ahitāya dukkhāyā ti, M. I.172.

[2] I.e. both corrupt and pure.

[3] Ye saṅkiliṭṭhā ... vitimissā cakkhusotaviññeyyā dhammā na te Tathāgatassa samvijjanti ... ye vodātā cakkhusotaviññeyyā dhammā samvijjanti te Tathāgatassā ti, M. I.318.

prior to and for the generation of belief (or faith). Elsewhere, doubting the teacher, the doctrine, the order, the training and being angry with one's co-religionists (satthari ... dhamme ... saṅghe ... sikkhāya kaṅkhati ... sabrahmacārīsu kupito hoti anattamano ..., M. I.101) are considered 'five obstacles or hindrances (to moral and spiritual progress) of the mind' (pañca cetokhilā ... cetaso vinibandhā, *loc. cit.*). This kind of doubt (vicikicchā) is regarded as one of the five impediments (pañcanīvaraṇā, M. I.269, 270) and it is said that one should 'clear the mind of this doubt, becoming certain of moral values' (akathaṃkathī kusalesu dhammesu vicikicchāya cittaṃ parisodheti, *loc. cit.*) but this doubt is apparently to be removed not by blind belief but by the conviction that dawns from a critical study and evaluation. After the above preliminary examination of the Tathāgata it is said that one would feel that it was worth listening to his teachings (evaṃvādiṃ ... satthāraṃ arahati sāvako upasaṅkamituṃ dhammasavanāya, M. I.319). After that 'he realizes with his own higher knowledge some of those doctrines and concludes that (they are true) and then reposes faith in the teacher, believing that the Exalted One was enlightened, his doctrine well-taught and the Order of good conduct' (tasmiṃ dhamme abhiññāya idh'ekaccaṃ dhammaṃ dhammesu niṭṭhaṃ agamaṃ, satthari pasīdiṃ: sammāsambuddho bhagavā, svākkhāto bhagavatā dhammo supaṭipanno saṅgho ti, M. I.320). It is said that 'the faith (saddhā) of him, which is thus fixed, rooted and established on these reasons, grounds and features is said to be a *rational faith* (ākāravatī saddhā), rooted in insight, firm and irremovable by recluse or brahmin, a god, Māra or Brahmā or anyone in the world' (yassa kassa ci ... imehi ākārehi imehi padehi imehi byañjanehi ... saddhā niviṭṭhā hoti mūlajātā patiṭṭhitā, ayaṃ vuccati ... *ākāravatī saddhā* dassanamūlikā daḷhā asaṃhāriyā samaṇena vā brāhmaṇena vā devena vā Mārena vā Brahmunā vā kenaci vā lokasmiṃ, *loc. cit.*). This rational faith which is a product of critical examination and partial verification is apparently contrasted with the '*baseless faith*' (*amūlikā saddhā*, M. II.170) which the brahmins have towards the Vedas and which the Buddha shows, does not bear critical examination (*v. supra*, 263). It is strange that no scholar has drawn our attention to this important distinction.

(667) We have so far come across saddhā (faith, belief) being used for different stages and types of acceptance of a proposition or doctrine. The first was that of accepting for the purpose of testing, the stage in

N*

which one 'safeguards the truth' (saccānurakkhaṇā, *v. supra*, 665). The stage in which one reposes faith in a person after realizing that he was honest, unbiased and intelligent (*v. supra*, 665) is perhaps the second. The next stage is the one in which there was a partial and personal verification of the doctrine (*v. supra*, 666) and it is at this stage that one is said to have a 'rational faith'. The word 'faith' here may seem less preferable than belief though we have used it to translate the word saddhā.

(668) It is this last stage that is greatly valued in Buddhism. The person who has developed this 'rational faith' seems to be identical with the person who is described as being 'emancipated by faith' (saddhāvimutto, M. I.478), who as Dr Gyomroi-Ludowyk has shown (*v. supra*, 652) is not emancipated at all since 'he has need of earnestness' (appamādena karaṇīyam, *loc. cit.*). This may be seen from the identity of the language used to describe the saddhā-vimutta with that of ākāravatī saddhā, viz. Tathāgate c'assa saddhā niviṭṭhā hoti mūlajātā patiṭṭhitā (M. I.478 = M. I.320).

(669) The concept of aveccappasāda- or 'faith resulting from understanding' (*v. supra*, 655) seems to be very close to if not identical with the above conception of ākāravatī saddhā. Dutt has, however, offered a different theory on this subject. In a paper whose object is 'to show how far saddhā in the former sense (i.e. as pasāda-) came to be regarded as the means for the attainment of Nibbāna'[1] he says that 'in a few places in the Nikāyas, saddhā is recognized as the third path[2] for the attainment of Nibbāna in spite of the fact that it does not go well with the rationalistic principles of which the Buddhists are the avowed champions. But this path which we may call the aveccappasāda- path or process is particularly important for the laity whose interest is almost ignored at the early stage of the religion and so, it is not improbable, that the third path came to be recognized only at a later date but in any case before the Pāli Canon was closed' (*op. cit.*, p. 640). In a later paper to this same journal he refers to this very same theory.[3] His *locus classicus* for the 'aveccappasāda- process' of salvation as he calls it, is the Vatthūpama Sutta.[4] But an analysis of the Vatthūpama Sutta hardly supports Dutt's contention. In the first place the

[1] 'Place of Faith in Buddhism' in IHQ., Vol. 16, p. 640.

[2] The other two paths mentioned are (1) the sīla-citta-paññā process, and (2) the sati-paṭṭhana process—a very arbitrary division.

[3] 'Popular Buddhism' in IHQ., Vol. 21, pp. 251–6.

[4] *v.* IHQ., Vol. 16, p. 644; cp. IHQ., Vol. 21, p. 252.

Sutta is addressed to monks (bhikkhave, M. I.36 ff.) and not to laymen. Secondly, the first mention of aveccappasāda- is after a detailed list of 'the defilements of the mind' (cittassa upakkilesā, M. I.36) are mentioned and all of them are said to be 'eliminated' (pahīno, M. I.37) by the monk. It is at this stage that the monk is said to 'be endowed with faith based on understanding in the Buddha', etc. (so Buddhe aveccappasādena samannāgato hoti, *loc. cit.*). But in eliminating the defilements of the mind, the monk has surely gone a long way in verifying the statements of the Buddha and it is therefore not surprising that he should at this stage have developed 'a faith based on understanding' (aveccappasāda-). This 'faith' is *inter alia* a belief that 'the doctrine (when put into practice) gives results in this life itself . . . and is to be personally verified by the wise' (dhammo sandiṭṭhiko . . . paccattaṃ veditabbo viññūhī ti, *loc. cit.*). Thirdly, the Sutta nowhere suggests that this faith is sufficient for salvation. Dutt's point is that the jhānic process of salvation is not mentioned here. But there seems to be an indirect reference even to this when it summarizes the stages in the sequence, viz. pamuditassa pīti jāyati pītimanassa kāyo passambhati passaddhakāyo sukhaṃ vedeti sukhino cittaṃ samādhiyati, i.e. to him who is glad, joy arises and the body of him who experiences joy becomes calm; with body becalmed he experiences happiness and with happiness his mind is concentrated. Dutt says that this 'skips over the processes of the third and fourth jhāna' (*op. cit.*, p. 645) but it is in the nature of all summaries to skip over details. Lastly, the Sutta states that the 'intoxicants' (āsavā) cease in the case of 'one who thus knows and sees' (evaṃ jānato evaṃ passato, M. I.38), unmistakably implying that it is knowledge and not faith which finally helps in salvation. Dutt adds that 'another remarkable feature in course of this training is that there is no insistence on the observation of the Pātimokkha rules and as such can be followed by a person who has not embraced the austere life of a Buddhist monk. This latitude is particularly noticeable in the remark that a person following this course of life is free to take luxurious food as that will not be a hindrance to his spiritual progress' (*op. cit.*, p. 646). This is absurd. The Sutta is clearly addressed to the monks and although there is no explicit reference to the Pātimokkha rules as such, one has surely to presume that it was by the strict observance of this disciplinary and moral code that these monks got rid of their defilements. Besides, nowhere in the Vinaya is it said that the monk should not eat the luxurious food that he may find in the course of his alms. There is therefore hardly any basis for Dutt's theory.

(670) The faith of the saddhānusāri (the one who is led by faith), who is reckoned the last of those who have some spiritual attainment (M. I.439) is not of the same order as that of the saddhā-vimutta (*v. supra*, 668) and could not be considered to have reached the stage of 'rational faith' (ākāravatī saddhā, *v. supra*, 666). This is evident from the description which says that 'he has a mere faith or affection for the Tathāgata' (Tathāgate c'assa saddhāmattaṃ hoti pemamattaṃ, M. I.479). This is a condition which can lapse (*v. supra*, 652); here the acceptance is more out of affection (pema), which is considered a hindrance rather than a help to salvation (*v. supra*, 657) than out of a genuine desire for knowledge.

(671) Now faith or belief in the above sense is only considered a first step towards understanding. It is not even a necessary step for all and this is probably the reason why it is not included in the noble eight-fold path. It is said that 'there are two sources for the arising of the right view of life, viz. the propaganda of others and critical reflection' (dve . . . paccayā sammādiṭṭhiyā uppādāya: parato ca ghoso yoniso ca manasikāro, M. I.294). The acceptance of the right view on the basis of the propaganda of others, presumably of the Buddha and his disciples, is an acceptance out of saddhā, but the fact that we may adopt it as a result of one's own independent thinking shows that saddhā is not necessary at least for the few. There is no doubt however that according to the texts the majority need it.

(672) In the lists of virtues or requirements for salvation, in which saddhā occurs, we find that it is always mentioned as the first member, while understanding (paññā) is almost always the last, viz.

1. *saddhā*, sīla-, suta-, cāga-, *paññā*, A. II.66, III.6, 44, 181, IV.270, 271, 284, 288, M. I.465, II.180, III.99.
2. *saddhā*, viriya-, sati-, samādhi, *paññā*, M. I.164, III.99.
3. *saddhā*, sīla-, cāga-, *paññā*, paṭibhāna-, A. V.96.
4. *saddho*, appābādha-, asaṭha-, āraddhaviriya-, *paññavā*, M. II.128.
5. *saddho*, hirimā, ottāpi-, akodhano, *paññavā*, S. IV.243.
6. *saddha*-, hiri-, ottāpi-, viriya-, *pañña*-, A. III.4, 9, 352, V.123.
7. *saddho*, araddhaviriya-, upaṭṭhitasati-, samāhito, *paññavā*, A. V.329, 333, 335.
8. *saddho*, hiri-, ottāpi, bahussuta-, āraddhaviriya-, upaṭṭhitasati-, *paññavā*, M. III.23, A. II.218, A. IV.23, 38.

9. *saddho*, sīlavā, bahussuta paṭisallīna, āraddhaviriya-, satimā, *paññavā*, A. IV.85.
10. *saddho*, sīla-, bahussuta-, suvaca-, kalyānamitta-, āraddhaviriya-, upaṭṭhita-sati-, santuṭṭha-, appiccha-, sammādiṭṭhika-, A. V.153, 154.

This sequence cannot entirely be accidental and probably reflects the fact that while saddhā or belief was a preliminary requirement, it finally led to understanding (paññā) which was reckoned to be of the greatest value. Nāgārjuna, although he was writing centuries later, sums up beautifully the relationship between the two in his Ratnāvalī:

> śraddhatvād bhajate dharmaṃ prajñatvād vetti tattvataḥ
> prajñā pradhānaṃ tv anayoḥ śraddhā pūrvāṅgamāsya tu[1]

i.e. one associates with the doctrine out of faith but one knows truly out of understanding; understanding is the chief of the two, although faith precedes. The stages from belief up to the first realization of the truth (saccānubodha-) are outlined in the Caṅkī Sutta (*v. supra*, 665, 666) as follows: 'With faith arisen, he approaches and associates with (the teacher); thus associating he gives ear, giving ear he listens to the doctrine, listening to the doctrine he bears it in mind; he then examines the meaning of the doctrines he has borne in mind, thus examining the meaning he approves of it, approving of it the desire (to try it out) arises; with desire arisen he exerts himself, having exerted himself he considers it; having considered, he puts forth effort; putting forth effort, he himself experiences the highest truth and sees it having penetrated it with his understanding'.[2] This first glimpse of the truth is followed by the stage of 'the attainment of the truth (*saccānupatti*), which results from the evoking of, culture and development of those mental states' (tesaṃ yeva ... dhammānaṃ āsevanā bhāvanā bahulīkammaṃ saccānupatti hoti, M. II.174). Thus *belief* (saddhā) is regarded only as a first step towards knowledge, with which it is replaced. It is not valuable in itself and bears no comparison with the final knowledge, which results from the personal verification

[1] Ed. G. Tucci, 'The Ratnavali of Nagarjuna' in JRAS., April 1934, p. 309.

[2] Saddhājāto upasaṅkamanto payirupāsati, payirupāsanto sotaṃ odahati, ohitasoto dhammaṃ suṇāti, sutvā dhammaṃ dhāreti, dhāritānaṃ dhammānaṃ atthaṃ upaparikkhati, atthaṃ upaparikkhato dhammā nijjhānaṃ khamanti, dhammanjjhānakkhantiyā sati chando jāyati, chandajāto ussahati, ussahitvā tuleti, tulayitvā padahati, pahitatto samāno kāyena c'eva paramasaccaṃ sacchikaroti, paññāya ca taṃ ativijjha passati, M. II.173.

of the truth. This greater valuation of knowledge over faith is clearly brought out in the following dialogue:

Nigaṇṭha Nātaputta: Do you *believe* in (*saddahasi*) the statement of the recluse Gotama that there is a jhānic state (trance) in which there is no discursive or reflective thought and there is a cessation of discursive thought and reflection (saddahasi tvaṃ samaṇassa Gotamassa atthi avitakko avicāro samādhi atthi vitakkavicarāṇaṃ nirodho ti?)

Citta: I do not accept this as a *belief* (*saddhāya*) (na khvāhaṃ saddhāya gacchāmi).

Nigaṇṭha Nātaputta: See what an honest, straightforward and upright person the householder Citta is . . . (passantu yāva ujuko c'āyaṃ Citto gahapati yāva asaṭho amāyāvi . . .).

Citta: What do you think? Which is better—*knowledge or belief* (taṃ kiṃ maññasi? katamaṃ nu kho paṇītataraṃ *ñāṇaṃ vā saddhā?*).

Nigaṇṭha Nātaputta: Surely, *knowledge is better than belief* (*saddhāya* kho gahapati, *ñāṇam eva paṇītataram*).

Citta: (I can attain up to the fourth jhāna) . . . *Knowing and seeing thus, why should I accept this on the grounds of faith* in any recluse or brahmin, that there is a trance in which there is no discursive or reflective thought . . . (so khvāhaṃ *evaṃ jānanto evaṃ passanto kassaññassa samaṇassa vā brāhmaṇassa vā saddhāya gamissāmi*, atthi avitakko avicāro samādhi . . .).

S. IV.298.

(673) The fact that it is better to have knowledge of something rather than faith or belief in it is often acknowledged. The general Sīha tells the Buddha that 'he does not accept out of faith in the Exalted One but has himself knowledge of the four visible fruits of giving alms, declared by the Exalted One' (yānimāni Bhagavatā cattāri sandiṭṭhikāni dānaphalāni akkhātāni nāham ettha Bhagavato *saddhāya gacchāmi*, aham p'etāni jānāmi, A. III.39, IV.82). The Buddha tells Ānanda on one occasion: 'You say this out of faith but it is a matter of knowledge for the Tathāgata' (pasādā kho tvaṃ . . . vadesi ñaṇam eva h'ettha Tathāgatassa, D. II.155, A. II.80). Faith or belief culminates in knowledge as is illustrated by the 'story of faith of the monk having faith' (saddhassa saddhāpadānaṃ, A. V.340). Such a monk, to begin with, is virtuous and observes the rules of the order (sīlavā hoti pātimokkhasaṃvarasaṃvuto . . ., A. V.338), becomes learned (bahussuto, *loc. cit.*), puts forth effort (āraddhaviriyo, A. V.339), develops the

four jhānas (catunnam jhānānaṃ ... lābhī, *loc. cit.*), acquires the faculty of retrocognition (anekavihitaṃ pubbenivāsaṃ anussarati, *loc. cit.*) and verifies the fact of rebirth, acquires the faculty of clairvoyance and verifies the fact of karma (dibbena cakkhunā ... satte passati cavamāne upapajjamāne ... yathākammūpage ..., A. V.340) and then himself realizes with his higher knowledge the emancipation of mind and the realization through understanding and attains to and abides in this state (... cetovimuttiṃ paññāvimuttiṃ ... sayaṃ abhiññā sacchikatvā upasampajja viharati, *loc. cit.*). These last three kinds of knowledge constitute 'the three-fold knowledge' (*v. infra*, 754) which the Buddha himself claimed to have attained (*v. infra*, 801). At this stage his faith or belief with which he started is replaced by direct personal knowledge. It is therefore not surprising that the Arahant is described as 'one devoid of faith' (assaddho, Dh. 97) and it is often pointed out that the Arahant must be in a position to claim the highest knowledge without having to rely on faith (cp. *aññatra saddhāya* ... aññaṃ vyākareyya, S. IV.138).

(674) Barua has tried to give a picture of the concept of faith in Buddhism which in some respects is the reverse of the one we have outlined above. This has been partly criticized by Dr Gyomroi-Ludowyk (*v. supra*, 652) but there are certain respects in which Barua is not totally wrong in what he says and this fact has been missed by Gyomroi-Ludowyk, who has assumed without justification that the attitude to saddhā throughout the Pāli Canon is uniformly the same. Barua says that 'according to the Buddha Gotama the higher is the place of cognition ... the stronger are the expressions of faith. There are in other words degrees of faith corresponding to the degrees of knowledge' (*op. cit.*, p. 345). While we pointed out above that faith decreases in direct proportion to the increase in knowledge until it is entirely replaced by the latter, Barua seems to be saying that faith increases with knowledge so that when a maximum of knowledge is reached, there is a maximum of faith. Barua's conclusion is based mainly on a statement in the Saṃyutta, where it is said that the Arahant has his five moral faculties, of which 'the faculty of faith' (saddhindriyaṃ) is the first, fully developed: 'One becomes an Arahant as a result of these five moral faculties being fully and completely developed. I declare that he whose five faculties are not present at all in any respect stays an ordinary individual outside (this religion)' (imesaṃ ... pañcannaṃ indriyānaṃ samattā paripūrattā arahaṃ hoti. Yassa kho ...

imāni pañcindriyāni sabbena sabbaṃ sabbathā sabbaṃ natthi, tam ahaṃ bāhiro puthujjanapakkhe ṭhito ti vadāmi, S. V.202).

(675) This is a different conception of the Arahant from that outlined earlier (*v. supra*, 673). It seemed to be a later view which emerged at a time when the Buddha was claimed to be omniscient (*v. supra*, 649) and the concept of 'emancipation by intellectual knowledge alone' (paññāvimutta) had developed (*v. infra*, 798, 799). At such a time, there would have been a wide and unbridgeable gulf between the Buddha and the Arahant. The Arahant, in not developing the jhānas, could not and did not verify the fact of rebirth and karma, which he had to accept on faith and therefore almost the whole theory of Buddhism had to be accepted on the authority of the Buddha alone. The disciple developed only an intellectual grasp of the Four Noble Truths, which he accepted almost wholly on faith. Thus, in this situation, saddhā does not supersede paññā but goes hand in hand with it.

(676) When the Buddha was not just a person 'who had a three-fold knowledge' (tevijja-, *v. infra*, 801) but one whose range of thought was unthinkable, so much so that one thinking about it would tend to go mad (Buddhavisayo acinteyyo ... yaṃ cintento ummādassa vighātassa bhagī assa, A. II.80), there was little point in trying to verify the knowledge that Buddha claimed. The disinterest in jhāna (*v. infra*, 799) and the unverifiability of karma on the part of the paññā-vimutta, likewise seems to have led to the belief that 'the range of jhāna' (jhānavisayo, *loc. cit.*) and the 'range of karma' (kammavisayo, *loc. cit.*) were equally 'unthinkable and should not be thought about' (acinteyyo na cintetabbo, *loc. cit.*). This is not the earlier attitude of saddhā which said that 'the Buddha knows and I do not know' (jānāti Bhagavā nāhaṃ jānāmī ti, M. I.480) but I shall try to discover or verify this myself (*loc. cit.*), but the attitude which is represented in the Ratnakūṭa which says, 'Here the Tathāgata alone is my witness, the Tathāgata knows, I do not know; boundless is the enlightenment of the Buddhas'.[1]

(677) It is possible that this new conception of saddhā was accompanied by a dogmatism which condemned the free inquiry, which the earlier attitude was based on and encouraged. There is an element of dogmatism in the condemnation of Sunakkhatta, which seems to imply that anyone who examines the claims of the Tathāgata, but

[1] Quoted by Keith, *Buddhist Philosophy*, p. 36; *v.* fn. 2.

comes to conclusions which doubt these claims is liable to an unhappy lot in the next life[1] but it is just possible when we take the context of this statement that Sunakkhatta was condemned not because of his conclusions but because he made these statements out of malice (*v.* kodhano ... Sunakkhatto moghapuriso kodhā ca pan'assa esā vācā bhāsitā, M. I.68). This authoritarian dogmatic attitude seems to have emerged only in the latest stages of the Pāli Canon. The Mahaparinibbāna Sutta, which portrays the dying Buddha still represents him as being anxious that his seeming authority should not stand in the way of the doubts of the monks being dispelled by questioning. He reproves Ānanda for trying to prevent Subhadda from coming to question him (cp. alaṃ Ānanda mā Subhaddaṃ vāresi, D. II.150) and later says that 'if anyone would not question out of respect for the teacher let a person tell his friend' (satthugāravena pi na puccheyyātha sahāyako pi ... sahāyakassa ārocetu, D. II.155). This dislike of authority on the part of the Buddha is also seen where he refused to appoint a person as his successor after his death. 'There is no monk singled out by the Buddha so that he would be a refuge after his death' (natthi ... ekabhikkhu pi tena Bhagavatā ... ṭhapito: ayaṃ vo mam'accayena paṭisaraṇaṃ bhavissatī ti, M. III.9). Here it is said that not even the Order of Monks appointed a leader for this purpose.

(678) From the Mahaparinibbāna Sutta we gather that sometime after the death of the Buddha there was an authoritative collection of texts called the 'Sutta' and the 'Vinaya'. These collections became all important in view of the Buddha's remark that 'we are not without refuge, we have the refuge of the dhamma' (na kho mayaṃ ... appaṭisaraṇā sappaṭisaraṇā mayaṃ ... dhammapaṭisaraṇā, M. III.9). This meant that, as 'the four great references' (cattāro mahāpadesā, D. II.123) state, all statements claiming to be the authentic teaching of the Buddha had 'to be compared with and found compatible with this Sutta and Vinaya' (Sutte otaretabbāni Vinaye sandassetabbāni, D. II.124, 125) to be deemed authentic. But apart from this general claim to be an authoritative collection, there is no suggestion that the statements contained in it should be accepted without question.

(679) We shall next consider the rôle of reason within Buddhism. In doing so we have to examine the following questions. Does the Buddha arrive at his doctrine by reason? What kind of reasoning, if

[1] M. I.71; cp. Keith, *op. cit.*, p. 37.

any, is put forward in defence of his doctrine? Does the Buddha or his disciples criticize other doctrines on rational grounds and if so, what kind of reasoning do they employ?

(680) The Buddha has very often been called a rationalist.[1] But the reason for calling him a rationalist has differed from scholar to scholar and sometimes the same scholar has called him a rationalist for different reasons. At times, he is called a rationalist for being non-dogmatic. Thus Bhattacharya says, followed by Tatia,[2] that the Buddha 'was an out and out rationalist' (*op. cit.*, pp. 9, 10) since 'he would not like to give anything as dogmatic truth, but always based his views on the strong ground of reason' (*loc. cit.*). He quotes the Kālāma Sutta in support notwithstanding the fact that this Sutta rejects various forms of reason such as takka (*v. supra*, 436) naya (*v. supra*, 437), ākāra-parivitakka (*v. supra*, 439) and diṭṭhi-nijjhāna-kkhanti (*v. supra*, 440) as much as the various forms of authority. For Poussin, Buddhism was rationalist mainly because it was non-mystical; 'if we were asked to characterize in a word the old Buddhist discipline of salvation and the old Buddhism as a whole, we should say that it is a form of rationalism. Every idea and every practice made use of by Śākyamuni to build up his theory and his rule of religious life have been freed from any tinge of mysticism'.[3] Radhakrishnan too says of the Buddha that 'he is a rationalist since he wished to study reality or experience without any reference to supernatural revelation' (*op. cit.*, p. 359). Another reason why Buddhism is called a form of rationalism is that it is non-metaphysical. Thus Poussin says: 'it succeeded in explaining the cosmos and human destiny without recourse to any metaphysical agent' (*op. cit.*, p. 32); and again: 'The Buddhist psychology in sharp contrast with Brahmin psychologies—and, it may be said, with nearly all psychologies—avoids or pretends to avoid any metaphysical surmise' (*op. cit.*, p. 38). Keith, while rejecting the suggestions that the teachings of Buddhism were rationalistic (*op. cit.*, pp. 14, 26, 61), suggests as an implausible hypothesis that 'the Buddha himself was a true rationalist and absolutely declined to accept the dogma of transmigration' (*op. cit.*, p. 14). Radhakrishnan too in calling the Buddha a rationalist stresses his empiricism when he says that 'he relied on reason and experience' (*op. cit.*, p. 359). In the same breath, he also calls him a

[1] Poussin, *The Way to Nirvana*, pp. 30 ff.; Bhattacharya, *The Basic Conception of Buddhism*, pp. 9 ff.; Radhakrishnan, *Indian Philosophy*, Vol. I, p. 359; Keith, *op. cit.*, p. 14; Tatia, *Studies in Jaina Philosophy*, p. 7; Jennings, *The Vedantic Buddhism of the Buddha*, p. xxiv. [2] *Op. cit.*, p. 7. [3] *Op. cit.*, p. 30.

rationalist in the strictly philosophical sense (in which rationalism is opposed to empiricism) when he says that 'he wanted to establish a religion within the bounds of pure reason' (*loc. cit.*).

(681) It is clear that we cannot make any significant statements about the Buddha being a rationalist or not, unless there is a clear and consistent use of the term 'rationalist' and since we are trying to evaluate the thought of Buddhism philosophically it is desirable that we use the term in its strictly philosophical connotation. Rationalism is used in philosophical language in opposition to empiricism[1] and it is defined as 'a theory of philosophy in which the criterion of truth is not sensory but intellectual and deductive—usually associated with an attempt to introduce mathematical methods into philosophy as in Descartes, Leibniz and Spinoza'.[2]

(682) In trying to determine whether the Buddha was a rationalist in this sense we have to see whether the Buddha in any sense considered certain premisses as being self-evidently true and deduced the rest of his philosophy from them. Descartes, Spinoza and Leibniz are considered the typically rationalist philosophers, since they tried to evolve systems of deductive metaphysics on the basis of a few premisses, axioms and principles which they considered self-evident or true *a priori*. The closest approximation to this kind of rational metaphysics in the time of the Buddha were the systems evolved out of *takka*-, which were described as being 'beaten out of logic, based on speculation and self-evident' (takka-pariyāhataṃ vīmaṃsānucaritaṃ sayaṃpaṭibhānaṃ, *v. supra*, 434). Many of these rational theories were based on *a priori* reasoning (*v. supra*, 435).

(683) When we thus examine whether the Buddha was a rationalist in this sense, we find that he rejected such claims. It is stated that according to a contemporary of his, Buddha's doctrines were a product of pure reasoning and were not based on any extrasensory perception or extraordinary insight. Sunakkhatta, who left the order dissatisfied, observes that 'the recluse Gotama does not have a distinctive knowledge and vision more than that of (other) men; he preaches a doctrine, which is a product of reasoning and speculation and is self-evident' (natthi samaṇassa Gotamassa uttariṃ manussadhammā alamariyañāṇadassanaviseso, takkapariyāhataṃ samaṇo Gotamo dhammaṃ

[1] Ewing, *The Fundamental Questions of Philosophy*, p. 30.
[2] Runes, *The Dictionary of Philosophy*, *s.v.* Rationalism.

deseti vīmaṃsānucaritaṃ sayaṃpaṭibhānaṃ, M. I.68). The Buddha denies that it is so and it is a veritable denial that he was a rationalist in the above sense of the term. We have no reason to doubt this claim, since nothing in the Nikāyas suggests that any doctrines were taught or were considered to follow from premisses which were held to be true in an *a priori* sense. On the contrary, we always find the Buddha recommending doctrines which are claimed to be true in an empirically or experientially verifiable sense (*v. infra*, 794). We have already seen that the reason for the rejection of theories based on takka- was that the reasoning may be valid or invalid and even if the reasoning was valid and consistent, the theories may be true or false in the light of facts. Pure reason was therefore no safe guide for the discovery of truth.

(684) But this did not mean that takka- was not of limited value. The Sandaka Sutta classifies religious theories based on takka- as not necessarily false (*v. supra*, 436) and the statement addressed to Ānanda that 'so far as anything can be ascertained by reasoning (takka-), thou hast ascertained it' (yāvatakaṃ . . . takkāya[1] pattabbaṃ anuppattaṃ tayā . . . S. I.56) seems to imply that takka- was of limited value.

(685) The Cūlakammavibhaṅga Sutta appears at first sight to embody a rational ethical argument for rebirth and karma but it is probably a mistake to regard the passage in this light. The Buddha is asked the question: 'What is the reason and the cause for the inequality among human beings, despite their being human?' (Ko nu kho . . . hetu ko paccayo yena manussānaṃ yeva sataṃ manussabhūtānaṃ dissati hīnappaṇītatā? M. III.203) and replies, 'Beings inherit their karma and karma divides beings in respect of their (various) high and low states' (sattā kamma-dāyādā . . . kammaṃ satte vibhajati yadidaṃ hīnappaṇītatāya, *loc. cit.*). We may argue that this embodies the following rational ethical argument, consisting of an empirical and ethical premiss, viz. people are of unequal status, those of unequal status ought to be such only by virtue of their own actions—therefore, since this is not due to their actions in this life, it should be due to their actions in a prior life. This means that both karma and rebirth is the case. But as we have shown (*v. infra*, 787–91) there is little ground apart from this passage to show that the concept of karma arises in Buddhism as an attempt to

[1] The Comy. explains 'takkāya' here as 'anumāna-buddhiyā' (SA. I.113), i.e. by the rational intellect.

rationally explain human inequality and we have therefore no right to assume a hidden ethical premiss, on which the entire argument rests.[1]

(686) Although there is little evidence that any of the basic doctrines of Buddhism are derived by reason, we sometimes meet with the Buddha recommending his doctrines on rational grounds. This is particularly evident where his sermons are addressed to the viññū or the élite, who seem to represent the open-minded rationalist (*v. supra*, 638). Thus, in the Apaṇṇaka Sutta we find such an appeal to reason. It is addressed to the brahmin householders of Sāleyyaka who are said 'not to have developed even a rational faith towards any teacher' (natthi . . . satthā yasmiṃ no ākāravatī saddhā paṭiladdhā, M. I.401). To them the Buddha recommends 'the following infallible dhamma' (ayaṃ apaṇṇako[2] dhammo, *loc. cit.*). Here the 'infallibility' is purely logical and rational. The Buddha says that there are these two doctrines, the one denying survival and moral responsibility and the other diametrically opposed to this (ujuvipaccanīka-vādā, M. I.402) which asserts survival and moral responsibility. The Buddha says that in this situation 'a rational person' (viññū puriso, M. I.403) would reason as follows: If a person (adopts the first alternative) and there is no next world (sace . . . natthi paro loko, M. I.403), then he will have no cause for regret (. . . sotthiṃ attānaṃ karissati, *loc. cit.*) but if there is a next world (sace . . . atthi paro loko, *loc. cit.*) he would suffer (apāyaṃ . . . upapajjissati, *loc. cit.*). In any case, he would be reproved in this life as an immoral person and a disbeliever (diṭṭhe va dhamme viññūnaṃ gārayho: dussīlo . . . natthikavādo ti, *loc. cit.*). If there is a next world he would stand to lose in both worlds (ubhayattha kaliggaho, *loc. cit.*). Thus, in adopting this alternative he is depending on one possibility (ekaṃsaṃ pharitvā tiṭṭhati, *loc. cit.*). On the other hand if a person (adopts the second alternative) and there is a next world (sace . . . atthi paro loko, M. I.404) he would be happy after death (param maraṇā . . . sugatiṃ . . . upapajjissati, *loc. cit.*). In any case, he would be praised in this life as a virtuous person and believer (. . . diṭṭhe va dhamme viññūnaṃ pāsaṃso: sīlavā . . . atthikavādo, *loc. cit.*). If there is a next world he would stand to gain in both worlds (ubhayattha kaṭaggaho, *loc. cit.*) and in adopting this alternative he is taking both alternatives into account (ubhayaṃsaṃ pharitvā tiṭṭhati, *loc. cit.*). We may represent

[1] On this kind of argument *v.* Broad, *Mind and Its Place in Nature*, Ch. XI, 'Ethical Arguments for Survival'.

[2] *s.v.* PTS. Dictionary: 'certain' 'unquestionable' = *aprasnaka (Weber and Kuhn) = ekaṃsika-, aviruddha-, niyyānika-, J. I.104.

this 'wager argument', which reminds us of a similar argument of Pascal,[1] as follows:

	If p is true	*If not-p is true*
We wager *p*	We are happy in the next life	We are praised by the wise in this life
We wager not-*p*	We are unhappy in the next life	We are condemned by the wise in this life.

The conclusion (logical) is that it would be better to wager p than not-p because in this alternative we win whatever happens, while in choosing not-p we lose whatever happens. The two theories that are contrasted above are the theories of atthikavāda and natthikavāda, between which it was urged on rational grounds that it would be better to choose the former, irrespective of their truth-value. In the course of the Sutta we find similar arguments to show that it would be better to believe in the kiriyāvāda (M. I.407) than the akiriyāvāda (M. I.406) or the hetuvāda (M. I.409) than the ahetuvāda (M. I.408).

(687) This appeal to purely rationalist considerations is, for instance, in utter contrast to the spirit of the Tevijja Sutta, where the Buddha addressing the brahmins appears to take the brahmin Weltanschaung for granted and preaches 'the path leading to companionship with Brahmā' (Ayam pi . . . Brahmānaṃ sahavyatāya maggo, D. I.151). It is this character of the Buddha in adjusting his sermons to suit the predilections and temperament of his listeners that comes to be known as the *upāya-kauśalya* or 'the skill in (devising) means (to convert people)' (*s.v.* BHS. Dictionary) which Edgerton says is 'extremely common everywhere' (*loc. cit.*) in the BHS. literature. There is a reference to upāya-kosallaṃ in the Canon as well (D. I.220); it is not clear whether this refers to the Buddha's technique of preaching but reference is made to 'the ability to comprehend the predilections of beings' (sattānāṃ nānādhimuttikataṃ yathābhūtam pajānāti, M. I.70) as one of the intellectual faculties of the Buddha (*v. infra*, 805). The content of these different methods of preaching is however self-consistent as far as the Nikāyas are concerned. The brahma-loka (world of Brahma) is part of the Buddhist cosmos as described in the 'thousand-fold world-system' (cūlaṇikā-loka-dhātu, A. I.227, 228, IV.59, 60) and it is not incompatible with the Buddhist thesis to say that all that reason can do is to point out that it is better to adopt the sammādiṭṭhi (the

[1] *v.* W. Kaufmann, *Critique of Religion and Philosophy*, London, 1958, p. 122.

right view) than its opposite, without being able to demonstrate that this was true. This means that reason was of limited value.

(688) The Buddha's attitude to the numerous theories which were being propagated and defended on rational grounds at this time (*v. supra,* Ch. V) seems to have been to ignore them. The evidence of the texts indicates that he refrained from joining issue with these dialecticians and rational metaphysicians in debate as far as possible, like some of the Sceptics (*v. supra,* 169) though he seems to have accepted the challenge when they came to him with questions for the purposes of debate (*v. supra,* 350 f.). The attitude of the Buddha is probably summed up in his own statement that 'when a debate has arisen the sage does not enter it' (vādañ ca jātaṃ muni no upeti, Sn. 780). It is probably this attitude of shunning debates in public assemblies on the whole, which earned for the Buddha the rebuke of the brahmins that 'the recluse Gotama utters a lion's roar, but he utters it in the empty house and not in the public assemblies' (sīhanādaṃ kho samaṇo Gotamo nadati, tañ ca kho suññāgāre nadati no parisāsu, D. I.175). Even when people wished to know from the Buddha his views on or criticisms of others' doctrines, he generally refrains from expressing any view and is content to teach his own doctrines. When Subhadda mentions the famous teachers of his time and wants to know whether 'they all understood, none understood or some understood and some did not' (sabbe te . . . abbhaññaṃsu, sabbe'va na abbhaññaṃsu, ekacce abbhaññaṃsu ekacce na abbhaññaṃsu, D. II.150, 151), the Buddha says, 'enough, Subhadda, leave these questions aside . . . I shall teach you the dhamma . . .' (alaṃ, Subhadda, tiṭṭhat' etaṃ . . . dhammaṃ te . . . desissāmi, *loc. cit.*). When two brahmins come to him and state the contradictory views expressed by Pūraṇa Kassapa and Nigaṇṭha Nātaputta on the extent of the cosmos (*v. supra,* 393) and wish to know which of them was true, his reply was the same (A. IV.429). This attitude probably explains why there is very little rational criticism even of doctrines which Buddhism opposed, in the Pāli Canon.

(689) The Buddha's rejoinder to the brahmin rebuke that his 'lion's roar' was to be heard only in empty houses was that 'the recluse Gotama does utter his lion's roar and does so in public assemblies' (sīhanādañ ca samaṇo Gotamo nadati parisāsu ca nadati, D. I.175). This statement too may have an element of truth, especially when we find positive claims that the Buddha 'participated in hundreds of assemblies'

(anekasataṃ parisaṃ upasaṅkamitā, M. I.72), in which perhaps he was more interested in preaching his own doctrines and defending them against criticism than in criticizing the theories of others. But the failure in general to mention the reasons against doctrines which are opposed may also be due to the style of the Pāli Suttas which often fail to give the reasons put forward in defence of a certain theory as much as the reasons against. For example, we find the following theory, which is opposed, mentioned in the Cūladhammasamādāna Sutta. It is said that 'there are some recluses and brahmins who are of the view and put forward the theory that there is no harm in sensual pleasures' (santi . . . eke samaṇa-brāhmaṇā evaṃvādino evaṃdiṭṭhino: natthi kamesu doso ti, M. I.305). Now from a few statements in the Nettippakaraṇa we gather that this theory was held on rational grounds by people who considered it 'wrong to refrain from sensual pleasures, holding that sensual pleasures should be enjoyed and multiplied' (bhuñjitabbā kāmā . . . bahulīkātabbā kāmā ti kamehi veramaṇi tesaṃ adhammo, 52). Their reasoning was as follows: yo kame paṭisevati, so lokaṃ vaḍḍhayati; yo lokaṃ vaḍḍhayati, so bahuṃ puññaṃ pasavati, 110.

I.e. he who indulges in sensual pleasures enriches the world
SaM(Minor premiss)
he who enriches the world accumulates great merit
MaP(Major premiss).

(690) From this the conclusion follows: he who indulges in sensual pleasures accumulates great merit, SaP(Conclusion). We have here (along with the conclusion) a syllogism in Barbara in the first figure (except that the Major premiss is stated earlier than the Minor premiss), giving the reason for the above theory, but the reason is not given in the Nikāya version.

(691) As we have said (*v. supra*, 688), the Buddha did reason with those who came to debate with him. He is also reported to have 'known the trick of turning (his opponents over to his views) with which he converted the disciples of heretical teachers' (āvaṭṭaniṃ māyāṃ jānāti yāya aññatitthiyānaṃ sāvake āvaṭṭetī ti, M. I.375, A. II.190). The Upāli Sutta, which gives a concrete illustration of this trick (māyaṃ) shows the Buddha arguing in Socratic fashion[1] with Upāli and defeating him with a series of simple dialectical arguments. The Buddha

[1] Cp. Oldenberg, *Buddha*, Tr. Hoey, p. 189.

starts with an assumption of his opponent and by a series of questions leads him to a position in which he contradicts himself and it is pointed out that 'what he said earlier is not compatible with what he has said later and *vice versa*' (na kho te sandhīyati purimeṇa vā pacchimaṃ pacchimeṇa vā purimaṃ, M. I.376, 377, 378). This is considered a disproof of his opponent's original proposition.

(692) The bulk of the arguments against other theories (with the possible exception of the criticisms of Jainism—*v. infra*, 788A), do not seem to belong to the earliest stratum of the Nikāyas. They occur for instance in the Sandaka Sutta of the Majjhima Nikāya, the Payāsi Sutta of the Dīgha Nikāya[1] and also in such works as the Jātaka. These arguments may belong to an earlier period though recorded later (as in the example we cited, *v. supra*, 689, 690) or it may have been the case that while the Buddha confined himself on the whole to the exposition of his own doctrines rather than to the criticism of his opponents, this was no longer possible when Buddhism had become a full-fledged missionary religion and had to fend with its opponents.

(693) It is significant that almost all these arguments are of the form *modus tollendo tollens* (*v. supra*, 134). Thus, in the Therigāthā, it is argued that 'if water-baptism can free one of evil karma (p), then the fishes, tortoises, frogs, etc. . . . straight to heaven will go[2] (q)'. But q is absurd or evidently false, implying the falsity of the implicans p. This idea is at best only barely suggested in the Udāna verse which says 'there is no (spiritual) purification from water; many are the folk who bathe here' (na udakena suci hoti, bahv ettha nhāyati jano, Ud. 6).

(694) The Pāyāsi Sutta is devoted to meeting the arguments of Pāyāsi, who denies survival. We have stated Pāyāsi's arguments in Ch. II (*v. supra*, 136–8). The counter arguments of Kumāra Kassapa make the point that although Pāyāsi's negative conclusions were inevitable they do not imply the falsity of the belief in survival. One of the main arguments (*v. supra*, 90) was that if Pāyāsi expected to see the person surviving, then obviously no such person could be observed with the naked eye but this did not imply the non-existence of the person surviving, for it did not follow from p (I do not see X) that q (X does not exist) was true. Kassapa thus denies the truth of the implicative premiss, $p \supset q$, on which Pāyāsi's arguments are based.

[1] The views expressed in the Sandaka Sutta are only indirectly represented as the views of the Buddha; for the Pāyāsi Sutta, *v. supra*, 135 f.

[2] Therīgāthā, 240–41.

(695) In the Sandaka Sutta, Ānanda uses an argument to prove that Materialism (M. I.515), Amoralism (natthi ... pāpaṃ ... natthi puññaṃ, M. I.516), Non- (Moral) Causationism (natthi hetu ... saṅkilesāya ... visuddhiyā, M. I.516) and Determinism (M. I.517, 8) were false. It is argued that if these theories were true (*p*), then it would not matter what people did (*q*).[1] It is then implied that *q* is false since even those who believed in *p* behaved as if what they did mattered and not as if 'the nakedness, the shaving of the head, the exertion in squatting (in practising vows), the plucking out of the hair of the head and the beard, on the part of such a teacher was superfluous'.[2] This argument would have appeared plausible only in the context in which all those who put forward the above theories, including the Materialists were species of ascetics.

(696) In the Jātaka we find this same *modus tollendo tollens* used against the main theories which opposed Buddhism at this time. In the Mahābodhi Jātaka we find the Bodhisattva criticizing the doctrines of five ministers, who represent five heretical doctrines. The context is one in which the five ministers accuse the Bodhisattva of having killed a monkey and thus committed an evil act. The rebuttal consists of showing that according to the theories of each of these ministers, killing would not be a crime (an evil act) and therefore on the one hand they have no right to accuse him, while on the other hand, these theories are false (it is assumed that the statement 'it is wrong to kill' is true).

(697) The first theory to be criticized is that of the Non-Causationist (ahetuvādi, J. V.237). It is said that 'if acts are uncaused, who is responsible (*lit.* affected by) for an evil deed?' (akāma-karaṇīyasmiṃ kuvidha pāpena lippati, *loc. cit.*). The argument is that if *p* (one acts without will, akāmā ... kubbati, *loc. cit.*) is true, then *q* (no one is responsible for the evil (na koci pāpena lippati, *loc. cit.*) is true. But *q* is considered to be evidently false, implying the falsity of *p*.

(698) The second theory taken up is that of the Theist (issara-kāraṇa-vādi, J. V.238). It is argued that the truth of Theism implies that man is not responsible for his actions (which is assumed to be

[1] The text says, 'both of us (i.e. those who believe in p and those who believe in not-p) would be alike and would have attained the fruits of recluseship' (ubho pi mayaṃ ettha samasamā sāmaññappattā, M. I.515, 516, 517, 518).

[2] atirekaṃ ... imassa bhoto satthuno naggiyaṃ muṇḍiyaṃ ukkuṭikappadhānaṃ kessamassulocanaṃ, *loc. cit.*

false). 'If God designs the life of the entire world—the glory and the misery, the good and the evil acts—man is but an instrument of his will and God (alone) is responsible.'[1] Elsewhere in the Jātakas, the argument from evil is used to disprove the truth of Theism by means of the same *modus tollendo tollens*: 'If Brahmā is lord of the whole world and creator of the multitude of beings (*p*), then why (i) has he ordained misfortune in the world without making the whole world happy (not-*q*), or (ii) for what purpose has he made the world full of injustice, deceit, falsehood and conceit (not-*q*), or (iii) the lord of beings is evil in that he ordained injustice when there could have been justice' (not-*q*).[2]

(699) The next theory criticized is that 'everything is caused by past actions' (sabbam pubbekatahetu, J. V.208)—a species of Determinism. 'If one experiences happiness and misery as a result of past actions (*p*), a person is paying off the debts of his past sin and being a payer off of past debts, is not responsible for his evil actions (*q*).'[3] Here again *q* is assumed to be evidently false implying the falsity of *p*.

(700) The Materialist is similarly disposed of. 'If the soul is alive only in this world and is destroyed at death and the world (consisting of) the fools and the wise perishes (*p*), then the world perishing, one is not responsible for one's evil actions.'[4]

(701) Lastly, the Machiavellian philosophy is dismissed. 'Fools thinking themselves learned say that there is the "rule of might" (khatta-vidhā) in the world (*p*); one may destroy mother, father, elder brother, children and wives, if such a need be there.'[5] Here what is meant is that if might is right (*p*), then one may kill mother, father, etc., when it is expedient to do so (*q*). But *q* is held to be an evidently false proposition, implying the falsity of *p*.

[1] Issaro sabbalokassa sace kappeti jīvitaṃ iddhivyasanabhāvañca kammaṃ kalyānapāpakaṃ niddesakāri puriso issaro tena lippati.

[2] Sace hi so issaro sabbaloke Brahmā bahubhūtapati pajānaṃ, (i) kiṃ sabbaloke vidahi alakkhiṃ sabbalokaṃ na sukhī akāsi . . . (ii) māyāmusāvajjamadena c'āpi lokaṃ adhammena kimatth'akāsi . . . (iii) adhammiyo bhūtapatī . . . dhamme sati yo vidahi adhammaṃ, J. VI.208.

[3] Sace pubbekatahetu sukhadukkhaṃ nigacchati, porāṇakaṃ kataṃ pāpaṃ tam eso muccate iṇaṃ, porāṇakaṃ iṇamokkho kuvidha pāpena lippati, J. V.208.

[4] Idh'eva jīvati jīvo pecca pecca vinassati, ucchijjati ayaṃ loko ye balā ye ca paṇḍitā, ucchijjamāne lokasmiṃ kuvidha pāpena lippati, J. V.239.

[5] Ahu khatta-vidhā loke bālā paṇḍitamānino, mātaraṃ pitaraṃ haññe atha eṭṭham pi bhātaraṃ haneyya putte ca dāre, attho ca tādiso siyā, J. V.240.

(702) The logical form of the above arguments in the *modus tollendo tollens* is not clearly depicted but in the Kathāvatthu, we get a conscious formulation of this form of argument.

(703) Bochenski in criticizing Randle's opinion that the author of the Kathāvatthu had little knowledge of logic[1] has quite rightly remarked: 'Denn es ist in unserem Text klar zu sehen, dass die Diskutierenden ganz bewusst bestimmte formallogische Regeln nicht nur anwenden, sondern fast ausdrücklich formulieren'.[2]

(704) There is, however, a difference of opinion between Bochenski and Schayer[3] as to what exactly these formal logical rules were. According to Schayer the Kathāvatthu tells us about 'a few theorems of the propositional calculus' (einiger Theoreme des Aussagenkalküls, *op. cit.*, p. 91), namely the definition of Implication (Definition der Implikation, *op. cit.*, p. 92) and the law of Contraposition, which Schayer calls the 'law of Transposition' (Gesetz der Transposition, *loc. cit.*). He does not say that these formal rules of the propositional calculus are explicitly formulated but that the author of the Kathāvatthu shows an awareness of them: 'Ich glaube, dass wir die Kenntnis dieser beiden Gesetze dem Verfasser des Kvu mit grosser Wahrscheinlichkeit zuschreiben dürfen' (*loc. cit.*). But according to Bochenski, Schayer goes too far (so scheint er zu weit zu gehen, *op. cit.*, p. 488) when he speaks of 'Antizipationen der Aussagenlogik' in the Kathāvatthu (*loc. cit.*). For him the relations established are not relations between propositions but between terms or concepts. So we are concerned here with rules which correspond somewhat to 'termlogical formulae' (termlogischen Formeln, *op. cit.*, p. 489) and not with the rules of propositional logic (aussagenlogische Regeln, *loc. cit.*).

(705) This in fact was the very ground on which Schayer criticized Aung's original symbolical formulation of the argument in the 'Points of Controversy' (pp. xlviii ff.) which Bochenski seeks to reinstate:[4] 'Wie man sieht, entspricht diese Formel dem stoischen *modus tollendo*

[1] *Indian Logic in the Early Schools*, pp. 13 ff.

[2] I. M. Bochenski, *Formale Logik*, Germany, 1956, p. 488.

[3] St Schayer, 'Altindische Anticipationen der Aussagenlogik' (Studien zur indischen Logik, II) in *Bulletin de l'Academie Polonaise des Sciences et des Lettres Cracovic*, 1933, pp. 90–96.

[4] Except for the fact that Bochenski's formulation makes use of only three terms, viz. A, B and C (*v. op. cit.*, p. 489, 51.022 and 51.032), while Aung's formulation makes use of four terms A, B, C and D. Bochenski is nearer the logical if the term-logical analysis is correct.

tollens, das sagt aber Shwe Zang Aung nicht und schafft ausserdem durch die unnötige Einführung von Namenvariabeln die grundsätzlich falsche Suggestion, als ob es sich um Relationen zwischen den fier Begriffen A, B, C and D handelte. Tatsächlich sind die Elemente, mit denen die Logik des Kathāvatthu operiert, evidenterweise nicht Namenvariabeln, sondern Aussagenvariabeln ...' (*op. cit.*, p. 91).

(706) We find that the evidence from the Kathāvatthu favours Schayer's exposition rather than that of Bochenski. As Bochenski himself has shown (*v. op. cit.*, p. 489, 51.021 and 51.031), if we treat 'puggalo upalabbhati saccikaṭṭhaparamaṭṭhena' (a person is known in a real and ultimate sense) as a proposition (say, *p*) and 'yo saccikaṭṭho paramaṭṭho tato so puggalo upalabbhati saccikaṭṭhaparamaṭṭhena' (a person is known in a real and ultimate sense in the same way in which a real and ultimate fact is known) as another proposition (say, *q*) we can clearly translate the argument of the Kathāvatthu without distortion of its form as it appears in the original:

Theravādin: Is *p* true?[1]
Puggalavādin: Yes ($\vdash p$).
Th.: Is *q* true?
P.: It is not true[2] ($\sim q$).

Th.: (1) Acknowledge defeat (ājānahi niggahaṃ): if *p* is true, then *q* is true ($p \supset q$).
(2) The assertion that *p* is true (*lit.* ought to be asserted, vattabbe) but not *q*, is false ($\sim(p . \sim q)$).
(3) If *q* is not true, then *p* is not true ($\sim q \supset \sim p$).
(4) is identically the same as (2).[3] Bochenski has rightly omitted it (*loc. cit.*) as this repetition is of no logical significance. Schayer includes it and refers to the 'four assertions' (vier Festellungen, *op. cit.*, p. 92) but the Kathāvatthu itself speaks of 'the five assertions (*lit.* the pentad) in direct order' (anulomapañcakam, *loc. cit.*), apparently considering the preamble also as a unit. (4) was probably repeated because it is the only assertion that ends in 'micchā' (false) and would have appeared to the debater to clinch the issue.

[1] We are taking the assertion of p as equivalent to 'p is true'.
[2] *lit.* one should not say so (na h'evaṃ vattabbe, Kvu. 1).
[3] Aung and Mrs Rhys Davids have given a false impression to the reader by giving different translations of (4) and (2), *v. op. cit.*, p. 9.

(707) The four-fold rejoinder proceeds as follows:

P.: Is p not true?
Th.: Yes ($\vdash \sim p$).
P.: Is q not true?
Th.: It is not the case that it is not true: $\sim(\sim q)$.
P.: (1) Acknowledge the rejoinder (ājānahi paṭikammaṃ): if not-p is true, then not-q is true: $(\sim p \supset \sim q)$.
(2) The assertion that not-p is true but not not-q, is false: $\sim(\sim p . \sim(\sim q))$.
(3) If not-q is not true, then not-p is not true: $\sim(\sim q) \supset \sim(\sim p)$.
(4) = (2).

(708) The argument is thus quite clear, when stated in the propositional form, whereas the analysis of the propositions into its terms or into subject–predicate form not only makes the argument less clear but tends to obscure the fact that truth or falsity is here predicated of propositions and not of terms. The Kathāvatthu is certainly familiar with the concept of 'term'[1] as the section on the 'clarification of terms' (vacana-sodhanaṃ, Kvu. 25) shows, but it may be seen that when the Kvu. uses the word *micchā* (false), it is used as the predicate of a proposition, e.g. (2) above, i.e. *micchā* $(p. \sim q)$ where $(p. \sim q)$ has to be taken as a compound proposition. Besides, the Kvu. is familiar with the term for a proposition, viz. *paṭiññā* (= Skr. pratijñā) and is using the word in this sense in these discussions; cp. etāya patiññāya h'evam paṭijānantānaṃ, Kvu. 2, rendered by Aung and Mrs Rhys Davids as 'you, who have assented to the very *proposition* ...' (*op. cit.*, p. 10). In addition, there are discussions in which Bochenski's term-logical analysis breaks down and fails to bring out the fact that it were the propositions, which are regarded as equivalent:

Th.: Is the person known in the sense of a real and ultimate fact?[2]
(Propositional analysis—p?; term-analysis—Is A B ?)
P.: Is the person *always* (sabbadā) known in the sense of a real and ultimate fact?[3]
(Propositional analysis—q?; term-analysis—Is A B, always?)

Here $p \supset q$, since q is only a restatement of p, a general proposition being true 'at all times' (sabbadā). But if it is a relation between the

[1] Not in the modern sense in which a proposition is composed of terms and relations.
[2] Puggalo upalabbhati saccikaṭṭhaparamaṭṭhena ti, Kvu. 8.
[3] Sabbadā puggalo upalabbhati saccikaṭṭhaparamaṭṭhena, *loc. cit.*

terms A and B, it need not be so, since Socrates may be well today (A is B) and ill tomorrow (A is not B).

(709) Now Bochenski himself says that it is noteworthy that 51.03 originates from 51.02 by substituting 'A is not B' for 'A is B' and also by substituting 'A is not C' for 'A is C' (*v. op. cit.*, p. 489). But surely, this is because 'A is B' and 'A is C' were considered as units or propositions in place of which other propositions (the negative forms) could be substituted.[1] In the circumstances, it is not possible to agree with Bochenski's contention that in attributing an awareness to the author of the Kvu. of two of the theorems of the propositional calculus, the rules of Implication ($p \supset q. \equiv \sim(p. \sim q)$) and Contraposition ($p \supset q. \equiv \sim q \supset \sim p$), one is ascribing to Indian thinkers a faculty of abstraction (Abstractionsfähigkeit, Bochenski, *op. cit.*, p. 489), which they did not possess. For one has to rely on the factual evidence in this matter and not on hypothetical possibilities of what can or cannot exist.

(710) It would not, of course, be correct to say that the author of the Kvu. formulated these rules since he does not actually *equate* (1) and (2) (Implication) nor (1) and (3) (Contraposition), but merely assumes their identity. And we do not think Schayer goes too far when he says, 'Ebensowenig sagt er expressis verbis, obwohl er dies zweifelsohne im Sinne hatte, dass die Thesen: $p \supset q$, $\sim (p. \sim q)$ und $\sim q \supset \sim p$ als äquivalent zu betrachten sind'. (*Op. cit.*, p. 92.)

(711) The presence of eight refutations (Kvu. 1–11) has no logical significance and the use of the word niggaha- (refutation) only up to the number eight (cp. aṭṭhako niggaho, Kvu. 11) is arbitrary, since the subsequent discussions also constitute refutations (*v.* ājānahi niggahaṃ, pp. 14 ff.).

[1] Note that Bochenski himself says, 'und das könnte die Vermutung nahelegen, dass es damals schon einige bewusst angewandte aussagenlogische Regeln gab' (*op. cit.*, p. 489).

CHAPTER IX

THE MEANS AND LIMITS OF KNOWLEDGE

(712) In this final chapter we propose to examine the means and limits of knowledge as recognized in the Pāli Canonical texts.

(713) In Chapter IV, we noticed that when the Buddha classified his predecessors and contemporaries in respect of the ways of knowledge emphasized by them as the Traditionalists, the Rationalists and the 'Experientialists' (*v. supra*, 250), he identified himself as a member of the last group (*v. supra*, 249). In his address to the Kālāmas and to Bhaddiya Licchavi, where he criticizes six ways of knowing based on authority (*v. supra*, 251) and four ways of knowing based on reason (*v. supra*, 314) on the ground that beliefs based on authority or reason may turn out to be true or false (*v. supra*, 283, 308, 436, 442), he ends on the note that one should accept a proposition as true only when one has 'personal knowledge' (attanā va jāneyyātha, A. II.191) of it, taking into account the views of the wise (*v. supra*, 662).

(714) This emphasis on personal and direct knowledge is found throughout the Nikāyas and in trying to determine the ways of knowing recognized in the Canon, it is necessary to see clearly what was meant by this kind of knowledge.

(715) The fact that the Buddha claimed to be 'one of those' (tesāham asmi, *v. supra*, 249) recluses and brahmins, who had a 'personal higher knowledge' (sāmaṃ yeva . . . abhiññāya, *loc. cit.*) of a doctrine not found among 'doctrines traditionally handed down' (pubbe ananussutesu dhammesu, *loc. cit.*) is clear evidence that the Buddha did not claim or consider himself to have an unique way of knowing denied to others. It ranks him in his own estimate as a member of a class of recluses and brahmins, who claimed to have a personal and a 'higher knowledge' of doctrines not found in the various traditions. Who could these 'recluses and brahmins' be, in the light of our knowledge of the historical background? (*v.* Chs. I, II, III).

(716) We saw that the brahmin thinkers fell into three types on epistemological grounds—the Traditionalists of the Vedas and Brāhmaṇas, the Rationalists of the Early Upaniṣads and the 'Experientialists' of the Middle and Late Upaniṣads (*v. supra,* 76, 244). Since the Buddha dissociates himself from the first two classes (*v. supra,* 246) we may presume that he identifies himself among others with the brahmin thinkers of the Middle and Late Upaniṣads. From the time of the Early Upaniṣads, newly discovered doctrines not found in the traditional Vedic learning, were being taught. Śvetaketu had 'learned all the Vedas' (sarvān vedān adhītya . . . Ch. 6.1.2) but had to be instructed by Uddālaka with a doctrine 'whereby what he has not heard (presumably in the Vedic teaching) is heard' (yenāśrutam śrutam bhavati, Ch. 6.1.3). Such doctrines as well as the doctrines constituting the 'higher knowledge' (parā vidyā) of the Middle and Late Upaniṣads (*v. supra,* 75) have to be reckoned among 'the doctrines not traditionally handed down' (ananussutesu dhammesu) referred to in the Pāli passage. The brahmin Rationalists have to be excluded from the class of thinkers, with whom the Buddha identifies himself, also for the reason that they did not claim to have a 'higher knowledge' (abhiññā) based on any kind of contemplative or meditative experience (dhyāna =P.jhāna, *v. supra,* 31), unlike the Middle and Late Upaniṣadic thinkers.

(717) We have observed that these latter thinkers claimed a kind of knowledge, which was a matter of directly 'seeing' or intuiting ultimate reality (*v. supra,* 73) and which was usually described by the word *jñāna* (*v. supra,* 74). In a sense, the emphasis on *jñāna* or knowledge was common to all the Upaniṣadic thinkers, since knowledge came to be valued as the means of salvation at least from the time of the Āraṇyakas onwards (*v. supra,* 16). Thenceforth, there was a cleavage in the Vedic tradition between the *karmamārga* or 'the way of ritual' and the *jñāna-mārga* or 'the way of knowledge'. Early Buddhism is aware of this distinction, for the Suttanipāta mentions the *yañña-patha* or 'the way of ritual' (*yañña-pathe* appamattā, Sn. 1045) as against the *ñaṇa-patha* or 'the way of knowledge' (ñaṇa-pathāya sikkhe, Sn. 868). But it is also necessary to emphasize the distinction between the two ways of knowledge recognized within the Upaniṣads – the intellectual or rational knowledge of the Early Upaniṣads and the intuitive knowledge of the Middle and Late Upaniṣads. Of these two, it is the latter way of knowing that Buddhism values.

o

(718) There is more evidence that Buddhism recognizes the validity of the means of knowledge upheld by this latter class of thinkers, although its valuation of it and what was known by it was not the same. We noted that jñāna was upheld in the Middle and Late Upaniṣads, where knowledge was described as one of 'seeing' (*v. supra,* 73). In the Nikāyas it is said that the Buddha is a jñāna-vādin[1] or a jñānin[2]. He is described as one who 'knowing, knows and seeing, sees having become sight and knowledge' (jānaṃ jānāti passaṃ passati cakkhubhūto ñāṇabhūto, M. I.111). 'The knowing and seeing One' (jānatā passatā, M. II.111) is a characteristic description of the Buddha and it is usually said of what he claims to know that he both 'knows and sees' (tam ahaṃ jānāmi passāmī ti, M. I.329). The central truths of Buddhism are 'seen'. One 'comprehends the Noble Truths and sees them' (ariya-saccāni avecca[3] passati,[4] Sn. 229). Even Nirvāṇa is 'seen' (nibbānaṃ passeyyan ti, M. I.511) in a sense analogous to the seeing of a man born blind after a physician has treated him (*loc. cit.*). The Buddha is one who 'has knowledge and insight into all things' (sabbesu dhammesu ca ñāṇa-dassī, Sn. 478) and 'the religious life is led under the Exalted One for the *knowledge, insight,* attainment, realization and comprehension of what is not *known,* not *seen,* not attained, not realized and not comprehended'.[5] It is said that the statement 'I know, I see' is descriptive of one who claims to be a *ñāṇavādin* (ñāṇavādaṃ . . . vadamāno janām'imaṃ dhammaṃ passām'imaṃ dhamman ti, A. V.42, 44) and ñāṇavādam or the claim to such knowledge is closely associated with *bhāvanā- vāda* or the claim to mental culture and development through meditation.[6]

(719) There is no doubt that 'knowledge and insight' (ñāṇadassana) or 'knowing and seeing' (jānāti passati) in the above sense is mainly though not exclusively (*v. infra,* 721) a by-product of 'mental concentration' (samādhi) in jhāna or yoga. It is said that there is a causal relation between the attainment of mental concentration and the

[1] Cp. *Samaṇo pi Gotamo ñāna-vādo,* aham pi ñāṇa-vādo, ñāṇa-vado kho pana ñāṇa-vādena arahati *uttarimanussadhammā* iddhipāṭihāriyaṃ dassetuṃ, D. III.12. Note the connection between *ñāṇavāda-* and *uttarimanussadhamma-* (paranormal).

[2] Ñāṇī ti . . . Tathāgatassa etaṃ adhivacanaṃ, A. IV.340. [3] *v. supra,* 655.

[4] Cp. Paramasaccaṃ sacchikaroti, paññāya ca ativijjha passati, M. II.112, 173.

[5] Yam . . . aññātāṃ adiṭṭhaṃ appattaṃ asacchikataṃ anabhisametaṃ, tassa *ñāṇāya dassanāya* pattiyā sacchikiriyāya abhisamayāya Bhagavati brahmacariyaṃ vussatī ti, A. IV.384.

[6] Ñāṇavādañ ca . . . vadamāno bhāvanāvādañ ca jānām'imaṃ dhammaṃ passām'imaṃ dhammaṃ . . ., A. IV.42, 44.

emergence of this knowledge and insight (*v. infra,* 724). This shows that it is qualitatively similar to the Upaniṣadic 'knowing' and 'seeing' which was also a result of dhyāna (cp. dhyāyamānaḥ, *v. supra,* 73).

(720) This kind of direct intuitive knowledge was also claimed by some of the Ājīvikas (*v. supra,* 213) and at least the leader of the Jains who professed omniscience (*v. supra,* 311). The direct knowledge and vision of omniscience is in fact called ñāṇa-dassana (M. I.482, 519). Pūraṇa Kassapa and Nigaṇṭha Nātaputta, who claimed omniscience, are called Jñāna-vādins or those who professed to have this kind of direct intuitive knowledge (cp. ubhinnaṃ *ñāṇa-vādānaṃ* . . ., A. IV. 429). This is confirmed from what we learn from the Jain scriptures, where knowledge is said to consist of jñāna and darśana. On this Tatia observes: 'The hoary antiquity of the Jain conception of *jñānāvaraṇa* and *darśanā-varaṇa* points to the antiquity of the distinction between *jñāna-* and *darśaṅa-*. The Jain Āgamas use the terms *jāṇāī* and *pāsāī* in order to express the two faculties of the soul.'[1] These Ājīvikas and the Jain leader may therefore be reckoned among the Samaṇas with whom the Buddha identified himself (*v. supra,* 249, 715).

(721) Though we left out the Materialists for the obvious reason that they did not claim any higher knowledge (*v. supra,* 142) there is good reason to believe that when Buddhism used the expression 'knowing and seeing' (jānaṃ passaṃ), it meant by it the direct knowledge gained by sense-perception as well. We find that the expression, 'I know . . . I see' (jānāmi . . . passāmi, *v. supra,* 90) was placed in the mouth of the Materialist who claimed to know only what could be directly perceived. We find this expression used in the Nikāyas to denote the direct knowledge derived from sense-perception. Thus in a context, where the conditions under which one's memory is said to become defective are stated (*v. infra,* 732), we find the following simile: '. . . just as if a man possessed of sight were to observe the reflection of his face in a basin of water disturbed, shaken, tossed about by (gusts of) wind and full of ripples, but fail to *know and see* (his face) *as it really is*'[2] (*yathā-bhūtaṃ* na *jāneyya* na *passeyya*).

[1] *Studies in Jaina Philosophy,* p. 71.

[2] Seyyathā pi . . . udapatto vāterito calito bhanto ūmijāto tattha cakkhumā puriso sakaṃ mukhanimittaṃ paccavekkhamāno yathābhūtaṃ na jāneyya na passeyya, S. V.123.

(722) Now Keith seems to have noticed the essential affinity between the way of knowing of the Middle and Late Upaniṣads and that of Early Buddhism; he makes the following observation: 'The view of intuition as the source of true knowledge, and at the same time a decisive cause of emancipation from rebirth is characteristic of Buddhism as of the Upaniṣads, and explains why in neither do we find any serious contribution to epistemology. The Buddha, like the sage of the Upaniṣad, sees things as they truly are (*yathābhūtaṃ*) by a mystic potency, which is quite other than reasoning of the discursive type. The truth of his insight is assured by it alone, for it is obviously incapable of verification in any empirical manner.'[1] He qualifies this statement when he adds that 'the Canon does not treat intuition (paññā) as being wholly distinct from, and unconnected with discursive knowledge . . . it is allied to deliberate and searching mental appreciation (yoniso manasikāro)' (*op. cit.*, p. 90).

(723) While we agree with Keith's comparison between the way of knowledge accepted in Buddhism and the Upaniṣads, in the light of the evidence that we have shown above, we cannot subscribe to his other remarks. Despite the qualitative similarity between the means of knowledge in the Middle and Late Upaniṣads and Buddhism, it is necessary to note that the latter gives a different orientation to and evaluation of this means of knowledge. This tends to present this knowledge in a different light altogether and makes less obvious the gap between the empirical and the mystical.

(724) In the Upaniṣads one's knowledge and vision is not, in the final analysis, due to one's efforts but to the grace or intervention of Ātman or God (*v. supra*, 73). The emergence of this knowledge is conceived as something inexplicable and mysterious. This character warrants it being called a kind of mystical knowledge. But in the Buddhist account the mental concentration (samādhi) which is a product of training and effort, is a causal factor (upanisā) in the production of this knowledge: '. . . in the absence of right mental concentration and in the case of one not endowed with right mental concentration, the cause is absent (for the production of) the knowledge and insight of things as they really are' (. . . sammāsamādhimhi asati sammāsamādhivipannassa hatūpanisaṃ hoti yathābhūtañāṇadassanaṃ, A. III.200). It is a natural and not a supernatural occurrence: 'It is *in the nature of things* (dhammatā) that a person in the state of (meditative) concentration knows and sees

[1] *Buddhist Philosophy*, p. 90.

what really is. A person who knows and sees what really is, does not need to make an effort of will to feel disinterested and renounce. It is *in the nature of things* that a person who knows and sees as it really is, feels disinterested and renounces. One who has felt disinterested and has renounced does not need an effort of will to realize the knowledge and insight of emancipation (vimutti-ñāṇadassanaṃ). It is *in the nature of things* that one who has felt disinterested and renounced, realizes the knowledge and insight of emancipation'. (*Dhammatā* esā . . . yaṃ samāhito yathābhūtaṃ jānāti passati. Yathābhūtaṃ jānato passato na cetanāya karaṇīyaṃ 'nibbindāmi virajjāmī' ti. *Dhammatā* esā . . . yaṃ yathābhūtaṃ jānaṃ passaṃ nibbindati virajjati. Nibbinnassa . . . virattassa na cetanāya karaṇīyaṃ 'vimuttiñāṇadassanaṃ sacchikaromī' ti. *Dhammatā* esā . . . yaṃ nibbinno viratto vimuttiñāṇadassanaṃ sacchikaroti, A. V.3, 313.) Here the 'knowledge and insight' (ñāṇa-dassana) which is a means to an end and is often called paññā (*v. infra,* 797) as well as the final 'knowledge and insight of emancipation' (vimuttiñāṇadassana-), which is the end itself, are considered to be natural causal occurrences.

(725) This difference in valuation is clearly brought out when we compare the views of Pūraṇa Kassapa and the Buddha on the nature of knowledge. Both claim to belong to the same class of thinkers on epistemological grounds. Pūraṇa Kassapa is a ñāṇa-vādin (*v. supra,* 720) and so is the Buddha (*v. supra,* 718). But their theories with regard to the genesis of knowledge are utterly different. Pūraṇa holds that 'there is no cause or condition for the lack of knowledge and insight . . . or for the presence of knowledge and insight' (natthi hetu natthi paccayo aññāṇāya adassanāya . . . ñāṇāya dassanāya, S. III.126), while the Buddha holds that 'there was a cause and reason' (atthi hetu atthi paccayo, *loc. cit.*) for both. This is partly due to the fact that Pūraṇa was a niyati-vādin or a Strict Determinist (*v. supra,* 199), but even the Middle and Late Upaniṣadic thinkers in claiming that the arising of the final intuition of reality was due to the grace of Ātman or God (*v. supra,* 73) subscribe to a similar view.

(726) In outlining the causes and conditions for the emergence or non-emergence of this (kind of) knowledge it is said: 'When one dwells with one's mind obsessed with and given to passion and one does not truly know and see the elimination of the passion that has arisen, it is a cause of one's failure to know and see . . . (likewise) ill-will, sloth and torpor, excitement and perplexity, and doubt (are causes

of one's failure to know and see).'[1] On the other hand, the cultivation of the seven factors of enlightenment (sattabojjhaṅga) is said to be a cause and condition for the arising of knowledge and insight.[2]

(727) The five factors outlined above as what causes the lack of knowledge and insight are in fact the same as what is commonly known in the Pāli Nikāyas as 'the five impediments' (pañcanīvaraṇa-, D. I.73). According to the Buddhist theory, the elimination of these five factors is said to clear the way for the development of the jhānas or the meditative states of the mind: 'When these five impediments are eliminated he looks within himself and gladness arises in him and with gladness, joy; with his mind overjoyed his mind becomes at ease and with his body at ease he experiences happiness; being happy his mind becomes concentrated.'[3] Then follows a description of the first up to the fourth jhānas.[4] It is at this stage, on the attainment of the fourth jhāna 'when the mind is concentrated, pure, cleansed, free from blemishes, purged of adventitious defilements, supple, pliant, steady and unperturbed' (evaṃ samāhite citte parisuddhe pariyodāte anaṅgaṇe vigatūpakkilese mudubhūte kammaniye ṭhite ānejjappatte, D. I.76) that he is said to 'turn and direct his mind to knowing and seeing' (ñāṇa-dassasāya cittaṃ abhinīharati abhininnāmeti, *loc. cit.*). The mind in this state is said to observe introspectively but directly one's consciousness associated with the body.[5] In this same state he turns and directs his mind to 'psycho-kinetic activity' (iddhi-vidhāya, D. I.77), to 'clair-audience' (dibbāya sotadhātuyā, D. I.79), to 'telepathic knowledge' (cetopariya*ñāṇāya*, D. I.79), to the 'retrocognitive knowledge of past existences' (pubbenivāsānussati*ñāṇāya*, D. I.81), to the 'knowledge of the decease and survival of beings' (sattānaṃ

[1] Yasmiṃ . . . samaye kāmarāgapariyuṭṭhitena cetasā viharati kāmarāgaparetena uppannassa ca kāmarāgassa nissaraṇaṃ yathābhūtaṃ na jānāti na passati ayam pi . . hetu ayam paccayo aññāṇāya adassanāya . . . byāpāda- . . . thīnamiddha- . . . uddhaccakukkucca- . . . vicikicchā-, S. V.127.

[2] Katamo pana bhante hetu, katamo paccayo ñāṇāya dassanāya, kathaṃ sahetu sapaccayo ñāṇaṃ dassanaṃ? Idha . . . satiṣambojjhaṅgaṃ bhāveti . . . pe . . . upekkhāsambojjhaṅgaṃ, S. V.127, 128.

[3] Tass' ime pañcanīvaraṇe pahīne attani samanupassato pāmujjaṃ jāyati, pamuditassa pīti jāyati, pītimanassa kāyo passambhati, passaddhakāyo sukhaṃ vedeti, sukhino cittaṃ samādhiyati, D. I.73.

[4] These correspond to the 'bhūmi-s' or the levels of consciousness described in the Akṣyupaniṣad, as studied by Przyluski and Lamotte; 'Bouddhisme et Upaniṣad' in BEFEO., Vol. 32, pp. 160 ff.

[5] Ayam me kāyo rūpī . . . idañ ca pana me viññāṇaṃ ettha sitaṃ ettha paṭibaddhan ti, D. I.76.

cutūpapātañāṇāya, D. I.82), to the 'knowledge of the destruction of defiling impulses' (āsavakkhaya*ñāṇāya*, D. I.83). These six came to be known as the 'six (kinds of) higher knowledge' (chaḷabhiññā, *v. infra*, 752) in the Pāli Nikāyas but since the first is a case of 'knowing how' and not of 'knowing that'[1] it came to be dissociated from the rest and these latter were known as the 'five (kinds of) higher knowledge' (pañcābhiññā, *v. infra*, 752).

(728) We note here the operation of a causal process. The elimination of the impediments makes the mind concentrated in meditation and this in turn makes it possible for it to have knowledge and insight of things as they are (yathābhūtañāṇadassanaṃ). This is why it is often said that 'mental concentration is the cause of knowing and seeing things as they are' (yathābhūtañāṇadassanassa upanisā samādhi, S. II.30). One first 'obtains the attainment of virtue' (sīlasampadaṃ ārādheti, M. I.200); this is followed by 'the attainment of concentration' (samādhisampadaṃ ārādheti, M. I.201) and subsequently by 'the attainment of knowledge and insight' (ñāṇadassanaṃ ārādheti, M. I.202).

(729) Now the word paññā (wisdom) is often used to denote this 'knowledge and insight' which results from concentration in so far as it pertains to salvation (*v. infra*, 797). It normally has a wider connotation and is used to denote 'intelligence comprising all the higher faculties of cognition.[2] The five impediments (pañcanīvaraṇa-) are often defined as 'defilements of the mind and factors which weaken wisdom' (cetaso upakkilese paññāya 'dubbalīkaraṇe, M. I.181, 270, 276, 521; II.28). The alleged observation on which this theory is based is that, as we saw above (*v. supra*, 727) 'when the mind is emancipated from these five defilements, it is supple, pliant, lustrous, firm and becomes rightly concentrated for the destruction of the defiling impulses' (yato ca . . . cittam imehi pañcahi upakkilesehi vimuttaṃ hoti, taṃ hoti cittaṃ mudu ca kammaniyañ ca pabhassarañ ca na ca pabhaṅgu sammā samādhiyati āsavānaṃ khayāya, A. III.16, 17). In this state it is said that 'he directs his mind to those things which have to be realized by one's higher knowledge in order to realize them by one's higher knowledge' (*abhiññā*-sacchikaraṇīyassa dhammassa cittaṃ abhininnāmeti *abhiññā*-sacchikiriyāya, *loc. cit.*) and here we find enumerated the usual six kinds of higher knowledge he is capable of (sace ākaṅkhati, *loc. cit.*) having (A. III. pp. 17–19).

[1] On this distinction, *v.* G. Ryle, *The Concept of Mind*, Ch. II, pp. 25–60.

[2] PTS. Dictionary *s.v.*; on this term see Mrs Rhys Davids, *Buddhism*, 1914, pp. 94, 130, 201; *Compendium of Philosophy*, pp. 40, 41, 102.

(730) We find here the simile of gold-ore, which is compared to the mind. Gold-ore is said to have the defilements (jātarūpassa upakkilesā, A. II.16) of iron, copper, tin, lead, and silver (ayo, lohaṃ, tipu, sīsaṃ, sajjhaṃ, *loc. cit.*) but when it is purified, it shines with its natural lustre (cp. also S. V.92, 93). In a Brāhmaṇic context a simile of this sort, functioning as an analogical argument (*v. supra,* 14), would have constituted the proof of the statement that the mind shines forth with its natural lustre and acquires the faculties of extrasensory knowledge and vision, when purged of its defilements. But in the Pāli Nikāyas, unlike in the Jain literature (*v. suprā,* 243) *upamā* or 'comparison' is not considered a separate means of knowledge but only as an aid to understanding. It is often said that 'a simile . . . is employed in order to make clear the sense' (upamā . . . katā atthassa viññāpanāya, M. I.155; III.275; It.114) or that 'some intelligent people understand the meaning of what is said by means of a simile' (upamāya idh'ekacce viññū purisā bhāsitassa atthaṃ ājānanti, A. IV.163).

(731) Since sīla or 'virtue' is a prior requirement for the development of samādhi or 'concentration' (*v. supra,* 728), a causal relationship is established between sīla and paññā (wisdom). This explains the saying that 'wisdom becomes brighter with conduct' (apadāne sobhati paññā, A. I.102) and also the statement that 'wisdom is cleansed by virtue and virtue is cleansed by wisdom—where there is virtue there is wisdom and where there is wisdom there is virtue' (sīlaparidhotā . . . paññā paññāparidhotaṃ sīlaṃ yattha sīlaṃ tattha paññā yattha paññā tattha sīlaṃ. D. I.124).

(732) The five impediments (*v. supra,* 726) constituting the emotional factors as well as mental and physical lassitude (thīnamiddha) not only prevent the mind from being concentrated and thus affect the emergence of jhānic (extrasensory) perception but affect our cognitive faculties even in normal consciousness. A brahmin named Saṅgārava comes to the Buddha and asks the question: 'What is the cause and reason why at times even hymns which have been recited for a long period do not clearly appear (before one's memory) not to speak of hymns not so recited, while at other times even hymns not recited for a long time are easily remembered, leave alone hymns recited for a long time?'[1] It is replied that this happens when the mind is affected by one

[1] Ko nu kho . . . hetu ko paccayo, yen'ekadā dīgharattaṃ sajjhāyakatā pi mantā na ppaṭibhanti, pageva asajjhāyakatā? Ko pana . . . hetu ko paccayo, yen'ekadā dīgharattaṃ asajjhāyakatā pi mantā paṭibhanti, pageva sajjhāyakatā ti? A. III.230.

or more of the five impediments which tend to cause forgetfulness (A. III.230–6).

(733) Not only was the origin of knowledge conceived differently (*v. supra,* 725) in Buddhism despite the qualitative likeness in the way of knowing between the Early Buddhist and the Upaniṣadic thinkers (*v. supra,* 719), but there was no agreement regarding the content of knowledge as well. The Upaniṣadic thinkers conceived of the Ātman or the ultimate reality as being seen or perceived (dṛṣtam), heard or learnt (śrutam), mentally conceived (mataṃ) or rationally understood (vijñātaṃ) (*v. supra,* 70, 71), while in the Middle or Late Upaniṣads the Ātman or Brahman was 'attained' (prāptaḥ, Kaṭha, 2, 3.18) by the yogic process. But all that is claimed to be known by these means, including the last, is rejected in Buddhism, e.g. yam p'idaṃ diṭṭhaṃ sutaṃ mutaṃ viññātaṃ pattaṃ . . . manasā: tam pi n'etaṃ mama, n'eso'ham asmi, na m'eso attā ti (M. I.136). This is probably the reason why we find in the Buddhist texts an apparently ambivalent attitude towards ñāṇa. On the one hand, it is valued as a means of knowledge necessary for salvation (see, however, *infra,* 798, 799), while on the other hand what is directly known by it is discarded as not being the knowledge of the ultimate reality. Thus while it is said that 'the one who is sceptical should train himself in the path of intuitive knowledge —the Recluse has proclaimed his doctrines after intuitively understanding them' (kathaṃkathī ñāṇapathāya sikkhe, ñatvā pavuttā Samaṇena dhammā, Sn. 868), we also find statements which criticize ñāṇa—as inadequate for salvation, e.g.:

> Passāmi suddhaṃ paramaṃ arogaṃ
> diṭṭhena saṃsuddhi narassa hoti
> etābhijānaṃ 'paraman' ti ñatvā
> suddhānupassī ti pacceti ñāṇaṃ.
> Diṭṭhena ce suddhi narassa hoti
> ñāṇena vā so pajahāti dukkhaṃ
> aññena so sujjhati sopadhīko
>
> Sn. 788, 789.

I.e. 'I see the pure and the transcendent, without defect—by seeing is man's salvation; knowing this, seeing the pure and apprehending it as the transcendent, he falls back on intuitive knowledge. If man's salvation is by 'seeing' and he abandons sorrow by intuitive knowledge, he is saved in a different way (from the true way), being still subject to limitations (also cp. Sn. 908, 909).

(734) This is not a contradictory attitude. It only means that this kind of knowledge is necessary but not sufficient for salvation. This is made clear by the statement that 'the Exhalted One had declared that there is no salvation from belief, hearing (or learning) or intuitive knowledge . . . nor does he say that it is possible by the absence of belief, hearing (or learning) or intuitive knowledge' (na diṭṭhiyā na sutiyā na ñāṇena . . . ti Bhagavā visuddhim (*v.* l) āha, addiṭṭhiyā assutiyā aññāṇā . . . no pi tena, Sn. 839). What this means is that belief (=saddhā, sammādiṭṭhi- *v. supra,* 672), learning or hearing from a teacher (*v. supra,* 672) and the development of knowledge or the verification of what is accepted as a belief, are necessary but not sufficient conditions for salvation. Even 'the knowledge and insight of things as they are' (yathābhūtañāṇadassana-, S. II.30; V.432; A. IV.336), which is had by means of ñāṇa- is only a means to an end and not the end itself, which is 'salvation' (cp. sammāñāṇassa sammāvimutti pahoti, M. III.76) or 'the knowledge and vision of salvation' (vimuttiñāṇadassana-, M. I.145, A. III.81, S. V.162).

(735) There is yet another difference, which is apparent in the Early Buddhist attitude towards the data of intuitive experience, which differentiates it from that of the Middle and Late Upaniṣadic thinkers. The Buddhist considered it possible to misinterpret this experience and draw erroneous inferences from it (*v. infra,* 790). We thus find that Buddhism does not make the claim of the mystic that this knowledge was derived from a supernatural source in an unaccountable manner but that it is a product of the natural development of the mind, and due to the operation of causal processes. It does not regard the content of this experience (like the mystic) as identical with ultimate reality. Buddhism also believes that erroneous inferences could be drawn from these experiences. At the same time it does not decry normal perception but like the Materialists draws many of its conclusions on the basis of it (*v. infra,* 784). It would be misleading to call this mystical or intuitive knowledge in the context of Buddhism in view of the utterly different attitude to and evaluation of it. We shall, therefore, refer to this kind of knowledge as 'extrasensory perception' in the Buddhist context.

(736) When it was said that this knowledge was to be had 'personally' or 'individually' (sāmaṃ) it is necessary to point out that what is meant is not that this knowledge was incommunicable or subjective. The primary reason for the frequent use of 'sāmaṃ' to qualify the verb from √dṛś in these contexts, seems to be to emphasize the fact

that this knowledge is to be had by directly seeing 'oneself' and not indirectly by hearing it from some source (as in the Vedic tradition). Thus it is said that a 'monk does not hear that in such and such a village there was a beautiful girl or woman but has *himself seen* her' (Idha . . . bhikkhu na h'eva kho suṇāti amukasmiṃ nāma gāme . . . itthi vā kumārī vā abhirūpā . . . api ca kho *sāmaṃ passati*, A. III.90). The distinction is drawn as to whether 'one has seen it oneself or has heard it from a tradition' (sāmaṃ diṭṭho vā hoti anussavasuto vā, M. I.465). At a time when a statement would have appeared authoritative only if it was handed down by a long line of teachers (*v. supra*, 294), the Buddha emphasizes that 'he has seen it by himself . . . and that he is not saying so after having heard from another recluse or brahmin' (diṭṭhā mayā . . . taṃ kho nāññāssa samaṇassa vā brāhmaṇassa sutvā vadāmi, It. 58). 'Would it be proper', he says, 'for him to say so . . . if he had not known, seen, experienced, realized and apprehended with his wisdom' (mayā c'etaṃ . . . aññātaṃ abhavissa·adiṭṭhaṃ aviditaṃ asacchikataṃ aphassitaṃ paññāya . . . vadeyyaṃ, api nu me etaṃ . . . patirūpaṃ abhavissā ti, M. I.475). He preaches what he has himself verified to be true but he claims that he could instruct an honest and intelligent person to verify for himself what he had verified: 'Let an intelligent person come to me, sincere, honest and straightforward; I shall instruct him and teach the doctrine so that on my instructions he would conduct himself in such a way that before long he would himself know and himself see . . .' (etu viññū puriso asaṭho amāyāvi ujjujātiko: ahaṃ anusāsāmi, ahaṃ dhammaṃ desemi; yathānusiṭṭhaṃ tathā paṭipajjamāno na cirass'eva *samāñ ñeva ñassati sāmaṃ dakkhiti*, M. II.44). 'The dhamma' is described as 'bearing fruit in this life before long, an invitation to "come and see", leading to the goal and verifiable by the wise' (. . . dhammo sandiṭṭhiko akāliko ehipassiko opanayiko paccattaṃ veditabbo viññūhi, M. I.37). This shows that this knowledge was not claimed to be a private experience, which could not be communicated.

(737) We saw that while the Vedic brahmins upheld hearing (the scriptures) or testimony as the supreme source of knowledge the main school of the Materialists upheld perception and probably what could be directly inferred from it (*v. supra*, 93, 94) as the only means of knowledge. It is true that even in the Vedic tradition when it came to a matter of deciding between the testimony of sight and hearing, the decision was in favour of the former (*v. supra*, 69) and the Maitrī

Upaniṣad takes the stand that perception was the most reliable means of knowledge (*v. supra,* 69), but it was the Materialists who underlined the importance of perception even to the extent of discarding other means of knowledge. The Buddhists seem to have been influenced by the Materialists in their emphasis on perception, although perception here is both sensory as well as extrasensory. 'Who would believe', it is said, 'that this earth and the majestic mountain Sineru would be consumed by fire, *except on the evidence of sight*' (ko saddhātā ayañ ca paṭhavī Sineru ca pabbatarājā ḍayhissantī ti . . . *aññatra diṭṭhapadehi,* A. IV.103).

(738) The Buddhist theory of truth (*v. supra,* 596) also makes it clear that truth and therefore knowledge is objective, as telling us the nature of 'things as they are' (yathābhūtaṃ). The knowledge of things as they are consists in knowing 'what exists as "existing" and what does not exist as "not existing" ' (santaṃ vā atthī ti ñassati asantaṃ vā natthī ti ñassati, A. V.36). 'Knowing things as they are', it is said, 'wherever they are, is the highest knowledge' (etad anuttariyaṃ . . . ñāṇānaṃ yadidaṃ tattha tattha yathābhūtañāṇaṃ, A. V.37). What is taught by the Buddha is claimed to be objectively valid: 'Whether the Tathāgata preaches the dhamma to his disciples or does not preach it, the dhamma remains the same' (desento pi Tathāgato sāvakānaṃ dhammaṃ tādiso va adesento pi hi dhammo tādiso va, M. I.331).

(739) The importance of eliminating subjective bias and of getting rid of habits of mind that cause people to fall into error is often stressed. It was the Sceptics who paid the greatest attention to this subject. The first school of Sceptics said that truth cannot be arrived at and it was always a subjective factor such as attachment (chando), passion (rāgo), hate (doso), or repulsion (paṭigho), which makes one accept a proposition as true (*v. supra,* 159). We have already seen that the Buddha's attitude to the debate (*v. supra,* 688) was similar to that of the Sceptics, most of whom avoided debate because of the vexation that it caused (*v. supra,* 338). We similarly see the influence of the above doctrine of the Sceptics where it is said that there are 'four ways of falling into injustice' or untruth (agati-gamanāni, A. II.18), namely out of attachment (chanda-), hatred (dosa-), ignorance (moha-), and fear (bhaya-); the arhat or the 'ideal person' in Buddhism is not misled in any of these four ways (D. III.133). The difference from Scepticism is that this does not result in Buddhism in total scepticism with regard to the possibility

of truth. One's emotions, whether it be one's likes or dislikes, can distort the truth and the Buddha warns his disciples: 'If others were to speak ill of me, the Dhamma and the Order, do not bear any hatred or ill-will towards them or be displeased at heart . . . for if you were to be enraged and upset, will you be able to know whether these statements (criticisms) of others were fair or not?'[1] On the other hand, 'if others were to speak in praise of me, my Dhamma or my Order, you should not be happy, delighted and elated at heart . . . for if you were to be happy, delighted and elated, it will only be a danger to you . . .'.[2] The Buddha himself claims to be neither pleased at the praise of others nor displeased at their abuse. He encourages his disciples to develop this same attitude (tatra ce . . . pare Tathāgataṃ akkosanti . . . tatra . . . Tathāgatassa na hoti āghāto . . . tatra ce . . . pare Tathāgataṃ sakkaronti . . . na hoti ānando . . . Tasmātiha . . . tumhe ce pi pare akkoseyyuṃ . . . tatra tumhehi na āghāto . . . karaṇīyo . . . pare sakkareyyuṃ . . . tatra tumhehi na ānando . . . karaṇīyaṃ, M. I.140). When Sāriputta, his own disciple, says in praise of him: 'I have such faith in the Exalted One that I do not think that there ever has been, nor will there ever be a recluse or brahmin who has greater understanding and knowledge than the Exalted One',[3] he quietly rebukes him with the remark, 'have you examined the minds of the perfectly enlightened Exalted Ones of the past . . . the future . . . or my own mind in the present'.[4] To this Sāriputta replies that he has not. The Buddha thereupon remarks, 'then why have you uttered a statement so grand, bold, made a categorical claim and uttered a lion's roar to the effect that "I have such faith . . ."'[5] This incident displays the basically objective attitude of the Buddha, who demanded that for statements to be significant and true, they must

[1] Mamaṃ vā . . . pare avaṇṇaṃ bhāseyyuṃ dhammassa vā avaṇṇaṃ bhāseyyuṃ Saṅghassa vā avaṇṇaṃ bhāseyyuṃ, tatra, tumhehi na āghāto appaccayo na cetaso anabhiraddhi karaṇīyā . . . tatra ce tumhe assatha kupitā vā anattamanā vā api nu tumhe paresaṃ subhāsitaṃ dubbhāsitaṃ ājāneyyāthā ti? D. I.3.

[2] Mamaṃ vā . . . pare vaṇṇaṃ bhāseyyuṃ dhammassa vā vaṇṇaṃ bhāseyyuṃ Saṅghassa vā vaṇṇaṃ bhāseyyuṃ tatra tumhehi na ānando na somanassaṃ na cetaso ubbillāvitattaṃ karaṇīyaṃ . . . tatra ce tumhe assatha ānandino sumanā ubbillāvitā tumhaṃ yev'assa tena antarāyo, *loc. cit.*

[3] Evam pasanno aham bhante Bhagavati, na cāhu na ca bhavissati na c'etarahi vijjati añño samaṇo vā brāhmaṇo vā bhiyyo'bhiññātaro, D. I.99.

[4] Kin nu . . . ye te ahesuṃ atītam addhānaṃ arahanto Sammāsambuddhā, sabbe te Bhagavanto cetasā ceto paricca viditā . . . kiṃ pana ahaṃ te etarahi . . . cetasā ceto paricca vidito, D. III.100.

[5] Atha kiñ carahi te ayaṃ . . . uḷārā āsabhī vācā bhāsitā, ekaṃso gahito, sīhanādo nadito, evaṃ pasanno ahaṃ . . ., D. III.100.

be based on evidence that warrants their assertion and not on the grounds of our subjective prejudices.

(740) The impact of desire on belief is clearly recognized in Buddhism. One of the causal statements made is that 'on account of desire there is clinging' (taṇhāpaccayā upādānaṃ, M. I.261). This 'clinging' is described as four-fold, viz. clinging to sense-pleasures (kāmupādānaṃ), to rituals (sīlabbatupādānaṃ), to *metaphysical beliefs* (*diṭṭhupādānaṃ*) and to *soul-* (*or substance-*) *theories* (*attavādupādānaṃ*). We are here only concerned with the latter two. This means that we believe in certain metaphysical theories and soul- or substance-theories because we are impelled by our desires to believe in them.[1] These desires are analysed as three-fold, viz. the desire for sense-gratification (kāma-taṇhā, M. I.48, 299; III.250), the desire for personal immortality (bhava-taṇhā, *loc. cit.*) and the desire for annihilation (or the desire for power?[2] vibhava-taṇhā, *loc. cit.*). These specific desires are not correlated with any particular beliefs in the Pāli tradition, but most probably it would have been thought that those whose desire for personal immortality (bhava-taṇhā)was strong would have believed in 'a theory of personal immortality' (bhava-diṭṭhi, A. I.83), while those who had a strong desire for annihilation (vibhava-taṇhā) would have believed in an 'annihilationist (Materialist) theory' (vibhava-diṭṭhi, M. I.65). The beliefs in soul and substance thus not only have their origins in our linguistic habits (*v. supra,* 133, 533) but is also rooted in a craving in us to believe in them. The acceptance of a causal impact of our desires on our beliefs did not, however, result in scepticism with regard to the possibility of knowledge, since according to the Buddhist theory, causation was not deterministic (*v. infra,* 764) and desires therefore did not necessitate all our beliefs. The stress laid on the importance of eliminating subjective bias is therefore probably due to a realization of this impact of desire on belief. The objectivity that should be achieved in introspection after attaining the fourth jhāna is described as follows:

[1] Cp. Stebbing, *op. cit.*, pp. 404–5, 'there seems to be a deep-rooted tendency in the human mind to seek what is identical, in the sense of something that persists through change . . . Hence the search for an *underlying* entity, a persistent stuff, a substance . . . Hence the popularity of substance theories in science . . .'.

[2] Both interpretations are possible since 'vibhava' means both 'power' and 'annihilation' in the Nikāyas (*s.v.* PTS. Dictionary). The latter is the usual interpretation given in the commentaries (see Dialogues III.208). At D. I.32, we find vibhava- used as a synonym of uccheda- (annihilation) and vināsa- (destruction): sato sattassa ucchedaṃ vināsaṃ *vibhavaṃ*.

'Just as one person should objectively observe another, a person standing should observe a person seated or a person seated a person lying down, even so, should one's object of introspection be well-apprehended, well-reflected upon, well-contemplated and well-penetrated with one's knowledge'.[1] This emphasis on the importance of getting rid of our prejudices and habits of mind, which make us fall into error reminds us of Bacon's 'idols',[2] which according to him interfere with the objectivity of our thinking.

(741) We may next inquire as to what means of knowledge constitute this alleged objective 'knowledge and vision' (ñāṇadassana-) or 'knowing and seeing' (jānāti passati). We may dismiss verbal testimony since the above 'seeing' was sharply distinguished from it (*v. supra*, 736) and we have ample evidence (*v. supra*, Chs. IV and VIII) that it was not considered a genuine means of knowledge. We may also dismiss reasoning in the sense of takka- (indirect proof, or *a priori* proof) as an unsatisfactory means of knowledge according to Buddhism. This is probably the reason why 'the dhamma' is said to 'fall outside the scope of *takka-* but be verifiable by the wise' (dhammo . . . atakkāvacaro . . . paṇḍitavedanīyo, M. I.167). Since comparison or upamā is also not recognized as a means of knowing (*v. supra*, 730), we are left with perception (normal and paranormal) and inference based on perception (in the sense in which this was understood by the second group—group (2)—of Materialists, *v. supra*, 94). By examining the terminology and descriptions of knowledge in the light of the claims of knowledge, we find that it was these means of knowledge, which are denoted by the phrase 'jānāti passati' and the word 'ñāṇadassana-'.

(742) We have already observed that the phrase 'jānāti passati' was used to denote the knowledge derived from perception on the part of the Materialists (*v. supra*, 721) and the yogic intuition of the Mystic (*v. supra*, 719). If we take the words for 'seeing' we find that they are used in the Nikāyas to denote normal as well as extrasensory perception. Thus at A. III.208 (cp. 299) the word 'diṭṭhaṃ' is used for what is 'observed' by sight;[3] at Ud. 68, 'diṭṭha-' is used to denote what is

[1] Seyyathā pi . . . añño vā aññaṃ paccavekkheyya, ṭhito vā nisinnaṃ paccavekkheyya, nisinno vā nipannaṃ paccavekkheyya, evam eva . . . paccavekkhanānimittaṃ suggahītaṃ hoti sumanasikataṃ sūpadhāritaṃ suppaṭividdhaṃ paññāya . . ., A. III. 27.

[2] *v.* Russell, *A History of Western Philosophy*, p. 566.

[3] Api nu tumhehi *diṭṭhaṃ* vā sutaṃ vā ayaṃ puriso pāṇātipātaṃ pahāya . . . tam enaṃ rājāno gahetvā hananti.

'perceived'[1] by the touch of blind men. At It. 58, 'diṭṭha-' is used to refer to what is 'seen'[2] by the Buddha by means of extrasensory perception. It is necessary to note that 'diṭṭhi-' (belief) is sharply distinguished from diṭṭha- in the sense of what is perceptually observed, e.g. diṭṭhi-gatan ti etaṃ apanītaṃ etaṃ Tathāgatassa. Diṭṭhaṃ etaṃ Tathāgatena, M. I.486). The Niddesa which belongs to the Nikāyas, commenting on the verb 'addakkhi' which means 'he saw' says it could mean 'he saw with his telepathic knowledge . . . retrocognitive knowledge . . . his human eye or divine eye' (paracitta-ñāṇena vā addakkhi, pubbenivāsānussatiñāṇena vā . . . maṃsacakkhunā vā . . . dibbena cakkhunā . . . Nd. 1.323). This means that 'see' may denote normal or paranormal (extrasensory) perception. Likewise dassana- is used for 'visual perception' (A. III.325) as well as in a wider sense of 'perception' which includes both sensory and extrasensory perception (e.g. āsavā *dassanā* pahātabbā, M. I.7). Ñāṇa-dassana-, as we saw (*v. supra*, 719) was used generally to denote the knowledge derived from extrasensory perception. When the Buddha says that 'there arose in him the knowledge and insight that Uddaka Rāmaputta had died the previous night' (ñāṇañ ca pana dassanaṃ udapādi: abhidosakālakato Uddako Rāmaputto ti, M. I.170), we have to presume that this knowledge and insight was had by means of extrasensory perception, although the Comy. tries to make out that omniscience is here intended.[3]

(743) It may be observed that ñāṇa-dassana- is also used to denote the knowledge of salvation which is normally distinguished from it and is called 'the knowledge and insight of salvation' (vimutti-ñāṇadassana-) as opposed to 'the knowledge and insight of things as they are' (yathābhūta-ñāṇadassana-) (*v. supra*, 724), e.g. 'there arose in me the knowledge and insight that my salvation is unshakable, that this is the last birth and that there is no further birth' (ñāṇañ ca pana me dassanaṃ udapādi: akuppā me vimutti, ayam antimā jāti natthi dāni punabbhavo, M. I.167; III.162). Ñāṇa-dassana- in this sense is equivalent to *aññā* (final knowledge), a term which is exclusively used to denote this knowledge of final salvation (e.g. idha bhikkhu aññaṃ byākaroti, M. III.29; aññāya nibbutā dhīrā, S. I.24; sammadaññā vimuttā, M. II.43).

(744) The psychology of perception in the Nikāyas has been studied by Dr Sarathchandra, who is impressed by the empiricist approach

[1] *Diṭṭho* . . . jaccandhehi hatthi. [2] *Diṭṭhā* . . . mayā sattā apāyaṃ upapannā.
[3] Ñāṇañ ca pana me ti mayhaṃ sabbaññutañāṇaṃ udapādi, MA. II.186.

to the subject found here. He says that 'what is most interesting in the analysis of mind contained in this literature is its empiricist approach and the fact that this approach produced results which are strikingly similar to those produced by modern psychologists using introspective methods . . . I believe that these are the first speculations putting forward a naturalistic view of mind and the closest in the ancient world to present-day psychological theories'.[1] The *raison d'être* of this new theory of perception according to Dr Sarathchandra is that 'Buddhism having cast aside the current conceptions about the soul, had to advance an alternative hypothesis to explain such functions of the senses as seeing, hearing, smelling or tasting which, in the Upaniṣadic philosophy, were activities of the Ātman residing in the respective sense-organs' (*op. cit.*, p. 3).

(745) In our opinion, this explanation puts the cart before the horse. It is not that Buddhism casts aside the concept of the soul and then evolves a completely new theory of perception altogether but that the approach of Buddhism results on the one hand in the elimination of metaphysics and on the other in the retention and development of some of the empiricist findings in the Upaniṣadic theories of perception. Let us illustrate this. The Buddhist account gives a strictly causal explanation of the origin of sense-cognition without recourse to any of the Upaniṣadic metaphysical concepts. Visual cognition, for example, results from the presence of three conditions (1) an unimpaired internal sense-organ of sight (ajjhattikaṃ . . . cakkhu aparibhinnaṃ hoti, M. I.190), (2) external visible forms entering into the field of vision (bāhirā ca rūpā āpāthaṃ āgacchanti, *loc. cit.*), and (3) an appropriate[2] act of attention on the part of the mind (tajjo ca samannāhāro hoti, *loc. cit.*). When these conditions are satisfied, it is said that 'there is a manifestation of this kind of perception' (viññāṇa-bhāgassa pātubhāvo

[1] *Buddhist Psychology of Perception,* The Ceylon University Press, Colombo, 1958, Introductory Note, p. viii. This was originally presented as a Ph.D. thesis, viz. The Psychology of Perception in Pali Buddhism with special reference to the theory of *bhavaṅga,* Ph.D. (London), 1948.

[2] Tajjassa ti tadanurūpassa, i.e. tajja- means appropriate to it, M.A. II.229. Sarathchandra says that 'samannāhāro' here can refer to either 'an automatic act of sensory attention' or a 'deliberate act directed by interest' (*v. op. cit.*, p. 21). He prefers the former and adds that 'the Sanskrit is preserving the original meaning of the term' (*op. cit.*, p. 22) but the Śālistamba Sūtra (quoted by him) merely has 'tajja- manasikāram pratītya', i.e. on account of the reflection resulting from it (*v.* ed. N. A. Śāstri, Adyar, 1950, p. 15; cp. Mādhyamaka Vṛtti, ed. Poussin, p. 567.

hoti, *loc. cit.*). All the above conditions, it is said, must be satisfied for the production of the above result. If condition (1) is satisfied but not (2) and (3), or if conditions (1) and (2) are satisfied but not (3), the result will not take place (*v.* M. I.190, lines 20 to 28). All this is in accordance with the Buddhist causal theory (*v. infra,* 766) but nevertheless the elements of the above hypothesis are traceable to the Upaniṣads and this Dr Sarathchandra (*op. cit.*, pp. 21, 22) does not seem to have noticed. Taking the ten sensory and motor organs together the Kauśītakī Upaniṣad points out that 'the material elements cannot exist without the cognitive elements nor the cognitive elements without the material elements and from either alone no form would be possible'.[1] Except for the fact that the 'cognitive elements' are here metaphysically conceived as the agents of the sensory functions, there is a recognition of the mutual causal dependence of sensible objects and their respective cognitions. Likewise the importance of attention for sense-cognition is recognized in the Upaniṣads where it is said, 'my mind was elsewhere, I did not see; my mind was elsewhere, I did not hear, for with the mind does one see and with the mind hear'.[2]

(746) While we have rendered viññāṇa- in the above passage (i.e. M. I.190) as 'perception' Sarathchandra translates it as 'sensation' (*op. cit.*, p. 21) and has a theory about it. He says that viññāṇa- in these contexts has been often 'interpreted to mean cognition' (*op. cit.*, p. 4) but that it meant 'not full cognition, but bare sensation, a sort of anoetic sentience' (*loc. cit.*); later he says that 'viññāṇa in the earliest texts was almost synonymous with saññā' (*op. cit.*, p. 16). This interpretation is based on the analysis of a single context (M. I.111, 112) and the alleged confirmation of this sense from the Abhidhamma (*op. cit.*, pp. 4, 25). Sarathchandra promises to 'analyse the various meanings of 'viññāṇa' (*op. cit.*, p. 4) but this promise is not fully kept (*v. op. cit.*, pp. 16–21) since he has failed to discuss those contexts in which viññāṇa- and the verbal forms of vi + √jñā have a distinctly cognitive connotation.

(747) Let us examine some of these contexts. The sense of 'knowledge' for viññāṇa- is quite clear where it is said that 'the Tathāgata should be examined in order to *know* (viññāṇāya, *lit.* for the knowledge of),

[1] Yaddhi bhūtamātrā na syur na prajñāmātrāḥ syur, yad vā prajñāmātrā na syur na bhūtamātrāḥ syuḥ, na hy anyatarato rūpaṃ kiñcana sidhyet, 3.8.

[2] Anyatra manā abhūvaṃ nādarśam, anyatra manā abhūvaṃ nāśrauṣam iti manasā hy eva paśyati, manasā śṛṇoti, Bṛh. 1.5.3.

whether he is perfectly enlightened or not'.[1] Defining viññāṇa- it is said that 'one discriminates (by means of it), therefore is it called knowledge' (vijānatī ti . . . tasmā viññaṇan ti vuccati, M. I.292); 'what does one discriminate—one discriminates the pleasurable from the painful and the neutral' (kiñ ca vijānāti: sukhan ti pi . . . dukkhan ti pi . . . adukkhamasukhan ti pi, *loc. cit.*). Paññā, a term which means 'understanding' and has a clearly cognitive import is placed on a par with viññāṇa-. It is said that 'the states of paññā and viññāṇa are intermingled; it is not possible to analyse and specify the difference—what one understands, one knows and what one knows, one understands' (yā ca paññā yañca viññāṇaṃ ime dhammā saṃsaṭṭhā no visaṃsaṭṭhā, na ca labbhā imesaṃ dhammānaṃ vinibbhujitvā vinibbhujitvā nānākaraṇaṃ paññapetuṃ. Yaṃ pājānāti taṃ vijānāti, yaṃ vijānāti taṃ pajānāti, M. I.292). It will be seen that vijānāti is used synonymously with pajānāti, a word which is employed to denote the 'cognizing' of the four truths.[2] A difference between the two words is, however, mentioned—'paññā- is to be cultivated and viññāṇa- comprehended; this is the difference' (paññā bhāvetabbā viññānaṃ pariññeyyaṃ, idaṃ nesaṃ nānākaraṇaṃ, M. I.293). In other words, viññāṇa- seems to be the general term for 'cognition', while paññā is more or less restricted in connotation to the cognition of spiritual truths. In a Sutta, which says that 'man is composed of six elements' (chadhāturo'yam . . . puriso, M. III.239), the statement is made that 'it is with viññāṇa- that one understands something' (tena viññāṇena kiñci jānāti, M. III.242). This is in fact a continuation of the sense in which we find the word used in the Upaniṣads (*v. supra,* 70).

(748) The context on which Sarathchandra bases his interpretation of viññāṇa- reads as follows: cakkhuñ ca paṭicca rūpe ca uppajjati cakkhu-viññaṇaṃ, tiṇṇaṃ saṅgati phasso, phassapaccayā vedanā, yaṃ vedeti taṃ sañjānāti, yaṃ sañjānāti taṃ vitakketi . . . We may translate this as follows: 'Dependent on the eye and forms arises visual perception, the concurrence of the three is contact, dependent on contact is sensation, what one senses one recognizes and what one recognizes one thinks about. . . .' Sarathchandra's argument is that 'knowledge comes later' (*op. cit.,* p. 4) in the above process. This interpretation assumes that there is a temporal succession in the above states; viññāṇa- is assumed to be a state occurring earlier than even vedanā or saññā

[1] . . . Tathagate samannesanā kātabbā, sammāsambuddho vā no vā iti viññāṇāyā ti, M. I.317.

[2] Pājānāti pajānātī ti . . . kiñ ca pajānāti, idaṃ dukkhan ti pajānāti . . ., M. I.292.

(*v.* sañjānāti) and hence it is 'bare sensation' or 'anoetic sentience'. But this interpretation is arbitrary since it is possible to argue that sensation (vedanā) and the rest arise simultaneously along with contact (phassa) and not in temporal succession. This is in fact how the Comy. construes it, saying 'on account of that contact, there arises dependent on contact, hedonic experience, etc. (vedanā), in a *co-nascent manner*'[1] (tam phassaṃ paṭicca *sahajātādivasena* phassapaccayā vedanā uppajjati, MA. II.77).

(749) Dr Sarathchandra also appeals to the Abhidhamma in support of this meaning of viññāṇa: 'In the Abhidhamma, viññāṇa- is defined as bare consciousness or sensation as yet undiscriminated by the selective activity of the mind. It is the awareness of the presence of objects. It does not produce knowledge of any sort' (*op. cit.*, p. 25). In support of this he quotes two statements from the Comy. to the Vibhaṅga (i.e. VbhA. 405 and 321: *op. cit.*, p. 25, fnn. 1 and 2). Neither of these statements in our opinion supports his conclusion. The Vibhaṅga, it may be noted, enumerates the 'five kinds of sense-cognition' (pañca-viññāṇaṃ) in the section and chapter dealing with knowledge (*v.* ñāṇavibhaṅga, ñāṇavatthu, p. 306). Now the Vibhaṅga states that 'with the five sense-cognitions one does not apprehend anything[2] other than what enters their sensory field' (pañcahi viññāṇehi na kañci dhammaṃ paṭivijānāti . . . aññatra āpāthamattā, Vbh. 321). Sarathchandra has quoted only part of this passage (from the Comy.) leaving out the other part. Naturally, it appears to mean the opposite of what it says. It is the same with the other quotation (VbhA. 405). When stated fully it reads: 'Even a very learned person does not apprehend a single act of good or evil other than the visual objects, etc., which come into his field of vision. Visual cognition here is mere visual perception. Auditory cognition, etc., (consists of) mere hearing, smelling, tasting and touching'.[3] In the light of the above evidence we can hardly agree with Sarathchandra's theory. We may take the 'six kinds of viññāṇa-' (cha . . . viññāṇakāyā, M. I.53, 259; III.216, 281) spoken of in the Nikāyas as comprising the five kinds of sensory perception and internal perception or introspection (manoviññāṇaṃ, *loc. cit.*).

[1] This is suggested even at M. I.190, where the five constituents are said to be present in a visual perception.

[2] The Comy. explains, 'one does not comprehend anything good or evil' (kusalaṃ akusalaṃ vā na paṭijānāti, VbhA. 405).

[3] Supaṇḍito pi puriso ṭhapetvā āpāthagatāni rūpādīni aññaṃ kusalākusalesu ekadhammaṃ pi pañcahi viññaṇehi na paṭivijānāti. Cakkhuviññāṇam pan'ettha dassanamattam eva hoti.

(750) As we have seen, in addition to normal perception, there is a recognition of paranormal[1] or extrasensory[2] perception, as a valid means of knowledge. The theory behind this was that when the mind is cleansed of its 'impurities' (upakkilesa-) or defilements, it acquires these faculties (*v. supra*, 729, 730). 'When the defilements of the mind are eliminated and the mind is prone to dispassion and is developed by dispassion, it becomes supple as regards the things verifiable by higher knowledge' (. . . cetaso upakkileso pahīno hoti nekkhammaninnaṃ c'assa cittaṃ hoti nekkhamma-paribhāvitaṃ cittaṃ kammaniyaṃ khāyati abhiññā sacchikaraṇīyesu dhammesū ti, S. III.232). The defilements (upakkilesā) of one who is engaged in developing the higher mind (adhicittaṃ anyuttassa) are said to be three-fold, gross (oḷārikā), medium (majjhimikā), and subtle (sukhumā). The gross defilements consist of misconduct with regard to body, speech or mind (kāyaduccaritaṃ, vacī°, mano°); the medium defilements are sensuous thoughts (kāmavitakka-), thoughts of destruction (vyāpāda-), and ill-will (vihiṃsā); the subtle defilements consist of attachment to one's race (jāti), country (janapada), egotism (avaññatti). Spiritual thoughts alone remain (dhammavitakkā avasissanti); when these defilements are got rid of, the mind is stayed within (cittaṃ ajjhattaṃ santiṭṭhati) and he directs it (abhininnāmeti) in the exercise of the six forms of higher knowledge (A. I.254, 255). These experiences are had 'after attaining the supreme perfection of equanimity and mindfulness' (anuttaraṃ upekkhāsatipārisuddhiṃ āgamma, M. I.367), which is characteristic of the fourth jhāna.[3] While we may be inclined to suspect the veridical character of these experiences, it was probably believed that 'since the mind was clear and cleansed' (citte parisuddhe pariyodāte, D. I.76) in this state, it was possible to have a clearer insight into the nature of things by means of this knowledge, than by normal perception.

(751) Poussin has emphasized the importance of 'abhiññā' (higher knowledge) in Early Buddhism.[4] Demiéville has made a comparative study of 'retrocognitive knowledge' (pubbenivāsānussatiñāṇa-) as mentioned in the Pāli Nikāyas and the Āgama (Chinese) literature.[5]

[1] Atikkanta-mānusaka-, *lit.* going beyond the human, D. I. 82; in this context, it is used only of dibba-cakkhu.

[2] Later in Indian thought we find the use of atīndriya-pratyakṣa-, *lit.* extrasensory perception.

[3] Cp. Upekkhāsatipārisuddhiṃ catutthajjhānaṃ, M. I.22; *v.* S. Lindquist, *Siddhi und Abhiññā*, Lund, 1935, p. 78.

[4] 'Le Bouddha et les Abhiññā' in *Muséon*, 1931, pp. 335–342.

[5] 'Le Memoire Des Existences Antérieures' in BEFEO., Vol. 27, pp. 283–98.

The most thorough study so far is by Lindquist who has made a comparative analysis and examination of the concepts of siddhi (P. iddhi) and abhiññā, as they occur in the Pāli Buddhist and Brāhmanical literature, especially Yoga.[1] He has occasionally compared this material with Western parallels and studies bearing on them. We shall, therefore, not go over trodden ground but confine ourselves to those aspects of abhiññā (higher knowledge), which concern the epistemology of Buddhist thought.

(752) The word abhiññā, as the PTS. Dictionary states[2] (*s.v.*), has an 'older wider meaning of special supernormal power of apperception and knowledge to be acquired by long training in life and thought'. Later, it exclusively means one of the six powers (*v. infra*), all of which are mentioned in all strata of the Pāli Canon. They are claimed to have been attained by the Buddha (M. I.69) as well as by his disciples (S. II.217, 222). It is said that 'out of five hundred monks, sixty have attained the six-fold higher knowledge'.[3] The six are as follows:

1. iddhividha-, i.e. psychokinesis (levitation, etc.)
2. dibbasotadhātu, i.e. clairaudience
3. cetopariyañāṇa-, i.e. telepathic knowledge
4. pubbenivāsānussatiñāṇa-, i.e. retrocognitive knowledge
5. dibbacakkhu, i.e. clairvoyance; also known as cutūpapātañāṇa (D. I.82), knowledge of the decease and survival of beings.
6. āsavakkhayañāṇa-, i.e. knowledge of the destruction of defiling impulses.

Of these, the first is strictly not a cognitive power in the sense of a 'knowing that' (*v. supra*, 727). It consists according to the Visuddhimagga in various manifestations of the 'power of will' (adhiṭṭhānā iddhi) in jhāna (*v.* Vm. 405) and have been dealt with at length by Lindquist (*op. cit.*, pp. 12–65). The sixth too is partly a case of 'knowing that'. Of the second (*v.* Lindquist, *op. cit.*, pp. 72–4), it is said that 'with one's clairaudience, clear and paranormal, one hears two (kinds of) sound, human and divine, far and near' (so dibbāya sotadhātuyā visuddhāya atikkantamānusikāya ubho sadde suṇāti, dibbe ca mānuse

[1] S. Lindquist, *Siddhi und Abhiññā*, Lund, 1935; cp. S. Lindquist, *Die Methoden des Yoga*, Lund, 1932, pp. 169–87.

[2] Cp. G. C. Pande, *Studies in the Origins of Buddhism*, University of Allahabad, 1957, p. 37.

[3] Pāncannaṃ bhikkhusatānaṃ . . . saṭṭhi bhikkhū chaḷabhiññā, S. I.191.

ca, ye dūre santike ca, D. I.79; M. II.19). This implies not only the alleged ability to perceive sounds even at a distance without the intervention of the physical media of hearing but the claim to be able to appreciate the sounds of non-human spirits. It is an expansion of auditory perception (without the medium of the sense-organ) both in extent as well as in (what may be called) depth. The Buddha is said to have heard the brahmin Bhārādvāja's conversation with the wandering ascetic Māgandiya at a distance by means of this faculty (M. I.502). Sunakkhatta confesses to Oṭṭhaddha that just three years after following the training of the Buddha he has the ability (in jhāna) of 'seeing celestial figures . . . though he cannot hear their voices'.[1]

(753) The other four forms of abhiññā, it will be noticed, are called specific forms of knowledge (ñāṇa-). Lindquist has not given the definition of 'the (paranormal) knowledge of another's mind' (ceto-pariyañāṇa-) as it appears in the Pāli Canon[2] and has also failed to see that two different kinds of telepathy are spoken of in these texts. Ceto-pariyañāṇa- corresponds to manaḥparyāya-jñāna- (Ard. Mag. manapajjavanāṇa-) in Jainism. According to the earliest account of this faculty it would appear that by means of it one would know only the general state of the mind of another. It is said, 'he comprehends with his mind the mind of other beings and individuals as follows: he knows that a passionate mind is passionate, (likewise) he knows a dispassionate mind, a mind full of hatred and free from hatred, ignorant and devoid of ignorance, attentive and distracted, exalted and unexalted, inferior and superior, composed and not composed, emancipated and not emancipated'.[3] This is compared to observing one's face in a mirror (ādāse) or a pan of water (udakapatte) and noticing whether there is a mole or not (sakaṇikaṃ vā . . . akaṇikan ti jāneyya, D. I.80). This description seems to imply that only the general character of another's mind is known in telepathy. But in the same stratum of thought it is said that 'one can read the mind, the states of mind, the thoughts and the trains of thought of other beings and individuals' (. . . parasattānaṃ para-

[1] Dibbāni hi kho rūpāni passāmi piyarūpāni . . . no ca kho dibbāni saddāni suṇāmi, D. I.152. [2] *Op. cit.*, pp. 75–7.

[3] So parasattānam parapuggalānaṃ cetasā ceto paricca pajānāti—sarāgaṃ vā cittam sarāgañ cittan ti pajānāti, vītarāgaṃ vā cittaṃ . . ., sadosaṃ vā cittaṃ . . . vītadosaṃ vā . . . samohaṃ . . . vītamohaṃ . . . saṅkhittaṃ . . . vikkhittaṃ . . . mahaggataṃ . . . amahaggataṃ . . . sauttaraṃ . . . anuttaraṃ . . . samāhitaṃ . . . asamāhitaṃ . . . vimuttaṃ . . . avimuttaṃ, D. I.80, 81.

puggalānaṃ cittaṃ pi ādisati cetasikam pi... vitakkitam pi... vicāritam pi..., D. I.213). At M. II.169, the Buddha claims to know by this means 'a specific thought' (parivitakkaṃ) in the mind of a brahmin student. In the Aṅguttara Nikāya (A. I.170, 171) it is said that one can know another's mind (ādesanā-pāṭihāriyaṃ) in both the normal and paranormal senses in one of four ways, viz. (i) by observing external signs (nimittena) (*v. supra,* 153), (ii) by getting information from others or from a mediumistic source, (iii) by listening to the vibration (vipphāra-saddaṃ) of the thoughts (vitakka-) of another as he thinks and reflects (vitakkayato vicārayato), and (iv) by comprehending with his mind the mind of another and observing how the mental dispositions are placed in the mind of a particular individual (manosaṅkhārā paṇihitā imassa cittassa antarā), on the part of one who has attained the state of concentration free from cogitative and reflective thought (avitakkaṃ avicāraṃ samādhiṃ). It will be noticed that (iii) and (iv) here represent two types of telepathy—*indirect telepathy,* had in normal consciousness where the 'thought-vibrations' of the other person are received and interpreted and *direct telepathy* had in jhāna. The Jain texts likewise distinguish between two kinds of telepathy; the Sthānāṅga Sūtra speaks of *ṛjumati* and *vipulamati* as the two types,[1] but the nature of the distinction is not clear.[2]

(754) The other three kinds of higher knowledge are of special concern to Buddhism since it is by means of them that 'the three-fold knowledge' (tisso vijjā) is attained (*v. infra,* 801). Demiéville deplores the lack of an original and well-established Buddhist theory on the memory of previous existences (*op. cit.,* p. 298) but the Pāli Nikāyas are apparently not interested in accounting for this memory by a theory but in merely stating that it is a faculty that can be evoked. It is said that as one directs one's mind, when it is supple and pliant after attaining the fourth jhāna (*v.* Lindquist, *op. cit.,* p. 78), 'he recalls his manifold past existences, one birth, two... for many periods of world-evolution and dissolution as follows, "I was in such a place with such a personal and family name, such a status, having such and such food, such and such experiences and such a term of life. Dying there I was born in such and such a place; there too I had such a name... Dying there I was born here". Thus he recounts his manifold previous

[1] *v.* Tatia, *op. cit.,* p. 66.

[2] It will be seen that the interpretations of these two terms by Umāsvāti (*op. cit.,* p. 66) and Pūjyapāda (*op. cit.,* p. 68) are different.

existences in all their aspects and details'.[1] This is compared to a person going on a journey from village to village being able to recall the details of his journey (D. I.81).

(755) Clairvoyance (*v.* Lindquist, *op. cit.*, pp. 82–8) is directed towards gaining a knowledge of the decease and survival of beings and acquiring an understanding of karma: 'With his clear paranormal clairvoyant vision he sees beings dying and being reborn, the low and the high, the fair and the ugly, the good and the evil, each according to his karma. . . '.[2] It is also by its means that one sees contemporaneous events beyond the ken of normal vision. Thus the Buddha claims to see the group of five monks dwelling in Benares in the deer-park of Isipatana (M. I.170) or Veḷukaṇḍakī Nandamātā giving alms to monks led by Sāriputta and Moggallāna (A. III.336). Anuruddha, who is considered the chief among those disciples who had attained clairvoyance (A. I.23), was believed to have the power of 'seeing a thousand worlds' (sahassaṃ lokānaṃ voloketi, M. I.213). This faculty resembles Jain *avadhi* (*v. supra*, 241) with the difference that the latter makes the vision of things possible irrespective of the time factor as well (*v.* Tatia, *op. cit.*, p. 61).

(756) With the last, i.e. the knowledge of the destruction of the defiling impulses, he is able to verify the Four Noble Truths as well as the origin and cessation of the defiling impulses: 'He knows "this is the truth of suffering", "this is the cause of suffering", "this is the cessation of suffering" and "this is the path leading to the cessation of suffering", "these are the defiling impulses", "this is the cause of the defiling impulses", "this is the cessation of the defiling impulses" and "this is the path leading to the cessation of the defiling impulses".'[3]

(757) Along with perception, both normal and paranormal, seems to have gone inference (anumāna). The word 'anumāna' occurs apparently

[1] So anekavihitam pubbenivāsaṃ anussarati—seyyathīdaṃ ekam pi jātiṃ dve pi jātiyo . . . aneke pi saṃvaṭṭa-vivaṭṭa-kappe. 'Amutrāsiṃ evaṃ-nāmo evaṃ-gotto evaṃ-vaṇṇo evam-āhāro evaṃ-sukkha-dukkha-paṭisaṃvedī evam-āyu-pariyanto. So tato cuto amutra upapādiṃ. Tatrāpāsiṃ evaṃ-nāmo . . . So tato cuto idhūpapanno' ti iti sākāraṃ sauddesaṃ aneka-vihitaṃ pubbenivāsaṃ anussarati, D. I.82.

[2] So dibbena cakkhunā visuddhena atikkantamānusakena satte passati cavamāne upapajjamāne hīne paṇīte suvaṇṇe dubbaṇṇe sugate duggate yathā-kammūpage . . . 'D. I.82.

[3] So 'imaṃ dukkhan' ti yathābhūtam pajānāti, 'ayaṃ dukkhasamudayo'ti . . . 'ayaṃ dukkha-nirodho' ti . . . 'ayaṃ dukkhanirodhagāminīpaṭipadā' ti . . . 'ime-āsavā' ti . . . 'ayaṃ āsava-samudayo' ti . . . 'ayaṃ āsava-nirodho' ti. 'ayaṃ āsava-nirodha-gāminī-paṭipadā' ti, D. I.84.

in the sense of 'inference' despite Mrs Rhys Davids' statement that '*anumāna* apparently does not occur at all' in the Piṭakas (*v.* ERE., Vol. 8, p. 133, fn. 4). In the Anumāna Sutta (M. I.95 ff.), the principle is laid down that one should not do unto others what one does not wish others to do unto you. This is said to be based on the knowledge that what is generally disliked by oneself is likely to be disliked by others as well; this knowledge is said to be due to inference: 'Here one should oneself *infer* (*anuminitabbaṃ*) as follows: "An evil person who is swayed by evil thoughts is disagreeable to and disliked by me; now if I were to be evil and swayed by evil thoughts, I too would be disagreeable and disliked by others".'[1] This embodies the following two inferences:

(i) I dislike an evil person.
X (i.e. any person other than me) is like me (as a person).
Therefore, X (probably) dislikes an evil person.[2]
(ii) X dislikes an evil person (conclusion of (i)).
I am an evil person
Therefore, X dislikes me.

(758) We also meet with the term 'anvaye ñāṇaṃ' (S. II.58, D. III.226, Vbh. 329) meaning 'inductive knowledge' in both the Nikāyas as well as in the Abhidhamma. By this is meant the inferential (inductive) knowledge that a causal sequence or concomitance observed to hold good in a number of present instances would have taken place in the (unobserved) past and will take place in the future. In the Saṃyutta Nikāya are described a number of causally correlated phenomena such as that 'with the arising of birth there is the arising of decay and death, and with the cessation of birth there is the cessation of decay and death', etc. (jātisamudayā jarāmaraṇasamudayo jātinirodhā jarāmaraṇa nirodho . . ., S. II.57). Knowing these causal correlations or sequences is called 'the knowledge of phenomena' (dhamme ñāṇaṃ, S. II.58). Then it is said, 'This constitutes the knowledge of phenomena; by seeing, experiencing, acquiring knowledge before long and delving

[1] Tatra . . . attanā va attānaṃ evaṃ anuminitabbaṃ: yo . . . puggalo pāpiccho pāpikānaṃ icchānaṃ vasaṃgato, ayaṃ me puggalo appiyo amanāpo; ahaṃ . . . pan'assaṃ pāpiccho pāpikānam icchānaṃ vasaṃgato, ahaṃ p'assaṃ paresaṃ appiyo amanāpo ti, M. I.97.

[2] This is an inductive inference from one particular instance to another; cp. A. J. Ayer, *The Problem of Knowledge*, Penguin Books, 1957, p. 72, 'The inference may be from particular instances to a general law or proceed directly by analogy from one particular instance to another'.

into these phenomena, *he draws an inference* (nayaṃ neti) *with regard to the past and the future* (atītānāgate, *loc. cit.*) as follows: 'All those recluses and brahmins who thoroughly understood the nature of decay and death, its cause, its cessation and the path leading to the cessation of decay and death did so in the same way as I do at present; all those recluses and brahmins who in the future will thoroughly understand the nature of decay and death . . . will do so in the same way as I do at present—*this constitutes his inductive knowledge* (idaṃ assa anvaye ñāṇaṃ, *loc. cit.,*)'.[1]

(759) These inductive inferences are based on a belief in causation,[2] which plays a central rôle in the thought of the Pāli Canon. It would be desirable to study this concept of causation in the Pāli Canon before we examine the use made of inductive reasoning in it.

(760) In the Ṛgveda there is a conception of order in the universe but not of a causal order, though we can trace the origins of the activity view of causation to the primitive animistic beliefs.[3] Explanations were given by assuming the existence of wills behind natural phenomena. The conception of ṛta (the course of things) comes closest to a conception of a natural physical order (*v. supra,* 12) but ṛta itself was considered to be the law of Varuṇa.[4] There was no doubt the search for first causes in trying to explain the origin of the cosmos, but often these were anthropomorphically conceived (*v. supra,* 5). In the Brāhmaṇas the order of the universe was mechanical but magical.[5] In the Aitareya Āraṇyaka, where the origin of the world is traced to Water, we find the earliest use of two words for cause and effect, namely mūla (*lit.* root) and tūla (*lit.* shoot) (*v. supra,* 64). Similarly, we find mūla and śuṅga (*lit.* shoot) used for cause and effect respectively in the Chāndogya

[1] Idamassa dhamme ñāṇaṃ; so iminā dhammena diṭṭhena viditena akālikena pattena pariyogāḷhena atītānāgate nayaṃ neti: ye kho keci atitam addhānaṃ samaṇā va brāhmaṇā vā jarāmaraṇaṃ abbhaññaṃsu, jarāmaraṇasamudayaṃ . . . jarāmaraṇanirodhaṃ . . . jarāmaraṇanirodha-gāminiṃ paṭipadaṃ . . . seyyathāpāhaṃ etarahi . . . ye hi pi keci anāgatam addhānam samaṇā vā brāhmaṇā vā jarāmaraṇaṃ abhijānissanti . . . seyyathāpāhaṃ etarahī ti, idam assa anvaye ñāṇaṃ.

[2] *v.* A. J. Ayer, *The Problem of Knowledge,* p. 72, 'In all such reasoning we make the assumption that there is a measure of uniformity in nature; or roughly speaking that the future will in the appropriate respects, resemble the past'.

[3] *v.* Stebbing, *op. cit.,* p. 293.

[4] *v.* Radhakrishnan, *Indian Philosophy,* Vol. I, p. 78 f.

[5] Radhakrishnan, *Indian Philosophy,* Vol. I, pp. 99 ff.

Upaniṣad, viz. 'understand this (body) is an effect which has sprung up, for it could not be without a cause' (tatraitac*chuṅgam* utpatitam ... vijānīhi nedam *amūlam* bhaviṣyatīti, 6.8.3). In the same context is mentioned a causal series: Being caused Heat, Heat Water, Water Food and Food the Body (Ch. 6.8.4). In the Kaṭha Upaniṣad (1.3.10, 11), there is a gradation of things starting with the senses (indriya-) and ending with the Person (Puruṣa) but this cannot be regarded as a causal series although it resembles to some extent the Sāṅkhya series.[1]

(761) The first true conceptions of natural causation seem to have arisen amongst the Ājīvikas, who were preoccupied with the problems of time and change (*v. supra,* 198, 208). We find two mutually opposed theories of change among them, Indeterminism or yadṛcchāvāda (*v. supra,* 199) and Strict Determinism or niyativāda (*v. supra,* 198), both of which are mentioned in the Śvetāśvatara Upaniṣad (1.2). The former maintained that all events were fortuitous and the latter that they were rigidly determined.

(761A) Another theory which was prevalent at this time was the theory of 'inherent Nature' (svabhāva-, Svet. 1.2; *v. supra,* 211). According to the Sarvadarśanasaṃgraha, it was adopted by the Materialists and was opposed to Indeterminism: 'If one says some things happen owing to chance, this is not right since it arises from inherent nature for it is said—fire is hot, water is cold and wind is even to the touch; by whom is this designed; it is fixed by inherent nature.'[2] Its relations with Determinism are not clear, but in common with it, human effort was considered to be of no avail: 'since everything is due to inherent nature, effort is useless.'[3] This svabhāvavāda did away with animistic, anthropomorphic, theistic and indeterministic explanations of events and tried to account for the changes which took place in terms of the inherent constitution of things. In doing so, it recognizes minor uniformities of nature,[4] e.g. fire is hot. In giving natural explanations and recognizing minor uniformities (though not a general causal order

[1] Radhakrishnan, *Indian Philosophy,* Vol. II, p. 250, referring to this passage in the Kaṭha Upaniṣad, Radhakrishnan says, 'Yet this is the earliest account of cosmic evolution which seems to have been utilized by the Sāṃkhya thinkers.'

[2] Ākāsmikaṃ syād iti cet—na tad bhadram svābhāvikād eva tad utpatteḥ tad uktam agnir uṣṇo jalaṃ śītaṃ samasparśas tathānilaḥ, kenedaṃ citritaṃ tasmāt svabhāvāt tad vyatiṣṭhitaḥ, ed. Abhyankar, 1951, p. 23.

[3] Svābhāvikaṃ sarvaṁ idañ ca yasmād ato'pi mogho bhavati prayatnaḥ, *Buddhacarita,* 9.58, Ed. Johnston, Vol. I, p. 102.

[4] Stebbing, *op. cit.,* p. 259.

of events) it paves the way for the idea of universal causation. We also noticed that causal arguments which presuppose a concept of causation were being used at this time particularly by the niyativādins (*v. supra*, 206) but it is not possible to identify a theory of causation with any of the non-Buddhist schools during this period.

(762) It is with Buddhism that we, for the first time, meet with a clear-cut theory of causation in the history of Indian thought.

(763) Causation as understood in Buddhism stands midway between the Indeterminism of yadṛcchāvāda and the Strict Determinism of niyativāda. The Buddhists seem to have coined the term adhicca-samuppanna- to denote the concept of yadṛcchā. These Indeterminists (adhicca-samuppannikā) are said to be of two types on epistemological grounds, (1) those who base their theory on (jhānic) observation, and (2) those who base their theory on reasoning (D. I.28, 29). The former, it is said, learn to recollect their past with their retrocognitive vision 'up to the moment of the arising of consciousness but not further' (saññuppādaṃ anussarati, tato paraṃ nānussarati, D. I.28, 29) and argue as follows: 'I did not exist before, but now not having existed, have come into existence' (ahaṃ hi pubbe nāhosiṃ, so'mhi etarahi ahutvā sattatāya pariṇato, *loc. cit.*). We see from this description the indeterminism of the theory—the belief that an event takes place with no relation to its past. The P.T.S. Dictionary derives the etymology of the term from Skr. * adhṛtya > P.adhicca (from √dhṛ, to bear, support) but it appears more likely that this word was coined on the analogy of paṭicca- (in paṭicca-samuppāda-, paṭicca-samuppanna-) in order to distinguish this concept from the latter. If so, the term is derived from adhi+ √i+(t)ya (gerundive) meaning 'having come on top of' as compared with prati+ √i+(t)ya meaning 'having come on account of'.

(764) The Buddhist theory likewise differed from Strict Determinism (niyativāda) in holding that 'the effort of the individual' (atta-kāra-) was sometimes a factor in causal processes and this was not strictly determined. The proof of this was the empirical fact that we feel free to act and exercise our effort, called our 'initiative' (ārabbhadhātu) in many situations[1] (A. III.337, 338). At A. I.173–5, three non-causationist

[1] Cp. Kathaṃ hi nāma sayaṃ abhikkamanto sayaṃ paṭikkamanto evaṃ vakkhati, natthi attakāro . . . ti? i.e. How can one walking up and down with one's own effort say that there is no personal effort . . ., *loc. cit.*

theories are criticized. One of these was a determinist theory which held that everything that happens is 'due to what one did in the past' (pubbekatahetu, *v. supra*, 211); the other was a theistic form of determinism, which held that everything was 'due to the creation of God' (issara-nimmāṇahetu) (*v. supra*, 211). The third theory that is criticized here is that everything happens 'without cause or reason' (ahetu-appaccayā); this could be a reference to an indeterminist (adhicca-samuppanna-) theory or to the determinism (niyativāda) of Pūraṇa Kassapa (*v. supra*, 199). Buddhism was also opposed to the quasi-determinism of svabhāvavāda (*v. supra*, 211).

(765) The words expressing causation in the Pāli Canon are too many to be recorded. As Stebbing says 'most transitive verbs except those that express emotional attitudes express causation' (*op. cit.*, p. 260). Buddhaghosa gives a list of synonyms meaning 'cause': 'paccaya-, hetu-, kāraṇa-, nidāna-, sambhava-, pabhava-, etc. . . . have the same meaning though the words are different'.[1] These are among the words frequently found denoting a 'cause' in the Pāli Canon; we may add the word 'upanisā'[2] (S. II.30, 31) to this list. Hetu and paccaya are the commonest and are used synonymously and together to denote 'cause' in the Nikāyas (M. I.444, 516; A. IV.151; S. IV.68, 69) but in the Abhidhamma Piṭaka, hetu is only the first of twenty-four paccayas (conditions) and denotes the psychological motives of an action.[3] The necessity for this distinction and change in meaning is foreseeable in the examples given of causation in the Nikāyas.

(766) We have already seen that in the account given of the causal genesis of sense-perception, three conditions were considered to be individually necessary and together sufficient for the production of the effect (*v. supra*, 745). To take a case of natural physical (biological) causation, it is said that if 'the five kinds of seed' (pañcabījajātāni)—the cause—are to 'sprout, grow up and attain maturity' (vuddhiṃ virūḷhiṃ vepullaṃ āpajjeyyuṃ, S. III.54)—the effect, three conditions have to be satisfied, viz. (1) the seeds have to be unbroken, not rotten, not destroyed by the wind or sun and fresh (akhaṇḍāni apūtini avātātapa-hatāni sāradāni, *loc. cit.*), (2) they must be well-planted (sukhasayitāni,

[1] Paccayo hetu kāraṇaṃ nidānaṃ sambhavo pabhavo ti ādi atthato ekaṃ vyañjanato nānaṃ, Vm. II.532.

[2] Cp. Sphuṭārthābhidharmakośavyākhyā, Vol. 1, p. 188, 'hetuḥ pratyayo nidānaṃ kāranaṃ nimittaṃ liṅgam upaniṣad iti paryāyāḥ.

[3] *v.* Nyanatiloka, *Guide Through the Abhidihamma Piṭaka*, p. 118.

loc. cit.), and (3) they must have the benefit of the earth and water. It is said that conditions (1) and (2) without (3) do not bring about the result, nor (1) and (3) without (2) but only when all three conditions are satisfied. The total cause thus consists of several conditions, each of which has a different relationship to the effect and is, therefore, a different type of condition. What the Paṭṭhāna does is to analyse and define these various conditions.[1] Sometimes the relationship between cause and effect may be one of mutual dependence, in which case we would prefer not to talk of a cause or effect for there is no priority of the cause. Thus one of the relationships subsisting between 'the psychophysical individual' (nāmarūpa) and his 'consciousness' (viññāṇaṃ) is such that 'the psychophysical individual is dependent on the consciousness' (viññāṇapaccayā nāmarūpaṃ, D. II.56) and 'the consciousness is dependent on the psychophysical individuality' (nāmarūpapaccayā viññāṇaṃ, *loc. cit.*). This relation is defined in the Paṭṭhāna as 'the condition of mutual dependence' (aññamañña-paccaya-)[2].

(767) Buddhaghosa commenting on the word samuppāda- (in paṭicca-samuppāda-=causation) says that the word denotes the presence of a plurality of conditions and their occurrence together (in bringing about a result): 'Samuppanna- means when arising, it arises together, i.e. co-ordinately, not singly nor without a cause' (uppajjamāno ca saha samā ca uppajjati na ekekato na pi ahetuto ti samuppanno, Vm. 521).

(768) Causation in Early Buddhism is not subjective and is not a category imposed by the mind on phenomena. Its objectivity is emphasized: 'Causation is said (to have the characteristics of) objectivity, necessity, invariability and conditionality' (tathatā avitathatā anaññathatā idappaccayatā ayaṃ vuccati . . . paṭiccasamuppādo, S. II.26). The Comy. explains these terms as follows: ' "Objectivity", etc., are synonyms of what is characteristic of causation. As those conditions alone, neither more nor less, bring about this or that event, there is said to be "objectivity"; since there is no failure even for a moment to produce the events which arise when the conditions come together, there is said to be "necessity"; since no event different from (the effect) arises with (the help of) other events or conditions there is said to be "invariability"; from the condition or group of conditions,

[1] *v.* Nyantiloka, *op. cit.*, pp. 118–127, for an account of these various relations as defined in the Paṭṭhāna.

[2] *v.* Nyanatiloka, *op. cit.*, p. 120.

which give rise to such states as decay and death, etc., as stated, there is said to be "conditionality".'[1]

(769) That a causal sequence or concomitance occurs independently of us and that all we do is to discover this, is implied in the following description of causation: 'What is causation? On account of birth arises decay and death. Whether Tathāgatas arise or not, this order exists namely the fixed nature of phenomena, the regular pattern of phenomena or conditionality. This the Tathāgata discovers and comprehends; having discovered and comprehended it, he points it out, teaches it, lays it down, establishes, reveals, analyses, clarifies it and says 'look!" (Katamo ca paṭiccasamuppādo? Jātipaccayā . . . jarāmaraṇaṃ; uppādā vā Tathāgatāṇaṃ anuppādā vā Tathāgatānaṃ ṭhitā va sā dhātu dhammaṭṭhitatā dhammaniyāmatā idappaccayatā. Taṃ Tathāgato abhisambujjhati abhisameti; abhisambujjhitvā abhisametvā ācikkhati deseti paññapeti paṭṭhapeti vivarati vibhajati uttanīkaroti passathā ti cāha, S. II.25).

(770) This causal cosmic order (*v.* sā . . . *dhātu dhamma*ṭṭhitatā . . . idappaccayatā, *loc. cit.*) was known as the dhamma-dhātu, which is claimed to be thoroughly comprehended (suppaṭividdhā, M. I.396) by the Buddha. Its causality is denoted by the term 'dhammatā' which literally means 'the nature of things'. Thus it is said, 'it is in *the nature of things* (dhammatā) that the absence of remorse is present in a virtuous person. A person who has no (feelings of) remorse need not determine in his mind that joy should arise in him. It is of *the nature of things* (dhammatā) that joy arises in a person who lacks remorse. A person who is joyful need not determine in his mind that delight should arise in him. It is of *the nature of things* that delight arises in a joyful person.'[2] Here by the term 'the nature of things' (dhammatā) are meant the causal psychological processes. But as we have seen, causality is not

[1] Tathatā ti ādīni paccayākārass'eva vevacanāni. So tehi tehi paccayehi anūnādhikeh'eva tassa tassa dhammassa sambhavato tathatā ti. Sāmaggiṃ upagatesu paccayesu muhuttam pi tato nibbattānaṃ dhammānam asambhav'-ābhāvato avithatā ti, aññadhammapaccayehi añña-dhammānuppattito anaññathā ti. Yathā vuttānam etesam jarāmaraṇādīnam paccayato vā paccayasamūhato vā idappaccatā ti vutto, SA. II, 41; cp. Vm. 518.

[2] Dhammatā esā . . . yam sīlavato . . . avippaṭisāro uppajjati. Avippaṭisārissa . . . na cetanāya karaṇīyam 'pāmujjam me uppajjatū' ti. Dhammatā esā . . . yaṃ avippaṭisārissa pāmujjaṃ uppajjati. Pamuditassa . . . na cetanāya karaṇīyam 'pīti me uppajjatū' ti. Dhammatā esā . . . yaṃ pamuditassa pīti uppajjati, A.V. 2, 3, 312; cp. for more examples, M. I.324, A. II.21.

confined to psychological processes. We mentioned an example of the operation of the causal process in the organic world (*v. supra*, 766). Likewise, when it is said that among the causes of the failure of rain are the disturbances of temperature and pressure (wind) in the upper atmosphere,[1] we notice an attempt to give a physical causal explanation of the phenomenon of rain (although mythical and ethical reasons for rain are also mentioned in this context).

(771) Those occurrences which are causally connected are considered to have the following relation, namely that (1) 'whenever A is present, B is present' (imasmiṃ sati idaṃ hoti, Ud. 2; M. I.264), and (2) 'whenever A is absent, B is absent' (imasmiṃ asati idaṃ na hoti, Ud. 2; M. I.264). This means that B does not occur unless A is present and occurs only when A is present. Thus a one-one correlation is established between the conditions constituting the cause and their effect. This is a scientific view of causation as opposed to the practical common-sense view.[2] (1) and (2) constitute the two main principles of causal determination as stated in the Pāli Nikāyas.[3] From the above abstract formula may be distinguished the concrete formula, which has reference to the world of change. 'From the arising of A, B arises; from the cessation of A, B ceases' (imass'uppādā idaṃ uppajjati . . . imassa nirodhā idaṃ nirujjhati, Ud. 2, M. I.263, 264; S. II.70).

(772) We find many applications of this formula. We have already noticed the explanation of psychological and physical processes (*v. supra*, 770) in terms of causation. We likewise find a causal explanation given of the origin of consciousness in order to reject the belief in an unchanging substratum of consciousness[4] (M. I.256–60). Similarly, we find a causal account of the genesis of the five constituents, we cling to.[5] Causal explanations are offered to repudiate the theory that

[1] *v.* . . . ime vassassa antarāyā . . . upari ākāse tejodhātu pakuppati tena uppannā meghā paṭivigacchanti . . . puna ca paraṃ . . . upari ākāse vāyodhātu pakuppati, tena uppannā meghā paṭivigacchanti, A. III.243.

[2] *v.* Stebbing, *op. cit.*, p. 264, 'The practical agent, however, is content with a relation that is determinate only in the direction *from* cause *to* effect; *wherever X occurs, E occurs.* But the scientific investigator wants to find a relation that is equally determinate in either direction, that is, he seeks a one-one relation: *wherever X occurs, E occurs, and E does not occur unless X has occurred.*'

[3] *v.* Stebbing, *op. cit.*, p. 319.

[4] Cp. O. H. de A. Wijesekera, 'Vedic Gandharva and Pāli Gandhabba' in UCR., Vol. 2, p. 93.

[5] Paṭiccasamuppannā kho pan'ime pañcūpādānakkhandhā . . . M.I.191. .

everything is strictly determined by our own actions in the past (S. IV.230), to disprove the belief that moral degradation and purity is due to fortuitous circumstances (S. III.69), and to show that the experience of pleasure and pain was not due to the work of metaphysical agents (S. II.38), etc.

(773) These general applications of the causal principle have in turn to be distinguished from the special application in what is called 'the Chain of Causation' after Burnouf.[1] This has been practically the only aspect of causation in Buddhism discussed by many scholars.[2] They have thus given a distorted view of the rôle of causation in these texts. Keith says that 'the chain of causation is essentially an explanation of misery; it tells us nothing regarding physical causes . . .'.[3] He concludes that 'to assign to Buddhism faith in the uniformity of the causal process or of nature is absurd' (*op. cit.*, p. 113), but it will be seen that this latter observation is without basis in the light of the evidence that we have adduced so far. Keith has failed to take sufficient note of the general formula of causation (*v. supra*, 771) or the two principles of causal determination, the mention both of psychological as well as of physical causal processes (*v. supra*, 770) and the conception of the cosmos as a causally ordered whole (*v. supra*, 770) in the Pāli Nikāyas.

(774) To discuss the problems raised by this 'Chain of Causation' and its treatment at the hands of scholars would divert us from our task. We shall therefore confine ourselves to making a few observations pertinent to our purpose. Almost all scholars have said that the purpose of this 'Chain' is to explain misery.[4] This is only partly true. From the evidence of the texts, it appears to have been used primarily to explain rebirth and karma without recourse to the metaphysical ātman-hypothesis of the Eternalists and without falling into the other extreme of Materialism. The Eternalists of the Upaniṣads explained rebirth and karma by assuming a self-identical soul which passed on from existence to existence as the agent of all actions and the recipient of reactions

[1] *v.* Thomas, *History of Buddhist Thought*, p. 58.

[2] Kern, *Manual of Buddhism*, pp. 46–9; P. Oltramare, *La Formule Bouddhique des Douze Causes*, Geneva, 1909; Poussin, *Théorie des Douze Causes*, Gand, 1913; Thomas, *History of Buddhist Thought*, pp. 58–70, 78–80; Stcherbatsky, *The Central Conception of Buddhism and the Meaning of the Word 'Dharma'*, London, 1923, pp. 28–31.

[3] *Buddhist Philosophy*, p. 112.

[4] *v.* Thomas, *History of Buddhist Thought*, p. 58, 'The Formula is held to expound the two truths of the origin of pain and the cessation of pain'.

(cp. Maitri, 3.1; Śvet. 4.12). As an Empiricist (*v. infra*, 793) the Buddha could not posit the existence of a soul. At the same time he could not, like the Materialists, deny the continuity of the individual after death and the responsibility of the individual for his actions. The *raison d'être* of the 'Chain of Causation' lies therefore mainly in the fact that it gives a causal account of the factors operating in maintaining the process of the individual and thereby of suffering. This is clear from the following statement: 'In the belief that the person who acts is the same as the person who experiences . . . he posits Eternalism; in the belief that the person who acts is not the same as the person who experiences . . . he posits Materialism. *Avoiding both these extremes* the Tathāgata preaches the doctrine in the middle. On ignorance depends our volitional acts (saṅkhārā)[1] . . . In this manner there arises this mass of suffering . . . does there cease this mass of suffering'.[2] Another purpose for which the 'Chain' was employed was to substitute an empirical causal explanation of the (relative) origin and development of the individual in place of an explanation in terms of metaphysical first causes or final causes. Thus, after enumerating the causal process of the genesis and development of the individual, the Buddha says: 'Would you, O monks, knowing and seeing thus probe (*lit.* run behind) the prior end of things . . . or pursue (*lit.* run after) the final end of things?' (api nu tumhe bhikkhave evaṃ jānantā evaṃ passantā pubbantaṃ vā paṭidhāveyyātha . . . aparantaṃ vā ādhāveyyātha, M. I.265). In the face of this evidence it is surprising that many scholars (Kern, Jacobi, Pischel, Schayer) should have tried to explain this 'Chain' as a 'kosmische Emanationsformel',[3] comparing it with the Sāṅkhya series. In fact it is expressly implied that 'ignorance' (avijjā) is not a first cause: 'The first beginning of ignorance is not known (such that we may say), before this there was no ignorance, at this point there arose ignorance' . . . but that ignorance is causally conditioned can be known' (purimā . . . koṭi na paññāyati avijjāya 'ito pubbe avijjā nāhosi, atha pacchā sambhavī' ti . . . Atha ca pana paññāyati 'idappaccayā avijjā' ti, A. V.113).

[1] For a detailed discussion of the meaning of this term, *v.* K. N. Jayatilleke, 'Some Problems of Translation and Interpretation I', UCR., Vol. 7, pp. 213–23.

[2] So karoti so paṭisaṃvediyatī ti . . . sassatam etaṃ pareti. Añño karoti añño paṭisaṃvediyatī ti . . . .ucchedam etaṃ pareti. Ete te . . . ubho ante anupagamma majjhena Tathāgato dhammaṃ deseti; avijjāpaccayā saṅkhārā . . . evam etassa kevalassa dukkhakkhandhassa samudayo hoti . . . evam etassa kevalassa dukkhakkhandhassa nirodho hotī ti, S. II.20, 21.

[3] *v.* Thomas, *History of Buddhist Thought*, p. 79.

(775) From the use made of causation in the Nikāyas, one could see that causal empirical explanations were everywhere substituted (e.g. theories of perception, knowledge, consciousness, etc.), for prevalent metaphysical theories. What about the theory of causation itself? Was it metaphysical or empirical? A comparison with some of the theories of causation in the Hindu philosophical schools is not without value for this purpose, in order to see more clearly where the Buddhist theory stood. We may list these theories as follows:

1. Śaktivāda (the theory that the cause is a kind of force)—Pūrva Mīmāṃsā.
2. Satkāraṇavāda = Vivartavāda (the theory that everything has Being as its cause and is a manifestation of Being)—Vedānta.
3. Satkāryavāda (the theory that the effect is contained in the cause)—Sāṅkhya.
4. Asatkāryavāda = Ārambhavāda (the theory that the effect is not contained in the cause and is something new)—Nyāya-Vaiśeṣika.

(776) Of these the Śaktivāda, which resembles an Activity theory[1] of causation, is criticized in the BHS. text, the Śālistamba Sūtra. Here it is said that although the 'element of heat' (tejodhātuḥ) is a causal factor in making a seed grow, it does not do this out of its own will: 'It does not occur to the element of heat, "I shall bring this seed to maturity" ' (tejodhātor api naivam bhavati, 'aham bījam paripācayamī' ti, Ārya Śālistamba Sūtra, Ed. Śāstri, p. 5). This sentiment, it may be noted, was already expressed in a psychological context in the Nikāyas, when it was said for instance that 'a person who lacks remorse need not *make an act of will* (saying), "*Let joy arise in me*". It is of the nature of things that joy arises to one who lacks remorse' (avippaṭisārissa na *cetanāya karaṇīyaṃ 'pāmujjaṃ me uppajjatū'* ti. Dhammatā esā ... yaṃ avippaṭisārissa pāmujjaṃ uppajjati, A. V.2; *v. supra*, 724). We may observe from this that even in psychological causation, a conscious act of will was not always considered necessary in bringing about a subsequent psychological state. This constitutes a criticism of the animistic and activist conception of causation.

(777) Although the Satkāryavāda, which is an Entailment theory[2] holding that the cause necessarily brings about its effect, which is contained in it and the Vedāntic Satkāraṇavāda are not mentioned as

[1] *v.* A. C. Ewing, *The Fundamental Questions of Philosophy*, pp. 169–72.
[2] *v.* Ewing, *op. cit.*, pp. 162–9.

such, we meet with foreshadowings of these two theories in pre-Buddhistic thought. In the Aitareya Āraṇyaka, where it was said that Water was the cause and the world the effect (*v. supra*, 760), we find the statement, 'whatever there is belonging to the son, belongs to the father; whatever there is belonging to the father, belongs to the son',[1] meaning by 'father' and 'son' cause and effect respectively. This seems to imply both that the effect (son) is contained in the cause (father) and that the cause (father) persists in the effect (son). This resembles the Satkāryavāda. Similarly in the thought of Uddālaka we found that Being (sat) was the ultimate substance, which manifested itself in the variety of the forms of nature (*v. supra*, 25); this is analogous to the Satkāraṇavāda. Now it seems to be this kind of belief of theory, which implies the presence of the effect in the cause or the immanence of the cause in the effect, that is criticized in the Poṭṭhapāda Sutta (Dīgha Nikāya). Here in the causal sequence 'milk, curds, butter, ghee, etc.', it was pointed out that one should not consider 'milk' to persist in 'curds' or 'curds' to exist in 'milk' in some mysterious manner (*v. supra*, 534), this is the kind of claim made in the above two theories. One may observe that according to the Satkāryavāda, 'the oil exists in the sesamum, the statue in the stone, *the curd in the milk*'.[2] The Asatkāryavāda, the least metaphysical theory, was in fact later confused with the causal theory of the Buddhists.[3]

(778) The Buddhist theory is therefore empirical since it spoke only of observable causes without any metaphysical pre-suppositions of any substrata behind them. It closely resembles the Regularity theory[4] except for the fact that it speaks of the empirical necessity (avitathatā, *v. supra*, 768) of the causal sequence or concomitance and does not seem to hold that all inductive inferences are merely probable (*v. supra*, 758). At the same time it is necessary to note that the Buddhist theory of causation was not deterministic (*v. supra*, 764), since it included mental decisions among the causal factors and these were not considered to be strictly determined. Thus, it is said that 'a person who knows and sees things as they are, need not make an effort of will (saying), "I shall become disinterested"; it is of the nature of things that a person who knows and sees becomes disinterested'.[5] But

[1] Aitareya Āraṇyaka 2.1.8.1; SBE., Vol. 1, p. 212.

[2] *v.* Das Gupta, *A History of Indian Philosophy*, Vol. 1, p. 257. [3] *Ibid.*

[4] *v.* Ewing, *op. cit.*, pp. 160–2.

[5] Yathābhūtaṃ . . . jānato passato na cetanāya karaṇīyaṃ 'nibbindāmī' ti. Dhammatā esā . . . yaṃ yathābhūtaṃ jānaṃ passaṃ nibbindati, A. V.313.

elsewhere it is said that if a person 'being ardent gains knowledge and insight, is pleased and satisfied with his knowledge and insight and because of it praises himself and looks down on others'[1] (M. I.195), he would not progress on to the next stage of his spiritual development (*loc. cit.*). So what is 'in the nature of things' (dhammatā) is only a probability and not a necessity, when psychological factors are involved.

(779) It is evident that causation plays a central rôle in the Nikāyas. It is claimed to be the truth about the universe discovered by the Buddha in the final stage of his enlightenment (Ud. 1, 2; Vin. I.1, 2). It is expressly identified with the dhamma: 'He who sees (the nature of) causation, sees the dhamma (i.e. the teaching) and he who sees the dhamma sees (the nature of) causation' (yo paṭiccasamuppādaṃ passati so dhammaṃ passati, yo dhammaṃ passati so paṭiccasamuppādaṃ passati, M. I.191). A stanza of great antiquity found both in the Pāli and the BHS. literature reads as follows:

Pāli: ye dhammā hetuppabhavā tesaṃ hetuṃ Tathāgato āha,
tesañ ca yo nirodho evaṃvādī Mahāsamaṇo.[2]
Buddhist Sanskrit: ye dharmā hetuprabhavā hetuṃ teṣām
Tathāgato' vadat,
teṣāñ ca yo nirodha evaṃvādī Mahāśramaṇaḥ.[3]

I.e. the Great Recluse says that the Tathāgata has spoken of the cause of things, which arise from causes and also of their cessation. Besides, it is said that the recluse Gotama in preaching his doctrine makes statements which are 'meaningful' (sappāṭihāriyaṃ, M. II.9) and 'causal' (sanidānaṃ, *loc. cit.*). Apart from this, there is much inscriptional evidence for a widespread belief in causation in the Buddhist world.[4]

(780) In the light of the above evidence, we cannot subscribe to Thomas' belief that in Buddhism causation was never applied as a 'universal philosophical principle',[5] to a similar view of Keith to which

[1] . . . Appamatto samāno ñāṇadassanaṃ ārādheti. So tena ñāṇadassanena attamano hoti paripuṇṇasaṃkappo. So tena ñāṇadassanena attān'ukkaṃseti paraṃ vambheti, *loc. cit.*

[2] Vin. I.41.

[3] The Laṅkāvatāra Sūtra, Ed. Nanjio, p. 444; Āryapratītyasamutpāda Sūtra, printed in Ārya Śālistamba Sūtra, ed. Śāstri, p. 26.

[4] *v.* S. Konow, *Corpus Inscriptionum Indicarum*, Vol. 2, Part I, 1929, pp. 152 ff. H. Johnston, 'The Gopalpur Bricks', JRAS., 1938, pp. 549 ff.; B. C. Law, 'The Formulation of the Pratītyasamutpāda', JRAS., 1937, pp. 290 ff.

[5] *Life of the Buddha*, p. 199.

we have already referred (*v. supra*, 773) nor with R. E. Hume's remark that 'neither Buddha nor the Buddhist writings had any interest in problems of ... scientific causation'.[1] Kern's criticism that in the 'Chain of Causation' 'the difference between *post hoc* and the *propter hoc* is utterly ignored'[2] is invalid, since the mention of the two principles of causal determination shows an awareness of the difference between coincidental and causal sequences. Thomas' observation that to say that 'birth is the cause of old age' is 'like calling day the cause of night'[3] is the kind of objection that has been levelled against the Regularity theory even in its modern form.[4]

(781) Mrs Rhys Davids has said that 'the only general principle of thought put forward in Europe which harmonizes with Buddhist axioms is that "Principle or Law of Sufficient Reason" for which certain logicians notably Leibniz claimed equal rank with the three named above, namely that "nothing happens without a reason why it should be so rather than otherwise". This comes very near to the idappaccayatā (this is conditioned by that) of Buddhist causality'.[5] This is a very misleading suggestion for the two have nothing in common. It is true that according to Leibniz's law of sufficient reason 'nothing happens without a reason',[6] but the reason is best known to God, who creates the best of all possible worlds, in which whatever happens necessarily contributes towards making it the best. This is the sufficient reason for all contingent truths and it lies in (the goodness of) God, who chose out of his free will to create this world in preference to every other possible world, which was relatively less perfect.[7] Since the knowledge of these reasons involves an infinite analysis of possible facts, in the light of their contribution to the goodness of possible worlds (and/or compossibility[8]), the reasons cannot usually be known by men.[9] This is an attempt to explain things in terms of final causes.[10]

[1] 'Miracles in the Canonical Scriptures of Buddhism' in JAOS., Vol. 44, p. 162.
[2] *Manual of Indian Buddhism*, p. 47. [3] *History of Buddhist Thought*, p. 62.
[4] Stebbing, *op. cit.*, p. 282. [5] 'Logic (Buddhist)' in ERE., Vol. 8, p. 133.
[6] B. Russell, *The Philosophy of Leibniz*, p. 32.
[7] R. L. Saw, *Leibniz*, Penguin Books, London, 1954, p. 36.
[8] Russell has suggested that in an esoteric account of his philosophy, Leibniz tries to account for existence by purely logical considerations, with no mention of God or creation, *v. A History of Western Philosophy*, p. 617.
[9] R. L. Saw, *op. cit.*, pp. 32, 33.
[10] Russell, *The Philosophy of Leibniz*, p. 34. 'Thus the law of sufficient reason, as applied to actual existents, reduces itself definitely to the assertion of final causes ...'.

It will be seen that this conception is theistic, metaphysical and relates to final causes. It is, therefore, utterly opposed to the conception of empirical causation as we find it in Buddhism.[1]

(782) Mrs Rhys Davids hailed the appearance of the causal theory of the Buddhist texts for the first time in Indian thought as an evolutionary moment in the history of ideas in one of her earlier works.[2] She distinguished between the 'formula of causation in general'[3] from the 'Chain of Causation' in her article on 'Paṭiccasamuppāda' in the ERE.[4] But when she changed her views about what constituted the message of original Buddhism and the methodology of discovering this, we find her anxious to dismiss causation as playing a very minor rôle in Early Buddhism.[5] She tries to make out that the causal theory was a contribution of the monk Kappina, suggests the flimsiest of evidence for this and ends up by admitting the weakness of her own surmise.[6] She then tries to play down the importance of causation by suggesting that 'Gotama was a Way-mandater, not Cause-mandater' (*op. cit.*, p. 146), that the applied formula . . . was not included in the list of sayings adduced as a final charge to his men by the dying Founder' (*op. cit.*, p. 152) and such considerations, none of which contradict or explain the important place that causation has in the Pāli Canonical texts. Her whole theory has to be dismissed on methodological grounds. She starts with certain *a priori* assumptions as to what Original Buddhism ought to have taught, picks out what appears to support her views (after a good deal of misinterpretation at times) and dismisses the great bulk of the material as monkish editing. When a statement occurs too frequently it is discarded as a 'stereotyped phrase'.[7] If it occurs rarely, it is likewise rejected when it does not

[1] Russell speaks of two principles of sufficient reason, the general and the special (*The Philosophy of Leibniz*, p. 30), the former applying to possible existents and the latter to actual existents (pp. 30, 36). He says that the former is 'a form of the law of causality asserting all possible causes to be desires or appetites' (p. 30). Even this conception of causality is opposed in Buddhism (*v. supra*, 776).

[2] *Buddhism*, Williams and Norgate, London, 1912, pp. 105, 106.

[3] 'Paṭiccasamuppāda', ERE., Vol. 9, p. 672.

[4] We find this distinction drawn even in *Śākya or Buddhist Origins*, London, 1931, p. 152, where she speaks of 'the abstract statement' and 'the concrete application'.

[5] *Śākya or Buddhist Origins*, pp. 133, 162.

[6] *Op. cit.*, p. 143, 'Save for the opening lines, I do not see that these verses, imputed to Kappina, strengthen my surmise, that in him we have a man chiefly responsible for Śākya becoming, in repute, a religion based on causation'.

[7] *v. Śākya or Buddhist Origins*, p. 136, 'Further, the prose rejoinder of Sāriputta is a *stereotyped phrase* occurring elsewhere in the Piṭakas'.

agree with her assumptions or what they imply.[1] On the basis of such a method of purely imaginative reconstruction, there is no limit to the number of largely speculative theories, which can be claimed to be the original message of Buddhism. For this reason, such speculations are of little value for scholarship, since no objective methodological criteria and rules of interpretation are adhered to.

(783) Inductive inferences in Buddhism are therefore based on a theory of causation. These inferences are made on the data of perception, normal and paranormal. What is considered to constitute knowledge are direct inferences made on the basis of the data of such perceptions. All the knowledge that the Buddha and his disciples claim to have in 'knowing and seeing' (*v. supra*, 741), except for the knowledge of Nirvāṇa, appears to be of this nature. For reasons of space we cannot examine all the doctrines of Buddhism in order to see whether they could be explained on this basis. Nor is this necessary, for we are concerned only with the epistemological foundations of the thought of the Canon. We shall therefore merely illustrate by taking a few samples, how the doctrines of Buddhism may be considered to be epistemically derived from direct inferences based on perception, normal or extrasensory.

(784) Let us first take some examples of direct inferences based on the data of normal perception:
(1) The statement that 'on account of birth there is decay and death' (jātipaccayā . . . jarāmaraṇaṃ, S. II.25) is an empirical generalization based on the observation (by perception) that all those who are 'known and seen' to be born eventually grow old and die. From the observed cases the inductive inference (anvayañāṇa-) is made that all those who are born, whether in the past or in the future, grow old and die.
(2) The statement that 'all conditioned things are impermanent' (sabbe saṅkhārā aniccā, M. I.228) is a similar empirical generalization. Quoting this example, Professor Wijesekera has observed that 'this is not given as a result of metaphysical inquiry or of any mystical intuition but as a straightforward judgment to be arrived at by investigation and analysis. It is founded on unbiased thought and has a purely empirical basis'.[2]

[1] *v. op. cit.*, p. 136, 'Further, the verse found in inscriptions on ruins at Benares and elsewhere occurs nowhere else in the Piṭakas'.
[2] O. H. de A. Wijesekera, *The Three Signata*, Kandy, 1960, pp. 2, 3.

(3) When it is asked whether the Buddha holds that the statement 'grief, lamentation, mental agony, sorrow and anxiety arise from and originate from attachment' (piyajātikā ... sokaparidevadukkhadomanassupāyāsā piyappabhavikā, M. II.108), he says 'yes' (evam etaṃ, *loc. cit.*) and adds that 'it should be understood in this way' (tad aminā p'etaṃ ... pariyāyena veditabbaṃ, *loc. cit.*). He then enumerates a series of observed historical instances of people in Sāvatthi, who because of their deep attachment to their loved ones, were given to grief when they died and lost their senses. He also recounts a case where a person killed his betrothed and committed suicide in the hope of reuniting with her in the hereafter, when she professed not to love him.[1] (4) The statement that 'among human beings there aren't the usual characteristics, which constitute species' (n'atthi manussesu liṅgaṃ jātimayaṃ puthu, Sn. 607) or in other words that the human race was biologically one species, is based on a keen observation of nature.[2] It is said that the grasses, trees, worms, moths, ants, four-footed creatures, serpents, fishes, birds have 'characteristics that constitute species' (liṅgam jātimayaṃ, Sn. 601–6) and that therefore there are 'different species' (aññamaññā jātiyo, *loc. cit.*) among them. But this is not the case with human beings, who do not have such characteristics in respect of their hair, head, ears, colour, etc. (*loc. cit.*); the difference among men is said to be only nominal (vokārañ ca manussesu samaññāya pavuccati, Sn. 611).

(785) Statements were not only justified on the basis of empirical evidence but were rejected as false when they conflicted with what was empirically observed. Thus the statement held by certain recluses and brahmins to the effect that 'so long as a person is young one is endowed with intellectual capacity ... but this is lost with old age' (yāvad evāyaṃ bhavaṃ puriso daharo ... tāvad eva paramapaññāveyyattiyena samannāgato hoti yato ... ayaṃ ... vayo anuppatto ... atha tamhā paññāveyyattiyā parihāyatī ti, M. I.82) is said to be incorrect. In support of this the Buddha points to his own example and to 'four *centenarians* (cattāro ... vassasatāyukā, *loc. cit.*) in the Order who are endowed with the highest intellectual capacity despite their old age. Likewise, the proposition held to be true by certain recluses

[1] Atha kho sā itthi sāmikaṃ etad avoca: ... ahañ ca taṃ na icchamī ti. Atha kho so puriso tam itthiṃ dvidhā chetvā attānaṃ uppāṭesi: ubho pecca bhavissamā ti, M. II.109, 110.

[2] For a detailed account of this argument, *v.* G. P. Malalasekera and K. N. Jayatilleke, *Buddhism and the Race Question*, UNESCO, 1958, pp. 35–7.

and brahmins to the effect that 'all those who kill living creatures experience pain and sorrow in this life itself' (yo koci pāṇaṃ atimāpeti, sabbo so diṭṭh'eva dhamme dukkhaṃ domanassaṃ paṭisaṃvediyati, S. IV.343) is said to be false since some people are honoured in this very life if they kill the king's enemies (*loc. cit.*).

(786) We find at the same time that many of the doctrines of Buddhism are claimed to be inductive inferences based on the data of extrasensory perception. In this respect, extrasensory perception is treated at the same level as normal perception and it is considered possible to make both valid and erroneous inferences on this data (*v. infra*, 790). It may be asked whether the claims to extrasensory perception belong to the mythical and miraculous element in the Canon and whether these claims were actually made by the Buddha and his disciples. There is reason to believe that these claims were actually made. There is no doubt that yoga-practices prevailed among the thinkers of the Middle and Late Upaniṣads, the Jains, some of the Ājīvikas and the Buddhists. Claims of this kind were common to all these schools. They are not considered miraculous but the result of the natural development of the mind in the Buddhist texts (*v. supra*, 724) and have a close connection with the central doctrines of Buddhism (*v. infra*, 797). Some of these experiences such as ante-natal retrocognition[1] have been claimed by people under deep hypnosis.[2] For others such as telepathy and clairvoyance, it is believed that there is a certain amount of experimental data which tends to confirm the existence of such faculties.[3] We have reason therefore to believe that genuine claims were made about having these experiences. The other question is whether these experiences were veridical or delusive. This falls outside the scope of our study and we do not propose to examine it here.

[1] Cp. a similar but less explicit claim attributed to Pythagoras, *v.* Kirk and Raven, The Presocratic Philosophers, p. 223.

[2] *v.* Th. Flournoy (Professor of Psychology, University of Geneva), *Des Indes à la Planète Mars*, Geneva, 1899; W. McDougall, *An Outline of Abnormal Psychology*, Sixth Edition, London, 1948, p. 510 ff.; cp. Charles A. Cory (Associate Professor of Philosophy, Washington University), 'A Divided Self' in *Journal of Abnormal Psychology*, Vol. XIV, Boston, 1919–20, pp. 282, 283; cp. also Ian Stevenson, *The Evidence for Survival from Claimed Memories of Former Incarnations*, Thamesmouth Printing Co. Ltd., Essex, 1961, and C. J. Ducasse, *The Belief in a Life after Death*, Illinois, 1961, p. 241–299.

[3] *v.* J. B. Rhine, *New Frontiers of the Mind*, Penguin Books, 1950; cp. by the same author, *The Reach of the Mind*, London, 1948; also, R. Tischner, *Telepathy and Clairvoyance*, London, 1925.

(787) Prominent among the doctrines derived as an inductive inference on the basis of the data of extrasensory perception, is *karma* as taught in the Pāli Canonical texts. There is said to be a general as well as a specific correlation between the kind of life led in this world and one's state of survival. Now it is said that 'the decease and survival of beings is to be verified by one's (clairvoyant) vision' (sattānaṃ cutūpapāto ... cakkhunā sacchikaraṇīyo, A. II.183). But with this clairvoyant vision one is also said to notice a correlation between the character of a person and his state of survival: 'He sees some beings endowed with bodily, verbal or mental misconduct, who reproach the holy men, hold false views and act in accordance with false views born in a state of decline, in an unhappy condition, in a state of downfall and a lower state at death on the dissolution of the body; and (he sees) other beings, who are born in a happy state, in a heavenly world at death on the dissolution of the body'.[1] It is this correlation between good character and a happy state after death, and bad character and an unhappy state after death that is called *karma*. For a person who has this clairvoyant vision is said 'to know how these beings fare according to their karma' (yathākammūpage satte pajānāti, *loc. cit.*).

(788) In the Mahāsīhanāda Sutta, Majjhima Nikāya, the Buddha claims to test this in a way analogous to the testing of an hypothesis. The Buddha says that he first examines by means of his telepathic powers the mind of a certain individual in order to gauge the general tone of his character. From this knowledge in the light of the karma-hypothesis he expects the individual to be born in a certain state after death. At a later time he observes this individual with his clairvoyant perception to see in what state he has survived and finds that the prediction made in accordance with the above hypothesis is confirmed, thus verifying the truth of the hypothesis. The text reads as follows: 'Here I observe with my mind the mind of a certain person as follows: "This person so conducts himself, behaves in such a way and follows such a path that at death on the dissolution of the body he would be born in an unhappy state ...; at a later time I observe him by means of (my) clear paranormal clairvoyant vision, surviving in the unhappy

[1] So ... passati ...: ime ... sattā kāya-duccaritena samannāgatā vacī° ... mano-° . . . ariyānaṃ upavādakā micchā-diṭṭhikā micchā-diṭṭhi-kamma-samādānā. Te kāyassa bhedā paraṃ maranā apāyaṃ duggatiṃ vinipātaṃ nirayaṃ upapannā. Ime vā pana ... sattā kāyasucaritena samannāgatā vacī° ... mano-° ... ariyānaṃ anupavādakā . . . te kāyassa bhedā paraṃ maraṇā sugatiṃ saggaṃ lokaṃ upapannā ti. D. I.82.

state and experiencing extremely unpleasant sensations. Just as if someone with sight were to observe a pit full of coals, without flames or smoke ... and a tired person walking on the only road leading to this pit and say, "this person surely walks and moves in such a way and follows such a road that he will fall into this pit"; at a later time he would see him fallen into that pit of coals experiencing extremely painful sensations'.[1]

(788A) The Buddha criticizes the Jain ascetics for not personally verifying the truth or falsity of their karma-theory. He approaches some Jain ascetics who were practising self-mortification in the belief that self-induced suffering was an expiation of past sins, which become exhausted as a result (M. I.92, 93). He finds that the theory on which these practices were based, was accepted on the basis of the omniscience of their teacher, but was not individually verified by them. He asks them the following questions to all of which the Jain ascetics gave negative answers. Do you know 'whether or not you existed in the past' (ahuvām'eva mayaṃ pubbe, na nāhuvāmā ti, M. I.93)? Do you know 'whether you did or did not do any evil karma in the past' (akarām'eva mayaṃ pubbe pāpaṃ kammaṃ, na akarāmā ti, *loc. cit.*)? Do you know 'what kind of evil karma you did in the past' (evarūpaṃ vā pāpaṃ kammam akarāmā ti, *loc. cit.*)? Do you know 'what amount of suffering (due to sin) has been spent, what amount remains to be spent and what amount of suffering was altogether necessary (for expiation)' (ettakaṃ vā dukkhaṃ nijjiṇṇaṃ ettakaṃ vā dukkhaṃ nijjaretabbaṃ ettakamhi vā dukkhe nijjiṇṇe sabbaṃ dukkhaṃ nijjiṇṇaṃ bhavissatī ti, *loc. cit.*). The example of the Jain ascetic was apparently contrasted with the personal verification of his past karma on the part of the disciple of the Buddha (see, however, *infra*, 798, 799).

(789) The correlations worked out between different kinds of acts

[1] Idāhaṃ ... ekaccaṃ puggalaṃ evaṃ cetasā ceto paricca pajānāmi: tathā' yaṃ puggalo paṭipanno tathā ca iriyati tañ ca maggaṃ samārūḷho yathā kāyassa bhedā param maraṇā duggatiṃ ... upapajjissatī ti; tam enaṃ passāmi aparena samayena dibbena cakkhunā visuddhena atikkantamānusakena ... duggatiṃ ... upapannaṃ ekantadukkhā tippā kaṭukā vedanā vediyamānaṃ. Seyyathā 'pi ... aṅgārakāsu ... pūr'aṅgārānaṃ vītaccikānaṃ vītadhūmānaṃ, atha puriso āgaccheyya ... kilanto ... ekāyanena maggena tam eva aṅgārakāsuṃ paṇidhāya, tam enaṃ cakkhumā puriso disvā evaṃ vadeyya: tathā'yaṃ bhavaṃ puriso paṭipanno tathā ca iriyati tañ ca maggaṃ samārūḷho yathā imaṃ yeva aṅgārakāsuṃ āgamissatī ti; tam enaṃ passeyya aparena samayena tassa aṅgārakāsuyā patitaṃ ekantadukkhā ... vedanā vediyamānaṃ, M. I.74.

and the expected consequences in a subsequent human existence are presumably to be verified in the same manner. Some of these correlations are as follows: (1) a person who kills living creatures (pāṇātipāti, M. III.203) . . . tends to be short-lived (appāyuka-saṃvattaniko, *loc. cit.*), while a person who refrains from killing living creatures (pāṇātipātā paṭivirato, *loc. cit.*) . . . tends to be long-lived (dīghāyuka-saṃvattaniko, *loc. cit.*), (2) a person who harms creatures (sattānaṃ viheṭhakajātiko, M. I.204) . . . tends to be sickly (bavhābādhasaṃvattaniko, *loc. cit.*), while a person who refrains from harming creatures (aviheṭhakajātiko, *loc. cit.*) . . . tends to be healthy (appābādhasaṃvattaniko, *loc. cit.*), (3) a person who is angry and irritable (kodhano . . . upāyāsabahulo, *loc. cit.*) . . . tends to be ugly (dubbaṇṇasaṃvattaniko, *loc. cit.*), while a person who is not so, tends to be beautiful (pāsādikasaṃvattaniko, *loc. cit.*), etc.

(790) However, it is said that some of the inferences based on one's clairvoyant vision may be invalid. The Mahākammavibhaṅga Sutta, Majjhima Nikāya, takes the following four examples:

(1) The first is that of a recluse or brahmin who attains a state of mental concentration, in which he sees with his clairvoyant vision a certain person who has misconducted himself born in an unhappy state after death. On the basis of this experience he forms the following conclusions, viz. (i) there are evil acts (atthi . . . pāpakāni kammāni, M. III.21), (ii) there is an evil consequence for misconduct (atthi duccaritassa vipāko, *loc. cit.*), (iii) that all those who kill living creatures, steal, etc. . . . are born in an unhappy state after death (yo . . . pāṇātipātī adinnādāyī . . . sabbo so . . . paraṁ maraṇā . . . duggatiṃ . . . uppajjati, *loc. cit.*), (iv) that those who assert (i), (ii) and (iii) are right and the others wrong (ye evaṃ jānanti, te sammā jānanti. Ye aññathā jānanti, micchā tesaṃ ñāṇan ti, *loc. cit.*). It is said that 'what he has himself known, himself seen, himself experienced' (sāmaṃ ñātaṃ sāmaṃ diṭṭhaṃ sāmaṃ viditaṃ, *loc. cit.*) he dogmatically claims to be 'the only truth, all else being false' (idam eva saccaṃ mogham aññaṃ, *loc. cit.*).

(2) The second example is that of a person who similarly attains a state of mental concentration, but sees with his clairvoyant vision a person who has done evil in this life born after death in a happy state. He comes to conclusions which are diametrically opposed to those of (1), viz. (i) there are no evil acts, (ii) there is no evil consequence of misconduct, (iii) that all those who kill living creatures, steal, etc. . . .

are born in a happy state after death, and (iv) that those who assert (2) (i), (ii) and (iii) are right and the others wrong.
(3) and (4) Two other examples are given to illustrate the other two possibilities, namely, that of a person who sees a person of good conduct born in a happy state and in an unhappy state respectively.

(791) In the course of this Sutta, it is pointed out that the Buddha does not deny the validity of the claims to have observed what they did claim to observe (M. III.212–15; e.g. Yañ ca kho so evam āha: apāhaṃ puggalaṃ addasaṃ idha pāṇātipātiṃ adinnādāyiṃ . . . param maraṇā . . . sugatiṃ . . . upapannan ti—idam assa anujānāmi, i.e. I grant his claim to have seen an individual who kills and steals, born after death in a happy state). But he denies the validity of some of the inferences made on the basis of these experiences. It is shown, for example, that all four generalizations made from a single instance are mistaken, e.g. yañ ca kho so evam āha: yo kira bho pāṇātipātī . . . sabbo so . . . duggatiṃ . . . uppajjatī ti, idam assa nānujānāmi, i.e. I do not approve of his claim that all those who kill . . . are born in an unhappy state. This shows a realization of the fact that one cannot make generalizations on the basis of one (or a few) instances.[1] But at the same time, the general rule that good acts tend to make one's future state of survival happy and vice versa is not denied for the apparent exceptions (2 and 4) are explained as due to the performance of good or evil deeds, as the case may be, sometime or another in one's past lives (cp. pubbe vā'ssa taṃ kataṃ hoti . . . pacchā vā, M. III.214, 215) or due to a change of heart at the moment of death (maraṇakāle vā'ssa hoti . . . , *loc. cit.*).

(792) Not only, therefore, does Buddhism not give a theistic or metaphysical interpretation to these experiences, but considers it necessary that we draw the right inferences from them in the same sense in which it was necessary for us to be right about our inferences from sense-experience.

(793) We have tried to show that perception (normal and paranormal) and inductive inference are considered the means of knowledge in the Pāli Nikāyas. The emphasis that 'knowing' (jānaṃ) must be based on 'seeing' (passaṃ) or direct perceptive experience, makes Buddhism a form of Empiricism. We have, however, to modify the use of the term somewhat to mean not only that all our knowledge is derived from

[1] *v.* Stebbing, *op. cit.*, p. 247.

sense-experience[1] but from extrasensory experience as well. This extension we believe is justified in the light of the reasons that we gave earlier (*v. supra,* 735). The definition of the term in Runes' Dictionary of Philosophy also allows us to use the term 'empiricism' to include the entire conscious content of the mind and not merely the data of the senses: 'That the sole source of knowledge is experience. . . . Experience may be understood as either all conscious content, data of the senses only or other designated content' (*s.v.*). Its empiricism is also seen in its attitude to the problems of substance (*v. supra,* 535), cause (*v. supra,* 778), the *a priori* (*v. supra,* 429, 436), perception (*v. supra,* 744), meaning (*v. supra,* 536 f.) and lastly metaphysics (*v. supra,* 377 ff.; *infra,* 816).

(794) Early Buddhism should therefore be regarded not as a system of metaphysics but as a verifiable hypothesis discovered by the Buddha in the course of his 'trial and error' experimentation with different ways of life. We agree therefore with Dr Warder when he says that 'the Buddha legend synthesizes the quest for truth on scientific principles regardless of past traditions: observation of life, experiments in asceticism (under various teachers and independently), final deduction of a way to end suffering'.[2] We also agree with him when, comparing Buddhism with Epicureanism, he says, 'Both attacked old superstitions and sought knowledge of nature, knowledge which we may characterize as scientific on account of its basis of *perception, inference, verification,* etc.'[3] (italics mine).

(795) In the Nikāyas, it is stated, how the Buddha left the household life in his youth (yobbanena samannāgato, M. I.163) for his 'noble quest'[4] (ariyā pariyesanā, M. I.162) for happiness, immortality, supreme perfection, security and Nibbāna (asokaṃ amataṃ asaṃkiliṭṭhaṃ yogakkhemaṃ nibbānaṃ, M. I.163). He seems to have tried out the various methods practised by the Jains, Ājīvikas and the thinkers of the Middle and the Late Upaniṣads. He says that he experimented with the four kinds of religious practices of penance

[1] Empiricists usually mean by experience, sense-experience, *v.* Ewing, *The Fundamental Questions of Philosophy,* p. 39; Russell defines 'Empiricism' as 'the assertion, "all synthetic knowledge is based on experience"', *Human Knowledge,* p. 516.

[2] *Op. cit.,* p. 57. [3] *Ibid.*

[4] The 'ignoble quest' (anariyā pariyesanā) is described as the quest of what is subject to birth, decay, death, etc., being subject to them, while the 'noble quest' (ariyā pariyesanā) is the quest of what is not subject to birth, decay and death, etc.

(tapassī), self-mortification (lūkha-), avoidance (jegucchha-) and seclusion (pavivitta-) (M. I.77). Here 'avoidance' appears to be a reference to Jainism for it is said 'I used to walk up and down conscientiously extending my compassion even to a drop of water, praying that even the dangerous bacteria in it may not come to harm' (so ... sato va abhikkamāmi sato paṭikkamāmi, yāva udabindumhi me dayā paccupaṭṭhitā hoti: mā'haṃ khuddake pāṇe visamagate saṅghātam āpādessan ti, M. I.78). The rest of the practices which are numerous and are described in detail (M. I.77–9) are of the kind practised by the Ājīvikas.[1] In this context are mentioned a few other theories he tried out. One of these was that 'salvation was by ritual' (yaññena suddhi, M. I.82), well known in the Vedic tradition.[2] Another was 'salvation, by food' (āhārena suddhi, M. I.80) held by certain recluses and brahmins who seem to have believed that salvation resulted from eating a special kind of food and gradually reducing it to the point of starvation. This was based on the theory that 'when the blood becomes dry, the bile and phlegm dries up and when the flesh wastes away, the mind becomes exceedingly clear'.[3] But he found that 'by this mode of life and conduct, by these ascetic practices, he did not attain any extraordinary spiritual knowledge and insight' (tāya ... iriyāya tāya paṭipadāya tāya dukkarikārikāya nājjhagamaṃ uttariṃ manussadhammaṃ alamariyañāṇadassanavisesaṃ... M. I.81). So when the Buddha says that neither 'the addiction to sense-pleasures' (kāmamucchā, M. I.241) nor the 'self-induced torture of the body' (opakkamikā dukkhā tippā ... *loc. cit.*) tend to produce knowledge and insight (ñāṇāya dassanāya, *loc. cit.*), it has an empirical basis in his own experiences.

(796) The Buddha also seems to have learnt the technique of yoga, found in the Middle and Late Upaniṣads, under the teachers Āḷāra Kālāma and Uddaka Rāmaputta. Before this, he seems to have tried certain other yoga practices with the idea of curbing his mind (cetasā cittaṃ abhiniggaṇheyyaṃ, M. I.242) or stopping his breathing (appāṇakaṃ jhānaṃ jhāyeyyaṃ, M. I.242) by the sheer effort of will. But these efforts were a failure. He is reported to have left Āḷāra Kālāma and Uddaka Rāmaputta dissatisfied (nibbijja pakkamiṃ, M. I.166) but what he learnt from them seems to have been of some

[1] Basham, *op. cit.*, pp. 96–7, 118–9, 169–71.

[2] Cp. Bṛh. 1.5.2., 'By offering with milk for a year one escapes repeated death' (Hume, *The Thirteen Principal Upanishads*, p. 87).

[3] Lohite sussamānamhi pittaṃ semhañ ca sussati,
mamsesu khīyamanesu bhiyyo cittaṃ pasīdati, Sn. 434.

value. For when he attained enlightenment he immediately thinks of preaching to these two, saying that they were 'wise, intelligent and with little defilements ... and were likely to comprehend his teaching very soon' (paṇḍito ... medhāvī ... apparajakkhajātiko ... so imaṃ dhammaṃ khippam eva ājānissatī ti, M. I.169, 170). His enlightenment is not considered to be a mysterious single act of intuition but the discovery by means of the developed natural faculties of the mind of the cause and cessation of suffering (Ud. 1–3). Knowledge of salvation is had only as the final phase of a gradual process of discipline and not in a sudden act of intuition: 'I do not say that one can win the final knowledge at the very beginning; it is had from a gradual discipline, a gradual mode of action and conduct' (nāhaṃ ādiken'eva aññārādhanaṃ vadāmi api ca anupubbasikkhā anupubbakiriyā anupubbapaṭipadā aññārādhanā hoti, M. I.479, 480).

(797) The method of verification of the Four Noble Truths is stated in detail in a number of similar passages which recur throughout the Nikāyas. Briefly, it consists in the practice of the virtuous life (ariyena sīlakkhandhena samannāgato, M. I.346) followed by the restraint of the senses (indriyasaṃvara-, *loc. cit.*), the development of mindfulness (satisampajañña-, *loc. cit.*), and the elimination of the five impediments (pañcanīvaraṇe pahāya, M. I.347). This results in the possibility of attaining the first up to the fourth jhāna, in which there is 'a perfection of equanimity and mindfulness' (upekkhāsatipārisuddhiṃ, *loc. cit.*). In this state there would be manifested the six-fold higher knowledge (abhiññā, *v. supra*, 727). Of the six only three are necessary for the saving knowledge. The first is retrocognition with which he verifies the fact of pre-existence (*v. supra*, 754). The second is clairvoyance, with which he verifies the fact of karma (*v. supra*, 755). The third is 'the knowledge of the destruction of the defiling impulses' (āsavānaṃ khayañāṇa-, M. I.348). With this he verifies the Four Noble Truths (*loc. cit.*). 'As he thus knows and sees, his mind is emancipated from the inflowing impulses of sensuous gratification, personal immortality and ignorance; along with this emancipation arises the knowledge that emancipation has been attained.'[1] The above stages are often described as the stages of moral excellence (sīla-, M. I.145), mental concentration (samādhi, *loc. cit.*), spiritual knowledge (paññā, *loc. cit.*), emancipation (vimutti, *loc. cit.*) and the knowledge and vision of emancipation (vimuttiñāṇadassana-, *loc. cit.*).

[1] Tassa evaṃ jānato evam passato kāmāsavā pi ... bhavāsavā ... avijjāsavā pi cittaṃ vimuccati, vimuttasmiṃ vimuttam iti ñāṇaṃ hoti, M. I.348.

(798) Not everyone, however, was capable of verifying the doctrine in this manner. We have seen that only sixty out of five hundred were capable of attaining the 'higher knowledge' (*v. supra*, 752). '*The rest*' are said to be 'emancipated by knowledge alone' (... *itare* paññāvimuttā, S. I.191). The question is asked: 'Why is it that some monks gain the emancipation of the mind, while others have only emancipation through knowledge' (atha kiñcarahi idh'ekacce bhikkhū cetovimuttino ekacce paññāvimuttino ti, M. I.437). The reason given is that it was due to the 'difference in their faculties' (tesaṃ ... indriyavemattataṃ, *loc. cit.*).

(799) The mention of this kind of emancipation raises a number of questions. It meant that the doctrine was not fully verified by the disciple but was accepted on trust, even if the conviction of emancipation was real and directly experienced. The doctrine of rebirth and karma and the greater part of the theory of Buddhism would have had to be accepted on faith by such a person since he did not have within him or develop the power of verifying them. This explains the conception of the saint with faith (saddhā) in the Pāli Canon (*v. supra*, 674 f.). Such a person need attain only the first jhāna (M. I.435; A. IV.422; A. V.343) after which he reflects that the five constituents in it are 'sorrowful ... empty and devoid of substance' (dukkhato ... suññato anattato samanupassati, M. I.435). So he turns his mind away from these states (so tehi dhammehi cittam paṭivāpeti, *loc. cit.*) and directs it to the element of immortality (amatāya dhatuyā cittaṃ upasaṃharati, M. I.436) thinking 'this is peaceful and excellent namely the cessation of all processes, the abandoning of all limitations, the elimination of desire, dispassion, cessation, Nibbāna. Established on that he attains the destruction of the inflowing impulses'.[1]

(800) We may next turn to the question of the limits of knowledge. Is knowledge unlimited in scope? Is omniscience possible? Is it the case that certain things cannot be known? These questions appear to have been posed at a time when Scepticism was rife.

(801) It is important to note that what the Buddha claimed was 'a three-fold knowledge' (tisso vijjā). He does so in a Sutta in which he disclaims omniscience in the sense of knowing all at once all the time:

[1] Etaṃ santaṃ etaṃ paṇītaṃ yadidaṃ sabbasaṅkhārasamatho sabbūpadhipaṭinissaggo taṇhakkhayo virāgo nirodho nibbānan ti. So tattha ṭṭhito āsavānaṃ khayaṃ pāpuṇāti, M. I.436.

'those who say that the Recluse Gotama is omniscient and all-seeing and professes to have an infinite knowledge and insight, which is constantly and at all times present to him, when he walks or stands, sleeps or keeps awake—are not reporting him properly and misrepresent him (as claiming) what is false and untrue'.[1] Asked how he should be correctly reported he says: 'in proclaiming that the Recluse Gotama has a three-fold knowledge, one would report him properly and not misrepresent him'.[2] This three-fold knowledge consists of (1) unlimited (yāvad eva ākaṅkhāmi, M. I.482) retrocognition, (2) unlimited clairvoyance, and (3) knowledge of the destruction of the inflowing impulses (*loc. cit.*). It will be seen that it was the same knowledge which the disciples who verified his teaching claimed to have (*v. supra*, 727). On the evidence of the Nikāyas themselves this is too narrow a definition of his field of knowledge for it fails to include the other forms of higher knowledge, such as telepathy, etc. (*v. supra*, 727), which both the Buddha and his disciples claimed to have. The probable reason for this restriction was the fact that it was this three-fold knowledge that really mattered.

(802) This very statement in which he claims only 'a three-fold knowledge' would have thus left the door open for speculation as to what the real extent of his knowledge was. At another place, the Buddha is credited with the statement: 'those who assert that the Recluse Gotama denies that there is any recluse or brahmin who was omniscient or all-seeing, are not stating the truth and are falsely accusing me of saying what is not true'.[3] He then says that what he stated was that 'there is no recluse or brahmin, who would know and see everything all at once'.[4] This means that it is possible for someone to know everything but not all at once. This is in fact the sense in which omniscience is ascribed to the Buddha in the Milindapañha

[1] Ye te evam āhaṃsu: Samaṇo Gotamo sabbaññū sabbadassāvī, aparisesaṃ ñāṇadassanaṃ paṭijānāti: carato ca me tiṭṭhato ca suttassa ca jāgarassa ca satataṃ samitaṃ ñāṇadassanaṃ paccupaṭṭhitan ti, na me te vuttavādino, abbhācikkhanti ca pana man te asatā abhūtenā ti, M. I.482.

[2] Tevijjo Samaṇo Gotamo ti . . . byākaramāno vuttavādi c'eva me assa na ca maṃ abhūtena abbhācikkheyya, *loc. cit.*

[3] Ye te evam āhaṃsu: Samaṇo Gotamo evam āha: natthi so samaṇo vā brāhmaṇo vā yo sabbaññū sabbadassāvī aparisesaṃ ñāṇadassanaṃ paṭijānissati; n'etaṃ ṭhānaṃ vijjatī ti; na me te vuttavādino abbhācikkhanti ca pana maṃ te asatā abhūtenā ti, M. II.127.

[4] Natthi so samaṇo vā brāhmaṇo vā yo sakid eva sabbañ ñassati sabbaṃ dakkhiti n'etaṃ ṭhānaṃ vijjatī ti, *loc. cit.*

(pp. 102 ff.). In the parable of the Siṃsapā leaves, the Buddha takes a handful of leaves in the Siṃsapā forest and says that what he has taught is like the leaves in his hand and what he knew but did not teach is like the leaves in the forest (S. V.437). This means that he claimed to know much more than he taught but he did not claim omniscience. Nor does he in the Nikāyas deny omniscience in the sense of knowing everything but not all at once. Yet it is clear that according to the earliest accounts in the Nikāyas, the Buddha did not claim (an unlimited) precognitive knowledge. In the Pāsādika Sutta, Dīgha Nikāya, it is said, 'It is possible that other heretical teachers may say "the Recluse Gotama has a limitless knowledge and vision with regard to the past but not with regard to the future" ...'.[1] The Buddha goes on to explain that 'with regard to the past the Tathāgata's consciousness follows in the wake of his memory' (atītam addhānaṃ ... ārabbha Tathāgatassa satānusārī viññāṇaṃ hoti, *loc. cit.*). He recalls as much as he likes (so yāvatakaṃ ākaṅkhati tāvatakaṃ anussarati, *loc. cit.*). 'With regard to the future the Tathāgata has the knowledge resulting from enlightenment that "this is the final birth ..." '[2] This appears to be an admission that the Buddha did not claim to have (at least an unlimited) precognitive knowledge of the future. This fits in with his disbelief in Strict Determinism (*v. supra*, 764).

(803) While the Aggi-Vacchagotta Sutta mentioned that the Tathāgata had a three-fold knowledge, we find it mentioned in one place in the Aṅguttara that 'there are six intellectual powers of the Tathāgata' (cha yimāni ... Tathāgatassa Tathāgatabalāni, A. III.417). The six constitute, in addition to the three-fold knowledge, the following: (i) 'the Tathāgata knows, as it really is, what is possible as possible and what is imposible as impossibie' (... Tathāgato ṭhānañ ca ṭhānato aṭṭhānañ ca aṭṭhānato yathābhūtaṃ pajānāti, *loc. cit.*), (ii) 'the Tathāgata knows as it really is, the effects according to their conditions and causes, of the performance of karma in the past, present and future' (... Tathāgato atītanāgatapaccupannānaṃ kammasamādānānaṃ ṭhānaso hetuso vipākaṃ yathābhūtaṃ pajānāti, *loc. cit.*), and (iii) 'the Tathāgata knows, as it really is, the corruption, perfection and arising from contemplative states of release, concentration and

[1] Ṭhānaṃ ... vijjati yaṃ aññatitthiyā ... evaṃ vadeyyuṃ-Atītaṃ kho addhānaṃ ārabbha Samaṇo Gotamo atīrakaṃ ñāṇadassanaṃ paññāpeti, no ca kho anāgataṃ ..., D. III.134.

[2] Anāgatañ ca kho addhānaṃ ārabbha Tathāgatassa bodhijaṃ ñāṇaṃ uppajjati —Ayam antimā jāti ..., *loc. cit.*

attainment' (... Tathāgato jhānavimokkhasamādhisamāpattīnaṃ saṃkilesaṃ vodānaṃ vuṭṭhānaṃ yathābhūtaṃ pajānāti, *loc. cit.*).

(804) The knowledge of possibility and impossibility is illustrated at great length in the Vibhaṅga (335–8). Some of the impossibilities seem to be logical, e.g. 'it is impossible for two universal monarchs to be born simultaneously in the same world' (aṭṭhānam etaṃ ... yaṃ ekissā lokadhātuyā dve rājāno cakkavattī uppajjeyyuṃ, Vbh. 336). Others are causally impossible, e.g. 'it is impossible for a good consequence to arise for one whose conduct is evil' (aṭṭhānam etaṃ ... yaṃ kāyaduccaritassa iṭṭho ... vipāko nibbatteyya, Vbh. 337).

(805) 'The ten (intellectual) powers' (dasa ... balāni, M. I.71) of the Tathāgata mentioned in the Nikāyas and the Vibhaṇga (335–44) add the following four to the above list of six: (i) 'the Tathāgata knows, as it really is, the mode of life leading to all states (of survival)' (Tathāgato sabbatthagāminiṃ paṭipadaṃ yathābhūtaṃ pajānāti, *loc. cit.*), (ii) 'the Tathāgata knows, as it really is, the world with its various and diverse elements' (Tathāgato anekadhātunānādhātulokaṃ yathābhūtaṃ pajānāti, *loc. cit.*), (iii) 'the Tathāgata knows, as it really is, the various predilections of beings' (Tathāgato sattānaṃ nānādhimuttikataṃ yathābhūtaṃ pajānāti, *loc. cit.*), and (iv) 'the Tathāgata knows, as it really is, what goes on in the senses and faculties of other beings and individuals' (Tathāgato parasattānaṃ parapuggalānaṃ indriyaparopariyattaṃ yathābhūtaṃ pajānāti, *loc. cit.*). Despite the apparent progress from three to six and six to ten, it is difficult to say that there is genuine change in the conception of the intellectual powers of the Buddha. The seven powers added to the list of three are commonly attributed to the Buddha throughout the Nikāyas and it is difficult to say that the transition from three to ten represents a change in stratum.

(806) But the position is different, as we pointed out (*v. supra*, 649) in the Paṭisambhidāmagga, where we notice that the Buddha is credited with 'knowing all the future' (sabbaṃ anāgataṃ jānāti, p. 131) and is omniscient (*v. supra*, 649).

(807) We may next turn to the problem of the unanswered (avyākatāni) questions. The list is enumerated in paragraph 378 (*v. supra*, 378). Professor Murti has translated avyākatāni as 'the Inexpressibles': 'The Inexpressibles (avyākata, Skt. avyākṛtavastūni) occur in very many dialogues. They are invariably enumerated as fourteen and

practically in the same order'.[1] This translation is not literally correct. Vyākaroti is used of answering or explaining a question (*s.v.* PTS. Dictionary); vyākata-, the past passive participle would therefore mean 'explained, answered' and the negative form a-vyākata-, 'unexplained, unanswered'. Dr Murti is also not correct in saying that these questions are 'invariably enumerated as fourteen'. Only ten questions are mentioned in the Pāli Canon[2] and it is in the Buddhist Sanskrit literature that the list is extended to fourteen.[3] The Pāli citations mention only two possibilities with regard to the duration and extent respectively of the universe, while the list of fourteen mentions four possibilities.

(808) The problem is on what grounds these questions were unanswered. Were they in principle answerable though left unanswered? If so, were they unanswered because the Buddha did not know the answers to them (Scepticism, Naïve Agnosticism) or was it because although he knew the answers, they were not relevant to the central problems of religion (Pragmatism). On the other hand, were they in principle unanswerable? If so, were the solutions beyond the grasp of the human intellect, transcending the limits of knowledge (Rational Agnosticism) or were the questions (logically) meaningless and therefore not admitting of an answer (Logical Positivism). We may exhibit these alternatives in a table on the following page.

(809) The above possibilities have not been carefully distinguished by scholars in their endeavour to explain why the Buddha set aside these questions. The above alternatives need not, however, be mutually exclusive for the following situations are possible, (i) that some questions were set aside for some reasons and others for other reasons, (ii) that on some interpretations the questions were answerable and on others not, (iii) that the Pragmatist solution need not necessarily imply that the Buddha knew the answers. It is possible that the Buddha did or did not know the answers or that the questions were unanswerable but that he still adopted the Pragmatist attitude to them. Let me call this the Pragmatist solution in the weak sense.

(810) Now solution (1) has been given by Keith. He combines with this the Pragmatist solution in the weak sense. It has also been suggested by Jacobi that Buddhism was influenced by the Sceptic's

[1] T. R. V. Murti, *The Central Philosophy of Buddhism*, London, 1955, p. 36.
[2] *v.* D. I.191; M. I.426, 484–5; S. III.257; A. II.41.
[3] *v.* Murti, *op. cit.*, p. 36, fn. 2.

attitude to these questions, which is also the same as (1).[1] Keith says: 'It is quite legitimate to hold that the Buddha was a genuine agnostic, that he had studied the various systems of ideas prevalent in his day without deriving any greater satisfaction from them than any of us today do from the study of modern systems, and that he had no reasoned or other conviction on the matter'.[2] 'He is silent, not merely because knowledge of these matters does not tend to Nirvāṇa, but

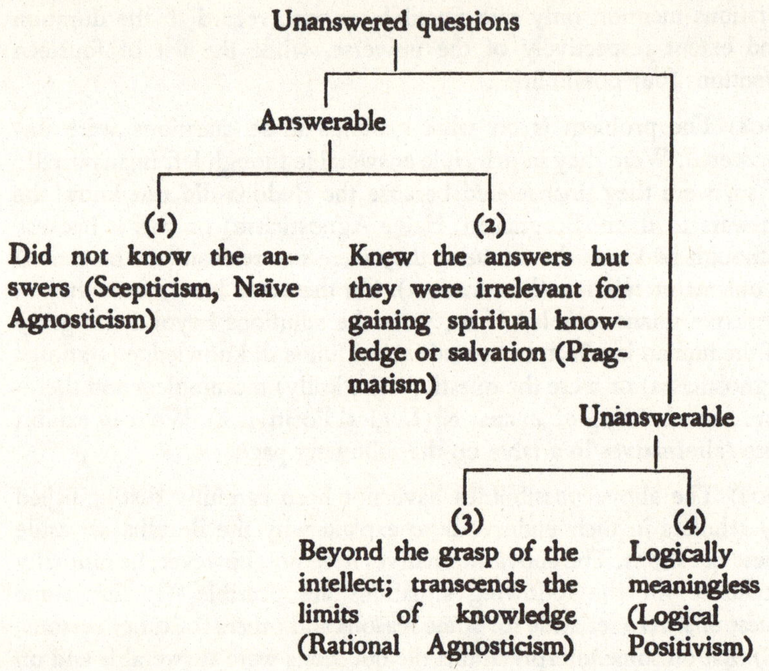

because men hold various opinions regarding them.'[3] 'This leads clearly to the conclusion that agnosticism in these matters is not based on any reasoned conviction of the limits of knowledge; it rests on the two-fold ground that the Buddha has not himself a clear conclusion on the truth on these issues, but is convinced that disputation on them will not lead to the frame of mind which is essential for the attainment of Nirvāṇa.'[4] In other words, the Buddha was a Naïve Agnostic who did not know the answer to these questions.

[1] *v.* SBE., Vol. 45, p. xxviii. [2] *Buddhist Philosophy*, p. 63.
[3] *Op. cit.*, p. 44. [4] *Ibid.*, p. 45.

(811) It is necessary to point out that whichever of the above solutions be true, the Buddha had a Pragmatist reason in the weak sense (as defined above) for rejecting these questions. This is clear from his often repeated remark: 'These (questions) are not connected with the goal, with the teaching nor with the fundamentals of the religious life and do not conduce to disinterest, dispassion, cessation, tranquillity, higher consciousness (*v.l.* higher knowledge[1]), realization and Nirvāṇa'.[2]

(812) But Keith's solution that the Buddha rejected these questions out of ignorance is not only not supported by the texts but appears in fact to be contradicted by them. Keith's statement that the Buddha was silent regarding these questions 'because men hold various opinions regarding them' is not true. The Buddha certainly says that men hold various views regarding these questions, which result in violent controversy (Ud. 67, *v. supra,* 377) but he does not say that he left them unanswered because of this. Keith gives three references in support of his explanation of the silence of the Buddha—'*Udāna,* p. 11; SN. V.437; DN. i.179' (*op. cit.,* p. 44, fn. 3). Of these instances, the subject is not even discussed at *Udāna,* p. 11 and DN. i.179 (i.e. D. I.179). SN. V.437 (i.e. S. V.437) suggests the very opposite of what Keith is saying, since it is stated here (the parable of the Siṃsapā leaves, *v. supra,* 802) that the Buddha knows much more than he has taught and he has not taught certain doctrines out of pragmatist reasons. Māluṅkyaputta put the question directly to the Buddha in regard to his failure to answer these questions, 'it is the honest (*lit.* straightforward) thing to say, "I do know or see this" if it is the case that one does not know or see this' (ajānato kho pana apassato etad eva ujukaṃ hoti yadidaṃ: na jānāmi na passāmī ti, M. I.428). The fact that the Buddha did not answer this question may also be considered as evidence against the correctness of solution (1) since we would otherwise have to say that the Buddha was dishonest and was evading the issue.

(813) There is a superficial similarity between the attitude of the Sceptic and that of the Buddha towards these questions. Sañjaya like the Buddha refuses to give a definite answer to four of the ten

[1] The word 'abhisaññāya' occurs at D. I.191 and abhiññāya elsewhere (e.g. M. I.431).

[2] Na h'ete . . . attha-saṃhitā, na dhamma-saṃhitā, na ādibrahmacariyakā, na nibbidāya, na virāgāya, na nirodhāya, na upasamāya, na abhisaññāya (*v.l.* abhiññāya), na sambodhāya, na nibbānāya saṃvattanti, D. I. 191; M. I.431; S. V.437.

'unanswered questions'.[1] But this is said to be 'due to his stupidity and ignorance' (mandattā momūhattā, D. I.27) unlike in the case of the Buddha. The very fact that Scepticism was distinguished from Buddhism points to the difference of the Buddhist solution.

(814) The parables of the arrow (*v. supra*, 603) and Siṃsapā leaves appear to support solution (2). The parable of the arrow seems to imply indirectly that questions regarding who shot the arrow, etc., can in principle be answered though they are irrelevant for the purpose of a cure. The parable of the Siṃsapā leaves (*v. supra*, 802) states that what the Buddha knew but did not preach was comparable to the leaves on the trees of the Siṃsapā forest, while what he taught was as little as the leaves in his hand; it is said that he did not teach the rest because it was irrelevant for our purpose. The statement that if the soul was identical with the body or different from it, then the religious life would be impossible,[2] implies that the theses 'the soul is the same as the body' and 'the soul is different from the body' were both in a sense known to be false. But it is possible that these statements were considered to be false only on one interpretation and not on the strict interpretation (*v. supra*, 478) that was given to them. Likewise, one cannot read too much into the parable of the arrow; and the parable of the Siṃsapā leaves does not necessarily imply that the ten questions were meaningful ones to which the Buddha knew the answer. There is, therefore, no decisive evidence in support of solution (2).

(815) The third solution has been suggested by Beckh[3] and offered by Murti, who sees in these questions a parallel with the Kantian antinomies. Murti says, 'The similarity of the avyākṛta to the celebrated antinomies of Kant . . . cannot fail to strike us'.[4] 'The formulation of the problems in the thesis-antithesis form is itself evidence of the awareness of the conflict in Reason. That the conflict is not on the empirical level and so not capable of being settled by appeal to facts is realized by Buddha when he declares them insoluble. Reason involves itself in deep and interminable conflict when it tries to go beyond phenomena to seek their ultimate ground.'[5] The similarity in fact

[1] I.e. 'does the Tathāgata exist after death'? (hoti Tathāgato param maraṇā, D. I.27) in accordance with the four possibilities.

[2] Taṃ jīvaṃ taṃ sarīran ti vā . . . diṭṭhiyā sati . . . aññāṃ jivaṃ aññāṃ sarīran ti vā . . . diṭṭhiyā sati brahmacariyāvāso na hoti, S. II.61.

[3] *Buddhismus*, Berlin und Leipzig, 1919, Vol. I, p. 120.

[4] *Op. cit.*, p. 38.

[5] *Ibid.*, p. 40.

extends beyond the subject-matter and 'the formulation of the problems in the thesis-antithesis form'. We have seen that both the theses and anti-theses were proved to be true by the debaters at that time (*v. supra,* 378 ff.). Besides, with regard to the problem of the origin of things, the Buddha clearly recognized that no empirical answer was possible since the earlier we went back in time there was a possibility of going back still farther and no ultimate origin of 'phenomenal existence' (saṃsāra) could be found empirically (*v. supra,* 10,774). Was this because the universe had no beginning in time (like a negative infinite series, viz. -1, -2, -3, etc.) or because the origin could not be discovered by extending one's paranormal memory backwards because of its remote ancestry in the past? The BHS. literature seems to have adopted the former alternative in turning anamatagga- into anavarāgra-, i.e. 'without beginning or end' (*s.v.* BHS. Dictionary). If we confine ourselves to the Pāli Nikāyas there seems to be a recognition of the limitations of empiricism and of the impossibility of discovering the truth about this question by empirical investigation.

(816) While this rational agnostic solution remains a possibility with regard to the problem of the origin, duration and extent of the universe, the other six questions appear to have been discarded on the grounds that they were (logically) meaningless, as we have already shown (*v. supra,* 474 f., 478 f.). This clearly resembles the solution of the Logical Positivist of such questions (*v. supra,* 476 f.).

(817) It is necessary, however, to draw a distinction between the solution of the Logical Positivist and that of the Buddhist. The Buddhist while saying that is meaningless to ask whether one exists in (hoti), does not exist in (na hoti), is born in (upapajjati), is not born in (na upapajjati) in Nirvāṇa, still speaks of such a transcendent state as realizable. The meaninglessness of these questions is thus partly due to the inadequacy of the concepts contained in them to refer to this state. This is clearly brought out in a verse in the Suttanipāta. The Buddha was asked the question: 'The person who has attained the goal—does he not exist or does he exist eternally without defect; explain this to me well, O Lord, as you understand it?'[1] The Buddha explains: 'The person who has attained the goal is without measure; he does not have that with which one can speak of him'.[2] The

[1] Atthaṃgato so, uda vā so natthi, udāhu ve sassatiyā arogo, taṃ me munī sādhu viyākarohi, tathā hi te vidito esa dhammo, Sn. 1075.

[2] Atthaṃgatassa na pamāṇam atthi, yena naṃ vajju taṃ tassa natthi, Sn. 1076.

transempirical cannot be empirically described or understood (*v. supra*, 480) but it can be realized and attained. The Tathāgata freed from the conception of form, sensation, ideas, dispositions and consciousness is said to be 'deep, immeasurable and unfathomable, like the great ocean' (gambhīro appameyyo duppariyogāho seyyathā pi mahāsamuddo, M. I.487). 'Whereof one can speak of him—that he does not have' (yena naṃ vajju taṃ tassa natthi, Sn. 1076) and hence one has to be silent. In this respect alone it resembles the Positivist's outlook: 'Whereof one cannot speak, thereof one must be silent'.[1] This attitude has, however, to be distinguished from Agnosticism.[2] It was not that there was something that the Buddha did not know, but that what he 'knew' in the transcendent sense could not be conveyed in words because of the limitations of language and of empiricism.

[1] L. Wittgenstein, *Tractatus Logico-Philosophicus*, 1933, 7, p. 189.

[2] This does not mean that the theistic interpretation is the correct one; cp. S. Radhakrishnan, 'To me the silence is not a proof either of denial or agnosticism ... Silence is on occasions the only language of true worship ... Our thoughts of God are always images though they may not be graven images.' ('The Teaching of Buddha by Speech and by Silence', *The Hibbert Journal*, Vol. XXXII, pp. 350 ff.); cp. also R. L. Slater, *Paradox and Nirvāṇa*, Chicago, 1950, p. 121.

APPENDIX I

(818) Criticizing Oldenberg's view that the Upaniṣadic concept of Brahman (neuter) becomes in Buddhism the God Brahmā,[1] Thomas says, 'the idea of Brahma (neuter) in the old Upaniṣads is said to have been hypostatized in Buddhism into a personal God Brahmā. But this rather implies that the older philosophical idea had been known to the Buddhists and this has been transformed into a much less philosophic conception. We have no evidence that Early Buddhism even knew it' (History of Buddhist Thought, p. 90). Of the Tevijja Sutta, Thomas says: 'The Tevijja Sutta, the discourse on the three-fold knowledge, the Vedas, undertakes to discuss the value of sacrifice and the brahmins are represented as holding that it leads to life in the Brahma world. But the Brahma world as described belongs purely to the Buddhist conception of the universe. It is a definite region above the heavens of sense pleasure . . .' (*op. cit.*, p. 86). Thomas' conception seems to be that the neuter Brahman is 'the chief conception' (*op. cit.*, p. 87, fn. 1) of the Upaniṣads and likewise that the Brahmaloka in the Brāhmaṇas and Upaniṣads was a state attainable on earth and not a place to be reached after death. Our contention is that the idea of a personal Brahmā and of Brahmaloka as a place is the dominant conception of both the late Brāhmaṇas and the Early Upaniṣads and that the Tevijja Sutta is criticizing these beliefs and not the impersonal concepts which dominate the Middle and Late Upaniṣads. We have already shown how Brahmā (masc.) is used along with Brahman (neuter) in the Brāhmaṇas and the Early Upaniṣads, which do not strictly distinguish them in usage and where the personal concept prevails and is even carried over to the Late Upaniṣads (*v. supra*, 269).

(819) It is the same with the concept of the Brahmaloka. It is the highest world in the Brāhmaṇas. In the Kauś. Br. (20.1) the world of

[1] *Die Lehre der Upanishaden und die Anfänge des Buddhismus*, p. 286.

Brahman is the most real[1] (sattamam) of the worlds and is the heaven above the world of the gods, fathers, the living, the world of Agni, of Vāyu, of Indra,[2] of Varuṇa and of men. In the early Upaniṣads it is still the highest and the seventh world from the world of men (Bṛh. 4.3.33). It is definitely a place to be attained only after death and by journeying there (Bṛh. 6.2.15, Ch. 4.14, 5–6, 5.10.2). The conception of the Brahmaloka as a state attainable in this life emerges only sporadically in the Early Upaniṣads, where a special theory is put forward such as, for instance, when it is suggested that we enter the Brahmaloka in deep sleep (Ch. 8.3.2). But even in the later Upaniṣads where Brahman is clearly a state attainable in this life, the earlier view of the Brahmaloka was still too strong to be put aside altogether. We see this clearly in the Muṇḍaka Upaniṣad, where the earlier idea of the 'meritorious Brahmaloka won by good works' (punyas sukṛto brahma-lokaḥ, 1.2.6) is criticized as an insecure goal (*op. cit.*, 1.2.7) even though those who attain the imperishable Brahman (*op. cit.*, 2.2.2) are still represented as departing 'through the door of the sun to where the immortal puruṣa is' (sūrya-dvāreṇa ... yatrāmṛtaḥ sa puruṣaḥ, *op. cit.* 1.2.11) as at Bṛh. 6.2.15 and Ch. 4.15 5–6, and attaining immortality in the Brahma-worlds (brahmalokeṣu) only at the end of time (parāntakāle, *op. cit.*, 3.2.6). When therefore it is said in the Buddhist texts that Sāriputta thought 'the brahmins were obsessed with the idea of the Brahma world' (ime kho brāhmaṇā brahmalokādhimuttā, M. II.194) and decides to preach to them 'the path to companionship with Brahmā' (brahmānaṃ sahavyatāya maggaṃ, *loc. cit.*) it is a reference to a genuine Brahmanical belief and not a fanciful Buddhist conception as Thomas seems to think, when he says commenting on the Tevijja Sutta: 'What is expounded here is not the brahmin theory at all but the possibility of attaining to the Brahma-world as the Buddhists conceived it to exist, that is by the practice of the Brahma-vihāras' (*op. cit.*, p. 87). According to the Buddhist texts there are five types of brahmins mentioned in the Vedic literature of which one is said to be those who follow tradition but develop mettā (compassion) (A. II.225). That the practice of mettā leads to the Brahma-world is not a later Buddhist conception, but one found in the Early Upaniṣads. In

[1] The text has 'saptamam' (the seventh) but this is a mistake as Keith has said (*v.* Ṛgveda Brāhmaṇas Translated, HOS., Vol. 25, p. 457, fn. 3).

[2] . . . devalokaṃ pitṛlokaṃ jīvalokaṃ . . . agnilokaṃ . . . vāyulokaṃ . . . indralokaṃ . . . varuṇalokaṃ mṛtyulokaṃ . . . Brahmaṇo lokaṃ *nākaṃ saptamaṃ* lokānām . . .

the Chāndogya where Vedic knowledge is said to be handed down from Brahmā, it is said that those who learn and teach the Vedas and practise ahiṃsā to all creatures except at holy places (ahiṃsan sarvabhūtānyanyatra tīrthebhyāḥ) reach the Brahma-world (brahmalokaṃ abhisampadyate, 8.15.1).

(820) The reference made to Brāhmaṇical ideas in the Tevijja Sutta can easily be illustrated from Brāhmaṇic and Early Upaniṣadic passages. The Tevijja Sutta speaks of the brahmins of the three Vedas worshipping (āyacanti thomayanti pañjalikā, D. I.240) the sun and the moon at their rising (yato uggacchanti, *loc. cit.*) and setting (yattha ca ogacchanti, *loc. cit.*) and of talking of the path leading to companionship of the moon and sun (candimasuriyānaṃ sahavyatāya maggaṃ, *loc. cit.*). It also speaks of their turning round in worship at the turn of the sun and the moon (pañjalikā namassamānā anuparivattanti, *loc. cit.*). In the Kauśītaki Upaniṣad we are told that Kauśītaki used to worship the rising sun (udyantam ādityamupatiṣṭhate, 2.7) and similarly the setting sun (astaṃ yantaṃ, *loc. cit.*). He turns himself with the turn of the sun (adityasyāvṛtam anvāvarta, 2.8.9; cp. P. anuvattati) and likewise worships the moon (2.9). In the Tait. Br., Indra teaches Bhāradvāja a universal science (sarvavidyā) which is a new version of the three-fold knowledge (eṣa u eva trayī vidyā . . . , 3.10.11.5), which makes it possible for him to become immortal and attain to the companionship of the sun: taṃ sa viditvā amṛto bhūtvā svargaṃ lokaṃ iyāya *ādityasya sāyujyam* amṛto ha eva bhūtvā svargaṃ lokaṃ etyādityasya sāyujyaṃ ya evaṃ veda eṣa u eva *trayī vidyā* (*loc. cit.*). The ideal here is sāyujya (companionship) which is accurately conveyed by the Pāli sahavyata-, 'fellowship'. That the brahmins of the three Vedas pray to (avhayāma, D. I.244) Indra, Soma, Varuṇa, Īśvara, Prajāpati, Brahmā, Maharddhi and Yama, the Vedic gods and expect to be born in the highest heaven as a result (D. I.244) is again a common conception of the Brāhmaṇas. The Brāhmaṇic schools mentioned in the Tevijja Sutta (D. I.237) are the main early Brāhmaṇical schools as Wijesekera has shown.[1] The 'Bhavyārijjhā (*v.l.* Bahvarijā, *v.* Rhys Davids, SBB., II, p. 303) brāhmaṇā' are the earliest brahmins of the Ṛgvedic school, known as the Bahvṛcas, whose brāhmaṇa text Keith surmises was the single tradition from which the Aitareya and the Kauśītaki Brāhmaṇas were composed.[2] The

[1] 'A Pāli Reference to Brāhmaṇa-Caraṇa-s' in *Adyar Library Bulletin*, Vol. 20, Parts 3–4, pp. 294–309. [2] HOS., Vol. 25, p. 22; cp. JRAS., 1915, pp. 493–8.

'Chandogā brāhmaṇā' are the Chandogas of the school of the Sāma Veda and whose brāhmaṇa text which included the Chāndogya Upaniṣad is mentioned in the Kātyāyana Śrauta Sūtra (xxii), the Parāśarasmṛti (i.38/39.4.28) and by Pāṇini (4.3.129). The 'Addhariyā brāhmaṇa' are the Adhvaryus, which, as Weber says, is the old name for the brahmins of the school of the Yajurveda.[1] The 'Tittiriyā brāhmaṇā' are the brahmins of the school of the Black Yajurveda, who had the Taittirīya Brāhmaṇa. There is apparently a significant omission of the school of the White Yajurveda to which the Bṛhadāraṇyaka Upaniṣad and the Śathapatha Brāhmaṇa, which contains this Upaniṣad, belongs. Wijesekera argues that this is because this Brāhmaṇa (and presumably this school) was of a later date than the Tevijja Sutta or was too new to be designated by the masculine plural, which should be used to denote the teachings of the older Brāhmaṇas (purāṇa-prokta- brāhmaṇa-) according to Pāṇini (4.3.101; 4.2.64). In our opinion, a simpler and a more probable explanation is that the school which was responsible for the Śathapatha Brāhmaṇa is denoted by 'Addhariyā brāhmaṇā'. For as Weber has shown the Śathapatha Brāhmaṇa applies the term Adhvaryus to its own adherents whilst their opponents are called Carakādhvaryus who are the objects of censure.[2] So the brahmanical schools mentioned in the Tevijja Sutta are the earliest and main schools of the Vedas,[3] viz.

School	*Text*
Ṛgveda-bavhārijā brāhmaṇā (Bahvṛcas)	Bahvṛca Brāhmaṇa (lost) but incorporated in the Aitareya and Kauśītaki Brāhmaṇas.
Sāmaveda-chandogā brāhmaṇā (Chandogas)	Chāndogya Brāhmaṇa
Yajurveda-tittiriyā brāhmaṇā (Taittiriyas)	Taittirīya Brāhmaṇa
Yajurveda-addhariyā brahmaṇā (Adhvaryus)	Śatapatha Brāhmaṇa

(821) The above evidence, we believe, should suffice to show that the brāhmaṇical conceptions criticized in the Tevijja Sutta are not a

[1] *The History of Indian Literature*, p. 86.

[2] *Ibid.*, p. 87; cp. *Indische Studien*, III, p. 454.

[3] i.e. leaving out the 'chandāvā' a name of obscure significance. Wijesekera identifies them (*op. cit.*, p. 299) as candānā=Skr. cāndrāyanāḥ mentioned in J. Brough, *The Early Brāhmaṇical System of Gotra and Pravara*, pp. 82, 124.

fanciful creation of the Buddhists, but are the genuine Brāhmaṇical beliefs found in the main streams of the Vedic tradition. The conception of Brahmā (masc.) is not a hypostatized version of the Upaniṣadic Brahman (neuter) as Oldenberg surmised, but the personal conception of Brahmā which emerges at a certain stage in the evolution of the Brāhmaṇas and is found in the Early Upaniṣads. Inasmuch as the Vedas were derived from this Brahmā in the Brāhmaṇical and Upaniṣadic tradition, the Buddhist criticism that none of the earlier seers or their successors had seen Brahmā amounts to a denial of the very foundations of the Vedic tradition. It seems to deny that the Vedic tradition can claim to be a revelational tradition at all.

CHRONOLOGICAL TABLE OF SCHOOLS

The following is a table of the schools discussed, according to their relative chronology. The dates given are very tentative.

	Vedic Schools	*Non-Vedic Schools*
1200–1000 BC	Ṛgveda (*v.* Ch. I)	
1000–800 BC	Brāhmaṇas and Atharvaveda (*v.* Ch. I)	
800 BC	Āraṇyakas (*v.* Ch. I)	
800–600 BC	Early Upaniṣads (*v.* Ch. I)	
		Materialists (Lokāyata; referred to in Kaṭha Upaniṣad, *v.* Ch. II)
	Middle Upaniṣads (*v.* Ch. I)	Sceptics (P. Amarāvikkhepikā=Ard. Mag. Aṇṇāṇiā=Skr. Ajñānikāḥ; independently referred to in Jain and Buddhist texts, *v.* Ch. III)
		Ājīvikas (Śvetāśvatara Upaniṣad mentions school having niyati—destiny—as central concept; *v.* Ch. III)
		Jains (mentioned in Early Buddhist texts as pre-Buddhistic school; *v.* Ch. III)
	Late Upaniṣads (*v.* Ch. I)	Early Buddhism (referred to in Maitrī Upaniṣad; *v.* Ch. I, sections 79–81).

BIBLIOGRAPHY

I. ORIGINAL SOURCES

A. *Pali Texts and Translations*

Abhidhammatthasaṅgaha, Tr. S. Z. Aung and C. A. F. Rhys Davids, *Compendium of Philosophy*, London, 1910.

Abhidhammāvatāra, Ed. A. P. Buddhadatta Thera, PTS. London, 1915.

Abhidhānappadīpikā, *v*. Secondary Authorities A.

Aṅguttara Nikāya, Ed. R. Morris and E. Hardy, 5 Vols., PTS. London, 1885–1900. Tr. F. L. Woodward and E. M. Hare, *The Book of the Gradual Sayings*, 5 Vols., PTS. London, 1932–36.

Atthasālinī, by Buddhaghosa, Ed. E. Müller, PTS. London, 1897.

Dhammapada, Ed. S. Sumangala Thera, PTS. London, 1914.

Dhammasaṅgaṇi, Ed. E. Müller, London, 1885.

Dīgha Nikāya, Ed. T. W. Rhys Davids and J. E. Carpenter, 3 Vols., PTS. London, 1890–1911. Tr. T. W. and C. A. F. Rhys Davids, *Dialogues of the Buddha*, SBB., Vols. 2, 3 and 4, O.U.P., London, 1899–1921.

Itivuttaka, Ed. E. Windisch, PTS. London, 1889.

Jātaka, Ed. V. Fausböll, 6 Vols. and index, London, 1895–1907.

Kathāvatthu, Ed. A. C. Taylor, 2 Vols., PTS. London, 1894–97.

Kathāvatthuppakaraṇa, Aṭṭhakathā, Comy. to Kathāvatthu, Printed in JPTS., 1889, pp. 1–199.

Khuddakapāṭha, Ed. H. Smith, PTS. London, 1915.

Mahāniddesa, *v*. Niddesa.

Majjhima Nikāya, Ed. V. Trenkner and R. Chalmers, 3 Vols., PTS. London, 1948–51. Tr. I. B. Horner, *Middle Length Sayings*, 3 Vols., PTS. London, 1954–9. Tr. R. Chalmers, *Further Dialogues of the Buddha*, 2 Vols., PTS. London, 1888. Tr. K. E. Neumann, Die Reden Gotamo Buddho's aus der mittleren Sammlung Majjhimanikāyo, Bande I und II, Leipzig, 1896–1900.

Manorathapūraṇi, Comy. to Aṅguttara Nikāya, Ed. M. Walleser und H. Kopp, 5 Vols., PTS. London, 1924–56.

Milindapañha, Ed. V. Trenkner, London, 1928.

Nettippakaraṇa, Ed. E. Hardy, PTS. London, 1902.

Niddesa, I-Mahāniddesa, Ed. L. de la V. Poussin and E. J. Thomas, 2 Vols.; II-Cullaniddesa, Ed. W. Stede, PTS. London, 1916–18.

Papañcasūdanī, Comy. to Majjhima Nikāya, Ed. J. H. Woods, D. Kosambi and I. B. Horner, 5 Vols., PTS. London, 1922–38.

Paramatthadīpanī, Comy. to Khuddaka Nikāya, Part III (to Petavatthu), Ed. E. Hardy, PTS. London, 1894.
Part not mentioned, Comy. to Udāna, Ed. F. L. Woodward, PTS. London, 1926.

Paramatthajotikā II, Comy. to Suttanipāta, Ed. H. Smith, 3 Vols. in II, PTS. London, 1916–18.

Paṭisambhidāmagga, Ed. A. C. Taylor, PTS. London, 2 Vols., 1905–7.

Puggalapaññatti, Ed. R. Morris, London, 1883.

Puggalapaññatti Aṭṭhakathā, Comy. to Puggalapaññatti, Ed. G. Landsberg and C. A. F. Rhys Davids, JPTS., 1914, pp. 170–254.

Saddanīti, Ed. H. Smith, *La Grammaire Palie D'Aggavamsa,* London, 1928.

Sammohavinodanī, Comy. to Vibhaṅga, Ed. A. P. Buddhadatta Thera, PTS. London, 1923.

Saṃyutta Nikāya, Ed. L. Feer, 6 Vols., PTS. London, 1884–1904. Tr. C. A. F. Rhys Davids and F. L. Woodward, *The Book of the Kindred Sayings,* 5 Vols., PTS. London, 1917–30.

Sāratthappakāsinī, Comy. to Saṃyutta Nikāya, Ed. F. L. Woodward, 3 Vols., PTS. London, 1929–37.

Sumaṅgalavilāsinī, Comy. to Digha Nikāya, Ed. T. W. Rhys Davids, J. E. Carpenter and W. Stede, 3 Vols., PTS. London, 1886–1932.

Suttanipāta, Ed. D. Anderson and H. Smith, PTS. London, 1948. Tr. V. Fausböll, SBE., Vol. 10, Part 2, Oxford, 1881.

Thera- and Therīgāthā, Ed. H. Oldenberg and R. Pischel, PTS. London, 1883. Tr. C. A. F. Rhys Davids, *Psalms of the Early Buddhists,* 2 Vols., PTS. London, 1903–13.

Udāna, Ed. P. Steinthal, PTS. London, 1948.

Vibhaṅga, Ed. C. A. F. Rhys Davids, PTS. London, 1904.

Vinaya Piṭaka, Ed. H. Oldenberg, 5 Vols., London, 1879–83.
Tr. T. W. Rhys Davids and H. Oldenberg, SBE., Vols. 13, 17, 20, Oxford, 1881–5.

Visuddhimagga, by Buddhaghosa, Ed. C. A. F. Rhys Davids, 2 Vols., London, 1920–21.

Yamaka, Ed. C. A. F. Rhys Davids, M. C. Foley, M. Hunt and M. Smith, PTS. London, 2 Vols., 1911–13.

B. *Prakrit Texts and Translations*

Āyāraṃga Sutta, Ed. H. Jacobi, Part I (Text), London, 1882. Tr. H. Jacobi, *Jaina Sūtras,* Part I—Ācārāṅga and Kalpa, SBE., Vol. 22, Oxford, 1884.

Bhagavatī Sūtra, with the Comy. (vṛtti) of Abhayadeva, Ed. S. C. P. Jhaveri and S. Keśarīmalajī, 2 Vols.; Vol. 1, Surat, 1937; Vol. II, Jamnagar, 1940.

Nandī Sūtra, by Devavācaka (Devarddhi Gaṇi), with Cūrṇi of Jinadāsa Gaṇi and Vṛtti of Haribhadra, Ed. Vijayadāna Sūri, Indore, 1931/2.

Samavāyāṅga Sūtra, with the Comy. (vivaraṇa) of Abhayadeva, Ed. N. Nemachanda, Ahmedabad, 1938.

Sthānāṅga Sūtra, Ed. V. Suracandra, 2 Vols., Bombay, 1918–20.

Sūtrakṛtāṅga, with the Comy. (vivaraṇa) of Śīlāṅka, Ed. A. S. Sūri and C. Gaṇīndra, 2 Vols., Bhāvanagara, 1950–3. Tr. H. Jacobi, *Jaina Sūtras*, Part II, Uttarādhyayana and Sūtṛakrtāṅga, SBE., Vol. 45, Oxford, 1895.

Uttarādhyayana Sūtra, Ed. R. D. Vadekar and N. V. Vaidya, Poona, 1954. Tr. H. Jacobi, *Jaina Sūtras*, Part II, Uttarādhyayana and Sūtrakṛtāṅga, SBE., Vol. 45, Oxford, 1895.

C. *Sanskrit Texts and Translations*

Abhidharmakośa, Ed. R. Saṅkṛtyāyana, Benares, 1955.

Aitareya Āraṇyaka, Ed. A. B. Keith, Oxford, 1909. Tr. F. Max Müller, *The Upaniṣads*, Part I, SBE., Vol. 1, Oxford, 1879.

Aitareya Brāhmaṇa, Ed. Pandit S. Sāmaśrami, 4 Vols., Bibliotheca Indica, Calcutta, 1894–1906.

Āryapratītyasamutpāda Sūtra, Printed in Āryaśālistamba Sūtra, *q.v.*

Āryaśālistamba Sūtra, Ed. N. A. Śāstri, Adyar, 1950.

Arthaśāstra of Kauṭalya, Ed. Ṭ. G. Śāstri, 3 Vols., Trivandrum, 1924–5.

Aṣṭādhyāyi of Pāṇini, *v.* O. Bohtlinck, *Pāṇini's acht Bucher grammatischer Regeln*, Bande I und II, Bonn, 1839–40.

Atharvaveda Saṅhitā, Ed. R. Roth and W. D. Whitney, Berlin, 1924.

Bodhisattvabhūmi, Ed. U. Wogihara, Tokyo, 1930–6.

Bṛhadāraṇyaka Upaniṣad, *v.* PU. With Comy. of Śaṅkara, Ed. K. S. Āgāse, A.A.S. No. 15, 1914.

Buddhacarita, Ed. E. H. Johnston, Part I, Calcutta, 1935.

Caraka Saṃhitā, with Ayurvedadīpikā of Cakrapāṇidatta, Ed. N. N. Śāstri, 2 Vols., Lahore, 1929.

Chāndogya Upaniṣad, *v.* PU. With Comy. of Śaṅkara, Ed. K. S. Āgāse, A.A.S. No. 14, 1913.

Gopatha Brāhmaṇa, Ed. R. Mitra and H. Vidyabhushana, Bibliotheca Indica, New Series Nos. 251, 252, Calcutta, 1872.

Harivaṃsaparvan, Ed. R. Kinjawadekar, Poona, 1936.

Īśā Upaniṣad, *v.* PU.

Jābāla Upaniṣad, *v.* PU.

Jñānaprasthānaśāstra, by Kātyāyanīputra, Ed. and Tr. S. B. Śāstri, Vol. I, Santiniketan, 1955.

Kaṭha Upaniṣad, *v.* PU. Ed. and Tr. J. N. Rawson, *The Kaṭha Upaniṣad*, O.U.P., 1934.

Kauśītakī Brāhmaṇa=Śāṅkhāyana Brāhmaṇa, Ed .G. R. V. Chāyā, A.A.S. No. 65, Rajkot, 1911. Tr. A. B. Keith, Ṛgveda Brāhmaṇas Translated, HOS., Vol. 25, Cambridge Massachusetts, 1920.

Kauśītakī Upaniṣad, *v.* PU.

Kena Upaniṣad, *v.* PU.

Laṅkāvatāra Sūtra, Ed. B. Nanjio, Bibliotheca Otaniensis, Vol. I, Kyoto, 1923. Tr. D. T. Suzuki, The Laṅkāvatāra Sūfga, London, 1932.

Mādhyamakavṛtti (Mūlamādhyamakakārikās), by Nāgārjuna, Ed. L. de la V. Poussin, Bibliotheca Buddhica, Vol. 4, St Petersbourg, 1913.

Madhyāntavibhāgaṭika, by Sthiramati, Ed. S. Yamaguchi, Nagoya, 1934.

Mahābhāratam, Ed. T. R. Krishnacharya and T. R. Vyasacharya, 18 Vols., Bombay, 1906–10.

Mahāvyutpatti, *v.* Secondary Authorities A.

Maitrī Upaniṣad, *v.* PU.

Māṇḍūkya Upaniṣad, *v.* PU.

Manusmṛti, with Comy. of Kullūka Bhaṭṭa, Ed. Pandit G. S. Nene, Benares, 1935. With Comy. of Medhātithi, Ed. G. Jha, 3 Vols., Calcutta, 1932–9.

Mīmāṃsā Sūtras, by Jaimini, Tr. G. Jha, SBH., Vol. 10, Allahabad, 1916. Tr. Pandit M. L. Sandal, SBH., Vol. 27, Part I, Allahabad, 1923–5.

Muṇḍaka Upaniṣad, *v.* PU.

Nighaṇṭu and the Nirukta, Text, Ed. L. Sarup, University of Panjab, 1927. Tr. L. Sarup, The Nighaṇṭu and the Nirukta, O.U.P., 1921.

Nyāyabhāṣya, *v.* Nyāya Sūtra.

Nyāyabindu, by Dharmottara, Ed. T. I. Stcherbatsky, Bibliotheca Buddhica, Petrograd, 1918.

Nyāyamañjarī, by Jayanta Bhaṭṭa, Ed. Pandit S. S. N. Sukla, Kāśi Sanskrit Series, Benares, 1936.

Nyāya Sūtra, with Nyāyabhāṣya of Vātsyāyana, Ed. D. N. Josi, A.A.S. No. 91, 1922.

Nyāya Sūtras of Gotama, Ed. and Tr. S. C. Vidyabhusana, SBH., Vol. 8, Allahabad, 1913.

Praśna Upaniṣad, *v.* PU.

Raghuvaṃsa, by Kālidāsa, Ed. M. A. Karandikar and S. Karandikar, Bombay, 1953.

Ratnāvalī, by Nāgārjuna, Ed. and Tr. G. Tucci, 'The Ratnāvalī of Nāgārjuna' in JRAS., April 1934, pp. 307–325.

Rāmāyana, by Vālmiki, Vol. 2, Ayodhyākāṇḍa, Ed. S. S. Kaṭṭi, Bombay, undated.

Ṛgarthadīpikā, on Ṛgvedasaṃhitā, by Mādhava, Ed. L. Sarup, 2 Vols., Lahore, 1939.

Rigvedasaṃhitā, with Comy. of Sāyaṇa, Ed. F. Max Müller, 6. Vols., London, 1849–74. Tr. R. T. H. Griffith, *The Hymns of the Ṛgveda*, 4 Vols., Benares, 1889–92. Tr. K. F. Geldner, *Der Rigveda*, Vol. I, Gottingen, 1923. Tr. H. H. Wilson, *Rigveda Saṅhitā*, Vol. 2, Poona, 1925.

Ṣaḍdarśanasamuccaya, by Haribhadra, with Guṇaratna's Tarkarahasyadīpikā, Ed. L. Suali, Calcutta, 1905.

Sāṅkhya Kārikā, by Īśvarakṛṣṇa, Ed. S. S. S. Śāstri, University of Madras, 1948.

Śāṅkhya Pravacana Bhāṣya, Ed. R. Garbe, HOS., Vol. 2, Harvard University, 1895.

Śāṅkhya Pravacana Sūtra, *v.* Sāṅkhya Pravacana Bhāṣya.

Sālistamba Sūtra, *v.* Āryaśālistamba Sūtra.

Sarvadarśanasaṃgraha, by Sāyaṇa Mādhava, Ed. V. S. Abhyaṅkar, Second Edition, Poona, 1951. Tr. E. B. Cowell, The Sarvadarśanasaṃgraha, London, 1882.

Sarvasiddhāntasaṃgraha, by Saṃkara, Ed. M. Raṅgācārya, Madras, 1909.

Śathapatha Brāhmaṇa, Ed. V. S. Gauḍa, C. Śarma and S. V. Śāstri, 2 Vols., Kasi, 1922–37. Tr. J. Eggeling, *The Śathapatha Brāhmaṇa*, 5 Parts, SBE., Vols. 12, 26, 41, 43, 44, Oxford, 1882–1900.

Sphuṭārthābhidharmakośavyākhyā, Ed. U. Wogihara, 2 Parts, Tokyo, 1932–6.

Śrīmānmahābhāratam, *v.* Mahābhāratam.

Śrīmānmahābhāratam Harivaṃsaparvan, *v.* Harivaṃsaparvan.

Švetāśvatara Upaniṣad, with Comy. of Śaṅkara, A.A.S. No. 17, 1905.

Taittirīya Āraṇyaka, Ed. B. S. Phaḍake, Second Edition, 2 Vols., A.A.S. No. 36, 1926–7.

Taittirīya Brāhmaṇa, Ed. N. S. Goḍabole, 3 Vols., A.A.S. No. 37, 1898–1938.

Taittirīya Upaniṣad, *v.* PU.

Tāṇḍyamahābrāhmaṇa, Ed. A. C. Śāstri and P. Śāstri, 2 Parts, Kāśi Sanskrit Series No. 105, Benares, 1935–6.

Tarkarahasyadīpikā, by Guṇaratna, v. Śaḍdarśanasamuccaya.

Tarkasaṃgraha, Tr. A. Foucher, *Le Compendium des Topiques D'Annambhaṭṭa*, Paris, 1949.

Tattvasaṃgraha, with Tattvasaṃgrahapañjikā of Kamalaśila, Ed. E. Krishnamacharya, 2 Vols., Gaekwad Oriental Series Nos. 30 and 31, Baroda, 1926.

Tattvasaṃgrahapañjikā, *v.* Tattvasaṃgraha.

Tattvopaplavasiṃha, by Jayarāśi Bhaṭṭa, Ed. S. Saṅghavi and R. C. Parikh, Gaekwad Oriental Series No. 87, Baroda, 1940.

Upaniṣads, Ed. and Tr. S. Radhakrishnan, *The Principal Upaniṣads*, London, 1953. Tr. F. Max Müller, *The Upanishads*, Part I, SBE., Vol. 1, Oxford, 1879. Tr. R. E. Hume, *The Thirteen Principal Upanishads*, Second Edition, O.U.P., 1934. Tr. P. Deussen, *Sechzig Upaniṣad's des Veda*, Leipzig, 1921.

Vaiśeṣika Sūtras, by Kaṇāda, Tr. N. Siṅha, SBH., Vol. 6, Allahabad, 1911.
Vajrasūcikā Upaniṣad, *v.* PU.
Yogabhāṣya, Ed. P. S. R. Śāstri and S. R. K. Śāstri, Madras Oriental Series No. 94, Madras, 1952.
Yogasūtras, Ed. and Tr. R. Prasāda, Third Edition, SBH., Vol. 4, Allahabad, 1924.

II. SECONDARY AUTHORITIES

A. *Reference Books*

Abhidhānappadīpikā, Ed. M. Jinavijaya, Ahmedabad, 1923.
Buddhist Hybrid Sanskrit Dictionary, Ed. F. Edgerton, New Haven and London, 1953.
Critical Pali Dictionary, Ed. V. Trenckner, D. Anderson, H. Smith and H. Hendriksen, Vol. I, Copenhagen, 1924–48.
Concise Oxford Dictionary, Ed. H. W. Fowler and F. G. Fowler, Fourth Edition revised by E. McIntosh, Oxford, 1959.
Concordance to the Principal Upaniṣads, by G. A. Jacob, Bombay, 1891.
Dictionary of Pali Proper Names, Ed. G. P. Malalasekera, 2 Vols., London, 1937–8.
Dictionary of Philosophy, Ed. D. Runes, London, 1945.
Dictionary of Philosophy and Psychology, Ed. J. H. Baldwin, 3 Vols., New York, 1940–9.
Encyclopaedia of Religion and Ethics, Ed. J. Hastings, 12 Vols., Edinburgh, 1908–26.
Mahāvyutpatti, Ed. I. P. Minaev, Bibliotheca Buddhica, Vol. 13, 1911.
Nyāyakośa, Ed. B. Jhalakīkar, Bombay, 1875.
Pali Text Society's *Pali-English Dictionary,* Ed. T. W. Rhys Davids and W. Stede, London, 1921.
Sanskrit-English Dictionary, Ed. M. Monier-Williams, Oxford, 1899.
Sanskrit-Worterbuch, Ed. O. Böhtlinck and R. Roth, 7 Vols., St Petersburg, 1855–75.
Vedic Concordance, by M. Bloomfield, Cambridge, Massachusetts, 1906.

B. *Monographs*

Ayer, A. J., *Language, Truth and Logic,* 17th Impression, London, 1958.
The Problem of Knowledge, Penguin Books, 1957.
Bagchi, S., *Inductive Reasoning—A Study of Tarka and its Rôle in Indian Logic,* Calcutta, 1953.
Bareau, A., *Les Sectes Bouddhiques du Petit Vehicule,* Saigon, 1955.
Barua, B. M., *A History of Pre-Buddhistic Indian Philosophy,* University of Calcutta, Calcutta, 1921.
Basham, A. L., *History and Doctrines of the Ājīvikas,* London, 1951.

Beckh, H., *Buddhismus*, Vol. I, Berlin und Leipzig, 1919.

Belvalkar, S. K. and Ranade, R. D., *History of Indian Philosophy*, Vol. 2, Poona, 1927.

Bhattacharya, V., *The Basic Conception of Buddhism*, Calcutta, 1934.

Bloomfield, M., *Religion of the Veda*, New York and London, 1908.

Bochenski, I. M., *Formale Logik*, Germany, 1956.

Böhtlinck, O., *Panini's Acht Bücher Grammatischer Regeln*, Bande 2, Bonn, 1839–40.

Bradley, F. H. *Appearance and Reality*, Second Edition, London, 1906.

Broad, C. D., *Mind and its Place in Nature*, London, 1937.

Brough, J., *The Early Brahmanical System of Gotra and Pravara*, Cambridge University Press, 1953.

Burnet, J., *Early Greek Philosophy*, London and Edinburgh, 1892. *Greek Philosophy*—Thales to Plato, London, 1943.

Chattopadhyaya, B., Lokāyata, *A Study on Ancient Indian Materialism*, New Delhi, 1959.

Colebrook, H. T., *Miscellaneous Essays*, Vol. I, London, 1873.

Das Gupta, S. N., *A History of Indian Philosophy*, Vol. I, Cambridge University Press, 1922; Vol. III, Cambridge University Press, 1940.

Deussen, P., *The Philosophy of the Upanishads*, Tr. A. S. Gedden, Edinburgh, 1906.

Ducasse, C. J., *The Belief in a Life after Death*, Illinois, 1961.

Dutt, N., *Early Monastic Buddhism*, Second Edition (Revised), Calcutta, 1960.

Ewing, A. C., *The Fundamental Questions of Philosophy*, London, 1958.

Flew, A. G. N. (Ed.), *Essays on Logic and Language*, Second Series, Oxford, 1953.

Flournoy, Th., *Des Indes à la Planète Mars*, Geneva, 1899.

Frauwallner, E., *Geschichte der indischen Philosophie*, 2 vols., Salzburg, 1953–6.

Garbe, R., *Philosophy of Ancient India*, Chicago, 1899.

Geiger, W., *Pali Literatur und Sprache*, Strassbourg, 1916.

Glasenapp, H. von, *Der Jainismus*, Berlin, 1925.

Goldstücker, T., *Pāṇini*, London, 1881.

Guerinot, A., *La Religion Djaina*, Paris, 1926.

Hiriyanna, M., *Outlines of Indian Philosophy*, Second Impression, London, 1951.

Hopkins, E. W., *Ethics of India*, New Haven, 1924.

Hume, David, *A Treatise of Human Nature*, 2 Vols., Everyman's Library Nos. 548, 549, London and New York, 1949.

Hume, R. E., *The Thirteen Principal Upanishads*, *v.* Upaniṣads.

Jayatilleke, K. N. and Malalasekera, G. P., *Buddhism and the Race Question*, UNESCO, 1958.

Jennings, J. G., *The Vedantic Buddhism of the Buddha,* Oxford University Press, London, 1947.

Johnson, W. E., *Logic,* Part I, Cambridge, 1921.

Kant, Immanuel, *Critique of Pure Reason,* Tr. N. K. Smith, London, 1933.

Kaufmann, W., *Critique of Religion and Philosophy,* London, 1958.

Keith, A. B., *Buddhist Philosophy in India and Ceylon,* Oxford, 1923. *Indian Logic and Atomism,* Oxford, 1921. *Religion and Philosophy of the Vedas,* 2 Vols., HOS., Vols. 31 and 32, 1925.

Kern, H., *Manual of Indian Buddhism,* Strassburg, 1896.

Kirk, G. S. and Raven, J. E., *The Presocratic Philosophers,* Cambridge, 1960.

Konow, S., *Corpus Inscriptionum Indicarum,* Vol. 2, Part I, Calcutta, 1929.

Lindquist, S., *Die Methoden des Yoga, Lund,* 1932. *Siddhi und Abhiññā,* Lund, 1935.

Lüders, H., Varuṇa, 2 Vols., Gottingen, 1951–9.

Ludwig, A., *Der Rigveda oder die heiligen Hymnen der Brāhmaṇa,* Band III, Prag, 1878.

Malalasekera, G. P., *Buddhism and the Race Question, v.* K. N. Jayatilleke.

Macdonell, A., *A Vedic Grammar for Students,* Oxford, 1916.

McDougall, W., *An Outline of Abnormal Psychology,* Sixth Edition, London, 1958.

McKenzie, J., *Hindu Ethics,* O.U.P., 1922.

M'Crindle, J. W., *Ancient India,* Westminster, 1901.

Mill, J. S., *A System of Logic,* London, New York, Toronto, 1941.

Mishra, U., *History of Indian Philosophy,* Vol. I, Allahabad, 1957.

Moore, C. A. and Radhakrishnan, S., *A Source Book of Indian Philosophy,* Princeton University Press, 1957.

Muir, J., *Original Sanskrit Texts,* 5 Vols., London, 1872–4.

Murti, T. R. V., *The Central Philosophy of Buddhism,* London, 1955.

Nowell-Smith, P. H., *Ethics,* Penguin Books, 1954.

Nyanatiloka, *A Guide Through the Abhidhamma Piṭaka,* Colombo, 1957.

Ogden, C. K. and Richards, I. A., *The Meaning of Meaning,* London, 1923.

Oldenberg, *Buddha,* Tr. Hoey, London and Edinburgh, 1882; Calcutta, 1927. *Buddha, Sein Leben, Seine Lehre, Seine Gemeinde,* 13 Auflage, Stuttgart, 1959. *Die Lehre der Upanishaden und die Anfänge des Buddhismus,* Gottingen, 1915. *Religion des Veda,* Stuttgart und Berlin, 1917.

Oltramare, P., *La Formule Bouddhique des douze Causes,* Geneva, 1909. *L'Histoire des Idees Theosophiques dans l'Inde—La Théosophie Bouddhique,* Paris, 1923.

Pande, G. C., *Studies in the Origin of Buddhism,* University of Allahabad, 1957.

Pap, A., *Semantics and Necessary Truth,* Yale University Press, New Haven, 1958.

Pischel, R., *Leben und Lehre des Buddha*, 2 Auflage, Leipzig, 1910.

Poussin, L. de la V., *L'Abhidharmakosa De Vasubandhu*, Paris, 1923–5. *Bouddhisme*, Third Edition, Paris, 1925. *Theorie des Douze Causes*, Gand, 1913. *The Way to Nirvāṇa*, Cambridge University Press, 1917.

Prasad, J., *History of Indian Epistemology*, Second Edition, Delhi, 1958.

Radhakrishnan, S. and Moore, C. A., *A Source Book of Indian Philosophy*, v. C. A. Moore.

Radhakrishnan, S., *The Principal Upaniṣads*, v. Upaniṣads. *Indian Philosophy*, Vol. I, London, 1941; Vol. II, London and New York, 1931.

Ranade, R. D., *A Constructive Survey of Upanishadic Philosophy*, Poona, 1926.

Ranade, R. D. and Belvalkar, S. K., *History of Indian Philosophy*, Vol. 2, v. S. K. Belvalkar.

Randle, H. N., *Fragments from Diṅnāga*, London, 1926.
Indian Logic in the Early Schools, O.U.P., 1930.

Rapson, E. J. (Ed.), *The Cambridge History of India*, Vol. I, Cambridge, 1922.

Rhine, J. B., *The New Frontiers of the Mind*, Penguin Books, 1950. *The Reach of the Mind*, London, 1958.

Rhys Davids, C. A. F., *Buddhism*, Williams and Norgate, Home University Library of Modern Knowledge, London, undated, 1912? 1914? *Buddhist Psychology*, Second Edition, London, 1924. *Śākya or Buddhist Origins*, London, 1931. *Wayfarer's Words*, 3 Vols., London, 1940–2.

Rhys Davids, T. W., *Buddhism*, London, 1917.

Ruben, W., *die Philosophen der Upandishaden*, Bern, 1947. *Geschichte der indischen Philosophie*, Berlin, 1954.

Russell, B. A. W., *A History of Western Philosophy*, 3rd Impression, London, 1948. *Human Knowledge*, London, 1948. *The Philosophy of Leibniz*, Fourth Impression, Second Edition, London, 1951.

Ryle, G., *The Concept of Mind*, London, 1950.

Sarathchandra, E. R., *Buddhist Psychology of Perception*, Colombo, 1958.

Śāstri, G., *The Philosophy of Word and Meaning*, Calcutta, 1959.

Saw, R. L., *Leibniz*, Penguin Books, 1954.

Schayer, St., *Vorarbeiten zur Geschichte der Mahayanistischen Erlösungslehren*, München, 1921.

Sharma, C. D., *A Critical Survey of Indian Philosophy*, London, 1960.

Sinha, J., *A History of Indian Philosophy*, 2 Vols., Calcutta, 1952–6.

Slater, R. L. *Paradox and Nirvāṇa*, Chicago, 1950.

Smart, N., *A Dialogue of Religions*, London, 1960.

Stace, W. T., *A Critical History of Greek Philosophy*, London, 1950.

Stcherbatsky, Th., *Buddhist Logic*, Vol. I, Leningrad, 1930. *The Central Conception of Buddhism and the Meaning of the Word 'Dharma'*, London, 1923.

Stebbing, L. S., *A Modern Introduction to Logic*, London, 1945.
Stevenson, Ian, *The Evidence far Survival from Claimed Memories of Former Incarnations*, Thamesmouth Printing Co. Ltd., Essex, 1961.
Tatia, *Studies in Jaina Philosophy*, Banaras, 1951.
Thomas, E. J., *The History of Buddhist Thought*, London, 1953. *The Life of the Buddha*, New York, 1927.
Tischner, R., *Telepathy and Clairvoyance*, London, 1925.
Toynbee, A., *An Historian's Approach to Religion*, O.U.P., 1956.
Ui, H., *The Vaiśeṣika Philosophy*, London, 1917.
Vidyabhusana, S. C., *A History of Indian Logic*, Calcutta, 1921.
Warnock, G. J., *Berkeley*, Penguin Books, 1953. *English Philosophy since 1900*, O.U.P., 1959.
Weber, A., *History of Indian Literature*, London, 1878. *Indische Studien*, Bande 18, Berlin und Leipzig, 1850–98.
Welton, J., *A Manual of Logic*, London, 1922.
Wijesekera, O. H. de A., *The Three Signata*, Kandy, 1960.
Winternitz, M., *A History of Indian Literature*, Vol. 2, University of Calcutta, 1933. *Geschichte der indischen Litteratur*, 3 Vols., Leipzig, 1909–20.
Wittgenstein, L., *Tractatus Logico-Philosophicus*, *London*, 1933. *Philosophische Untersuchungen*, Tr. Philosophical Investigations, 2 Vols., Oxford, 1953.
Woozley, A. D., *The Theory of Knowledge*, London, 1959.

C. *Articles*

Bahm, A. J., 'Soes Seven-Fold Predication Equal Four-Cornered Negation Reversed' in *Philosophy East and West*, Vol. 7, pp. 127–130.
Barua, B. M., 'Ājīvika—What it means', ABORI., Vol. 8, 1927, pp. 183–188. 'Faith in Buddhism' in *Buddhistic Studies*, Ed. B. C. Law, Calcutta, 1931, pp. 329–49.
Bevan, E. R., 'India in Early Greek and Latin Literature' in *The Cambridge History of India*, Ed. E. J. Rapson, Vol. I, pp. 391–425.
Bloomfield, M., 'The Marriage of Saraṇyū, Tvaṣṭar's Daughter' in JAOS., Vol. 15, pp. 172–88.
Brough, J., 'Logic', ERE., Vol. 8, pp. 127–32.
Burnet, J., 'Sceptics', ERE., Vol. 11, pp. 228–31.
Chalmers, R., 'Tathāgata' in JRAS., 1898, pp. 103–15.
Charpentier, J., 'The Kāṭhaka Upaniṣad' in *Indian Antiquary*, November 1928, pp. 201–7.
Cory, C. A., 'A Divided Self' in *Journal of Abnormal Psychology*, Vol. 14, Boston, 1919–20, pp. 281–91.
Das Gupta, M., 'Śraddhā and Bhakti in the Vedic Literature' in IHQ., Vol. 6, pp. 315–33.

Demiéville, P., 'Le Memoire des Existences Antérieures' in BEFEO., Vol. 27, pp. 283–98.

Dutt, N., 'Place of Faith in Buddhism' in IHQ., Vol. 16, pp. 639–46. 'Popular Buddhism' in IHQ., Vol. 21, pp. 251–6.

Ewing, A. C., 'Meaninglessness' in *Mind*, 1937, pp. 347–64.

Faddegon, B., 'The Catalogue of the Sciences in the Chāndogyopaniṣad' in AO., Vol. 4, pp. 42–54.

Foley, C. A., 'The Vedalla Sutta as illustrating the Psychological Basis of Buddhist Ethics' in JRAS., 1894, pp. 321–33.

Glasenapp, H. von, 'Vedānta und Buddhismus' in *Abhandlungen der Geistes- und Sozialwissenschaftlichen Klasse*, 1950, pp. 1013 ff.

Gyomroi-Ludowyk, E., 'The Valuation of Saddhā in the Early Buddhist Texts' in UCR., Vol. 5, pp. 32–49.
'Note on the Interpretation of Pasidati' in UCR., Vol. 1, pp. 74–82.

Hacker, P., 'Āṇvikṣiki' in *Wiener Zeitschrift fur die Kunde Sud- und Ostasiens und Archiv für indische Philosophie*, Band II, 1958, pp. 54–83.

Haug, M., 'Vedische Räthselfragen und Räthselsprüche' in *Transactions of the Munich Academy*, 1875, pp. 7 ff., *v.* p. 40, fn. 1.

Hoernle, A. F. R., 'Ājīvikas', ERE., Vol. 1, pp. 259–68.

Hume, R. E., Paper on 'Miracles in the Canonical Scriptures in Buddhism' in JAOS., Vol. 44, p. 162.

Jayatilleke, K. N., 'A Recent Criticism of Buddhism' in UCR., Vol. 15, pp. 135–50. 'Factual Meaning and Verification' in UCR., Vol. 13, pp. 1–16. 'Some Problems of Translation and Interpretation I' in UCR., Vol. 7, pp. 212–23. 'Some Problems of Translation and Interpretation II' in UCR., Vol. 8, pp. 45–55.

Jacobi, H., 'Der Ursprung des Buddhismus aus dem Sāṅkhya-Yoga' in *Nachrichten von der Königliche Gesellschaft der Wissenschaften zu Göttingen, philologisch-historische Klasse*, Göttingen, 1896, pp. 43–58. 'Zur Frühgeschichte der indischen Philosophie' in *Sitzungberichte der Preussische Akademie der Wissenschaften*, Berlin, 1911, pp. 733 ff.

Jaini, P. S., 'The Vaibhāṣika Theory of Words' in BSOAS., Vol. 22, Part I, 1959, pp. 97–107.

Johnston, H., 'The Gopalpur Bricks' in JRAS., 1938, pp. 547–53.

Keith, A. B., 'Āpastamba and the Bahvṛca Brāhmaṇa' in JRAS., 1915, pp. 493–98.

Kern, H., Toevoegselen op't Woordenboek van Childers, 2 Parts, Amsterdam, 1916.

Law, B. C., 'The Formulation of the Pratītya-samutpāda' in JRAS., 1937, pp. 287–92.

Lewy, C., 'Why are the Calculuses of Logic and Arithmetic applicable to Reality' in PAS., Vol. 20, 1946, pp. 30–39.

Niyamoto, S., 'The Logic of Relativity as the Common Ground for the Development of the Middle Way' in *Buddhism and Culture*, Ed. S. Yamaguchi, Kyoto, 1960, pp. 67–88.

Przyluski, J., 'Dārṣṭāntika, Sautrāntika and Sarvāstivādin' in IHQ., Vol. 16, pp. 246–54.

Przyluski, J. and Lamotte, E., 'Bouddhisme et Upaniṣad' in BEFEO., Vol. 32, pp. 141–69.

Poussin, L. de la V., 'Dogmatique Bouddhique' in JA. Tome 20, 1902, pp. 237–306. 'Documents D'Abhidarma—les Deux, les Quatres, les Trois Verites, Extraits de la Vibhāṣā et du Kośa de Saṃghabhadra' in *Mélanges Chinois et Bouddhique*, Vol. 5, pp. 159–87. 'Faith and Reason in Buddhism' in *Transactions of the Third International Congress for the History of Religions*, Vol. II, 1908, pp. 32–43. 'Le Bouddha et les Abhiññā' in *Muséon*, 1931, pp. 335–342. 'On the Authority (Prāmāṇya) of the Buddhist Āgamas' in JRAS., 1902, pp. 363–76.

Radhakrishnan, S., 'The Teaching of Buddha by Speech and by Silence' in *The Hibbert Journal*, Vol. XXXII, pp. 342–356.

Raju, P. T., 'The Principle of Four-Cornered Negation in Indian Philosophy' in *Review of Metaphysics*, Vol. 7, pp. 694–713.

Ryle, G., 'Categories' in *Logic and Language*, Ed. A. G. N. Flew, Second Series, pp. 65–81.

Rhys Davids, C. A. F., 'Logic' (Buddhist), ERE., Vol. 8, pp. 132–3. 'Paṭiccasamuppāda', ERE., Vol. 9, pp. 672–74.

Robinson, R. H., 'Some Logical Aspects of Nāgārjuna's System' in *Philosophy East and West*, Vol. 6, pp. 291–308.

Ruben, W., 'Uber den Tattvopaplavasiṃha des Jayarāśi Bhaṭṭa eine Agnostizistische Erkenntnis kritik' in *Wiener Zeitschrift für die Kunde Sudund Ostasiens und Archiv fur indische Philosophie*, Band, II, 1958, pp. 140–53.

Sadaw, L., 'Some Points in Buddhist Doctrine' in JPTS., 1914, pp. 115–63.

Schayer, St, 'Altindische Anticipationen der Aussagenlogik' in *Studien zur indischen Logik II*, Extrait du Bulletin de l'Academie Polonaise des Sciences et des Lettres Cracovic, 1933, pp. 90–96.

Thomas, E. J. 'Buddhism in Modern Times' in UCR., Vol. 9, pp. 215–25.

Tucci, G., 'A Sketch of Indian Materialism' in PIPC., 1925, pp. 34–43.

Warder, A. K., 'Early Buddhism and Other Contemporary Systems' in BSOAS., Vol. 18, 1956, pp. 43–63.

Wijesekera, O. H. de A., 'A Pali Reference to Brāhmaṇa Caraṇa-s' in *Adyar Library Bulletin*, Vol. 20. pp. 294–309. 'Upanishadic Terms for Sense Functions' in UCR., Vol. 2, pp. 14–24. 'Vedic Gandharva and Pali Gandhabba' in UCR., Vol. 3, pp. 73–95.

INDEX